C000132920

THE LIBRARY OF HOLOCAUST TESTIMONIES

Memoirs from Occupied Warsaw, 1940–1945

The Library of Holocaust Testimonies

Editors: Antony Polonsky, Martin Gilbert CBE, Aubrey Newman, Raphael F. Scharf, Ben Helfgott

Under the auspices of the Yad Vashem Committee of the Board of Deputies of British Jews and the Centre for Holocaust Studies, University of Leicester

My Lost World by Sara Rosen
From Dachau to Dunkirk by Fred Pelican
Breathe Deeply, My Son by Henry Wermuth
My Private War by Jacob Gerstenfeld-Maltiel
A Cat Called Adolf by Trude Levi
An End to Childhood by Miriam Akavia
A Child Alone by Martha Blend
I Light a Candle by Gena Turgel
My Heart in a Suitcase by Anne L. Fox
Memoirs from Occupied Warsaw, 1942–45
by Helena Szereszewska
Have You Seen My Little Sister?
by Janina Fischler-Martinho
Surviving the Nazis, Exile and Siberia by Edith Sekules
Out of the Ghetto by Jack Klajman with Ed Klajman
From Thessaloniki to Auschwitz and Back 1926-1996
by Erika Myriam Kounio Amariglio
Translated by Theresa Sundt
I was No. 20832 at Auschwitz by Eva Tichauer
Translated by Colette Lévy and Nicki Rensten
My Child is Back! by Ursula Pawel
Wartime Experiences in Lithuania by Rivka Lozansky Bogomolnaya
Translated by Miriam Beckerman

Memoirs from Occupied Warsaw 1940–1945

HELENA SZERESZEWSKA
Translated by Anna Marianska

VALLENTINE MITCHELL
LONDON • PORTLAND, OR

Published in 1997 in Great Britain by
VALLENTINE MITCHELL & CO. LTD
Newbury House, 900 Eastern Avenue
London IG2 7HH

and in the United States of America by
VALLENTINE MITCHELL & CO. LTD
c/o ISBS, 5804 N. E. Hassalo Street
Portland, Oregon 97213-3644

English language translation copyright © Anna Marianska 1997
Reprinted in 2000

British Library Cataloguing in Publication Data
Szereszewska, Helena
 Memoirs from Occupied Warsaw, 1940–1945 – (The library of
 Holocaust testimonies)
 1. Szereszewska, Helena   2. Jewish women – Poland – Warsaw –
 Biography   3. World War, 1939–1945 – personal narratives,
 Jewish   4. Jewish ghettos – Poland – Warsaw
 I. Title
 940.5'318'092

ISBN 0-85303-313-7

ISSN 1363-3759

Library of Congress Cataloging-in-Publication Data
Szereszewska, Helena
 [Krzyż i mezuza. English]
 Memoirs from Occupied Warsaw, 1940–1945 / Helena Szereszewska :
 translated by Anna Marianska.
   p.   cm. — (The Library of Holocaust testimonies, ISSN
 1363-3759)
   ISBN 0-85303-313-7 (pbk)
   1. Szereszewska, Helena.   2. Jews—Poland—Warsaw—Biography.
 3. Holocaust, Jewish (1939–1945)—Poland—Warsaw—Personal
 narratives.   4. Warsaw (Poland)–Biography.   I. Title.   I. Series.
 DS135.P63S943713   1997
 940.53'18'094384—dc20   96-44956
                                                                     CIP

Typeset by Regent Typesetting, London
Printed and bound in Great Britain by
Antony Rowe Ltd, Chippenham and Reading

In memory of my grandson

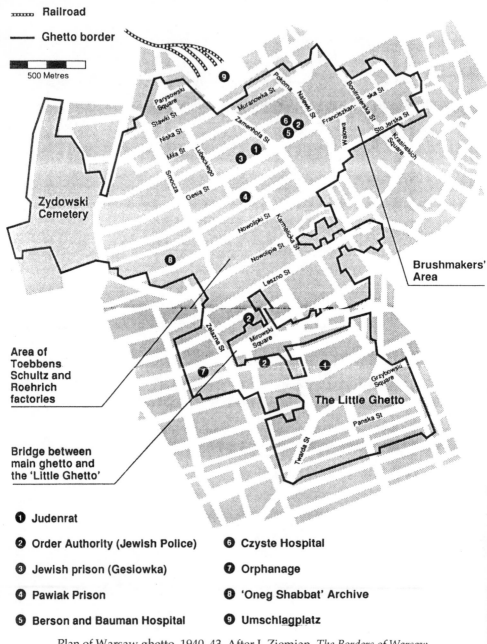

Railroad

Ghetto border

500 Metres

Zydowski
Cemetery

Parysowski
Square

Stawki St

Niska St

Mila St

Smocza

Gesia St

Lubeckiego

Muranowska St

Zamenhofa St

Pokorna

Nalewki St

Franciszkan-

ska St

Sto Jerska St

Bonifraterska St

Walowa

Krasinskich
Square

Nowolipki St

Karmelicka St

Nowolipie St

Leszno St

Zelazna St

Mirowski
Square

Twarda St

Grzybowski
Square

Panska St

**Brushmakers'
Area**

The Little Ghetto

**Area of
Toebbens
Schultz and
Roehrich
factories**

**Bridge between
main ghetto and
the 'Little Ghetto'**

❶ Judenrat

❷ Order Authority (Jewish Police)

❸ Jewish prison (Gesiowka)

❹ Pawiak Prison

❺ Berson and Bauman Hospital

❻ Czyste Hospital

❼ Orphanage

❽ 'Oneg Shabbat' Archive

❾ Umschlagplatz

Plan of Warsaw ghetto, 1940–43. After J. Ziemian, *The Borders of Warsaw Ghetto*, Jerusalem, 1971

Contents

Illustrations

Biographical Note

Helena Szereszewska, née Szpilfogel, was born in 1891 in Wola Krysztoporska, not far from Piotrkow Trybunalski, south of Lodz, on an estate which had been acquired by her grandfather. The author's upbringing was influenced by both the Jewish and the rural Polish traditions. Her parents spoke Yiddish to each other and Polish to the children.

The author attended grammar school in Piotrkow and then studied in Geneva. This was probably the happiest time of her life, but it did not last long. She became engaged to her cousin, Stanislaw Szereszewski and married him shortly afterwards. The young couple settled in Warsaw. Stanislaw Szereszewski, an intelligent and energetic man, worked in the yeast industry. In the household all decisions were made by him. The author was more content to read and write than to look after the household and their three daughters. It was an assimilated home, but twice a year, on the Jewish New Year and Day of Atonement, the girls did not attend school.

In the autumn of 1939 when the Second World War broke out, her eldest daughter, Anna Maria (Marysia), was married with a three year old son, Macius. Her second daughter, Irena, had been studying medicine for a year in Grenoble, but managed to return to Poland. Janina (Nina), the youngest, had just matriculated from grammar school.

The German occupation changed the family's living conditions and lifestyle. First of all their belongings disappeared, plundered by the Germans. Then came the deaths of their closest relatives and friends. Before the ghetto was established the family was forced to exchange their spacious flat for a small three-roomed flat, and lived there until the first resettlement action in July 1942.

Stanislaw Szereszewski was a member of the Jewish Council and responsible for the Welfare Department, and later, before the destruction of the ghetto, for the Finance Department. His wife and daughters decided to learn a trade: Marysia learnt tailoring, Irena studied nursing, while Nina worked in the Jewish Council and after work she made hats. The author looked after the household and her grandson, and learnt corsetry.

In the first resettlement action the author lost her mother, sister and brother, as well as many more distant relatives. In the second resettlement action her eldest daughter's husband was deported to Treblinka. After this action Helena Szereszewska and her two younger daughters left the ghetto. Her eldest daughter Marysia was waiting for them on the Aryan side. She had lived for a year with her son in the Otwock ghetto and managed to escape before its liquidation in August 1942.

Stanislaw Szereszewski stayed in the ghetto. He was shot at the Umschlagplatz after the outbreak of the Rising in the ghetto in April 1943.

The author, her three daughters and grandson survived the war thanks to the help of Polish friends and acquaintances. After the end of the war they lived in Warsaw for a little under a year, and then left for Italy, from where Helena Szereszewska and her two older daughters and grandson emigrated to Israel, while her youngest daughter went to England. It was in Rome that the author started writing her memoirs of the five and a half years of war, and then continued writing them in Israel.

Fragments of the memoirs, which were written in Polish, were published in translation while the the author was still alive. A Yiddish translation of the second part, the description of the author's life on the Aryan side, was published in Argentina in 1959 under the title 'The Cross and the Mezuzah'. A Hebrew translation of the first part was published in Israel in 1968 under the title 'The Last Chapter – Memoirs From the Warsaw Ghetto'. This was followed by a Hebrew translation of the second part which was published in Israel the following year and was also entitled 'The Cross and the Mezuzah'. After the author's death in 1978 a Hebrew translation of the complete memoirs was published in Israel in 1980 and entitled 'The Last Chapter'. The memoirs were published in Poland in the original Polish in 1993 and entitled 'The Cross and the Mezuzah'.

The Yiddish translation of the memoirs was dedicated to the memory of the author's husband. All the other translations were dedicated to the memory of her grandson, Macius Robert, a lecturer in the Department of Economics of Jerusalem University, who was killed in 1967 on the first day of the Six Day War.

1 • 20 Narbutt Street

On 1 September 1939 we lived at 20 Narbutt Street in Warsaw. On the third floor of the annexe. It was a modern house with a beautiful flower-bed in the courtyard. There was a name plate on the door of our flat: Stanislaw Szereszewski, Engineer. We had an entrance hall with a phone in it. Paintings on the walls, carpets on the floors, curtains in the windows. It was our home. We were all still together: my husband, me and our three daughters. Marysia the eldest, nineteen year old Irena and seventeen year old Nina. She had just matriculated from school.

So Nina was with us. But the war caught Irena unawares in Grenoble where she was studying. She returned home on 8 September.

'Did you have to come back? You'd have seen the war through safer in France than here,' we said anxiously.

What a journey it had been. She kept telling us about it. 'Three of us came back. I sold a bracelet in Milan because I didn't have any money left for the ticket. What on earth would have happened if I didn't have the bracelet?'

That evening my husband sat by the gate of the house with Mr Fortini. They were on duty. Cannons were firing, you could hear them quite near. Mrs Lukasik, our caretaker, came up to them. 'You've got to dig trenches,' she said. 'There's an order. One person from each flat.'

Dig trenches? My husband was an older man. He could keep watch at the gate. But to go to a field outside Warsaw in the dark? So Irena went with Mrs Lukasik in her father's place even though she'd just arrived. They took some spades, put them over their shoulders and walked down Narbutt Street towards Pulawska Street talking all the way.

Irena had attended the grammar school run by Mrs Roszkowska and Mrs Popielewska and wanted to study medicine at Warsaw University. But when a fight broke out between Poles and Jews

1

during the exams she was beaten up too. So she went to France instead. 'Did you want me to stay there?' she asked. 'No, I couldn't stay there on my own.'

So now we were at Narbutt Street with Irena and Nina, and Warsaw was already being bombed. It was 8 September. In fact we'd only been at Narbutt Street for two days. Before that we'd been in our villa in the village of Wieliszew and that's where the war had caught us. We wanted to see the war through in Wieliszew. We had stocked up with flour, kasha and peas and we were so naïve that we had bought gas masks and sixteen blankets for an anti-gas shelter.

We had managed to take the blankets by horse cab to the Gdanski Station for the Warsaw–Zegrze train. At Marszalkowska Street (we were moving at a slow trot because there was so much traffic) Nina's nanny, Mrs Dobrzelewska, jumped onto the steps of the cab. Her hair was as white as snow and she was over seventy, but she was as energetic as ever even though she was very stout. What was she doing here? We gave her two blankets. She hugged us and jumped down. It was a very strange meeting.

We bought a crystal set as well as the blankets. So now we had a radio and a crystal set in Wieliszew. All day long we listened to the messages announcing air raids in Warsaw. But mainly we listened to the thunder of the cannons, quiet and distant at first and then louder and louder. 'Coming from the direction of Plonsk,' we said. Sometimes we thought it was Plonsk, at other times a different direction. Spurred by the thunder which was getting nearer all the time we quickly made an anti-gas shelter out of the blankets. Our neighbours also laid in supplies, built shelters and intended to see the war through in Wieliszew.

Marysia and Ryszard and their son, who was not quite three, were also with us. Ryszard had just completed his legal articles. On the whole in the first days of the war we still lived a relatively calm and normal life. We had electric lighting and the windows weren't blacked out yet as it was still only the beginning, three or four days after the war started. When we went into the bathroom or lavatory we turned the light on and turned it off again when we came out. One evening when we were having supper a soldier with a rifle entered.

'You're signalling to the enemy.'

'We're signalling?'

'The light's going on and off. On and off. You're signalling. That's treason.'

2

I can't describe how astonished we were. Ryszard was the first to recover. He got up from the table, went up to the soldier and started to explain that we hadn't meant to do anything wrong. The light couldn't stay on in all the rooms, but it couldn't be off all the time either.

'Let me show you round the flat.'

'Well then, cover the windows,' said the soldier as he was leaving.

Next day the German planes were dropping bombs from first thing in the morning. Onto the village of Wieliszew. Our neighbour was wounded in the chest by fragments and her tenant's son was gashed in the face. He was eighteen and a student in Edinburgh. When the war broke out he left Edinburgh on the last plane because he wanted to be with his family. Overcome by panic, the inhabitants of the village left for Warsaw on carts, leaving their villas to their fate.

So Irena was now with us at Narbutt Street. It was an odd period: strangers would come to our flat, ask for our advice and tell us their troubles. Sometimes they even stayed the night though we didn't know them. A certain Mrs Puchalska stayed for two or three nights on the sofa in the hall. She was terrified. She kept crying and moaning, and gave her husband no peace. They probably came from the provinces, we didn't know exactly where from. We said that she was sowing defeatism. Her surname reminded us of the Polish word for an owl and so we made puns about owls not being allowed in. We joked, masking our own fear.

Then, when the cannon fire and bombing became heavier and we didn't think that Narbutt Street was safe enough, we fled to my brother-in-law Leon Szereszewski's flat on Marszalkowska Street next to Wilcza Street. When the bombing was at its heaviest we went down to the caretaker's lodge or sat by the gate. We never went down to the cellars, we didn't trust the cellars. We had heard about cellars being covered with rubble and the people in them suffocating to death. We were joined in this flat by my husband's cousin from Lodz, Boleslaw Szereszewski, our caretaker from Wieliszew, Waclaw Taperek, and an eighteen-year-old boy from Krysztoporska Wola whose father was my mother-in-law's servant many years ago. Funnily enough, the last two spent day and night in the cellar as, according to them, that was the safest place to be.

When the Germans took Warsaw, Waclaw Taperek returned to Wieliszew. Then he showed up one day, bringing a suitcase with a few things in it. He said that everything in the villa had been plundered and the furniture removed, and our bitch Mucha, which we'd had since she was a puppy, had been shot by the Germans. 'This is a Jewish dog,' the German had said, 'so it's got to die.' That's what Taperek told us. But that was later, after Warsaw had been taken.

On Marszalkowska Street I went upstairs to the flat two or three times a day from the caretaker's lodge. I boiled water for tea and made a huge pan of soup once a day. I thickened the soup with kasha, flavoured it with some fat and shared it out among everyone in turn. Once I cooked some horseflesh which one of us cut off a dead horse and once our servant, who had stayed at Narbutt Street, brought us some potatoes, carrots and beetroots in a sack.

When Warsaw fell we returned to Narbutt Street. Marysia lived very close to us on Wisniowa Street. After Ryszard left Warsaw she got rid of her flat and moved in with us together with her son, her belongings and her furniture. Macius was two years nine months old at that time and exceptionally intelligent. Once when Nina was at her sister's, she chopped some wood and lit the stove in the kitchen. 'Nina chopped the wood,' he told us with delight, 'and she did it all with those tiny hands of hers that are only a little bigger than mine.'

So Marysia moved in with us and we had plenty of furniture and things in the flat. But not for long. Because the Germans started to take everything away bit by bit. Not only bedding and eiderdowns, but watches, rings and bracelets. 'Bist du eine Jüdin?' one of them asked me as he entered the flat. If I'd denied it he might have left. 'Ja,' I replied, 'ich bin Jüdin.'

'So, Jüdin, everything I'm taking you're giving me as a present. Verstanden?'

Others came too. Under the pretext that they were searching for arms they pulled out drawers and ransacked the baskets of things our relatives had left with us.

But that was later. When we returned to Narbutt Street there was no glass in the windows and no gas, and since we had a gas cooker we had nothing to cook on. So my husband got hold of some coal and a stove. He bought it on Graniczna Street or Bagno Street, where there were large warehouses with iron stoves and cookers. We put the stove-pipe into the rubbish chute and used coal to cook on.

My husband bought some glass too. The windows were glazed by Father Puder's brother. Although originally a Jew, he was the parish priest of All Saints' Church on Grzybowski Square. The glazier,

4

a tall slim young man with fair hair, did not look Jewish at all. He didn't convert, and he told us about his brother while he was puttying our windows.

From our dining-room window you could see an enormous red flag with a swastika blowing in the wind from the roof of a tall building.

Milk and meat were hard to get. Not all the shops were open and you couldn't buy everything you needed. One day Irena came back from town with a turkey on her back. She'd managed to get hold of a live turkey and that's how she brought it back. She had a canvas bag with straps with her and so she put the turkey into the bag and strapped it on her back. 'But it was gobbling in my ear,' she said, 'and people were staring at me.'

It was October now, very cold this year. It snowed half-way through the month and from our kitchen window you could see the graves of people killed by the bombs or cannon fire. I'll never forget how, at the beginning of the war, a few corpses were carried into our courtyard from the street. I gave the people who brought them a blanket to cover the corpses with. While they were lying there a dog ran into the yard and cocked its leg just where the heads were.

The Germans were now coming for our furniture almost every day. They had a team of Jews with them to carry the furniture downstairs and load it onto a lorry waiting by the gate. The Jews were rounded up on the street and it sometimes happened that people took their own furniture downstairs. My husband was rounded up on Marszalkowska Street and helped to load fur linings from Apfelbaum's shop onto a German lorry. A friend of ours, Mr Spinka, helped bring down his best friend's furniture.

One day we were all at home. An officer with a leather whip in his hand came and asked my husband, 'Geben Sie mir die Adressen von reichen Juden, von prominenten Juden. Wer ist hier in Warschau ein prominenter Jude?'

'Ich bin ein prominenter Jude,' replied my husband.

'Die Adressen!' threatened the German, lifting his whip.

'Ich gebe keine.'

The officer made as if to whip him but Nina threw herself at her father with a cry.

At this time there was a strange woman in Warsaw who attacked Jews. Once she attacked my husband as he was walking down the street. 'I know you, you Jewish aristocrat,' she shouted. Many of our friends had come across her.

5

More and more Jews were trying to leave. Some were going east and others west. At this time it was still possible to go west but you had to know how to organize it and who to turn to. It was said that the most important thing to do was to become a Christian. Ryszard's sister sent us a letter. Her husband was an Italian Catholic and they lived in Milan. She urged Ryszard, who had returned to Warsaw, to go to Milan with Marysia and the child, and likewise her sister, Tosia Lawendel, with her husband and son.

Tosia Lawendel had herself and her closest relatives christened without giving the matter much thought and without asking anyone. She settled the formalities and left for her sister's, taking her husband's nephew with her as well. But as for Marysia and her husband and child leaving, it all came to nothing because of the terrible way Ryszard's mother reacted. 'I'd rather see him among the dead than see him betray his religion,' she shouted.

That was at the very beginning of the occupation. We didn't know that in a few years' time you could simply buy papers where you'd figure as a Catholic and have a new name even if you'd never crossed the threshold of a church.

Not everyone was able to go abroad and not everyone had relatives in Italy or Spain, but hundreds of Jews were christened at this time, even people who couldn't speak Polish well, as they all thought that changing their religion would help them survive the war. The reason being that Jews had already started being repressed and arrested, mainly among the intelligentsia. From among our friends the Ickowicz brothers, who were architects and friends of Dr Radzinowicz, were arrested in a pension on Polna Street, and Teofil Konzon from Lodz was arrested at the same time. Hercman the engineer, Borensztein and his son, Moses Sobelman, Hilary Tempel, the lawyer Belkes, and Held were all arrested. It was said that they were sent to a camp in Stutthof near Gdansk and that they would return later. But none of them ever did.

When the order to wear white armbands with blue Stars of David was issued, we put them on our sleeves. So now the Germans could know for sure who was Jewish. They could now recognize me and my daughters, even though we didn't look very Jewish. There were hundreds and thousands of people like us. But take that old Jew of eighty, that old man with a white beard down to his waist, wearing a traditional Jewish hat and long coat. I met him on Pulawska Street, opposite Narbutt Street, and he lives in my memory like a photographic negative. Did he need this mark of recognition?

6

For a long time after the order some people deliberately stayed at home. They didn't want to make trouble for themselves, but they didn't want to put on a white armband. Walking along Narbutt Street there was a time when I could see the lawyer, Leon Berenson, sitting in the window of his ground floor flat every day. But I never met him on the street.

Some people from Lodz rented a flat on the second floor of the annexe of our house. There were two married couples. We knew they were Jewish and they looked like Jews. But they didn't wear armbands. They milled about Narbutt Street and Pulawska Street, went into shops and liked to talk to the neighbours. They were very sure of themselves. At that time it was easy to strike up acquaintances and so one day we asked them, 'How come you don't wear armbands?'

'We are allowed not to wear them,' they said and smiled. 'We've got Karaite papers.'

The Karaites were a Jewish sect but they were beyond the reach of German persecution. The Germans didn't consider them to be Jews, that we knew. But the very possibility of buying papers, and in this case papers which could be a defensive shield, astonished and intrigued us. After all, they hadn't said they were Karaites, only that they had Karaite papers. There weren't many Karaites in Warsaw. Most of them lived in the Wilno region of eastern Poland. But there were some in the Ukraine and the Crimea as well. Once when I was looking through statistics of Warsaw University I came across four students listed as Karaites. After we left Narbutt Street we heard that these Jews had died at the hands of the Germans even though they had Karaite papers.

Mr and Mrs Kalisz and their daughter Maryla and their son Mietek were refugees from Lodz and they rented a flat at 22 Narbutt Street. It was very easy to get to know people at that time, especially Jews, as we clung to each other because of our common misfortune. So I became friendly with Mrs Kalisz, and Nina with Maryla, who was her own age. One day when I was at Mrs Kalisz's I met some young men who were talking to Maryla and Mietek in German. She saw my surprise and when I was saying goodbye she whispered, 'They're school friends of Maryla's. Their fathers are German factory owners.' As it turned out, a few years later Maryla and her brother owed their lives to these school friends of theirs.

Yes, these were very hard times. But once something funny happened and amused us, although at the same time it terrified us because everything connected with the Germans was unsafe and could end up badly. My brother Leon, who was a musician, lived with us at the beginning of the occupation and when he shaved he used to leave some hair on his upper lip, creating a moustache. When he was crossing Pulawska or Narbutt Street (this was before we had to wear armbands) the German soldiers he met saluted him, thinking he was German. All because of his moustache which was just like Hitler's.

About half-way through November the Germans issued a decree ordering Jews to hand over their gold. Anyone who failed to comply would be executed. I had inherited 500 gold dollars from my father who had died before the war. I took the gold to the Polish Bank on the corner of Danilowiczowska Street and Bielanska Street and handed it in to the German authorities in return for a receipt on a small piece of pink paper. An old man who looked like a worker was standing behind me in the queue and he said to me, 'Taking gold to the bank? The best bank is your own pocket.'

I didn't say a word. I knew he was right. When I got home I gave the receipt to my husband and he slipped it into his waistcoat pocket. At that time he was still director of the Henrykow distillery and yeast factory and was still driving – although more often than not he went on foot – to the offices on Elektoralna Street. Or to Czacki Street where the offices of the yeast business were. But you couldn't call it work. Jews were being removed from higher positions everywhere and Jewish businesses were gradually going into German hands. But he still went to Elektoralna Street. It might have been out of habit. So when he was stopped by two Gestapo men on Marszalkowska Street he said, 'I have given the German authorities my property in gold dollars but you're arresting me all the same.'

'Where's the proof?' they asked.

He looked in his waistcoat pocket, found the pink paper and gave it to them. They let him go and he came home. But they kept the receipt. If at first we'd regretted handing over the gold dollars, now we thanked God we'd done so. Perhaps they saved his life. 'There was a time when we wanted to bury them under the paved terrace in Wieliszew but we didn't do it because we kept thinking that Waclaw Taperek was spying on us,' we said on Narbutt Street now.

So my husband still went to Elektoralna Street. It was a long way from Narbutt Street to Elektoralna Street. But he walked all the same. Ryszard worked at the Jewish Council. One day Irena announced, 'If I can't be a doctor then I'll be a nurse,' and enrolled at the nursing school at the Jewish Hospital, 'na Czystem'. 'I get there on a tram with a star of David on it,' she told us.

Marysia had completed three exams for her higher degree, but she enrolled on a tailoring course at Mrs Natkin's. 'You've no idea what an expert she is,' she told us with delight, 'but it's not surprising because she studied at the tailoring academy in Paris.'

Our motto now was: change our habits and learn a trade. And so Nina went to the Chwats who had a well-known hat shop on Kredytowa Street and learnt millinery there. Even I learnt corsetry from a certain Miss Marta who drove over from Zelazna Street in the afternoons. I could see that the general situation was getting worse every day.

In the mornings I looked after Marysia's little boy. I held his hand and we walked along Pulawska Street and Rakowiecka Street, then we turned into Wisniowa Street where he used to live before the war. He always recognized his house. We both liked unusual sights and unusual situations. We walked along the streets looking for something unusual, hoping to come across something we would remember for a long time. One day we saw a horse on a cart. Wasn't that unusual? And so we looked curiously at the horse and talked about it for a long time. Another time we saw a porcelain dachshund in the window of a small sweet-shop on Rakowiecka Street. Macius was delighted. 'I can see an elongated dog,' he said. We remembered the dog for a long time as well.

Sometimes we dressed Macius in Nina's apron for fun and he wiped the plates in the kitchen dressed as a girl. He didn't have a lot of fun, and nor did we, and so he took the place of the theatre and concerts, our former amusements. That child with the curly fair hair, and grey eyes which were so comprehending and so interested in everything, never cried. He gravely watched the German officer walking around our flat as if it were the floor of a stable. The officer didn't greet us when he entered, he didn't say goodbye when he left. Once he took an eiderdown, which he'd snatched from an unmade bed. Another time, he opened the wardrobe himself, took what he fancied out of it and put it all in his pocket.

At this time, when we heard about people leaving for abroad and the mysterious manipulations which preceded their journeys, we thought that in time we might manage to emigrate as well. Bronek Kornblum visited us nearly every day. He was a lawyer and a colleague of Ryszard's. He had a brother who was an architect in

Brazil and as he'd always wanted to join him there he had learnt Spanish. 'It would be good to learn Spanish from Bronek,' we said, 'it might come in useful if we manage to go to Brazil. Who's got the time? Who could learn quickest?' They said I could. Yes, I was to learn from Bronek, it might come in useful for all of us some day.

Bronek brought a textbook and I had lessons from him regularly until he was caught by the Germans. He dug ditches in Falenty. When he returned to Warsaw a month or two later, Spanish lessons were out of the question. Later the Goralskis, who had come from Lodz, told us that Portuguese is spoken in Brazil, not Spanish. The Goralski family managed to escape to the west via Katowice as early as the beginning of April 1940, to Brazil.

My husband's sister longed to leave and had the means to do so. She also wanted her younger brothers, Edward and Leon, to leave with their families. But they had an eighty-year-old mother who lived with us. Could they leave her behind? They discussed and debated the matter for ages, and in their thoughts they went and returned, and in the end they stayed. Because there was no incentive, no order from their old mother to go. The plans were never discussed in front of her so she had no idea what was going on. She had no inkling that they'd perish if they stayed.

Round the corner of Narbutt Street, just next door on Pulawska Street, was Mr Cetnarowicz's large grocery shop. We sometimes bought food there. I went there one day holding Macius by the hand, and sitting at the till I saw Halinka, the daughter of my cousin Marian who was in Lwow with his wife at that time. Halinka wasn't wearing an armband. I gathered that she must have married Kazik Cetnarowicz if she was sitting so openly in his father's shop. When I was paying she told me that she had taken a two roomed flat at 20 Narbutt Street, in our house. Her father was joint owner of the house.

Kazik was tall and blond, and a handsome boy despite a disfiguring scar on his face. He got it when he was injured in a car accident. They came to visit us sometimes. We toasted General de Gaulle over a bottle of fruit wine, saying, 'Long live de Gaulle'. So now because Kazik Cetnarowicz had entered the family we could ask him more boldly to take some of our things and look after them. We were always very embarrassed when asking people. We asked him to take three kelims, otherwise they were bound to fall into the hands of the Germans. He agreed and took them to his father's villa in Skolimow.

One evening Marysia's friend Olek Bernstein dropped in. He had left Warsaw when the war started and was staying in Baranowicze. He'd come back for his parents. He was urging Marysia and Ryszard to go with him. He spent the night on the sofa in the hall so they had a lot of time to talk. Olek was a good-humoured and amusing boy. He never stopped talking about Baranowicze. Ryszard was prepared to go with Marysia and the child. But we were worried about Macius. The journey was so difficult – in the dark and maybe in the rain as well. 'So it's no,' said Olek as he was leaving. 'Well then, so long.'

So some people were leaving for Russia, others via Italy for Brazil, and some via Japan for the United States. And there were even some who managed to get to Palestine, via Wilno, Odessa and Constantinople. Rysio Bychowski, a colleague of Nina's, Dr Bychowski's son, was one of the people who went to America via Wilno and Japan. Everyone knew that he was in love with Nina. On 30 November he came on his bike to say goodbye to her. My husband had been arrested the day before and taken as a hostage to the Academic House on Grojecka Street. Scores of men, both Poles and Jews, were taken at that time. On the anniversary of the November Rising the Germans were expecting anti-German demonstrations. They threatened to kill the hostages if there were any disturbances.

Rysio wrote to Nina in the ghetto through the Red Cross until the time when the Jews started being deported. Then all postal communications were interrupted. Nina kept the letters and always carried them in her handbag. They were her amulets. She imagined that they protected her at this dangerous time. Rysio enrolled at a university in California and worked as his professor's servant to earn his keep. Then he went to England and joined the Air Force. By chance he became friendly with our niece, Irena Radzinowicz née Szereszewska. Years later she told us that he worried whether Nina would survive the war in Poland. As it turned out, it was Nina who survived the war although she was often only a hair's breadth away from death, while he died over the English Channel.

Dulman was a cobbler who lived on Wisniowa Street in a tiny house, in fact a tiny whitewashed hut. He had a fat wife with black eyes and black hair, and three small children. Most of his customers were Poles because there were few Jews on Wisniowa Street. He mended our shoes too. The Germans took nothing from Dulman. On the contrary, they even gave him something. They gave him leather for beautiful officers' boots. But most of the leather disappeared into

11

the darkness of the cellar under the kitchen with its hatch covered with a faded carpet, or into one of the many stores or outbuildings to be found in the yard behind Dulman's wooden house.

I can safely say that while we were becoming poorer, Dulman was getting richer. He didn't mend shoes for anyone any longer. We were his only customers. He did our shoes out of friendship, out of the goodness of his heart, out of neighbourliness. He liked to natter and complain about the Jewish fate, but mainly to speak his mind about the ways of the world. Because Dulman believed that Fortune governs human affairs, and he continued to believe it right up to the end. He used to finish a conversation saying, 'Don't worry, Mrs Szereszewska. There'll be a wood where there used to be a wood, rye will grow again where it used to grow, and grass will grow and flowers will bloom again where the meadows used to be.'

Our Polish servant Genia cooked on the iron stove with the pipe stuck into the rubbish chute in the wall. Genia was a happy girl. We inherited her from our cousin Witold Szpilfogel who had gone over to the Russian side with his family. By chance, by accident, he didn't get to Wilno like other relations of ours but lost his way and went to the small town of Telechany in the Pinsk region, and he was killed there later together with his wife and daughter by the Germans.

It often surprised us that Genia wanted to work for Jews. Especially in such a large family where there was so much work. We thought it was due to the fact that she knew us from the days when we walked along the streets sure of ourselves, when we didn't feel German fists on our backs, and we didn't wear the humiliating sign on our sleeves.

We had only lived on Narbutt Street for two years. Before that we lived at 3 Poznanska Street. The engineer Marek Lichtenbaum lived on the floor below us together with his wife and two sons. A Polish servant who was a friend of our Genia's had worked there for 20 years. She was called Antosia. One day Genia came home with her shopping basket very excited.

'Do you know what? I met Antosia on Narbutt Street. They live two or three houses away from us.'

'So what?'

'I talked to her. She said that even if there's a ghetto she's going with them. That's what she's decided.'

Rumours were already in the air. People were already talking about it anxiously. Some believed the rumours, others didn't. But there was no denying that the Germans were building walls. They'd build them one day, then knock them down the next and put them up somewhere else. Naturally they built them using Jewish labour. But even the workers didn't know if families suffering from typhoid or other people were going to live within the walls, because the part of town surrounded by walls was going to be called Seuchengebiet.

'So what did you say, Genia?'

'I said I'd do the same. We talked and both agreed. If anything happens we're both going to the ghetto.'

2 · 6 *Walicow Street*

On 10 July 1940 we moved from 20 Narbutt Street to a three-roomed flat at 6 Walicow Street, number 12 on the fifth floor. We acquired the flat after long and difficult negotiations conducted by young Jakub, the assistant administrator of this enormous house. The owner of the flat, Izaak Mayzner, had moved out to his father's house on Chlodna Street. The flat was empty, bomb damaged and full of rubble.

We signed the contract in May. The most important clause was our undertaking to return the flat to Izaak Mayzner as soon as the war was over. It took a month to repair the flat. We had to rebuild the damaged walls, repair the broken stoves, glaze the windows. Young Jakub was to look after all this. He was tall and slim with a long face and a calm voice. He used to come to Narbutt Street with a file and spread the documents out on the table.

'I'm simply being careful,' he said, running his pencil along rows of figures. 'One day the flat is sure to be in the ghetto everyone's been talking so much about lately.'

It was meant to be in the ghetto, but for the time being Walicow Street wasn't separated from the other Warsaw streets. Poles and Jews walked along it freely. So on 10 July we moved into the flat. In fact it was half a spacious six-roomed flat. All the windows of our three rooms looked out onto the courtyard, while the windows of the other half looked out over the street.

Marysia and Ryszard and their son took the first room, Nina and my mother the second room, and the third room, the dining room, was also our bedroom. Our middle daughter, Irena, didn't live with us. She was at the nursing school on the corner of Panska Street and Marianska Street. But she came to see us every day. When she crossed the long wide hall she would glance at the clock in the corner and the glass-fronted bookcase full of books.

In the dining room, apart from the bed and the couch, we placed the ash sideboard, the table with folding wings, the birch chest of drawers with a mirror, and the veneered birchwood wardrobe. The

14

balcony window shone with new panes in its yellow frame. It was in a deep niche that made the room dark and sad in the day time. Outside the window there was a narrow balcony with a round railing. When you stood there you could see blue-grey roofs at various heights and deep down below the yellow courtyard paved with small cobbles.

Diagonally across the courtyard an old grey-haired man sat in an armchair on a fifth-floor balcony from morning till evening. He was said to be a Soviet citizen. A fair-haired woman with an American passport lived on the fourth floor on the street side. She didn't mind showing her passport. 'Would you like to see it? Here it is.' From the windows of her flat you could see Walicow Street with its narrow uneven pavements, grey entrance doors and shabby shops. Genia occupied the servant's room. She slept there under a flowery eiderdown.

So now we were on Walicow Street. We had followed young Jakub's advice and had taken the precaution of getting a flat within the anticipated ghetto. And sure enough, four months later Walicow Street found itself within the ghetto walls. Until that happened I took Marysia's son for a walk along Twarda Street and Zelazna Street as far as Aleje Jerozolimskie every day and nobody stopped us. I held his hand and we looked at the shop windows with their toys, kitchen-ware and haberdashery. A white armband with a blue star was sewn onto the sleeve of my jacket.

Then we returned home the same way. The child was quiet and calm. He never asked for a toy or a cake from the shop windows. He looked at the German soldiers gravely and silently. 'Are you tired?' I asked. 'No,' he replied. Every day we passed the tea shop on Zelazna Street. By a strange coincidence the sign had my maiden name on it. We turned into Twarda Street where the barbed wire still was.

The ghetto was only closed half-way through November. Until then a hawker, a Polish woman from near Warsaw, used to come via the kitchen entrance and sell us butter, eggs and even hens. Our dressmaker from Powisle once came to the front door and sold us some smoked bacons. She had taken up hawking as she couldn't live off dressmaking. We were surprised that she had been able to find us.

One day a young Pole who was a complete stranger to us came through the kitchen door and returned my sister's identity card. She had lost it in the courtyard of the house at 25 Marszalkowska Street.

She lived there until she rented a room in the annexe at 6 Walicow Street. Also just before the ghetto was closed my husband's former clerk, Miss Rembielinska, came to the front door to say goodbye and return thirty zlotys he had once lent her.

'I'm giving you back the thirty zlotys, you might need them.'

'Please keep them, I don't need them yet.'

She had tears in her eyes. She stood in the hall leaning against the bookcase. She wouldn't stay and rest, not even for a moment. She didn't know any of us apart from him.

We weren't the only ones who moved into the house on Walicow Street. Other members of the family gradually moved in too from various Warsaw streets and some even came from Lodz. Some of them rented flats, others sub-rented rooms, and others still moved into the adjacent streets.

One day my brother-in-law Leon Szereszewski came from Sliska Street and brought his stamp albums along for safe-keeping. 'Hide them for me,' he said, 'they'll be safer with you.' We started looking around for a good hiding-place. In the end we lifted up the ornamental top of the bookcase, a low rectangle which was hollow inside, and slid Leon's stamps in there.

Opposite stood the tall, black clock. It had a nice chime and that was why we brought it with us from Narbutt Street. It stood diagonally in the corner and so there was an empty space behind it. We fastened some string in there and on it we hung the smoked bacons we'd bought from the dressmaker. You couldn't see anything at all. We also hung up a piece of pork fat that was already going yellow. We'd bought it from the tenant on the third floor. We thought it was such an excellent hiding-place that we now looked at the clock through completely different eyes than before when we only wanted to know the time. We wondered what else we could use it for.

We had been plundered so often by the Germans in our old flat that we were searching for a safe hiding-place for the rest of our jewellery in the new flat. One of us said, 'Let's hide it between the springs and the cogs in the clock's mechanism.' But another of us pointed out that the clock would seize up and stop chiming. It won't chime? We looked round the rooms, looked at the pelmets, the stove, the chairs, the pot with the shrivelled plant on the balcony. We finally hid some gold bracelets, brooches and earrings we had inherited from our grandmothers, and which were of sentimental value, in a box of beans which stood in the dresser. We put two gold

16

twenty-dollar coins into a cardboard box under the medicine bottle. You could be sentenced to death for possessing gold dollars and our flesh crawled when we looked at them.

Taught by experience in the flat at Narbutt Street we were sure that we would be harassed here by the Germans as well. How much thought, how much imagination we had to develop in order to conceal our property. You might think that sewing jewellery into an upholstered chair is an excellent idea. But it isn't, because there might come a time when you have to leave the flat there and then, and in the panic you won't be able to recognize the right chair. Hadn't we heard about cases like that? We were told the story of a certain Jew who only just managed in time to pull a diamond out of a wall he had plastered it into.

We had an antique footstool covered with faded tapestry. We wanted to sew our jewellery into that, but had second thoughts. The father of one of our daughter's friends came up with an extremely clever idea. He sewed all his valuables into an old, worn sofa cushion. The dirty horsehair cushion couldn't be of any interest to the Germans. And if he had to leave the flat quickly all he had to do was take the cushion with him and nobody would find it odd. An old man carrying a small cushion, nothing unusual. But what about us? Could we carry the footstool and go into the unknown with it?

The same went for the flowerpot with the shrivelled plant which attracted us for a while. It belonged to Artur Mayzner and had always stood in the corner of the balcony. We had heard about people who concealed their valuables in flowerpots. We were stopped from doing so by the fear that the servant – we still had a servant at that time – might throw the useless flowerpot away one day.

Even though Jews were being plundered by the Germans they didn't always do the sensible thing. One lady pressed a diamond into a piece of soap and placed it on the soap-tray by the kitchen sink. When the Germans came, one of them saw the soap and as it was a valuable commodity at that time he took it and slipped it into his pocket. We heard how Goldfarb the lawyer made a false bottom in a small plain cupboard and hid his wife's jewellery there. But the Germans took a fancy to the cheap little cupboard and ordered it to be carried out together with the other furniture. It might even have been Goldfarb who carried out his own furniture, taking the valuable cupboard with a heavy heart.

17

So we decided to use the box of beans and we had no misgivings, although we knew that at our relatives' the Germans had poured all the preserves out of their jars onto the floor and had even looked for gold in the baby's nappies.

The kitchen corridor was behind the dining room. Four doors led off from the corridor: to the servant's room, the kitchen, the bathroom and the toilet. A black gas meter hung high up on the wall. Opposite was a deep shelf where we put our empty cases and sacks. We found a telephone on the shelf. The previous tenant had concealed it in the darkest corner. A telephone with a receiver, covered with dust and plaster. We examined it very curiously. Genia came out of the kitchen and examined the telephone attentively as well. Then we threw it back onto the shelf. It described an arc in the air, hit the wall mutely and disappeared behind an old brown suitcase.

The coal stove which we had brought with us from Narbutt Street stood in the middle of the small kitchen. Although it was in the way here we wouldn't part with it for anything because it was so useful at this critical time. There was gas and electricity at Walicow Street and a clerk came every month and we paid him the bill, but the war was still on and nobody knew what tomorrow would bring. The stove was our mainstay. We believed it would help us again when the time came.

The gas and electricity people came every month. They were both Poles. A third Pole was the stove maker. The stove in the hall wasn't drawing and so we got hold of a stove maker. He brought a bucket of clay, took the grate out of the stove, sealed the holes and gaps and put the grate back. Although the ghetto wasn't closed yet it was strange to see that Pole kneeling in front of our stove. The fourth Pole who came was the collector whom we paid five zlotys a month for the electric floor polisher we had bought on instalments just before the war. It lay on the shelf and was completely useless because we didn't look after the floors now.

Apart from the Poles who came legally, we saw a fifth one too. We met him in the entrance door of our house when he slipped in sideways and didn't look anyone in the face. He wore a tram driver's cap and came to see his Jewish girl-friend who lived on the ground floor.

We kept the front door on a chain, if we remembered. When the lock jammed, the door wouldn't close and so it stayed ajar. Beggars came to the kitchen door and the front door. Once when we forgot the chain they stole father's warm coat.

As I've already said, the ash sideboard, which had once stood in my grandmother's flat, stood in the dining room now. We kept our supplies in it. On top was sugar, tea, milk powder, and jam, and underneath were the two tin boxes of beans where we had hidden our jewellery. Next to it there was a narrow wall cupboard where we arranged a.few porcelain figures from Saxony, three old cups and a crystal carafe. In this solid house with its square of sky above the roofs, these delicate knick-knacks were strangely conspicuous because they were so unusual and subtly beautiful. So we often said, 'The Germans are sure to take them if they come. Let's sell them.' But my husband replied, 'No. We might have our own house again one day.'

Yes, we had the flat. We lived in it and breathed in its walls. We were still a family in it and had a place of our own within its strong walls. Strong walls. We knew how to appreciate them. From one of our windows we could see a huge hole in the wall of the side-annexe. Two spinsters lived there and through the hole we could see them moving around the room. They never had it repaired.

So on 10 July when we arrived at 6 Walicow Street on a large cart full of furniture, our Polish Genia came with us too. She was still with us in August and September. She managed to make supper for Tietz, the German administrator who had taken over the yeast factory which belonged to our family in Henrykow. My husband was the director of this factory and before the ghetto was closed he once invited Tietz for supper. Tietz was a German but one of us, as it were. He came from Lodz and spoke very good Yiddish. The strangest thing was that he never concealed it. His parents had a dry-cleaner's on Piotrkowska Street or some other street. Tietz accepted the invitation and even brought his wife along, a slim, quiet and melancholic woman.

Genia roasted two chickens and made some borscht with dumplings. With the meat she served mashed potatoes and cold, soured red cabbage. Then she brought in a large bowl of fruit compote. Tietz was jovial and amusing. He drank and ate with moderation. His wife was immersed in sad thoughts and didn't say a word all evening.

When notices appeared on the walls of houses in the ghetto at the beginning of November announcing that all Polish servants and all Poles in general had to leave the Jewish district, Genia protested. She announced that she would stay with us. She wasn't the only

19

one because the wife of the engineer Lichtenbaum also had a Polish servant who'd worked for her for 20 years. ' "I won't leave her for anything", that's what she told me today, because I met her on Prosta Street.'

Then the ghetto was closed. So in order to make it easier for Genia to decide what to do, we regretfully said to her, 'We've paid you sixty zlotys a month regularly up to now. But we don't know if we can keep on paying the same in future. We're not sure.' So Genia packed a suitcase and a bundle and Marysia accompanied her along Panska Street and Sliska Street as far as Sienna Street, to the wall bristling with glass.

After Genia left Mrs Jelen worked for us. She came from Kalisz and liked to talk about her wealthy life before the war. 'I had a large flat with a balcony on the main street, and my two grown-up daughters played the piano.' Neither of them was with her now. The older one went to the Caucasus and the younger one married a Pole and lived in the country. The younger one's Persian lamb coat was hanging up in our kitchen cupboard. Mrs Jelen was about forty-five and short-sighted. She always wore glasses. She spoke Polish in an odd way. Every sentence she said contained the little word 'then', it was probably a characteristic of the region she came from. She never mentioned she had a husband and we were convinced she was a widow. One day we opened the door to the servant's room by accident and were surprised to see a collection of bread and a short, squat, poorly dressed man.

'Who's that man?'

'Then that's my husband,' she replied. 'He sells bread.'

We considered. We conferred. One of us said, 'It's November now. We're using the stoves. Perhaps it's just as well. He can bring coal and wood up from the cellar. At least we know who he is.'

One minute Mrs Jelen was worried that her daughters weren't with her and then the next minute she was pleased that they were free. The fact that her son-in-law was a Pole didn't bother her. She quickly accepted the marriage. She watched the fur coat like a hawk. It hung in the brush compartment of the kitchen cupboard. At first her husband only came in the mornings, then we saw him in the evenings as well. We found out that he stayed the night. 'Kaziu', that's what she called him. He didn't reply. He was usually silent. 'Kaziu, bring two buckets of coal from the cellar. Don't look for the key, you've got it on you.' He didn't say anything. Shortly afterwards it came out that he was taking and selling our coal. When we told our caretaker he smiled. He smiled as if he'd known about it for a while.

At that time there were no Polish caretakers left in the ghetto any longer. After the memorable announcement about all Poles having to leave the Jewish district, the caretakers moved out and not a single one stayed. Their places were taken by Jews who fought over the jobs and moved heaven and earth to get them. We heard of cases where lawyers were working as caretakers. You had to have a whole heap of friends in the right places to obtain the position.

The caretaker at 6 Walicow Street was called Zysie Fligelman. He was thirty-two. Tall and strongly built, he had an enormous nose and looked typically Jewish. In fact he was ugly, but he was engaging because he liked to laugh and joke. Before the war he had worked as a chauffeur on my family's Wola Krysztoporska estate. He used to wear a brown leather jacket, a leather peaked cap and boots. He worked conscientiously and he was trusted. He was proud and never accepted tips. He was called Zygmunt then. Most of the house at 6 Walicow Street belonged to our family, so that's how he got the job. He immediately started using his Jewish name again. He wasn't a snob. He was now living only among Jews so he stopped using the name Zygmunt because there was no sense in it in the closed ghetto.

He occupied the flat that the Polish caretaker, Mateusz or Mikolaj his name was, had lived in, to the left of the gate. He had a small, dark and cold room with a window overlooking the square courtyard. He immediately found himself an assistant, a thin lad with red hair, and gave him a broom. He always had a broom as well and was rarely seen without it. He didn't wear a smart jacket or semi-military cap any longer, just a plain, blue cap pulled right down over his ears. He was said to have luck with women, and people often joked about it in his presence. He didn't admit it but just laughed. His smile reached from ear to ear. But there must have been some truth in the rumours because a Polish girl came to live with him in the ghetto shortly afterwards. He had charmed her when he lived in Wola Krysztoporska.

She was twenty-eight, an attractive, dark girl who looked Ukrainian. It turned out later that their relationship had been going on for years. Her younger brother had been married for a long time but she hadn't got married and everyone knew why. She turned up one day with a small suitcase and lived in the caretaker's lodge as Fligelman's wife. She put a white armband with a blue Star of David on the sleeve of her Zakopane sheepskin and got hold of a yellow ration card which she used for getting food rations. People called her Mrs Fligelman and she used the name too. Apart from our family I don't think anyone else knew her secret. She had a round childish face, black hair and thick eyebrows over grey eyes. She had a calm manner and didn't talk much. She wore a tight blue woollen cap from morning till night. She must have been cold in the caretaker's lodge. Her name was Zofia Margasinska and her father was a mechanic in Wola Krysztoporska. Fligelman was good to her, but if he was pleased that she was with him, he was pleased inside. He wasn't in the habit of showing his feelings.

One day she went to her parents. We were sure she wouldn't come back. We often joked about it in the cellar when Fligelman was helping us stack the wood or remove shoots from the potatoes. But Zosia did come back. We could imagine what sort of a battle she must have fought at home. Her sisters were crying. Her father in gloomy silence. Her mother with the youngest child on her knee, 'Zocha, Zocha, your life's in danger. People are saying the Germans are going to finish the Jews off.' Zosia didn't show them her white armband. She had hidden it carefully by sewing it into the sleeve of her coat under the lining. If she entered the ghetto again – through the lawcourts on Leszno Street or allowed through by a guard who turned a blind eye – she could immediately put it on again.

The cellars at 6 Walicow Street were solidly built. Low but comfortable with long barred windows. The house had a lot of cellars. We had two, one for coal, the other for wood, potatoes and sauerkraut. If Fligelman didn't have the time, the caretaker from number five on the other side of the road bought wood and coal for us. He was called Abram Sobelman. Before the war he was a driver and had a taxi. He was a relative of ours, a cousin three times removed, but we didn't know him at all.

My husband once got into his taxi by chance on the corner of Pulawska Street and Narbutt Street. Suddenly he heard, 'Hello. We're related, you know. I'm Sobelman from Henrykow.'

'So you're Sobelman? I knew your father and grandfather very well.'

Now he was a caretaker in the ghetto. As luck would have it, he was opposite the house we lived in. Sobelman had thick black hair, an energetic face and large strong hands. The odd thing was that although he was the right height and well-built, he had a hump on one shoulder. We didn't know him at all before the war. But here, in the ghetto, we were often surprised at how important these blood relationships had become. He had two rooms and a kitchen on the street side of the ground floor. He might have installed himself earlier than Zysie Fligelman. Or the flat might have been his from before the war. His wife was a painter and he was proud of it. But she was ill. She was always in bed and looked at her easels by the window from her bed.

I went there a few times to sort a few small matters out. The house was old and gloomy with a paved courtyard and gave off damp and the sour smell of poverty. When I greeted his sick wife I could catch her sad glance directed at a still life she had started. A jug, a book, two apples and a rose. Will I finish the picture, said her eyes? Then his mother and sister moved in with him. He didn't have a father any more, he had been deported by the Germans to a camp in the first months of the war and had never returned.

The sister had a Polish boyfriend, a railwayman from Pruszkow. She lived with him for a while but when she became ill with her lungs she came to the ghetto, to her brother's. And the mother came after her. So now there were four of them. Interestingly enough the Polish railwayman didn't forget his lover. He would be seen from time to time on Walicow Street, knocking on the door of Sobelman's flat. Although she was at death's door he still wanted her to come and live with him, and the mother too. But she wasn't interested in anything any more by that time, and she didn't want to go with him.

It's curious that this relationship between a Pole and a Jewish girl didn't interest anybody now. Before the war it would have angered her family and friends greatly. Sensitivity had become blunted. People had become indifferent. People lived for the hard present and had a vague foreboding of worse times yet to come. Things like this were excused and tolerated. They were nothing compared with the reality which was becoming increasingly threatening all the time.

Some people might even have thought it was a pity she fell ill. If she'd been his wife she might have survived the war peacefully. They both died on 10 November 1941. Pinkiert's hearse took Abram Sobelman's wife and sister away at the same time. The hearse stood on the street, poor and dilapidated, harnessed to a grey horse. It stood in the middle of the road between two houses. The gates of both these houses were wide open. My mother-in-law, Michalina Szereszewska, died the same day and she was taken to the cemetery in the same hearse. She was eighty-three years old and had died on her birthday. And so when we followed her in the hearse we were also following Sobelman's wife and sister, and other dead people

23

the undertaker had collected on the way. They had no names or family names, not even numbers.

When Abram Sobelman returned from the cemetery he washed his hands in the kitchen sink, took the broom and swept the courtyard, just like he used to do every day. His mother opened the windows and washed the floors in the whole flat. There were just the two of them now. They accepted their fate quickly.

The hawkers we bought from at that time could be divided into two categories, the front door hawkers and the more lowly ones who used the kitchen door. The kitchen door was used by professional hawkers such as Rachela and Sara whom we bought meat from. Beef at first, then only horseflesh. The kitchen door was also used by a woman who lived in the attic in the house opposite and whose husband was in Russia. She used to bring her four-year-old daughter along with her. 'No news from your husband?' 'None.' We bought butter and cheese from her and sometimes a piece of pork fat. She lived with a thin, dark woman who earned her living taking in washing.

The front door was used by society ladies who had taken up hawking because of circumstances. Stefa Pinus, for example. She sold us pork fat, and sometimes socks and sometimes packet soups. Her sister was the wife of our cousin who had gone to Russia with his family when the war started.

'Have you heard from them?' She hadn't.

'But we've received a letter through the Red Cross,' we said. 'Here it is.'

Her sister wrote that her husband was working in a sawmill as a book-keeper. That they were living with a peasant, that the accommodation was poor but the food was plentiful. She had recently gone to Lwow by canal. She had toothache so she had gone to the dentist. The canal journey was beautiful, 'but I'd like to come back to Warsaw. We feel strange here all the same and we miss the family.'

'She should stay there if she's doing well. She can miss us all she likes but she should stay all the same.' We were angry with them for knowing so little about us and perhaps even thinking that life in the ghetto was peaceful and secure.

The front door was used by Zofia Moscibrodzka, a sempstress who had made curtains for our family for years. She used to have a workshop on Twarda Street but she closed it and was now selling underwear and bedding. I bought two pairs of stockings from her and four sheets for 'after the war'. Strange how little we understood the situation in the first year after the ghetto was closed and how we still believed in surviving. And yet thousands of Jews had already been taken to camps we knew nothing about, including many acquaintances, and even friends.

Mrs Markowicz also came, my cousin's widow. Now she was selling soap, but before, when she could still receive parcels from her brother in Copenhagen, she used to sell smoked pork fat. She lived with distant relations and left a married daughter behind in Lodz. The second daughter managed to leave for Palestine with her husband and child. Her youngest daughter and her lawyer son were in Nowogrodek. 'Would you like to see their photographs?'

One day Mrs Lau, the music teacher, came to the front door. Her husband was an officer in the Polish Army and had been captured or killed, she didn't know. He was a smart man, an engineer. She was a real Rose of Sharon – black eyes, dark skin. They had one daughter, beautiful Martuska. Now she sold packet soup. Martuska looked after children on Karmelicka Street in return for her keep and a bed. 'Yes, times have changed. My husband hasn't come back from the war, unfortunately.' She was poorly dressed and gave off the smell of poverty.

Mr Widerszal, the engineer, lived underneath on the third floor. He set up an electrical repairs workshop in his flat. I once took him a kettle to be mended. 'My sister sells pork fat,' he said. 'Of course it's only for the time being, you understand.' She came to the front door one day and it would have been rude to refuse even though the fat was yellow and rancid. We flavoured soup with it and some of us fell ill.

The kitchen door hawkers said 'goodbye' and closed the door. We didn't have to fuss over them. The front door hawkers were offered tea and sometimes soup. They could use the toilet. We saw them to the door and sometimes continued our conversation when the door was already open.I saw Zofia Moscibrodzka to the landing. She was no longer young but she was good-looking and pleasant to talk to. I had known her for many years and she had never married. Now she suddenly did. At a time like this. That's why she needed money. 'Would you like to buy a sewing-machine from me?' she asked. 'I've got a few, one of them's even electric.'

The only exception was the woman in the green coat who also sold us horseflesh but came to the front door all the same. 'I can't risk meeting any of the competition at the kitchen door. I've got a child. I must earn some money.'

25

Our child – Marysia and Ryszard's son – still had his white cot and slept peacefully in it while the Germans were closing the ghetto. He was called Macius. He had grey eyes and blond curls. He kept his toys in the corner behind the bookcase. Puzzles, lotto, a trumpet, a doll's house. He liked the doll's house best. A friend of Nina's left him it when she was leaving for Lwow. The doll's house, the trumpet, and an opera hat. Ryszard's father had once brought him his old opera hat to play with. He used to run round the flat wearing a tight pullover, long white gaiters and the opera hat, trumpeting or singing his favourite song, *Du kleiner Offizier*.

He learnt the song from the gramophone which we'd brought with us from Narbutt Street together with our record collection. Listening to records was our greatest amusement at that time and we liked *The Jewish Wedding* most of all. Even Genia loved the music with its Hasidic songs. She stood in the door and clapped her hands with us. Our records were very popular. We often lent them out. They were always being borrowed by Mr Epsztein who used to own two linen shops on Nalewki Street. He was the man who hit on the clever idea of concealing all his valuables in the dirty old sofa cushion. 'Good morning,' he said, 'I've come for the lecords.' He came from Russia and didn't pronounce Polish correctly. 'Uncle Lecord's come,' shouted Macius.

The gramophone stood next to the balcony door on a kitchen stool covered with a cloth. One day two German officers came to the flat. They studied the gramophone and records for a long time. We thought they'd take them away but they didn't. They didn't take anything that time.

Ryszard used to recite *Ordon's Bastion* while he was shaving. Macius learnt a few excerpts from the poem. He knew almost the whole of *Alpuhara* by heart as well. We played with the child like a toy. We used to change the words of *Alpuhara* round for fun. Instead of saying 'Almanzor and a handful of knights' the child recited 'Fligelman and his red-haired assistant', which amused us greatly. When Ryszard's parents visited us they were speechless out of their love for the child. They watched him in silence with tears in their eyes. 'Maciula', sighed his granny.

They still lived on Sienna Street at that time, which was their first move from Marszalkowska Street. When Sienna Street was removed from the ghetto they moved to Wronia Street and then to Dzika Street, but they couldn't get used to it there at all. 'Is Maciula well?' Ryszard's mother used to ask, wiping her eyes with a handkerchief.

'Is he really well? We can't stand it here.' So Ryszard looked around and rented a room for them, just one room, in a huge house on the corner of Zelazna Street and Chlodna Street, in a flat with Hanka Chwat who had the hat shop.

'Is Maciula well?' Ryszard's mother asked at Chlodna Street. 'Is he really well?' She cried. This nomadic life had made her really nervous. She kept leaving her furniture behind every time she moved, it was old-fashioned and not worth much but she was attached to it with all her heart. She left her tall dresser at Sienna Street, her linen cupboard at Wronia Street, and her chest of drawers and kitchen cupboard at Dzika Street. All she took to Chlodna Street was the beds, just to be able to survive until the war ended.

Ryszard had a law degree and at this time he worked for the Jewish Council. He went from Walicow Street to Grzybowska Street every day. Marysia went to Nowolipki Street to a workshop producing dresses. She worked day after day for a Mrs Neumann and when she came home she ate her bowl of bean soup or pearl barley soup and a piece of horseflesh with potatoes. She still had the beautiful wide bed bought at Szczerbinski's, the low armchair with the down cushion, the oval walnut table and the old secretaire. The three gold twenty-dollar coins lay hidden in an almost inaccessible hiding place in the secretaire.

While Marysia was sewing in the workshop I took Macius for walks along the ghetto streets. I held his hand and we walked slowly along Prosta Street and Twarda Street. We passed the shop with horseflesh, then the shop window of the laundry with just the one dusty collar always displayed in it. I still had my husband's collars starched and ironed at that time and I used that laundry because it was the nearest. Past the laundry there was a rickshaw stand on the corner of Ciepla Street, and the wooden kiosk where Broncia from Poznanska Street sold vegetables. Then the bakery. I sometimes bought bread there but I didn't carry it in my hand any longer because of an incident with some boys who knocked me over. I put the loaf into the bottom of my basket and covered it with an apron.

We walked towards Grzybowska Street one time, and another time towards Zelazna Street as far as the barrier which divided the street. The Jewish district ended here. How could you amuse a sensitive and intelligent child on a walk past the miserable ghetto shops? No trees, no benches. A passing rickshaw or truck; a piece of coloured tape in the corsetière's window; the window of the

27

chemist's shop. That was all. So when he saw the little boy dressed up as a policeman and wearing a cap with a yellow rim, a belt and a wooden sword, he wanted a costume like that too. It was very popular in the ghetto. Then Macius ran round the flat in a policeman's hat waving his sword and wearing a yellow band on his sleeve, and he didn't play with his grandfather's opera hat for a while. About this time a play-group was formed. Macius was in it too. There were four children: Macius, Piotrus Szereszewski, Jerzyk Tempel and Izrael First's little girl, a beautiful girl with blonde plaits. Her mother brought her along. Then the group moved to the Firsts on Twarda Street.

Irena didn't live with us. She lived in the nurses' home on the corner of Panska Street and Marianska Street. But she came every day. She wore a cotton dress with pink stripes, a wide white apron, a navy blue cape and a white cap with a velvet ribbon. A year before the war she had started studying medicine at Grenoble university but when the war broke out she returned to Warsaw on a roundabout route via Milan and Lwow. The trains were already being bombed and she often had to jump out of the carriage and hide in a potato field with the other passengers.

At that time we lived on Narbutt Street. 'You shouldn't have come back,' we said, 'you'd have survived the war safer in Grenoble than we will here.' But since she had come back, she enrolled in the nursing school in Czyste. When the Germans requisitioned the hospital in Czyste the school moved to Panska Street. The bursar of the school was the engineer Weissblatt, the director was Mrs Bielicka. Dr Szejman taught chemistry, anatomy and physiology, Dr Minc pharmacology, Dr Apfelbaum internal medicine, Dr Syrkin-Birsztein hygiene, Dr Borkowski surgery, Dr Wilk diseases of the eyes, Dr Wdowinski psychiatry, Dr Mosciskier laryngology, Dr Sztein pathology, Dr Przedborski paediatrics, Dr Herman neurology, Dr Zmigryder-Konopka bacteriology. There were about 80 students.

She lived and studied there, and at the same time she did her practical training in the Bersons and Baumans children's hospital on Sienna Street, and then later in the hospital on Stawki Street, which she reached using the Jewish tram with its blue Star of David. It wasn't far from Panska Street to Walicow Street. Irena came home almost every day, until she got scabies and then fell ill with mumps and had tetany complications.

A lot of the students went down with typhus when the epidemic

28

broke out. Irena received Weigel's anti-typhus vaccination. You could buy these vaccinations, and they weren't cheap. A lot of them were fake. Next to the nursing school was a bacteriological laboratory where the vaccinations were checked. Dr Fejgin worked there and everyone in the ghetto knew that she carried out the investigations scrupulously. A vaccinated doctor worked with her, but died of typhus all the same. The vaccinations didn't give complete protection, only assuaged the worst of the fever.

Several of Irena's friends died of typhus at this time. Irena didn't go down with it although she came into contact with the sick every day and didn't protect herself. She nursed patients with typhus and dysentery for four months in the hospital on Stawki Street. The conditions were frightful – two to a bed – and the mortality rate was very high. One day in the hospital on Stawki Street Irena was reprimanded by her teacher in the presence of the patients. 'Is it the first time you've seen a corpse?' she mocked, 'or do dead people upset you? The way you work is a real disgrace.' Then one of the patients, a veritable ghost, sat up on her bed and raised her fist. 'Hold your tongue, you cow! If you all worked like this girl does then things would look different here.'

'But don't tell anyone about it', said Irena when she told us the story at Walicow Street.

All our daughters had attended the grammar school run by Mrs Popielewska and Mrs Roszkowska on Bagatela Street in Warsaw. Nina was not yet seventeen when she received her matriculation certificate. When we lived in Walicow Street she worked for the lawyer Maslanko in the legal department of the Jewish Council and learnt millinery at the same time. She went to the Chwats after dinner. Mrs Chwat had a hat shop before the war and was the sister of Nina's best friend Krysia.

Nina even managed to earn a few zlotys when she made a hat for our neighbour, the one with the American passport. Dome shaped hats were fashionable at that time and Nina made them by hand. Not only for our neighbour, since my husband's niece wore a black fur-trimmed hat which Nina had made as well. And everyone said how well it matched her grey fur coat. It might seem strange that in the poverty and cramped conditions of the ghetto, women wanted to wear hats. Yet everyone wore them, apart from poor women who tied a headscarf round their heads. I wore a brown narrow-waisted coat trimmed with fox fur, and a small brown hat with a short veil, and didn't feel in the least embarrassed. Later – during the resettlements – you could even see crowds of women wearing hats on the *Umschlagplatz*.

Hania Pakszwer and Stella Jonas learnt millinery together with Nina. Hania was the wife of the young doctor who vaccinated us with the Weigel vaccine and she was a rare beauty. Stella was a short-sighted blonde who always wore glasses. She didn't have a mother. She lived with her father on Panska Street. Our neighbours, the Jonas family, were relations of hers. Although Hania and Stella were both older than Nina they were friends of hers and sometimes came to our flat to sew hats together. They sat down round the table by the balcony window and took out needles, scissors and pieces of felt wrapped up in paper. They talked about people they knew. Sometimes they turned the gramophone on. At dusk they put the light on.

Leon Wyszewianski sometimes came over from the flat opposite in his policeman's uniform. He was our niece's husband. He entered the room quietly and stood by the lamp or the table. He could stand like that for an hour. He was of medium height, good-looking and had an intelligent face. He had studied chemistry at Zurich Polytechnic. He didn't take his eyes off the lovely Hania. At that time falling in love with other people's wives and husbands was a common occurrence. Maybe because of the lack of amusements or maybe because of the monotony of the passing days.

And the strangest thing was that nobody condemned these affairs. Against the background of the insecurity and temporary nature of life at that time, murders on the ghetto streets, the activities of informers – the so-called Thirteens or Jewish Gestapo – and poverty, epidemic and depression, the private lives of individuals were of no concern to anybody. Least of all to Nina. Because Nina had an emotional life of her own and it engrossed her completely. At that time she still received letters through the Red Cross from her friend Ryszard Bychowski. First from Moscow, then Japan, then New York and finally California. She always carried the letters in her beige handbag together with a few mascots that she never parted with.

What amusements did Nina have? Some cafés had opened in the ghetto but she didn't go there. She may once have gone to the concert given by Marysia Ajzensztadt in a small garden on Nowolipki Street, she may have gone to a concert in the Femina cinema on Leszno Street, and she may have attended a concert in the Judaic Institute on Tlomackie Street. But nothing else. She didn't make herself any dresses. She once had a blue dress of Marysia's remade at a dressmaker on Sliska Street. When she collected it she found a louse on it. 'Big deal. Don't make a fuss. Even father found two lice on his collar.'

She had a winter coat made out of her father's old coat at a tailor's on Panska Street. He was a quiet and patient man who was bowed by the weight of his troubles, but at the same time he was extremely amusing. To tell the truth, fittings at the tailor's were real fun for Nina. She told us afterwards what he had said and we laughed, forgetting our own troubles for a moment. 'I must do the shoulder again,' he used to say, 'I can't leave it like that.'

She was reading the best book in the world, a book we loved and tore out of each other's hands, Thornton Wilder's, *The Bridge of San Luis Rey*. And today she has received a letter from California and has added it to the other letters in her beige handbag. The last one? Yes, the last one. Because after that the letters stopped coming. Nina was reading. She sat with her back to the lamp at the ash table with its wings unfolded. The lamp hung in the middle of the room but the table stood at the side by the sofa which was covered with a brown, flowery material. We seated all the relatives, friends and business visitors who came to see us on the sofa, as we considered it the most comfortable and most prestigious place of all.

This is where my cousin Tyla Goralska sat when she came over one evening from the Aryan side. She lived there disguised as a Pole together with her daughter and granddaughter. The flat belonged to a family of office clerks. 'I hung a huge cross on the wall opposite the door so they could see it through the keyhole, because they're sure to · be spying on us,' she said. I walked back with her. We walked along Prosta Street and Panska Street. And although the ghetto wasn't shut off yet and none of the passers-by paid us any attention in the darkness, she addressed me formally as if I were a complete stranger.

Mrs Wanda Kraushar sat on the sofa, shattered and shivering. 'Let me come and live here,' she said. But we didn't understand what her strange words meant. She rented a room on Sienna Street – the ghetto was closed by then – a room-cum-passage with a false corridor made out of a curtain. From morning until night she could hear the footsteps of people milling about the flat, but that wasn't what got her down. She was christened. She got herself christened at the beginning of the war together with hundreds of others who all had the same idea – that it would protect them against the Germans.

I visited her at that time in her flat on Chocimska Street. She was ill. She lay in an antique mahogany bed and above the bed hung a cross. We talked about everyday matters although we had other things on our minds. She was a widow. She came into the ghetto while her married daughter stayed on the Aryan side. But even that wasn't the reason for her depression. She had hidden a few thousand dollars in a flowerpot on the balcony and told the Pole who took over her luxury flat what she had done. She had trusted him.

'Dollars? First time I've heard of them. You're imagining things,' he said when she asked for them.

It wasn't far from Walicow Street to Sienna Street. I often called in to see her. I took her by the arm and we walked along Panska Street and Sliska Street. On the corner of Marianska Street she went into the chemist's shop and bought a phial of Luminal.

'What do you need that for?' I asked.

'I sleep so badly', she replied.

Another person who sat on the sofa was Hildebrandt, our tailor from Hoza Street, who mended my husband's suits. The ghetto was closed off by that time and a police force was being organized. Three thousand policemen were being recruited and everyone was convinced that they would survive the war – they and their families.

'Mr Szereszewski', he said, 'you've known me for a long time. Could you please use your influence so my son gets into the police?'

'Where do you live, Mr Hildebrandt?'

'On Leszno Street. On the corner of Leszno Street and Zelazna Street. Before the war there was a hostel for Jewish students in the house.'

The daughter of our former landlord on Poznanska Street had the same request. She brought her son along. He was no more than eighteen years old. He was a student at Edinburgh University. He came back just before the war started. And on the very first day he was wounded by a fragment of shell in front of the house where they had a summer flat in the country. You could still see deep gashes on his face. And my brother-in-law, Witold Szereszewski, who was an architect, made the same request, on behalf of a worker he had employed in his office before the war.

Councillor Kupczykier was known to be organizing the police. My husband didn't have anything to do with the police. But there was such a rush to get taken on that people tried to make use of contacts with anyone they thought might have some influence.

Later on, Councillor Rabbi Eckerman sat on the sofa. At that time he still had his own teeth, his beard, his wife and seven children. Among the other matters discussed that afternoon they also brought up the question of the two Jews from the Kutno ghetto who had come as delegates from the Judenrat there. They had spoken to my husband too because he was one of the directors of the Jewish Aid Organization. They told us about the tragic situation of the Kutno Jews. They were locked into a sugar beet plant which had been unused for twenty years. The plant's huge shops and large yards were surrounded by barbed wire and formed a ghetto for thousands of Jews, not only from Kutno and the surrounding towns but also for Jews from Pomorze. They lived there in indescribably cramped conditions.

In 1941 a typhus epidemic broke out and decimated them. They didn't have enough doctors. The hospital was directed by the regional doctor who was a Pole and Dr Weinzaft from Krosniewice. Dr Weinzaft was the only doctor who lived in the ghetto. His wife, a Polish woman, didn't want to live there with him. A young doctor called Brzoza returned to Kutno with the delegation. He perished later in Chelmno during the final liquidation of the ghetto there.

Our relation Stefa Pinus, the hawker, sat on the sofa as well. One evening she brought along a young Jew from Wilno. He was tall and blonde and spoke excellent Polish. He had managed to make it from Wilno to Warsaw and brought news of the mass shootings of Jews. He had come as a messenger and was returning to Wilno. As a rule people didn't believe him. When he said he had lost his wife and child, they questioned his veracity all the more. 'He's lost his wife and child and tells us about it so calmly.' It was unbelievable. Things like this didn't fit into the frame of normal thought and so they could hardly penetrate our consciousness.

After Mrs Jelen left Regina worked for us. She was quite young and attractive but hard of hearing. We had to talk to her very loud. She worked in a loose dressing gown and when she served at table she used a bra as a belt. That was her way. Times were hard, the ghetto was sealed off by then, and a bra instead of a belt was a trivial matter in comparison with everything else. We didn't pay it any attention. Sometimes we laughed behind her back.

We made bean soup almost every day. We still had gas and so we used that in order to save coal. We did have gas, but it was poor quality and didn't give enough heat. Everyone complained about having 'cold' gas. Later we didn't even have 'cold' gas. There was a

33

time when there wasn't any gas during the day, only at night. So we cooked at night, at two or three or four o'clock.

Regina was a distant soul and we never knew what she was thinking. Genia had been like an open book, Mrs Jelen a sly fox. But nobody knew how to sum Regina up. She did her own thing and we did ours. She didn't live with us but alongside us.

'Regina, how's the soup doing?'

She couldn't hear.

'Is the soup ready?'

'The gas is cold today,' she replied.

The horseflesh broth cooked much quicker. My husband couldn't get used to horseflesh for a long time. We cheated him and told him it was beef. Then he got used to it. The whole ghetto ate horseflesh, only people who were very rich ate other meat. Everyone adapted to necessity quickly. The best propaganda was made by the doctors: they said that horseflesh was very good for children. With her bra for a belt Regina served horseflesh chops with mashed potatoes. We ate fried onions for supper every day. At that time we could still get as many onions as we wanted and beetroots, carrots and cabbage as well.

It was now 1941. Regina was our servant at the time when the thieves came to our flat at nine o'clock one evening. There were four of them. They immediately took up their positions just as if they were under orders – one in the hall by the front door and one by the kitchen door, while the other two sat down at table with us. Regina was asleep and they didn't enter her room at all. Ryszard, Marysia and the child were in bed and they didn't go there either. They were well dressed. They wore hats and coats with fur collars. They didn't wear armbands – they were Poles. They weren't Jews from the ghetto underworld (which the painter who lived in the attic was said, rightly or wrongly, to belong to), and they weren't Germans. Polish thieves.

That evening my uncle who lived in the annexe and my brother-in-law Witold, his sub-tenant, had come to see us via the attics and dark corridors, using a torch to light their way. And the two strangers sat down next to them and calmly carried on a conversation as if they were part of the family. But they had their eyes on them, you could feel it. One of them said that they were sure to hang him after the war. 'They're sure to hang me on the first lamppost, I'm prepared for that. I've got too many sins on my conscience.' The second man talked politics.

They both took their hats off and behaved like gentlemen. But the one standing in the hall didn't take his hat off. He was wearing a thin casual coat with a leather belt. He opened the bookcase and went through the books. He was looking for money among the pages. We were afraid that he'd lift the ornamental top of the bookcase and find Leon's albums. Then he went to the dining room. I had a good look at him by the light of the lamp. He was young and fair with a lean face, handsome. He wore a pince-nez and looked like an intellectual. He was looking at the old birchwood cupboard. And while the other two were engaging us in conversation he found the two secret drawers and slid them out in a trice. We had 20,000 zlotys hidden there. He put the money calmly into his pocket. While the other two kept on talking, just glancing to check that nobody had jumped up to raise the alarm with the neighbours.

Then the one in the casual coat went over to the sideboard, opened the bottom door, calmly took out the tin box of beans and spilled them out onto the floor. We were terrified to see our gold bracelets at his feet. He placed them all on the table in front of his bosses. He entered the room where my mother was asleep, silently searched her cases and removed all the money. They also took the diamond ring which I had in a little bag round my neck. They told me to undo my blouse. They knew I had the little bag. Their behaviour was very correct.

'And now we're going to buy everything back, aren't we?' They said they'd return the bracelets for a certain sum of money and named the sum. We didn't have the money because what the man in the belted coat had taken didn't count any more. The diamond ring was out of the question as well. They pretended they'd lost it and even looked under the table. So uncle and Witold said that they would bring some money from home and pay out on our behalf, and they agreed. Regina slept as if nothing was happening. Some light was showing through the glass above Marysia's door but they weren't interested in those two rooms at all, as if they knew they wouldn't find anything there.

Suddenly the bathroom door opened and out came Nina in a willow-green dressing gown. She had been having a bath and didn't know what was happening. She passed through the room, exotic and lovely, embarrassed to see so many men there. She thought they were friends of her father's and was surprised they had come so late. They were startled. That was obvious. They had mounted guard on the entrances. They had grounded everyone. Nobody had left any of the closed rooms. And suddenly here was Nina. But Witold and uncle were getting up from the table. Nobody followed them. The man by the kitchen door moved aside and let them both through. They went up a few stairs to the attic and then disappeared into the darkness of the corridors. They didn't have to come back. But the men were sure they would. After all the money was needed for us.

Finally the thieves said goodbye very politely. Just as if they were leaving a social gathering. The one who had talked politics and the one who had said he'd be hung after the war shook hands with all the men. The one with the belt stood aside, grave and silent. He didn't take part in the conversation. The light from the lamp was reflected in the lenses of his pince-nez. He looked like a teacher or a clerk. Then finally the fourth one showed up. The one who had guarded the kitchen door. Squat and coarse with a cap on his head. He was the only one not wearing a hat. He had smallpox scars on his face.

And then they were gone. The door closed quietly after them. We put the chain on. And Regina was asleep. Who had put them onto us? For a fraction of a second we thought it was Mr Jelen. But what was the connection between Jelen and Polish thieves? We didn't know.

Our ration cards were yellow with a Star of David. They were for bread, sugar, jam and fat. They were registered at Szafran's food shop. The same Szafran who had a shop selling dairy products on Piekna Street before the war. And when we lived on Poznanska Street we were his customers for many years. At first we couldn't get over our surprise at having Szafran so near again. He could have opened a shop on Leszno Street or Karmelicka Street but fate had seen to it that he set up on Walicow Street no less, and at number six at that. 'Do you know that Szafran's with us again?' we said, or, 'Szafran's treading on our heels.'

We always considered him honest. Because when our maid cheated us on the milk, he told us about it. We had known his stout wife and two children well. She was no longer alive and the children had grown up. The son had gone to Russia and nothing was known about him, while the daughter worked in the shop. She was a big girl with fair skin and was called Helena. On her head she wore a scarf tied up like a turban.

Szafran was fair-haired with a red face. He soon married a second time. She was quite a young woman and had a son of three. His first

36

wife had been a normal shopkeeper and had stayed in her role, while the second one wasn't interested in trade. Although she came to the shop from time to time, she didn't help. In fact her help was completely unnecessary. The shop was run by twenty year-old Salka, a girl like lightning.

Szafran ran the shop on Walicow Street in partnership with his brother who had a few daughters. The husband of one of them, Wasser, was a lawyer and worked in the Statistics Section of the Jewish Council. The youngest was fifteen and was called Ciunia, a strange name. Salka was the third or even the fourth. She wore men's shoes and a sheepskin. On top of the sheepskin she wore a white overall with long sleeves, and a white woollen shawl on her head. A round face, a snub nose, brown eyes and dimples. There was nobody like her in the whole world. She sometimes came to us on the fifth floor if she had a pot of honey that had been smuggled over from the Aryan side. The Szafrans themselves didn't smuggle. They stood slightly to one side in the shop and kept their hands in their coat pockets. They didn't serve the customers. The shop was completely ruled by Helena and Salka, mainly Salka. The Szafrans stood with their hands in their pockets, watched the door and waited.

Suddenly the door would open wide and in would rush a smuggler in a cloud of frosty dust. He wore a cap pulled low over his ears, thick gloves and boots. He rushed in and threw a sack or crate down in front of him. Sometimes he clapped his shoulders to get warm or pounded the floor with his feet. Then he went out, without a word, or taking any money. All that was left after him was a puddle of water, some wet snow and a grey fog which disappeared into the muddy floorboards as it slowly descended.

Opposite our house was the small shop belonging to the cobbler who sometimes mended our shoes. It was a dark and miserable place. The workshop was under a muddy window which looked out onto the narrow tramped pavement. In the middle of the shop stood a primitive iron stove on long legs, and the cobbler's wife looked after it and moved the pans around on it. You might think that this thin, drawn and silent little man would die of hunger in his miserable workshop one day. Yet the miserable workshop was only a smokescreen. He organized large-scale smuggling and had a whole team working for him. Many of the tenants in the house, including us, stocked up with flour and kasha at the cobbler's. He thought he had a better chance of surviving if he pretended to be poverty stricken.

At 8 Walicow Street there was a butcher's shop where Ryfka sold meat. You could buy a few bundles of wood from her as well because the shop was big but there wasn't much meat and the counter was enough for all there was. In fact Ryfka kept the meat under the counter, nothing ever hung on the hooks. She arranged the wood around the walls right up to the ceiling. She wore a head-scarf, a sheepskin and men's shoes and warmed her hands over a tiny stove which stood on the empty counter. She didn't have any horseflesh. Only beef, kosher too, expensive, she could vouch for it.

'I can vouch for it,' she said, 'I can swear in front of the rabbi any time. Can't you see? My fat is white, the other is as yellow as wax. Even a child can recognize horseflesh by its yellow fat.'

When rumour had it that doctors recommended horseflesh because it's healthier than beef, specially for small children, we believed it. We stopped going to Ryfka's at number 8. We opened the door wide for Rachela and Sara who sold horseflesh.

There was a food shop on Prosta Street and it even had a shop window. I sometimes went there and bought some ersatz coffee, breadcrumbs and sweets. The shopkeeper, an attractive and pleasant woman, had three sons, the oldest nineteen and the youngest fifteen, and an eight-year-old daughter. The whole family including the father was always in the shop. I couldn't understand when they cooked, cleaned or washed. The youngest son, tall and slim with flaxen hair and long hands, never left his mother's side. 'Look, Mrs Szereszewska, he clings to me from morning till night.' The three boys didn't go to school. 'Circumstances, you understand', she sighed.

Sometimes when I entered the shop the oldest or middle boy wasn't there.

'Where's your oldest?'

'At his friend's.' Or, 'He's at his uncle's.' But the youngest was always there. And the girl, who had dark hair and eyes, and wore a red shawl on her head, usually stood in front of the shop and chewed pumpkin seeds. When I crossed Prosta Street I slowed down in front of the shop and looked in through the shop window. The youngest was always there. I looked at him and thought to myself that he was suffering. He might have had a foreboding, or could see images which tormented and alarmed him.

Opposite the shop on exactly the other side of the road lived a girl who mended laddered stockings. She sat in the window of the ground floor flat from morning to night. You didn't even have to go into the flat. She opened the little window and handed you the stocking rolled up into a ball. 'How much?' 'Ten', she replied and stretched out her hand.

Everything in the ghetto was well thought out. You didn't have to go far! Everything was at hand. From her window it wasn't more than five steps to the chemist's on the corner of Prosta Street and Twarda Street. The chemist's on the corner, next to the chemist's a beggar had his pitch. The chemist's had a high threshold and once you were inside it was clean and airy, with two light shop windows. The chemist was called Seret. He had a wife and a ten year-old son. His wife came from Bendzin. Née Potok, Salomon Potok's daughter.

Behind the chemist's there was a soap shop. On the corner of Panska Street and Twarda Street. In the soap shop a tall, old Jew in a cloak, with a long, white beard. We bought soap and soda from him. At the beginning of December my mother and I went to him to find out when the anniversary of my father's death would be. 'The fifth day of Kislev, so when will that be?' He took a Jewish calendar out of his pocket and flicked through a few pages. 'On Thursday. This coming Thursday.'

One day I came across a little girl crying bitterly in front of the soap shop. She told me a boy had snatched her glasses off her face and she didn't have them any more and she didn't know if she'd ever get them back.

The chemist on one corner, the soap shop on the second corner, and on the third corner a shop where they sold bread. Nothing but bread. The smell of bread greeted you in the street, it smelled of bread just like it smells of mown hay in meadows. The fair-haired shop assistant resembled a field of rye. A four year-old boy in a woollen cap knelt on a chair behind the counter. She stroked his head with a floury hand. When I asked her where her husband was she didn't reply immediately. It was as if she was recalling an already faded picture, recreating it, digging it up out of her memory.

'We lived at Okecie. My husband worked at the airport. There were Poles and Jews in the group, and they shot them for no reason. I went there at night, and found him and buried him myself. I dug his grave myself, with these hands.' She stretched out her hands in front of her. She turned both palms up and held them like that for a moment. One winter day when I left the shop with a loaf of bread two small boys threw themselves under my feet. I fell down and the bread rolled into the mud. They grabbed it and ran away. I got up

39

from the ground and leaned groggily against a notice-board. On it there was a notice about the murder of Igo Sym.

Next to the bread shop a shop with potato pancakes. On winter days, frosty and damp, the frozen passer-by could drop in for pancakes. They were fried in a black pan from morning till night. The pan stood in the shop window on a gas flame and everyone could see them being fried. They were fried by a woman wearing a white overall over her sheepskin. She held an earthenware bowl and poured the grated potatoes into the pan. The shop was so busy that the door never closed. Even though it was frosty, it stood wide open. Small boys with caps pulled down over their ears and their hands in their pockets didn't leave the window from morning till night. The woman kept threatening them with a tin spoon.

And so, a chemist's shop, a soap shop, bread and pancakes, the notice-board, and next door a tiny little ironmonger's shop. This had nails, hooks, files and nuts, hammers and screws. One day I bought a tool for prising out the stove tiles in there. In fact it was a stove-setter's tool. A long, narrow rectangle sharpened at both ends. The shopkeeper wasn't surprised at all. She handed me the tool indifferently as if I'd asked for a padlock. I bought the tool the week after the thieves raided our flat and we had to buy our things back so expensively. We found out afterwards that the best hiding place was the opening in the stove when you removed a tile. After I paid for the tool the shopkeeper wiped a stool with her apron and when I sat down by the counter she told me the story of her aunt. What's interesting is that in those times the relationship between shop-keeper and customer was unceremonious, almost as if you were a member of the family. Together with his goods the customer received the confidence of the most intimate troubles, like it or not.

'She lived with me and I let her stay until one night I threw her out. The bread was being stolen, that's a fact. I told myself there was a thief in the house. I didn't go to bed and hid behind the cupboard. At three in the morning I heard a rustling. Someone was stepping quietly in the darkness and opening the sideboard door. In the morning I saw some bread had gone. I hid again the second night. More rustling, more footsteps. I jumped out from behind the cupboard, grabbed the thief by the hand and took the bread off her. It was my aunt, my dear, the aunt I'd taken in. "Out of my flat, aunt," I shouted, "you thief!"'

Everything was to hand and close by in the ghetto. On Twarda Street before you reached Ciepla Street there was a small laundry with just one stiff collar in the shop window. And the strangest thing was that the children even gaped at that collar. A miserable shop window. An old dilapidated house. A huge door with a rotting threshold. Sad windows with old-fashioned blinds on each floor. Dr Koenigstein, the laryngologist, lived in that house. He had typhus.

Then Ciepla Street and the corner house, on the wall a notice announcing the death of Mrs Iberal, the dentist. We had known her from before the war. 'Did you say she's died?' they said at home, surprised. Past Ciepla Street on Twarda Street lived Mrs Moscibrodzka who embroidered and sewed for us. It was just one minute to her place from Walicow Street. In the past it took us so long to get there and we wasted so much time. Opposite was a wooden hut and in the hut a small food shop. You can see Broncia in the shop. Our Broncia from Poznanska Street. She moved her shop here, just here, to this hut knocked up out of planks of wood.

Many of the shops we knew from before the war had been scattered far and wide but now they came to the ghetto in our wake. They all had miserable premises and displays now, and the worst one of all was the shop belonging to the Brylant brothers who used to own the beautiful food shop on the corner of Koszykowa Street and Piekna Street. I entered their little shop on Sliska Street by chance one day. When they saw me they were surprised and moved. I had been a long-standing customer and I knew their father, red-haired Brylant.

Behind them was Kleinsinger, the antique dealer from Swietokrzyska Street. A few old plates, two silver sugar-bowls, a string of amber and a Turkish scarf in a tiny window. Also an ivory miniature and next to it a chess set. There was nothing to look at. All the same I sometimes stopped in front of the shop and looked at these knick-knacks which were of no use to anyone and so out of place in the raw reality of the ghetto.

The only shop I couldn't find again was the paper shop from Piekna Street. It belonged to a tall orthodox Jew with an exceptionally beautiful and noble face. On 18 January 1943, when on a frosty and sunny day, I was standing among thousands of other people on the *Umschlagplatz*, after I'd been picked up on Muranowska Street, a cart drove up. Suddenly I saw him standing there on the cart. It seemed as if he was all alone, even though thousands of people were there, all pushed and crammed together. His tall black silhouette stood out so clearly against the blue sky that I couldn't see anyone else.

41

Sometimes when I took Mrs Moscibrodzka or another of the 'society' hawkers to the front door, we stood on the landing and talked about this or that. We could often hear the neighbours quarrelling. We didn't know which ones because three families lived in the three rooms which had been cut off from our flat. A policeman with his mother in the first room, a young man with his mother in the second, and the Jonas family in the third. One day the first door opened and to our surprise the policeman appeared in his long-johns and threw a man out onto the stairs. 'Raus! Raus! Raus!' he shouted. We never found out who he was and why he was thrown out of the flat. So we had the nervous policeman in the first room, and the Jonas family in the third room, relations of fair-haired Stella, the one who made hats with Nina.

Before the war Mr Jonas had a jeweller's shop in the Hotel Europejski. He must have had a beautiful flat and high-class customers. He and his wife were an elderly couple who loved each other deeply. She was stout and asthmatic and he looked like a doctor or a professor. A carefully dressed man who was going grey. Mrs Jonas never went out shopping. Her husband brought her everything. It was strange and moving to see him slowly climbing up to the fifth floor dragging a shopping bag full of cabbage, beetroots and carrots. They must have had friends on the Aryan side to whom they'd given some of their property because they kept ringing them.

In the attic lived a painter who had a phone. To reach his room you had to be very familiar with the topography of the attic and its corridors, corners and strange passages. Rather than go down from the fifth floor to the courtyard and then go up again to the painter in the attic through the side entrance of the annexe, it was much simpler to go through our flat and get to the attic the moment you left the kitchen door and went up a few stairs. 'May I go through your flat?' 'Of course.'

If it was Mr Jonas, he bowed and thanked us with exquisite elegance. In these times when human dignity was so degraded it was nice to see an older man with such charming manners. But usually it was Mrs Jonas who crossed our flat. In a flowery dressing gown, unbelievably fat, and breathing like a fish. When she appeared out of the dark hall she merely nodded her head in greeting and disappeared into the kitchen corridor. Once outside the kitchen door she turned on an electric torch and shining and then extinguishing the torch she was swallowed up by the darkness of the attic labyrinths.

42

If Mrs Jonas came in the evening I didn't detain her. If she came in the daytime I asked her to sit down on the divan-bed for a chat. It was pleasant to natter with Mrs Jonas and listen to her singsong Polish. She came from Poltawa and hadn't lost her Russian accent even though she'd lived in Poland for so many years. She once confided to me that she wore a corset with gold dollars sewn into it. 'I wrapped each piece up in cloth and then sewed them all into the corset. I don't even take it off at night', she said in a whisper, even though there was nobody in the room. She must have trusted me since she told me such a great secret. Everyone knew that you could be executed for having gold or paper dollars.

The policeman's mother passed through our flat almost every day. She was still quite a young woman and crossed the room coquettishly. The policeman never came. He never greeted us on the stairs either. His face was always harsh and strange. Obviously he didn't want to know us. Once when his door wasn't completely shut I saw him squatting over an iron stove. The stove was in the middle of the room and the pipe went up, then bent at a right angle and disappeared into some plywood in the window. He was wearing his mother's apron and was holding a frying-pan and blowing into the stove. His cheeks were distended and his eyes were shut. The room was grey with smoke. We assumed that his mother had contacts with the Aryan side as well. She used to knock at our door three times and ask if she could come through.

Sometimes when she was crossing the room towards the kitchen she met Mrs Jonas going the other way. Then the neighbour from opposite, small red-haired Mrs Ferhendler who was the wife of a police officer, was knocking at the door. Sometimes Nina opened the door, sometimes Ryszard.

'Could I go through your flat?' She blushed to the roots of her hair. 'Sorry it's so late.' It really was late but her small daughter had only just gone to sleep. Mrs Ferhendler had a grand piano and played beautifully. There's no doubt that she was a very gifted pianist. Before the war she dreamed of fame and of playing to thousands. Who knows, perhaps the world would have heard of her? But here, in this fortress of a house, in the heart of the so-called small ghetto she played only for herself. And that had to suffice.

Even so you might think that this woman's life had taken quite a happy course. She had a good and handsome husband, a lovely child, filigree beauty and a noble instrument. But she wasn't happy. She had a widowed mother who had been paralysed for many years. The engraved, brass name-plate on the door showed that she had lived there before the war. She couldn't walk or talk or read. She sat on the balcony from morning to night wearing a colourful dressing gown. You could see her looking out of the window at any time of day. She needed nursing like a baby. She had to be fed, dressed and put to bed. She was an attractive woman, not at all old, and aware of her misfortune. If her son-in-law, the police officer, crossed our flat *en route* to the attics we asked him to sit with us, if only for a few moments. He always had something interesting to tell us about the life of the ghetto, something that shattered us. Unfortunately it was not so often he could tell us anything to bolster our spirits.

Ryszard had an extraordinary memory, a rabbinical memory as it's said, (his great-grandfather really was a rabbi in Lublin). He could name all the forty-eight states of America without hesitation. He was just repeating the latest news bulletin. He had either heard it himself on a clandestine radio or had been told by one of the people listening. Benghazi. The word was repeated many times in the latest bulletin and filled us with hope. It was our contribution – the news we exchanged for Ferhendler's news.

The fair-haired woman from the fourth floor, the one with the American passport, passed through our flat just as frequently as Mrs Jonas. She had a common name, Rozenberg or Rotblatt. We treated her very politely because she was Nina's client. We were fascinated by her American citizenship. When she entered the hall we saw her passport with all its stamps first of all and only afterwards the person. 'May I come through?' she asked. Her voice was young and charming, and her Polish was excellent.

As time went by even people we didn't know at all crossed through our flat. And not only *en route* to the phone, but also to the tenants on this side of the house. Sometimes they asked for permission and at other times they crossed in silence as if it were a public footpath trodden by the force of habit. Some days we noted a fall in frequency, and on others an increase. Particularly at the time when the Germans confiscated Jewish furs. Between seven and nine in the evening it wasn't even worth closing the door. Sometimes one of us would grumble impatiently, 'What's going on? We don't know what private property means any more. Is the flat ours or not?'

The painter who lived in the attic was a secretive man. Nobody had ever seen him in workclothes, with a bucket of lime, a brush or a ladder. So how did he make his living? He left the house early and came back late. He was even suspected, rightly or wrongly, of being mixed up in shady dealings. He had a short, fat, dark-haired wife and a twelve year-old niece who always wore a blue woollen cap. You never saw the girl in the courtyard. She stood in the round attic window all day long and threw pieces of plaster at the red-haired boy who was the caretaker's helper. She didn't seem to do anything else all day long, as if that was her only occupation.

Apart from the painter in the attic, Mr Migdal, the tenant in the fourth floor flat at the front, also had a phone. Mr Migdal was the owner of a gas-meter factory so he wasn't a nobody. He was respected. He was a tenant from before the war, like our paralysed neighbour. It was out of the question to use his phone and pay him for the call. No-one would have dared. If he'd let anyone ring it would have been out of politeness. That's why everyone went to the painter's. Everyone with the exception of Mr Koenigsztein who also owned a factory like Mr Migdal, but was richer still. Mr Koenigsztein wasn't a tenant from before the war. You could even say that Mr Koenigsztein had come from a palace to the ghetto.

So Mr Migdal had gas-meters and Mr Koenigsztein had paper-works. But in fact neither of them had anything. The Germans had already requisitioned all Jewish factories a long time ago. They left Migdal his wife, a small fair-haired woman, and twelve-year-old daughter, Rutka, while they left Koenigsztein his eleven-year-old son, Oles, and his tall, slim, elegant wife with her aquiline nose and narrow lips, née Landsberg. I remembered her from my childhood. She was his second wife in fact, and not so young when she married him. But she gave him a son, a charming and beautiful boy who was the leader of the children in our courtyard.

The courtyard of our five-storied house was paved with yellow cobbles and on rainy or cloudy days it resembled the bottom of a well. Nevertheless Oles rode a bike round and round the courtyard from morning until night, playful, laughing and happy. 'Oles! Oles!' shouted the children from the balconies. 'Oles!' tall slim Mrs Koenigsztein shouted through the window. 'Can you see Oles?' I asked Macius. He gripped the iron balcony railings and although he longed to see him he couldn't manage because he was tiny. But when I lifted him up and Oles was passing on the opposite side of the courtyard then he could see him. Rutka, Migdal's dark daughter, could stare at Oles all day long. She had a lot of time because she didn't go to school. There weren't any schools at that time, so we could always hear her voice. She was short like her mother and dark

45

like her father. Migdal's Rutka, we used to say. Neither Mr Migdal nor Mr Koenigsztein ever came to our flat.

There wasn't a day or a single hour free of trouble. The troubles were both common and private. The common ones worried all the Jews enclosed in the ghetto, and the private ones only concerned our family. But our private troubles could also be divided into large and small ones. It started in the morning. The moment we woke up we again suffered the news we'd heard the day before. Another Jew had been caught on the Aryan side and killed, or a non-Jew, christened from birth. The Germans had arrested or shot someone again. The smaller troubles might include Mr Jelen's dishonesty, for example. For over a week we wondered how much of our coal he had managed to take and sell. We lost faith in the couple and sacked Mrs Jelen.

Times were hard. Against that background the theft of coal was a trivial matter and the shoots growing on the potatoes in the cellar were trivial too. All the same it was something to worry about. 'The potatoes are getting spoilt. We've got to go down to the cellar and check them. We'll take Fligelman with us.' In the end we went down one evening. We lit a candle and by its flickering light we tore the long, yellow shoots off the potatoes in the low cellar, some of us stooping and some on our knees.

'The cellar's too warm,' one of us said.

'If we open the window the potatoes will freeze.'

'What will happen to the cabbage? It's going bad in the barrel.'

There was a lot of trouble with the cabbage as well. We decided to make cabbage soup every day and flavour it with the fat of dubious quality which we couldn't not buy from our neighbour. But even cooking every day didn't solve the problem. One trouble led to another. Since we cooked more than we could eat we gave the leftovers to a beggar. First to one and then to a second whom he brought along. After a week there were over a dozen of them. They thought it was a canteen for the poor. They were impatient, beating the door with their fists and cursing us. The worst thing was that they soiled the stairs. 'They're using the stairs as a toilet,' shouted Fligelman, craning his neck up from the courtyard and looking at our balcony.

In fact it was trivial. Real trouble descended on us when the Germans issued the order about Jewish furs. What? Hand our furs over to the Germans of our own free will? We thought up endless schemes to avoid doing so. Polish and Jewish traders, both with Jewish armbands, immediately appeared on the streets and bought up the furs for next to nothing, or nothing at all. Stefa Pinus came flying over, her cheeks aflame, shaking all over. She wouldn't even sit down for a moment. 'I know a Polish woman who'll take your furs into safe-keeping. She's waiting on Ceglana Street. Give me your best furs as quickly as possible.'

'What! This minute?'

'There's no time to lose. Every second counts.'

Her agitation is hard to describe. It seemed as if a spark was flying out of every hair on her head. Her eyes were nearly popping out of their sockets. She was panting because she'd run up the stairs, and there were five flights of them. I unstitched a large, black, Persian lamb collar from a coat for her Polish friend to look after. She didn't tell me her name or her address. So how would I find the collar again after the war?

'You won't find it,' said my husband that evening. 'But Guzik knows some Poles in Swider and he's prepared to take our furs there together with his.'

'What if the guard finds the furs and the Germans start to investigate who they belong to? That'll be the end of us.'

'Don't worry about the furs!' he replied – he was an optimist all his life – 'we'll buy some more after the war. The main thing is that the children are well.'

So in the end Fligelman took all my husband's furs to the Jewish Council while I sold my black Persian lamb coat to a Polish trader at a give-away price. The fur trimmings from our costumes and my mink collar we burnt in the coal fire.

At about this time people in the ghetto started whispering about Aryan papers. That was the first time we'd heard about them. Ryszard brought the news about Aryan papers. You could always learn something new and unexpected from Ryszard. During supper that evening, while he was spreading fried onions on his bread, he said, 'A man called Orzech has got himself some Aryan papers and is living quietly in his own flat on Aleje Jerozolimskie or some other street.' His words knocked us off balance for a long time. What are these papers called? Aryan? And he's living quietly on them? It was too good to be true.

We recalled the first weeks of the German occupation when that Jewish family moved into our house on Narbutt Street. They came from Lodz, or some other place. One day they told us, without making a secret of it, that they were going to get themselves some documents, that they were Karaites. Now we were curious to know what had happened to them – whether they'd moved into the ghetto or had been allowed to stay on the other side.

We also remembered what my niece Anusia had said. 'One of my friends has got himself some Italian papers. He might have bought them. He uses an Italian name and lives on the other side. He's Italian now. But he comes to see us in the ghetto.' I knew the boy by sight, he was dark-skinned and black-haired. I'd seen him in a group of young people on the roof of the annexe of our house, on the terrace between the chimneys. You reached it using an iron ladder from the attic.

There wasn't a single moment in the day when we weren't thinking about Mr Orzech. We admired his boldness and envied him. He was passing himself off as a Pole. What nerve! Later we found out that our cousins who had come to Warsaw from Lodz, mother, daughter and small granddaughter, had also bought Aryan papers. All three of them had an excellent appearance, it's true. They didn't look Jewish at all. They altered their names. The mother was called Tyla. In the false papers she was Otylia. Her parents were called Judel and Golda. Now they were Julian and Gizela.

My brother-in-law Witold Szereszewski lived on the fourth floor of the annexe of our house. He administered four houses on Muranowska Street. There were a lot of administrators like that in the ghetto, with a German *Reichsdeutsch* woman, Mrs Sabart, in charge of them. Her office was on the Aryan side, but she came in person for her Jewish administrators' accounts and reports.

As time went by her official attitude to Witold and his wife became friendly, even cordial. She visited them more and more often, not only on matters concerning the four houses, the four blocks as they were called, but for friendly talks. She once told them that she didn't support Hitler, and also that her husband was Jewish and she had him in hiding in Warsaw. We were surprised that she told Witold and his wife such a secret. She promised to get them Aryan papers if they decided to leave the ghetto.

'If the Germans catch you with false papers they take you to the ghetto and shoot you. They've just shot someone called Toeplitz although he was christened a long time ago, it might even have been when he was a baby,' Ryszard told us a week later. When we heard that we didn't envy Orzech any more, and we didn't believe in that quiet living of his any longer.

Shortly afterwards new troubles came. My niece Anusia stopped going to school when the war started. In the ghetto she learned to sew in a workshop on Nowolipie Street. When Többens' workshop was opened she went there with her mother and worked in the tailoring department. They lived at 6 Walicow Street, in the annexe, at Mrs Berman's. Anusia was 17. She was an attractive girl with Tatar looks, tall and graceful. The war, and in particular the ghetto, had a bad influence on her. Her mother couldn't control her any longer. Not a day passed when one of our relatives didn't tell me, 'I met Anusia on Panska Street. She was with a strange-looking boy. He was short, dark and thin, leaning on a stick and limping.' Or they would say something similar. It turned out that he lived with his mother and was very poor, although there was nothing wrong with that. But we suspected that he'd latched on to Anusia because he thought she was rich. He walked with a stick and was said to have tuberculosis of the bones.

'Harry is twenty-two,' said Anusia. It was obvious that it impressed her to have a boy-friend who was so much older than she was.

'Can't you explain to her? The boy looks poverty-stricken. But that's not the point. The trouble is he looks suspicious.'

No argument could prevail. You'd meet the couple on all the neighbouring streets – Twarda, Ciepla and Sliska. But it wasn't as tragic as all that, as it later turned out. Now it was just a worry, another reason for concern. An added anxiety was when Irena caught scabies and then went down with mumps with complications shortly afterwards. Yes, mumps with complications was quite serious. There was a lot of running from Walicow Street to the nurses' school before she got up out of bed again. After that Macius went down with pleurisy and that was the worst. All our troubles until then had been nothing compared with that.

Two months later Dr Brokman the paediatrician sent him to Otwock. At that time you could still go there if you had the ways and means. The 'Zofiowka' psychiatric hospital had opened a recuperative sanatorium on its premises. You used a white ambulance with a Blue star of David to get there. It was such an effort before Marysia and Macius finally entered the white ambulance with their suitcase. Would they get there safely? Wouldn't the Germans turn them back when they were half-way there?

They arrived. Even though the wood was surrounded with barbed wire, it did have pine needles and cones on the ground, and squirrels disappearing among the branches, woodpeckers and cuckoos. What a contrast to the crowded, miserable streets of the ghetto. In surroundings like this the child should get better soon. Marysia received permission to go from a Polish doctor from Poznan who was ordered to work in the ghetto by the Germans. He was said to be a good man who helped Jews. He was also said to be the friend of one of the nurses who worked in the Berson and Bauman hospital. So this load was removed off our minds.

While Marysia was at Otwock she caught typhus even though she'd had the Weigel vaccine. 'Get some sheets ready, four or six, or even more. Ryszard will take them to Otwock.'

'What's happened?'

'Marysia's got typhus.'

Fortunately it wasn't bad. She was attended by the young hospital doctor, Dr Frydman.

Was there any time at 6 Walicow Street for joy? Yes, despite everything there was. What was it like? What did it remind us of and what longings did it kindle? What recollections, what memories? Joy in the closed ghetto had to be meagre. On Saturday mornings we often saw small girls in the neighbouring streets carrying double-handled pans. The pans were cauldron shaped, covered with tightly fitting lids and then tied up in tautly stretched cloth. The pans contained chulent. We really felt like having some. But we knew it was hard to digest. Potatoes with peas and kasha, stewed in fat, in a hot bread oven. Yes, chulent was out of the question for us. Not for my family and not for me. But when I was small and went to visit my grandmother who lived on Swiety Jakub Street in Lodz I used to eat chulent every Saturday. Brown potatoes and beans with pearl barley served in a deep salad bowl by Gitla the cook, an old woman with down in her hair.

'If we can't have chulent,' said Mrs Jelen who was our cook at that time at Walicow Street, the lenses of her glasses flashing, 'if we can't have chulent, then at least we can eat macaroni kugel.'

She put some boiled macaroni into our biggest enamel dish, beat some egg whites, added the yolks, sugar and lots of beetroot jam, and took it to the bakery on Twarda Street. So that Saturday we ate a large kugel and our enjoyment had almost a pre-war measure. To complete our satisfaction we played the record of *The Jewish Wedding*. Because here at Walicow Street we considered that *The Jewish Wedding* was the most beautiful of all our records. 'It improves our tempers,' as Irena put it. Irena had always paid attention to her temper, even when she was a child. 'You spoiled my temper last summer,' she might say accusingly. There were six records. Ryszard's father once gave them to us before the war when he came to the village of Wieliszew where we spent the summer.

In the first days of April 1941, the day before the first Passover meal in the ghetto, we were sent a bundle of red radishes wrapped up in paper and some leaves of lettuce so young it hadn't formed heads yet. 'It's from Toporol', we said happily. The Toporol Association was organized in the ghetto by the agronomist Dobrzynski and attracted young people from all social classes. Its aim was to make allotments on every inch of waste ground, in the ruins of bombed houses and even in the cemetery. It was in the cemetery that the scientific and experimental work was carried out, preparing the patches of ground, sowing and planting. The red radishes were grown in the cemetery.

We sat down very emotionally that evening for the Passover meal. A copy of the Haggadah lay in front of every place setting. We collected Haggadahs and had a lot of them. From the most primitive to the most elaborate with coloured illustrations. The Haggadah lay in front of everyone and everyone turned its pages. Those who could read a few sentences in Hebrew did so, but not many of us could apart from my husband, and Ryszard too, but Ryszard was at his parents' this evening and was spending the night there.

Our daughters didn't know any Hebrew, apart from Marysia who ought to remember what her grandfather Maurycy Szereszewski taught her when she was a child. 'Marysia', he used to say, 'we're going to have a lesson.' The clever girl with her fair hair was the apple of his eye, his beloved granddaughter. He used to lay the Haggadah open in front of her on the table and she imagined its huge letters were composed of rectangular and square bricks. 'They're bricks,' she said.

'No,' he explained, 'they're letters. That's *aleph* and that's *bet*.' She could say 'the cat jumped over the fence' and 'the horse is pulling a small cart' in Hebrew. Later she learnt Hebrew with Miss Lis for a while and then it came to an end, because grandfather died and there was no more incentive or time.

After we'd eaten a hard-boiled egg and radishes dipped in salt water and drunk a glass of wine, Mrs Jelen brought in a plate with an imitation fish. It was made of yolks mixed with beaten egg-whites and matzo flour, cooked with onions and carrots: then a compote of stewed apples. Then the seder meal was over.

How different the seder meal at my father's had been, on the special dinner service with its dark red rim. The dinner service was only used for eight days in the year. For the rest of the year it stood in the wall cupboard. The wide stripe of dark red matched the dark red of the borscht, and in the borscht were dumplings made by the Jewish cook. The cook was called Estera, and the maid was Hinda, the seventeen-year-old daughter of Zlata the hawker from the village of Parzniewice – the one whose husband was killed by lightning on the Day of Atonement, when going out of the synagogue wearing his prayer shawl to breathe some fresh air for a moment under a tree in the stormy morning.

The concert Marysia Ajzensztadt gave in the garden on Nowolipki Street can be described as a real experience, if you apply the measure of those times. We walked from Walicow Street, over Leszno Street to Karmelicka Street. It was a long way and we crossed the bridge on the corner of Chlodna Street and Zelazna Street. A huge crowd was flowing in both directions along these streets. Most people were poorly dressed. The bridge was the one and only artery leading from the small to the large ghetto. Absorbed into this human flood we immediately became like drops of its waters, losing our individuality and becoming grey like the surrounding crowd.

The garden on Nowolipki Street contained a few trees, benches and a platform. On the platform there was a piano and the accompanist. At the piano, wiping her dusty eyes with a handkerchief, a girl of not more than nineteen was singing French songs. She was the daughter of the cantor at the synagogue on Tlomackie Street. Listening to the concert I thought of *Dybuk*, the opera which had been performed with such veneration in the Teatr Wielki before the war. The Italian composer's work had been played to a full house. To give the performance the most realistic and artistic framework, the producer had hired the boys' choir which performed synagogue works under the baton of the cantor Ajzensztadt. The boys were all between ten and thirteen and the choir was renowned for its excellence.

The concert in the Femina cinema on Leszno Street was no less an experience for us. The orchestra had its faults of course because it was incomplete and the playing wasn't of the highest order, but at the time it was a spiritual feast for all of us enclosed in the ghetto, and we remembered it for a long time afterwards.

At about this time Ryszard held a party for his lawyer colleagues and Nina held a birthday party. They were poor dos in comparison with the ones we used to hold for our daughters before the war. Ryszard had about twenty guests, including the lawyer Maslanko, who was a friend of his even though he was older, and Popower, Szenfeld and Friedman. The mainstay of the party was a bigos of sauerkraut and kosher ghetto sausage, strongly spiced with garlic, salt and pepper. It was more like dynamite than bigos. The strange thing was that they wanted to eat it and were able to do so.

The main dish at Nina's birthday was ice-cream which she made herself in the ice-cream maker. Nina pulled the machine out from under the suitcases and sacks on the shelf, got hold of half a bucket of ice, bought some coarse salt, creamed some sugar with egg yolks and added some milk. It was meant to be a surprise for her guests, her teachers Hanna and Dawid Chwat, the beautiful Krysia, dark-skinned Mark, and the lovely charmer Hania. Stella wasn't there. She didn't come. But Irena took a few hours off from the nursing school and came, and so did Anusia Laskowska, my niece. The ice-cream was a flop because it didn't set at all and was eaten in its liquid state, but the birthday party was quite merry all the same. They sang and even danced to our unfailing favourite, *The Jewish Wedding*.

House committees organized dance evenings every now and then but Nina and her guests didn't attend them for various reasons. Firstly, they weren't in the mood, so they said. Secondly, they didn't want to meet strangers, they had enough of them on the crowded ghetto streets. 'There isn't a day goes by,' said Mrs Chwat, 'when I don't find lice on my clothes, and what's more, in places where I'd least expect to find them, in my shoe, for example.' At this time there was hardly a flat where someone wasn't ill with typhus. In fact, at 6 Walicow Street the entire house committee, including the secretary, died of typhus. It amazed us. It seemed like a bad joke but it was true.

Could people possibly attend balls during an epidemic? But they did and the balls continued to take place, in various houses in turn. Anusia Laskowska went dancing on Panska Street, but she was the only one of us who did so, although she made no secret of the fact. It was a place where young people danced under the direction of a dancing teacher, and sometimes without him too. It didn't cost much to enter. That's where she met Harry. He often went there although he didn't dance because he was lame.

To sum it all up, we didn't have a lot of pleasure at Walicow

Street. When I mention the singing of the courtyard singer, the one we called 'Lovely Voice', the picture will be complete. When we heard her voice we all ran to the windows and down in the courtyard below we could see a woman of forty-five in a brown coat and a straw hat, arm in arm with a man in black glasses. Perhaps he was blind. The man opened a violin case. She sang arias from *Aida*, *Tosca* and *The Pearl Fishers* in a voice so beautiful it took your breath away. Who was she? An opera singer? Or a street singer? And who was the old man she brought along with her? Words can't describe the joy her singing brought us. We all had tears in our eyes and there was more sadness and nostalgia after she left than there was before.

In the late spring of 1942 a military car drove up to the gate of our house. Two elegant SS men jumped out. They entered the flat of the fair-haired woman on the fourth floor, examined her American passport and ordered her to pack. 'A few things in a suitcase and you're coming with us.'

She started to cry. 'Where to? I've got a husband and a six year-old daughter. Who will I leave them with?

'We're interning you,' they said. 'You're going to Germany, to a camp. Your husband and daughter will join you in a month or six weeks.'

They were even relatively polite to this client of Nina's. They addressed her as 'Sie' and were quite patient when she was getting her things together. She was throwing clothes into a suitcase and then pulling them out again and changing them. She was crying because her daughter, a slim girl with curly black hair who looked just like her father, was terrified and wouldn't let go of her. They even calmed the woman down, saying, 'Gleich schreiben Sie an ihnen eine Postkarte.'

In the end, seeing that she couldn't hide or run away, she shut the suitcase and hugged the child. She put on her pale-grey coat. It had threads on the collar where she had unstitched some Persian lamb trimming that winter, and handed it in to the Germans or sold it or burnt it. She put her hat on and went out onto the stairs behind them. Suddenly she remembered something. 'Can I say goodbye to my neighbours?'

'You can.'

She knocked at our door. 'I'm going away. I'm being interned. The SS is taking me.'

Before a week has passed a military car drives up in front of the gate of our house again. Two SS men jump out. They enter the front door. 'Where's the caretaker?' He's just coming with his broom in hand and with his cap over his ears. The Germans are in the house again. They're not afraid of typhus. What's up?

'Hey you, caretaker! Do you know this name? Take us to this person.'

'I know the name,' says Zysie Fligelman, 'it's him.' He points to a balcony with his broom. Then he takes them there; up the stairs of the other annexe to the fifth floor. An elderly man in glasses who looks like a doctor or a professor sits there in an armchair on the balcony all day long, reading. Sometimes he writes on white cards. There's a brown blanket on his knees. No-one knows his name but it's rumoured in the house that he's a Soviet citizen. They order him to dress and pack a suitcase as quickly as eins, zwei, drei. They address him as 'Sie'. Curiously enough they don't say 'Jude'. 'Sie sind interniert als Sowietischer Bürger.'

All this is terrible and incomprehensible. Fligelman is standing in the hall and can hear everything they're saying, whether he wants to or not. The man's daughter or niece – or maybe the woman is no relation to him and he only rents a room from her – brings a suitcase and helps him pack. Fligelman can hear her crying. 'Ruhig,' they say to her, 'gleich schreibt er eine Postkarte.' The professor or doctor, an old man no matter what he is, doesn't say anything. But his hands are shaking and he's turned white. And he's become hunched and smaller, as it were. He follows the Germans to the door. Fligelman carries his suitcase and the door slams. And that's how they go down the five flights of stairs, with the old man breathing loudly because he's got a heart complaint. But who cares about that? Nobody. Then they get into the car, shut the door and they're gone. It starts to rain, people take shelter in entrance doors, a strong gust of wind catches up a wisp of straw that has fallen off a cart.

This was the time of the greatest hunger and mortality in the Warsaw ghetto. One day when I was going to Szafran's shop I saw the body of a poorly dressed woman next to the gate of our house. She wasn't covered with anything, no rag, not even a newspaper. The crowd of people walked past her indifferently with their muddy complexions and sunken eyes. But two or three women stopped. Perhaps they knew her.

'She owned some houses in Plock or Ciechanow and she was rich,' one of them said to me. 'But she didn't have anything to live off here. She was weak from hunger and died.'

Further along Prosta Street I saw a corpse covered with newspapers. I thought it was the body of a child. But when a gust of wind blew the paper off, it turned out to be an old man, dried and shrivelled. Faded rags or newspapers held down with stones lay here and there in front of entrance doors. Families threw out their dead without registering the death and thanks to that they could keep on using the ration cards.

A small girl, swollen with hunger and covered with scabs, sat on the pavement on Sliska Street with her hand outstretched. Her mother or father or guardian brought her there to arouse the pity of passers-by because of her awful appearance. An attractive boy with sad eyes, eight years old or so, came to our kitchen in a white sports jacket and stood at the door in silence. A boy in rags always sang the same Ukrainian song in the courtyard. It was strange that a voice so powerful and moving should issue out of the mouth of a boy with such a small frame. When I crossed Walicow Street or the courtyard of our house the melody of his song always sounded in my ears.

Two teenage girls, probably sisters, lay by the wall on Prosta Street, swollen with hunger. They didn't have the strength to beg. They were dying in front of the very eyes of the passers-by. Once when I opened the front door I saw Johanna, one of the Jews expelled from Gdansk, lying on the landing with a wounded leg. She had dragged herself to our door.

My husband was one of the directors of the Jewish Welfare Organization at that time. One day a huge crowd gathered in front of the building. Hungry people were demonstrating against the members. He came home depressed. 'It's a bottomless pit, we can't do more than we're doing,' he said.

'What's happened?'

'They threatened and cursed me. But one of them stood up for me. "This man's hands are clean," ' he told them. As he was saying it, he put both his palms flat on the table. We looked at his hands. A stranger had vouchsafed them. He had vouchsafed the honesty of my husband, the father of our daughters.

In the second half of July 1942 notices appeared asking for volunteers for resettlement in the east. The east was a vague concept. Where could these camps be? In the Minsk region? In Polesie? No-one knew exactly, although the population of the ghetto, schooled by experience, didn't usually believe the Germans, there were many who, in their simplicity, believed these promises.

What was incredible was that one of the first was our washerwoman, a fit and energetic woman of 50. She was a widow and had one daughter who she'd fallen out with. 'So there's nothing to tie me down and I've got nothing to regret. I'll see how my life works out in these camps.' The day before her departure she visited the people she used to work for and told them what she was taking in the way of luggage and food. The housewives all wished her a safe journey and gave her a few zlotys as well. 'Are you taking your quilt?' they joked. 'That's the first thing I'm taking,' she replied.

At that time you could see lots of people with sacks on their backs in the ghetto streets because there were many more like our washer-woman. You could even see children with sacks. The sacks were made of grey cloth and had the owners' names visibly sewn on them. I met Mrs Iberal on Twarda Street, the mother of a school friend of one of our daughters. She was carrying one of these grey sacks on her back with her name and surname clearly sewn on. She was an intelligent woman but all the same she said to me, 'I've volunteered to go.'

Her husband was dead. Her sister-in-law had been a dentist and had also lived with them but she was dead too. I'd seen her death announced on the wall on the corner of Ciepla Street and Twarda Street. Her son and daughter were in Russia. 'So really there's nothing to keep me and I've nothing to regret,' she said, shaking my hand.

You could see Jews with not just sacks on their backs but their whole workshops too. They took their cobblers' tools or a lathe or some other machine because they were allowed to take the tools of their trade. 'You can take the tools of your trade', that's what the posters said. People took them in good faith, believing they would come in useful when they were resettled. The announcements even stipulated the exact weight of baggage permitted. Fifteen kilograms, not a gram more. Warm things were permitted, valuables too. So people weighed their sacks and bundles, repacked them and con-sidered what to take and what to leave so that they wouldn't weigh more, God forbid, than the announcements said.

Our relative, Abram Lichtenbaum, was a doctor and to be really sure he weighed his suitcase on a precision scale for new-born babies. He was the husband of Natalia, the paediatrician, so he had some scales in his room. Most of what he packed in his suitcase consisted of medical instruments such as a thermometer, a sphygmomanometer, a stethoscope and probably a stomach pump as well because he was a gastrologist.

It's worth mentioning that at this critical time we still received a visit from the agent who took the instalments on the electric floor polisher. My husband was also still able to send our former neighbour 500 zlotys, the sum we paid him each month for safe-keeping our paintings, carpets, antique candelabra and silver. It was the last instalment we paid. We couldn't pay any more.

The gasman came too. He read the meter, sat down at the table, took a fountain pen out of his pocket and wrote out an account, which I paid. It's hard to believe but it's true all the same. That morning I had been stopped on Twarda Street by two Jewish policemen. They told me to go with them, which meant they were rounding people up off the streets. I showed them the document made out for me by the Jewish Council. They looked at it suspiciously for a long time and kept glancing at me. I was still furious about it and said to the gasman, 'How can we live? Every time we go out on the street we're in danger. And is the house safe? It might not be in a day or two.' He agreed with me while writing the bill. He seemed to be sympathizing, as if he was silently think-ing, yes, this life of theirs is hard. He didn't say anything. He wrote the bill in accordance with all the regulations and signed it under-neath. He was Polish and worked for the gas board. There was a strange discrepancy between this prosaic bill left on the table and the dramatic atmosphere outside.

When the Jews stopped volunteering, the 'non-productive elements' came into the first line of fire for compulsory resettlement. People from welfare aid centres – the old, the sick, and anyone not employed. People with luck, influence or money got themselves put down as workshop employees. If not as a working employee, then as a fictional one. They were listed, but in reality they didn't work. That's how our former landlords at Poznanska Street, Mr and Mrs Walchowicz, and our niece's parents-in-law, Mr and Mrs Wyszewianski, and our relatives, Elkun Szereszewski and his wife, got themselves listed in Többens' workshop. It cost a lot of money and the Szereszewskis were protected by their son-in-law who was in charge of the materials department at Többens.

You could only be taken on at a tailoring workshop if you had your own sewing-machine, so the price of sewing-machines increased out of all proportion. There were crowds in front of the workshops. Young Hartzylber and his wife managed to get listed in a workshop thanks to the sewing-machine belonging to their brother-in-law, Witold Szpilfogel, the machine we took with us to the ghetto from the flat they left. But Hildebrandt, the tailor who lived on Hoza Street before the war and often mended my husband's suits, didn't have to present a machine in order to gain admittance to the workshop. People like him were accepted immediately because he was a master, a craftsman. Hildebrandt had an unusual surname – the same as the famous medieval German poet. He was a religious Jew, a man of great presence. He wore a black Jewish cap and a long coat, and had a son in Palestine. And so when the list for emigration to Palestine appeared, Hildebrandt was the first to volunteer. 'My son's out there,' he said, 'and I'm the first.'

Huge crowds queued to sign up. But he was first. The second was Mira Konstantynowska, my sister-in-law's mother. She had two daughters in kibbutzim, one near Chadera and the other in the Bet-Shan valley. She showed the letters she received from them, to prove it was true. They came to their senses a week later. Some of them said, 'God only knows what's behind it.' Others said, 'They'll deport us, murder us and rob us and we'll never see Palestine.' So they queued all over again. Now they removed their names from the lists in exactly the same way as they had previously feverishly entered them, including Mrs Konstantynowska and probably Hildebrandt the tailor too because they remained in the ghetto until the end.

At this stormy time Elkun Szereszewski sent his four-year-old grandson over to the Aryan side. He was helped by someone he knew in the Jewish police who had contacts with Poles. He sent the child to Sulejowek, to Marylka Muszol who was the fiancée of his student son, Leon. She had a Jewish father and a German mother. But the child soon came back. He looked Jewish and was unruly – he kept running out of the house and that could have attracted attention to himself and brought misfortune onto the whole family. So they sent him back to the ghetto. But Leon stayed with Marylka. They'd left the ghetto together, Leon and the child. Elkun thanked God that at least his son had stayed on the other side.

One afternoon we heard terrible screams coming from Többens' workshop. Our bathroom window looked straight out onto the courtyard of the workshop. I looked out and saw crazed mothers. The women workers at Többens brought their small children with them every day. They played in the garden in the care of a nurse while the mothers were working. That day a German lorry drove up unexpectedly and took all the children away, including young

59

Tempel who attended the play-group together with our Macius as his mother worked at Többens.

What happened to the two eight-year-old twin sisters who lived in one of the annexes in the workshop courtyard? They wore tartan dresses. Everybody knew them. You always saw them standing in front of the gate together. Were they taken away as well?

The first time our house was blockaded I was taken to the *Umschlagplatz* but managed to return. Standing in the crowd I could see from afar how a mother was voluntarily taking her small children in a crocodile to the *Umschlagplatz*. They all had a large red cushion strapped to their backs. I saw the children at the *Umschlagplatz* later. They were squatting down next to each other and eating jam with their fingers out of paper packings. Because, apart from the work that was promised, every person who volunteered for resettlement received a loaf of bread and a packet of jam for the journey. It was stated clearly in the announcements.

In front of me elderly women in hats sat on their suitcases chatting peacefully. Some of them had tiny dogs on leads. They behaved exactly like passengers in the waiting room at a railway station. A young woman whose name was Domb said, 'My name is Domb. I've just given my daughter away. I don't know the woman but she's staying behind. My daughter's a year old.' I didn't know her. I don't know what made her tell me her name and her heartfelt trouble unasked. She was laughing and crying simultaneously, happy that the child would stay and dying of sorrow at having so easily given her away forever.

An SS officer was milling in the crowd and he accidentally touched the shoulder of an old Jewish woman. I saw him stop and shake his hand with disgust.

At that time we had a servant called Klara. She was just washing some shirts belonging to my husband and Ryszard when we heard the whistle in the courtyard. So we went to the *Umschlagplatz* with the column of people. I marched next to a young woman from our courtyard whose husband had gone to Russia. She was carrying a small child and gave me the child to hold. A few rows in front of me Klara was marching next to Ita, who used to be my deceased mother-in-law's nurse. They were both wearing worn slippers. When I managed to get back home from the *Umschlagplatz* I finished washing the shirts. I wrung them and hung them up. In the evening Klara's brother came and took a basket with her things. Klara was the last servant we had.

When our house was blockaded again the next day and we were taken back to the *Umschlagplatz*, our column contained scores of other residents from our house. Mr and Mrs Loewensztein, Dr Kirszenbaum's brother, the tailor from the ground floor, the two spinsters from the bombed flat. Just about everybody apart from the old lady whom I saw on the roof with her arms round the chimney. She might have been shot. Everyone who had hidden the previous day and everyone who had managed to return from the *Umschlagplatz* was picked up the second time. Because, as it turned out later, the Germans were clearing the house for Többens' workers and none of the residents could remain there.

Zofia Margasinska died during the blockade, the one who was the friend of our caretaker, Fligelman. She had a rucksack on her back. I was surprised that she had a rucksack ready too. She worked at Többens but that day she was on another shift. She stood there calmly, confident that she would be reclaimed.

Mr and Mrs Walchowicz's sixteen-year-old son also died. They were the ones who were listed at Többens. His parents left him at home in bed. He was either ill or feigning illness. So did Migdal's wife and daughter, Oles Koenigsztein and his mother, née Landsberg.

Mr Loewensztein from the fourth floor was a tall, handsome man who looked a hundred per cent Aryan. There was a letter with seals and the Swedish coat of arms on the door of his flat because he was the representative of Swedish trading companies. The letter safeguarded him against having his furniture requisitioned and perhaps against having his money and valuables stolen by the Germans, but it didn't protect his family from being resettled. The day before the Germans took his eighteen-year-old son and twenty-year-old daughter. It was said that during the selection the boy must have been sent to a transit camp, a so-called *dulag*. He was tall and very handsome and it was unthinkable that a boy like that should perish. But did his parents believe it?

Now Mr Loewensztein was marching with his wife in the column. She had small regular features and she looked Aryan, which she might have been. She was wearing one of those tight, white, woollen caps so popular in the ghetto. He was leading her by the hand and they were walking along together. When he entered the *Umschlagplatz* he showed the SS men his documents. They looked at them and handed them from one to the another. 'Sie sind frei,' they said.

'What about my wife?'

'She isn't.'

Then he took her by the hand again and together they followed the others, all destined to perish. I was looking at his back when he turned and I saw how the two of them walked forward.

We returned thanks to a miracle this time as well. This time it was thanks to my neighbour Ferhendler. Tired and panting he jumped off his bike and handed the SS men a letter of authority with a seal. When we got back home we were sitting at the table, very depressed, when suddenly there was a knock at the front door and Mr Koenigsztein entered. He sat down on the sofa without greeting anyone and without saying a word. A moment later Mr Migdal came in, unshaven, dishevelled, the same as Mr Koenigsztein. He sat down with us in silence without greeting anyone.

They were both out when the house was blockaded. They might have been on the Aryan side in their factories, as the Germans still ordered them to work there. When they returned to the ghetto no-one was there any more. There was a terrible eloquence in their silence and in the fact that they had come at all. Because they'd never ever been before. But we understood that the two fathers had to come to someone who still had a family, if only to sit for a moment in silence.

After the second blockade of Walicow Street, when we returned to the empty house, we finally understood that the Germans needed our house for Többens' workers and no-one could stay in it. So where were we to go? To Irena's. That was our first thought. Irena lived in the nursing school on the corner of Panska Street and Marianska Street, next door to the ruins of a bombed house.

The ruins of a bombed house. There were ruined houses in every single street in the ghetto, but those ruins had special significance. Not for everybody, just for me. Because they remained engraved in my memory from the time when I saw the eminent Warsaw cardiologist Dr Semmerau-Siemieniecki crossing them .– no, not Marianska Street but the ruins. He was being led by a Jew in an armband. He must have come from the Aryan side to a sick patient, a very sick patient, having been asked or begged to come. It wasn't a safe thing for him to do. I was so moved at the sight of the doctor that I always connected him with the nursing school and the ruins of the house. The same thing happened now. In my mind's eye I immediately saw an indivisible knot of images.

So we'll go to Irena's. It was late afternoon already because after we were freed from the *Umschlagplatz* we didn't go home straightaway. We sat on some planks in Landau's sawmill for a while. Then on Gesia Street we met an official we knew and we stopped for a moment. He was walking behind us, dragging along behind. We kept turning round to look at him. What had happened to make him walk so strangely? 'I saw my mother off,' he said when he caught up with us. That's exactly what he said. 'I saw my mother off. I watched her leave.'

It was already getting dark as we ran along Prosta Street. We passed Többens' workshop, then the food shop where the three boys and the girl in the red scarf had spent their time all day long until so recently. Then the chemist's window appeared in front of us, then the ironmonger's and the shop where they fried pancakes in winter. At last we ran along deserted Panska Street and reached the corner of Marianska Street. I glanced at the ruins and saw in my mind's eye Dr Semmerau and the Jew in the armband, and we rang the bell.

The director, Mrs Bielicka, was sitting behind a desk in the hall. Behind her there was a window covered with a curtain. A telephone box stood in the corner and that seemed strange. In front of us hung a portrait of Weissblatt, the engineer, in a dark frame. He was the administrative director.

'Can you put us up for the night? Just for one night. We've just come back from the *Umschlagplatz*.'

To come back from the *Umschlagplatz* lent you a sort of legitimacy. It engendered surprise, disbelief, astonishment and even respect. People who returned from the *Umschlagplatz* were like the dead resurrected. They had to be treated with consideration. Could she refuse? She couldn't.

The school was still functioning despite everything. The students' coats were hanging on pegs. One of the professors even had a lecture that day. Women from the staff in white aprons milled about the corridors and asked the director for instructions. But all the same you could already feel the place slackening. Student nurses Margolis, Olomucka and Bielenki had gone over to the Aryan side. Zofia Turkoenig had gone to Otwock where her mother worked in the Brijus sanatorium. The director's two children, a boy and a girl who you could always see in the hall, didn't come any more. Where were they?

She took us to a narrow room with two beds. Its one and only window had no curtain. A short pelmet hung on the window frame.

The room was on the lower ground floor and any passing German patrol or Polish policeman could see us at once. We didn't sleep a wink all night. We tossed and turned on the beds. We had lost many members of our family and we were shattered.

In the morning I saw a cart passing by through the window, harnessed to a horse. Not even a truck, just a plain large peasant's cart. Men, women and children were standing on it crushed tightly together. I recognized my sister-in-law Stefania Szereszewska's elder sister, Janina Majde. She was wearing a blue dress with large bunches of flowers, or was it a dressing-gown? It could have been because it was seven o'clock, not yet eight. Janina could still have been in her dressing-gown and picked up by the Germans like that. Sometimes they even threw people out of bed and took them away in their night-clothes. Nobody on the cart was wailing or protesting or defending themselves. Everyone was indifferent and determined. Janina Majde's face was immobilised by surprise.

I once saw a girl being taken to the *Umschlagplatz* in a rickshaw. She was wearing a night-dress and had fainted. Perhaps it was out of embarrassment and humiliation. Our neighbour, paralysed Mrs Kaczor, was carried out onto a truck in a shoddy dressing-gown and trodden down slippers. She recognized me and I could see on her face how embarrassed and upset she was.

Once I witnessed something extraordinary. A girl standing next to me in the column was wearing old, thin, flat patent slippers on her bare feet, they didn't even have a leather sole. Plucking up her courage she started complaining to the German gendarme. 'I didn't even have time to change my shoes,' she said, 'let me nip back home and take these old things off and I'll be back in a minute.'

The odd thing was that he let her. She jumped into the entrance door like a wild goat. She hid in the cellar or somewhere no-one else knew about. There must still have been a spark of human pity twitching in the gendarme's heart because of course he knew she wouldn't come back.

We took Irena with us and walked towards Grzybowska Street in the direction of the Jewish Council. Crossing Ciepla Street we met Mrs Lewkowicz with her daughter, Nina's school friend. They had rucksacks on their backs. 'We're going to the Aryan side,' they told us.

'Which way?'

'Though the lawcourts.'

At that time you could still get through the lawcourts from

64

Leszno Street to Ogrodowa Street, this section of which was on the Aryan side. People crossed over that way if they had contacts on the other side.

'What about your husband?'

'He's over on the other side already.'

Ciepla Street! It linked Twarda Street and Grzybowska Street and was one of the most important arteries, one of the most frequented routes in the ghetto. Relatives, friends and acquaintances met on this street, either on foot or in rickshaws. The inhabitants of the ghetto didn't stay at home much but usually walked along the streets, like ants, restless ants. Everyone felt that the ghetto was like an anthill. On Ciepla Street we suddenly meet Olga. How is it possible? Olga? She was our Nina's nanny many years ago – a German Jew from Wroclaw. We hadn't seen Olga for over ten years and we'd forgotten all about her. It was she who recognized us. 'I'd recognize you even after a hundred years, Mr Szereszewski.'

'What are you doing in the Warsaw ghetto?'

'I'm in charge of a workshop.'

That's what she said. We were surprised. Director of a workshop? How come? But we didn't ask, we simply accepted it as something completely normal. All we said was, 'Where do you live?'

'Here, on Ciepla Street. My daughter's with me. Do you remember I had a daughter?'

I did remember. She placed the child in an orphanage while she worked with us. Her husband was a tailor. He was a young man and was still living with his parents. His parents didn't want to know her. I also remembered that she was a poor worker. She was talkative and self-assured and often used to go and play chess at the Kleszcz patisserie on the corner of Marszalkowska Street and Nowogrodzka Street. Who did she meet there? It didn't matter any more. Now, in this terrible time, when only a workshop could save your life, perhaps we should make use of this contact and get Irena and Nina listed in Olga's workshop?

'Here's my workshop,' she said, pointing to a gate. Inside was a cobbled courtyard and then a row of buildings. In the corner of the courtyard, not far from the gate, lay a pile of German steel-helmets. We looked at them, fascinated. She invited us into her flat. 'You'll know where I live,' she said, 'and you'll see my daughter.'

We followed her willingly. She lived on the corner of Twarda Street and Ciepla Street, on the dark ground floor. Not at the front, but in the dark courtyard full of rubbish and scraps. We thought that she lived quite modestly seeing as she was the director of a workshop. A girl with blue eyes and light curly hair came out opposite us. She looked like a sun-filled picture in the gloomy frame of that background. Then I understood why Olga wanted to show us her daughter so much. We didn't say a word about what we were thinking and planning. We knew where her workshop and her flat were. For the time being it was enough.

The Jewish Council headquarters were at 26 Grzybowska Street in an old house which remembered the Council's first president. The last president, Mayzel, went east and crossed the River Bug when the war started and died in a town on the Polish-Soviet border. His wife died of typhus in the ghetto in the autumn of 1942. The building was so large that before the war it housed a trade school. The school was closed down when the war broke out. The older students were called up into the Polish Army, some went to Russia and the rest stayed in the ghetto.

As you approached Graniczna Street you crossed Grzybowski Square and the church of All Saints. That's the church where Father Puder was, the christened Jew. The christened Jews in the ghetto were gathered round him and the church. Many of them lived in buildings attached to the church, in the presbytery. One of the people who lived there was Dr Weinkiper, the laryngologist. A sewing shop where christened Jewish women worked, older women mainly, was opened in the basement. Many of them were neophytes who felt spiritually safe under the wings of a new religion. When the resettlements started all the christened Jewish women from the sewing shop at All Saints were taken to the *Umschlagplatz*, as were all the christened Jews who lived in the presbytery. I don't know what happened to Father Puder, whether he managed to survive or whether he perished with the others. His brother was a glazier and we even knew him. At the beginning of the war, after the bombing, he glazed some windows for us.

When Wanda Kraushar committed suicide, a requiem mass for her soul was said in this church. It was attended not only by friends and relatives from the ghetto but also by her daughter and cousins from the Aryan side. One of her cousins was kneeling on a hassock immersed in prayer. The Jews thought it strange. The exaggerated fervour of this neophyte was by no means an exception.

The Jews who had converted to Protestantism gathered round a Protestant church on Leszno Street. Leon Fejgin's wife and her small son hid in that church. She worked as the pastor's house-keeper.

The hall, corridor and rooms where the officials of the Jewish Council worked were dark and gloomy. The walls were cracked and hadn't been painted for a long time. Cigarette ends were every-where, the floors unwashed, there were dirty windows, dusty and fly spattered portraits of former chairmen and benefactors. In these uncertain times it didn't bother anyone. Every day could be your last so who was going to pay any attention to things like that? Who cared about the appearance of the place or even the sanitary conditions? It was trivial compared to other problems a hundred times more important.

A crowd of people on business and officials with tired faces and eyes sunken from lack of sleep and anxiety milled about the hall and wide corridor. The harsh expressions on these faces were at odds with the street basking in the July sunshine and the indifferent blue of the sky unfolded between the houses. Many of them had already lost a father or a brother; typhus had claimed many a beloved child. But no-one talked about it and nobody asked.

Czerniakow was no longer among the living. It was only the week before that, after talks with the Germans in his office, he had asked for a glass of water and had taken cyanide. He left a note for his wife on his desk. Just a few words: 'remember our boy'. That was all. Janek Czerniakow managed to escape to Russia when the war started and is said to have died of hunger somewhere in Samarkand. For a long time his mother kidded herself that he was alive and would return. After her husband's death she went over to the Aryan side and lived in hiding with a Polish friend. Now the chairman of the Jewish Council was Marek Lichtenbaum.

When we walked along this noisy wide corridor we didn't yet know that the wife of Councillor Rozensztadt's brother had been taken to the *Umschlagplatz*. She didn't return. The news caused con-sternation and panic. Until then people believed that Jewish Council workers and their families were protected against being resettled. 'Have a look. He's the one by the window behind the desk. The one with his head down.' It was strange that he was sitting so calmly, that he wasn't weeping or shouting or cursing.

We sat down in a room where some women were typing. One of them was called Hirszberg and came from Lodz. Her husband, an army doctor, was a prisoner of war in Russia, somewhere near Kozelsk. She took her seven year-old son with her to the Council every day. He was red-haired, just like her. There was one thing she wanted – to send him over to the Aryan side where she had some friends. He'd gone over with the work team that morning. That's why she was crying as she typed. 'Andrzejku!' she called out after him once more. He didn't turn round. He just waved to her with one hand, one of the team was holding him by the other hand. Then they crossed the check-point. She told me about it when I sat down next to her.

There was a long table covered with a green cloth in front of us and some officials were sitting at it. We were sitting at a small table next to the door. We were sitting there and looking at the cracked walls and the tall windows with six panes and a casement, when in comes Wika, Baumberg's daughter. Baumberg the engineer, a colleague of my husband's. Is this the same Wika I knew when she was two years old? Yes, the same – but she's eighteen now, tall and well-built. Her hair is as light as corn and she doesn't look Jewish. Why has she come? I can hear her saying that her father died a year ago and the Germans took her mother and brother away. She managed to hide and so she saved her life. 'But I'm going to the Aryan side today and I'd like some money.'

I look at her and think how neglected she looks. Her skirt is crooked and creased and her hair is dishevelled. I wonder where she spent the night. What hide-out was it? I can hear her say, 'I want to go to the Ciechanow area and work on the land there.'

They give her 500 zlotys. 'Here are 500 zlotys for you.' They bless her: go with God and survive the war. 'You've got every chance of surviving.' Every chance means her flaxen hair. I think about her flaxen hair and then she's gone. She slipped the money into her pocket and walked through the room with strong, sure steps. She had sandals on her bare feet.

Now a poorly dressed, middle-aged woman comes in with her seventeen-year-old daughter. It's the wife of Rabbi Eckerman, one of the hostages the Germans are holding. 'I'm going to Minsk Mazowiecki with the children,' she says. 'It's still quiet there. I need some money.'

'How will you get to Minsk?' they ask.

'We're being picked up by a cart. I've arranged it with a peasant. He's coming for us.'

Rabbi Eckerman has been imprisoned by the Germans together with about ten other hostages and no-one knows how they're treating him. But she's got seven children. The eldest, Hilary, is staying in the ghetto because he's married and his wife is pregnant. She's taking the younger children with her. There aren't any resettlements in Minsk Mazowiecki. Life flows normally there. They give her some money. Tomorrow at dawn she'll be rattling along in the cart, not on the main road but on side roads, and she might arrive there safely.

'Mrs Eckerman,' they say, 'go in health. Go with God and go in health.'

She takes the money from the table and puts it away into a leather bag. The blessings she takes and puts away into her heart. She is a sober and provident mother. She has to make decisions for herself and her husband now. She's leaving 'because death is lurking here on every street and in every house.' But in Minsk Mazowiecki the death she was evading caught up with her and they all perished. When Rabbi Eckerman returned from prison he found no-one in his family alive except Hilary, the one who was married and had stayed in the ghetto.

The rabbi's wife hasn't left the room yet, she's still putting on her jacket and closing her bag, when an official we don't know comes into the room. Maybe he's just a passer-by from the street? His face is red and he's breathing loudly, we can see he's been running fast. He doesn't greet anyone, it must be something important.

'What am I to do with the linen from Dr Korczak's orphanage? There are heaps of vests, aprons and towels. Who shall I give it all to? Tell me what to do with it.'

'I saw it,' says Irena. Irena is saying something! Always so quiet but now she's clearly affected by what this man is saying. 'I saw Dr Korczak and his orphans walking along the street. The Jewish policemen were clutching his clothes. "Don't go," they said, "you can save yourself" '.

'On Sliska Street,' the man says, 'it's there, all the linen left behind after the murdered children. The orphanage is empty. But there's still a pile of linen in the store-room.'

The words of this unknown person make an incredible impression on us all. Because the children's linen is still there. It testifies mutely that the children once existed. After a while one of the people sitting at the table asks, 'Where did Dr Korczak get the money for the orphanage from in the last few months?'

'From the Thirteens,' says Irena. 'I heard that the Thirteens covered the orphanage's costs for some time.'

Suddenly Bronislawa comes in. My sister-in-law, Bronislawa Szereszewska, Edward's wife. It seems strange that she's suddenly come to the Council holding two children by the hand, her boy of eight and girl of six. 'I've escaped from the house. I was scared they'd blockade it. I've been trailing round the streets. I came across the Germans on Panska Street. We ran into the nursing school and hid in the telephone box.'

She stayed for fifteen minutes, not a moment longer. Then she jumped up from her chair and took the children by the hands again. She said she was going to the Aryan side, maybe as early as today, but definitely tomorrow. 'Stay well,' she said, opening the door.

'Where's Edward? Where's your mother?' we called after her.

'I don't know. They're all saving themselves the best they can.'

We spent the night on the floor in the Council, on coats. We lay on coats on the floor and our daughters lay on the table with the green cloth. The shooting outside the walls lasted all night long. Endless shooting day and night. One wall was quite near – past Ceglana Street was the Aryan side.

The next day we were allocated a room in a house belonging to Mr Tarasiewicz on Grzybowska Street. The one-storey house was between Ciepla Street and Walicow Street. An old and inconspicuous house, it had no more than four flats and two or three shops on the street side. Everything was empty now. We didn't know who had lived here before.

Tarasiewicz didn't live in the house himself. It was the same Tarasiewicz who owned the shops selling 'Pluton' coffee all over Warsaw.

We were allocated a room on the first floor. This was long and narrow with one window which looked out onto a neglected garden. The room contained two beds and a small oval table with chairs, and our two sacks of bedding. On the other side of the staircase was a room allocated to Dawid Weintraub, the Council's book-keeper. When we come up the stairs he's standing in front of the door as if he's waiting for us. Weintraub is standing in front of the door and behind him we can see the head of his wife and the head of the child she's carrying. His wife's hair is flaxen. She's standing behind him. You can tell at a glance that she's shy and helpless. Her husband is the brains of the family. He makes the decisions and protects the other two.

'Mr Szereszewski,' he says, 'we'll bring you some tea and we can let you have half a loaf of bread.'

His suit is creased and stained and his hair is dishevelled. He is small and slim with fair hair like his wife. His mouth is half open and he's got buck teeth. And we see that the child's mouth is half open too and it looks like she can't shut it.

'What's she called?'

'Arianka,' says her mother in a voice as quiet as a whisper.

Arianka? How odd. She must have read about Ariana and given the child the same name. They follow us, all three of them. Our two sacks of bedding have already been brought from the Council for us. We open them and put the pillows on the beds.

'Mrs Koral lives on the ground floor,' says Weintraub. 'Do you know her?'

Nina knows her. She's the aunt of a school friend of hers. But where did Weintraub live before we became neighbours? Judging by his appearance and clothes we can tell that he's been in hiding somewhere with his family for some days. They might have spent the night in a cellar or in an attic, and maybe that's why his wife is following him so closely and her eyes are so full of fear.

'We don't know how long they'll let us stay here and we won't be able to sleep at night, that's for sure. They're shooting non-stop.' Weintraub does all the talking. His wife doesn't say anything. She is standing behind him with the child and looks at us speechless. There is a small oval table by the door and two chairs. We sit down.

'Do you need anything else?'

'We don't need anything else.'

They go out. The door slams behind them. When we're on our own the shooting outside the window seems to be getting more and more frequent and nearer all the time. Then Natalia comes in – Natalia the doctor, our cousin.

'Natalia,' we shout. 'How did you find us? Where did you get the address from?'

'In the Council.' She asked someone who works there. Her voice is colourless, her eyes exhausted. She is sitting on the chair in a state of desperation.

'Has something bad happened?' we ask in a whisper.

'They took us both to the *Umschlagplatz* this morning,' she replies.

Both – that means Natalia and her husband. He took the suitcase he had weighed so many times. In front of the carriages she was reclaimed because she's a doctor allocated to a block of houses and he could have been reclaimed for the same reason. The train was just moving off. Whatever came into his head? He jumped in,

71

of his own accord and of his own free will, and waved his hand to say goodbye.

'He waved his hand to say goodbye,' says Natalia, 'as if he was going on holiday. Then the train moved off and he was gone.'

That's how she tells us about her husband. Now she's getting ready to go. That's all she wanted to say. 'I just want you to know that's how it happened. That's why I came.'

She doesn't even say goodbye. There's no room for that word in the ghetto today. Here we live on life's border. 'Is this the last time we're meeting?' That's what we should say. So Natalia leaves without saying goodbye. The shooting lasts all night, then the new day dawns.

At six in the morning I'm standing in front of the gate already and I can see a huge crowd of workers, men and women, hurrying to their workshops. They're carrying shoulder-bags and in them a slice of rye bread with dripping, jam or mock honey, and a flask of ersatz coffee. They'll get a bowl of soup in the workshop at noon but they have to provide their own bread. The shoulder-bags are made of grey cloth by wives or sisters. Sometimes, though less often, by daughters, though they could be made by daughters as well. But if there isn't a woman to make it, if she's been taken, then the bag is made clumsily with thick uneven stitches by the man.

While I'm standing in front of the house I see a relation of mine in the crowd, Felicja Zychlinska. I didn't know she was in the ghetto. Her son was on the Aryan side, and it was even said he'd married a Polish girl. I was surprised that he wasn't looking after his mother and hadn't got her out and into the country somewhere. She was carrying a shoulder-bag and walking energetically. I didn't call out to her. I watched her from afar. I was looking at her face – her real face – concentrated, closed and severe.

One day, as I was standing next to the stalls on Ciepla Street, I was watching my cousin Roza Mayzner in the crowd in exactly the same way. She was walking along the narrow pavement next to a ruined house, deep in thought. I stood at a distance and looked at her real face, completely different from her normal everyday face, closed and severe.

Then a horse-cab passed and in it young Hartzylber's parents. The parents in the horse-cab and on the platform at the driver's feet a small suitcase with their things. Where are the Hartzylbers going so early, I thought astonished? And although I knew them and had visited them in their house I didn't call out to them or stop the horse-cab. When I returned home with a loaf of bread the family immediately asked where I'd bought it.

'On Walicow Street not far from Chlodna Street. I saw a cowshed there in the courtyard. A lot of women came with jugs for milk. Pity I didn't have a jug, they might have sold me some too.'

'Did you see anyone we know?'

'I saw Felicja Zychlinska on her way to her workshop, and the old Hartzylbers in a horse-cab. When I was buying the bread that Jew from Plonsk drove past in a peasant's cart, that old bachelor who farmed with his old sister. What's his name?'

No-one knew. Everything that had just taken place had knocked us completely off balance and his name had escaped our memory.

That evening a woman we didn't know came to our room. We'd never set eyes on her before. 'I'm Natalia's landlady. She lived in my place. She rented two rooms.'

'What is it?'

'They did a blockade today and took her away and she hasn't come back.'

That's all she wanted to tell us, that's why she came. She turned round, closed the door behind her and was gone. We glanced at the oval table – at the table-top where Natalia's hands had rested yesterday – and we thought we could still hear her saying, 'He waved his hand to say goodbye and then the train moved off and he was gone.'

On 9 August the news went round that everybody in the small ghetto had to move into the main ghetto. Only workshop employees were to remain in the small ghetto. The Jewish Council was to move too, and with it all the officials and workers, to Zamenhof Street, Dzika as it used to be called. This time we were going to spend the night at Ignacy Baumberg's, the lawyer, in his flat on Chlodna Street.

Chlodna Street on the even side was the Marszalkowska Street of the ghetto. Adam Czerniakow had lived here. The finest shops were here. People met friends here on sunny Saturday afternoons. It wasn't a long way from one end to the other, from Zelazna Street to Biala Street, but the pavement was wide at this point and the ghetto's high life walked along it. Gutnajer's antique shop; a delicatessen shop; Forbert the photographer; cosmetic treatment at number 8. A wall ran along the middle of the street and you crossed into this section from the small ghetto by a wooden bridge.

At five in the afternoon we got hold of a cart, loaded our sacks of bedding, and in an incredible squash, moving at a snail's pace, we arrived at Chlodna Street at the house where Baumberg's numerous family lived on the first floor. Baumberg went to Lwow at the beginning of the war. He met a young widow there and married her. She had a son of eleven. Shortly afterwards they all returned to the Warsaw ghetto where Baumberg got a job in the Jewish Council housing office. We'd known him for many years.

That evening at supper – the main course was potato soup flavoured with flour fried with onions – there were twelve people at table. Ignacy Baumberg wore a stiff white, celluloid collar. Next to him were his wife and stepson, then his wife's parents, then the two of us and two of our daughters. There were also Baumberg's two sisters, Jadwiga Benkel and Aniela, and his youngest brother Aleksander. His wife's son was called Oles. He had something that was a real treasure in those days – an 'Iskry' almanac, a children's magazine, bound in red cloth. The calendar was passed from hand to hand and aroused much interest.

'What's in it?' they asked Oles.

'Everything. All about Columbus, Nelson, Copernicus and Alexander the Great.'

'Do you read it?'

'I read it every day. And when I reach the end I start again.'

He was tall and slim and had dimples. When I looked at this Oles I thought of the other Oles at 6 Walicow Street. He was the same age and had the same charm and even looked similar. And he had the same name. I also thought, when I looked at him, that perhaps God would protect this boy since he didn't protect the other one.

Jadwiga was the wife of Benkel the lawyer whom the Germans had taken to a camp in the first months of the war. At that time from among our friends they took: the two Ickowicz brothers, Teofil Konzon, Hercman the engineer, Hilary Tempel, Borensztein and his son, Mojzesz Sobelman, the father of our caretaker at Walicow Street. People said they were in Stutthof and waited for letters from them. At the beginning of the war people were so naïve that they expected to get letters from everyone the Germans took away. Jadwiga was a doctor. In the first year she waited for letters just like the rest. But now she doubted whether her husband would ever come back. Aniela was a clerk. She had many Polish friends. She was sour and sad and had no connections with Jewry. She longed with all her heart to be on the Aryan side.

Someone said, 'A christened Jewish woman died in our house

74

and we saw the funeral through the window. A small, black hearse with one horse drove up to the courtyard. A dozen people or so, family and friends, accompanied her to the check-point. Then the hearse drove off alone.'

I thought of Wanda Kraushar. 'Take me,' she had cried in our flat at Walicow Street and no-one knew what her strange words meant. She was accompanied to the same check-point. The hearse moved at a snail's pace through the ghetto and then the horse received a flick of the whip and moved forward at a sharp trot.

The next morning the cart with our bedding rolled through the crush and crowd again. Along Zelazna Street, Leszno Street, Karmelicka Street until it reached Zamenhof Street, in front of the Jewish Council headquarters. We sat down on our sacks in the wide entrance hall of the building waiting for somewhere to live. There was feverish movement here. The door was wide open and many people were coming in from the street. Some milled about for a while, looked into adjacent rooms and then went out again. Others sat down next to us and waited patiently for something or someone.

We sat like that for hours, and next to us was the family of Zundelewicz the lawyer, his wife, daughter and twelve-year-old son. We were so tired we couldn't keep our eyes open. We were like nomads resting after a long journey on foot. One of the people who came into the hall and then went out again was a friend of Irena's from the nursing school. She had a rucksack on her shoulder and a scarf on her head.

'Madzia,' said Irena, pleased to see her. 'Are you going somewhere?' She thought she was going to the Aryan side, like Margolis and Bielenki.

'Yes. I'm going to the *Umschlagplatz*. They took my parents away yesterday. I might find them.'

'Don't go,' said Irena in alarm, 'if it calms down the school might carry on again.'

'School? It was blockaded today at noon and they took all the staff, even Weissblatt. When I got there everyone had gone.'

She milled around for a while. She looked through an open door into the room where the engineer Sztolcman was working at his desk, nodded her head and went out. People later said that Weissblatt, an old man of seventy, went to the *Umschlagplatz* with all his staff wearing his best suit. Interestingly enough the detail about the suit was stressed. At the *Umschlagplatz* he committed suicide.

When evening came everyone sitting in the hall started moving

75

their bundles and preparing a place to sleep for the night. We were convinced that we'd spend the night on the concrete floor or leaning against one another in chairs. Then Popower and his wife came over. Popower worked in the Council and his younger brother was a friend of my son-in-law, Ryszard.

'We live nearby at 7 Lubecki Street. We'll take you to our flat for the night.'

We went willingly. They let us have their bedroom with its two wide beds and they slept on the sofa in the dining room.

'We don't know how to thank you,' we said, very moved.

'Don't thank us. We're just as homeless as you are. In fact we shouldn't be living here because this whole side of the street has already been resettled. We had a miraculous escape. We're still wandering from place to place.'

'You could write a book about the various stages of our journey,' said Mrs Popower. 'We even returned to our own flat. It attracted us like a magnet.'

We shuddered. We thought of our flat at Walicow Street in the empty house we had run away from in panic. We went to bed by moonlight and starlight because we didn't put the light on and didn't even light a candle for fear of the Germans.

When we came back to the Council we were told that Chlodna Street had been blockaded the day before and Baumberg's family had been taken to the *Umschlagplatz*. His sister, Jadwiga Benkel, committed suicide. Aniela was said to have managed to get over to the Aryan side. Ignacy Baumberg was reclaimed at the *Umschlagplatz* and could have saved himself but he didn't want to be separated from his wife and went with her of his own free will.

We had been told Roman Kramsztyk, a famous painter, was shot during the blockade on Chlodna Street. He was running down the stairs, he wanted to hide in the cellar. He ran straight into a German.

3 • The Day of Deliverance

In the middle of August 1942 when the small ghetto was liquidated and the Jewish Council moved from 26 Grzybowski Street to 19 Zamenhof Street, my husband was allocated a flat at 6 Lubecki Street. My husband, Stanislaw Szereszewski, was at that time the director of the Finance and Budget Department of the Jewish Council.

Lubecki Street connected Pawia Street and Gesia Street. All the residents of the houses on both sides of the street had been resettled. Now, after the small ghetto was liquidated, the houses on the even side of the street could be lived in again. The houses on the odd side were completely deserted. Deserted?

An electric light burned in the cellar of number 7. It was as if someone careless lived there and you wanted to tell them to turn the light off. The light was on all day and all night long the whole time we lived there. The deserted and silent street was only a cover. A lot of people were still in hiding in cellars and attics and on the mezzanines of empty flats. I often saw my neighbour looking around quickly and entering the gate of an empty house. She was taking food to relatives who were hiding in the cellars.

The corpse of a girl with a smashed skull lay in the gate of the house. 'Shut your eyes!' I shut my eyes but all the same I remembered the shape wearing a grey dress and with her hands wide apart. We crossed the girl and went upstairs. I dragged myself up the stairs. Wasn't that dead girl a bad omen? Why was she killed?

'She probably wanted to save herself and jumped out of the column into the gateway. Don't think about it.'

There were no panels in the door of our first floor flat as they had been smashed with rifle butts. Instead there were a few planks and you could slide your hand in through them and turn the key. We stood in front of the door and hesitated. We could take the flat on the ground floor with its normal strong door. But it was dirty and poor. In the large room there was a table covered in scraps of leather and with a small hole punching machine nailed to it. The flat must have been lived in by a craftsman who produced belts, handbags and satchels.

A woman was hovering around the flat. 'There's a hide-out in the kitchen,' she told me quietly, 'a cubby-hole where you can hide from the Germans. You should take the flat.' I entered the kitchen and found the hide-out in an alcove made of part of the bathroom behind the kitchen. It had been separated off and the entrance was through the alcove in the kitchen. But we moved into the first floor flat. A three-roomed flat with water, gas and electricity.

We had a few beds and mattresses of our own. One room was for me and my husband, while Irena and Nina slept on a mattress on the floor of the second room. The small, third room was still in a mess. It was on the courtyard side. There was a heap of bedding, men's clothes, dresses and coats on the floor. When we swept the rooms we found identity cards in the corner. The former owner must have been a lawyer or civil servant. In the room the girls slept in were two huge old-fashioned sideboards that reached to the ceiling and two velvet bags containing prayer shawls lying high up on a shelf in one of them.

From the objects we found we recreated the lives of the people who had lived here before us and who had been been deported to annihilation. In the kitchen under the window there was a medallion of Our Lady, which meant they had had an Aryan servant. In the pantry a whole collection of brown earthenware pots – they must have pickled cucumbers and made sauerkraut, borscht and jam. In one of the drawers of the huge sideboards lay syringes, medications and bottles of cheap perfume – therefore their daughter had worked in a chemist's shop. There was a row of textbooks and exercise books on a shelf, so they must have had a son of school age. We found a box of plumber's tools including picklocks, a flat wooden box with cupping glasses, and a scrap of material, a cutting left over from a suit. The material went over to the Aryan side with us and two years later, in Sulejowek, I made a pair of trousers for my grandson out of it.

The next day a relative of the former owners of the flat came for their things. A round-faced, corpulent woman called Mrs Jankiele-wicz. She brought a man with her and they took the sewing-machine. There was a tall basket full of dirty linen in the kitchen next to the alcove and they took it just as it was. They started feverishly taking bowls, pans, plates, the teapot and frying-pans.

The man stood in the hall with an open sack and she was just going up to him with a bucket and a scrubbing brush.

Then my husband said, 'Stop!' He lifted up his hand with the palm facing outwards. 'Mrs Jankielewicz, this is not right. The household we left at 6 Walicow Street was just as well furnished. How are we going to cook and clean if you take everything?'

I was standing by the sink and scrubbing a burnt saucepan with ashes. She put the bucket and scrubbing brush down without saying a word and walked out of the kitchen. In the evening when we were sitting at the kitchen table eating supper my husband said, 'Mother's worrying again.'

'Why is our mother always so bitter?' asked Irena.

'We've got a bitter mother. And she's in the habit of worrying in advance,' said Nina.

'There are seven of us,' I said. 'Winter's coming and we've only got two warm coats. In the course of all our moves we've lost father's coat, Ryszard's coat, Nina's, Marysia's and the coat Macius wore.'

Then my husband got up from the table. He went into the room where Mrs Jankielewicz's things were still piled up on the floor and brought out a coat. Grey-green with a black thread running through it. 'Hide it and there'll be a coat for one of us. There must be another dozen coats lying there. It's the law of war.'

Mrs Jankielewicz and the man came a few more times until they had taken everything. We didn't say a word about the coat. We hung it up in the wardrobe.

We threw the things we didn't need out of the window into the courtyard, just like everyone else. The pile of furniture, pillows and mattresses reached as high as the first floor. We threw two folding beds, two old mattresses, a settee and a few prints in wide frames out of the small room. We preferred to throw suspicious-looking beds out rather than sleep on them. We swept the room. A low, white kitchen dresser with glass panes stood against one wall and a white painted chest against another. We left the dresser and chest. We spread some netting and a mat from Marysia's bed out on the floor and when my brothers-in-law Witold or Edward came they slept there. Marysia was on the Aryan side with her son.

The flat was full of bugs and countless fleas. Our sheets, pillow-cases and night-dresses were spattered by fleas. Every evening we stretched a washing line between the window and the door and hung our washing up on it. There was no glass in the windows of the rooms at the front. There was no black-out material either. The Germans used to fire at windows whenever they noticed a crack of light, so we didn't turn the lights on in these rooms. We went to bed in the dark.

Our life revolved round the tiny kitchen with its window overlooking the courtyard. We covered the window with a thin, red kelim with beige flowers. We never took it off. We only moved it aside a little in the daytime. We cooked, ate, did the washing and received visitors in the kitchen. A smallish, rectangular table stood by the wall just next to the door. Above the table there was a shelf. On it hung two frying-pans, a grater, a colander and some keys. The hands of the good housewife who was no longer there had carefully hung the keys underneath the shelf. And they stayed like that. There were twelve of them, all various sizes. They might have been for the attic, the pantry, the cellar, the kitchen, or for padlocks and suitcases. We didn't need the keys but we didn't throw them out of the window. They stayed with us.

Our relatives, Dr Meir Mayzner and his wife, sat in this kitchen on stools. She told us calmly and impassively about her two sisters. They had died together with their husbands. She didn't shed a single tear while she was telling us about it. She took a piece of butter wrapped up in paper out of her coat pocket and ate it with a spoon. 'I bought it from a caretaker on Gesia Street, the one with the Aryan-looking wife.'

Then he told us that his brother had died. He was a doctor but had worked in a workshop as a manual worker, while his ninety year-old father had survived and had come nearly all the way from Otwock on foot. He took one of the velvet bags with the prayer shawl and tefilim which we had found in the sideboard for his father.

Stefa Pinus was sitting on a stool in our kitchen. She worked as a typist for the police on Ogrodowa Street. Her mother was no longer alive. She had been been put to sleep by her daughters. The same thing had happened to Anna Zuk, the mother of my sister-in-law, Celina Szereszewska. As soon as Stefa entered the kitchen she placed a pot of dripping on the table and asked, 'Can I leave this here for a day or two?' I was looking at her and thinking: she killed her mother. She and her sister Zofia who lived with her mother.

'I've brought the dripping here because it's my greatest treasure. Can I leave it here?'

'Yes. Where do you live?'

'I'm moving right now and it might get lost in the move.'

'What about your sister Wanda and her husband, Mieczyslaw Hartzylber?'

'They were deported from the workshop.'

I didn't ask her anything about Zofia or her husband. Zofia was lame. I had met Mieczyslaw Hartzylber's parents on Grzybowska Street at the end of July during the first days of the resettlements. They were riding to the *Umschlagplatz* in a horse-cab just as if they were going to the railway station. Their suitcase stood by the driver's feet. They loved each other very deeply. They were afraid they'd be separated so they went of their own free will.

'Do you remember, Stefa, what old Hartzylber always used to say?'

' "I've got one wife, one son, one daughter, one daughter-in-law, one son-in-law, one granddaughter, and one God." Do you mean that?'

'Yes, that's it.'

Edward Drabienko now lived on the third floor in our house. Before the first air raid he lived on the corner of Lubecki Street and Gesia Street. But when the house was hit by a bomb and a large crack appeared in the ceiling above his head he moved into number 6. His brother Stefan worked in a workshop on Leszno Street. He often visited Edward and they both came to see our daughters. They sat at the kitchen table. We gave them tea and kasha. They taught our daughters a new way of washing shirts, a system they had thought up. The system saved on soap and labour. The shirts washed themselves. Stefan left his parents' trunks and suitcases with us, and a crate of food and even two folded beds and mattresses. We also had my brother-in-law Witold's sack of food and two enormous baskets belonging to my other brother-in-law, Edward.

One day Mrs Konstantynowska came, Edward's mother-in-law. She sat down at the kitchen table as well.

'You haven't come across Stefa Pinus, have you?' I asked her. 'She left a pot of dripping here. No-one's seen her at all.'

'No, I haven't seen her.' She was silent and then she added, 'my daughter and the children are on the Aryan side now. They crossed at the check-point on Leszno Street.'

Olga Liwszyc was listed at the workshop on Niska Street, the steam laundry. Her two daughters, Danusia and Irka, worked in Többens' workshop in the small ghetto and lived at 6 Walicow Street in the flat my sister used to live in. One day Irka came to see us. I sat her down on the stool at the kitchen table, sat down on the other stool and looked at her. She was fifteen, tall, dark and very pretty. She was wearing a red pullover which used to be my sister's. She had died in the small ghetto. 'What's happened to my mother? She worked in the laundry on Niska Street. Have you heard anything about my mother?'

I couldn't take my eyes off my sister's pullover. It was a long way from Többens' workshop to Lubecki Street, and dangerous too. No-one was allowed to cross from the small ghetto to the large ghetto. Only policemen, but even they couldn't always cross. The journey was ensnared with traps. The number of times she must have had to dive into gateways before she reached us! Such a long way. She ate a bowl of soup, then lay down on the bed and fell asleep immediately. She got up after an hour and started getting ready to go home. I wanted her to stay the night but she couldn't. She had an aunt on Pawia Street and had to call in to see her.

Witold Szereszewski sometimes called in the evening and stayed the night. Both he and his wife were also listed at the steam laundry on Niska Street. We sat talking for a long time at the kitchen table. My husband's younger brother Edward also came and stayed the night. At this time everyone had severe enteritis.

One evening my husband asked, 'Has Stefa Pinus taken her dripping?'

'Yes, but only today.'

'Thank God. I thought she'd never come again.'

Every visit was accompanied by great danger. Mass resettlements were being carried out. It wasn't safe to go out on the street. People only left their houses in the evenings, and even that wasn't fail-safe. My relations, the Mayzners, left their workshop on Nalewki Street with a group of workers at eight o'clock when it was dark. A large column of people was just passing on their way to the *Umschlagplatz* to be deported. The Germans put them in the column as well, even though they all had work cards. Many people spent twenty-four hours in their workshops because that's where they felt safest.

There was a small balcony outside our bedroom. A few rods round the sides and top formed a pergola or bower. Climbing up the rods were a vine, a morning glory and sweet peas. And there were plants in pots. This little balcony must have been the pride and joy of the family which no longer existed. The father had fixed the rods and fastened wires for the climbing plants. He had done it himself, helped by his small son. He used the pliers, hammers and nails in the box we found. The vines in their pots were thick and twisted. That meant the bower was built a long time before the war. The vines were watered by the Aryan servant, the one whose medallion of Our Lady we found on the kitchen floor on the first day. The daughter who worked in a chemist's shop gazed at the starry sky on spring and autumn evenings, and leaning against the balustrade she dreamed of love. We found her love letters. Carefully arranged and lying in a square, wooden box from Zakopane with a flower carved on the lid.

The mother – busy, careful housewife that she was – whose keys hung under the shelf above the kitchen table came here and sighed. On Saturdays and holidays visitors were proudly shown this poetic corner. The boy brought the chairs, and the girl brought the tea. The visitors stayed long, warming themselves in the sun and looking at the balconies on the other side of the street. I liked to sit on the balcony. In front of me were the empty houses on the odd side of Lubecki Street and the constantly burning electric light in the cellar of number 7.

A book I had found in the ample depths of the sideboard lay on my knees. I found it very moving. It was called *The Biography of My Son*. By his father Samuel Maliniak. He had published it privately. Writing archaically but with great simplicity the father related his son's childhood, his school years, his military service in the Caucasus and finally his illness and death. One of my aunts was related to the Maliniak family and in the book I came across names I knew from her stories.

From our balcony I could see another balcony. In line with ours, at number 4, where there was a police station belonging to the Polish police. They must have lived there with their families because women sat out on the balcony. An old woman sat there for a long time and I looked at her grey hair.

One day I saw a woman with two tiny children. They came out of Gesia Street and turned into Lubecki Street. The woman was dragging huge sacks. The children both had a pillow strapped to their backs. They sat down to rest in the gate of number 7, where the light was on in the cellar all day and night. A car of German officers drove past like an arrow. They didn't notice the woman and the children. After a while the woman got up, went in the direction of Pawia Street and disappeared. The children sat on the sacks and waited patiently. Suddenly they jumped up terrified and started looking for their mother. They left the things and ran to the corner of Gesia Street, came back and ran to the corner of Pawia Street. Then they came back again. They ran around many times in a circle like that until she finally came back. Then all three of them walked towards Pawia Street, the wooden soles of their shoes clattering loudly on the pavement.

From our balcony you could see part of Gesia Street and the columns walking along it to the *Umschlagplatz*. After a column had gone past pillows, parcels and rucksacks lay scattered on the street. In their tiredness people had thrown off everything that was weighing them down. The old or sick sat down on the pavement. Then the Germans shot them. Hearses followed every column. The best known was Pinkiert's hearse. It picked up everyone the Germans had killed. Sometimes a hearse stopped under our balcony, in front of the gate. The driver lived in our house. The cemetery workers wore caps with black rims and white edging. Their wives and the women who rode beside them on the hearses wore similar caps. Zygmunt Hurwicz was responsible for the Cemetery Department in the Council. He wore a cap with a black rim and white edging as well.

So first of all you could hear steps. Like a drum silently beating. Rhythmic and constant. Then the column appeared. I saw an old man with a sack. He sat down on the kerb and put his sack down beside him. He couldn't go any further. Then I heard a shot. My husband often said, 'Don't sit on the balcony. The Germans will walk past and fire at you.' Then he added, 'Can't you see there's no-one on the balconies or in the windows.'

When I saw the Germans approaching I ran in from the balcony. I sat on the bed and waited until they had passed. I could hear their steps and every word of their conversations.

A huge wardrobe stood against the wall. Two baskets of Edward's were arranged one on top of each other next to the balcony. There were our two beds and between them the small, oval table. One bed by the window, the other nearer the wardrobe. They were covered with net curtains made of Greek tulle. The property of the family who had lived here before us and who had been deported to be exterminated. Each curtain was a different colour, the one on my bed was white and the other was cream.

A loose pile of papers wrapped up in newspaper lay in the wardrobe. It was the chronicle of our family. It fell off the cart during the move and the pages got scattered and dirty. On top lay the chapter about my grandmother and a photograph of an old woman wearing an amber necklace, a dress with leg of mutton sleeves and an old fashioned head-dress. Opposite the wardrobe, between the window and the balcony, hung an enlarged photograph in an oak frame. An old Jewish woman in a wig, with earrings, wearing a dress with leg of mutton sleeves, pinned at the neck with a brooch. On her head she had an old fashioned head-dress made of velvet ribbons and lace, just like my grandmother.

Next to the wardrobe was the door. It opened onto the corridor to the kitchen. A second door right next to the baskets opened into the room where the two huge sideboards stood side by side. Sometimes when I lay in bed I remembered that I had left something on the table in the other room. I got out of bed and stepped carefully so as not to tread on my daughters sleeping on the floor. And when I was walking like that in the darkness, in my night-dress with my hands stretched out in front of me, the light from the stars or the moon was reflected in the brass doorknob or the glass or the metal ornament on the sideboard, and trembled quietly in the dim glow. Wasn't that someone's shadow brushing against my hair or the tips of my fingers? If the shadows of the people torn out of this nest and exterminated return anywhere, then it must be here. Should I be scared of these shadows? Or on the contrary – will they be well-disposed and good to us?

There was a mezuzah on every door. The four Sabbath candlesticks, two large and two small, that Mrs Jankielewicz didn't take stood high up behind the dresser rail. So they were religious. Here, in these walls, their thoughts turned to God. They had their worries and their joys, their sicknesses and their funerals. Here's the knob they touched so often, the light switch they turned on, the threshold they crossed, and the window they looked out of every day. God! When will we free ourselves of these people's shadows? In their furniture, in their things, in their vapour – we survive and live their lives without knowing it.

I lie on the bed their mother worried in. She sighed and couldn't get to sleep for a long time. Then father woke and lifted his head and said, 'Du slufst nis, tajerenkie'. I can't sleep either and I sigh and my husband wakes and lifts his head just like the other one and says, 'Aren't you asleep, darling?'

Our neighbour on the kitchen side was Izaak Giterman, the director of Joint, the American welfare organization. He occupied a

85

small flat with his wife and son and never left the house. Opposite, on the front side of the house, Henryk Gliksberg, the engineer, occupied a three-roomed flat with his wife and two sons, Tadeusz and Stefan. Tadeusz was twenty and Stefan fifteen. Tadeusz's movements, posture and behaviour were just like his father's. He was grave and reticent. He crossed to the Aryan side with the 'Brandenburg' work team. Stefan was incredibly charming. He had light-brown eyes and brown hair. He was tall and agile, and was always smiling and good-natured.

The Gliksbergs moved from Polna Street into Ogrodowa Street in the ghetto where they had such a lovely flat that was so beautifully furnished that the Germans filmed it, with Mrs Stefania Gliksberg sitting at an antique table. They were making a propaganda film to document how well the Jews lived in the ghetto.

So the Gliksbergs were our neighbours. They lived in flat 3 while we lived in flat 2. They brought their own beautiful furniture with them, antique tables, secretaires, a drinks cabinet, chairs, armchairs, carpets and paintings. Once, when I was sitting there in a low, club armchair the old clock, which stood on legs and had a dial behind glass, struck four quarters, then three o'clock and finally played a carillon. 'That's a real gem,' I said in delight.

'It's my grandfather's clock,' said Mrs Gliksberg. She put her hand on the clock caressingly. Then she rang. Ada came in, a strong, dark girl who helped in the house. She was wearing a white apron and was carrying two cups of tea on a tray. Mrs Gliksberg was still the lady of the house at Lubecki Street and ran the household just like before. Drawn curtains shaded the windows. She had ordered Ada to wash the floors, windows and doors and had mentally prepared herself for a long stay.

They had their own furniture, so they threw a lot of things they didn't need out of the window, and placed the sideboard on the staircase. They occupied two rooms and gave the third to Dr Steinsapir and his wife. They owed the doctor a debt of gratitude as he had cured Henryk Gliksberg of a serious heart complaint when they lived at Ogrodowa Street.

Dr Wielikowski lived on the second floor with his wife and daughter. He worked for the Jewish Council too, just like Gliksberg and my husband. His daughter didn't leave her mother's side. The Wielikowski's oldest daughter was in Brazil. 'If only we could go there,' said Mrs Wielikowska sometimes. After the final liquidation

86

of the ghetto they were deported to Poniatowa and managed to escape from there. They are now in Brazil.

Melamud, the Council's cashier, lived on the ground floor in the flat that had a hide-out in the kitchen and where the leather-goods workshop used to be. When she moved in, the first thing Mrs Melamud did was to throw the heaps of multicoloured scraps of leather out of the window, and then she threw out the iron hole-punching machine that was screwed to the table. Finally, a few days later, they threw the table out and carried in a different one from another flat. The Melamuds spent most of their time in the kitchen with its carefully covered window, just like we did. The hide-out made them feel safer. They kept opening the door and looking in curiously. In the evenings the two of them sat at the kitchen table pining for their sons who were in France.

At first their sister-in-law lived with them with her small child. She was a widow or else her husband was in Russia. She didn't have a work card because she didn't work and no-one could provide cover for her. She and the child died during the first selection.

On the ground floor on the courtyard side was the Union of Pharmacists with its director, Henryk Gliksberg. Our son-in-law Ryszard worked there. On the first floor above the Union of Pharmacists the Finkielszteins, Ryszard's parents, shared a flat with Mr Noz and his family. Noz worked in the Union of Pharmacists too. A few days later Ryszard's father got hold of a small shop on Gesia Street. It was meant to be a fuel distribution point. He threw all the rags, scrap-iron, smashed jars and broken bits and pieces on the floor out into the street, and hung a sign above the door. I noticed the freshly painted sign when I was walking past one day and looked inside. The shop was empty. There wasn't a single lump of coal or a single spadeful of turf in it. Jakub Finkielsztein sat on a box, next to the box stood a bucket and in the corner was a broom propped up against the wall.

One morning there was a selection in the gate of our house. That's when Melamud's sister-in-law died. The Germans questioned Finkielsztein's work certificate. Then Ryszard and his father went to Gesia Street with one of the Germans and Ryszard showed him the sign and the shop – his father's place of work. So Ryszard's father sat from morning till night in the empty shop, and the sign was his defensive entrenchment. When he sat there alone gazing at the wall or the broken window various melodies he had heard in his life must have passed through his head, because he was very musical. He liked to tell us about the concerts he had attended before the war and about famous conductors. He was very proud of Bronislaw Szulc, a relation of his who was a conductor and had emigrated to Palestine.

In the course of three years Ryszard's mother had had to move from Marszalkowska Street to Sienna Street, then to Wronia Street, then to Dzika Street, from Dzika Street to Chlodna Street and finally to Lubecki Street. She was tired out by the frequent moves, but even so she kept calm and stayed as good-humoured as ever. She had lost her hair-grips and combs and her hair was tied up at the back with a piece of tape. Ryszard asked a team worker he knew to buy some hair-grips and combs for his mother. They lived together with Mr Noz and his family. Mrs Noz was a French Jew with two children, a son of fifteen who crossed over to the Aryan side with the 'Brandenburg' work team together with Tadeusz Gliksberg, and a red-haired girl of twelve, Tala. Mrs Finkielsztein often said, 'She's such a brave girl. She can even make the pastry on the pastry board on her own.' But although she was brave Mrs Noz never let her out onto the courtyard. We never saw her.

The two flats on the courtyard side were occupied by Popower and his wife and Mr Wojdyslawski, a tall, thin official who had lost his wife in the first days of the resettlements. They both worked in the Finance Department. In the flat Wojdyslawski was allocated he found a wardrobe full of clothes left behind by the former resettled owners and he wore a different suit nearly every day.

By a strange coincidence the Popowers' former flat was opposite the house where the cellar light was on all day and all night long. That side of the street had to be emptied of residents and the Popowers couldn't stay there. We knew the flat because they had let us stay the night there once when we were sitting in the Jewish Council with nowhere to go. Late in the evening Mrs Popower went down to the cellar with a pan of soup and a loaf of bread. One of her friends or relations was in hiding in the cellar. We heard rustling and noises on the landing and gathered that someone was in hiding there as well. Things like that happened so often that we didn't take any notice and asked no questions.

On the right-hand side of the courtyard lived Mr and Mrs Kowalski with their son and daughter. Oles had fair, curly hair and was seven or eight. Their charming sixteen-year-old daughter had curly hair and mulatto features. Oles was the only small child in our courtyard. There might have been more but they were kept hidden.

I used to see Oles on pyramids of furniture next to a flowerpot with a shrivelled palm and a portrait of a man with a moustache. The portrait was in a wide velvet frame and stood leaning crookedly against a rusty basin.

He was looking for treasure just like boys do. There were paints and paintbrushes in a box and if he wanted he could take them. If he wanted to, he could put a bowler hat on his head or wrap himself in a prayer shawl or put on a pair of galoshes and imagine he was in seven-league boots. There were heaps of various shoes and sofa cushions lying scattered down there. The cushions were embroidered with butterflies, pierrots and roses and were the first things to go flying through the windows.

The noise of falling objects and the crash of broken glass could be heard from morning till night. Lamps, photograph albums, rocking horses, old suitcases, baskets, wooden stakes from the flowerpots that Oles sat on, provided they could still be sat on – all this lay in the courtyard. All day long I could hear Oles shouting, 'Nora! Nora!' or 'Norka! Norka!' and Nora's voice from inside the flat shouting, 'Oles! Oles!' That's how the two of them called to each other. I also met Oles in the gate where the hearse was often kept. He looked at the spokes of the wheels and tried out the reins. I even met him on the street in front of the gate. Walking along the street was really dangerous.

Mr Kowalski worked for the Council. Mrs Kowalska and a helper brought two buckets of soup every day for our house from the kitchen at 4 Lubecki Street. She stood in the courtyard and called, 'Soup! Soup!' We came down with pans. She ladled the soup into the pans and distributed black bread. Once when Mrs Kowalska was in the courtyard with the buckets a German soldier came in. He was carrying two loaves of bread under his arm. 'Are there any children in this courtyard?' he asked in German. 'Are there any children here?'

There was very little bread at that time. But Mrs Kowalska said, 'There aren't any children in this courtyard. No, we haven't got any children.' Her heart was thumping when she returned to her flat.

There was water, gas and electricity in every flat on Lubecki Street, and also in other streets in the main ghetto. The gas office with its Polish workers was still on Zamenhof Street. Some of the residents of our house wanted to go there and have the meters put in their names. Wojdyslawski went there one day. 'I'd like you to put the meter in my name,' he said politely.

89

'We haven't been told to do that,' said the official.

'You haven't been told to do that? I've taken the place over. The meter's ticking away. I want to pay.'

'You can't pay.'

'But the meter's ticking away.'

'Well then, go and kiss the meter.'

That's what they said to him and that's how it finished. The whole time we were there no-one ever asked us to pay for the gas and electricity. Strange, isn't it?

My youngest daughter, Nina, worked as a clerk for the lawyer Rozensztadt in the Legal Department of the Jewish Council. At that time the Legal Department was on Gensia Street. The lawyers Goldfarb, Maslanko, Szarogroder, and Goldwasser and the articled clerks Lewkowicz and Aleksander Lewi worked there too. At the beginning of the war Aleksander Lewi went to Lwow with his father. His mother stayed behind in Warsaw and committed suicide. In the end they both returned from Lwow but the mother wasn't alive any longer. The father went over to the Aryan side and the son stayed in the ghetto. He was quiet and sad and friendly with Nina. He lived on Pawia Street so I sometimes saw him from the balcony, turning from Gensia Street into Lubecki Street and then walking towards Pawia Street.

I often asked Nina, 'Why don't you invite Aleksander Lewi over? He lives very close.'

'I've asked him a few times but he doesn't like being with people,' she replied.

He committed suicide by taking cyanide on the turbulent night before the great selection in the ghetto. He left a letter asking to be buried together with his mother but I don't know if his request was carried out. The same night Edward Drabienko descended on a rope into Przejazd Street from the roof of a house on Leszno Street and escaped from the ghetto.

So Nina worked in the Legal Department and after work she came back home.

All the shops along Gensia Street were destroyed. The doors were broken, the windows were smashed and there were rags, old iron and rubbish everywhere. But new shops were already opening. One or two distribution points, a coal store, a tiny shop with a jar of cucumbers in the window. You had to walk along the street carefully. Make sure you can't see any Germans. Listen for the stamping of feet. Because a column on its way to the *Umschlagplatz* might suddenly appear out of a side-street and they'll immediately include you in it. That's exactly how Fogel's wife died. She didn't dive into a gate, she didn't take cover in time.

Nina is walking down the street. Above her the blue sky. Under her the asphalt of Gensia Street. Everything around her is deserted and silent. Not a single passer-by. Suddenly she stands rooted to the ground. She hears a shout and in front of a gate she sees a German with his back to her beating a Jew with a rubber truncheon. The Jew has curled up and sat down. A bike is leaning against the wall and by the bike a dog is howling quietly, waiting for a sign from its master. Nina's grey short-sighted eyes didn't see all this from a distance. Now she can see it. But at the same time she can also hear a distant, deafening, rhythmic stamping. There's a gate! A saviour! She dives into it. Then from the gate into the courtyard in the direction of the cellar. Two murdered Jews are lying on the ground in the courtyard, without shoes or jackets. She passes them carefully. In the cellar corridor she waits a while with a few other women. Then she continues walking. She walks and walks. Now she's passing the house where the nursing school is. Her sister Irena is a student there. Nina looks up. Will she see Irena in the window? But there's no-one in the window.

Before the liquidation of the small ghetto the nursing school was in the insurance building on the corner of Panska Street and Marianska Street. Here on Gensia Street there were no more lectures or regular work during the resettlements. Irena spent the days at school but slept at home. The director, Mrs Bielicka, worked as a nurse in Schultz's workshop. I saw her sometimes from the balcony coming back from work in her nurse's cap and navy-blue cloak. The students had to make their own arrangements for meals. They pulled a cart with cabbage or bread along the street. The German soldiers watched them kindly and addressed them in German.

Now Nina is passing the gate of the house where a two-year-old girl was left behind when her family was resettled. The people who moved in afterwards got the child together with the flat. A few Germans knew about the child. They came every day to ask if she was eating, if no harm was coming to her and if there was anything she needed.

Here's the prison on Gensia Street. The wife of the lawyer Ruff was there at the time. She was sent to prison from the Aryan side. Jan Ruff was sent to Auschwitz and died of dysentery shortly afterwards. Mrs Ruff didn't admit to being Jewish and was sent to Ravensbrück. She came back to Poland after the war. There were a lot of gypsies in the prison at the time. One night a hundred of them escaped. Gypsies were resettled just like the Jews.

The Union of Pharmacists opened a chemist's shop on the corner of Lubecki Street and Gensia Street. Mr Seret, who had previously run a chemist's shop in the small ghetto on the corner of Prosta Street and Twarda Street, worked there. One day his wife and ten year-old son were taken from their home. When he heard about it he ran to the *Umschlagplatz* and never returned.

In the September sun, her head uncovered and wearing a navy-blue blouse with white spots, Nina passes the chemist's shop and turns into Lubecki Street. She's twenty years old, with soft, black hair, grey eyes, a round, childish face. She is slim and graceful. She steps lightly. In her hand a bag. In the bag letters. Apart from the letters a cuddly rabbit and a felt duck, her two mascots.

The light is on in the cellar of number 7. She has to glance over there. Then she turns into the gate, climbs up to the first floor and stands in front of the door of flat number 2. The unwanted sideboard thrown out of the Gliksbergs' flat is standing on the staircase. In it are plates, glasses, and even crystal vases and a canteen of cutlery. The drawers have been ripped out with an axe. She stands in front of the door which has been smashed by rifle butts; in front of the door with no panels. Crossed boards and pieces of wood cover the opening. She knocks. Then I come out of the kitchen and open the door.

I left Nina at home and went to the butcher's on Pawia Street with Stefania Gliksberg. Our neighbour had told us that we could get some horseflesh in the third house from the corner, in flat number 1. We went downstairs and stopped in front of the gate. When we looked right we saw Jewish policemen on Gensia Street riding past on bikes. The prison courtyard gate was wide open. We couldn't take our eyes off it. Then Stefania said, 'My husband told me that two men and a child were killed there. They shot the mother in the neck. She's in hospital, but she's probably going to live.'

'Is it true they entered the flat because they could see some light through a crack?'

'They saw a table set for supper. They found a large supply of food. Wine and tins. It enraged them. But don't let's talk about it any more.'

We turned left out of the gate and walked along Lubecki Street. Here's the shop in the basement. Here's the gate of number 4 with the kitchen where Mrs Kowalska brought food from. I looked up at the balcony on the first floor. The grey-haired woman was sitting motionless on the balcony. On the corner of Lubecki Street and Pawia Street was the prison. There was silence all around. Not a single face in the windows. 'That's Pawiak,' whispered Stefania. 'That's it.' The first two houses on the corner of Pawia Street were occupied by doctors. Kupczykier from the Jewish Council also lived there. He had typhus.

Through the dark gateway into the courtyard. From the courtyard turn right. In the narrow, ground floor room a skinned horse hung on the wall. Pieces of meat lay on the counter. A man with a cloth wrapped round him was beating the bones with an axe. Stefania and I both bought half a kilogram of horseflesh.

When we returned home I saw Nina's school friend Krysia Braun sitting at the kitchen table. She had lost her mother and grandmother. She saved herself by hiding in the chimney. She and a friend had got their names down in a workshop and she was just on her way there. 'You're wearing a smart coat,' Nina said.

'When I get bored with it I'll go into an empty flat and find another one. I'll leave this one. I wear a different dress every day. There are wardrobes full of dresses in the empty flats.'

She shared some of the soup that Mrs Kowalska brought along in the bucket, shouting 'Come and get your soup!' in the courtyard. 'Nora! Nora! Bring a pan and get some soup!' Mrs Finkielsztein, Mrs Noz, Mrs Popower, Mrs Giterman and Mrs Melamud came down to the courtyard. Even the caretaker's wife took the soup although she was well off. Her husband sold smuggled food, just like the other caretakers. Only the undertaker didn't take any soup. He cooked fish and meat. He had butter, cheese and eggs. He scorned Mrs Kowalska's soup. Undertakers used their hearses to engage in large-scale smuggling.

At dusk we heard a clattering coming from Gensia Street. Some rickshaws stopped in front of the house. There were quick footsteps on the stairs and then a knock at the door. Three Jewish policemen entered, and Lichtenbaum the Jewish Council chairman, his son Mieczyslaw, First and two others I didn't know. They didn't take their hats off, they didn't greet my husband or me or my daughters, they didn't apologise, they went through the flat like a whirlwind, looked into the bathroom and toilet, checked the kitchen door and went out onto the front stairs. We could hear their footsteps on the upper floors. Doors being opened and closed. The sounds of conversations. Fifteen minutes later the rickshaws drove off.

Surprised and dazed we knocked at the Gliksbergs' door. 'Were they here too?'

'Yes, they were. They went to Melamud's and Wielikowski's and to the third floor. They checked the whole house. Lejkin was waiting downstairs in a rickshaw. Don't you understand what's going on? They're still living on Zelazna Street but they've got to move nearer the Council so they'll probably throw us out of our flats.'

'Do you know that the chairman didn't even take his hat off? He didn't greet us and didn't apologise either.'

'Pigs,' said Gliksberg.

We didn't say anything. We were embarrassed. Our humiliation and degradation were so intense that our hearts couldn't take in the enormity of it.

We weren't thrown out of our flats. The people who lived on Zelazna Street were informed in confidence that it wasn't worth moving. They were told that they would be moving again immediately afterwards so they could miss out on this move. They were told that the ghetto was going to be narrowed down again in about ten days' time and they would move straight into houses allocated to them, for the final phase.

Late in the evening my daughters were washing their father's shirts in the kitchen. They placed a small, white, washing-up bowl on the table. They had found a small washboard and were rubbing the shirts on it. Then they soaked the shirts overnight in soapy water, in accordance with Edward and Stefan Drabienko's system. The shirts had blue stripes, brick-red stripes and grey checks. Father was sitting in his usual place between the table and the dresser. The red kelim on the window was lowered. Water for tea was boiling on the gas cooker. Suddenly he said, 'Mother's thinking about something again. What's she thinking about now?'

'According to one school of thought, events turn full circle. Everything always happens again and is repeated in an eternal circle,' I said.

'What about it?'

'In a hundred thousand or five hundred thousand years, or a million years, your daughters will be washing your shirts just like they're doing today in a kitchen just like this and you'll be asking what I'm thinking about and I'll reply in exactly the same words.'

'So we'll experience this hell once more and a hundred times more and a thousand times more?' asked Irena in terror.

'Yes,' I replied, 'if the wheel comes full circle then everything will be repeated.'

'If I knew,' said Nina, 'that there was even a grain of truth in that Indian philosophy then I'd be screaming in desperation.'

It was nine o'clock. After nine. Suddenly we heard awful shouting coming from the direction of Gensia Street, and the sounds of blows. Someone was being beaten. Someone was being horribly beaten. It was forbidden to go out on the streets after nine o'clock in the evening. We listened. Then a shot. Then silence. And then there was no more shouting. After a while father said, 'Our family reached its peak before the war but it's definitely dying out now together with this dying ghetto. In this case I can really see that the wheel is turning.'

'Daddy,' said Nina, 'what about our family chronicle? It would be so good if it survived.'

He smiled and said, 'If we're not here any more, if we're all gone, our mothers, our fathers, our brothers, our sisters, our young people, our children, it would be good if at least the chronicle survived us.'

Next day as I was walking along Gensia Street with my husband to the Jewish Council we met Tyller, the engineer from Lodz, by the chemist's. He worked in the Building Department that Edward and Mieczyslaw the sons of chairman Lichtenbaum were in charge of. My husband greeted him and then said, 'My brother was a well-known architect in Lodz. He's listed in the steam laundry on Niska Street. Could he work in the Building Department?'

'I know him personally. I didn't know he's in the ghetto. I'll let you know tomorrow,' replied Tyller.

And thanks to his efforts Witold got a job as a store-keeper in the Building Department and received a room in the ground floor annexe on Gensia Street, which is where the employees of that department lived.

We said goodbye to Tyller and walked on. Above us was the blue sky, below us the asphalt of Gensia Street. In front of us and behind us was a long chain of grey houses. A dozen people hurrying to work. They were walking carefully. They were looking carefully to see if there weren't any Germans about. They were listening to hear if there wasn't any distant tramping of feet.

Abraham Gepner was standing on the pavement next to the Council. He was wearing a black coat and a ski cap. I knew him from before the war so I was pleased to meet him. He was an exceptionally noble man and I had a very high opinion of him. He was the director of the Provisions Office on Franciszkanska Street and lived there with his wife. He perished during the final liquidation of the ghetto. His wife was taken to Majdanek and died there. We talked for a moment and then went on.

The building at number 19 on the corner of Gensia Street and Zamenhof Street was once a magnate's palace. Until 1918 when Warsaw was under Russian rule it housed a prison. In the ghetto it was the Jewish post office. Now it was the seat of the Jewish Council. It had a deep gateway and then a courtyard. Beyond the courtyard, surrounded by annexes and former stables, other courtyards, then more outbuildings. They had been burnt at the beginning of the war but were still standing. The windows were all gaping and empty. The courtyards were overgrown with grass and weeds. Further on there were empty yards, rubbish and rubble.

On the left-hand side of the gate some dirty, wooden stairs led up to the other floors. The rooms on the second floor were low with mansard ceilings. On one side of the staircase was the flat occupied by the lawyer Warman, the Council secretary, and on the other side the office of the Finance and Budget Department. The employees worked in two rooms, one of which was enormous with windows at each end. Popower's and Wojdyslawski's desks were in the small room where my husband worked. Behind this room there was another one which was going to be renovated. In the meantime the two-year-old daughter of the head book-keeper, Dawid Weintraub, lived there. There was also a kitchen with a stove which ran on paper and books.

I went to the Council building and sat by my husband's desk every day. It was the same with all the Council staff – unless the wives and children worked they sat by their husbands' desks. Rozental had his only child with him, his beautiful, eighteen-year-old daughter. She looked as if she was cut out of an English print. His wife and Aryan servant were taken to the *Umschlagplatz* as they were walking along the street. Sitting next to Jaszunski were his wife and very young daughter-in-law. Next to Zundelewicz were his wife, daughter and son. Next to Wielikowski, his wife and daughter.

Everyone provided cover for their families. But only when the families were near at hand. The Germans could pick them up off the street or from their flats at any time. My neighbour, Mrs Popower, sat by her husband's desk constantly. It was the same on other floors. There were even a lot of fictitious marriages where employees were married off to redundant staff. But the best cover of all was the police force. People paid large sums of money for fictitious marriages with policemen. I heard of one case where 8,000 zlotys were paid over.

Because Maslanko worked in the Disciplinary Commission he was allowed to wear a policeman's cap. So he wore the cap thinking it would save his father. But he lost his father all the same. Everything was only good for as long as it lasted. Two wives of Council members were resettled. Rozen was shot by an Ukrainian not far from the Council as he was going to the *Umschlagplatz* in a rickshaw to save his sister.

The time came when the policemen's families were taken away, and even the undertakers' families too. They were the most privileged caste of all because they were the most needed. Finally the time came when the Germans tore the caps off the heads of policemen on the *Umschlagplatz*, which made them into ordinary people, part of the grey crowd, and pushed them into the wagons. They carried out selections among them too. There were 3,000 of them, then 1,000, and in the end only 300 were left.

The policy of the Germans was to kill the Jews by the hands of other Jews. From time to time they issued an order: every policeman had to bring five 'heads' to the *Umschlagplatz* or else the Germans would take their own families. Through the window I saw a rickshaw with five tiny children, a few months old. Tiny children, no-one else. Their heads were swaying from the movement of the rickshaw. None of them was crying.

I saw how they grabbed a seven-year-old boy. It was just opposite the Council. He kicked and shouted and defended himself so vigorously that they let him go. He ran away quickly down the street and hid.

There was a very pretty six-year-old girl in the chairman's office for a while. She had been found deserted in an empty flat and taken to the Council.

For a long time I could see nappies drying on the first floor balcony opposite the window I looked out of. No-one took them off the line. They hung there rain or shine, blowing in the wind, drying in the sun, getting wet in the rain. No-one took them off the line. But sometimes a head appeared for a moment in the window of an empty flat. The head of a woman or a man. It appeared and then

97

disappeared for days on end. One day an old Jew with a long beard and a prayer shawl on his head looked out of the window for a moment and his eyes met mine.

When a column was going to the *Umschlagplatz* you should never look out of the window because the Germans fired when they saw faces. A woman in the column was carrying a child in one hand and a heavy bundle of things in the other. She didn't have enough strength and while other people were throwing down their pillows, rucksacks, and suitcases, she carried on walking with the heavy bundle and left the child on the pavement.

You should never look out of the window, but once when I was sitting by my husband's desk someone called out to me, 'Your daughter's in the column!' I threw myself at the window. The students from the nursing school were going to the *Umschlagplatz*. Then they passed. I saw them from behind. They looked like white birds. With their pink dresses, wide, white bibbed aprons gathered at the waist and their stiff, white caps. They came back. Many of them were without their caps and aprons. The Jewish policemen tore their caps and aprons off them. In that way they saved other women, taking money for it, but they weakened the chances of the nurses as they became just ordinary girls without their uniforms, and faced deportation. Irena came back. But from then on I had no peace until she promised that she would stay with her father in the Council, by his desk.

From time to time Brandt came, the Gestapo boss responsible for Jewish affairs. He went from floor to floor and from room to room. He held a rubber whip in his hand and looked like an angry mastiff.

'Who is this woman?' he asked.

'That's my wife.'

'Who is this girl?'

'That's my daughter.'

He looked suspicious. 'So this is your wife?'

'Yes.'

'And this girl is your daughter?'

'Yes.'

'All right, all right,' he said quietly, as if what he really meant was – all in good time.

I was sitting by my husband's desk and my neighbour, Mrs Popower from Lubecki Street, was sitting by the next desk when Popower pointed at his wife and said, 'That's the most valuable book in my library.' Popower liked jokes and puns. There was always someone who asked him why. He would explain that his wife's maiden name was the same as the Polish word for book.

So the wives were still sitting by those two desks but no-one sat by Wojdyslawski's desk. He had lost his wife in the first days of the resettlements and lived alone. One day his niece came. She was wearing a pullover and ski trousers. She had fair hair and was tall with regular features. When the house she lived in was blockaded she hid in the attic. Suddenly a Ukrainian came up and found her there. He looked at her and said, 'You're so young and pretty, it's a shame to send you to the *Umschlagplatz*.' And that's how she stayed alive. Her husband was ill in hospital on Leszno Street and so she didn't have a moment's peace. She sat next to the desk anxiously, leaned her head on her hand and whispered with Wojdyslawski for a long time. He took a bread roll, a piece of sausage and some butter wrapped up in paper out of his drawer. He cut the sausage into thin slices with a penknife and they both had something to eat.

The councillor Stolcman's wife was in charge of the kitchen at the Council. All the staff received soup. Sometimes Mrs Stolcman came to our department's kitchen followed by someone with tins of condensed milk in a flat box. Twenty or thirty tins. You opened the tins, poured the contents into a pan, added water and shared the milk out.

In my husband's drawer there was a mug, a plate, a knife and a teaspoon. Some sugar in a tin box. Some tea. A piece of bread. Some rice in a bag. When he was ill I cooked rice or kasha in the kitchen and brought it to him in a pan. Pans stood on every burner. Someone was always cooking something. Under the window stood a long bench. Tired women and children sat on the bench or stools from morning till night. The families of the staff. The sink was in the kitchen. A box of books and papers that were used as fuel, and a blue painted dresser.

Beyond the kitchen there was a small, dark corridor. Then a bathroom, with a toilet, which you closed with a hook. There was often water on the floor in the bathroom and the corridor, and the toilet was often out of order. Once during an inspection in the Council the family of one of the staff hid in the bathroom. They assumed the Germans wouldn't want to cross the dark, dirty, flooded corridor. And they weren't wrong either.

One day a slim clerk in glasses was standing in the kitchen by the blue dresser. He had put both his hands on the dresser and pushed his head back and was weeping aloud. His wife and little boy had been taken from home while he was at work. His neighbour dropped in to tell him. He then bent forward and quiet again he returned to his desk. He sat down, dipped his pen in the ink-well and continued writing.

A pale, young woman in high, brown, laced shoes hovered around in the kitchen. Her name was Mrs Zylberberg. Her family was in Hrubieszow. She looked after Wojdyslawski's tea, and all the pans belonging to Mr Katz, Mrs Reizman, Mrs Kopelewicz, Miss Herzberg, and Mrs Hirszberg. She looked after Weintraub's daughter, little Arianka, if his helpless fair-haired wife went out for a moment.

Weintraub was short and fair like his wife and wore an old, stained suit. He was exhausted. He milled about the office and always had a pen behind his ear and a payment order or a pan of kasha in his hand. Or he was carrying Arianka, pressing her head to his unshaven face. The child was beautiful, fair and bright. Her mouth didn't shut properly, just like her father's, but she was lovely all the same. Mrs Weintraub followed her husband.

'Dadek,' she said, 'you feed her. She'll eat if you give it to her. The child looks poorly today. And then put her in the pram and you might get her to go to sleep.'

Mrs Reizman was sitting at the other end of the room. 'Weintraub!' she said in surprise, 'why don't you send the child over to the Aryan side? Don't you know anyone who'd want to take her?'

'I know a caretaker on Zlota Street. But he wants to keep the child for good. He'll never give her back. That's the condition he made.'

A relation of Popower's worked in the Finance Department, a boy of eighteen. Tall, dark-haired, handsome and intelligent. The Germans picked him up one day and he died together with his parents. Mrs Popower sat at her husband's desk in despair, indifferent to everything. Then young Popower came, he was her brother-in-law, a lawyer. He was in love with Irena, the oldest daughter of Councillor Hurwicz. He sat down and read the latest bulletin. Mrs Popower didn't even look at him.

Then Fliederbaum from the hospital on Leszno Street came for a payment note. Rabbi Spira and Rabbi Stokhammer came. Karabanow the policeman came. Then Dr Frendler, our neighbour from Walicow Street. The Germans had taken his wife to the *Umschlagplatz* and his son who was also a doctor had just gone there. The father had dived out of the column into a gate without being seen by the Ukrainian guard and had saved himself.

100

The door was open and my brother-in-law's brother, Mieczyslaw Laskowski, fell into the room. He was dishevelled, his clothes were in a mess and he looked terrified. 'They've taken my wife to the *Umschlagplatz*. What am I to do?'

'Is Karabanow still here?' asked my husband.

'He's here,' shouted Mrs Reizman, 'he's sitting here with me.'

'Go with him, Mr Laskowski.'

Mrs Popower didn't lift her head. She was used to scenes like this. She was lost in her own despair. Suddenly Mrs Kowalska appears. Mrs Kowalska from our courtyard. The one with the bucket of soup. The mother of Oles and Nora, the girl with the curly hair. Her hair is curly too and her lips are slightly protuberant. Her eyes are crying but her mouth is smiling. 'They picked my husband up on the street and took him to the *Umschlagplatz*. But he's back already.' That's all she wanted to say. She stayed a moment and then left. Wojdyslawski looked at her in surprise, his neck sticking out.

Mr Kowalski worked in a completely different department and each department was a world of its own. But in her joy she announced the news all over.

'Mrs Popower! Did you hear? Mr Kowalski came back from the *Umschlagplatz*. Pull yourself together!'

Who said that? Was it Wojdyslawski? Or was it the man who'd just come into the room? Small and stocky with a thick neck and short arms and a common face, a Jewish policeman called Brzezinski. Brzezinski? Mrs Popower pulled herself together at once. She knew him.

'How could you let it happen? Such a wonderful boy. No-one in the world like him. With his parents too. Oh God. Where were you, Mr Brzezinski? Why didn't you save them?'

He pulled his chair up close to her, bent his head towards her and explained something to her. He talked for a long time. Then he got up and said goodbye. They shook hands. He shook Wojdyslawski's hand too.

'Do you know who that was?' asked Popower. He was silent for a moment and then he said quietly and clearly, 'That was Brzezinski. He loads the wagons. That's his job. You have to be on good terms with him. He might come in useful.'

The next day when I was sitting next to my husband as usual Mrs Popower said, 'Let's go up to the attic. Let's see what's up there.'

She was calmer now. On our way up to the attic she turned round and asked, 'Where's your eldest daughter?'

'On the Aryan side,' I said quietly.

'My daughter's in Paris. I don't get letters from her now. She married a Polish communist.'

Suddenly she started talking about something completely different. 'What do all these people write in those big books? All those typewriters, what do they write? The files are full of cards but what's on the cards? The books are full of the names of everyone who paid their dues, but the people aren't there any longer. They transfer all these empty names from one book to the next. They tidy them up, transfer them, and segregate them. They have to pretend they're working.'

Here's the attic. It's so long that we can't see the end. There are some rags lying on the floor and it looks as if it's lived in. We trip over a pan, a bottle, a bucket. The attic turns right and left. We turn left and keep coming across signs of life. Here's a mattress with a quilt on it. Here's a bit of candle stuck to a rafter. A piece of bread wrapped up in paper.

We keep going. The attic is tall. Low, long windows along the sides. Suddenly there's a wall in front of us. Stop! A red-brick wall. The end of the attic on this side. We'll have to turn back. But we don't. We stand and look at the wall. Because in the wall there's a hole, the bricks have been removed and then delicately replaced. We easily remove a few bricks and put our heads through the hole. We are struck by a blast of sunlight, the blue of the sky, the warm wind and the open space. We can see large patches overgrown with grass and weeds, heaps of rubbish, fences and rubble. You could jump at this point because of the slope. It was no more than three or four metres high There – beyond those open spaces, beyond those fences, beyond those heaps of rubbish – was the Aryan side.

At two o'clock we heard a terrifying whistle in the courtyard.

'The Germans!' shouted Mr Popower. 'They must be going to check if there's anyone here who doesn't belong to the Council.'

'We've got to go down to the courtyard!' shouted someone from the room next door.

Everyone was seized with anxiety. As usual, there were about a dozen outsiders in the kitchen, relations or friends of staff. It must have been the same on the other floors. Some of them ran up to the attic. We went down to the courtyard. There were husbands with their wives and children. A woman we didn't know ran out of the kitchen and when she saw Wojdyslawski going down the stairs alone she took his hand. We stood in the courtyard. Each department separately. Three Germans and the chairman, Lichtenbaum, stood in front of our department.

'Wer ist dieser?' asked one of the Germans.

'Das ist unser Finanzleiter, Ingenieur Szereszewski, seine Frau und Tochter.'

'Gut. Weiter. Wer ist dieser?'

'Das ist der Buchhalter der Abteilung, Popower und seine Frau.'

'Weiter.'

'This is the department's second book-keeper, Weintraub, and his wife and child.'

'Weiter.'

'The department's typist.'

'Weiter.'

'The accounts clerk.'

'Stop! He isn't needed. He can go.'

'No, sorry. He is needed. The office couldn't function without him.'

'Good. He can stay. But the other one isn't needed. Off with him.'

'He's the best employee in our office. We can't work without him.'

'Donnerwetter! And who's this one?'

'This one? He's invaluable, unsere Kapazität. He's the best and most talented employee in the whole Council.'

He didn't know him. He might never have seen him before. He didn't know his name. He was replying to the Germans in a calm and even voice. The staff walked past in turn. He recited their virtues and assured the Germans that they were indispensable. But here too they took a dozen away all the same. The German hit a lot of people with his rubber truncheon, including Miss Polikier who worked one floor lower and always came to my husband with papers. He hit her in the eye. The black marks stayed on her face for a long time.

When we returned to the building and I found myself near Chairman Lichtenbaum, I said to him, 'You talked to them as if you were their equal, completely fearlessly. Aren't you afraid of them?'

'I know for sure they'll shoot me one day. Sooner or later. I don't value my life and that's why I'm not afraid of them.'

But we were terrified about Nina. How had she survived the selection at Councillor Rozensztadt's, in the Legal Department on Gensia Street? But no selection was carried out there. When she came over to our department she didn't know what had happened.

We went home together. My husband looked very ill that day. He had toothache and a bad stomach. He walked along indifferent and silent, and we walked next to him. Above us was the sky, below us the asphalt, and behind us and in front of us a chain of grey houses and wide, black gates opening into cluttered courtyards. Nina was walking a few steps behind us and crying all the way.

'Why is the child crying?' asked my husband, 'she never cried when she was small.'

'Why are you crying?' asked Irena. 'We're coming back whole and in one piece, aren't we?'

Nina was looking at her father's back and thinking about how he'd been carrying us so far. Was this her father, this sick man in front of her? What had happened to her happy, energetic and confident father? No. This isn't him. This is an old Jew from the ghetto, tired and suffering. She saw thousands of Jews like that in the columns, resigned and passive. They sat down on the pavement if they didn't have the strength to go any further and put their sacks down next to them. If father is as dejected as this then we won't survive and we'll all perish. Another day had passed and we were still together.

On 5 September at two in the morning the Jewish police knocked at our door. They knocked and shouted, 'All councillors are summoned to the Council for a meeting.' They took my husband, Wielikowski and Gliksberg from our house and accompanied them to the Council. All three of them came home at seven in the morning. They told us that the residents of the house were ordered to go to the Council together with their families, as quickly as possible.

We quickly made up a few parcels – some food. I took my winter coat. We went down the stairs slowly. We stopped for a moment in the gate. There was an empty shop in the basement on the left-hand side. The day before Mrs Popower had said, 'There's a cellar in the shop in the basement. The entrance is covered with an old carpet. It might come in useful.'

Perhaps we should hide in the cellar? Not go to the Council. The Gliksbergs weren't to be seen. They had stayed at home. Someone said, 'Come on, let's not stand so long.' We walked along Lubecki Street and turned into Gensia Street. There were a lot of people in front of us and behind us. Everyone was carrying a suitcase, a bundle, a bag or a basket. Every face was worried. No-one knew why they were going and if they'd return. Some people disobeyed the order, like the Gliksbergs, and hid in cellars and attics.

The Jewish Council building. We entered the gate. Then went left up the stairs. On the first floor, two policemen always used to stand next to the entrance to the chairman's office. They were exceptionally tall, one was called Litmanowicz and the other Liliental. That morning only Litmanowicz was on duty. Liliental and his wife had committed suicide during the night.

We went to the second floor, to the Finance Department, to the room my husband worked in, and placed the things we'd brought behind his desk. Arianka lived in the long room next door now. She had enteritis and lay exhausted and motionless in her pram. Dr Kirszenblum, our neighbour from Walicow Street, came with his wife. They sat down next to us. He kept calming his wife down, 'Milusia, calm down, everything will be all right.' She had a limp. She was his brother's wife first. He loved her very much.

Three thousand. The Council staff and their families were allocated three thousand numbers – to stay alive. But it doesn't mean that all the others had to perish. Three thousand numbers were permitted. Three thousand people could stay alive legally. The others could hide in empty houses, could even hide in the cellars at the Council, or they could escape to the Aryan side. Many people escaped through the hole in the wall in the attic. You could jump out onto the heaps of rubble, into the empty spaces. Life showed that most of the people who survived were the ones who went into hiding at the beginning and didn't believe in any papers or numbers. An infallible instinct ordered them to hide and that was the best way.

Every department had a committee to draw up a list. The lists of names went to a main committee for confirmation. It consisted of the lawyer Grodzienski who was the councillor responsible for personnel, the lawyer Rozensztadt and the lawyer Zundelewicz. All three of them perished together with their families four months later.

Dr Lipszyc, an acquaintance of ours, didn't receive a number. He shouted in despair. During the night he went over to the Aryan side but he perished there some time later. The typist, Mrs Hirszberg, didn't receive a number either. She'd been absent for two days. She'd tried to get over to the Aryan side where her little boy was, but she didn't succeed. So she came back but it was too late. The list was already drawn up.

The nursing school received twenty numbers. There weren't as many students as that in the school any longer. Some had gone to their parents in the country, some had gone to workshops as nurses or just as workers. The director's two children, her 11-year-old daughter and four-year-old boy, were also on the list.

Some people received a number but weren't entitled to get one for their wives. Dr Steinsapir, our neighbour from Lubecki Street, lost his wife during this selection even though she should have been entitled to get a number because she was the wife of a hostage.

At the end of July, as soon as the resettlement action had started, the Germans had taken thirty Jews as hostages. They were people the Germans considered prominent – meaning the most important. They were picked up from the Council or from their homes, and some were picked up on the street. The Germans held up rickshaws and picked them up from the rickshaws. Generally they took people who were well-dressed. The hostages included Councillor Zygmunt Hurwicz and his wife and daughter, Irena. Grodzienski, the lawyer, and his wife, Eckerman, Dr Steinsapir and many others. Also Goldfarb, the owner of a fuel store, our neighbour from Poznanska Street from whom we used to buy coal. A month later they were set free. They said they were beaten and humiliated. Eckerman returned with no beard and no teeth. He had seven children, and only one son survived, Hilary, who worked in the Hospital Department.

As I was crossing the courtyard I saw my brother-in-law Witold and his wife Celina. They were sitting on the grass in the shadow of the walls. Celina had received a number as Witold's assistant in the Building Department stores.

'Is there a kitchen anywhere?' they asked. 'Can we get some soup?'

We went together. The kitchen was full of people. But in the end we got some soup in tin bowls. Renia Lichtenbaum was sitting at one of the long, low tables, like the tables in the shelters. She was a relation of the chairman's. She was crying. Her mother was standing next to her with a rucksack.

'I can't get to him,' she said in a broken voice, 'I can't do anything. If only one of the staff or a policeman would marry my mother. But I can't arrange it.'

I stood there helpless too. Fictional marriages were of no importance any longer. My son-in-law's mother hadn't received a number either. His father received a number from the Supplies Department.

At dusk a huge cart harnessed to percherons drove into the courtyard. It contained the undertakers' families. The women were shouting at the tops of their voices, maddened by despair. The crowd parted fearfully before the hooves of the terrified horses.

In the evening Witold and Celina came. We spread coats on the floor, placed bundles under our heads and lay down next to each other. It was hard and uncomfortable and we kept getting up. The air was stuffy and full of dust. My daughters lay down on Wojdyslawski's table. Popower and his wife lay down on their own table. Dr Kirszenblum and his wife spent the whole night on chairs leaning against each other.

While this selection was being carried out in the Council, another selection was happening in the workshops and also in the Police Department. Stefa Pinus worked as a typist in the Police Department and perished. All workshop workers had to go to Parysowski Square. Stefan Drabienko was also there together with the workers of his workshop and he got through the selection, but Mieczyslaw Laskowski and his wife and son died. On the third day in the morning we saw a column of workers through the window. They were going in the other direction and carrying a banner saying 'Printers'. Then we saw more and more columns like it. They returned to their workshops.

The same day everyone in the Council who had received a number was summoned to a distant courtyard that was part of the property. All the outbuildings were burnt out. A lot of people who hadn't received numbers hid in the ruins. We were ordered to form sixes. Each of us had a yellow number pinned to our chest on the left side. Each department formed a separate column. Mieczyslaw Lichtenbaum and First walked along the columns wearing boots, and in the German style they carried whips and arranged, ordered and shouted.

The wife of Warman, the secretary of the Jewish Council, died of tuberculosis in the ghetto leaving an eighteen-month-old daughter. He was carrying her. The child was slight and sickly and wore a blue coat with a blue hood. She had a small, yellow number pinned to her coat. Warman was extremely tall and he carried this tiny thing, this little mite, with the greatest care, just like the most tender mother.

Now the column of workers from the Building Department is passing by. Going evenly and bravely, in sixes like soldiers, towards the exit. Witold and Celina are in this column. The Germans are

107

standing there, in the first courtyard, and they're going to count the sixes. Not more than 3,000. That makes 500 sixes.

The Supplies Department column goes past. My son-in-law's parents are in it. Ryszard's mother has thrown a coat over her shoulder on the side where her number should have been pinned. She walks beside her husband in a six like everyone else. The column steps quickly and bravely. The Germans count, and she gets through unnoticed.

Now the first column of Council officials. Dawid Weintraub with his fair-haired wife. She's carrying a suitcase, he's got a rucksack on his back. The Germans mustn't know that Arianka is in the rucksack. A child without a number. Sick Arianka who's unconscious because they drugged her with a sleeping pill. There goes Councillor Kupczykier who's got typhus. He looks like a ghost. He was pulled out of bed in a fever, he's supported on one side by his wife and on the other by his sister. He describes a great semi-circle with the column as it heads towards the exit. His eyes are shining, his face is yellow, he's breathing hoarsely through the mouth, he's stepping like a puppet on wooden legs. If he doesn't fall he's got to be a brave infantryman right up to the end. The Germans mustn't know he's got typhus.

Now our column. My husband, Nina and me. Irena went with the school in her nurses' uniform, her pink-striped dress, her long, white, bibbed apron, her cap and navy-blue cape. We stand next to Councillor Zundelewicz, his wife, daughter and twelve-year-old son. Councillor Hurwicz is standing a few rows in front of us wearing the black cap of an undertaker. He's holding his wife and daughter Irena by the hand. She's the one young Popower's in love with. Mrs Hurwicz is wearing a large elegant hat. She's the only one wearing a hat in the courtyard. Next to them Councillor Rozental with his beautiful daughter. He's both father and mother to her now. His wife, the doctor, died together with their Aryan servant who accompanied them to the ghetto of her own free will.

'Keep even,' Mieczyslaw Lichtenbaum calls out.

'Line up,' shouts First and turns red with the effort.

They're very big. They're important. Everyone is as scared of them as of the Germans.

A boy runs in from the entrance. Tall and very slim. He's running breathlessly. He works in the Finance Department. He's eighteen. He lost his parents not long ago. There's a yellow number pinned to his chest – 3,001. 'They let another 100 in!' he shouts. 'That's 3,100 altogether.'

'March!' shouts First.

The column sways. We move, evenly, like soldiers. Energetically and quickly. We pass the second courtyard, now we're entering the first one. Two Germans are counting the sixes. A third German, a handsome, elegant man in gloves, is standing to one side. It looks as if he's only a spectator. As if he's just come along to have a look. He has fair hair and we don't know what he's thinking.

It turned out later that the Germans hadn't allowed a hundred extra numbers to be given out at all. At first they didn't notice, then they stopped the last hundred and didn't let any more through. They were from the Supplies Department.

We go out of the gate and turn right, but not at once, into Gensia Street. First we go straight towards Zamenhof Street and then we turn right. We reach the crossroads and now at last, dazed and not knowing where they're taking us, we turn right again at a sharp angle into Gensia Street. It's empty. Now we walk more slowly. Now we're feeling tired. As we walk people drop out of the column and enter gates. It must be where their flats are. Now we're on the corner of Lubecki Street. We're passing the chemist's. Then the gate to number 6. On the first floor we stop in front of the door. It's wide open.

It was the work of the Polish police at number 4, so it's said. Not only our things have been stolen but everything belonging to the Drabienko family and all the things my brothers-in-law Witold and Edward left with us. In fact a lot of flats in the ghetto were broken into then. Our suitcases were stolen as well. The less valuable things were thrown out onto the floor. The coat that we had kept and not given to Mrs Jankielewicz was stolen too.

'Children, they've stolen the coat that we stole,' joked my husband.

'Maybe it's God's punishment,' said Irena, 'maybe God punished us for it and that's why we've been robbed.'

'No. There's no God in the ghetto. Even the Germans say so.'

Everybody had heard how on the day before the New Year a delegation went to the director of Többens' workshop asking for an empty room they could use for a religious service.

'What do you want to do?' asked the German in surprise.

'We want to pray,' they said.

'Who do you want to pray to?'

'To God.'

'To God? God's got you in his a— Can't you see what's happening?'

Late at night there was an English or Russian air raid. We were already in bed, exhausted by what had happened. It was ten o'clock. The noise of the shattering bombs and the blinding light of the flares comforted the Jews. This is the reply! They're thinking of us! They'll smash the *Umschlagplatz*. That's for us! No Jew in the ghetto went down to a shelter during the bombing. Death by bombing held no terrors. My daughters and Ryszard stood the whole time in the balcony door.

A house on Gensia Street was hit by a bomb and part of the wall was ripped out. Another bomb hit the roof of the house at 4 Lubecki Street. The rush of air threw me out of bed onto the floor. The window panes were shattered and my bed which stood near the window was covered with glass. Wasn't that strange? Stranger still was that a bomb hit Schultz's workshop killing and badly wounding about fifty people. No-one believed that the Jews were being avenged any longer. The bombs fell blindly. Our fate was of no interest to anyone. The ghetto was like a galley forgotten by God and man, straying over the ocean and condemned to destruction.

Then I fell ill with enteritis. I had a high temperature and was in pain so they called Dr Swieca. The young doctor told us how he'd worked in Schultz's workshop all night rescuing the badly wounded.

There was a small, oval table next to my bed. Irena was ironing nurses' caps on it, using the electric iron which we hadn't given to Mrs Jankielewicz. While she was ironing she said that she'd like to go with a work team to Spala. There were work teams like that, groups of Jews who worked on estates near Rembertow and Spala. Every team had a doctor and nurse or just a nurse. I didn't want her to go. But she was so keen that she bought some ski boots, prepared a rucksack and went to the Labour Office on the corner of Leszno Street and Zelazna Street several times on the matter. Despite her strenuous efforts she didn't manage to go. In late autumn all these teams were brought back to Warsaw and sent to the *Umschlagplatz*.

Once, when I was alone in the flat, I was seized by anxiety. I went to the kitchen and looked out of the window. There was no-one there. The courtyard was tiny and bisected by a wall. In it were piles of furniture, mattresses, baskets and paintings. A narrow path led between these heaps of rejected things from the gate right up to the door on the left, where the Union of Pharmacists was and where Ryszard's parents lived on the first floor.

There was no-one there. I couldn't hear a sound. I opened the kitchen door onto the narrow balcony. In the corner stood two flowerpots and a tall, round, metal rubbish bin. The window from the Gitermans' kitchen opened onto this balcony. The window was closed. I couldn't see anyone behind the glass. I ran to the hall and opened the door. The huge sideboard which stood on the staircase flashed its crystal pane. There was silence here too. Everything was quiet. Will Irena come back safely from the Labour Office? Will Nina come back home? Will I see them again?

Then I rushed to the balcony on the street side and saw Stefania Gliksberg on the balcony of flat number 2. She was leaning on the balustrade with her face turned towards Gensia Street. She stood for a while strained and listening. When she saw me she said, 'I'm terrified. My Stefan is at the *Umschlagplatz*. Someone came and told us and my husband's gone there.'

We both stood there. Each on her own balcony. It was seven o'clock. Mrs Gliksberg's hair was golden in the rays of the setting sun. Her hand lay on the parapet. It was trembling. Suddenly we saw Stefan on the bend in the road by the window of the chemist's shop. He was walking with his father. He was merry and happy. He had reddish hair like his mother, and her brown eyes. They entered the gate. The hearse was right behind them. It stopped in front of the gate as well. The horse lowered its head and the undertaker jumped off the cab and started removing parcels and bundles from under the seat. He lived in our house – a tall, handsome, broad-shouldered man called Michelson. He'd brought back some smuggled goods.

Irena and Nina came home shortly afterwards. First one and then the other. Their yellow numbers were pinned on their chests. 'Why are you so late?' I asked.

'Do you know,' said Irena, 'it's impossible to wear these numbers. People tear them off in the street. They jump out of gates and tear them off. It's happened a few times already. You have to carry them in your bag.'

'But why are you coming back from the Labour Office so late? Did you call in to see someone on the way back?'

'If that's how it is then I'm taking my number off right now,' said Nina.

111

She unpinned the number, put it in a drawer, fiddled about and went out. I ran out on the stairs after her.

'Where are you going now?'

'Nowhere. Just to the courtyard. I want to see where Ryszard's parents live. I might go and see them.'

She went to the courtyard, lifted her head and started looking at the windows. She was searching and thinking: where do they live? While she was standing there looking round like that a German soldier entered the courtyard through the gate and stood in front of her. 'What are you doing in this courtyard?' he asked her.

'I live here.'

'Why haven't you got a number? Come with me immediately.'

'I left my number at home. My father is a councillor in the Jewish Council.'

That didn't interest him.

'You're going with me. You haven't got a number. You've come here from somewhere. Give me your bag.'

He searched her bag. There was a bracelet in it. He took it and put it in his pocket. He noticed she was wearing a watch. He took it. He looked at her closely, then turned and left. Nina came back home and didn't say anything. She went to bed and suddenly ran a temperature of 40 degrees. She didn't say anything. When her father returned she told him everything.

'We'll ask Dr Steinsapir,' he said. He knocked at the neighbour's door and returned immediately.

'It's a nervous shock. Don't worry. It'll pass,' said Dr Steinsapir.

The next day she didn't have a temperature. And life rolled on.

In August I worked for a while in the communal kitchen on Gensia Street, not far from Lubecki Street. The entrance to the gate was blocked by a huge heap of rubble, old pans and rags. When I entered the courtyard for the first time through the dark, deep gate I didn't know where the kitchen was. There was no sign or notice anywhere. The huge courtyard was surrounded by the ruins of burnt out houses. An old man, with string for a belt, was ineptly chopping up an ash cupboard. He lifted his head and looked at me with watery eyes. His hair was white as snow, and he was wrinkled and hunched. He must have been ninety. An old woman was sitting next to him on an upturned bucket. She was as like him as two drops of water and was chewing a crust of black bread.

They must have been in hiding in the ruins and come out for a moment to drink some water, eat a bite of bread, breathe some air

112

and then disappear, hide themselves again in the heaps of bricks and stones. It was one of the paradoxical things you saw in the ghetto and it was surprising and moving at the same time.

'Where's the kitchen?' I asked.

He pointed silently with his axe. I entered the dark hall and then went up the dirty stairs. There was a wide open door on the first floor and through it I saw a sink and two women in wide aprons carrying a washing-up bowl full of chopped cabbage. I was given an apron too and a big knife, and I sat down at the table to slice cabbage.

Inside the kitchen was a store-room, a small room with sacks of salt, onions, dark flour, bran and kasha, and there was a work room where the vegetables were cleaned and pastry for macaroni was made, and a small kitchen in the hall with a new cooking pot set on brick walls. Six of us worked there. Also a store-keeper, a house-keeper and a woman who took out the ashes, fetched wood, mixed food in the huge pot and performed other strenuous tasks.

We cooked 450 dinners. They all went to the *Umschlagplatz*. A cart came every day and picked up soup in closed containers. The Germans demanded thick and tasty soup. We often wondered who ate the soups. People worked at the *Umschlagplatz* after all. Workmen who repaired the water supply, the boilers and the lighting. Perhaps the soups were for them.

The husband of one of the women was a lawyer in England. She was a young, fair-haired woman who was always good tempered and smiling. She'd been at the *Umschlagplatz* once and had bought herself out with a gold five-rouble piece. She lived in the same house, in a two-roomed flat on the courtyard side which was reached by climbing up a ladder. Someone from the Council lived in one room and she lived in the second room with an older woman who had sons in very good jobs in America. She managed to escape during a selection at the Council. She was shot in the hand. She had nowhere to go for a while and now the two of them were together. But this morning she swallowed some poison. 'Can you hear her moans?' We stopped cutting cabbage and rolling pastry for a moment. In the ensuing silence we heard a prolonged moan. 'That's her. She didn't take enough. Or else it wasn't strong enough.'

The husband of a pale, black-eyed woman also worked in the Council. She was from Wilno herself and sang in Jewish theatres there. She sang for us too in a low, throaty voice while peeling carrots and grating beetroots. She sang 'The little town of Belz' and we listened. Through the open window overlooking the courtyard we could see the blue of the sky and the flashes of swallows in flight. She looked at the window, blinking. We knew she was homesick for Wilno when she sang about Belz.

The woman who did all the heavy work listened, leaning against the frame of the door leading into the kitchen. Her hands were lowered, her face painful. The mezuzah hung above her head like an exclamation mark. We knew that she had her own town in front of her eyes when she listened to the song about Belz.

There were some small, square tables joined together in the room. We worked two on one side of the tables, two on the other and two by the window. The ones by the window made the pastry and rolled it into wide circles. We laid the circles out to dry on benches which stood round the walls. Swarms of flies settled on the rolled out pastry. We kept chasing them away. We chopped cabbage, peeled carrots and grated beetroots. Sometimes cauliflowers or tomatoes were delivered. But we never received 'potatoes. Potatoes were smuggled into the ghetto and were very expensive.

One of the two women rolling the pastry was the wife of the store-keeper. She was short and dark. The store-keeper, a trained engineer, was short and dark too. They had a twelve year-old daughter. They had lived in France for a long time and spoke French among themselves and to the child. The child was slim, frail and delicate with a transparent little face. She cut the pastry into macaroni with us. Her mother didn't take her eyes off her. 'Blanche, you haven't said good morning to the lady.'

'Bonjour,' said the girl. She reddened and curtseyed.

Before they came into the ghetto they lived on Szosty Sierpnia Street. They earned their living by baking cakes in an iron stove and selling them. The mother came from Poltawa. In the ghetto, during the resettlements, they hid in a walled up room which was entered through the kitchen dresser. You pushed aside a piece of hardboard at the bottom of the dresser and that was the entrance. There were twenty-five people hidden in there. One day someone moved the hardboard aside and the head of a Jewish policeman wearing a cap with a yellow band suddenly appeared in the hole in the wall. Behind him was another head. The Jewish police were experts at finding disguised rooms. They could discover a flat's lack of proportion at a glance. The first policeman slid through the hole into the room. Behind him the second one. Would he be followed by any Germans?

114

Then the mother said, 'This girl is an orphan. She doesn't even live here. Take her out on the street and she can go. We don't know her at all.' She wanted to save the child and hoped they'd take pity on her. But the terrified child cried out, 'O non, maman, ce n'est pas vrai,' and cuddled up to her.

None of us ever asked her what happened to the rest of the people in the disguised room. It was enough for us to have the mother making pastry among us, the girl in the faded velvet dress, and the father who was just locking the store-room and coming towards the kitchen.

His keys jangled as he walked and he was followed by the house-keeper holding a frying-pan of fried onions. There was no burner on the range in the kitchen so she fried the onions in the flat opposite and was just about to season the soup. Behind her the kitchen helper was carrying buckets of peelings down to the courtyard. She was poorly dressed with a scarf wound round her head. She never smiled. She didn't talk to us. We didn't know her voice. Her eyes were always sad. She had the stigmata of suffering on her face, almost as if a seal. She sometimes brought her child with her, a boy of twelve months with red, curly hair. She sat him down on the floor in the corner of the kitchen and gave him a spoon to play with. He never cried.

One day I went to work to the kitchen as usual. Just like yesterday there was soup again today, with macaroni made of dark flour. I cut the pastry into short strips, placed them on a tray and sprinkled them with flour. Then I threw them into the pan. As I went from the room into the kitchen with a tray of macaroni I could hear the house-wife asking the woman, 'Hena, are you from Stobnica?'

So her name was Hena. I stood with the tray in the dark hall and listened.

'No,' she replied unwillingly.

'Are you from Sobolew? Or Krasnystaw or Krasnik?'

She was silent for a long while. I didn't think she'd say anything and I was about to go. Suddenly it was as if a dam had burst inside her. Her voice made me think of a person who's been running for a long time and is out of breath.

'I'm from Zarnow. I hid in a flour bin with the child. I gagged him with a rag. When I got out of the bin it was night-time. My husband was dead on the floor by the bed. I took a sheet off the bed and covered him. I put a candle in a candlestick by his head, but I was scared and I didn't light the candle. I was afraid they'd see the light through the window and kill me and the child. Then I left the town and walked for a long time.'

When she fell silent again I went into the kitchen and looked at her. Her head was lowered, she was pale and shaking like a leaf in the wind. The child never cried but he was wailing now, terrified by the violence of his mother's words. That woman and probably all my fellow workers, including the housekeeper, were not registered, they were non-registered persons. They had saved themselves from being selected. They had hidden. Non-registered persons didn't have the right to a flat, and when ration distribution points were set up they didn't have the right to ration cards. But life showed that people got round this regulation.

We worked from eight in the morning to two. We each received half a kilogram of black bread and a bowl of soup. What was most important, we each had a piece of paper stating we were cooks employed in the kitchen on Gensia Street. After work I used to go to my husband's office at the Jewish Council or back home. In my pocket I had a document on thick pink paper with a photograph stating: 'Wir bestätigen, daß Szereszewska Helena, Gattin des Mitglieds des Judenrates – Ing. Stanislaw Szereszewski – ist in der Küche N. 4 als Köchin beschäftigt.'

At the end of September 1942 the Germans ordered the ghetto to be narrowed down again. A lot of streets were not to be included in the ghetto any longer: Lubecki Street, Pawia Street and Dzika Street as far as Gensia Street and the odd side of Gensia Street. And the Council staff were again allocated other blocks of houses to live in. When Gensia Street was no longer in the ghetto and was divided into two by the ghetto wall, Kurza Street became a vital artery. The Building Department received its blocks there. The Building Department was considered to be the most important department in the Council, mainly because it worked for the Germans and was directed not just by the chairman's sons, Edward and Mieczyslaw Lichtenbaum, but also by First and he was the link in the Building Department between the Germans and the Jewish Council.

The director of the Health Department was Dr Milejkowski and his staff received a block on Kurza Street too. The Supplies Department headed by Councillor Abraham Gepner stayed on Franciszkanska Street. The Union of Pharmacists transferred its stores to the Council building and wound up the chemist's on the corner of Lubecki Street and Gensia Street. Council staff were allocated houses at 38, 40 and 42 Muranowska Street. When we heard about this order we were terrified. We knocked at the Gliksbergs' door and held a conference with them.

'Do we have to live on Muranowska Street?' asked Stefania Gliksberg. 'Let's look for a flat somewhere else.'

'They're pushing us nearer and nearer the *Umschlagplatz*, that's for sure,' replied Henryk Gliksberg.

'Come on! Let's look for a flat now. Don't let's wait until they're all taken. Let's go!' called Stefania.

She took a colourful scarf, tied it round her head and put her coat on. We called our children and were soon walking along Gensia Street in a flat-hunting fever. Our daughters walked in front of us. It was Saturday, we weren't working. We walked along the street, impatient and anxious. We were sorry about leaving the flats that had been so hard to get used to at first. Now, when our souls had seeped into them and they had become ours, we would have to leave them.

Tadeusz Gliksberg turned round and said, 'Why don't we go to 65 Niska Street? It's a modern house.'

'Niska Street,' replied Stefania surprised. 'But that's even nearer the *Umschlagplatz*. Who lives there?'

'Giterman and the Kowalskis and Himmelfarb, the lawyer.'

She thought it over. Then she said, 'No. As far away from the *Umschlagplatz* as possible. Let's go to Franciszkanska Street first.'

As we were walking along Gensia Street a tall, stout, fair-haired woman with her hair done in curls joined us at the gate of number 37. She was wearing a long, grey, pleated coat with a hood. It was Mrs Grinberg, the wife of someone at the Union of Pharmacists. The gate at 37 was wide open. Through it we could see the courtyard piled high with things and the burnt out ruins of the adjacent annexe. The kitchen I worked in was in that house. The kitchen and its new range were on the odd side of Gensia Street and so it wasn't part of the ghetto any longer. I had stopped working. All the non-registered workers in the kitchen stopped working too.

When she saw us Mrs Grinberg said, 'It's good the resettlements have stopped. You can walk along the street in peace now.'

'We're going to look for a flat,' said Stefania.

'I'll go too.' She sailed forward like a ship in her magnificent coat. I couldn't take my eyes off her, she looked so strange against the background of grey walls and streets.

There were no flats on Franciszkanska Street. Since the Supplies

117

Department had not moved, their staff had already occupied the best flats. We entered the houses and came across total wrecks. We tripped over bricks and stones and heaps of loose gravel. Broken doors, smashed windows, and burnt out doors and window frames everywhere. In fact we didn't look at any flats at all. We only entered the gates and came out again. It stunk of emptiness, damp and excrement.

'We can't live here,' said Mr Gliksberg. 'Let's go further on.'

'You mean, let's go nearer,' said Stefania with a sad smile.

So we turned back. We crossed Nalewki Street which had been badly bombed, part of Gensia Street, and then turned into Dzika Street and walked towards Kurza Street. Kurza Street looked amazing. The right-hand side was piled up with heaps of pillows, quilts and mattresses. Some of the pillows were ripped and the feathers were coming out. Most of the pillows were without pillowcases as they had been taken by the young Jews who worked on the Aryan side and sold to Poles. Clothes and bedding was what they usually took from empty flats. It was called taking the rags out.

At first the flats of resettled Jews on Kurza Street were taken by the women who worked in one of the workshops. Now, after the ghetto had been narrowed down, the workers had to move somewhere else and their flats were to be occupied by the Building Department staff. There was a certain logic in these constant changes. After every move you became poorer. Having to get used to new surroundings was tiring and morally destructive. Moves were part of the system. Just like shooting all day and all night during the resettlements was part of the system too.

When we turned out of Dzika Street into crowded and noisy Kurza Street Stefania said, 'We've been walking for ages but we haven't seen any beggars anywhere. Just think, we can't see any beggars and there used to be so many of them before.'

'Nowadays nobody sings "Ich hob nis ka mues" and "Di bone, di bone",' one of us said.

Suddenly the music of these courtyard songs sounded in our ears. I remembered the courtyard at Walicow Street and the singer we used to call 'Lovely Voice'. There were two of them, a man and a woman. He played the violin and she sang. Arias from *Faust*, the *Pearl Fishers* and *Carmen*. The courtyard of that five-storey house was like a deep well. Her voice echoed against the walls and trembled on angels' wings. Heads looked out of every window. People threw her money and bits of bread wrapped up in news-

118

paper. When she sang, our suffering and longing were boundless and it seemed as if only death would soothe us. We all had the same thoughts as we walked along but no-one voiced them.

We couldn't see any corpses covered with newspapers beside the gates either. They were carried out of flats during the night. They lay there until the hearse came and picked them up and took them to the cemetery. No-one knew who had died. People did it so as not to lose their ration cards.

A woman was standing by the gate at number 6. She was watching the end of Kurza Street. The wind was blowing her hair. She looked forlorn and anxious. 'It's Mrs Lerner,' I said, 'the wife of Lerner, the engineer from Wilcza Street. Our children know her daughters.'

I went up to her.

'I've lost my husband,' she said, 'and now I'm waiting for my daughters. They work in the workshop. They should be back soon.'

They worked in the workshop, Mirka and her sister, and lived here on Kurza Street. When they move out, the Building Department staff will occupy their flats. They'll have to get used to another one, full of ghosts.

We entered the gate to number 10 and looked at the flats on each floor. As we were crossing the empty rooms we saw a man crouching next to the bathroom in one of the flats and stoking a fire in an iron stove. He lifted his head and looked at us, and his eyes flashed in a smile. He knew my husband from before the war. He was a yeast merchant and my husband worked in the yeast industry.

'What are you doing here?' asked my husband.

'I'm non-registered,' he replied, and laughed. Then he added, 'Are you looking for a flat? It's cold and dark here. And it's damp.' He was crouching the whole time he was talking to us. Won't he stand up? Or can't he stand up because the damp has got into his bones? He said goodbye and wished us good luck. Good luck? Has he gone mad? What we said with a bitter smile in the ghetto was: may you survive. And people asked: do you believe in life beyond the wagons? Then there was a joke about the last two Jews who met at the funeral of the third one.

We went down the stairs to the dark entrance and stood on the pavement. The Gliksbergs and the woman in the grey coat with a hood came out of the entrance next door. We walked along together again, back along Kurza Street towards Dzika Street.

'So we're going to Muranowska Street,' said Mr Gliksberg.

119

This time Mrs Gliksberg was silent. She had an aversion to that street because it was so near the *Umschlagplatz*. But there were no other flats so she had to bow to necessity. The next street was Niska Street and then Stawki Street. And the *Umschlagplatz* was on Stawki Street. To live on Muranowska Street meant to live on the edge of the ghetto, on its borders. We went to the houses at 38, 40 and 42. Once more we went into entrances and up stairs. There were three and four-roomed flats on the street side and in the annexe but they were all occupied. We went from floor to floor. Drawers and bedding were lying on the floor everywhere, and unmade beds. We trod on plates, candlesticks, photograph albums, and Hannukah lamps. It was incredibly disordered. As if a wild beast had passed through.

The caretaker was standing in the gate. He was holding his little boy by the hand. The child was sucking a sweet. We knew the care-taker from Gensia Street. We bought butter or cheese from him on our way home from the Council. His wife looked so Polish that for a long time we thought that she'd entered the ghetto out of love for him. She was of medium height and fair-haired with light eyes. Her voice was throaty. She talked loud and fast in the purest Polish. I thought she was a girl from Powisle. He worked for the post office before he became a caretaker. He was said to have a very bad heart.

'Mr Szereszewski,' he said, 'there are two five-roomed flats free in the adjacent annexe on the second floor. And on the first floor there's a large six-roomed flat that Alter, the owner, lived in before he was resettled. The veranda, you can see, belongs to the flat. It's like a bower for the Feast of the Tabernacles, the ceiling is movable.'

We all looked at the veranda. It looked like a swallow's nest.

'We'll have a look,' said Mr Gliksberg and we were already cross-ing the courtyard and then we were engulfed by the door of the adjacent annexe. A smashed, black safe lay wide open on the cement floor.

The caretaker was following us and he said, 'That's the Alters' safe, they lived on the first floor. It was thrown out of the flat and it's here now.'

As we were going up the stairs a door opened slightly. We could see the head of an old woman through the narrow crack. She was watching us curiously.

'That old woman is all alone. It's her flat. She lost everybody. She hid in a cupboard and they didn't open it. It's a small flat with one room. The window overlooks Niska Street,' explained the caretaker.

The woman closed the door quietly. Her curiosity was satisfied.

On the second floor we quickly passed through the two spacious five-roomed flats. They were almost empty. The odd piece of furniture, a chair or cabinet, still stood against the walls.

'I am taking both these flats for the Union of Pharmacists,' said Henryk Gliksberg.

We all looked at him. He said the words in a clear and solemn voice. Ages ago, discoverers must have spoken like that when their brigantines reached islands where no human had ever set foot before. 'I am taking this island for the Queen of England.'

Finally we went down one floor lower. Rags, kitchen equipment and old shoes lay on the floor. Our footsteps echoed in the deserted rooms and resounded against the walls. They still had a few pictures hanging on them.

Then the caretaker spoke again, 'This is the flat where Alter lived before he was resettled. You can share it. Two families.'

There were stoves with pipes and burners in the rooms. So a family had lived in each room. Maybe his sister with her children, maybe his sister-in-law or mother-in-law. In the dining room there was a neat, white stove similar to the one we bought at the beginning of the war when we still lived on Narbutt Street. The number of the flat was 28.

We all remembered the time when the Germans surrounded the houses at 38, 40 and 42 Muranowska Street during the night on 4 August and took all the residents out of bed to the *Umschlagplatz* – apart from the people who didn't lose their heads and had time to hide. So for the second time we're occupying a flat whose owners have been resettled. If the caretaker stops talking and the children are quiet and we hold our breath for a moment we might hear them sighing. Because if the ghosts of people seized by force and destroyed return anywhere, then this is where everyone ripped out of this nest will return.

Just like on Lubecki Street, there was a mezuzah on every door in this flat too. A grimy, dust-covered Hanukkah lamp gleamed on the old-fashioned, white kitchen dresser. Hebrew books spilling out of the bookcase, the glazed veranda with its skilfully opening roof, the roll of parchment in a cardboard cover which my daughter found in the corner of the cupboard – all this testified that pious Jews had lived here. So here, in these walls, their thoughts turned to God. They had their worries and their joys, their sicknesses and their funerals. They celebrated the seder at this table. Sitting on the stove side they had the huge black sideboard which looked like coffins knocked together in front of them. Sitting on the opposite side they faced the stove, with its ornate moulding and as high as the ceiling.

I tripped over the candelabra they used on the Day of Atonement and on the anniversary of their relatives' deaths. Alter's wife closed her eyes and swayed over the candles. The old mother shuffled round the rooms before old age forced her to take to her bed for good. She will have worn an old-fashioned head-piece made of lace and ribbons, and long earrings of red coral. And as she shuffled the warm smell of baked chollahs reached her from the now cold and empty kitchen.

On the glazed veranda is a large, wooden chest with a lid. The lock has been torn off and is lying next to it. The chest is full of books, law and chemistry and a few dictionaries. There are also two large photographs, the sort you'd have in a cabinet: a handsome young man and a beautiful young woman.

'That's Alter's daughter,' said the caretaker, 'I heard he had a daughter and son-in-law.'

So that's his daughter and that's his son-in-law. She studied chemistry and married a lawyer, or she studied law and he studied chemistry.

In a narrow room opening onto the veranda there was a grey ash cabinet by the wall and a table with a glass top. The remains of her trousseau. This was her room, hers and her husband's. This is where they wove their plans for the future. They looked at this ceiling when they woke every morning and put this light out every evening. I looked towards Stefania. Our eyes met. And in her pupils I could read the same thoughts.

Two non-registered women came to wash the floors, the windows and doors. Two sisters who were no longer young. They used to own a pension in Otwock. Saved from selection they didn't have the right to a flat. And they really didn't have a flat. They slept any old where, in an unoccupied room of a deserted house, or simply on a pile of rags in the cellar. On Muranowska Street, like on other streets, there were many deserted houses with flats piled high with things and feathers ripped out of quilts and pillows. Non-registered persons lived with their families or on their own somewhere in small cubicles under a cloud of feathers. They didn't light fires, they went out at night. The dirtier and more piled up the entrance, the more certain it was that the Germans wouldn't come.

Many people lived in cellars all the time and that's where they felt safest.

Two days later Stefan Gliksberg was sent to see if the flat was ready and came back with the news that the stove in the dining room had been stolen. Who could have taken it? Not just the care-taker but everyone in the house and even the people who were going to move in must have known that we had taken the flat. This trivial matter affected us deeply. The stove had to be found and replaced. We talked about nothing else all day long. Ryszard had contacts on the Aryan side and he phoned and asked for a cart. It made the journey a few times. It brought all the Gliksbergs' furniture and things, and our things and everything belonging to the staff of the Union of Pharmacists.

We didn't have any furniture of our own apart from four beds, and there wasn't much left in the Alters' flat, so we brought the small oval table, the white dresser and three coal crates with us. The crates were clean inside and used for keeping food in. But we were terrified because winter was approaching. It might be hard to get coal, the cellars might be broken into. We wanted to have a supply of coal in the flat. We also took the two enormous baskets belonging to my brother-in-law Edward. They were almost empty after the last robbery.

During the move we lost two umbrellas which we put on the cart with all the things instead of holding them. 'What'll happen now? How will you go to work when it's raining?' I asked my husband.

'I'll tell the staff in the office. They might know someone who wants to sell an umbrella.'

So now we were living in the new flat on Muranowska Street. We shared the dining room. The table was for all of us. The Gliksberg family sat on one side and we sat on the other. Between the table and the stove was a bed that Ryszard slept on. By the sideboard a funny, pink sofa. It was round with a very high back. We called it the 'horned' sofa. You used to see sofas like that in the waiting-rooms of provincial railway stations. It was so extraordinary that on the very first evening Stefan started looking for treasure in it. He turned it upside down and examined all its nooks and crannies to see if there wasn't anything hidden in it. He didn't find anything. He turned it right side up again, sat down on it and started thinking.

But now a searching fever came over him. He got up again a moment later, bent down and then he was under the table. He knocked all over the under-side of the table-top, slid his hand under the place where the boards crossed over and pulled out a round box made of strips of wood. He was very pale while he was opening it. It was empty.

Now it was Tadeusz's turn to be infected and he started knocking on the walls, room by room. In the meantime Stefan ran onto the balcony with a spoon, his face aflame. Green, wooden, flower tubs stood there. They all contained the shrivelled stems of plants which no-one had watered. He dug through all the tubs with the spoon, but he didn't find anything and came back into the room. He moved the table over to the stove, put a kitchen stool on it, and a chair on top of that. He jumped on the chair and threw everything from the top of the stove onto the floor, raising a cloud of dust. The non-registered women hadn't dusted the top of the stove at all. He found a small, framed print depicting a stall-keeper or hawker. Also a large album with drawings of children's underwear. An inscription on the cover: 'course in underwear'. Everyone looked at the drawings curiously. Even Stefania came and had a look. And Ada, who helped Stefania, came straight from her pastry board in the kitchen where she was making macaroni.

'I made a discovery today,' said Stefan. 'The table with the glass top is the bottom part of a modern drinks cabinet. I found the glass shelves from the grey cabinet under the wardrobe in our room, and on top of the wardrobe the upper part of a desk.'

'And what did you do with these discoveries?'

'I've made a guess. They deliberately took their furniture apart and scattered it over the flat in order to save it from the Germans. I heard about a man who chopped up the sides of some beautiful cupboards with an axe. The sides of the cupboards were damaged and so the Germans didn't take them.'

'Now I'm going to have a look at the kitchen hall,' declared Stefan.

There was a store cupboard high up on the wall. He dragged the table out of the kitchen, placed a chair on it and opened the cupboard. It had three shelves crammed with things. On the highest shelf he found a few large porcelain bowls and a huge, brass plate encrusted with coloured stones, similar to a medieval shield.

'It's made by Becalel! It's a plate from Jerusalem!' exclaimed Stefania.

'Alter visited Palestine and brought the plate back with him. Or else his daughter and son-in-law brought it back for him as a present from their honeymoon. They hid it from the Germans among all the junk,' said someone.

The plate was passed from hand to hand and in the end it was put on a cloth covered coal-crate which stood in the deep door recess in the dining room. We also placed an enlarged oval photograph of my husband's mother on it. Michalina Szereszewska died in the small ghetto in 1941 at the age of eighty-three. She was fifteen in the photograph. Her hair was arranged in curls on both sides of her childish face. Her eyes were large and shining, her mouth smiling. Her dress fastened at the neck with a star-shaped brooch. The photograph stood in the middle. On the right the Becalel plate, and on the left the Alters' Hanukkah lamp. At each end we placed the tall candlesticks of thin silver which we found in the courtyard. We took them as they might come in useful when there was no light.

The Gliksbergs took two rooms overlooking Stawki Street and the *Umschlagplatz* for themselves and their sons. The first room had three windows and ornate plasterwork on the ceiling and was the Alters' living room, and the room next to it was their bedroom. The third room, a narrow room in line with the others, was taken by Dr Steinsapir who lived with the Gliksbergs here, just like he did at Lubecki Street. The fourth room in the row, a spacious room with a window and a balcony, was taken by Irena and Nina. I entered this room with a shudder. From it you could see the *Umschlagplatz* as if it were on the palm of your hand.

It was a large square and in the middle was a modern building with terraces. There was a school in that building before the war. Before the resettlements there used to be a hospital with wards for nervous illnesses, internal medicine and infectious diseases in the ghetto. Irena went to the hospital from the nursing school on Panska Street. It was a long way from Panska Street to Stawki Street. She took the tram from Zelazna Street through Leszno Street, Karmelicka Street and Dzika Street. There was only one tram-line in the ghetto for the Jewish population and the trams had a blue star painted on them. Then the hospital was closed down. The Germans built a railway siding behind the school and linked it to the main track. When resettlements were being carried out wagons were brought to this siding and the Jewish population was deported. Now the square was empty. But of course in my mind's eye I could still see thousands of people there.

I didn't like going into the Gliksbergs' room either, even though it was like an old print. It had antique furniture of light-coloured

125

wood, a secretaire, a work-table, a cupboard-cum-bar, soft arm-chairs. There were paintings, Persian carpets, silk curtains and two ash beds and wardrobes to match the colour of the antiques. The wardrobes stood diagonally in two corners of the room. They kept food behind them so as to hide it there from the Germans.

Our room was narrow and tiny, like a ship's cabin, and had dark-red wallpaper. When we entered it for the first time, there was a mirror in a wide, green, velvet frame leaning against the wall. We carried it out onto the landing. Someone knocked a hook into the corner between two walls and hung it up. So it hung there. When we left the house we could check in the mirror to see if we hadn't forgotten the white armband with the blue star. I covered the beds with two coloured table-cloths. I cut up the curtains the beds used to be covered with before, made some curtains for the windows of the glazed veranda and hung them up. I placed a table and two chairs in the middle of the veranda. I loved our room. Precisely because it was so small. I felt safe in it. I sometimes thought that I was in the cabin of a ship sailing over the sea.

For the black-out we hung the red kelim we'd brought from the previous flat on the veranda door. Every day at dusk I climbed onto a chair and hung the kelim up on hooks. The kitchen window was also covered with a kelim. A beautiful kelim from the Caucasus, out of Stefania's trunk. It was a large Venetian window with square panes. It caused us much worry as it wasn't double glazed and we were worried that it would be cold in winter. We even wanted to make a frame and glaze it, but it would cost too much. We each had our own household in the kitchen. Even the dresser was divided into two halves.

The sun was still very warm until the middle of October. When we had time Stefania and I sat on the veranda and sewed. We talked and even laughed. Separated from the whole world by the curtains, we feasted on the rare moments of peace and quiet.

'I'll tell you a secret,' said Stefania one day. 'Tadeusz has got a girl-friend on the other side. He gets letters from her.'

She was proud that she had a grown-up son and he had a girl-friend. She was pleased. Within the confines of the tragedy we were experiencing there was sometimes something that was a cause for joy. Except that our joy was never complete, belonging as it did only to a given moment.

Apart from fundamental worries many anxieties and secondary worries nested in all our hearts. Some of them assumed catastrophic proportions, for example the loss of our warm coats, what with winter approaching. Of course the worrying thought that we might not survive until the winter always cropped up in the innermost recesses of our minds. We might die before winter so what's the point of worrying about losing our coats? Smaller but very painful worries included losing our umbrellas, the theft of the stove or the missing window frame.

Isn't it in the attic somewhere?' asked Stefan, 'or maybe it's leaning against the wall in the passage in the cellar and we don't know it's there. Let's go and see. It's got to be somewhere because there are hinges on the frame.'

They went but didn't find it. Ada said it was all the same to her. She would freeze all the same whether the window was double-glazed or not. She couldn't have a bed. Every evening she unfolded a deck chair she'd found in the courtyard in the kitchen and in the daytime she folded it up and hid it behind the dresser. She wasn't allowed to sleep with us. She was a non-registered person. It was an offence punishable by death to provide such a person with somewhere to sleep. Previously she lived with her parents on Panska Street in the small ghetto. She had attended the eight grade Jewish grammar school before the war. She knitted attractive pullovers and costumes and Stefania, who was an elegant woman, wore the clothes she made. Ada's father died of dysentery and her mother was deported. After the small ghetto was liquidated she came to the Gliksbergs and stayed with them as their helper.

There was a wash-basin in the kitchen hall. Above it hung a mirror and next to the mirror, a first-aid cabinet. One day Irena put two tubes of veronal into the first-aid cabinet. A lot of people in the ghetto always carried poison on them. 'I'm putting two tubes of veronal in there,' she said, 'remember.'

There were also two boxes for dirty linen. One day when Stefania was counting the linen that was scattered over the floor she said, 'I'll show you something. Look what's here.' Something was shining in the box in among the linen. She bent over and lifted up a Torah crown crafted in an old-fashioned way. Then she took out the rolls of the Torah in a purple cover with gold embroidery. Finally, a chased silver page mark for holding the pages when the Torah is being read.

'These are our family's treasures,' she said. 'I'm hiding them here from the Germans. I believe they'll bring us luck.'

She closed the box and went into the bathroom. There was a round gas fire in there but it was broken. In our long line of worries

127

we also had the worry about the bathroom. How would we heat it in the winter?

'We'll try to get hold of an iron stove, just a plain little stove. We'll burn turf.'

'But where will we get the stove from? Everything's already been taken.'

'My brother Witold is the store-keeper for the Building Department,' said my husband. 'We'll ask him for a stove. But first we must get someone in to seal up the stoves and check that the pipes are in order.'

The stove-setter came. He was a tall man with unusually handsome and aristocratic features. He worked at the *Umschlagplatz*.

'He's a stove-setter?' said Stefania. 'He's a diplomat or a prince in disguise! I wonder what his wife's like.'

'Yes, I have got a wife,' he said, 'and I did have a mother and three sons.' He was silent for a moment and then he continued, 'One day when I was repairing a stove on the *Umschlagplatz* I looked out of the window and saw my mother in the crowd carrying my youngest child. My three-year-old son was standing next to her. I flew down the stairs just as I was and still holding my bucket of clay. "What's happened?" I shouted. "Your wife gave me the child to hold," replied my mother, "and went out to buy something and took the oldest with her. But they blockaded the house in the meantime and took me and the children." One child's lost, I said, I can't rescue two. I threw the clay out of my bucket, got hold of the older boy under the shoulders and put him in the bucket. The child huddled up in there. I picked a dirty rag up off the ground and covered the bucket with it and carried him off the *Umschlagplatz*. The Germans thought I was carrying clay. Since then I can't forgive my wife for giving my mother the child to hold. My mother was old and so her life was in the greatest danger.' He finished his work. He pushed the bucket aside, stood up and then said, 'My child was wasted. And I loathe her because of it.'

It's still early, we haven't eaten our breakfast yet, Stefania hasn't taken off her dressing-gown with the green and black stripes yet, but Mrs Cukier is already entering. She sells horseflesh.

'No,' says Stefania, 'we're buying from the others today.'

'Mrs Cukier,' I say to her, 'do you remember what I asked you? Can you find out about a coat for my eldest daughter?'

After breakfast the other hawkers come to the kitchen door. My husband has already gone to the Council. Nina has gone to Kurza Street where Councillor Rozensztadt's legal office has moved to. Irena has gone to the hospital on Gensia Street. Tadeusz Gliksberg works with the *Werterfassung* team now. The team collects and segregates for the Germans the things that resettled Jews have left in their flats. Tadeusz walks with the team or drives in a lorry to the small ghetto and brings back a lot of English books and periodicals. He's specially interested in chemistry so he collects books and periodicals in that field. Any novels or poetry he finds he brings for Nina. The Council sends carts out on the street to collect Jewish and Hebrew books from empty flats. Special staff are designated to segregate them and arrange them carefully on shelves.

'They're here already,' shouts Stefania. 'They've already come.'

I go into the kitchen. Two women are standing on the stairs. One of them is wearing a tight cap on her head, the other, who is older, is bare-headed. The younger one worked as a shop assistant in the Warszawiak company's porcelain shop on Mirowska Street before the war. She has lost her mother, husband and seven-year-old son. The Germans picked them up when she was out. She lost someone else as well but she didn't admit to it.

'I've lost my mother, my husband and my son,' she said and looked straight in front of her, tightening her mouth.

The second woman stood there, sad and silent. Only once when she came on her own she said, 'And a ten-month-old daughter. But it won't pass through her lips, she can't talk about it.'

They lived together now. They got to know each other one day in a cramped hide-out when they were hiding from the Germans. Although they were non-registered they occupied the basement at 44 Muranowska Street. You could buy butter and cheese from them as well as horseflesh. So we're buying horseflesh from these two women, and, while we pay, Stefania chats with the younger one. 'Well? Did you find out about a hairdresser in our part of town?'

'On Mila Street. Not on the left side of Dzika Street but on Mila Street on the right side. You walk all along Mila Street until you see a ruined house. The hairdresser lives just next door.'

Stefania goes to the hairdresser's immediately after dinner. Two hours later she comes back with her hair fashionably done and tells us, 'In the room where my hair was being done a woman was

129

cleaning the scales off a carp on the table. She was making a pan of soup. When she finished, she grated a few raw potatoes, made some potato dumplings and put them in the soup. Then they offered me a bowl of soup. I felt completely at home.'

For the next few days Stefania made soup with potato dumplings every day. But then she returned to carrots with kugel stuffed with jam, which is what we cooked mostly. It was our favourite dish, ours and the Gliksbergs. We eat together at a large square table. We don't use a tablecloth, just oilcloth. They use half the table and we use the other half. Ryszard eats at his parents. Ada brings in a large tureen of steaming soup and places it on the stove, the same stove that disappeared and then turned up again. Stefania uses it during meals as an additional piece of furniture.

We sit down. Stefania at the head of the table. Her husband on one side of her and Dr Steinsapir on the other. Tadeusz sits next to him, and Stefan sits next to Mr Gliksberg. Dr Steinsapir eats with the Gliksbergs. He is a renowned diagnostician and typhus specialist but in everyday life he is reticent and unpleasant. He always comes to table with a metal tin containing sugar.

Stefania often asked my advice, 'How much should I charge him? He asks me every day and I don't know what to say.'

I didn't know either. His daughter was a doctor. She lived in Nowe Miasto near Warsaw and had just had a baby. His son-in-law was a doctor as well. Dr Steinsapir was always thinking about his daughter and her baby.

Just like him, there was no day and no hour when we didn't worry about our eldest daughter and her son in hiding on the Aryan side.

Marysia went to Otwock at the end of summer 1941 with her sick four-year-old son, Macius. When the Germans started liquidating the ghetto in Otwock half-way through August 1942 she managed to escape to Warsaw in an ambulance at the last minute. She got out at the edge of the city and drove in a horse-cab to Nowy Zjazd Street where her former grammar school teacher, Mrs Janina Poniatowska, lived. Mrs Poniatowska was the wife of an university professor. She cared for our daughter and her child really sincerely, helping her in everything. She advised her and taught her how to behave so as not to arouse suspicion, and helped her get some Aryan papers. Marysia was registered as Maria Swiencicka, from the small town of Marki.

Professor Stanislaw Poniatowski went for a walk with Macius

every day. He held his hand and talked to him endlessly. The boy was attractive and fair-haired, alert and receptive. Since both the professor and his wife were members of the underground resistance movement, Mrs Poniatowska was worried about informers and so she advised Marysia to move in with her sisters Zofia and Wanda Lubecki who lived one floor lower in the same house. The older sister worked in the Town Hall, the younger worked as a librarian at the University Library. Professor Meir Balaban, who was ordered by the Germans to do some research, went to the library every day from the ghetto. He had a pass. He lived on Muranowska Street, in our courtyard. He was sixty-eight. He had a bad heart and was hard of hearing.

So Marysia lived with Zofia and Wanda Lubecki. She had her own room and paid 250 zlotys for it. The same price as Poles paid. She cooked for herself and the child. Every few days she went to a café, a different one each time, or to a shop where they didn't know her and rang the Jewish Council. 'Is that Mr Szereszewski?' she asked her father and he asked about the child. They talked about this and that, about their health, something or nothing. They were afraid the line was bugged. Yes. Worry about our daughter and her child were our daily bread.

Irena finished the nursing school and received her diploma. She worked in the hospital at 6 Gensia Street which started up after the hospital on Leszno Street was closed down. The nurses who worked there prepared it all themselves; they washed the doors and windows and scrubbed the floors. The director was Dr Jozef Sztein. Dr Borkowski, Dr Amsterdam and Dr Rothaub were in charge of the surgical ward. Dr Bielenki and Dr Munwes were in charge of the medical ward. Dr Rothaub's assistant was Dr Kajzer. However, 300 doctors had already been sent to the *Umschlagplatz*.

Irena works shifts, a week of nights and then a week of days. She often has afternoon shifts as well. Sometimes she comes home in the evening with the wife of Mr Kornfeld who works in the Council. She's also a nurse and lives in our courtyard. When she's working nights she puts on her warmest pullover. She takes a thermos of hot coffee and always takes a candle in case the light goes out. In the evenings it's dark and empty on the ghetto streets at eight o'clock. The nurses always come back in groups.

One day Irena was working late and the others had already gone home. A German patrol stopped on Dzika Street opposite the Council. She wanted to show her pass but one of them had already

131

hit her on the head and back with a rubber truncheon and ordered her to go with him to the check-point. Then the other one came up and read her pass and asked, 'Where do you live?'

'42 Muranowska Street.'

'I'll see you home.'

He accompanied her to the gate. Since the door was closed early he waited until the caretaker came and opened it. Then the German bent over and kissed her hand. She crossed the courtyard. Then she entered the door and went upstairs. She stopped in front of the mirror hanging on the landing, lit her torch and looked at her pale face.

Every day when my husband came home from work he knocked at the door twice and then quickly three times. So we knew it was him. It was our family's pre-arranged signal. The Gliksbergs knocked differently. We open the door. 'Children,' says my husband on the threshold, 'it's raining. Leave my umbrella to dry.'

He's got an umbrella now. It belonged to Mr Neusztadt who used to work in Joint and was married to the artist Klara Segalowicz. Since both of them had foreign citizenship they had been taken to Pawiak during the resettlements and no-one knew what happened to them. Mr Neusztadt's sister lived at 44 Muranowska Street. When she heard that we needed an umbrella she brought her brother's umbrella. At first she didn't even want to take any money. 'I promise to give the umbrella back if your brother turns up,' said my husband.

'Did Marysia ring?' I ask.

'No,' he answers, 'she didn't. But my pass has been renewed. I'll be able to go over to the Aryan side, and Ryszard has got a pass as well.'

We sit down to supper. While we're sitting round the table Stefan starts telling us something. He likes being listened to. 'Something strange happened in my friend's family. In the evening when they were all at table, a woman they didn't know came in. She didn't say a word, only crossed the room, opened the window, removed a brick, took something valuable out of it and ran out of the flat.'

'Don't be silly,' said Stefania. 'You're going soft. Daddy doesn't know that you spend days on end looking for valuables that the Alters left behind when they were deported.'

'Mummy, it's true,' says Tadeusz. 'She must have been a non-registered person who used to live there. She came to get her property. I heard today that some new people were clearing up a flat they'd moved into and when they moved the dresser aside two furs fell on their heads.'

'Didn't Mrs Cukier, that woman who sells horseflesh, say that her neighbour, who's non-registered, opened the stove and found some Persian lamb wrapped up in a dirty rag?' said Stefan.

During this conversation I thought of Christmas last year when the Germans issued the order about Jewish furs. You could be sentenced to death for even the tiniest scrap not handed in. Many Jews smuggled their furs over to the Aryan side or sold them dirt cheap to Poles or even burnt them in their stoves to avoid handing them over to the Germans. I heard that some people plastered their furs up in the walls. There were many Poles wearing Jewish stars on their sleeves in the streets of the ghetto at that time. No-one escaped the German order. Poor people brought their moth-eaten fur caps and worn collars and least little scraps of fur to the Council. Anything over ten square centimetres – that's what the order said. Whole processions of Jews went to the Council with furs. Then the furs were sorted. The most beautiful went to Germany. Medium grade fur such as rabbit and sheepskin, and children's furs, were used for army greatcoats, while collars and trimmings were used for gloves and warm hats. The Jews made them in workshops in the ghetto.

'You've got to hand in your rabbitskin coat as well,' Marysia told her son.

'What for? Have they got such little soldiers?' replied Macius.

Every evening a young boy of twenty called Olek Nimcewicz visited Nina. He was a guard at the brush works on Bonifraterska Street, the biggest workshop in the ghetto and employing the most workers. At that time all the houses in the ghetto were connected via holes in the walls or holes in the attics. Nimcewicz left his workshop through the attic and walked along several streets using the attics. Workshop guards, Jewish policemen from workshops, or even German soldiers, stood at intervals and collected 'tolls'.

Olek Nimcewicz brought underground newspapers and news from the radio. His family had started building a house on Wisniowa Street in the Mokotow area of Warsaw before the war. When the building work was interrupted the cellars were already finished so they made themselves a shelter down there. The caretaker who guarded the building site was a person they trusted. Olek often asked Nina, 'If the need arises would you like to have a share in the shelter and live with us? If we're parted ring Mr Domanski on

Przejazd Street and ask about Olek and his sister.' He brought her all sorts of things he thought might be useful. He found them in the empty flats of deserted houses. A lampshade, a torch, and a weaver's bobbin which she carried around for a long time. It increased the number of her mascots, her comforters as she called them.

There was no time of day or night when Henryk Gliksberg wasn't thinking about his sister who was living on Aryan papers in Swider in a pension called 'Anulka'. He had lost his older sister and niece during the resettlements and was tormented by the fact that he couldn't save them. Stefania often said, 'He's tormenting himself because of his older sister and he can't sleep at night.' One day a tram driver visited us from the Aryan side and brought a letter from the pension. Stefania gave him a diamond ring for her sister-in-law.

'Can you trust him with something as valuable as that?' I asked.

'I trust him like a brother.'

The tram driver was the father of Tadeusz's school friend. He's the man who was hiding the girl Tadeusz was in love with and her mother. Together with the letter from the pension, the tram driver also brought a letter which Tadeusz looked at delightedly for a long time before opening and reading it.

'What does she say?' asked his mother.

'She wants to see me. I'll go over to the Aryan side tomorrow.'

Next day he joined a group of Polish workmen who worked in a factory on Muranowska Street. He paid the foreman fifty zlotys for the favour. He left the ghetto and returned the same way.

'You're back!' called Stefania. 'You're back! I was getting so worried.'

'Is it five o'clock yet?' asked Stefan.

Stefan's study group met three times a week at five o'clock. They were in the sixth year. Nora Kowalska was in the group too. She lived with her parents at 61 Niska Street. Adas, the son of the lawyer Himmelfarb, came with her. Stefania hovered among them anxiously. 'Sit down and calm down. The teacher will be here soon and then you'll have your lesson.' The noise continued. But when the old clock struck five and played its tune then it became quiet. And the clock played in the silence.

Two winter coats turned up at the Wyszewianskis on Walicow Street. They belonged to Ryszard and Nina. The house at 6 Walicow Street was in the small ghetto. The workers from Többens' workshop lived in it. And the Wyszewianskis, the parents of our niece's husband, worked there. Többens' workshop was now an island in the liquidated small ghetto which had become the Aryan side. They sent us the coats via their sons who were policemen and received passes from time to time. So, of the five missing coats, two had turned up.

It was November already and my husband was still wearing a summer coat, so in the end he bought a coat from the articled clerk Lewkowicz. It had belonged to his father who had been deported by the Germans. We paid 500 zlotys for it. Old Lewkowicz was a very large man and the coat was much too big. So Nagel the policeman, who was a tailor, came every day and remade the coat. I had a sewing-machine which Nagel used but since the material was thick he bent the needle and ruined it.

'You've ruined the needle,' I said worried. 'Where will I get another one from?'

'I'll ask around and find one.'

I had so many worries that this small, bent needle was the last straw. I would have preferred it if my husband's coat came from someone who was still alive and not from a man who was deported. When someone had been deported, wearing their clothes meant you'd die the same way. You died and attracted the next victim through your things. That's what people believed.

'Don't be superstitious,' said my husband. 'You don't really believe what you're saying, do you?'

I wasn't superstitious. But all the same I always looked at the coat and Neusztadt's umbrella with a certain amount of misgiving.

We still didn't have a winter coat for our daughter on the Aryan side. Where could we get one?

'There's a woman on the fourth floor with a coat for sale,' said Ada.

'The fourth floor? Up the kitchen stairs? The woman with a husband and stepson?'

'Yes. That's the one.' I went upstairs. The stepson opened the door, a boy of 17. The coat was cut the French way and was made of thin gaberdine so it wasn't suitable. When I told Nagel about it he asked, 'Have you or your daughters got a winter coat? If I find some wadding I can line it.'

'I've got an English coat. And there's some wadding in my dressing-gown.'

So Nagel remade the coat. When it was ready Ryszard got it

135

across to the Aryan side to a chemist's he knew on Krakowskie Przedmiescie and Marysia collected it from there.

Marysia sold the table silver which she had given her teacher Mrs Mikolajewska for safe-keeping at the beginning of the war. Every so often she sold some of our things that were in safe-keeping on the Aryan side and lived off the money. First of all she sold a Persian carpet. Then a Persian lamb coat. Tietz, the German agent in charge of the Henrykow yeast works, bought it for his wife. She sold it for 13,500 zlotys. Most of the money went on making Aryan papers for us and Ryszard. Since the Henrykow factory belonged to our family, Marysia got hold of some yeast from the agent. She took it to the market at Hale Mirowskie and sold it. She had what was called a 'good appearance' and that's why she went out on the streets. She was fair-haired with grey eyes and a fair skin. What could give her away? Her Polish was faultless. Her manner and behaviour as well.

'Only your eyes give you away,' said Mrs Poniatowska, 'and maybe the way you walk does a bit too. No, just your eyes, nothing else.'

Every evening before he went to bed Ryszard came to our room and sat down on the old-fashioned hatbox which stood next to the door.

'I was on the Aryan side today and saw Marysia.'

'Tell us. Where did you see her?'

'I was in her flat. At Nowy Zjazd Street. The professor's been arrested. Mrs Poniatowska is ill and she's been taken to hospital. The flat's been sealed.'

We didn't say anything. Then Ryszard said, 'Marysia's papers were stolen in the tram, but they've already been sent back. The thief kept 1,000 zlotys.'

'And what else did Marysia say?'

'She needs our photographs to have the papers made for us. I arranged that when I get some Zakopane shoes taken over for her I'll slip them under the lining. There's a photographer in Schultz's workshop.'

Then he said, 'I want Marysia to come back. It's peaceful here. Jews are coming back from the other side. It's much worse there than here. Round-ups and arrests all the time. What do you think, father?'

He sat for a while and then left. I asked my husband what he was thinking about.

'I've got a pass and I go to the Aryan side on Council business. What would happen if I suddenly met our grandson on Wierzbowa Street or Krakowskie Przedmiescie? I might not be able to restrain my tears and that could give him away.'

Next day the phone rang in the Jewish Council. It was Marysia.

'Any news, Mr Szereszewski?'

'Ryszard wants you to come back.'

'Does he? I'll think about it. Anything else?'

'He'll be at Alfred's tomorrow at three.'

Alfred Kaftal's father was Jewish and his mother was Aryan, from Vienna. Alfred passed himself off as a *Volksdeutsch*. He had married a peasant girl and had a son of thirteen. Tall, stout, short-sighted and talkative, he used to teach Marysia German, which he had studied. He was thin and poor then. His parents and brother had lived with him in a poor and tiny flat. While he gave lessons he lived in poverty. In the end he took to trade. He traded with Jews, entering the ghetto through the lawcourts bordering the ghetto and the Aryan side. There were entrances to the courts from Ogrodowa Street on the Aryan side and from Leszno Street in the ghetto. In the ghetto he put on a white armband with a blue star. He sold stockings and knitted goods.

In the evening Ryszard came and sat down on the hatbox.

'I went to Kaftal's and saw Marysia.'

'And what?'

'She told me that a Jewish work team removed the furniture from Professor Poniatowski's sealed flat. She stood there in the door and couldn't believe her own eyes when she saw Jews legally crossing to the Aryan side like that. She stood there and forgot that she was cooking carrots and burnt the lot.'

'What else?'

'I told her to come back. I know a Jewish family who've done up a three-roomed flat on Nalewki Street. A lot of Jews are returning from the Aryan side. She says that the Wilno ghetto has been completely liquidated and the Lubecki sisters don't advise her to come back. I don't know if I won't take the child off her if she won't come back.'

When the door closed behind him I said to my husband, 'You know, I don't like what Ryszard said about the child one bit.'

He didn't say a word. He just sat staring and lost in thought.

But then when the tailors were deported from the workshops in

137

the ghetto to Lublin – which was something the Jews really couldn't understand because you were considered to be untouchable if you worked for the Germans – we finally decided that despite everything it was safer on the other side. And we stopped weighing up whether our daughter should stay or come back.

Hancia from 38 Muranowska Street came to do the washing. The day before wash-day Stefania counted the linen in the kitchen hall. She kept the linen in a small, wooden box. When she'd turned everything out onto the floor she said, 'Come and see what's on the bottom of the box.'

I knew what was there as she'd already shown me. But I wanted to see it again. It shone silver and gold. Carefully she took out and lifted up a crown for a Torah – yes, a crown. An old silver chalice with a Hebrew inscription and a chased silver page marker for reading the Bible. It was in the shape of an outstretched finger. I knew that now she'd say: 'I'm hiding it here so it doesn't disappear. I watch it like a hawk. I believe it'll bring me luck.' She was so pleased to get a washerwoman at last that she wanted to give her a pair of shoes. They were old but still in good condition. But Hancia laughed. 'You're joking. I've got thirty pairs at home. Come and see for yourself. I've got beautiful glass and china too. I went into empty flats and took what I wanted.'

She ordered potato soup for her morning meal and supper. Without any vegetables, just potatoes and some fat. That's how she liked it best. She took her blouse off to do the washing. Her neck and hands were as white as snow. Her eyes and hair were black. 'If only you knew what a beautiful daughter I've got. She's eighteen and works in Hallmann's workshop.'

She was happy that she'd managed to get her daughter into the workshop. She talked about it all the time. She also talked about our caretaker who dealt in food. She had done the washing there for four days on end and couldn't praise the food she had there highly enough. 'I had lamb and tripe. For supper they gave me sausage and curd cheese.'

Hancia did the washing in our kitchen for three days. Then she hung washing lines on all the balconies and in the kitchen, high up under the ceiling. The kitchen ceiling was hung with washing lines in every direction. To reach the highest one Hancia stood on the table, then got on a chair and then placed a stool on the chair. No-one hung their washing in the attic any more. Attics didn't serve that purpose any longer. The attics were all connected by means of holes in the walls and they'd become trails. They'd become paths, beaten tracks used by the Jews to avoid being seen by the Germans.

After that we didn't use Hancia to do our washing any more. My cousin Marek Szpilfogel moved into 4 Muranowska Street. He was a doctor of chemistry. He and his wife Erna both worked in the steam laundry in the former Britannia Hotel at 10 Nowolipie Street. The laundry was for the Germans. Marek and Erna came to us with rucksacks and took our washing and the Gliksbergs' washing and we paid them per item. They also took Dr Steinsapir's washing. It used to be done by a washerwoman from Niska Street who had a small soap shop and when the doctor handed over his washing he used to bring back some paraffin in a bottle. When there was no electricity he lit a lamp and the paraffin would sputter because it was mixed with water.

He tidied his room and made his bed. He hated it if Ada came in to tidy up. Sometimes when he was out Stefania grabbed a broom and swept the room because she couldn't stand the mess. She showed me the piles of cigarette-ends. Dr Steinsapir was the doctor for the block. He was in charge of the sanitary arrangements for a few houses on Muranowska Street, or blocks as we called them. He went to the Health Department at 10 Kurza Street every morning. He received patients in his room in the flat between five and seven. However one day someone knocked at our front door at six in the morning.

'Who do you want?'

'Dr Steinsapir,' replied one of the two men standing there. We didn't know them.

He came out to them in his dark red and brown striped dressing-gown. He opened the door but didn't let them in. He stood on one side of the door and they stood on the other. He looked at them suspiciously with his hand on the handle ready to slam the door. They asked him to go to Schultz's workshop. To see someone with typhus.

'We've got a pass for you to enter the workshop. We've got a cart ready harnessed. We'll take you there and bring you back.'

'I can't,' he said. 'Forgive me, but I can't.'

'But we've got a signed pass! And the stamp is real. It's got a bird on it.'

'I believe you. But I'm scared, that's what it is. That's how I am. I can't overcome it.'

They promised him the moon. He didn't go. He was terrified of the Germans. He had a thing about it from the time when he was held hostage for a month. That was in July at the beginning of the resettlement action. From time to time a friend of his daughter visited him with her husband. They were his only friends. They came dressed like team workers, both of them wearing ski trousers and pullovers and jackets. They worked in the workshop on Stawki Street opposite the Transavia workshop. Their workshop bore the name Serejski, Slucki and Wisniewski. He was a lawyer and she was a doctor. Dr Steinsapir never smiled. And he never said a word to anyone apart from the Gliksbergs.

When we heard that his daughter and son-in-law had been deported from Nowe Miasto Stefania couldn't sleep for fear that he'd commit suicide. At two in the morning I heard her footsteps in the hall and I quietly opened the door.

'Well, what's up?' I whispered.

'He's sitting at the table all the time. Not in his room but in the dining room. He's leaning his head on his hands and he's deep in thought. When I speak to him he doesn't reply. Is he going to do himself some harm?'

Shortly afterwards he was informed from the Aryan side that the child was alive. The woman who was the chemist's servant brought the baby to Warsaw in a suitcase. Sometimes we believed the story. At other times we thought that the whole business was thought up by dishonest people who wanted to swindle him out of money for bringing up the child.

After a while Ada stopped working as a maid and got into the *Werterfassung* work team. She worked in areas that had previously been part of the ghetto. That meant Chlodna Street, Grzybowska Street and the part of Nalewki Street that had been excluded from the ghetto. Poles were gradually beginning to settle into flats and shops that Jews used to have and the area was now called the Aryan side. We used to say that Ada was going to the Aryan side. When the *Werterfassung* work team was collecting goods from haberdashery shops Ada brought us brooches, belts or artificial flowers. Sometimes she brought a blouse or a silk night-dress or a pair of stockings.

On the Aryan side she bought milk, sausage, butter and bread and sometimes even some meat. You placed an order with her and she added a certain amount to the cost of each item for her earnings. So she brought food into the ghetto and earned money on it, and

140

took clothes and linen out of the ghetto for the Jews living on the Aryan side. She was paid for that as well. A woman who had worked as her parents' servant lived on Ogrodowa Street. She waited for Ada at an arranged place. Ada entered the gate, took off her coat and dress and underwear and handed it all over to the woman. The woman took the things to her flat and then people came to collect the clothes. Nothing ever went missing.

That was how Ada took over many clothes for Henryk Gliksberg's sister. She took things for Mrs Hurwicz' younger daughter and she also took my suit which my daughter came to collect. Ada was doing well. She ate eggs and drank milk. When Ada left, Stefania found someone else to help her. There was an old woman who lived alone on the ground floor of our flight of stairs. She had lost all her children and was on her own. She took in a fifteen-year-old girl from Legionowo with fair hair and blue eyes. She called her Blumcia. When the Legionowo ghetto was being liquidated she managed to escape and hide in a house, where she was kept for a few months by the Polish woman who lived there. She and her husband knew she was Jewish. They treated her well.

'She called me Wandzia,' said Blumcia. 'If anyone came I had to go to the end room and sit there quietly.'

'What did you do there?'

'I knitted pullovers and helped with the housework.'

'Why didn't you stay longer?'

'Because she said she didn't have any food to give me.'

Stefania didn't have a lot of joy out of Blumcia. After her there were two girls, Hania and Rachelka. And then at the very end there was Sabinka who lived in the cellar because that's where she felt safest. When the resettlements started Sabinka lived on Gensia Street. When the house was blockaded her mother hid in the corner of the room under a pile of rags and linen. Sabinka hid under the bed. A Ukrainian entered the room and pulled her out from under the bed. She stood there, pale. She pulled a ring off her finger. It was made of thin silver and had a blue stone, and she handed it to him in silence. He looked at her face. At her slender, trembling fingers. Perhaps he had a sister like her because he said, 'I'm going, you stay here.'

He pushed her hand aside and said, 'You might need it.'

So that's how she stayed alive. She and her mother managed to get to 38 Muranowska Street and they hid in a cellar which had a window into Niska Street. They found a Jew in a prayer shawl and

141

his wife, who had typhus down there. All four of them were dying of hunger. They had nothing left to eat. Then Sabinka decided to betray the hiding-place, so she jumped onto a box, opened the window and stretched out her hand.

On the corner of Dzika Street and Niska Street there was a police station used by the Polish police. Niska Street was fenced off and a shed stood there, and next to it stood two policemen. Niska Street was a district of workshops and blocks inhabited by work teams. They were only allowed to leave the place in groups, never individually unless they had a special pass. The Germans trusted the Polish police completely and used them to guard the workshops. One of the policemen noticed the outstretched hand and realized that some Jews were hiding in the cellar. He waited for the right moment, hid a bottle of water and a loaf of bread under his coat, and then walked along the side of the wall and gave the hand the bread and water. 'He fed us for a long time,' said Sabinka, 'until it calmed down.'

All the time we lived at Muranowska Street we could see that police station from the balcony of our flat. They might not have been the same policemen any more. But whenever I hung the washing out I looked at them and thought: is that the one who gave Sabinka the bread?

I once went to the cellar where she lived, through the passage full of stinking puddles. She wasn't there. Only her sick mother, lying in bed. She slowly turned her head towards me. Next to her was a second bed with another woman lying on it. And a Jew was standing there, with a long beard, fully dressed for prayer.

'This isn't a prayer time,' I said in surprise.

'He dresses like that from morning till night. I've never seen him in anything else,' said Sabinka's mother.

My husband's brother, Witold, was allocated a room in the houses for the Building Department staff on Kurza Street. He was given a room in house number 8, on the second floor, in a large flat that used to be lived in by wealthy Jews before they were deported. The entrance was from the kitchen because the front door was nailed up and never used. He received the dining room, a table, a large, dark sideboard and two beds by the wall. Two women from a work team slept in the same room on a two-person sofa. They were sisters. The younger one was twenty. They went to Narbutt Street on the Aryan side with their team and, just like Ada, they brought bread, butter, milk, apples and meat into the ghetto and sold them. They shared the household with Celina, my sister-in-law, and found a hunchbacked girl to cook and wash for them.

Early one November morning Celina crossed to the Aryan side with them. She was dressed just like they were. She wanted to renew her Polish contacts because she was scared of the ghetto and intended to escape. She visited her friends, the Holzgrebers, in the Mokotow area of Warsaw, then she went to the Millers in Bielany and finally she visited her friend Mrs Sabart, the German administrator for Jewish property in the ghetto. In 1944, a year after the ghetto was liquidated, Mrs Sabart employed some Jews in her house on Twarda Street, including Fein, who was a draughtsman in Witold's office before the war. She was denounced for safe-keeping Jewish property. The Gestapo searched the house. She was arrested and shot.

Celina returned to Kurza Street with the same work team, unnoticed by the Germans. I sometimes went there at dusk. There were no more resettlements by then. But even in the daytime the streets were empty and you mustn't let the Germans see you, because the ghetto was a labour camp now. The only people to ride along the streets were the Jewish policemen on their bikes, and undertakers.

I went along Muranowska Street until you get to Dzika Street. Then along Dzika Street. The first junction is Mila Street, the second is Kurza Street. At dusk it was crowded and noisy. The work teams were returning. Boys with cigarettes and hawkers with bread stood on the streets and in house gateways. Everyone thought it was safer when it was crowded and noisy. As I was walking along Kurza Street I met Dr Alapin, our neighbour from Walicow Street.

'My wife,' he said, 'went to the Aryan side with our son but she came back.'

'Why was that?'

'She didn't have anywhere to spend the night.'

So there was that too. You didn't have anywhere to spend the night. So you had to prepare the ground on the other side very thoroughly before you left the ghetto. As I stood there lost in thought Mr Dulman, the cobbler from Wisniowa Street in Mokotow, the one who used to repair our shoes before the war and in the first months of the war, came up to us.

'Are your wife and children with you? Where do you live?' I asked.

143

'I've still got a wife and children and I live on Mila Street. What about you?'

'On Muranowska Street. My husband's shoes need mending. Will you do them?

'Yes. I'm in a team. But in the evenings I mend shoes.'

Here's the entrance to number 8. Turn right in the courtyard. I go up a few stairs and reach a small, dark hall and then the Building Department's stores where Witold is standing behind the counter. It's cold in the stores. Witold's wearing his coat. The collar's raised and he's got a cap on his head. Not a hat. No-one wore a hat in the ghetto any longer. There was an order saying Jews had to wear caps. It was a golden age for cap makers. People wore ski caps or large cycling caps. Nagel, the policeman, sold my husband a piece of material with grey checks and my husband, and then Ryszard too, ordered caps for themselves.

Witold weighed nails in the stores, counted rolls of wire and gave out tools to the workers if they had a requisition slip. 'I've come for a small stove. Just an iron stove to burn turf, and for a stove door because ours is broken.'

We talk. Then I say goodbye and leave. I cross the courtyard and go up to see Celina on the second floor. A hunchback is sitting at the table in the clean kitchen peeling potatoes. Mrs Rotmil, from the work team, is standing next to her weighing apples. She's thirty and divorced. Her ex-husband is in hiding on Aryan papers in Milanowek and she managed to get in touch with him. At the beginning of December she's going over to the Aryan side as usual with her sister at six in the morning and they won't come back. I find Celina sitting over a book, leaning her head on her hand and staring straight in front of her. Mrs Rotmil's sister is lying on the sofa, tired after her day's work.

'How can I live here with these ghosts?' Celina says to me. 'Tell me, how can I live here with these ghosts all around?' She gets up and opens the sideboard. 'They ate off these plates, drank out of these glasses, cut their bread with these knives. They sat by the light of this lamp in the evenings, just like we're doing now. They looked out of this window into the courtyard.'

She was talking about the ghosts of the people who had lived in the flat. But she was thinking about her two sisters who died, one of them during a selection at the Council and the other in Hrubieszow in eastern Poland. About her brother who died at the beginning of the war, and her mother who was put to sleep.

144

'Should I be afraid of these ghosts?' she asks and turns pale.

She's silent and looks at me. At me, even though I've lost my closest family just like she has. Then she whispers, 'But I'm afraid of them all the same.'

Then I go home. I make my way through the thick crowd. A cold wind is blowing. My head is wrapped in a scarf and bent low. I walk along, then I turn into dark Dzika Street and dark Muranowska Street. Standing in front of the entrance to 44 is Stanislaw Gans, the policeman, who knows our family. I stop and ask him, 'Is there any news of my uncle Adam Szpilfogel and his wife? I know they left Otwock for Warsaw, then went to Zyrardow and then to Piotrkow. Are they alive?'

'They walked into a resettlement action in Piotrkow. They took poison. She died but he was saved and deported.'

I enter number 42 and cross the long courtyard. All the windows are darkened. I enter the entrance to this annexe of the house. The Alters' safe is lying on the concrete floor. I go upstairs and knock at the door using our arranged signal, first two knocks and then three quick knocks. And I think: who will cry for them? Not one of Adam Szpilfogel's three daughters was still alive.

A candle is burning in the tall candlestick in the dining room because the electric light isn't working. The shadows of the people sitting round the table move on the walls. Boleslaw Szereszewski, my husband's cousin, Stanislaw Tempel, a relative of ours, and his father. The flame sways and small transparent tears flow down the candle. Izaak Tempel is seventy-three. His hair and eyebrows are yellow because he dyed his white hair so as not to look old. Since the ghetto has become a labour camp old people have lost the right to live. The Germans let him join the *Werterfassung* work team without knowing how old he really was. He lost his wife at the beginning of the resettlements. He lived alone at 6 Muranowska Street in the block where the team workers lived. Every morning at half past six he goes to 37 Leszno Street on the Aryan side with his team where there are huge stores of Jewish furniture. And while the other team members collect the furniture from flats and deliver it in lorries, Izaak Tempel is the store-keeper.

It's not heavy work. He gets soup and bread from the Germans. At dusk when he returns home he brings a few chopped up planks with him and burns them in an iron stove in his room. He has two sons. He hasn't had any news about his older son Marian who went to Wilno with his family and was arrested by the Russians and deported. His younger son Stanislaw is working in the Transavia workshop on Stawki Street where aeroplane parts are manufactured. There is a very close and loving relationship between father and son. The son is proud of his father for being in the work team. At the same time he worries about him living all alone and cooking for himself. He'd love to live with him but he's in another team. He goes to his father's every evening or else they meet at our place. It's not far from Stawki Street to Muranowska Street.

'You're pale,' old Mr Tempel says to me, 'did you get cold? There's a strong wind today.'

Shall I tell him or not? Probably not because he'll take it very much to heart. Adam's wife was his sister-in-law. I take some scissors and trim the wick of the candle. The shadow on the ceiling forms a dark moving circle. 'Do you need an iron? I can sell you one,' says Boleslaw. He's sitting with his back to the window.

'No. It'll be the same as it was with the electric cooker.'

Boleslaw is fifty-three. His hair and eyebrows are golden, just like Izaak Tempel's. He dyed them like everyone else with grey hair in the ghetto. He didn't work. He survived a selection. He's a non-registered person. He lived in Lodz and came to Warsaw in order to escape the ghetto there. All his family perished. He had a few things of Edward's, my brother-in-law, whom he lived with for a while. He was selling them with no scruples. He once sold us an electric cooker and a mincer without telling us whose they were. Edward's mother-in-law came over from the Aryan side one day, recognized both machines and took them back at once. Boleslaw was now living in a police house in a flat with a relative of ours, the engineer Leon Wyszewianski, and Leon Fejgin, who worked in the Supplies Department.

So of our relatives we still had: Witold and Celina on Kurza Street, Marek Szpilfogel and Erna on Muranowska Street, Izaak Tempel and his son, Leon Wyszewianski and Boleslaw Szereszewski. The rest of our relatives were on the Aryan side: my husband's brothers Leon and Edward with their wives and children, Marian Szpilfogel and his wife Julia, my uncle Maurycy Szpilfogel and his wife Helena and daughter Hanna Wyszewianska. And my niece Anusia Laskowska. Marek Szpilfogel's mother was also on the Aryan side. She was seventy-three and very ill. The person who got her out of the ghetto and who was to look after her often rang Marek in the Council. My husband took the calls.

146

'I'm speaking on behalf of mother as she's in hospital. She wants Marek to come and bring some money.'

When Marek and Erna returned to Muranowska Street from the steam laundry they called in to see us.

'There was a call for you,' said my husband. 'It's the same voice and he's asking for money.'

'I gave mother all my money,' replied Marek.

One evening, when Marek and Erna were visiting, my husband told them about the latest phone call from the Aryan side and finished by saying, 'There's a Jewish Bank on Nalewki Street. An official bank. I know that Szymon Szpilfogel had 20,000 zlotys on deposit there. Szymon and his family are dead. You need money. Write a promissory note saying: I authorize my nephew Marek Szpilfogel to withdraw 20,000 zlotys. Backdate it and forge Szymon's signature. Otherwise the money will be lost. You're the nearest relative so try it and you might succeed. In these terrible times you can't even call it a crime, even though it looks very much like a crime.'

I don't know if Marek managed to get the money. All I do know is that he spent a few evenings practising Szymon Szpilfogel's signature.

Late in the evening when everyone had gone I went up to my husband. Do you know, I wanted to say, that Adam and his wife are dead. Something drew them to Piotrkow to be nearer home and that's where they died. But I couldn't say a single word. I just looked at him. He already knew. Now he could see in my eyes that I knew too.

I took my husband's shoes to Dulman the cobbler. The courtyard of the house where he lived was cramped and muddy. I had to jump over puddles and take care not to twist my ankle in the piles of bricks. I could barely find the number of the flat in the long, dark hall on the ground floor. When I knocked Mrs Dulman opened the door.

'I saw you in a column on Smocza Street going to the *Umschlagplatz*,' she said. 'I was hiding in the attic with the children and I was looking out through a hole. I said to the children, "Look, there's Mrs Szereszewska going to the *Umschlagplatz*."'

There were two birchwood double beds in the room, a large wardrobe and an iron stove with a pipe. Next to the stove on a chair stood a pastry board and on it a pile of thinly cut macaroni. A pan of boiling water stood on the stove. She took some macaroni, shook it and threw it into the pan. Her children, a girl and two boys, watched her hands.

147

'Hanka! Wipe Elek's nose,' she shouted. 'Dulman, Mrs Szere-szewska's come with the shoes. You can go over to the workshop, Mrs Szereszewska, it's over there.'

Dulman was sitting in his workshop mending a shoe. An oldish grey-haired man was mending another shoe next to him. There were two bowls under a chair. The first one was full of pike and carp, the second contained beef and tongues.

'He brings it all back because he's in a work team on the Aryan side,' said Mrs Dulman, 'but he still makes shoes. And that's his partner. If you need any fish or meat we'll always sell you some. We're doing well. The children only eat white bread. Even Elek, who is four now has got money in his pocket too.'

A girl comes in. Eighteen or so, cleanly dressed, with her hair in curls and wearing lipstick. She takes a stool and sits down next to the oldish man.

'Do you recognize her?' asks Dulman. 'It's Mancia, Mrs Skorochodowa's daughter. She's my wife's sister. The whole family died in Zelechow and she's the only one left alive so she's come here to us. We married her to our partner, him over there with the shoe. What were we to do with her?'

'When will my shoes be ready?'

'I'll do them for the day after tomorrow.'

'Make sure you do them, Dulman,' shouts his wife, 'don't trouble Mrs Szereszewska for nothing. I'll see to it, don't you worry, Mrs Szereszewska.'

He didn't do the shoes for the day after tomorrow and not for next week either. I called many times and my husband even went once too. He did mend them in the end. The Germans were likely to come at any time. In order to pull the wool over their eyes he used his cobbler's shop as a cover for his smuggling activities, but he didn't have the time to think about mending shoes.

When we lived in the small ghetto on Walicow Street Dulman came to see us one Sunday. It was the first time I'd seen him since the ghetto was established. He was smartly dressed and holding his eight year-old son by the hand. Everything the child was wearing was new: his suit, his coat, his cap and his shoes, and he was even wearing gloves. It was early. My husband was sitting at the table eating his breakfast.

'Sit down, Mr Dulman. Where do you live and how are you doing?'

'I live on Pawia Street and I've got a shop. I'm doing well.'

148

He stayed a while. Suddenly he got up, came up to me and said quietly, 'Mrs Szereszewska, I've no secrets before you, just as if you were my mother. If you only knew how much gold I've got hidden.'

'So what's it about, Mr Dulman?' asked my husband.

'Mr Szereszewski, I've come for a grave.'

'A grave?'

'My father-in-law has died. I'm doing well so I can't have him being buried in a common grave. I'd like to buy him a grave of his own.'

'Mr Dulman, I don't run the cemetery. I work in a completely different department. Councillor Zygmunt Hurwicz is responsible for the cemetery.'

'Mr Szereszewski, I know very well that you're not in graves. But before I go to Mr Hurwicz I came to ask you, seeing as we know each other from Mokotow, if you can help me get it without paying too much.'

He stayed a bit longer and then he went. My husband said to me, 'He's a strange man, isn't he? He comes to ask me to use my influence and at the same time he says he's got a lot of gold hidden away.'

'How did he make so much money?'

'Don't you understand? When he made shoes for the Germans in Mokotow he stole the hides.'

The last time I saw Dulman he was in his new flat on the second floor on Mila Street. He moved there from his dark and damp ground floor flat. By that time he'd made so much money that he could have moved into a palace if he wanted to and if he could find one. But his wife continued to dress poorly and still wore the old skirt she was used to. She never wore a coat but always wrapped an old, grey shawl round her. She had black eyes, white teeth and a pleasant smile. But because she was fat she looked like Dulman's mother. She came from a small town. In Mokotow, they had Polish neighbours and always spoke Polish to the children. Ten year-old Hanka looked like her mother, while four year-old Elek had curly fair hair and thick lips and looked like his father.

This time I went there with my own shoes. The two birchwood beds and wardrobe now stood in a large, sunny room with two windows. The iron stove with a pipe stood there too and Mrs Dulman was frying potato cakes on it. Hanka was standing by the window, crying.

149

'Why's she crying?' asked Dulman who was sitting in his work-shop.

'She wants money for sweets again. I've already given her some today. She won't eat anything, just sweets.'

'Give her some money. Why do you begrudge her it? Let her have what she wants. We're going to die all the same and these poor children are going to die with us.'

'As soon as December came,' sighed Mrs Dulman, 'he started getting black thoughts. From morning to night all he says is that we're going to die, and he doesn't want to do anything. And when night comes he stares at the ceiling for hours and says he's amazed. He's amazed that we're still breathing, that we're still walking on the earth, that the sky is still above us. He puts his finger on Elek's head and says what a miracle it is that the child is so near him.'

'Mrs Dulman, why do you torment yourselves? You've got money. Your husband's dealing with Poles. He's got contacts. Go over there. Go over to the Aryan side and hide.'

Dulman heard and said, 'There are people in hiding on the other side who are giving everything up and coming back. It's hell over there, they say, the constant fear. Scared of the policemen, scared of the children and scared of the Germans. They say it's a thousand times worse over there than here.'

'Mrs Szereszewska,' Mrs Dulman comes up to me, 'do you remember the woman who was sitting next to the wardrobe the first time you came? She was on the Aryan side and she came back.'

'Goodbye,' I say. 'I've got to go now. Is Mancia still living with your partner?'

'Yes, she is,' says Mrs Dulman and comes out on the stairs with me. 'Mrs Szereszewska dear, nothing's happened yet, has it? It's quiet. We've got everything we want. We've got a good flat and we're not short of anything. But we can feel death. Yes, we can feel death. It's just above our heads.'

She lifted her hand and drew some circles over her head. And I understand that in her imagination she saw death as a bird which circles and circles until it finally swops and destroys.

The three-storey house at 42 Muranowska Street was built in such a way that it had four-roomed flats at the front, five and six-roomed flats opposite and two and three-roomed flats on the sides. Small flats were the most sought after. The larger ones had to be shared by two families. The flats on the sides of the house were occupied by

PLATE 1

Helena Szereszewska
a few years before
the War.

PLATE 2

Stanislaw
Szereszewski when
he was approximately
30 years old.

PLATE 3

Ryszard Finkielsztein
in the Warsaw Ghetto
in 1942.

PLATE 4

Maria Majewska's
identity card (*Kennkarte*).

PLATE 5

'Aniela Gologowska', photograph from her identity card (*Kennkarte*).

PLATE 6

'Maria Majewska' in Berlin in September 1944, photograph from her working card (*Arbeitskarte*).

PLATE 9
Children in
the Berlin
camp.
Macius is on
the left. The
picture was
taken by one
of the camp
guards.

PLATE 10
Macius in the
Berlin camp at the
beginning of 1945.

PLATE 11

Janina (Nina)
Szereszewska in
Italy after the
Liberation.

PLATE 12

Robert (Macius)
Szereszewski.

Councillors: Sztolcman the engineer, Grodzienski and Rozensztadt the lawyers, Professor Balaban and Mr Jaszunski, the director of the Post Office.

The other Jaszunski, Zundelewicz the lawyer and Hurwicz all lived at the front. Apart from us and the Gliksbergs, the side of the house was occupied by the Councillors Kupczykier and Wolfowicz on the third floor. Councillor Rozental lived opposite us with his mother and daughter. Other flats were occupied by Council staff: Kornfeld whose wife was the nurse, Mrs Politzer who still had a black eye from being hit with a rubber truncheon, Mucha, Lewin the engineer, and on the ground floor Fogel and Fiszhaut the dentist. Underneath us in two flats on the ground floor were two undertakers' families, and on the second floor Pozner the undertaker.

Dr Kirszblum, our neighbour from Walicow Street, lived at the front. His wife had already gone over to the Aryan side. Also Professor Nossig from the Gestapo with two secretaries. One of them was Aryan, and the other was called Epsztein. Professor Nossig was about eighty. He wore dark glasses and when he walked he held his Aryan secretary, a tall blonde, by the arm. It was no secret that he worked for the Gestapo. It even said so on his door. He wrote long reports for the Germans about the atmosphere in the ghetto. The Council paid him a salary, on German orders. He came to collect it regularly from Melamud the cashier. At the end of January, after the second resettlement, Nossig was shot by the Jewish Fighters' Organization [Jewish Underground Movement].

Engineer Marek Lichtenbaum, the chairman of the Jewish Council, lived at number 40 in a four-roomed flat with his son Mieczyslaw and his family. His second son Edward lived with Councillor Wielikowski. First and his wife and daughter also moved into number 40, as well as Rabbi Spira and Rabbi Stokhammer with their numerous families, and many policemen who were stationed at the Council. The flat by the entrance was occupied by the caretaker. He dealt in food, just like our caretaker and all caretakers in the ghetto.

The first thing all these people did, from councillor to caretaker, was to throw all the things they didn't need out of the window. The pile of things in our courtyard was getting higher all the time. Pillows, beds, mattresses, benches, tables, lamps. Sometimes wardrobes were thrown down from balconies with a loud smash. If a piece of furniture was difficult to carry out of the flat it was simply thrown out of the window or the balcony.

151

You could also take whatever you fancied from the courtyard. Ada took a deck chair and slept on it for a long time. Stefania took a few large bowls which were lying there unwanted. I found a brass candlestick and a velvet photograph album in the rubbish. Nothing but old, yellowed photographs of people I had never known. But I took it upstairs all the same, and enjoyed looking at it for a long time.

When the Hurwicz family moved into their flat they threw so many things out of the window that Mr Grodzienski couldn't cross the courtyard. Through the window I saw him coming out of the hall a few times and then going back in. In the end he lifted his hands up in the air and shouted for them to stop. The Hurwicz family poked their heads out of the windows, not understanding what he meant. After a while the caretaker made a bonfire of this heap of unwanted things. It burnt for several days. The smoke billowed low in the air and squeezed its way through doors and windows into our flats. Then it rained and the fire went out.

Shortly afterwards a shop was repaired on the ground floor at the front and a distribution point was opened. We received ration cards and bought artificial honey, jam and bread there. You could also buy sauerkraut and torches, needles, thread, toothpaste, and even mugs and glasses at reduced prices. A second distribution point with heaps of onions, cabbage, potatoes and beetroots on the floor was opened at number 44. It had barrels of pickled cucumbers too. I did the shopping there with Stefania.

In the same house on the street side Jakub Finkielsztein, Ryszard's father, opened and ran a fuel store. We received ration cards for turf which we used for heating the bathroom when we finally managed to install the stove that Witold got hold of for us in the Building Department.

The director of the distribution shop for our house was the wife of Councillor Rozen. He had been shot by Ukrainians as he was riding along in a rickshaw. She received a flat next to the shop. She had two aged mothers with her, her own and her husband's. And· she had two children, a boy and a girl. The girl wore glasses. She was 11 and the boy was eight. I saw them on the rubbish in the courtyard playing with the undertakers' children from our staircase.

First's daughter came through the hole in the wall from number 40. She was six and came to Fredzia, the daughter of Rela Warszawska who lived with her relative Councillor Kupczykier. Twelve-year-old Julek Stückgold also lived with his mother at

Councillor Kupczykier's but he and Tala, the twelve-year-old daughter of Mr Noz from the Union of Pharmacists, weren't often to be seen in the courtyard. Tala even worked in a chemist's as a packer and had a work card.

The caretaker's five-year-old son and the six-year-old son of Mucha who brought us coal from the cellar also played with the other children. We had two cellars, one was for the coal we were allocated, and the other was for potatoes. The windows of both cellars opened into Niska Street. I watched the children from behind white net curtains on my veranda. They shrieked and shouted, fell out and then made it up. They ran, laughed and cried. Watching them I thought about the children at 6 Walicow Street. The children there had also filled the well of the courtyard of that five-storey house with noisy life.

One day as I was waiting my turn in the distribution shop I saw Renia Lichtenbaum standing next to me. She's the one who had been weeping so desperately in the Council during the huge selection because her mother had to die.

'Do you still work in the post office?' I asked her.

'Yes, I'm still there. But I've got married.'

She was wearing a team worker's clothes, jacket and ski trousers. She took her pot of artificial honey and left the shop. The shop assistant who was now weighing out my shopping was a young man with a charming smile. 'I'm a fatalist,' he used to say. 'We're going to die. We've no right to live. Just think. If hundreds of thousands of innocent people have died, then why should we deserve to live? If we stay alive then it would have to cry to heaven for vengeance.'

When the honey was weighed he cut the number off the ration card with a pair of scissors. I took the pot and went into the courtyard, stepping slowly and carefully. It had snowed and the ground was like an ice-rink. I looked at the window of the small flat on the ground floor where the kitchen for the house was going to be.

The kitchen was opened half-way through November. It was in a two-roomed flat, with one room for stores and the second for cleaning vegetables, peeling potatoes and making pastry. There was a small cooker with a cooking pot. Potatoes were available in the ghetto now. The Supplies Department brought them in from the Aryan side. A large airy cellar in our courtyard was designated as the potato store for the kitchen.

The kitchen was run by Mrs Zylberberg, the same woman who made tea for everyone in the Finance Department. She was slim and pale and wore high, laced shoes. Her family had died in Hrubieszow. There were 350 portions of soup made in the kitchen every day for our courtyard and for the two neighbouring houses. Wood was burnt in the stove. People were specially designated by the Council to bring and chop wood and in return they received hot soup.

Eight to twelve women worked in the kitchen, including a teacher called Kalkstein and the tall, handsome daughter of Councillor Jaszunski who was the director of the Post Office. There was also a woman who had escaped from a work team in Rembertow and a seventeen-year-old girl from Krasnystaw. The girl brought her brothers and sister with her. Two brothers of six and four and an eighteen-month-old sister. For a long time they lived with a woman in Praga. In the end she was denounced, but she didn't admit she was Jewish. The six-year-old boy was beaten and his trousers were pulled down. She said he was born like that, and her younger brother, also beaten and maltreated, shouted that he wasn't Jewish. In the end they were shoved into the ghetto. She put the boys into the orphanage on Dzika Street and her little sister into a shelter for very young children and found herself somewhere to live on Kurza Street.

I observed this girl for three weeks, which is as long as she worked in the kitchen. The evolution she underwent was really amazing. Her features were extremely Semitic. Her nose was curved and her hair was curly. I couldn't understand how a girl looking like that could survive and reach Warsaw from Krasnystaw with three children.

The people who gave her food *en route* must have known who she was. They must have protected her out of pity for her fate. There were scores or even hundreds of good-hearted people like that, a chain of people of goodwill from Krasnystaw to Warsaw. They endangered their own lives but unselfishly contributed to the existence of these crumbs of humanity.

When she found somewhere to place the children she relaxed. She rested and her humour improved. She took more care over her appearance. A new being was born out of the depressed, sad and silent girl. She became more self-confident, and even stopped giving way and quarrelled with her workmates. After two weeks she started using lipstick and rouge and dressing in bright colours. After three weeks she threw the job in and didn't show up any more.

Blumcia from Legionowo also worked in the kitchen, the one who

154

lived with the woman on the ground floor of our staircase. The kitchen employed this woman to wash pans and scrub the floors. So she had something to do, and what's more important, the soup left on the bottom of the pans was hers. One day when she was washing the floor she slipped and fell down and broke her leg. She was at home to start with and then she was taken to hospital at 6 Gensia Street and Blumcia was on her own in the flat.

The only window of the flat opened into Niska Street. Blumcia looked at the window and thought about her 17-year-old sister whom she had managed to find again. Now that there were only the two of them left in the world Blumcia longed with all her heart to be together with her, but the sister lived with a man who wore high boots. Who wore high boots in the ghetto? Gestapo above all. Jewish Gestapo. What about the man who lived on the third floor at the front and had a fair-haired wife who was so beautifully dressed and cared for and made-up? Didn't he wear high boots? He dealt in food and had a lot of money and everyone said he was in the Gestapo.

There was no electricity in the flat and Blumcia didn't have the money for a candle. So she sat in the dark and pondered: should I go to my sister's even though she lives with a man in high boots, or stay here in this cold, dark room.

My daughter Irena nursed the woman with the broken leg who worked in our kitchen. She wrote letters to Blumcia on scraps of paper and sent them via Irena. Look after my flat, she wrote, I beg you by your dead mother to look after my things, and send me a white blouse and night-dress. Blumcia brought Irena the night-dress and white blouse wrapped up in paper. 'It's for her,' she said, 'it's for the old woman who broke her leg.'

The woman who escaped from Rembertow was thin. Her legs were as thin as sticks. Her face was like a skull. She never said a word. Not a single word escaped her lips from the first time I saw her. And she was silent right up to the end. Mrs Zylberberg swayed pale and ghostly among the workers. She weighed flour, chopped onions, stirred the pan, but her soul was in Hrubieszow stalking around her father, mother and brothers who were no longer alive. She would suddenly become lost in thought, she'd bend her head and listen. Maybe it was a moan or a complaint or a call for help.

Someone would speak to her. She would summon her soul back. Suspended in the trap of the flat in a small town, on the stove or on the menorah or on the Hanukkah lamp so close to her heart because

155

it was connected with her very first childhood memories, her soul had to return and flow over cold, unknown paths from Hrubieszow to Muranowska Street, the last boundary of the ghetto. Two huge zinc pots stood on the floor, full of peeled potatoes. I helped her cut them into squares. We took them out of the pots with large colanders. Our fingers were white with cold. I observed her and thought: she's not alive any longer. She's lost and destroyed and dead to the world. Her dead will drag her after them in their wake. I observed her hands which were still working and her eyes which were still shining. And I thought: if this is what your days are like, then what about your nights?

When dinner was ready everyone came with pans and took the soup. The councillors' wives who lived in the courtyard supervised the kitchen. Two of them worked every day, a different two each day, and helped with the work. Mrs Balaban came. She put on an apron and peeled potatoes together with the rest. Mrs Hurwicz came, always wearing a large beret. Pale Mrs Zundelewicz and majestic Mrs Rozensztadt. Only Stefania never came.

Then Ada the team worker moved into the kitchen. She got hold of a bed and unfolded it in the store-room for the night. Kornfeld, who looked after our kitchen, said, 'I don't like this sleeping in the kitchen. It's not hygienic.'

'But I'm guarding the store-room by sleeping here. It's on the ground floor and could be broken into,' replied Ada.

She admitted to us that she was dying of fright at night. Everyone knew that non-registered persons who were in hiding during the day came out at night. They sometimes broke into people's flats in their search for food. They crossed from one house to the next via the roofs or through the holes in the walls. 'It's fortunate I'm so tired after work,' said Ada. 'I fall fast asleep the minute my head touches the pillow.'

The Building Department kitchen on Kurza Street was much bigger than our kitchen. It prepared suppers as well as dinners. It was run by Mrs Lichtenbaum, the chairman's wife, and she was assisted by Mrs Jaszunska and Mrs Grodzienska who were both councillors' wives. A kitchen was also opened at 44 Muranowska Street and it was to be run by Professor Balaban's daughter-in-law.

But it was generally said in the ghetto that the best supplied and best run kitchen belonged to the Dustmen's Union on Franciszkanska Street. While the undertakers belonged to the most privileged caste, the dustmen were the richest. The undertakers carried on working long after the second resettlement, even though they had lost their families. The dustmen took rubbish to the Aryan side and so they were in contact with Poles. They all had special passes and a special green armband. They were paid by Jews to be taken to the Aryan side under the rubbish, and they smuggled goods in from the Aryan side. So they became rich. While the Dustmen's Union kitchen benefited from these smuggling activities, our kitchen was a humble institution on a small scale. We made some tripe soup once and once made some potato and mutton soup. These soups were rarities and we remembered them for a long time afterwards.

One December evening the councillors' wives came to our flat for a meeting. We were going to decide whether the kitchen should prepare more food. For a small payment there could be more for dinner. We invited Mrs Lichtenbaum as our honorary guest. She came just like any neighbour would. She knew all our kitchen's complaints and shortcomings. At first we had wanted her to be in charge of our kitchen but we couldn't get her to do it. She dropped in at the kitchen when she could spare the time and we felt honoured. She was short and dark-skinned and a bit fat, and she wore a black coat and a pointed, close-fitting cap made of red wool.

I'd known her for a long time. Before the war we'd been neighbours in the same house at 3 Poznanska Street for twenty years. When we moved to Narbutt Street she moved too and lived at 26 Narbutt Street. In the ghetto I saw her every day because she lived next door on Prosta Street. She did us the honour of coming to our meeting. I don't know if she used the gate or a hole in the wall. The meeting didn't take place in the dining room as usual but in Stefania's beautiful bedroom.

Mrs Balaban came, and quiet Mrs Zundelewicz and Mrs Rozensztadt who was really interested in our kitchen even though she didn't eat the dinners we made. The Rozensztadts got their dinners from Franciszkanska Street, from the dustmen's kitchen. It didn't go down well in our courtyard because it was felt that they scorned our kitchen and were taking advantage of their contact with Heiman, the leader of the Dustmen's Union. If it was true, then the contact dated back to the times before the resettlement when the dustmen in the ghetto were responsible to the Property Department which was directed by the lawyer Boleslaw Rozensztadt, who was also the department's Councillor. Perhaps that's

157

why his wife worked so hard in our kitchen, because she wanted to keep the rumours at bay.

Mrs Hurwicz didn't come to the meeting. She was busy preparing her daughter's wedding. Besides, she'd complained about her health recently. She came to see Dr Steinsapir and Irena gave her injections. So we met without Mrs Hurwicz. But a woman who lived at the front and had a policeman for a husband came. She was a relation of Mrs Rozensztadt's. She wore a black hat and lipstick.

Mrs Lichtenbaum and the councillors' wives behaved impeccably at the meeting. They didn't let anyone see how struck they were by the luxury of Stefania's room. They were calm, even indifferent. The chairs were arranged in a semicircle. We talked and discussed and then the meeting was over. A policeman detailed specially to escort Mrs Lichtenbaum stood in the hall. She never went out on to the street without a policeman. And it might have been because the woman in the hat was talking about literature that Mrs Lichtenabum asked, 'Have you by chance got anything my husband can read?'

Stefania opened the dining room door and said, 'Children, have you got any books the chairman can read? Have a look.'

Stefan jumped up and brought some books. He had a big supply of various books which he found in deserted flats or received from his brother who worked with the *Werterfassung* team.

Mrs Lichtenbaum was pleased. She said goodbye and left followed by the policeman. When the door closed behind them Stefan said, 'Do you know what I gave her?' He waited a moment so that his words would have greater effect. *The Dragon's Teeth*, *Lucifer's Revenge* and *Arch-fiend*. I've got nothing personal against the chairman. But I'd really love it if the books get into the hands of his son Mieczyslaw. Especially *Arch-fiend*. That's just right for him.'

A week later as I was going to the Council I met Mrs Lichtenbaum on Dzika Street and we talked. She admitted that Stefania's room had made a big impression on her. 'How can she in times like these?' she asked furiously. 'In my flat there are baskets in all the rooms. And I don't hang any net curtains up on purpose. I'm surprised,' she kept repeating, 'I'm still really surprised.'

One evening Mrs Berman's nephew came. She used to be a neighbour on Walicow Street. My husband met him outside the Council and asked him to visit us.

'Do you know who I met?' he said at home, 'you won't guess. Adek Grinberg from Walicow Street. I asked him to come over but he probably won't.'

But he did come. He was a handsome boy, fair-haired and tall. He used to have a mother and two sisters, Lola and Irka. They were both nurses. When we lived at Walicow Street the younger one nursed Ryszard when he had dysentery. Their mother was not in her right mind. She kept disappearing and they had to look for her. Or else she'd get into a rickshaw and have herself driven round and round.

When Irka and her mother were taken to the *Umschlagplatz* in the first days of the resettlement, Irka could have saved herself because she was a nurse. Nurses weren't being deported yet. They even worked at the *Umschlagplatz*, helping the people who were going to be deported. But one day their whole team was put inside the wagons together with everyone else and from then on there weren't any nurses at the *Umschlagplatz*.

While she was standing at the *Umschlagplatz* with her mother a Jewish policeman came up to her and said, 'You can save yourself because you're a nurse. Your mother can stay in the cellar until evening and so she'll save herself as well.'

Irka looked into the cellar and noticed it was dirty and fouled. She had a violent nature. She used to explode and raise hell over nothing. She shook all over and said, 'No! My mother isn't going to sit on shit! Not for a single second! I'd sooner she died instead!' And she went to the wagons with her. I met her sister Lola immediately afterwards on the corner of Walicow Street and Prosta Street and she wept as she told me about it.

'Well now, Mr Grinberg,' said my husband, 'what do you intend to do?'

'To get away from my work team on the Aryan side and get a Polish girl to fall in love with me and hide me. Any Polish woman will do, a girl or a widow, so long as she's got a two-roomed flat of her own. I'd live in the second room. If anyone came in I'd hide in the wardrobe or in a big basket. I'd love her out of gratitude.'

He was a handsome boy, there was no doubt about it, a high forehead, blue eyes, regular features. But dressed like a team worker with a scarf wound round his neck and his voice hoarse from working in the open air, he looked like a simple workman.

'Why does he talk so loud?' asked Stefania quietly. 'Has he learnt from the Germans?'

159

'Poor Irka,' I said. 'She could have saved herself then.'

'You remember?' asked Grinberg. 'She didn't want our mother to sit on shit. That's an ambition in its own way too.'

He stayed a bit longer and then left.

Another time Fels the policeman, a friend of the Gliksbergs, came round. He was terribly upset. He sat down at the table, hung his head and huge tears flowed down his face.

'Lejkin's been shot. He was my best friend. Czaplicki's been shot as well but he's going to live.'

We all looked at this huge man who wasn't ashamed of his tears. We were more sorry for him than for Lejkin who had been loathed in the ghetto. Lejkin was the director of the Order Service. He kept receiving threatening letters from the Jewish Fighters' Organization and notices often hung on the streets warning him. Now the sentence had been carried out.

Fels was about fifty. Before the war he'd been a member of the Animal Protection Association. He was a man with the heart of a dove. His wife was on the Aryan side. He had a nephew in the ghetto who was a lawyer. He'd known the Gliksbergs for a long time and often came to see them. He was a brilliant story-teller and once told us something extraordinary he'd witnessed with his own eyes. It happened during the resettlements on Mila Street. A boy of twelve who played the violin wonderfully lived there with his mother. When the Germans and Ukrainians formed the column to march to the *Umschlagplatz*, people said to the Germans, 'There's a small boy here, a real artist on the violin. That's him standing over there holding his violin case with his mother. It's a shame for him to die.'

'An artist on the violin?' asked the German in surprise. 'All right, let him play.'

The boy took his violin out of its case. Silence fell. A melody flowed into the silence. Everyone knew that the boy was playing for his life and his mother's life. The people in the column were crying. The Jewish policemen had tears running down their faces. Everyone could feel how the boy was trying to play as beautifully as possible in order to move the Germans. When he finished the people in the column looked up and looked expectantly at the Germans. Then one of them said, 'Yes, you played nicely. You're a good musician but you can march off now.' And the column moved off to the *Umschlagplatz* nearby.

When we sat looking at Fels weeping Stefania said, 'May the

160

ground be light for Lejkin. If he's dead then nothing will bring him back to life. But what about his wife?'

'She's just had a baby, a little girl.'

'Poor thing.'

In July 1945 a plainly dressed Polish woman stood next to me in the Jewish Committee offices at Targowa Street in Praga and said to the clerk, 'I want to ask about someone.'

'Who?'

'Mr Fels. Do you know if he survived and what happened to him?'

'What Mr Fels? I've never heard of him.'

Then I turned to the woman and said, 'A very tall man. Elderly. A very good man. A bit hard of hearing. I knew him in the ghetto. He used to sit at our table.'

'That's him. What happened to him? Is he alive?'

'He died. I was told he died in the ghetto. And I don't even know if I can say, "May the ground be light for him".'

When we lived in the small ghetto on Walicow Street a woman in a green coat used to come and sell us horseflesh. She knocked on the front door because other women with horseflesh came to the kitchen door. She had lost her husband, her three-year-old child and her family during the resettlement. She was all alone After the small ghetto was liquidated and we lived on Lubecki Street there was a time when I went to the Jewish Council every day, to the Finance Department my husband was in charge of. I sometimes looked out of the window onto the street.

'Do you know,' I once said, 'I saw the woman in the green coat again.'

Then we moved to Muranowska Street. In November I caught sight of her one evening on Mila Street. The work teams were returning and Mila Street and Kurza Street were crowded and noisy. At supper I said, 'I saw the woman in the green coat again, in the crowd on Mila Street.' Then I didn't see her again and didn't think about her.

At the beginning of January 1943 Councillor Kupczykier and I went to visit the orphanage on Dzika Street. It was Saturday, the day of rest. The Germans took great care that the Jews should observe it. Councillor Kupczykier was our neighbour. He came every evening, though never with his wife. They were such a badly matched couple that no-one would believe it, looking at them, that they were married. He was tall, distinguished, and exceptionally handsome, while she was thin, wasted and prematurely old. She lived in his shadow. He always came dressed as neat as a new pin. In his jacket pocket a snow-white handkerchief. Stefania was a smart woman and she really appreciated it.

'He dresses for us,' she said to me in the kitchen, 'for us, the women in this house. Do you know,' she stopped for a moment, 'it meant so little before the war but here, all cooped up and humiliated, it gives me more strength to survive. I'm grateful to him for it.'

When the police force was organized in the ghetto in 1941 Kupczykier was the councillor responsible for the police. He was important. Then he was pushed out. Now he was in charge of Welfare in the Jewish Council.

'I was in Schultz's workshop today,' he once said, 'and I bought 3,000 pairs of shoes for our team workers. One of the Hirszfeld brothers has opened a restaurant in the workshop just like before the war.'

'You looked in, of course. We heard that Brandt was at the Council again this morning,' someone said.

'Yes. He entered the room, looked at me and asked, "Hören Sie mal, wie heissen Sie?"'

'"Kupczykier."'

'"Wie?"'

'"Kup-czy-kier."'

'"Ja, ja," he said and threatened me with his finger.'

Henryk Gliksberg said, 'Perhaps he can't stand tall Jews. Warman is huge and one day he was standing with a file by the chairman's table when Brandt came in. "Was macht hier der lange Kerl?" he asked. "Das ist unser Sekretär," replied the chairman. "Warum arbeitet er nicht?" Meaning why isn't he carrying bricks? Or lugging stones? Or in a workshop? In his opinion intellectual work is no work.'

'At the beginning of the resettlements,' said Kupczykier one day, 'I lived on Panska Street in the small ghetto. I used to lock the door and not let the Germans enter. They hammered with their rifle butts but I didn't open the door.'

'But they could have broken the door down,' we said.

'I was counting on the fact that they're by nature law-abiding. They wouldn't want to damage a well-made front door. They could see that the door was closed so they went away.'

The orphanage was in the 'House of Death'. The name came from before the resettlements when it was occupied by Jews who'd been picked up from the neighbouring towns. They were decimated by typhus. There were so many people in the house that the beds, if you can call them beds, were piled up next to each other not only in the rooms but on the corridors as well. Now the house had changed beyond recognition. It was spotlessly clean all over. And quiet. We couldn't hear any chattering even though there were children in the house. Our footsteps echoed in the long corridors.

In addition to orphans in the ghetto, all the Jewish children from the Aryan side who had lost their parents were directed here too. When no-one would pay for their keep any more and their guardians couldn't or wouldn't keep them for nothing, they handed them back to the ghetto again. We entered clean and well-lit class-rooms with small benches and long, low tables. Cut-outs and engravings hung on the walls. The children were well dressed. They were divided according to age. The younger children had separate rooms and class-rooms. There was a teacher with the children in every class-room. There were about 200 children, all calm and well-fed. The orphanage was the Germans' pride and joy. They ordered the children to be well looked after and fed. Each child received a larger ration of bread than an adult in the ghetto.

We entered the kitchen and talked to the housekeeper for a moment. She was frying a mountain of pancakes filled with jam. Two 14-year-old girls, orphans too, were helping her. We were told about a little girl of five:

'What's your name?' asked the teacher.

'Barszczewska,' she replied. She stopped and thought and then added, 'and Basia too.'

'Don't be afraid,' the teacher cajoled her mildly, 'you're among Jews. You can tell us your real name without being scared.'

'Barszczewska,' the child replied stubbornly. She smiled, which meant that she wasn't afraid, but all the same she said the same thing.

'She never says anything else. She was told on the other side she's got to be called that. Her parents are dead. There was no-one to pay for her so her guardians gave her to a policeman,' her teacher explained.

The little girl was very fair-haired and had a red scarf on her head. She didn't look Jewish. I looked at her and thought: perhaps she isn't a Jewish child. Perhaps there's a tragic mistake.

There was a tall handsome boy of 13 in the boys' class. His appearance immediately attracted our attention. He had grey eyes and black, close-set eyebrows. The expression in his eyes was severe.

'His father was a teacher,' said the teacher, 'and his mother was a teacher too. They're both dead. The boy was on the Aryan side and he says he had some money. When his guardians found out his parents were dead they took it all and said they weren't going to keep him any longer. He's an intelligent boy.'

'And now,' said the teacher when we went out into the corridor, 'I'll show you a boy who brought three small children to Warsaw after the ghetto in Otwock was liquidated. They were all alone and they walked all the way. It took them a long time.'

He was ten. His father was probably a tradesman. The children he'd brought were much younger, a girl and two boys. They weren't related in any way and didn't know each other at all. I looked at the small captain and thought: what words did he use to encourage them? Children are so scared of the dark. When they were in a wood or a field at night surrounded by darkness, and their mothers weren't there, what words did he use to comfort them? Villagers must have guessed what kind of children they were. They must have gone up to people and begged after all. Many mothers shading their eyes with their hands will have watched them disappearing into the distance on the road.

'Women whose children are lost or dead come here,' said the teacher. 'They think they might find their children here. There's one who's lost hope now and wants to take another child and bring it up instead of her own. She comes every few days.'

He turned to the boy again. He said something, smiled and stroked his head. I was standing close by and I saw how the caress made the boy huddle up and turn pale. I thought: they give the children so much warmth and care and attention. Maybe the Germans will let them stay alive. I remembered looking out of the window at the Jewish Council during the resettlements. The orphanages were going to the *Umschlagplatz*. Long crocodiles of children holding hands. Wearing aprons and white collars. They all wore wooden-soled shoes and the clatter trembled for a long time in the air before it quietened down again.

I also remembered the day when one orphanage returned from the *Umschlagplatz*. Why it came back that day no-one knows. It was taken later all the same. It was said that the German officer who was in charge of resettling the orphanage said, 'If it goes on like this any longer I'll shoot myself.'

It was the orphanage from Gensia Street. From the part of Gensia Street near Nalewki Street.

As we were coming down the stairs, from the third floor to the second floor, and then from the second to the first, the woman in the green coat brushed against me. So it's her, I thought. She's going for a child. She's decided. She's going for it now. She's taking it. I could tell from her tight lips, the expression on her face, her lowered eyes. She didn't recognize me, didn't notice me, didn't see me.

The orphanage on Dzika Street turned out to be the usual German trap and the Jews in the Warsaw ghetto fell into it. Their vigilance was put to sleep and they started believing they'd survive. On 18 January 1943 the orphanage went to the *Umschlagplatz*. The children walked along a beaten track in a long crocodile holding hands and clattering with their wooden soles. The children were accompanied by their teachers and the caretaker and the housekeeper. Also among them were Basia Barszczewska, the teacher's son, the boy from Otwock and the three children he had brought to Warsaw.

Not long after Lejkin's death, First was shot. At seven in the evening, in front of our house door. He was walking along with his wife and sister-in-law; he was in the middle and they were on either side of him, when he was shot in the back. Just as with Lejkin, the Jewish Fighters' Organization had settled its accounts with First. After a week we stopped talking about it. Mr and Mrs Hurwicz's daughter was getting married and we all wondered who they'd invite. But no-one was invited to the wedding apart from the immediate family. The groom's sister who lived on Kurza Street and his elder brother with his wife. Also Ada, our Ada the team worker. She was invited not so much as a guest but as a helper.

When she came back from the wedding she had to tell us right down to the smallest detail what the bride and her mother were wearing, and the groom of course, because he was the younger Popower and we knew him. He was a colleague of Ryszard's, a lawyer just like Ryszard. Then she had to recount in turn all the dishes that were served. When she said there was a goose, we were stupefied. Someone said, 'It's incredible, it's impossible.' All we ate was horseflesh. The thought of goose didn't even enter our heads.

After the wedding the younger Popower moved in with the Hurwicz family. As with First's death, the wedding made a big stir in our courtyard. Then we stopped talking about it too and life rolled on.

165

Every morning Mrs Cukier came to the front door and sold us horseflesh, or cheese, or a piece of pork fat. Two other women came to the kitchen door, a young one and an older one, and also sold us meat and cheese. We saw more and more tired women wrapped in shawls on the kitchen stairs. They sat on the steps and chewed bread. Or they stood leaning against each other. They came from far away, they spoke Yiddish with a different accent. They came from small towns where the Germans had liquidated the ghettoes. Saved by a miracle, they came to the Warsaw ghetto because it still existed.

One of them was a girl from Biala Podlaska. She told us that she saved herself by hiding in the hay in the loft. She lay there all night and all day. The next night she came down the ladder and escaped. Some Jews, like the girl from Biala Podlaska and a boy of 17 from Buska, came to the ghetto of their own accord. Others were brought in from the Aryan side by the German police after being denounced. Of the people we knew who were in hiding on the Aryan side, Mrs Feilchenfeld and her daughter were brought back to the ghetto although they escaped again shortly afterwards, and Dr Anna Messing with her mother. They were sent to the prison on Gensia Street and then to the *Umschlagplatz*. But since there weren't any regular resettlements any more they managed to buy their way out of the *Umschlagplatz*. In December Anna Messing came to me on Muranowska Street and told me about her experiences in prison. A few weeks later she went over to the Aryan side with her mother for the second time.

Jews caught on the Aryan side were beaten mercilessly. One day my daughter Irena was walking through a ward in the hospital on Gensia Street, where she worked as a nurse, and she saw the lawyer Kon-Wojecki on a bed. He had been beaten by the Germans and thrown into the ghetto. He didn't recognize Irena and she pretended not to recognize him.

In those uncertain times people were drawn together searching for courage from each other. There wasn't a day that passed when one of our friends or relatives didn't come, or friends of the Gliksbergs. Maybe the reason why so many people came was because it throbbed with life in our flat where there were young people laughing and joking and Stefania radiating calm and confidence. That's why Councillor Kupczykier came every evening. He didn't have the same atmosphere at his place and so he came to us to drink hope like wine from a jug.

One day a friend of the Gliksbergs came and said that the Wilno ghetto had been completely liquidated. The news touched us to the quick, all the more because people in the Warsaw ghetto used to say how good it was in Wilno, in the ghetto there. 'Can you imagine it, they've even opened a theatre.'

We were still suffering from the shock when Kosower and Melnik came one evening. Before the war Kosower had a brick-built house and a small food store. A wife, a son and three daughters, beautiful girls. The Germans shot his wife. Where his daughters were he didn't know. He now worked in a work team with his son. Melnik came from Legionowo. He was in a work team just like Kosower and they both lived on Niska Street. They were happy to be sitting with us because it gave them courage and helped them throw the load off their hearts.

'When I come home from work,' said Melnik, 'I just cry and cry. My wife and my three children! There was a Pole who wanted to keep my little two year-old daughter but I didn't want to let him have her. God took my brains away.'

'What happened to Rozenkranc, the painter from Legionowo?' we asked.

'He died. His wife was shot on a cart just as she was leaving the place. They had a son of ten. When he saw his mother had been shot he threw himself into the Vistula.'

That's what they told us. They drank some tea, stayed a while and then left. While we were drinking tea with Kosower and Melnik, Danuta Fryde was at Stefania's. She'd come all the way from Többens' workshop where she worked. She came for courage too. She was a lovely girl with black hair and black eyes. We knew her from Walicow Street.

'I was once in a column going to the *Umschlagplatz*,' she said, 'and I thought that there was no way I could be saved when an SS man, who was walking past, saw me and pulled me out of the column. He grabbed me by the arm, like this, and tugged hard. So I stayed alive. But what of it? I haven't got anybody.'

Stefan Drabienko once came to see us from the workshop on Leszno Street which was also far away.

'Where are your parents?' we asked.

'They've been on the Aryan side for a long time. They live separately. My father lives with Edward. The Organization [Resistance Movement] got hold of documents for Edward. Do you know what he does? He works for the Germans as a chauffeur.'

'Yes,' we said, 'Marysia saw Edward on the Aryan side. He was in a car. Ryszard told us.'

'I'm in touch with an Aryan woman who's looking for work for me in the country. In a factory, maybe in the Ursus plant. If it's bad here then I'll escape,' said Stefan.

Sometimes we and the Gliksbergs and our daughters all had visitors at the same time. Each workshop was a world of its own and it was difficult for the people who worked there to get the time off. Their visits were dangerous too so they rarely came, perhaps just once, and then we didn't see them again. Olek Nimcewicz was the only exception. One evening two of Irena's friends from the nursing school came to see her, Irka Parczew and Irka Goldstein. Irka Goldstein came from Kutno and worked in Hallmann's workshop where toys were produced. She and her parents were on the workshop's list.

'I paint toys,' she said. Then she added, 'I got married recently.'

Irka Parczew was a nurse in Schultz's shop. Her father and sister were listed there as well. So the three girls with the same first name sat round the table happy to be together and seeing each other again. What's happened to Mrs Bielicka, the nursing school director? Who's gone over to the Aryan side? Poor Zofia Turkönig died in Otwock. One of the girls went to the *Umschlagplatz* of her own free will. Her parents had been taken away the day before and she wanted to join them. As they were sitting talking Olek Nimcewicz passed through the room. Nina saw him to the door and came back.

'I'll tell you something you don't know. It'll surprise you.' She was so shaken she didn't know how to begin. 'Olek's married to his own sister!'

We hadn't heard of anything like that before.

'Before he became a guard he used to be a policeman. And while he was a policeman the rabbi married the two of them. He passed her off as his wife and protected her that way. They live in the brushworks on Swietokrzyska Street.'

Late in the evening before we went to bed Stefan went up to Nina and quietly asked her, 'Can you bring the next volume of the civil code from the trunk?'

'Why? Is the other one finished already?'

'Yes, it is.'

She went to the veranda and opened the trunk. It still contained many law books that had belonged to Alter's deported son-in-law.

There were also his daughter's chemistry books but no-one touched them. All the time we lived at Muranowska Street we tore pages out of the civil code because we didn't have any toilet paper.

One morning we were shattered to hear that the Jewish Council's safe had been raided. Melamud, the Council's cashier, lived with his wife on Kurza Street. Someone knocked at the door at two in the morning. He was afraid to open the door so Mrs Melamud got up out of bed.

'Open up!' they heard someone shouting in Yiddish.

In the end she opened the door. Six of them came in and they each had a revolver. Melamud said to them from his bed, 'You're Jews, aren't you? What are you doing? Have you gone mad? Isn't it enough that the Germans . . .'

They didn't let him finish but put their guns to his head.

'Where are the keys to the safe?'

And when he'd handed them over they added, 'Right then, Melamud. Get dressed and come with us.'

They forced him to go with them. He opened the safe for them with his own hands. They took out 100,000 zlotys.

'Tell the chairman,' they said when they were leaving, 'that the Jewish Fighters' Organization has taken the money from the safe to buy machine-guns.'

The matter was discussed by everyone in the flat and analysed from every angle. Someone even said, 'Did Melamud get a receipt? Is there any note with the Jewish Fighters Organization's stamp? How do we know? Maybe he thought the raid up and pocketed the hundred thousand.'

'We don't doubt Melamud's honesty in the slightest,' said the others.

'What did the chairman say to all this?' asked someone.

'He was furious. He shouted like a German. See how this German way of doing things rubs off on us.'

After that raid, robberies in the ghetto increased. They were carried out under the guise of the Jewish Fighters' Organization. In the evenings passers-by were robbed and flats were broken into. Things were gradually becoming slack. The ghetto was sailing into the unknown like a rudderless ship.

In the first half of January 1943 Professor Balaban died of a heart attack. His son was a doctor and lived with him but was unable to save him. The funeral took place the next day. I waited in the crowd for them to carry him out. A thin and wasted elderly woman stood next to me all the time. It was Councillor Kupczykier's wife. When the hearse set off we set off behind it. From Muranowska Street to Dzika Street, then straight along Dzika Street until we passed the Jewish Council. At that time the wall divided Gensia Street into two halves. On the corner of Dzika Street and Gensia Street was a gate in the wall with German gendarmes standing beside it. We stopped here, by the check-point. Only the immediate family and the Councillors could accompany Professor Balaban to the cemetery. You could only cross if you had a pass. We stood for a while longer. Then we went home.

On 17 January none of us had any premonition of the tragedy which was to be played out the next day. Councillor Kupczykier came as usual. He showed us some photos of his daughter in France. Then he read us the latest war communiqué. Like Ryszard, he also knew someone who listened to the communiqués on the radio. He twisted the name Sidi-el-Barani in such a funny way that Stefania and I made an excuse to leave the room and laughed in the dark corridor.

'Well now,' she said in the end, 'that's enough joking. Let's go back.'

We went back. She sat down at the table still laughing. And instantly, like a fan, she diffused an atmosphere of calm and well-being. Councillor Rozental's lovely daughter was also there that evening. She lived opposite and came to see our children from time to time. She didn't say much, just sat and stared with her golden eyes. When she left someone said, 'The youngster comes here from time to time, but old "alle Juden werden erschossen" hasn't even come once yet.' That was Councillor Rozental's nickname. It dated from the time when he was in charge of the Work Battalions Department. He frequently came in contact with the Germans and they must have said it to him one day. Then he kept muttering it all the time: 'alle Juden werden erschossen'. So it became his nickname.

Stanislaw Tempel and his father visited us that evening as well. We had found out through Stanislaw Fiszhaut's sister who worked in a workshop and had contacts with Poles, that Marian, Izaak Tempel's older son, was in Palestine. We immediately informed them and they had come to hear the details. But we didn't know anything else apart from that. Later, when everyone had gone, we sat round the table and talked for a long time. Dr Steinsapir brought a microscope – where on earth had he got it from? – and we all took turns to look at a splinter and a scrap of paper. We started talking about books. The doctor was a learned man and had heaps of books in his room. We knew he was writing a dissertation on typhus.

'Since we're talking about books,' one of us said, 'I wonder what happened to the Hebrew books the Alters left behind when they were resettled. There were so many of them.'

'I took them out onto the landing,' said Stefan, 'and then they disappeared. Pozner, the undertaker, must have taken them.'

'Why Pozner?'

'Because he's an orthodox Jew. He's got a beard and wears a long coat. No-one else could have taken them.'

Then we started talking about something completely different. About bunkers. That's it, about bunkers. Tadeusz Gliksberg didn't work with the *Werterfassung* team any more. He worked in the Building Department and was even quite important there although he was only twenty.

'I saw something unusual today,' he said. 'I saw a bunker on Franciszkanska Street. The Supplies Department staff are building it for themselves.'

A bunker? That was something for us.

'There are bunker specialists in the ghetto, you know. Bunker engineers. It's a golden time for them now. A bunker has to be intelligently built – with gas, water, light and sanitation. The bunker on Franciszkanska Street is incredibly luxurious. It's got separate rooms, wash-basins, beds, and lighting. It cost a fortune. Gepner, the chairman, has got his own room there too and it's got everything.'

That's what Tadeusz told us. We listened very attentively. Ryszard who was sitting there with us said, 'You know that Solna Street is part of the Aryan side now, don't you? Well, Poles are slowly starting to move into the houses which used to be Jewish and stood empty for so long. I was told someone found a really unusual bunker. You went down through the stove door. But no adult could go down – the adults were already in the bunker. A small girl came in and out of the stove door and brought them food. The bunker was found by a Polish family who moved into the flat.'

'If so many people in the ghetto are building bunkers then perhaps we should build one too,' said Stefania. She thought for a moment and then added, 'Or maybe it's now time for our children to go to the Aryan side.'

The next day we woke at dawn. We had the strange feeling that

171

there was something in the air. It wasn't seven o'clock yet. But we could already hear footsteps in the hall. My husband opened the door.

'Has anything happened?' he asked.

At the same time we heard Ryszard's voice asking from the bed in the dining room, 'Has anything happened, father?'

Irena wasn't at home. She was on night duty. Nina opened the door in her night-dress.

'What's happened, daddy?'

'There are two German soldiers standing in front of the gate,' replied Henryk Gliksberg in a calm voice.

'I'll go and see why they're there,' said my husband. He got dressed and put on his coat and cap. He went out and didn't come back. I looked out of the window and saw Councillor Grodzienski. He was holding his wife by the arm and they were crossing the courtyard to the gate. They must have been going to the Council. They stopped and asked the soldier something. The soldier lifted up his hand and spoke to them. Then they carried on, but not right in the direction of the Council, only left. A moment later I saw Zygmunt Hurwicz with his wife and their daughter Irena and her husband. They wanted to go to the Council as well but the soldiers directed them to turn left. Some people crossed the courtyard from one part of the building to another.

We sat down to breakfast. Stefania had a large beret on her head, ready to go out. She poured out the coffee. Her husband and sons sat eating calmly. Dr Steinsapir came out of his room not knowing what was happening. He was holding a tin of sugar as usual A few moments later, seeing that Stefania had her beret on, he asked with surprise, 'Where are you going?'

'To our deaths.'

That's exactly what she said. He put his unfinished cup of coffee down on the table and looked at her.

'What's up?' he asked.

'There are soldiers in the gate. Can't you see?'

He approached the window and looked out. Then he understood.

'I'm going to the Health Department,' he said.

He put on his coat and ski cap and went out. I saw him crossing the courtyard through the window. When he was near the gate he became afraid of the Germans and turned back. Then he passed through the room in silence. Stefania went into her bedroom and opened the balcony door wide. In front of her was the *Umschlagplatz* and a crowd of many thousand Jews.

'If we could let ourselves down from the balcony onto Niska Street we could save ourselves. There aren't any Germans there at present,' she said.

Why didn't she think that the window of the woman who broke her leg looked out onto Niska Street? A ground-floor flat. You could even jump out of the window. No-one remembered. When you are in danger of losing your life a strange powerlessness overwhelms your soul. Only a few people developed a sharper instinct of self-preservation. Most people were simply resigned.

Why didn't we go down to the cellars via the kitchen stairs? The door was closed, yes. In fact it was frozen. We hadn't used the door at all for a week. Everyone, both the residents and the hawkers who came to us, used the front. But there was an axe for chopping wood in the kitchen. We could have smashed an opening in the door. Or some of the men could have taken the door off its hinges. Or we could even have left by the front door, crossed the courtyard and gone down to the cellars. The Alters' huge baskets and trunks were in the potato cellar – we could have hidden. Instead of that we both sat down on the sofa wearing our coats and ready to go out, and our children staggered around the flat in spiritual powerlessness.

'Have you got everything on you, your valuables and money?' I asked.

'At a time like this you've got to have everything on you,' she answered.

I entered the bedroom. We had English beds with metal bars that screwed together. One day we unscrewed them and saw that the bars were empty inside. We'd been plundered by the Germans so often that we hid the rest of our jewellery inside a bar. When I returned to the room I put a few pieces of bread into Nina's bag. Ryszard and his parents came. Ryszard's mother had a large beret on, just like Stefania. Everyone sat down and waited. Ryszard's father was restless and kept sighing. 'Calm down,' his wife said to him, 'sit still and wait.'

'Can't we hide in the bathroom?' asked Ryszard.

Tadeusz laughed. He'd seen strong bunkers the day before, so how could such a naïve idea fail to amuse him? A Jewish policeman and the Jewish Gestapo man who lived at the front entered through

173

the open front door. When they saw us all sitting together they asked, 'Didn't you have somewhere to hide?'

And then we saw a German soldier in a helmet right behind them. He was carrying a rifle. He stood next to the other two and didn't say a word.

Ryszard took me aside and asked, 'Have you got any money, mother?'

'No. Father's got the money on him.'

'He gave me 3,000 zlotys. Who knows what's in store. You mustn't be penniless.'

'What about you?'

'I've got some more.'

Why didn't it enter our heads to give the soldier a watch or some money? He might have accepted it and left. We hadn't hidden and so we could have bribed the German. We'd often heard about people buying their lives, hadn't we? We went downstairs calmly, passive and dazed. Dr Steinsapir. Henryk Gliksberg and his wife. Their sons. Ryszard and his parents. Nina and me.

Germans in front of the gate, and a harnessed cart. Next to it Councillor Rozen's wife, her two children and the two mothers, hers and her husband's. Both of the old ladies were bareheaded and without scarves. Just their unbuttoned coats thrown over their shoulders. It was a sunny but frosty day. I was standing near them and I could see their bare necks pulsating and the wind ruffling their hair.

A young girl on the cart was fighting hysterically with a policeman. She wanted to escape but he was too strong for her. Ryszard helped me onto the cart. Mrs Noz and the tall fair-haired woman with curls, wives of Chemists Union staff, were with us too. It was so packed on the cart that we drove standing and huddled together into one mass. At the beginning of the resettlements when we lived in the small ghetto on Walicow Street we once fled from our flat and spent the night in the nursing school on Panska Street. I happened to look out of the window and saw a cart going to the *Umschlagplatz*. People were standing on it huddled into one mass. Among them Janina Majde, the sister of my sister-in-law Stefania Szereszewska. She stood there calm and dazed. No-one on the cart was weeping or calling for help or shouting. And as I drove along, standing just like they had been, squashed and humiliated, I saw her in my mind's eye. And I could even clearly see the pattern on her dress. A blue dress – or was it a dressing-gown? – with large bunches of flowers.

It wasn't far from 42 Muranowska Street to the *Umschlagplatz*. Straight along Dzika Street next to the orphanage and then right and there it was.

'Will we find father and Irena there too?' I said to Nina.

When we got down off the cart we saw a crowd of five or six thousand people in front of us. A huge sea of heads. Then I was in among them. The first person I saw was Mrs Zylberberg, who was in charge of the kitchen on our courtyard, and all her workers, including Miss Kalkstein the teacher, Mr Jaszunski's daughter and the woman who'd escaped from Rembertow. They were arm in arm so as not to get lost. They smiled and nodded at me.

Tala, Mrs Noz's twelve-year-old daughter, was hugging her mother. She'd been picked up at the chemist's where she worked, together with all the other staff. Her mother had been picked up at home. But when, I thought, did Tala manage to leave the house for the chemist's? The gate was surrounded by Germans, wasn't it? And then I had the answer. She went out through the holes in the walls and crossed the neighbouring courtyards. The chemist's was on the corner in the third house at number 44. Her brother is standing next to her. He's sixteen and in the Brandenburg work team. He's even carrying a rucksack and the linen bag he keeps bread in. He's ready to go to the Aryan side with his team. Some strangers are telling him to go.

'Mr Noz', they say and point, 'the team workers are standing over there by the fence. He can save himself. The Brandenburg team is there.'

The dazed boy stands there and doesn't know what to do, whether to go over to his colleagues by the fence or to stay here with his father, mother and sister. I observe his battle and I think to myself in surprise: these people are facing death yet they want the boy to be saved. You might think that since they're dying they won't be interested in the boy's life. But it's not like that. 'Go,' they urge him. 'Save yourself. You've got the chance.'

I look up and I know all the faces I see. What is this? Have we gathered here to go on an outing together? All the staff from the chemist's on the corner of Dzika Street and Muranowska Street. All the staff of the distribution shop at 44 Muranowska Street standing behind their director, a tall, elderly man who looks Spanish. Behind us are all the staff from the distribution shop in our block. They're all together close to Mrs Rozen so as not to get lost. Suddenly her

175

daughter cuddles up to her crying. She's terrified by the crowd. I look at her and wonder if it matters that the child is only wearing a thin pullover on a frosty day like this? Does it matter if she catches cold? And I hear her mother saying to her, 'Don't cry.' These are her exact words, 'Don't cry. Daddy died and so we can too.'

Everyone is calm in this huge place and apart from this one girl no-one is crying. And one more, a little girl of eighteen months. Her father's a tradesman. He rocks her and comforts her saying, 'Sia, sia krojnele, met bald gajn a hajm.'

'Hilary Eckerman's here,' says Nina.

He was the son of Councillor Eckerman, the rabbi. His wife was standing next to him holding a new-born baby.

'Have you seen my husband, Stanislaw Szereszewski?' I ask him.

'Yes, I have. He should be here. Wait a moment and I'll find him,' he replies.

He goes and looks for him, and I wait. In a crowd six thousand strong. Is it possible he'll find him? He shouts, 'Szereszewski'. People in the crowd repeat the name. Then Hilary Eckerman comes back.

'No, I haven't found him, but I did see him before. He is here.'

'People are saying they saw him in the other direction. Let's go and look for him,' says Ryszard.

We go in the other direction. Then Ryszard turns back and I keep on going. And as Nina and I are making our way through these thousands of people a Ukrainian fires into the air and waving his gun he squashes the crowd into a corner near the fence. Now we have different people next to us. Melamud, the Council's cashier, is standing next to me with his wife. Mrs Melamud has got a scarf on her head, a gaudy rag. It keeps sliding off her head onto her neck. Mrs Melamud is so crushed in the crowd that she can't put it back on her head again. But he's still got a hand free. He carefully pulls the scarf back onto her head.

Here's Councillor Zundelewicz with his wife, daughter and son. They're all keeping together, holding each other tight, arm in arm. Mr Zundelewicz has been ill lately. How he's aged! And Mrs Zundelewicz, she's always pale and weak, but now her face is green. I see Councillor Rozensztadt with his wife and daughter. The daughter's husband is standing next to her. She only married him two days ago. They're standing arm in arm so as not to get lost, because that's what they're most scared of. 'My husband is a fatalist,' Mrs Rozensztadt often used to say. How right he was!

Next to them are Councillor Hurwicz with his wife and daughter Irena and the younger Popower, her husband. They're standing crammed together. It's so packed now that you can hear people saying, 'We're choking. Let's break the fence down. A couple of hundred people will die, but a lot will be saved.'

I stand there with despair in my heart and wonder whether people at the *Umschlagplatz* take poison at a time like this? And suddenly I realize that I've forgotten to bring the two tubes of veronal that Irena put in the first-aid cupboard.

Above us the sky. Under us the trodden snow. Behind us people with typhus, picked up straight from their beds in the hospital. They're wearing their night-gowns and are wrapped in blankets. Their eyes are watery, their faces red with fever. I can hear their rasping breathing. They're crowded together. They can't fall. And suddenly I feel that one of them has leaned his tired head against my neck.

'Your husband's over there,' says Councillor Hurwicz and shouts to him at the top of his voice. I am struck and surprised by the fact that he uses his first name. 'Your wife and daughter are here.'

I stood on the tips of my toes and thought I'd caught sight of him somewhere very far away in this sea of heads. But how was I to get there in this crowd? Then I saw an unusual sight: the Gypsies were coming to the *Umschlagplatz*. They were passing us, first the men, then the women. Old ones and young ones carrying children. And then came young girls. They were wearing gaudy skirts and had their hair in plaits, and as they walked they swayed their hips. There was an indescribable charm in the way these women walked. It looked as if they were walking to the rhythm of music. They stood out sharply against us and the background of the sky because they were so exotic. They walked calmly and quietly, without a word.

Then the crowd shudders and sways. The Ukrainians are shouting and shooting and we are driven into another courtyard. Walking behind all the others with Nina I suddenly notice my husband not far off. That one face that is so familiar and so close suddenly covers the whole *Umschlagplatz*. For a moment I can see nothing apart from that one and only face. I call him. We're tearing our way through these waves of people. All we want is to be together, nothing more. Just like everyone else.

'Hey,' I shout and grab him by the arm 'Have you seen Irena?'

Just then a Ukrainian hits me on the head with his gun. But I don't let go of my husband's hand and together we cross through the wide

177

open gate into the second courtyard. Now we have behind us the door to a modern building where the Jewish hospital used to be before the resettlements and which was a trade school before the war. In front of us is the fence. In the fence a narrow gate and a Polish policeman standing next to it. We've been driven here. We stop here. And as we stand I suddenly see that my husband is swaying.

'I fell down,' he says, 'and got trampled. I thought I'd be trampled to death. Have you got a piece of bread on you by chance?'

'I've got some bread, daddy,' says Nina and takes it out of her bag.

'Can I have some too,' asks an unknown man.

I can again see many familiar faces round me. People are talking and smiling. They're greeting each other and lifting their caps. I can see Leon Fejgin. I've known him since I was a child. He's standing with Miss Eliasberg and the daughter of Gamarnikow, the lawyer. He bows and smiles at me. But despite his calm behaviour his face is green just like Mrs Zundelewicz's. I see Mrs Syrkis-Binsztein, the doctor, and Dr Milejkowski who's in charge of the Health Department. And I can hear him telling all the people who are going to their deaths the latest war communiqué in his calm voice. And they're standing there and drinking in his words.

I think to myself that now I'm going to die with all the rest. Nothing will save me. I can see that things are not cut out on a human scale. If by chance I'm saved, then won't God kill me, just like inconvenient witnesses are done away with? And if I live, will I have breath enough? I will suffer in a search for words that should act as a lever, but of course I won't find them. And I realize with bitterness that I won't achieve anything because my words will be everyday and commonplace, like bread and salt.

'Brandt came,' says my husband. 'I asked him to release me but he just laughed. Hurwicz asked to be released. He said, "Yes, but not your wife." Jaszunski asked him and he hit him on the face with his stick instead of replying. I heard that Witold and Celina are in the building.'

Now Ryszard's standing near us. He points to the policeman by the gate and says, 'Someone's already gone to talk to him on behalf of the Union of Pharmacists.'

Suddenly people start moving. A Jewish policeman runs into the crowd and shouts, 'There are two Aryan women here! Where are they? Come forward!'

Two women step out of the crowd and follow him.

'Do you think they're really Aryans?' asks Ryszard with a smile.

And then they're shouting and shooting into the air and waving whips again and chasing us out of this courtyard as well. And as we're trotting, one behind the other, I can see that at the front they're starting to form columns to march to the wagons. A lot of people are standing there. At the very front the Gliksbergs, the Finkielszteins, Dr Steinsapir, the entire Union of Pharmacists. We go there. Faders, the German controller of the Building Department, is standing near the iron fence.

'I can see Faders,' says my husband.

'Go and ask him, he might release us.'

'I'm here with my wife and daughter,' my husband says to him. 'Can you release us?'

'You can go, but not your wife and daughter.'

'If that's the case I can't go alone.'

And he comes back to us. 'What did he say?' we ask.

'He can let me go but not you.'

'Well then go,' I say to him, 'there's still Marysia and the child. They'll need you.'

'Go, daddy,' says Nina. 'Perhaps Irena's not here.'

'Ask him once more,' I tell my husband.

So he goes back and asks a second time. Next to the fence where Faders is standing there's a shed-cum-check-point. The narrow door is open. I don't know what comes over Faders. No-one knows what impulse makes him do it. He deliberately turns his back to us. His hands are behind his back. He makes a sign with the palm of his hand in the direction of the shed. My husband grabs us both by the hand and pushes us in front of him.

Faders came to the *Umschlagplatz* to reclaim the Building Department workers he needed most. That day, out of five or six thousand people, twenty-seven were reclaimed by Brandt and Faders, including Melamud, the cashier. His wife stayed behind on the *Umschlagplatz*. Councillor Graf: his wife stayed behind on the *Umschlagplatz*. Tyller: his wife and son stayed behind on the *Umschlagplatz*. Wermund: his wife and daughter stayed behind on the *Umschlagplatz*. Eleonora Hopfenstand, the architect, was also reclaimed and Leon Tenenbaum with his wife and brother. Twenty-seven people altogether. Just one person from the Union of Pharmacists was saved, the man who'd been talking to the Polish

179

policeman by the gate. Also saved were the dentist Stanislaw Fiszhaut and his wife who was Professor Balaban's daughter. Goldfarb, the lawyer, wasn't facing resettlement yet because he was a policeman. But his wife and son were taken away. He went with them of his own free will.

Dawid Weintraub, the chief book-keeper of the Finance Department, was standing with his wife and daughter next to a man they didn't know. The man confided to him that he had 150 dollars in gold on him. Mrs Kopelewicz from the staff was also standing with them. Weintraub took the money and bribed the German gendarme. All five of them saved their lives. Yet so many people had money and gold on them but died nevertheless. It was said later that the man in charge of the distribution shop at 44 Muranowska Street had the entire contents of the safe on him, 130,000 zlotys, but he died all the same.

Mrs Rajzman, another staff member from the Finance Department, also saved her life. There were a few corpses lying by the fences on the *Umschlagplatz*. When she was near the fence she had enough presence of mind to fall down next to one of the corpses and pretend to be dead when she heard a shot. Every so often a hearse came and collected the corpses. One undertaker took her by the feet and the other by the shoulders, they swung her in the air and threw her onto the cart. That's how she left the *Umschlagplatz*.

At four o'clock a German sentry came and led the twenty-seven out of the shed. We were counted, arranged into rows and taken under escort to the Council. We left the *Umschlagplatz* with despair in our hearts.

Our eyes are closed, we don't look round, we don't want to see if the place is empty or if the columns formed for the wagons are still standing there. We've left so many of our nearest and dearest, Irena, Ryszard, Witold, Celina, the Gliksbergs, the Finkielszteins. On the way to the Council we keep meeting Ukrainians from the *Vernichtungskommando*. They heap insults on us. They threaten us with axes. Apart from firearms they all have axes for breaking down doors and smashing windows. They plundered shops and flats and ran wild in the ghetto.

We arrive at the Council at half past four. Exhausted and with all our strength gone we sit down at the table in one of the offices on the first floor and eat some bread and jam which a policeman has brought us.

'Mrs Sztolcman is making some soup,' he says. 'When it's ready you'll all get some.'

We sit and think: there are three of us now.

'We've got to ring the hospital,' I say to my husband.

'I'll ring at seven.'

He's putting it off. He wants that tiny spark of hope to keep burning. At seven o'clock he rings.

'Is nurse Irena Szereszewska in the hospital?' he asks. And waits. But of course he knows they'll say she's not there.

'Yes,' they say, 'she's here.'

He can't speak. They say something to him but he doesn't answer. They want to tell him something but he puts the receiver down. When he comes back to us there are tears in his eyes.

It's empty in the Council. We don't see anyone. The policeman comes every now and then and we can hear the echo of his footsteps for a long time. Melamud is sitting in the entrance behind a screen. I go up to him. I see that he hasn't turned the light on and he's sitting in the dark.

'I left her on the *Umschlagplatz*,' he says. 'I didn't have the strength to stay with her.'

Wasserman is sitting at the next table. He's in charge of the Registration Department. We know him from Walicow Street. He's not worried about his wife because he's got her over on the Aryan side. The phone rings. Wasserman picks up the receiver. 'It's for you, Mr Szereszewski.'

It's Stefania's sister. She works in Roerich's workshop. She came to Muranowska Street sometimes. She got a pass and stayed the night. The next day she got up at dawn and returned to the workshop. Her name was Tecia. Tecia Landau. 'Are my sister and brother-in-law and the children there?' she asks.

'No, unfortunately they're not,' says my husband.

There's no reply at the other end. It's silent. No reply.

Later on Irena arrives.

'What happened? Weren't you at the *Umschlagplatz*?' we ask her.

'It was a stroke of luck. I saved myself by chance.'

Some carts drove up to the hospital at seven in the morning. Two Germans came in, *Oberstumführer* von Bloescher and another one. 'Resettlement' they said and ordered the sick to be carried out onto the carts. She was working on the surgical ward. The doctors and nurses hurriedly poisoned the chronically sick patients by injecting them with large doses of morphine. Some of the patients didn't want

181

to go. 'Let them shoot us here on our beds', they said. The two Germans came and when they saw them lying on their beds, they shot them. When Irena was going downstairs one of the Germans blocked her path. He was waving his revolver and he shouted, 'Hast du Angst, Judin? Hast du Angst?' It was the same man who had stood aside during the great selection in the Council on 5 September and watched. 'Ist das ein Jammer!' ['Is that a wall!'] he had said.

A lot of the staff hid in the cellars. Even some of the typhus patients jumped out of bed and hid in the toilets and various cupboards. Out of sixteen midwives, one survived. When the patients had been driven away, the Germans summoned the staff for a selection. They formed them up in the courtyard. The doctors separately, the nurses separately, the orderlies separately, the office staff separately. Both the Germans were drunk. Von Bloescher noticed Irena first. 'Komm, komm,' he said and pointed with his finger. That was how she was the first to survive the selection.

The others who survived were the director Dr Jozef Sztein and his wife, Dr Wortman, Dr Heller, Dr Brandwein and the cashier, Amzel. But Dr Gelbfisz died. Two other nurses survived, Zenderman and Rochman. The ones who were driven away included the staff nurse Fried and nurses Pruzanska, Katz, Swierdzioll, Michelburg and Niemec. Nurse Jakobson was also taken but she escaped. There were two carts for the staff. Then they drove off.

'Then in the evening,' Irena tells us, 'I was warming myself by the stove in the empty ward. Dr Wdowinski came in. He was glad I'd survived. I was called to the phone. It was you, daddy, and I wanted to talk to you but you put the receiver down.'

She's telling us what happened. We're listening. As I sit at the table with my husband and my two daughters opposite me, Nina the youngest on one side and Irena the middle one on the other side, I wonder what happiness is. Within the confines of the tragedy I am experiencing I'm happy at this moment. We are happy, we four, in the whole meaning of the word. But not even for a single minute do we think that God had saved her. There is no God in the ghetto. There is only chance.

Then we go to the room which is the Building Department's office. The chairman's family is sitting there. His wife, two daughters-in-law, two granddaughters – a ten-year-old girl and a five-year-old girl – and both sons' mothers-in-law, Mrs First with her daughter, and Councillor Wielikowski's wife and daughter. Apart from them another ten or so people I don't know, probably policemen's families. Chairman Lichtenbaum comes into the room from time to time. He comes for a moment, just for one moment. Just so as to look at his beloved granddaughter, the younger one. To revel in her charm and clasp her head to his face. She's called Asia. She's wearing shoes from Zakopane. She's as lively and active as a sparrow.

Late in the evening hundreds of people crowd into the Council. There are no resettlements in the evening. Many of the people who managed to save themselves stay in cellars and hiding places for several days. Many come to the Council in the late evening, taking advantage of the relative peace and quiet.

The people who hid in the shelter of the artificial honey factory come too. The factory is on the territory of the Jewish Council property. The shelter is under a wide pavement made of concrete slabs. Down there the Germans' footsteps could often be heard overhead. You went down to the shelter from the factory. There were some shelves on the walls. One of them was movable. It turned and opened a gap which a person could slip through. Pans on the shelf masked the mechanism.

A few hundred Jews hid in the shelter. The ground was covered with strips of paper which everyone lay on. It was indescribably stuffy. A bucket stood in the corner. A sheet hung over some rope. In the evening everyone will go out to breathe some fresh air. Many of them will spend the night in the Council and go down to the shelter again in the daytime. Among the people hiding in the shelter are Councillor Zabludowski's daughter and the wife of Lewin, the lawyer who was a policeman and lived in our house. Our relative Leon Wyszewianski is also hiding down there even though he's a policeman.

I sit with Irena and Nina in the room which is now so crowded and noisy, and Amzel the policeman comes over to us. He's the husband of Dr Anna Messing.

'I'm so glad my wife's on the Aryan side again,' he says.

Mrs First hears and says, 'Anyone can go to the Aryan side at any time. All you need is money.'

'That poor Rela Warszawska,' someone says, 'was picked up in the Council. She fell down on her knees in front of the German, you know.'

'And Jaszunski's daughter-in-law, the very young one, she fainted. And they took her like that, while she was in a faint.'

'Bronek Kornblum's gone as well,' says a policeman we don't

know. 'I saw him on the *Umschlagplatz*. He was worried he'd lost his sister.'

They talk and we listen to them because we know everyone they're talking about. Adas Himmelfarb, Stefan Gliksberg's friend, comes into the room. He lives at 61 Niska Street with his family. The residents of that house had the foresight to prepare a bunker in a house that was being built next door and had just had its cellars built. They dug a passage from their own cellars. The house was started before the war. When the war broke out the building work was interrupted. Two hundred people hid there, including a few small children.

'The children,' says Adas and frowns, 'were given sleeping pills and slept like the dead. We thought they had died and would never wake up again.'

He also tells us that Icchak Giterman, the director of Joint, lived in the same house. His wife and son had already gone down to the bunker. Giterman stayed behind for a moment and then ran downstairs but he was too late. A German soldier was going upstairs and when he saw Giterman running he fired and killed him.

Adas had come on reconnaissance. To examine the situation. To see and experience with his own eyes what it was like in the Council.

'Now I'm going for my parents. I'll bring them in a minute. It's hard for them down there in the shelter,' he said.

Half an hour later they return: Lawyer Himmelfarb, his wife and Adas. It's now very late. Everyone settles down for the night. People sleep leaning against the wall or sitting at a table with their heads on their hands. Mrs First and her daughter are lying on a table. They're wearing white felt Zakopane shoes. We look at the shoes. High boots and felt shoes, the greatest chic in the ghetto.

'He was so proud of his daughter, my poor husband, for being so clever and intelligent, and so pretty,' Mrs First says to me.

The little girl has got blue eyes and flaxen hair in plaits. She looks like her father and is impulsive like him.

'Who could tell she's a Jewish child,' I say.

'Can you believe it,' replies Mrs First, 'a Polish policeman latched on to me one day on Leszno Street and asked what right I had to be taking a Polish child round the ghetto?'

So we all find a place for the night as best we can. We go with Himmelfarb and his family to look for a room. As we walk around various offices in the side annexes of the building, we see a sick boy of about ten on a mattress on the floor in one of the rooms. His father is sitting next to him, one of the Council staff. There's a very old sofa in the room and a second one in the room next door and we're just about to stay and settle down when the man suddenly speaks, 'You'd better go somewhere else.'

'What's the child got?'

'Typhus.'

'Where were you this morning?'

'I was sitting here all the time. They didn't come.'

And I wonder why the boy is lying on a mattress on the floor when there's a sofa? But I don't ask.

As we're leaving the room we meet a policeman who's looking for us. He's got the key to Gorny's flat for us, the Council store-keeper. Gorny was picked up by the Germans together with his wife and daughter but it's rumoured that he's not dead. They say he was reclaimed and is in hiding somewhere. So we go to Gorny's flat. And as we're going from floor to floor via different staircases, the articled clerk Lewkowicz suddenly comes out of a cellar he's been hiding in and stands in front of us. The same Lewkowicz who sold my husband the coat that used to belong to his resettled father. His clothes are creased and dirty, he's unshaven and his hair is unbrushed.

'I've lost my wife,' he says. He sighs and returns to the cellar.

Gorny's flat consists of two furnished rooms and a kitchen. There is a modern wardrobe and two beds, next to the door, a table with an electric ring. In the kitchen dresser a whole assortment of pots and china. Adas finds two folding beds. He slides them together and all three of them lie down. We lie down too. Irena and Nina on one bed. My husband and I on the other. Nobody has undressed. We lie down in our clothes. My husband takes his jacket off so as not to crease it. I lean my head against his back and listen to him breathing. He's alive, I think, his heart's beating. It hasn't stopped yet. And suddenly I can hear him saying, 'Witold was an older man. But it's Ryszard I'm grieving over.' He loved his older brother so much and yet that's what he said.

At about midnight we hear the rumble of lorries and people shouting in chorus. We can hear, 'Oh! Oh! Oh!' but we can't distinguish the words.

'What is it?'

'They've arrested some Poles,' says Himmelfarb. 'They're taking them to Pawiak.'

We lift our heads and listen. We heard afterwards that the lorries rumbled all night. We didn't listen long. We fell asleep.

Next morning I go down again to the room where the chairman's family is sitting. Nina goes to Warman's office. They're drawing up a list of people who were seen on the *Umschlagplatz*. They think they might still be able to save someone from there. Nina gives the names of all the people we saw. But apart from Gorny no-one has returned. While they're making the list Olek Nimcewicz comes from the brushworks. He's escorted, for safety's sake, by a German soldier. He's come to find out what's happened to us. He doesn't even see Nina. He talks to Councillor Wielikowski and finds out from him that we're alive. He only stays a moment and then leaves, relieved.

At nightfall Councillor Kupczykier comes with his family. His wife, sister, sister-in-law and twelve-year-old Julek. The whole five of them locked themselves into the lavatory in the flat and took the key out. The Germans passed through the flat but didn't look in there. That's how they survived.

'Now then,' says Kupczykier by way of greeting, shaking my husband's hand. His eyes are shining. He's so moved he can't say anything else.

'Brandt was in the Council this morning,' replies my husband. 'He said to the chairman, "Three will do. Lichtenbaum, Sztolcman and Wielikowski. The rest can clear out." '

'Didn't he come during the day today?' asks Kupczykier.

'Yes, he did. He saw me. He refused to release me when I asked him on the *Umschlagplatz*. I smiled when I saw him. He smiled too. It was an ominous smile. We were conducting a wordless conversation.'

I shudder as I listen. What was Brandt thinking about when he smiled? Wasn't he thinking: wait and we'll settle up.

'Who's survived from our house?' I ask Kupczykier.

'Rozental and his daughter. They hid in the cupboard behind the door. And the Wolfowicz family. They've got a disguised room in their flat.'

'Who else?'

'Rabbi Spira's family and Rabbi Sztokhammer's family at number 40. They hid in the cellar.'

He tells us and we listen.

Kupczykier is a Councillor so his family is to share the flat with us. Himmelfarb and his family go somewhere else. In the unheated flat it's just as cold this evening as on the street. The panes are

186

covered in frost. A policeman brings us a bucket of coke and my husband and Julek light a fire. We all gather round the fire. We warm ourselves up and then we light the range in the kitchen. The crackle of the coke and the brightness of the flames soothe our nerves. We stretch our frozen hands out to the fire and as we stand there it seems as if we're blessing the life-giving warmth.

'Let's make some supper,' says Kupczykier's wife. She goes into the kitchen followed by her sister and sister-in-law. They find some potatoes and carrots in a basket. They've brought some dripping with them from home. They fill the pan with water, move the rubbish bin, look for an onion, look for salt, rattle the pans. They return to normality. Rooting around in the flat they come across a pickled horse tongue on the window sill in the bathroom. But they don't touch property that's not theirs. Later on Gorny was surprised to find the tongue in exactly the same place as he'd left it. All they make is potato soup flavoured with dripping and onion, and when it's ready they share it out among us all.

Then they unfold the beds and lie down on them together with Julek. Kupczykier lies down in the other room on two armchairs. He's about to turn the light off when a member of the Council staff we don't know comes into the room with her mother. She says she lives in our house, they saved themselves by hiding in the cellar. The old woman is tall, thin and bony. She sits down on a chair and weeps.

'Why's she weeping?' I ask her daughter.

'She heard that her two nieces poisoned themselves in a cellar on Kurza Street.' She's silent for a moment and then says, 'I saw thieves in your flat. They lit a candle and were going from room to room. I saw their shadows moving.'

When the old woman hears this she stops weeping. She becomes animated and says, 'They put suitcases full of things in the court-yard. There must have been twenty cases.'

I look at her. She's older than my mother who died in the small ghetto. It always affects me when I see an older woman.

In the end they lie down on armchairs in Gorny's study as well. And we lie down on the beds again.

'Go to sleep Julek,' shouts Kupczykier from the next room.

'Leopold,' says his sister, 'I've got something to tell you.'

'Listen, Leopold,' says his wife.

'Are you asleep? Are you comfortable? How is it in there?' Kupczykier asks.

In fact they haven't got anything to tell each other. They're just calling out in order to hear each other's voices. They're happy beyond measure. They've escaped death.

Early next morning we go to the Finance Department office. We're in the long, narrow room that Weintraub's sick daughter once lived in. The room has recently been renovated. My husband's desk is here, this is his study. The window opens onto the courtyard and we can see a long, yellow painted one-storey building. We sit down at the desk in this room. Mrs Rajzman comes, and another member of staff who survived by hiding in the attic. Mrs Rajzman has got a black eye. She's blonde. Neither short nor tall. An Aryan type. She's full of *joi de vivre* and likes jokes.

'Can you believe it, Mr Szereszewski, I even received a proposition on the *Umschlagplatz*? One of the Polish policemen said he'd get me out if I'd live with him. But I didn't fancy him.'

We open all the drawers in the desk. Everything amuses us. Even the pink, artificial-horn pencil-sharpener which I carried around in my bag for a long time afterwards. Mrs Rajzman opens a drawer full of files and takes out a pile of letters which have come to the ghetto from the Red Cross.

'Read them if you've nothing to do, ladies,' she says.

The letters come from all over the world. From China, from Mexico, from Canada, and even from Australia and Africa. Children inquiring about their parents, brothers about their sisters, husbands about their wives. The people being inquired about have died a long time ago. There are letters from Palestine as well. I find a letter from my brother inquiring about our mother, and a letter from Abram Epstein, our Marysia's colleague. We thought he was dead. The letters we read are a cry from afar. Like an appeal.

On our way back we pass through the room with windows at each end. And we see that the door to the kitchen is blocked by a huge cupboard. There's no sign of the door. The cupboard is open. Suddenly some hardboard is moved aside at the bottom. A rectangular opening appears and Mrs Kopelewicz from the Finance Department, a huge woman, slides out of the opening like a snake.

'Aren't you ashamed to be crawling around on the floor like that?' jokes my husband. 'What were you doing there?'

'We disguised the kitchen. I live there with Weintraub and his wife and child.'

'But the kitchen's got another door that opens onto the corridor,' says someone.

188

'We flooded the corridor.'

'Weintraub, come on out!' calls Mrs Rajzman.

Out he comes. His wife and daughter behind him.

'Mr Szereszewski,' he says, 'not many of your staff are left. Just three clerks and the book-keeper.'

'Where's Popower?'

'He's gone to the Aryan side.'

'And Wojdyslawski?'

'He's dead.'

Weintraub is wearing his stained suit as usual but it's more creased than ever. His hair is dishevelled and standing on end. Seeing that my husband is shaved he asks, 'How did you manage to shave?'

'I sent a policeman to my flat to collect my shaving gear. But he brought me Grodzienski's things.'

Weintraub smiles understandingly. A minute later he says, 'I've got an idea. Why don't you use your influence to get a tunnel dug from the Council across Gensia Street to the cellars on the Aryan side. We can escape that way if necessary.'

'I'll think about it,' says my husband.

The tunnel was never made. In any case shortly afterwards Weintraub crossed over to the Aryan side with his wife and daughter.

In some workshops the Jews defended themselves during the selection and started shooting. But the Germans quickly overcame these attempts at resistance. On Kurza Street a grenade was thrown at the Germans as they were going down to the cellars. From then on they never went down to the cellars first. A Jewish policeman always went down first in front of them. Even on the second and third day we could still hear loud shooting from the direction of the Council. After three days everything quietened down.

Now when it's quietened down, they let us go home. As we go downstairs we meet Feliks Wyszewianski at the gate with his wife and son. They're incredibly dirty, all covered with soot. They hid in a chimney. We're lined up in rows and then we set off escorted by policemen. The escort is led by Felhendler who used to be an officer in the Polish Army and is now a Jewish policeman. We know him from when we lived in the small ghetto on Walicow Street. We owe him our lives. One day at the beginning of the resettlements we were taken to the *Umschlagplatz* but Felhendler rode up on his bike at the last minute and just managed to hand the Germans a card with an official stamp on it. We were released on the strength of that card.

189

We set off. While we're walking back I say to Felhendler, 'Do you know that Ryszard, and Witold and his wife aren't with us?'

'I know,' he says without turning his head. 'I know. I know everything.'

We walk along the empty streets. We look at the ransacked shops and broken windows and smashed doors. Is it possible, I think, that life is going on as normal just a few hundred steps away, on the Aryan side, while here we're crossing the desert? But we're already turning into Muranowska Street. The chemist's on the corner has been plundered. The distribution shop as well. We enter and cross the courtyard. Here's the gate to the side annexe. The Alters' smashed safe is still lying on the concrete floor. The stairs and the landing. In the corner on its hook the same mirror in its velvet frame where we checked that we'd not forgotten our white armbands with the blue star. At last we stop in front of the door to number 28. It's wide open.

We enter the flat in silence. It's so quiet that it seems we can hear our hearts beating. We haven't got the courage to enter the rooms yet. Out of reverence or fear. An unknown force detains us on the threshold. First we go into the kitchen. Cold and deserted. The potatoes we had peeled and left ready in the pan are frozen. The water in the bucket is frozen too. The window panes are covered with ice and frost and barely let the light through. We see that the boards have been chopped off the kitchen door. An axe is lying by the door.

'That's not our axe,' we say. 'Someone's left it. Must have been a Ukrainian.'

Then we enter the Gliksbergs' room. It looks like a hurricane has struck it. We look round and see that the wardrobes and drawers are open and completely emptied of clothes and linen. The quilts taken from the beds. The night-clothes are untouched and still lying just like they were before, on the creased unmade beds which still bear the shapes of the people who slept in them. It was a superstition among thieves in the ghetto. They didn't take night-clothes from beds. They believed they were the indivisible property of the people who had worn them. A night-dress could take its revenge.

Stefania's old clock which had chimed so beautifully was gone. It had been her grandfather's and she looked after it like the apple of her eye. And all her cases of linen and also the cases belonging to her resettled sister and Henryk Gliksberg's niece. All the food they kept hidden behind the wardrobe was also gone. We stand and look at this profanation of the beds and at the silent but eloquent signs of the family's existence. Here's Stefania's slipper, Henryk Gliksberg's tie and sock, Stefan's cap, Tadeusz's book. The candlestick with a candle butt, crushed by a heel. And letters and photos are everywhere. The thieves had thrown them on the floor as things of no value while they were ransacking the drawers. Three old, worn jackets are lying on the floor by the balcony. One on top of each other, a pile of rags. We wonder where they came from.

'They put on the Gliksbergs' coats and jackets and left their rags behind,' says my husband quietly.

'Let's throw them out,' suggest our daughters.

'Not all of them,' replies my husband. He picks out the worst coat, the one that's the most dirty and torn, takes it onto the veranda and puts it into the chest. 'It might come in useful,' he explains.

Then we return to the dining room and look at the bed Ryszard slept on. The quilt, his mother's lilac down quilt, has been stolen. The blue pyjamas he slept in are lying on the bed. I come closer. They still contain Ryszard's warmth and life.

It's the same in Dr Steinsapir's room. The wardrobe open, open drawers all empty, scattered things, the quilt taken, the bed stripped and on the sheet his night-shirt.

As we walk from room to room we see that only things belonging to the Gliksbergs and Dr Steinsapir, and Ryszard's quilt and alarm clock, have gone. Our bedroom where I'd made the beds before we left the house is untouched. The same with the room the girls slept in. Nina had made her bed in the morning and the room looked as if nobody had entered it. This discovery makes a deep impression on us. Who took the things? It must have been the non-registered, the first to come stealing via attics and holes in the wall from the deserted houses they lived in. No-one else would have left those old jackets behind. Thieves from our house would have come later. They will have known from the police that we were alive. They respected our property. But we're surprised that our property was not of any interest to the non-registered.

We all knew that everything left behind after people had been resettled became the property of the Germans. What else was the *Werterfassung* team for? Taking things that were left behind meant robbing the Germans. That's why no-one said 'steal'. What you said was 'take'.

We sit at the table. We don't take our coats off. It's as cold inside

191

the flat as outside. Nina goes to her room, opens the wardrobe and we suddenly hear her say, 'Daddy, they've taken something of ours as well. My rucksack which was in the wardrobe. There was a new pair of shoes in it, and a pullover and skirt.'

We run in. We see the made beds. The room is clean, no disorder. Only the rucksack is missing. It always stood in the corner of the wardrobe next to the Alters' Book of Esther which we kept to bring us luck. Then Blumcia comes. Yes, Blumcia's standing pale in the hall. It looks as if she's apologizing with all her soul for still being alive while they, the Gliksbergs, are dead. So beautifully dressed, living so beautifully, so gracious in every way. She's so moved she can't speak. She pokes her head into their room. 'Oh God,' she sighs.

'Where did you hide?' we ask her.

'I didn't leave the flat. I closed the door and took the handle off. They didn't come in because there was no handle.' She's silent for a moment and then she asks Irena, 'What about the old lady with the broken leg?'

'They deported her.'

She was asking about the woman who took her in, the one who used to work in our kitchen. The one who was in hospital after breaking her leg while washing the floor.

'They deported your old lady,' Irena repeats.

'Deported,' whispers Blumcia. Her eyes are round with terror.

'All the same we should put what's left tidily away,' I say. 'Stefania's sister might come from her workshop and take the things.'

There's an almost empty trunk in the boys' room. I slide it into the middle of the first room, open it and pack everything I can find into it. On the bottom of the trunk I can see some thick stamp albums. They weren't taken because no-one realized they were valuable. I put the Persian carpets and kelims which covered the boys' beds on top of them. I also put all the night-shirts from the beds into the trunk. Stefania's shoes, Henryk Gliksberg's ties, Stefan's red gloves which Nina knitted for him, the boys' albums, and odds and ends. Then I pick the letters and photos up from the floor. I look at them. On one yellowed photo I can see Stefania sitting at the piano. Her head is lowered and she's smiling. Henryk Gliksberg is standing next to her with his hand on her shoulder. I don't put that photo into the trunk. I keep it for myself. That one and a few more.

Then I close the trunk just like you close a coffin. It closes with a dry rattle. Is this room not a cemetery? And I wonder what it would be like if it was the other way round? If we had died and Stefania had survived. And I imagine her in our rooms gathering up the silent but eloquent signs of our existence. My husband's ties, my daughters' dresses, my old unwanted shoes, and our night-shirts. I can see her as she looks trembling at our beds which seem naked without their quilts and then she bends over and picks the scattered letters and photos up off the floor. I'll take them for her daughter on the Aryan side, she thinks. As she's picking them up she looks at them. Suddenly she sees a photo of me when I was twenty. She keeps it for herself. And a few others. Then she closes the trunk, the small, black trunk we used for hats, the one Ryszard always sat on, she shuts into the trunk the defenceless remains of our lives and of our existence on earth. The top closes with a dry rattle. And she wonders what it would be like if it was the other way round.

At nightfall we light a candle. We put it into the thin silver candlestick we found in the courtyard. The Becalel plate was taken but the candlestick was left because it was of no value.

Stanislaw Tempel comes from the Transavia workshop on Stawki Street. He's heard that we've come back and he's come to greet us. But how he's changed! His hair's a mess. He looks neglected.

'My poor daddy,' he says. His eyes fill with tears. He can't say anything else.

'This is your home too. Always. Any time,' we say to him, moved by his suffering.

In order to direct our thoughts and conversation along other lines, Nina goes to the first aid cupboard and takes out the two tubes of veronal.

'See this? We forgot to take them to the *Umschlagplatz*,' she says to him.

'Oh, I nearly forgot,' says Tempel and livens up. 'I've brought you a present. One each.' He hunts in his pockets and places four steel hack-saw blades on the table, thin and long. 'They're for sawing through the bars in the wagons.'

We pick up these fragile life-savers and look at them in the candle-light. Then we put them carefully down on the table again.

'Someone told me,' says Tempel, 'that about a dozen Poles were put into the wagons together with the Jews. They were in the underground resistance and were wanted by the police. They were hiding in the ghetto with some Jewish friends and died needlessly.'

We sit at the table and think about these Poles who died like the Jews because of a tragic mistake. They couldn't say they weren't

Jews because then they'd die for being in the underground. The Germans suspected that there were a lot of Poles in hiding in the ghetto, wearing white armbands with a blue star as a disguise. It was even said that Polish underground newspapers were printed in the ghetto. And now they had died in someone else's cause, not their own, when the houses were blockaded.

As we sit there lost in thought and staring into the swaying flame of the candle, the door opens. We haven't locked it. What for? What would be the point of locking the door? Young Frendler comes in, he's the son of the gynaecologist who used to live on Walicow Street. He's a doctor too, but now he's a workman in a workshop. A lot of doctors, lawyers and engineers were ordinary workmen in workshops because they thought it would help save them. He's unshaven and neglected just like Tempel. Covered in mud and lime. Dressed like a team worker, he has a jacket and ski trousers, and on top a coat that doesn't button up.

'I tried to get my father into the workshop and after a lot of difficulties I managed it in the end. But he died there during a selection, poor thing. I work as a presser in the same workshop. My wife and I hid in the ruins of a burnt out house for three days. We're still living there now.'

We take him into the kitchen. He looks at the door with the boards chopped out of it and picks up the axe. He lifts it up and shakes it. 'They've left their axe,' he says. 'Let me have it. It'll be my weapon for now.'

As he speaks his gaze meets Stanislaw Tempel's. And we see how these two men, staring at each other, are trembling with hatred and despair. Then he goes. He doesn't even say goodbye. He turns round and then he's gone. He shuts the door behind him, that's all.

Here comes Boleslaw Szereszewski, my husband's cousin. He's come because he heard we survived. He saved himself by hiding under a barrel in the cellar. He hid under it when the alarm first sounded. Hundreds of ordinary people with no documents hid like that. What happened was that during the second resettlement the majority of people who died were Council staff and people with work cards. The Councillors went to the Council that morning believing that nothing bad would happen to them. They even went to the *Umschlagplatz* believing that. They were sure they'd be reclaimed. Didn't everyone from the Union of Pharmacists gathered around Councillor Gliksberg believe they'd be reclaimed? Our kitchen helpers and the assistants from the distribution shops stood on the *Umschlagplatz* all believing the same thing. That's why they stayed together.

But the non-registered like Boleslaw believed only in their instinct which told them to hide. That's why people like Sabinka, everyone who was able to live in a cellar or a room full of feathers, managed to survive.

Boleslaw has brought a down quilt and an enormous bottle of eau-de-Cologne. He found the things in a deserted flat and took them with no scruples. If he didn't take them then someone else would. That was his line of thought.

'The eau-de-Cologne is for you,' he says to Nina and Irena, 'and hang on to the quilt for me until I take it.' He points to his rucksack and then brings another one in from the hall. 'These are my pillows.'

'Put the things into the Gliksbergs' room. They can stay there,' we tell him.

Shortly afterwards Mrs Giterman and her son come. They've brought a few cases and we put them into the Gliksbergs' room as well.

'We're moving to the workshop,' they say. 'Look after these things for us for a few days.'

In that way the Gliksbergs' room becomes a store-room where we keep other people's property.

As soon as Boleslaw Szereszewski leaves the flat, or perhaps a quarter of an hour later, a man we've never seen comes in. He says he knows that a down quilt and pillows belonging to him are to be found in our flat. He asks for them back. 'I've been hiding somewhere else and not in my own flat during the last few days. The flat was robbed in my absence because they thought I wouldn't come back. But I have come back.'

We return his things to him immediately and without a word. We even ask if the eau-de-Cologne is his. He says it isn't. It stays in the flat.

Marek Szpilfogel and his wife Erna come too. Marek!' we shout. 'Marek! So you're alive!'

They lay for three days in the cellar of the former Britannia Hotel where their laundry was. They escaped and hid as soon as the alarm was raised. They tell us they've been to Witold and Celina's flat on Kurza Street. Their things have gone. Someone's rags were in the room.

'I took a few coats to sell,' says Erna. 'But I found Celina's brooch on the floor. It would be good if her daughter could get it.'

195

She gives me the amber brooch set in silver which Celina wore on her dress. Will it get to Irka? It'll have a long journey before it gets to her.

'Listen,' I say to them. 'You've been robbed, haven't you? There's a good pair of shoes that used to belong to Dr Steinsapir. They might do for Erna.'

I bring the shoes and Erna tries them on.

'They're fine. I'll take them'.

'Go to the Finkielsztein's flat too,' we advise them. 'There might be some things there. You can sell them or keep them for yourselves.'

Erna goes to the flat but soon returns.

'There's nothing there apart from this dress.'

I look at the dress. It's made of navy blue taffeta. I look closely and recognize it. Ryszard's mother wore it on his wedding day.

All sorts of people come to the flat all evening. One person is leaving and the next is coming in. The residents of the house come twice and even three times. Suddenly Dr Wladyslaw Sterling enters through the kitchen door, his wife behind him. They're dirty, covered in soot and lime, terrified and helpless. They lived at number 44 and hid in the chimney. Can they stay the night? Yes, they can. So they go to Dr Steinsapir's room. We give them towels and night-shirts. When they've washed my husband asks, 'How is it possible? I didn't think you were still in the ghetto. Why aren't you on the Aryan side?'

'My wife is very nervous, as you probably know. I'm not sure that she wouldn't shout or cry or laugh while we were passing through the check-point. But now we definitely want to go.'

They stayed for three days. Then they moved to the second floor to the Union of Pharmacists' flat. They picked a comfortable and beautiful room. Mrs Grinberg used to live there, the tall fair-haired woman with her hair in curls. Mrs Sterling took Dr Steinsapir's pillows and blanket. She also took the coat which used to belong to his wife before she was resettled and which was hanging on a nail in the wall.

Next day when she came for a chat she said, 'I've got a dressing room up there. Lipsticks, powder and cream all over, serviettes and handkerchiefs. Who lived there? Was it a prostitute?'

Shortly afterwards they left the ghetto in a bribed German lorry and went to the Aryan side. A whole group of Jews left at the same time. The vehicle put them down on Twarda Street which was on the Aryan side by then. From there they dispersed in all directions.

196

The Day of Deliverance

The Sterlings died on the Aryan side, even though their appearance was excellent – they didn't look at all like Jews – and even though they'd been christened for a long time.

Even Piotrus Held came to us that first evening. We hadn't had any news about him for a long time. We only knew that he worked in a workshop on Niska Street and lived in a police house. He used to visit the Gliksbergs, not us. The boys were friends of his. Stefania looked after him when he came out of hospital.

'The door isn't closed,' he says. 'I touched the handle and it opened.'

We don't reply. Why shut the door? The thieves have already been. For the next few days no-one will take a single stitch of ours. There's a kind of unspoken agreement, seeing as we've survived. We may be robbed later. Marek and Erna Szpilfogel were robbed every few days and there was nothing they could do about it.

'The Gliksbergs aren't here,' we say. 'They didn't come back from the *Umschlagplatz*.'

He sits down at the table, heavy and saddened. He doesn't speak. A tall, dark boy who looks Ukrainian. First he lost his parents and then his grandmother. Now he's on his own. We give him a pair of pyjamas that used to belong to Dr Steinsapir and a few flannel shirts from the Gliksberg boys. I take the shirts out of the laundry box.

'Would you like some food?' I ask, bending over the box. 'There's a lot left.'

'Yes, please.'

I pour some of the pearl barley which Stefania always cooked into a box and some fine oatmeal into a sack. Then Piotrus goes: hunch-backed as if he is carrying a load that exceeds his strength. He closes the door and we don't see him again.

People come and go. Some have even been twice already. It seems as if we haven't got a flat of our own any longer. It belongs to everyone. It's not ours any longer. The two rabbis, Spira and Stokhammer, come through the hole in the wall from number 40. The candle has nearly burnt down so I put a new one into the candle-stick. We observe the two rabbis by candlelight. The shorter one, Rabbi Spira, has undergone a visible evolution in the last few months. At the beginning of September he wore a long coat and had a long beard. I used to see him when he came to the Finance Department. As time went by Rabbi Spira's coat and beard became progressively shorter. This evening he doesn't have a beard at all any longer, just a tiny moustache, and he is wearing a suit and tie.

197

They hid in cellars and survived. In April, during the Rising, they all died except Rabbi Spira. After the war he was said to have survived a concentration camp too. They come to see us. To look at a visible sign of God's mercy. To congratulate us on our survival.

'It's a miracle,' they say. 'God's miracle. We ought to light candles in the synagogue. But we haven't got a synagogue.'

We sit at the table together. My husband and I and our two daughters, and the two of them opposite us. While we're sitting there Councillor Rozental comes in and sits down next to us too. Not at the table but a little to one side. He sits and chews his moustache and says nothing. He's gone strange and become a hermit after losing his wife. We're surprised because he never came before, not even once.

'A nes,' they say. 'A nes. A miracle.'

They smile and nod their heads and move their hands. The shadows of their heads and hands lie on the walls in stains and move with the rhythm of their words. We drink in their words happily. This evening our hard and suspicious hearts bask willingly by the fire of their simple faith.

'We still have hope,' they say in the end. 'We haven't stopped hoping.' They fall silent, too moved to continue. Then they go. The door slams and they're gone.

We feel so lonely in this flat. What will our lives be like here? Every stick of furniture, every object reminds us of the Gliksbergs and their children, and Dr Steinsapir and Ryszard. We sit down to table in our old places. Their end of the table is empty. The chairs stand as if waiting for them. Those are their places. When Dr Steinsapir and Tadeusz sat here at table they faced that black sideboard of the Alters, which looks like three coffins joined together. While Henryk Gliksberg and Stefan faced the stove, which is as high as the ceiling, and has the ornate top-piece. Here is Stefania's place. This is where she sat in that green and orange costume of hers, which Ada, the knitting specialist, had made. The collar of the costume was fastened with a gold brooch shaped like a clover-leaf.

If I shut my eyes I can imagine that Stefania is getting up from her chair and going towards the kitchen. In the dark hall she stops in front of the chest containing the treasures she has shown me so many times. I can see her bending down and carefully lifting up the crown, yes, the crown for the Torah, and the old-fashioned silver chalice with a bird and vine leaves. Now it's our turn to be tormented and we don't know whether their ghosts will be good to us. Or will they drag us after them so that we die too?

My husband has gone to the Jewish Council. Irena and Nina have gone out too. As I walk all alone through these empty, cold rooms I realize that I won't bring them to life and heat them on my own. I'll go and get Sabinka, she can come and help us. I go to number 44. In the corner of the courtyard I go downstairs to the cellar. The corridor is full of puddles. My feet sink into wet, rotten feathers like into a bog. Does this mud and muck disgust me? It's Sabinka's defence, isn't it? Nineteen-year-old Sabinka.

Her mother is still in bed. 'Is Sabinka here?' I ask her.

'She's not here at the moment,' she replies. 'And when she's not here for a moment I die of fright. No, she won't come to you. I want her to stay in the cellar.'

The Jew in the prayer shawl is standing by the east wall. I point to him and ask in a whisper, 'Same as ever?'

'Same as ever.'

Then I call in on the woman who's got a food shop in this courtyard. I sometimes went there with Stefania and bought a piece of butter or cheese. There she is. And her two daughters and son are there too.

'Are you all here?' I ask. 'Where were you hidden?'

'In the flour bin,' she replies. Then she says, 'We're all here, thank God. I've only lost my twelve year-old boy.'

When I look round I see that the son of the shopkeeper on Prosta Street is sitting at the table. I knew the boy when we lived at Walicow Street. The owner of the shop had three sons and a small daughter. The youngest son was fifteen.

'When my mother and sister were taken away,' he says, 'our youngest boy flew after them of his own accord because he loved mother so much.'

'In our courtyard there was a woman,' says the shopkeeper, 'and she was ill in her flat with typhus. Her son was a policeman. When the Germans came to get her he went with her to the *Umschlagplatz* of his own free will. His mother was hopelessly ill and would have died in any case but the young man sacrificed himself for her.'

'As I was coming here I came across an old woman who must have been a hundred. No, more than that. Where could an old woman like that hide?' I ask the shopkeeper.

'That old woman,' the shopkeeper explains, 'lay for three days in a room full of feathers. When they found her she was clutching some salt. She sucked the salt and it kept her alive.'

I go back home. When my husband comes I say to him, 'We'll have to manage on our own. Sabinka won't come.'

'We'll talk to Mucha. He can light the fires for us. We'll give him food as payment.'

'Mucha told me yesterday,' I say, 'that both our cellars have been robbed. All the potatoes. There's a bit of coal left.'

'It'll be enough.' Then he says, 'Marysia keeps ringing the Union of Pharmacists and asking if Ryszard's there. They say he isn't. This morning they told her that Ryszard's gone away but they hope he'll be back.'

'She probably understands now that Ryszard is dead,' I say.

'She already knows for sure. When she rang me at two she didn't say a word about Ryszard.'

'What did she talk about?'

'She's urging us to go over. She's arranged the papers and somewhere to live. We've got to sit down and think it over. It's time for you to go to the Aryan side.'

'What about you, daddy?' asks Nina.

'I'm staying. You two go for the time being.'

In the evening when we're going to bed he says to me, 'Poor Edward rang this morning and asked about Witold. When I told him he shrieked and wept on the phone.'

Mrs Lejkin moves into the flat where Councillor Grodzienski lived before he was deported. They open the door wide in our courtyard and a cart full of furniture drives in.

'Who's moving in?' I ask Mr Kornfeld through the casement.

'Mrs Lejkin.'

After Lejkin was murdered her child fell very ill. She went to her husband's grave in the cemetery. The cemetery keeper saw her lying on the grave, her shoulders shuddering from her sobs. But the child died all the same.

Who'll move into the Gliksbergs' rooms now? We want someone to move in because the silence and emptiness behind the doors torment us. But the Germans leave the ghetto within its present boundaries, although it's rumoured that it'll be narrowed down again, and no-one moves in.

'Well now, how many of us are left? About 30,000.' That's what some people say.

Others say 20,000, and others still 10,000.

'They're sure to leave us alone now,' they say, 'if only for the sake of abroad.'

After the Sterlings, Ada occupies Dr Steinsapir's room. The day she moves her things in I hear a knock at the door at six in the evening and the husband of a friend of Dr Steinsapir's daughter comes in. The one who works in the Serejski, Slucki and Wisniewski workshop.

'Is the doctor dead?' he asks.

'Yes, he is,' I say.

He stands there undecided. I can tell that he wants to say something. His eyes are shining as if he's got a fever.

'Was he wearing a ski cap?'

'Yes, he was.'

'Where are his pillows?'

'His pillows?' I am surprised he is asking about his pillows. 'Mrs Sterling took them upstairs.'

'He had 8,000 zlotys sewn into his cap and 15,000 zlotys in his pillow.'

'Well then, go and see Mrs Sterling. She took the pillows this morning.'

'Are you sure he was wearing the ski cap? He wasn't wearing a different cap, was he?'

'It was definitely the ski cap.'

I am surprised. He and his wife were Dr Steinsapir's only friends. No-one else came to see him. Why doesn't he ask how he died? Why doesn't he say anything about him? He's standing next to the trunk which is covered with a cloth. In the candle-light his shadow is a large stain trembling on the wall. His eyes are shining. His eyes are burning. He says to me, 'He didn't have any other friends. He had no secrets from us. No-one's touched the bed, have they? He told us that he had a hiding-place there in case anything happened to him. I'll show you it. It'll prove I'm telling the truth.'

I take a candle and walk in front of him into the darkness of Dr Steinsapir's room. I lift the candle. He opens the bed, slides open a small board in the corner and takes a rouleau of gold dollars out of the hiding-place.

'Can I take it?' he asks and looks at me.

Why is he asking? Have I got the right not to let him? 'His daughter had a child. I'm sure you know. You'll be wanting to cross

201

to the Aryan side now with your wife. Promise me that you'll use the money to find the child and bring her up.'

He writes me a note stating that on his word of honour he undertakes to find the child and bring her up. In the evening when I show the note to my husband and Kupczykier they laugh at me. The next day he comes with his wife. A warm smoking-jacket made of dark cloth was left behind in Dr Steinsapir's room after the robbery.

'I'm taking the jacket,' says his wife. 'I went to the tailor's with him when it was made. Isn't there anything else left?'

'There was his wife's coat,' I reply. 'It hung on a nail on the wall. Mrs Sterling took it. And a pair of shoes. They were taken by my cousin Erna who works in the steam laundry. Piotrus Held took the striped pyjamas.'

'I'm taking the jacket,' she repeats. And she looks at me to see what I'll say.

Then they left and I didn't see them again.

One evening some people from our house come to see us. Some of them I know, others I don't. I know Kornfeld, Lewin and Mucha. The others I'm seeing for the first time. The two Wolfowicz's, Kupczykier and Rozental. I know them. They say they're collecting money to build a bunker.

'Not me,' says Mucha. 'I'm contributing to the undertaker's bunker under the councillor's kitchen. I've even put a bed into his cellar already. We share the same staircase.'

'Not you,' says one of the people I don't know. 'But the rest of us. We're making a bunker on the ground floor in the other under-taker's flat, the one who died with his family. We've already removed a square of the parquet. Now we have to wall up the cellar from the corridor.'

My husband pays his share. The next day they bring a pile of bricks, cement and lime. They arrange the bricks under the window in the courtyard and then take them to the cellars. I see women I don't know helping to carry them. I worry about the Jewish Gestapo man who lives on the third floor at the front, but has two windows looking out into the courtyard. Professor Nossig lives at the front as well, but he's got windows on the courtyard side too. We've often seen his secretary, Mrs Epsztein, sitting by the window. The pile of bricks is lying in full view next to the undertaker's flat.

Next evening they come and say, 'We're building the bunker.

We've cut off three cellars. The ladder's already there and we've got benches. There's light there so if the electricity's working we'll have light too. Are there any carpets here to make it warmer?'

We take them into the empty room. As I pass through I see that the room has gone grey from being all covered with dust, like brass turns black. The trunk is still standing in the middle of the room. There are two Persian rugs on the floor near the balcony. One of them is light-coloured, like milky coffee.

'We'll take both of them,' they say. They put the carpets over their shoulders and carry them out.

'I don't know these people,' I say. 'I don't know them at all. They must be non-registered.'

'No, they're not,' says Kupczykier. 'They're bunker engineers.'

One afternoon Dr Borenstein, the economist, comes. When we lived at Walicow Street he worked with my husband in the Jüdische Selbsthilfe [Jewish Self-help]. He's a handsome man with beautiful white hair. There are people in the room sitting at the table so he goes out into the dark corridor with my husband and closes the door behind him.

'Mr Councillor, I'm going to the Aryan side with my wife. The Organization has made us some documents. We're going tomorrow. Give me some photos of yourselves. I'll get some papers made for you and your family. It won't cost anything.'

We offer our visitors everything we've got. We open our best jars of preserves. We even open the two tins of condensed milk we've been guarding so carefully until now. We don't believe that our daughter's son will come back to the ghetto any more. We don't need our hoard of food any longer. In the evening we hold a conference.

'Girls,' says my husband, 'you've got to go over to the Aryan side. Irena and Nina, go as quickly as you can. We'll pack some things in sacks today and I'll get them taken over to the other side. I've got the address of the caretaker on Panska Street. Marysia will take them from there to Kaftal's or to Mrs Krasnodebska's. Fein will sort it out for me.' He stops talking and then he adds, 'I saw that man Mr Neujahr today, the one Olek Messing wrote about in his letter. He's on Bonifraterska Street in the ghetto, in the Dea shoe factory. Some Polish women work there too. They go home at five every day. The Germans count them at the check-point. Two of them will spend the night in the factory and you'll cross over instead. Kupczykier is interested too because his sister wants to go over.'

203

'Mrs Kornfeld told me that they're opening the hospital again,' says Irena. 'I don't want to go. I prefer to stay and work in the hospital.'

We don't pay her any attention. We don't reply.

'What did Olek Nimcewicz say today?' we ask Nina. 'Are things getting any better?'

'He didn't say anything about that. He was urging me to go to the shelter they're preparing on Wisniowa Street.'

'Please God, let's start packing,' says my husband. 'I'll pay Neujahr tomorrow. He's in touch with the foreman. Marysia rings every day. Olek Messing rang to say he's got the address of somewhere to live. He'll be waiting for you on Bielanska Street.'

We start packing the things into sacks. My husband's newest suit, his raincoat, a few pillows and quilts, some of Ryszard's shirts and his warm dressing-gown – the child can have it, it might come in useful for a coat. Two tiny Persian carpets which have survived, they can go into the sack as well, and a few aluminium pans, the first to hand. Some of them are Stefania's. We might need them on the other side. One of the sacks is ours. We take a second one from Dr Steinsapir's room. We take an empty suitcase too and my daughters pack their dresses and coats in it. Can we take my memoirs as well? Good God! We can't take them! They've got to stay in the ghetto.

Kornfeld comes. We can hear his footsteps. Now he's in the girls' room where the sacks are standing tied up with ropes.

'Our daughters are going to the Aryan side,' we say.

'What about you, Mrs Szereszewska?' And he looks at me. 'Save yourself if you can. You look Russian. Mr Councillor, I've come to tell you that there's news from the people who were deported.'

'What news?'

'Goldfarb's son jumped out of the train. He twisted his ankle and dragged himself to a doctor he knows in Praga. He rested there for a few days and then returned to the ghetto. He's in Schultz's shop. The news is from him.'

'What else?' we ask.

'Irena Hurwicz and her husband, young Popower, jumped out of the train and were killed.'

When he goes I ask my daughters, 'How would you sum Kornfeld up?'

'The eye, ear and conscience of our courtyard,' says one of them.

'I can't forget about his cousin who escaped from a camp in

204

December,' I say. 'He told me that Jews wear ridiculous striped clothes, specially to humiliate them. Do you remember him? He got frost-bite in his hand while he was escaping.'

Next morning we ask Mucha to come and say to him, 'Mr Mucha, here are two cases. One of them contains my daughter's letters. The bigger one contains our passports, our property deeds, my husband's diploma, school leaving certificates, photos, family papers and memoirs. Can you take a spade and bury both of them in the cellar? My daughters will go with you.'

I lift the lid and slide in a sheet of paper which says: a reward is promised to whoever finds these papers and returns them to any member of the Szpilfogel or Szereszewski families. Then I close the lid carefully, just like you close a coffin containing someone you loved very much. My daughters go to the cellar with Mucha. He digs a hole, puts the cases in and levels the ground.

At four o' clock Irena and Nina get ready to go. They put on three night-dresses and two dresses, and headscarves. Father takes them to the Dea factory.

'Goodbye,' they say to me, 'come over to us.'

I kiss them and they go. I can hear them going downstairs. Did they look at themselves in the velvet-framed mirror for the last time? Did they glance at the Alters' safe? They're not there any longer. They've gone.

There's an alarm that night. We get up and dress quickly. Kupczykier knocks at the door and we go down together to the bunker in the undertaker's flat. Pillows and quilts lie scattered on the floor in the large, empty and uninhabited room. Sacks with clothes stand there too. A square of parquet has been removed in the corner. That's the hole for going down to the cellar. We stand by the hole.

'What happens next?' we ask the man directing everyone going down to the cellar and keeping order.

'The last one down stands on the ladder and gets hold of the parquet square, making sure it's covered with a quilt. He puts the square back into place and the quilt disguises the entrance.'

I go down the ladder to the bunker as well. Behind me is young Rozensztadt, the councillor's nephew, with a large rucksack. He's lost his parents, sisters and brother-in-law and is all on his own. He comes down clumsily, the rucksack gets in his way. At the bottom an orderly shows him his place. Two eighty-year-old women come down after him. They grope in the dark to place their feet on the rungs of the ladder. It takes a long time. But everyone waits patiently. No-one shouts at them to hurry up. They're saving their lives. We all understand the value of life. Everyone has the right to save their lives.

We have to whisper in the bunker. There are three rooms with benches round the sides and adults and children sitting on them. I see two small boys sitting quietly on the benches. The old women are shown where to go. They sit down obediently without a word, shrink and fall asleep. I enter the cellar where the Gliksbergs' light-coloured Persian carpet is lying on the ground. I can see Councillor Rozental and his daughter on a bench, and next to them Professor Nossig, the Jewish Gestapo man. He was terrified by the alarm and so he has come down to the bunker too. He sits quietly like the others. No-one pays him any attention but I worry that he might betray our bunker to the Germans.

I go to the third room. Most of the people sitting on the benches are unknown to me. Among them are the clerk and her mother who came to Gorny's flat in the Jewish Council when we stayed there. Most of the people in the bunker are from the same staircase. So that they can hide more quickly. I realize it's only a test alarm. But there's a sentry at the front in Councillor Hurwicz's flat. The sentry is changed every two hours. His task is to watch the street. It's all part of the self-defence action that's been organized. I climb up the ladder and leave the bunker. It's three in the morning. We go back home. The others spend the whole night in the bunker.

A day or two later Professor Nossig was shot in the street by the Jewish Fighters' Organization. I saw a huge cart through the window and his Aryan secretary giving orders to the people bringing his furniture down. His other secretary, Mrs Epsztein, went over to the Aryan side.

My husband returns from the Jewish Council and says to me, 'Marysia rang. Olek Messing was waiting for Irena and Nina on Bielanska Street and took them to Kaftal's. They spent the night there and then went to the flat she's rented. It's on Chlodna Street. Of course I don't know the number.'

'What about you? Are you going, and if so, when?' I ask him.

'Don't worry. I'll manage. At a time like this a family is only a burden.'

'Brandt said you're not needed,' I say. 'You were condemned and you survived by chance. I don't want to be there alone.'

He doesn't reply. I look at him and think how he's changed. He's

206

become old. He's got so thin lately that his clothes don't fit him properly any more. He doesn't look after himself and wears Edward's old, brown, wadded jacket in the house.

Neujahr comes in the evening and my husband pays him 700 zlotys for me to go over. Councillor Kupczykier pays the same for his sister.

'I'm scared of the Aryan side,' I say. 'I don't know if I'll go over.'

'If only my wife survives as well,' Kupczykier says to me, 'for the sake of our daughter in France.'

Then Fein comes.

'What's up, Mr Fein?' asks my husband.

'My wife and child have already gone over. I'm having my things taken over now.'

In the evening when I go to bed I think that there are only three of us in this flat now, Ada and the two of us. My last night at 42 Muranowska Street. Next morning, 31 January 1943, my husband goes to the Council as usual. He won't talk to me. I want to ask him something but he's already gone. Things are happening despite me. I can't stop them.

I'm alone again. I walk around the flat. I open the door of the Gliksbergs' room and go into the boys' room. I touch Stefania's secretaire and look out of the window at Niska Street. The Polish police station is still there on the corner. And I suddenly remember that a German was shot as he was riding along Niska Street in a rickshaw on 18 January. He was even a decent German, so it's said.

Then I look out of the window at the courtyard. I look up and see the roof where the Germans shot the husband and stepson of the woman who had a coat to sell. And for some unknown reason I remember Pozner, the undertaker, who was said to have taken the Alters' Hebrew books.

Finally I go to the kitchen. I use the pork fat Stanislaw Tempel brought to make some soup.

We eat our last dinner together. It's four o'clock. I put layers of clothes on, just like my daughters did. Kupczykier comes and asks, 'Are you ready? My sister's waiting.'

I put my coat on. I tie a scarf round my head, go out and slowly shut the door behind me. We walk down Muranowska Street. Then we turn right until we reach Bonifraterska Street. I walk with Kupczykier's sister and the other two walk behind us. Suddenly I see that there's a hole in my husband's glove. 'Give me your gloves. Mine haven't got any holes,' I say to him.

The warmth of his hands is still in his gloves and when I put them on it seems as if he's holding my hand and leading me.

At nightfall the women leave the Dea shoe factory and I'm one of them. I march to the Aryan side with them, just as grey and colourless as they are. It's foggy. I look round. They're still behind us. Will I ever see you again? I walk next to a Polish woman I don't know. She tells me that she lives in Wola and she's got an old mother. I look round. They're still behind us. And as I walk with these women in this thickening fog, I wonder if I will ever see him again? I look round again. They're still behind us. Now I can see the checkpoint. They'll be counting us in a moment. I look round. I can't see anyone – just fog.

4 • Shadows

So I'm walking along with this team of Polish workers at nightfall, in the foggy, frosty, fast-falling evening. I'm walking and I don't recognize the streets. The streets where we're walking are divided by a fence or a wall into two sections: one is the Aryan side, the other – the ghetto. The wall is spiked with glass to stop people crossing from one side to the other. We walk alongside the wall and fence for a long time, then we turn and then we walk straight ahead again, finally we stop in front of a shed where the German sentry is.

'Do they search us?'

'Sometimes they do.'

All I've got is a black handbag. That's all. No photos in the handbag. They might recognize Jews from the faces on the photos. My money is under the lining of the bag. In my pullover pocket, wrapped in a white rag, my mother's brooches, and my grandmother's brooch and coral ear-rings. They're not worth much. I squeeze them in my pocket. When we get near the check-point I'm so terrified that I want to throw them onto the ground. But now they're counting us. They've counted thirty-nine. That's the number of workers who passed the check-point into the ghetto this morning. Thirty-nine.

Then we walk on. Where are the white armbands with the blue star? I keep looking anxiously at my sleeve but it's not there any longer. I took it off when the women were coming out of the factory.

'I don't recognize these streets,' I say to the woman next to me.

'We're on Nalewki Street. By Simons' Passage. We're nearly at Bielanska Street.'

'Could you take me to Zelazna Street?'

'Yes.'

'Good thing they didn't search me today,' one of the women says to me. 'I'm taking a heap of things over under my dress today. I get paid for it.'

A whole heap of things under her dress? Before we left the ghetto we also gave Ada our best things for her to take to the Aryan side.

She worked on Tlomackie Street next to the ruined synagogue, and the caretaker she knew on Ogrodowa Street was already waiting for her there.

Bielanska Street. Here, next to these ruins, Olek Messing was waiting for Irena and Nina. He nodded his head to them, turned away and walked in front of them, as if he didn't know them, and they walked behind him. As they were walking they bent their heads against the gusts of wind just like I'm doing now, and their thoughts, just like mine, returned obstinately to Muranowska Street, to flat number 28. They knew that while they were moving further away with every step they made, their father and mother were sitting at table by candlelight and could visualize them walking along Bielanska Street. Did Messing come on time, their parents were thinking, did nothing happen to him on his way there?

Now it's my turn to walk along Bielanska Street and I know that at Muranowska Street in candlelight . . . And as I struggle with my yearning, I hear the woman beside me say, 'Wake up. We're at Teatralny Square.'

A tram comes along. One of them gets in and waves her hand. 'I'm going to Praga,' she says.

Now we're walking along Senatorska Street. We pass Bankowy Square and walk into Elektoralna Street. Is this Elektoralna Street? If it is, then where's the wall that divided it into two? It extended as far as Zelazna Street. A high brick barrier bristling with sharp glass. The even side of Elektoralna Street was the ghetto and the odd side was Aryan. Polish or Jewish sentries stood at intervals along the wall and guarded it. But the policemen, even the German ones as well, were bribed. The bricks in the wall were movable. They would be moved aside, a hand would appear and pass food or other goods through. Smuggling. Smuggling was mainly carried out at night, but also took place in the daytime along the parts the Germans didn't guard so closely.

My cousin, Maria Lipszyc, lived at 4 Elektoralna Street in a small flat on the courtyard side. When she came out of the entrance door she could see the wall. The wall bristling with glass.

'I can't stand it,' she used to say. 'I'll go mad.' She was ill with ghetto nostalgia, like many people.

People pass us as we're walking along the dark street. Two young people are talking with an accent that makes me think. A woman appears in the darkness in front of us with a man beside her. They say a few words and again the accent makes me think. I've got the

210

feeling that they're Jews. They must be Jews who are in hiding and have come out to get some fresh air.

Here's Zimna Street off Elektoralna Street. There's no street, only ruins. The Warszawiak & Co. porcelain shop used to be here before the war. One of the shop assistants used to come to Muranowska Street and sell us horseflesh. The Holy Spirit hospital. The Union of Pharmacists was once behind the burnt out ruins of the hospital, at number 12. Ryszard worked there. Is this cellar I'm just passing the one where he hid our beds and our sack of food before the small ghetto was liquidated?

'Aren't you cold?' I ask the Polish woman next to me and bend my head against the wind.

'No. I wrapped myself up tight in my shawl.'

Solna Street. This is the street with the bunker Ryszard told us about. You went down to it through the stove door. Through the stove door – odd, isn't it? But adults couldn't get through. A small girl came in and out through the stove door and brought them food. Last year in this place, at this precise junction, I saw a group of German Jews as I was riding along in a rickshaw. They were walking rhythmically with towels on their shoulders and singing. They must have been returning from the baths. You often saw German Jews in thick shoes on Zelazna Street with spades. They worked outside the city. The groups included older people and quite young boys They all looked Aryan. It was said there were university professors among them too. They all died. Not a single one remained alive.

'Aren't you cold?' I ask again.

'No.'

She's not cold. She's wound a shawl round her neck. She's walking along ordinary streets with houses on each side. But I'm walking through the ghetto. The cloudy sky above us, darkness behind us, and fog in front of us. Under her feet is the pavement, but I entered the ghetto from a different side and so I see ghosts which don't exist for her.

Biala Street. Chlodna Street. 2 Chlodna Street. 4 Chlodna Street. I stop on the corner of Chlodna Street and Zelazna Street. Now I'll say goodbye to my companion. She's a good and honest woman. She knows I'm Jewish and she gave me courage as we walked along. But I don't want her to walk with me any further. She shouldn't know where I'm going. I've got to say goodbye here. I open my bag and give her a hundred zlotys.

'Be of good heart,' she says to me. She goes to Wolska Street where she lives. She'll go to work in the ghetto again tomorrow, to the Dea shoe factory, and she might bring another Jewish woman over to the Aryan side in the evening. She goes to Wolska Street and I go to Ogrodowa Street, to Alfred Kaftal's flat. He's my daughters' former German teacher. Mrs Kaftal opens the door.

'Come in and wait a moment,' she says in a quiet voice. 'I'll put my coat on and go with you.'

'Is it far?' I ask.

'No. It's just round the corner. On Chlodna Street.'

We enter the gateway. Then we cross the courtyard to a staircase in the corner. We go to the third floor. We stop on the landing to get our breath. A woman is coming downstairs. Perhaps she's not thinking about anything. Perhaps she just glanced at me automatically. But I'm seized by anxiety. She's bound to go the caretaker and say, 'I saw a stranger in a green headscarf on the stairs a moment ago. She's wearing a headscarf just like a hawker. But she doesn't look like a hawker to me.' And I listen out for heavy, male footsteps.

'I'm going home now,' says Mrs Kaftal, 'and you go higher. The door on the right. You're to knock. If they ask who it is, say you're Marysia's mother. It's been arranged.'

I go and knock. 'Who is it?' 'Marysia's mother.' The door opens a crack and I see the head of an old woman.

'Come in,' she says. 'Your daughters are over there.'

I pass through a dark kitchen and a narrow room with the light on and then enter another room, a garret. There is a sofa, a small table, two chairs and a bedside table. I see Irena and Nina on the sofa, covered with a quilt. When I enter they get up and look at me with sleepy eyes.

'Is this it?' I ask.

'It's only a poor worker's flat. We'll have to get used to it,' says Irena.

'What about the people in the flat?'

'An old mother with two sons. The older one is called Zenon and he's a carpenter. The younger one is dumb. And Zenon's wife Krysia. She's a hairdresser.'

'Is she the Krysia Ryszard mentioned?'

'Yes, she's the sister of that Ola who as working in the Epsteins' shop.'

'Have you got any documents?'

212

'We've got registration cards from Bednarska Street.'

'Marysia's buying a bed tomorrow,' says Nina. 'Tonight we'll spend the night sitting on the sofa. She's already bought an iron stove and had it installed. It gets hot quickly. Zenon's mother brings us coal.'

Then Zenon comes in and sits at the table with us. He's short and fair-haired and looks at us sideways. He doesn't say anything. So we sit in this strange room with this silent stranger.

'Mother's very tired,' says Irena.

'Yes,' he says. He gets up heavily. He doesn't say anything else. The door slams behind him.

In the morning Nina lights the fire. First she scatters some shavings from Zenon's workshop and then places lumps of coal on them carefully. She makes some coffee and looks at her soiled hands for a long time. We talk in whispers. We move silently. The door is shut. If anyone enters the flat we sit motionlessly and silently.

Marysia comes at nightfall next day. She stands in the open door and looks at us. We look at her coat trimmed with fur, black Persian lamb. When she was staying with the child in Otwock she got hold of Aryan papers in the name of Maria Swiecicka, born in the small town of Marki. In August 1942, twelve hours before the start of the action in Otwock, she escaped to Warsaw. We hadn't seen her for a long time. Now, at first sight, she seemed strange. Different, as if she wasn't ours. We couldn't tear our eyes off the fur on her coat, because it was the fur which we had stopped having in the ghetto that accentuated the difference.

'What about father? Is he coming?' asks Marysia.

We didn't know.

'Mrs Kaftal brought mother along here,' says Irena.

'When I was there last time,' says Marysia, 'she was sitting in the kitchen and crying. She said that her husband was betraying her with the wife of a captain and that she was sure of it. Can you imagine, she was crying over something as trivial as that? But then she's allowed to cry, it's only us who can't have eyes that have been crying. Remember that, won't you?'

'Is Chlodna a good street?' we ask. 'Do we know anyone who lives near here?'

'It's said to be full of informers. Stefa Szereszewska lives nearby.'

But she doesn't give us the number of the house because the fewer people know where anyone lives the better. Best if no-one

213

knows at all. Because you might get caught and be tortured by the Germans. Not everyone can stand it. A son once betrayed his own father. This is the advice and the lesson Marysia gives us, because how can we know all this otherwise?

She also tells us that when she was walking along the street one day she met Szternfeld from the Thirteens. She saw him on Wierzbowa Street. He looked into her eyes and she knew he recognized her. 'Will he follow me now,' she thought? 'Will he find out where I live? Will he tell a passing patrol about me?' To make him lose the trail she started dodging and weaving along the streets. She entered a courtyard, crossed it and left into another street. She looked round. No. No-one was following her. Szternfeld recognized her for sure but obviously he didn't want to harm her.

'I'm telling you this so that you know the sorts of surprises in store on the Aryan side.'

When Macius was ill and she was at the sanatorium in Otwock, Jewish Gestapo men often went there. They were called the 'Thirteens', because their headquarters was at 13 Leszno Street. They all wore high boots in the German manner. High boots and a rubber truncheon. And they had beautiful girl-friends. The Thirteens didn't wear armbands with a blue star.

'Tell us who else you've met,' we ask her.

She once saw Tamara Goralska, a relation of ours, on Chlodna Street, but she didn't go up to her. On Krolewska Street she met Maryla Kalisz. She was smartly dressed in a coat with a silver fox collar. Her brother managed to escape from the ghetto. She's hiding him in a wardrobe in her flat. She once saw Janka Szereszewska, a relation from Lodz, being taken to the police station by a Polish policeman.

'Why didn't you want to go up to Tamara but you spoke to Maryla Kalisz?' we ask her.

'I don't know. I'm asking myself the same question. I can't understand it.'

She tells us that she rang Mrs Kazimiera Brzezinska, father's former clerk. She asked about him very warmly. She'd like Nina to come over, she says she's got to meet his youngest daughter. Then Marysia told us about Mrs Janina Poniatowska, her teacher. She visited her in the Wolski hospital. She was very ill. She took her some apples. She was drowsy after an injection but recognized her. She only said one word to her, 'Father?' Nothing else.

'I've got to go now.' She gets up from the chair and goes over to

214

the window. We can see she's uneasy. 'Remember not to tell anyone what you're called now and what you're really called. Don't tell Zenon's mother or Zenon or Krysia. It's no business of theirs.'

Is that so? We didn't know. Good thing she told us.

'You should sort something out for yourselves now,' she says. 'This place is only temporary.'

'How much do we pay for it?' we ask.

'1,000 zlotys.'

'1,000 zlotys?'

'You don't know anything', laughs Marysia. 'You've no idea. A normal room costs 250 zlotys a month. That's what I pay the Lubecki sisters because they don't take advantage of the position I'm in. But Jews pay a thousand and more. They pay for the risk.'

We stand near her. We know she'll leave in a moment and the door will close behind her. We suddenly realize that we're as helpless as children lost in a forest. That we don't know any-thing and we might well get lost in the tortuous labyrinths of the Aryan side.

'So what now?' we ask.

'I'm seeing aunt Julia about Irena tomorrow and I'll ring Mrs Brzezinska about Nina. I'll buy you a few dishes and a bed. I'll send Hania to you, the woman who sorts out registrations and identity cards. I nearly forgot the most important thing. The baptism certificates you've got. Learn them by heart, your parents' names and your date of birth. And something else: I'll buy you a catechism so learn the prayers. Because if you were caught . . . They test you on religion. They caught a Jewish woman on Chlodna Street once and asked her when All Saints' Day is. She told them it was the second of November. She gave the wrong answer because the second is All Souls' Day and All Saints' is on the first. No, I won't buy you a catechism. Who buys books like that? Only Jews. I'll borrow one from someone.'

She turns the handle and is just about to go. She'll say goodbye in a moment and the door will slam behind her. And we don't know anything. There are so many things we still want to ask her about.

'What about Macius? How is he?'

'Well, there's a problem with him, because when I leave the house Macius waits for me by the door in the hall. He waits all the time and is terrified about me. And he cries. He must cry because his eyes are red. "I was very worried about you," he says when I get back. "I stood by the door and waited all the time." I keep explaining that I'd prefer to be at home with him and not go out at all. But I have to go out. Unfortunately I have to.'

That's how it is with her son. He's heard of round-ups and knows the dangers facing Jews, and he's afraid he might lose her. Although he's still only small, he plays his part well and has entered it completely. He accepts that the role is necessary. A picture of Our Lady hangs above his bed. Every evening he kneels and prays, and never forgets.

How can we fill the time shut up in this garret? In conditions like these every activity, even the smallest, has its own importance. First of all we hang up some washing lines. We look for hinges or nails, somewhere we can hook them over. Washing lines in the rooms you live in – we got used to that in the ghetto. We immediately wash our stockings and hang them up on the lines. Then we unravel a pullover, wind the wool into balls and then make strips, wash them and hang them up. While we're doing all this we walk on tiptoe, talk in whispers and move around without a sound.

'That Krysia's got black hair,' says Nina, 'just like me. But she doesn't think twice about it.'

Zenon's mother cooks on an iron stove which heats the narrow bedroom at the same time. Sacks of sawdust and planed shavings lie on the floor. A low door leads from this room into our garret. There are two iron hasps next to the doorknob and the door is closed with a padlock. I look at the door and say, 'If we hid it behind the wardrobe the garret would be disguised. The back of the wardrobe ought to be movable in that case.'

As I speak I remember Weintraub. That's how he disguised the kitchen where he lived with his wife and child and Mrs Kopelewicz. We still gravitate towards that side. Every situation brings a comparison to mind. It seems as if every object, every action and even every word we say finds an answer and an echo in the ghetto.

'What for?' says Irena. 'We don't need to disguise the garret. We'll leave here in the end and you'll stay and register. You'll be living here legally.'

But my thoughts return obstinately to the disguised kitchen and I can hear Weintraub's words in my ears when he said, 'A tunnel from the Council building under Gensia Street to the cellars on the Aryan side.'

This duality, this dissociation tormented us greatly. How long will it last? Can we live with it? And when I think about it I remember the woman in charge of the kitchen on Muranowska street, the one whose soul was in Hrubieszow. "My soul is in Hrubieszow," she used to say. She looked at us sleepily and smiled strangely. Her movements were slow and she spoke in a tired distant voice.

'Think about it,' says Nina. 'You'll be living legally. Now let's learn our baptism certificates by heart.'

I take my baptism certificate carefully out of my bag and smooth it out with the palm of my hand. Issued by the church of St Barbara in Warsaw in the name of Alicja Maria Biernacka. Parents' names: Wladyslaw Szymon and Maria Kazimiera. Maiden name of mother: Chrzanowska. It's an original certificate issued for the deceased Alicja Biernacka. The dates are more or less right. She's dead and now I'm going to live her life. I take out the faked marriage certificate. Name of husband: Stanislaw Majewski. Born in Lwow. Parents' names: Kazimierz and Anna née Kurkiewicz.

Marysia got hold of an original certificate in the name of Stanislaw Majewski for her father, just like she did for me. The dates tallied. Even the name tallied. The marriage certificate was drawn up on the basis of the other two. She had it done like that so that we could live as a married couple one day.

'Now me,' says Irena and reads: 'Aniela Gologowska. Born in Lwow in 1915. Parents' names: Mieczyslaw and Maria née Pawlowska. Look, Marysia's taken a certificate for me which makes me a few years older than I really am.'

'Too bad,' says Nina, 'you'll have to get used to it. I'm Jadwiga Tokarska, born in Warsaw. Parents' names: Stanislaw and Katarzyna née Barszcz. The dates are nearly right, I'm just a year older.'

'Wait. I can hear singing,' I say to my daughters.

Our window has a white embroidered curtain. An old darned rag. We go to the window and look out through the holes in the embroidery. An old man is standing there, a beggar with a sack. His hands are supported by a stick. He opens his toothless mouth wide and sings. We look at him. Our heads meet. We can never move the curtain aside. None of the neighbours must see any strange women in the garret. Every so often one of us looks out on the courtyard through the holes in the embroidery. We see a Gypsy. She wears gaudy skirts and a colourful shawl on her back. Plaits hang down the sides of her face and she's plaited silver coins into them. 'Read your palm!' she shouts. 'Read your palm.' We're surprised to see a

217

Gypsy on the Aryan side. And walking so openly along the streets. It was only a few weeks ago that so many Gypsies went to the *Umschlagplatz* after all. Has something changed? We look at her and we can't explain it.

We see a small boy with a little girl. They're blowing on their fingers and stamping their feet on the frozen snow. We can see they're cold. 'Oh farewell, farewell,' they sing, 'to my mother and family.'

When I look at these singing children, at these children with poor and probably hungry parents, I can see in my mind's eye the children in the courtyard at Walicow Street and the children begging in the small ghetto. Two little girls. The older one is beating a drum and singing. The younger one is eight or nine and she's dressed as a nymph, yes, a nymph, her long hair is loose and she's dancing. She runs round in a circle, bends over, lifts the hem of her long dress which is made out of paper. Then they both collect the coins and pieces of bread wrapped in newspaper that people have thrown from their windows.

I see a boy who sings a Ukrainian song, always the same one. His voice is mournful, moving and penetrating. People watched with astonishment to see such a thin and hungry child singing so loud and clear. What about the singing, old beggar women? Does anyone else remember them apart from me? They sang and danced, lifting their skirts high. The people who threw them money were appalled and didn't want to look at them.

My soul kept returning to the other side of the wall and it seemed as if nothing could loosen the bonds.

Marysia comes at nightfall. She brings a catechism. 'I've borrowed it from Mrs Voelnagel,' she says. 'At last I've got one.'

She tells us that Nina's certificate was no simple matter. She thought about it for a long time. She had the possibility of buying a certificate with a family. But according to the certificate Nina would have been seventeen. She couldn't decide. 'Just think, a family too. If Nina was ever stopped she could give her address and they'd say, "yes, she's a relation of ours, we know her."'

'Pity,' I say. 'You could have taken the certificate. Nina looks seventeen.'

'It's too late now. Too bad,' replies Marysia. She takes three thin aluminium saucepans out of her bag, three teaspoons, and a white milk jug. 'Guess what else I've got.'

We can't guess.

'A yellow fox fur for mother.'

She shows us a yellow fox with a tail and a head and lays it out in front of us on the table. We look at it terrified.

'I'll get a collar made. I've got the address of a furrier. I bought you some second-hand Persian lamb in the market, enough for collars. There's even enough to sew a trimming for Irena's coat from the top to bottom by the fastening. I'll take your coats in turn.'

'Give over. We'll do it ourselves.'

'No,' she says. It's got to be done smartly. It's got to be sewed with chic.'

Now she's saying goodbye. She can't stay a moment longer. Now she's gone. I run after her through the room with the light on where Zenon's mother is sitting hunched in front of the fire. I stop Marysia in the cold dark kitchen which no-one cooks in.

'Have you spoken to your father?' I whisper.

'Yes I have. He promised to come and see us. He's got a pass after all.'

'How will we know it's him when he knocks?'

'He'll say he's come to see Karolina.'

In the evening we make coffee in our own saucepan and put Zenon's mother's pan aside. We're so pleased with our pans! They're very plain, at forty zlotys they're the cheapest she could buy, but they're ours. Every evening we pay Zenon's mother for three dinners on the following day. Dinner means borscht with potatoes and kasha with mushroom sauce. Or cabbage soup with potatoes and noodles with mushroom sauce. Dinner costs thirty-five zlotys. Every morning Zenon's mother brings us a loaf of bread and half a litre of milk. We make our own breakfast and supper. We have to eat her dinners.

Zenon's wife Krysia comes every evening. We look at her black hair and think of Nina's hair.

'Can you bring us a library book?' we ask her.

'What shall I bring? There's a library next to the hairdresser's where I work.'

'*Quo Vadis*', we say. 'We'd like to read *Quo Vadis* again.'

Zenon's dumb brother comes too. He sits next to Nina, always next to Nina. He utters throaty sounds which we don't understand. He laughs and nods his head. He takes a pencil and a sheet of paper out of his pocket. He knows how to write. He goes to the institute for the deaf and dumb every day.

'Don't let him get used to us,' we warn each other. 'He's not normal. He might tell his friends in sign language that there are some women living in his flat.'

We talk in whispers. We walk silently on tiptoe.

A certain Mrs Domanska has a three-roomed flat on Wspolna Street overlooking the courtyard. She's a school teacher. Her mentally ill sister Zofia lives with her. There's a strong grille on the windows. Zofia jumps onto the window sill and gazes at the courtyard for hours. She stands there, shrunken and hunched, with her fingers fastened to the grille. Sometimes she's restless and throws chairs at the walls, smashes plates, tramples on the bedding and tears the sheets into fine strips. The knives and forks are hidden from her. Can she be left in the flat alone? While she's at school working Mrs Domanska suddenly remembers with terror that she hasn't put a box of nails away. Zofia might swallow a nail. She might eat the candles, pour the paraffin out, or what's worse, break the grille.

Something has to be found for Irena. Marysia asks Julia, her aunt Julia, who's like a second mother to her. She tells her about Irena and Julia in turn talks to Mrs Domanska whom she's known since before the war.

'Just think,' she urges, 'Irena is a qualified nurse. You're out at work and you won't have to worry about your sister. Besides, Irena's mother will pay you for her keep.'

Mrs Domanska is so upset that she turns pale.

'I couldn't take advantage of the girl just because she's Jewish. If she lives with me I'll pay for her keep. But I couldn't pay her for the work because I don't earn much.'

Julia and Marysia arrange to meet one evening in a small café on Wspolna Street. Julia is fifty. Short, with Semitic features, completely white hair and a fair, young face. Her husband, Marian, lives elsewhere, in Mokotow. They have two children, a son at Zurich Polytechnic and a daughter in the concentration camp in Majdanek.

'She agrees,' says Julia, 'but she doesn't want to register her. You'd better know that Irena's going to have her hands full with that mad sister of hers.'

They stand up and look at each other for a moment without speaking.

'See you here next week at the same time,' says Marysia.

'What about your father?' asks Julia.

Then they leave. First one and then the other. Each turns in a different direction. It's frosty and windy. The illuminated shop windows are reflected on the frozen snow. An informer stands on the corner of the street and looks sharply into the eyes of every woman who passes. Are they Jewish by chance? No, this one with the calm, fair face isn't Jewish.

The tram comes. It goes to Chlodna Street via Zelazna Brama Square. Marysia sits next to a woman holding a child, next to a policeman or next to a trader with a basket. She glances with lightning speed over the inside of the tram. She won't sit down next to a man who looks suspiciously Jewish. If she meets a Jew she knows she won't nod or glance in his direction. Because against someone else's background, the crumb of Semitism which is in her, will become clearer and more obvious to the eye. She has fair hair and a fair face but all the same there's something different in the way she walks, in her figure, in her movements, or in her eyes, and she can't let this difference be magnified.

This time she doesn't know anyone. She looks at the darkening windows of the tram and thinks her own thoughts to the knocking of the wheels. Who'll take Irena to Mrs Domanska's? Henryk will take her. Henryk Falencki. She gets off the tram at the corner of Chlodna Street and Zelazna Street. She makes a phone call to Saska Kepa from a phone in the food shop. That's where Henryk Frydman lives, a young doctor from Otwock. He managed to leave the Otwock ghetto when it was being liquidated and make his way to Warsaw.

'Can you come to where my mother lives on Chlodna Street at seven o'clock tonight? Irena's got a job. She's got a lot of cases so we'd like you to help take them to Wspolna Street.'

Will he understand, thinks Marysia as he puts the receiver down? She made up the heavy cases. It's fortunate that none of his landlady's daughters answered the phone because they're very jealous of him. She leaves the shop. Chlodna Street. Number 28. She crosses the courtyard. She goes upstairs, her hand moving slowly up the bannister. 'To see Krysia,' she says. 'Is Krysia at home?' Zenon's mother opens the door. The neighbour from opposite opens the door a crack and watches her closely in the dim light of a darkened light bulb hanging from the ceiling. She comes to where we are in our garret. All three of us are sitting at the table in silence. When Marysia stands in the door we look at her.

'Listen,' she says, 'I've got Irena fixed up. Mrs Domanska has agreed to take her. Henryk will take you there. He's coming at seven. Don't take anything with you. I'll bring you everything you need. The only thing is that I'm afraid you're going to have a hard life. If you can't stand it we'll look for somewhere different. You can't be together at Zenon's forever.'

Henryk comes at seven. He looks at us with a troubled smile. Irena ties a headscarf round her head. She opens her bag and checks to see if she's got her certificate and backdated registration for Bednarsha Street. The documents are there. Neatly folded, each one next to the other. Now she puts on her fur-trimmed coat. We stand around her and look at the narrow strip of fur which runs round her neck, down the fastening, along the pockets and around the cuffs. Made from the piece of black Persian lamb bought at the Hale Mirowskie. The fur should help her now, and safeguard and protect her.

'If father comes he won't see Irena,' we say.

'That's true,' says Irena. She jumps up and stands there thinking with one hand in the sleeve of her coat. 'I forgot about father in the ghetto.' Now they're leaving. The door closes behind them and we listen to their muffled footsteps moving into the distance. I run out after them to the dark kitchen.

'I must tell you something,' I say, catching my breath. Irena turns round and looks at me. But I just stand there from too much emotion and look at her without saying a word because I've forgotten what I wanted to say.

Irena sleeps in the same room as Zofia. She sleeps any old how, with no sheet and no quilt, covered with her coat. She'll have to manage until Marysia brings the pillows and sheets and a quilt. It's terribly cold in the flat. The stoves are never lit. The rooms are cluttered with furniture that used to belong to parents, grand-parents and relations. They smell musty. Heaps of school textbooks and exercise books lie in the corners. They're covered in dust and the mould of time. No-one removes them, no-one throws them away. The dedicated teacher hoards them year after year.

There's a lodger in the smallest room. An ordinary-looking young man. He leaves early and comes back late. He wears rubber soles and you can't hear his footsteps. Irena doesn't know anything about him. Sometimes he stands silently in the kitchen door and then he pretends that he can't see her and comes up to the sink, turns the tap on and pours some water into a bottle. Irena doesn't know what he's thinking.

Early in the morning on the third day Marysia brings her sister some bedding. Irena takes her into the kitchen. They sit down on stools by the sink. The kitchen is dark, smoky and dismal. A chipped mirror in a frame hangs crookedly on a hook above the sink. The handle of the rubbish bin is missing, the kitchen shelf is too high, the tap leaks, dusty bottles stand in the corner. The cotton curtain has frozen to the grille. There's a table with a drawer and a grey oilcloth, one wooden stool and a little footstool which Irena is sitting on now.

'I'll bring you everything,' says Marysia. 'Even coal so you have something to cook on. Try to take as little as possible from Mrs Domanska. I'll bring you some flour, potatoes, kasha and even vegetables. Now tell me how it's going.'

'So far so good,' replies Irena. 'I even like my Zofia. Our first meeting was funny. "I'm Aniela," I said to her. She threw herself round my neck. "You're my born sister, you're my darling Aniela." She hugged and kissed me. I do her hair differently every day. She's my doll. Come and see her.'

She opens the door to the room. Marysia is astonished to see, on the chest of drawers, on the table, and on the shelves, a huge number of boxes of all sizes, cigarette boxes, matchboxes and sweet boxes.

'What's this? Is it a shop? It looks like a shop.'

'No,' replies Irena. 'Zofia plays with them. Just like a child. Look, she's jumped onto the window sill again.'

Zofia is standing on the narrow sill, shrunken and hugging the iron grille, and is looking down into the courtyard.

'She once stood there for twelve hours,' says Irena. There was no way we could get her down. It was late at night when we got her down at last.'

'She looks like a bat,' says Marysia as she closes the door. They go back to the kitchen and sit down on the same stools.

'Have you phoned father?' asks Irena after a while.

'I saw father in the Kredytowy Bank on Fredro Street. What luck he's got a pass from the ghetto to the Aryan side.'

'You saw father!'

'Yes, I did. There's a trusty porter there. We were in an empty office. I didn't talk with him long but he promised to come to Zenon's one day when it gets dark. He'll knock and say he's come to see Karolina. I've arranged it with him. He was in a hurry and was worried about me. "Go now," he said.' Marysia is silent and then she asks, 'Do you go out to the shop or into the courtyard yet?'

'I took the rubbish out once but I was scared of the caretaker.'

'Everyone's scared of caretakers and children. Don't say you're

Jewish if they stop you. Don't trust anyone, not even people you think you can trust.' Marysia takes an old cloth bag from a hook. 'I'll bring you some coal,' she says.

She brings the coal, then goes out again and returns with a loaf of bread, some butter wrapped in paper, a piece of sausage, some kasha, potatoes and beetroots.

'It'll last you a while,' she says. 'I'm going now.'

They say goodbye and then Marysia leaves while Irena is left alone staring at the curtain.

One day Marysia found Irena crying.

'Why are you crying? Tell me.'

'I want to go back to the ghetto. The hospital's there. The doctors are still there. I can't get used to it here.'

'Can't you?'

'No. I can't.'

At seven o'clock in the morning – we're still asleep – the door suddenly opens and Marysia's standing there holding her six year-old son by the hand. She comes in. She's holding a heavy bundle in the other hand and she stands still for a moment without saying a word while Nina and I look at her. Something bad has happened, I think, because she's come unannounced and so early. I haven't seen Macius for nearly a year and he seems different, as if he's not ours. What's that coat he's wearing? So that's the coat from Hale Mirowskie that she told her father about on the phone.

'While I was here,' starts Marysia, 'Rachelka was waiting for me in front of the door of the house on Nowy Zjazd. Do you remember her? The waitress in Otwock. There was a locksmith's workshop in the basement with Polish workers. One of them saved her, brought her to Warsaw and now lives with her. "What are you doing here?" I asked her. "And who told you where I live?" "No-one told me. I watched you on the street."'

She watched Marysia on the street! She followed her. She didn't let her out of her sight. When Marysia turned right, she turned right as well. When Marysia stopped in front of a shop, she stopped too. She tracked her just like you track an animal to find its lair.

Marysia asked her what she wanted.

'I need Dr Frydman's address. I've got a three-year-old boy with me and he's very ill. I'm scared of an Aryan doctor. I'd like Dr Frydman to come and examine the child.'

'No, I can't give you the address,' Marysia said.

She turned round and carried on walking. Rachelka might have been telling the truth, but she might not have been. If she knows where Marysia lives then she can't stay there any longer. She'll be at her mercy and her life will depend on a nod of her head. Does she know Rachelka well? Perhaps the locksmith she lives with has told her to take advantage of the secret of where she lives and she's going to threaten to hand her over to the Germans. Who knows what she wants?

When Marysia came back later Rachelka wasn't there any longer. 'Wait,' we tell Marysia. 'Give the child something to drink.'

We get out of bed and throw our coats over our shoulders. We fiddle around aimlessly not knowing where to start. Macius doesn't say a word the whole time. He's indifferent and tired. He isn't pleased to see us and he isn't surprised at the poverty of the room. He holds his mother's hand all the time and looks sideways at the covered rectangle of the window. A frame with black paper stretched over it is placed in front of the window. It's so early that the light doesn't penetrate the paper. Marysia put the light on when she entered the room.

'What happened next?' we ask, shaking with cold, an internal cold that chills us through and through.

'It's the first time it's happened, but I panicked,' replies Marysia. 'I went into my room and started feverishly packing our things. I wanted to leave at once but it was already curfew time. I decided to wait until morning. I didn't get undressed at all. I lay down for a moment. I got up at four and packed this bundle, and left the house after five because the curfew's lifted by then.'

'Are we going out into the dark?' asked Macius. 'Yes, we are. We can't live here. Where we live has become unsafe, a hundred times more unsafe than it was before.'

But where are they to go? To the railway station for the time being. There are hundreds of travellers sitting there on the long benches. She'll sit down next to a woman with a basket and won't attract any attention. Macius will lean against her shoulder and sleep a bit more. So she goes there. Step after step. It's a long way from Nowy Zjazd to the railway station. The child walks next to her in the frosty February morning. When she arrived at the station and sat down among the travellers, traders with baskets and sacks, Macius leaned his head on her knee and immediately fell asleep.

Nina lights the fire with sawdust. When the coffee's ready we'll add the drop of milk left in the jug from yesterday. They should

225

both warm themselves up a bit. We take the blackout frame down from the window and turn the light off. The new day enters our garret even though the moon is still hanging over the chimneys on the roofs. We can already hear the first sounds of the day from the courtyard, a door being slammed, a dog barking, women quarrelling and shouting. We put Macius to bed, take his shoes off and cover him with a quilt.

'He's so pale,' we say. 'He's got dark rings under his eyes.'

'When I was sitting at the station,' continues Marysia, 'I noticed a man with a thick scarf round his neck some way away from me. When he passed me he didn't look at me at all but he was watching me from afar, it was obvious. I wondered if he was an informer and I suddenly saw a Polish policeman in a navy blue uniform in front of me. "What are you doing here?" he asked. "I'm waiting for a train," I replied, "I'm going to Lublin with the child." "You're Jewish," he said, "I'm taking you to the police station." "My papers are in order," I said. But I took Macius by the hand and followed him.'

'There were three Polish policemen at the police station. One was standing by the window, the second by the door and the third was sitting by the desk and writing. As soon as I entered the one who was writing said, "You're Jewish. I'm going to inform the appropriate authorities immediately." "Why are you detaining me? My papers are in order." "All right then. You don't want to admit it? We'll undress the boy." Macius was terrified and he started crying and then he choked from coughing. "Don't torment us," I said, "the child's ill. It's so cold that he's caught a chill."'

'"He'll get better in his grave," he replied. His words hit me like a bullet and I straightened up and said, "Many boys in our family entered the army of their own free will during the Great War to fight for Poland." Then I fell silent. I couldn't say anything else. I reached behind the fur cuff on my coat and tore out the bracelet I'd sewn in wrapped in a piece of white cloth. I took it out and placed it on the table in front of him in silence. "Not enough," he said. I undid my coat, reached into my bra, took out 2,000 zlotys and put them down in front of him in silence. "Where do you live?" he asked. "6 Nowy Zjazd," I replied. He waved me out. The other two, the one by the window and the one by the door, were looking at me indifferently when I walked past them.'

What could she do next? When she left the police station she suddenly realized that she'd given her real address. She could have thought up a different street and house number, couldn't she? Now

226

she really can't return to the flat. She's betrayed it. Where should she go now? To Zenon's? She'll go to Zenon's with the child, but only if the worst comes to the worst. The man's got a funny way of looking at you. And that silent mother of his. Perhaps she was in too much of a hurry and it was a mistake to rent the garret.

She knew the address of a certain pension on Wiejska Street near the Polish Parliament. The landlord was a Volksdeutsch called Elgiert who used to be a teacher before the war. The German textbook written by Lempicki and Elgiert was known in all secondary schools. His wife was Polish. He had a son of 17. He hid Jews in his flat in return for a good reward.

From time to time the alarm was raised in the pension. The Jews hurriedly left the flat and moved into spare rooms or to friends. That was when SS men came to the Elgierts for supper and when his son who was in the *Hitlerjugend* quarrelled with his father and threatened to go to the Gestapo and tell them about his Jews. He'd slam the door and leave the house and not show up for a few days. The father and son were arguing the day she went and no-one would even talk to her. So where should she go? What about Mrs Voelnagel who lent her the catechism? She should have gone there at once.

She got off the tram on the corner of Krolewska Street. As she was walking along Wierzbowa Street Macius started crying because he was tired, saying he wanted to go home. But they didn't have a home to go to. She was in complete despair when she rang Mrs Voelnagel's bell. 'I've got nowhere to go,' she said, 'I can't go home.' Mrs Voelnagel listened sympathetically but didn't discuss the matter. Marysia felt that she was prepared to help but it was clear she didn't want her to stay there.

Where was she to go now? To Bracka Street. She had the address of a pension there from a Polish doctor she knew. She went there. As soon as she entered the room she was shown to – she didn't even have time to take her coat off, all she did was take a roll wrapped in paper out of her bag and give it to the child, and then sit down tired on the chair – two men entered without knocking. They were both wearing caps and high boots. 'You're Jewish,' one of them said, 'we're taking you to the police station.' The other man didn't say anything. Perhaps he was new to the job and still felt a little uneasy, or perhaps it was he who'd tracked her down and had brought the other one along.

'I'm not going,' said Marysia, 'I'll give you 500 zlotys and please leave me alone.'

227

They took the money, pulled up some chairs and sat down.

'This place isn't sound,' the first one said. 'you'd better leave as quickly as possible. Who stays in a place like this? Only people like you when they haven't got anywhere safe to live any longer. Take my advice, won't you?'

The next day she got up while it was still dark. She left the money for the room on the table. She took her things, put her coat on, took the child by the hand and opened the door. Two men were standing in the hall by the door.

'How much?' she immediately asked. She couldn't even hear the sound of her own voice.

She glanced anxiously at the child. He was withdrawn and silent and he turned pale and suddenly withered like a plant.

'It's 200 zlotys,' said one of them. She paid at once, pleased not to have to pay more. Their fierce faces relaxed.

'You'd better get out of here as quickly as possible,' said the second one. 'I'll give you the address of a place where you can live peacefully and no-one will trouble you. I'm Polish and what I want is a free Poland' – while he was saying these words he struck his chest – 'and you can trust what I'm saying.'

She thought it over. She'd heard of many cases of Jews hiding with policemen or even secret agents in return for money. The black-mailer who preyed on Jews and hid Jews in his flat at the same time. But she didn't trust them. 'Thank you,' she said. As soon as they'd gone she left too.

Marysia spent the whole of the first day in bed. Macius gazed at the courtyard through the ragged net curtains covering the window. Through the holes in the embroidery.

'I can see a dog,' he suddenly says. No-one replies. We don't say much.

'I can see two dogs,' he says next.

'You've got to whisper,' Nina tells him, 'and don't walk around the room because your boots creak.'

'Marysia,' we say, 'buy him some slippers or some rubber-soled shoes because the neighbour might come as his boots are noisy. He'll give us away.'

'I'll buy some,' says Marysia.

Now Macius sits at the table in his creaking boots and draws.

'What is it,' asks Nina.

'It's a grenade exploding on a battlefield.'

'What's that?'

'Soldiers fighting on the front line.'

'Oh yes,' says Nina and thinks to herself that he's a soldier fighting on the front line, isn't he? She looks at his eyes, at the concentration on his forehead and at his fingers holding the pencil as if she's discovered a great truth.

That evening Zenon's mother said, 'Zenon said you're to lend him 3,000 zlotys because he needs some money.'

We decide that they want to take advantage of the position we're in. They've gathered that Marysia's left her flat for some reason or other. We pay 1,000 zlotys a month for the room. So 3,000 zlotys is three months in advance. Can we reckon on not being troubled for three months?

But Marysia is pursuing her own train of thought and she's worried about other things. 'That was too much,' she says. '2,000 zlotys for the blackmail in the police station was enough. It's a pity about the bracelet. I wasn't thinking clearly. I wasn't in control. It was all because of my meeting with Rachelka.'

We're silent for a long time. We weigh up what she's said. We're really sorry about the bracelet. We sent it over from the ghetto in December to a chemist's we knew on the Aryan side. It was sewn into a soft toy, a teddy bear. She could have sold it if necessary and lived off the money for quite a while.

At twelve o'clock Zenon's mother brings us our dinner as usual. Barley kasha with mushroom sauce and cabbage with potatoes. She doesn't look at us. She places the plates carelessly on the table and lays the table unwillingly. Maybe we're imagining it. Our hearts die and we wait anxiously for her to start talking about money. We don't enjoy dinner today at all. We swallow it with difficulty. What's been left unsaid hangs in the air like a grey curtain. She's collected the plates. She's at the door. Will she say anything about the money or not?

'Zenon's asking,' she says without turning her head, 'if he'll get the 3,000 zlotys. He needs the money.'

So she's said it. And she's waiting with her hand on the handle, with her back to us, for what we'll say.

'We'll discuss it. We've got to think about it.'

We don't say anything else. Mrs Jachimowicz comes at four o'clock. She's the one who arranges backdated registrations and the submission of documents for identity cards. She's a smart, fair-haired woman of thirty something. No-one knows she's Jewish. She's wearing a fashionable dark-red hat and a brown coat with a fluffy fox fur. She looks at each of us in turn with the eye of an expert.

'Jadwiga Tokarska and Alicja Majewska will collect their own identity cards. Aniela Gologowska too. But Stanislaw Majewski won't collect his. He'll receive a ready made one. It'll cost 5,000 zlotys.'

We pay her 2,000 in advance and give her our documents and photos. Marysia immediately asks her to get hold of new documents for her, including a marriage certificate with Ryszard Majewski. 'I've got to change my address,' she explains. 'I want to register at the new address under the name of Majewska, Alicja Majewska's daughter-in-law.'

Then Mrs Jachimowicz goes. We remain alone with our thoughts. Late in the evening the door opens and Zenon comes in without knocking. His eyebrows are drawn together threateningly. It seems to us that his face is saying: the fun's over now, we're going to have a serious talk. Nina jumps up from the sofa.

'Let's go to the kitchen and talk.'

They go to the kitchen.

'We haven't got a lot of money,' explains Nina. 'We'll pay you for next month even though this one isn't over yet. Here's 1,000 zlotys and 1,000 zlotys loan, 2,000 altogether. We can't give you any more.'

Next morning Marysia goes out. 'Don't forget to buy Macius some rubber-soled shoes,' we call after her.

First of all she goes to the food shop and rings the university library. Her landlady, Wanda Lubecki, is a librarian there.

'This is Marysia. Has anyone been and asked about me?'

'No. Nobody's been.'

'What shall I do now?'

'Wait a few days. The child can come back. Do you understand?'

'Yes,' she says, 'I understand.'

The minute she comes back we ask her, 'Did you buy the child some rubber-soled shoes?'

'I spoke to Mrs Lubecka,' replies Marysia. 'She'll have Macius back. But I've got to find myself somewhere else to live. I've got to start looking.'

Macius is with us in our garret on Wednesday, Thursday, Friday and Saturday. His boots squeak and he stomps about and talks noisily although we warn him not to. Marysia goes out every day to look for somewhere to live. She's so troubled that she keeps forgetting to buy him some shoes even though we keep reminding her about it.

On Saturday she says, 'I'll take Macius to the Lubecki sisters this evening.' Then she thinks it over. 'No, I'd better go early tomorrow morning. I don't want to steal into the flat. In fact I want the caretaker to see me.'

She walks through the still empty streets with Macius at seven o'clock on Sunday morning. Fog hangs in the air and grey vapours billow over the ground. It snowed in the night and the fine snow creaks underfoot.

'Are we going home?' asks Macius.

'Yes, we are.'

So she walks and the child walks beside her on this frosty February morning. As soon as Macius returned to the Lubecki sisters Marysia started feverishly looking for somewhere to live. She ran around all day long. She renewed all her former acquaintances.

'I rang Mrs Kazimiera Brzezinska,' she told us that evening. 'She's invited Nina to stay for a while. But it won't fix Nina up. Emilia is coming tomorrow morning at ten to look her over.'

'Where do you know Emilia from?' we ask.

'She's a good friend of Hanka Jachimowicz's, the one who came here. If she likes Nina she might let her live with her.'

Macius was back at Nowy Zjazd so that was one worry less. But there were so many left. Finding somewhere for Marysia to live and Zenon and us. Fixing Nina up.

'Have I got to leave?' asks Nina. She puts her head back and looks sideways at us. 'Father might come while I'm away.'

Emilia comes the next day at ten o'clock. She's a real lady. Zenon's mother shows her in respectfully. How old is she? Forty something with white hair and a young face. In the easy simplicity of her manner you don't feel any distance. She's a woman who attracts. While she's talking to us she keeps glancing automatically at Nina. She's observing her movements, listening to her accent and looking at her hair. And as I sit next to her I think to myself: this woman is sizing my daughter up with a strange measure. She's looking for Semitic features. Nina's black silky hair and her exotic beauty are unforgivable defects. Her beauty's got to be destroyed and transformed. We understand all this implicitly and know that there is nothing else in the way. Then Emilia gets up and says goodbye. 'I'll let you know,' she says, 'as soon as my tenant moves out.'

'I'm going out too,' says Marysia. I want to ring Mrs Brzezinska and tell her that I'll bring Nina along at nightfall today.'

Nina leaves at nightfall. At half past five, when the first lights are lit in the windows of houses. It's thawing. From our garret window we can see the fog hanging in the air. The fog will be Nina's ally as she walks around the Warsaw streets. The fog will disperse later and there'll be a fine rain and the rain will also be her ally. We wish for a storm with torrential rain because that would be her most effective defence. We believe in the beneficial power of storms and bombings, remembering the day in the ghetto when a few thousand Jews escaped from the buildings and courtyard of the *Umschlagplatz* one evening during the bombing.

Nina puts on her coat trimmed with the black Persian lamb bought in the market. She folds a woollen headscarf.

'Have you got your mascots with you?' we ask her.

She opens her bag and tips them onto the table: the velvet rabbit, the tiny duck with the huge beak and the weaver's shuttle which Olek Nimcewicz gave her in the ghetto.

'Macius is longing for a shuttle like that,' says Marysia. 'He's seen yours and wants it.'

'Not yet,' replies Nina. 'Not yet.'

She covers her black hair with the headscarf and carefully opens the garret door.

'Zenon's mother's out, Krysia's out, no-one's there and so I'll steal out quietly.'

She stands on the threshold deep in thought. She bends her head back and with that sideways look of hers she looks at the sloping ceiling, at the stove and at the stockings hanging on the line. She turns round and crosses the threshold. Marysia follows her and I'm behind her. As we're crossing the darkness of Zenon's room and then the darkness of the kitchen, I again want to tell this daughter of mine something very important concerning our future and the peace of our nights, but when Nina turns her head and waits for my words I forget what I wanted to say.

On 4 March at nightfall we were alone in the garret. There was no-one in: Zenon and his mother were both out. We were alone. Irena, Nina and Macius weren't there. Suddenly we hear someone knocking at the door. Marysia runs to the kitchen.

'Who is it?' she asks.

'I've come to see Karolina,' she hears.

Is it father? Marysia calls me to come. She calls quietly but I can hear her. I open the garret door and father has already come in. There's a foggy darkness in the room, the light from opposite suddenly strikes the pane and my husband seems unreal, as if he's flowed down from the foggy darkness. He smiles confusedly and looks round with surprise at the sloping ceiling of the mansard, at the poor uneven walls, and at the dark sharply delineated patch on the window. Did he imagine the place differently? Why doesn't he say anything?

'Your Nina has gone,' we tell him.

He's alarmed and shudders. At first he doesn't realize that she's gone to live somewhere else. We see how troubled he is. We can see something is tormenting him. He hasn't taken his coat off yet. He's standing there and thinking. In the end he sits down on the sofa. We tell him about Zenon because that's what's troubling us most. We tell him that he borrowed 2,000 zlotys from us and wanted more.

'We couldn't refuse him. What would you have done in our place?' We wait for an answer but he doesn't say anything.

We tell him about Irena. 'She's looking after a woman who's mentally ill. She hasn't got an easy life unfortunately but could she refuse an offer like that? Mrs Domanska is a really good woman. And Nina's at Mrs Brzezinska's. But she'll probably go to Emilia's shortly. Emilia came here and saw Nina. And you ought to know that we gave a Mrs Jachimowicz 2,000 zlotys deposit for your identity card. And there's a long story about Marysia and Macius,' and we tell him about Macius being in our garret for five days.

'What about you, daddy?' asks Marysia. 'Tell us when you're coming over to this side. Shall we look for somewhere for you to live now? You're not needed there, are you? Brandt laughed when he saw you, didn't he? He laughed because you were still alive.'

'I sometimes think,' replies her father and hesitates. 'I sometimes think that there's another reason why I should be in the ghetto. Something might happen to one of you or one of the family and then if I'm over there I could do something quicker.'

'That's nonsense,' Marysia interrupts. 'Nonsense.'

When we've discussed everything he tells us about himself. He doesn't live at Muranowska Street any more. He's moved to the Council.

'A fighting squad once came at ten in the evening.'

'What happened?' we ask.

233

'Nothing. I gave them 6,000.' He smiled. 'One of them took the shuttle out of the sewing machine but he replaced it.'

He also tells us that some of the people with passes spend the night on the Aryan side. They leave the ghetto in the evening and come back in the morning. They've got somewhere to live on this side.

'Remember,' we tell him, 'don't tell anyone here your name from your new certificate or what you're really called. It's not their business.'

'Yes, of course, I understand.'

He eats supper with us. The stove is red-hot and heats the garret up. So he take off his jacket and rolls up his shirt sleeves, and that's how he sits at table.

'It's 5 March tomorrow,' we tell him. 'Your birthday. We haven't forgotten.'

Then Krysia comes in. As usual she comes in without knocking. Father jumps up from the chair and introduces himself to Krysia. 'Szereszewski,' he says. But he sees our terrified faces. 'No,' he corrects himself, 'I'm Majewski.'

So he's betrayed us twice over. Should Krysia know our names? And what's more, what we're called now? The accommodation is temporary because even I don't want to stay at Zenon's. We think anxiously how weak and naïve and inexperienced he is. He doesn't know how to dodge the obstacles on this slippery ground. He's the one who needs looking after and encouragement, not us. And with a sudden flash we realize that he won't want to leave the ghetto. He'll always find an excuse for staying there.

He leaves next morning. He puts his coat on at half past eight. We follow him into the kitchen. In Zenon's dismal kitchen when I see he's about to open the door, I stop him. I want to tell him something that would sum up our life together but I just can't find the words. He lifts his hand and touches my hair. The door slams, and we listen to his receding footsteps. We run to our room and throw ourselves at the window. He's crossing the courtyard. We can still see him. Then the gateway swallows him up and he disappears inside it.

Two or three days later Nina came back to our attic. It was evening when she knocked. Zenon's mother opened the door.

'Are you back? Father came.'

'What? He was here and I missed him!'

She couldn't stay at Mrs Brzezinska's any longer because the ground was starting to burn under her feet. It was just about all right with the woman who came to do the cleaning. She wasn't to see Nina and so while she was working Nina locked herself into the servant's room. But the worst thing was that the room was requisitioned and a German clerk moved in immediately afterwards. So I was together with Nina again. Marysia found somewhere to live and left the garret.

One day a man from the electricity board came. He sat down at the table and wrote out the electricity bill. Zenon's mother was sitting next to him. The door to the garret wasn't closed. We could see his back and the back of his head. And suddenly he turned round and glanced at the door and his eyes met ours. What about it? Perhaps he didn't think anything of it. He saw two women sitting in the next room, an older woman and a young girl, relatives or guests. But when he'd gone Zenon's mother started grumbling. 'He saw you through the door. I was right then,' she said, referring to the key in the door.

Because as soon as we moved in to Zenon's the question of locking us in arose. 'I'm going to lock you in,' she said, looking at us sideways.

We wouldn't let her. 'What happens if there's a fire and there's no-one in? We won't be able to get out. We'll be burnt alive.'

Zenon's mother was a sullen old woman. Her narrow lips never smiled. All the time we were there we never saw so much as a ray of friendliness or even a shadow of goodness in her eyes.

She went to church on Chlodna Street at six o'clock every morning. Even though she was there at six, she wasn't the first. Other old women were always there before her. They had a severe old priest. 'Go away!' he told them. 'Go home. Wash the floors and play with the children.'

She told us about it one day in a moment of sudden sincerity.

As soon as Zenon came back she told him about the man from the electricity board. He sat on the bed and his face darkened. Perhaps he decided to take advantage of the incident. They whispered together. Then Zenon went out and was gone all evening. Krysia hadn't come back from work yet. She only came back at eight. But Krysia wasn't privy to plots like this, only Zenon and his mother. Perhaps they didn't trust her.

Next morning Zenon's mother said to us, 'Zenon said that the man saw you and guessed who you are. We've got to shut his mouth. We've got to treat him to a dinner'

'What dinner?' asked Nina. 'Who for?'

'For the man from the electricity board. A good dinner with drinks.'

'How much would it cost?'

'It will be 200 zlotys.'

She turned round and went out. She'd said what she had to say. She'd carried out her order. Then she brought our dinner. Always the same. Kasha with mushroom sauce and cabbage soup. She didn't say another word about the man or about the dinner. That was her way. She said something once and that was it.

We didn't turn the light on for a long time that evening. We sat at the table worrying. Krysia was the sister of Ola who had worked in Fira Epstein's shop before the war and Fira was a school friend of Marysia's. It was Ola who had given her Zenon's address. Ola was married and lived on Bednarska Street in the house where we were registered on false papers. If she was dishonest she could find out our real names and then make use of the information. Sometimes when we were depressed we started to worry about whether we could trust Ola. But we put it out of our minds.

Yes, that was Ola and this is her sister, but no-one knows Zenon or his mother.

'He'll squeeze the last penny out of us,' said Nina. She was nearly crying. 'We've got no choice. We've got to get out of this hole. It's lucky Marysia's found somewhere to live.'

A few days earlier when Marysia was walking along Chlodna Street she met a Polish school friend of hers, so she immediately told her she was looking for somewhere to live and asked her if she could help. It turned out that the friend's aunt lived on Lwowska Street and had some rooms to let. 'You can mention my name,' she said. 'She's called Wanda Grabowska.'

Marysia went there at once. Mrs Grabowska was in. 'Your niece told me to come. I was in the same class in school.' She kissed her hand as a sign of great respect. That's what the woman's niece would have done. But it was never the custom among Jews to greet anyone like that.

So the ice was broken. Mrs Grabowska had a suspicious nature and could sniff out an enemy in every stranger, but she took Marysia to her own room and asked her to sit down on a red-velvet armchair. Marysia told us afterwards that she'd never in her whole life seen such an overfurnished room. Everything was in it. A huge oak table covered with a velvet cloth, a plate of artificial fruit in the middle, a piano, two cupboards, a chest of drawers, a sewing-machine, a bed, a sofa and two low tables with albums on them.

There were holy pictures above the bed, the sofa and the tables. Mrs Grabowska revered St Anthony of Padua and there were figures of the saint on the chest of drawers. When she saw that Marysia was looking round the room she immediately said to her, 'I worship St Anthony, as you can see.' It didn't even enter her head that Marysia might not be Christian.

She rented her two adjacent rooms for 450 zlotys and Marysia moved in at once. So she lived on Lwowska Street: on the courtyard side on the first floor. She had to cross the courtyard to get to the flat. The caretaker lived by the gateway and his window opened on to the courtyard too. The window was an observation point for the caretaker and his wife and their three sons.

When Marysia came to see us she immediately noticed how sad we looked.

'Has something bad happened?' she asked.

We told her what had happened the previous day.

'You've got to leave. I'm convinced that Zenon didn't see the man at all. He's made it all up. It's just plain blackmail.'

She told us to pack some things, then poked her head out of the door.

'There's no-one in just now. I'll go and find a horse-cab. If Zenon or his mother come back in the meantime I'll go to Lwowska Street on my own and we'll wait for another occasion.'

She decided to take me with her to Lwowska Street and to take Nina to Emilia's at Zoliborz the next morning. For now she'd take her to Piusa Street, to Miss Rembielinska's. She ran downstairs. She went out onto the street and was immediately swallowed up by the darkness. It was drizzling and a grey fog hung in the air like a cobweb. She heard the clatter of hooves and an open horse-cab drove past. She hailed it. Then she ran upstairs again. We had our coats on and were ready. We turned the light off, closed the door behind us and ran downstairs. The horse-cab was standing in front of the entrance. Marysia and I sat on the front seat and Nina sat on the seat opposite.

'Where to?' asked the cab driver.

'Lwowska Street,' said Marysia. 'Stop at the corner of Piusa Street and Lwowska Street, please.'

'What if Miss Rembielinska isn't in?' asked Nina.

'You'll come and tell us. We'll wait for you in the cab.'

That's how we left Zenon's flat, taking nothing or next to nothing with us. We left our bed, our bed linen and our stove behind.

The cab stopped on the corner of Piusa Street and Lwowska Street. Nina got out and came back shortly afterwards. 'She's in,' she said. She nodded her head at us and dissolved into the darkness. The cab stopped on Lwowska Street. We entered the courtyard and then the hall in the side annexe. Did the caretaker see us? Probably not. It was so dark that he couldn't see anyone.

Marysia rang the bell. Two short, sharp rings. Is that what they'd arranged? When Mrs Grabowska opened the door she said, 'Don't be angry but I've brought my mother with me. She's not feeling well and I'd like her to stay with me for a while. She's very quiet and she won't cause you any trouble. There's no-one to look after her where she lives.' It looked as if Mrs Grabowska had only just got home. She was wearing a fur jacket and a black felt hat. She was holding the leather straps of a very old bag which was swinging like the pendulum of a clock. She was looking at me piercingly. But I could tell from her face that she hadn't guessed.

'Is she ill?' she asked. She must have been so pleased to get a tenant recommended by her niece in these uncertain times that she put up with my arrival. Or perhaps she was so surprised at Marysia's confidence and lack of constraint that she accepted it as normal.

'Go to bed,' Marysia said to me. She lowered the black paper blind and put the light on.

When I went to bed Mrs Grabowska came in. She was still wearing her fur jacket and holding the bag. She started fussing nervously round the room.

'I'm sorry but the room's not finished and there's no net curtain. I'll go and get the caretaker's son to put it up.'

She ran out of the room and shortly afterwards we heard the door shutting. The caretaker's son? We didn't have time to recover from our terror when he was already there in the room. And not just one son but two, one of eighteen and one of sixteen. They brought a ladder with them. They put it up by the window. One climbed it and the other handed him the frame with the net curtain pinned to it. They saw me. They kept turning their heads and looking at me. They thought it was odd to see a woman they didn't know lying in bed at eight o'clock. Marysia wanted to clarify the situation and so she came up to me with a glass of water and said, 'Do you want a drink, mummy? Are you feeling better? You can spend the night with me and then go home tomorrow.'

Then they left and took the ladder with them.

'The room will be habitable now,' said Mrs Grabowska. She was exquisitely polite. You might think that I was her guest. 'Shall I make you some semolina? Or an egg perhaps?'

So she didn't know yet. The time would come when she'd find out.

Nina stayed the night at Miss Rembielinska's, a clerk in my husband's office before the war. A young girl of twenty-three. She didn't have a responsible position. She was just a typist. She once needed some money and my husband lent her thirty zlotys. When the war broke out the office was closed down. After a while we moved to the ghetto. The walls were built and spiked with glass and the ghetto was going to be sealed off any day. It was November. In the last few days before the ghetto was closed Poles came to say goodbye to their Jewish friends. No-one came to us. None of the many people my husband worked with came. But Miss Rembielinska did. She came to say goodbye and to return the thirty zlotys he had lent her.

'You'll need the money now, Mr Szereszewski.' She had tears in her eyes.

My husband didn't accept the money. 'Please keep it,' he said.

Nina rang the bell of the ground floor flat where Miss Rembielinska rented a room. 'I'd like to see Miss Rembielinska,' she said. 'Is she in?' She was in. Nina went into her room, and stood in front of the white wall in her grey coat and with the blue scarf on her head.

'I'm Mr Szereszewski's daughter. Could I spend the night here? I'll leave tomorrow morning,' she asked shyly, bending her head back like she always did.

'Yes,' said Miss Rembielinska and quickly got up from her chair.

She was very hospitable. She didn't have a spare bed so she shared her bed with Nina. In the morning she went to work. But before she went out she pulled up a chair, covered the table with a serviette, put some bread and butter on a plate and a cup of cocoa next to it. When Nina woke up she was gone. Nina ate the bread and drank the cocoa and when she was putting the cup down it slipped out of her hand and smashed.

'I felt so sorry,' Nina told us afterwards. 'I hadn't even thanked her and then I went and broke her cup.'

Then she took the tram to Zoliborz. She got off at Wilson Square and went to the house where Emilia lived. There were already a few Jews in hiding there so it wasn't the safest of places to go but she didn't have any choice.

Mrs Grabowska was the widow of a retired official. She'd been on her own for many years and maybe that's why she was odd. She had a wealthy daughter but she didn't keep in touch with her. Layers of emotions had piled up in her heart and she found an outlet for them in religion. She was a devout Catholic and had a confessor in the Church of the Saviour. She went to confession every week. She was sixty-five and short and squat with greying black hair, a face that was marked by time, hunched shoulders and suspicious, piercing eyes. In the depths of her soul she might have been angry with her tenant for bringing her mother back without warning, but aren't Christians required to be merciful to the sick?

She spent as little as possible in order to save money. She ate very cheap dinners in a small canteen on Piusa Street near Aleje Ujazdowskie. The day after I arrived she brought me some tripe in an earthenware dish from the canteen. She really believed I was ill. She sat down beside me and handed me the dish covered with a clean cloth. It was probably an extra portion that she'd paid for. I tried not to accept but she insisted very wheedlingly.

'Please don't refuse,' she kept repeating.

She handed me a spoon and while I was eating I suddenly looked at her and noticed a change on her face. Her features had set, her eyes had become round. It lasted a second or two. But I knew at once that she'd guessed. She didn't let on at all. She was the same as before. She didn't give herself away with a single word or action.

She had only one key to the flat and as she often went out – it seemed as if she couldn't sit still – she left the key at the caretaker's. When she and Marysia both went out I was locked in. What happened next took place a few days after my arrival. I was lying in bed. The place had been empty for two hours. Suddenly I heard steps in the hall and then in Mrs Grabowska's room and then in the room next door as well, in the so-called reception room. At first I thought that one of them had come back, but I hadn't heard the key in the lock. So who could it be? Thieves?

The blood rushed to my head. What should I do? Get up and make a noise? The tenants will come out of their flats, the caretaker will come, the police will come. They'll say that I scared the thief off,

240

but then they'll ask who I am. They'll ask who I am and want to see my papers. But I haven't got any. There was no help for it. I lay in bed and listened to the rustling and the footsteps for about ten minutes. From time to time I could hear a chair being moved or the floor creaking. Then it was all quiet again. I was dying of fright that they'd enter the room I was in. But they didn't.

After a while Marysia came back. 'Do you know,' she said to me, 'I asked for the key but it wasn't there. I thought Mrs Grabowska had come back. I came upstairs and met the caretaker's son at our door. The youngest one. I knocked at the door but no-one opened it. I went to the caretaker's again and the key was back there again. Strange.'

I gathered from what she said that the caretaker's son was the thief. I told her what had happened. We were very concerned. Was this what we'd run away from Zenon's for, to risk an affair like this? Hadn't we jumped out of the frying-pan into the fire? We didn't know yet what had been stolen from Mrs Grabowska. She might even suspect me because I was alone in the flat.

She came home at one o'clock. She entered her room and saw the wardrobe and drawers open and everything in disorder. She ran into our room like a hurricane. 'I've been robbed – 36,000 zlotys have gone. What am I to do?'

'It's the caretaker's son,' said Marysia. 'I met him by the door.' She told her about the missing key.

'I'm going to the police station. I can checkmate them. I know they had a Jew in hiding. You'll be my witness.'

She looked at us and we could read on her face that she knew everything about us. She said something else too. Something that had nothing to do with the matter in hand – superficially at least. 'A Jew from the house opposite threw himself out of a window on the fifth floor today.'

'I must see father,' said Marysia when we were alone.

She put her coat on, went out and rang the Jewish Council from the shop she knew.

'Is that Mr Szereszewski?'

'Oh, it's you.'

'I'd like to see you tomorrow.'

'At nine o'clock in the same place as before.'

Next morning when Marysia was in the kitchen Mrs Grabowska said to her, 'Do you know I went to the caretaker's a few times yesterday and asked for Kazik, the youngest, the one you saw by the

241

door? He was out all day and he didn't come back for the night. He's run off. I must inform the police.'

'I'd like to talk to you,' said Marysia. And she laid out her cards. She told her everything, the whole truth. She gave her our real names and surnames. She told her about our troubles at Zenon's and how she'd run into her niece. Obviously she didn't want to have anything to do with the police. She was meeting her father at nine o'clock for his advice.

Mrs Grabowska replied just as honestly. She didn't want to mix the police up in the matter either. She had the money from selling some land in Milosna, but in fact she'd sold it illegally because she'd given a smaller valuation in order to pay less tax.

At nine o'clock Marysia was already in the bank on Kredytowa Street. The porter took her to a small room in the bank offices. Father was already waiting for her. He was anxious and in a hurry. He wanted her to go as soon as possible. He was worried about her. But he listened carefully.

'Don't mix the police up in it,' he said. 'I've got some plots of land in Wieliszew and I'll make one over to her. If she knows a notary she should get a deed of gift drawn up. I won't be able to give her the plot number because we buried the plan in the cellar on Muranowska Street. As soon as the deed is ready we'll arrange a meeting and I'll sign it. How's mother? Kiss her from me.'

Mrs Grabowska knew a notary so she asked him to draw up a deed of gift. She wasn't sure if the caretaker was mixed up in the robbery as well or only his sons. The youngest son had gone. He'd run off. The two older ones were still at home. Weren't they surprised that she hadn't called the police, that nothing had been written down and that their flat hadn't been searched? Marysia had come across one of them by the door, hadn't she? She could testify against him. So why had nothing happened?

It was a strange silence, full of insinuations. Each side spied on the other and drew its own conclusions. One week passed and then a second. The deed of gift was already signed by my husband with his real name and surname. Mrs Grabowska hid it in the cellar where she had a hiding-place. An ingenious and unique hiding-place, although why she didn't hide the money there that she received for the land I don't know.

It was a long time since I lay in bed pretending to be ill. I fiddled about the flat between our room and the kitchen. I didn't go out and didn't even approach the window. But every morning at seven o'clock I waited hidden behind the curtain. A Jewish work team from the ghetto passed at that time with armbands. Men and women. I didn't know where they were going. It might have been Narbutt Street or Pole Mokotowskie. There was a girl I knew from when we lived at 42 Muranowska Street in the group. She used to visit us sometimes.

When I heard the stamping of feet approaching I ran to the window. They came out of Noakowskiego Street into Polytechnic Square. They stamped noisily past our window. Then they turned into Polna Street and their footsteps became quiet in the distance. First I saw the grey mobile crowd with the white stains of armbands. Then I looked out for individual faces. Where is she? There she is, in a tight, blue, handmade cap. A moment later they disappeared round the corner. I could still see the backs of the people in the back row and then they were gone. They returned at five in the afternoon. And I watched them again, hidden behind the curtain.

Mrs Grabowska's flat was very strange. It seemed as if the furniture had been arranged without any consideration as to its usefulness. Our room was narrow with one window and contained a huge black desk which took up almost a third of the room. It served as a wardrobe for our clothes and linen, and as a pantry. There was another huge black desk in the so-called reception room. And a cupboard, but I don't know what it was for. It was like something you'd see in a chemist's. It contained a few books and old journals and a lot of various boxes and medicine bottles. Perhaps they were from Mr Grabowski's last illness and had remained as a souvenir.

The cupboard was made of yellow wood and had no door. It was unnecessary and useless and stood opposite the window. I looked at it and examined its contents in the same way as explorers examine islands they have discovered. I flicked through the twenty-five year-old journals, read the labels on the medicine bottles and guessed what illness they were meant to counter. There was a broken barometer on the wall. I could imagine the sick, coughing man looking at its pointers every morning.

In our room there was the bed that I slept on and Marysia's small folding bed. In fact it was more of a child's bed. Who used to sleep in it? It must have been Mrs Grabowska's daughter when she was small. I imagined that she was fussy and stubborn, never good and even-tempered. I imagined her lying in bed with her head on the pillow Marysia was now using. She probably slept under the quilt

I was using now. We'd left everything at Zenon's so we didn't have any bedding.

'We're really struggling,' Marysia sometimes said. 'We should get hold of our things and the new bed I bought recently. It would be really useful now.'

'Aren't you scared of going to Zenon's?'

'Yes.'

Now that I was living enclosed and my horizon had become small, shrunk to our room, the reception room, the hall and the kitchen, not only the furniture but even Mrs Grabowska became a source of incessant investigation. To tell the truth I didn't often see her. She was one of those women who is chronically busy. I knew she didn't have matters to attend to, it was all because of her nerves. I sometimes heard her talking to herself when the door wasn't properly closed.

Her room was a fortress. She didn't let anyone she didn't know into it. If the bell rang she approached the door stealthily on tiptoe and looked through the keyhole. If it was someone from the tax office, or any other office involving payments, she didn't open the door on principle. She watched through the keyhole until the caller gave up and left.

In order to save money she didn't use the kitchen range. It was hard to get coal. She got hold of a small iron stove, removed the lid and placed it inside the opening. In that way she could use the chimney draught with the minimum amount of coal. She talked Marysia into buying a stove like that for herself. I used the stove to boil water for washing, to make coffee for breakfast and soup for dinner. I flavoured the soup with fried onions but Mrs Grabowska couldn't stand the smell. 'What am I to do?' I asked, very put out.

'Don't worry about it,' said Marysia. 'I've seen her frying onions for herself. She can't stand the smell only when someone else is frying them.'

All our things, pans, glasses and milk jug, stayed behind at Zenon's. We had to start our household from scratch again. Mrs Grabowska gave us a shelf in the small kitchen cupboard. Marysia scrubbed it with soap and hot water. If she could she'd have planed it, she was so dubious about its cleanliness. What was the other side of the cupboard like? It was probably full of cobwebs because it hadn't been moved for years. She pushed it aside and what did she find? A white armband with a blue Star of David. She picked it up. Her fingers were trembling.

244

'Where did this armband come from?' she asked.

Mrs Grabowska was standing at her fuel-saving stove. She turned her head. Suddenly she blushed. She hesitated for a moment.

'It's mine,' she said at last. 'I went trading in the ghetto for a while. Through the courts on Ogrodowa Street.'

So she went trading as well? Many Poles milled about in the ghetto with white armbands. They bought goods and sold them on the Aryan side. It was forbidden. The Polish police caught traders like that but weren't able to recognize most of them. Amusing misunderstandings sometimes arose. My fifteen year-old niece was stopped by a policeman. She looked Aryan. He ordered her to show him her identity card. What he read was Anna Alicja Laskowska. No religion. He was sure she was Polish. She had difficulty in convincing him she was Jewish. My sister-in-law Stefania Szereszewska was stopped on Sliska Street. The policeman wouldn't believe she was Jewish. She took him to her flat. She rang the bell and her mother answered the door and said, 'Ah, you're back at last.' Then she saw the policeman behind her.

The discovery of the armband gave us a tremendous shock. It palpably brought us nearer to the ghetto. The small scrap of cloth contained a magical power because it took us back to the world we had left.

One evening Marysia went to Zenon's. 'We left your place,' she told him, 'because you were dragging us into expenses we couldn't shoulder. But you haven't lost anything on it. You took two months' rent in advance. I've come for our things, our bedding, our bed and our stove.'

He was furious and wouldn't listen.

'Didn't he threaten to hand you over to the police?' I asked when she told me what she'd done.

'No. He didn't say that. But he didn't want to let me have the bed or the stove, only the quilts and pillows. That's what I brought.'

Afterwards she regretted going. It was too risky.

She immediately returned the bedding Mrs Grabowska had lent us.

'What are we going to do with your mother?' asked Mrs Grabowska. 'Are we going to register her?'

It wasn't the first time she was asking. Registration. It was a problem. To register or not to register? If yes, then I'd have to go to the house administrator in person. But I didn't trust my appearance at that time. But I couldn't stay at Mrs Grabowska's without being registered any longer and endanger her and Marysia. I didn't want to either. Perhaps I should go somewhere else? Perhaps someone knows of somewhere I can live?

But first of all we should rent a room for my husband. That was the most important thing. He'd told us himself that some Jews from the ghetto had two places to live. The ones with passes even managed to spend the day in the ghetto and to sleep on the Aryan side. We wanted him to have somewhere to live in case he decided to leave the ghetto. In the end Marysia managed to rent a room in Zoliborz. It stood empty and waiting. It didn't wait long. Irena moved in. Marysia was informed that Irena should be got out of the way for a while.

Mrs Domanska belonged to the underground resistance movement. All sorts of people came to the flat and she closeted herself in her room with them. She brought underground newspapers back and Irena even read an article about the ghetto once. One of the people Mrs Domanska knew was arrested. Mrs Domanska was warned. She thought her flat would be searched. Irena went to Zoliborz and lived in her father's room. The owners' son, a young boy, brought her books from the library. He started borrowing money from her. His parents can't have known. He borrowed hundred zlotys from her twice.

Marysia saw her aunt Julia. She met her every Thursday in a small café on Wspolna Street. That's what they had arranged. She went straight to the point. 'Irena's got to leave Mrs Domanska's. It might be temporary or for good. She's living in the room I rented for father. I visited her and she feels terrible there. It looks as if the owners' son is blackmailing her so would it be possible to fix her up somewhere else?

'Yes. I'll give you Ada's address. You know who, the Swedish woman.'

'Shall I give you my address?'

'Your address? God forbid. I don't want to know.'

They finished their coffee and got up. Julia stood up first. She nodded her head and went out. Marysia left a few minutes later.

Ada Albin had a modern three-roomed flat in Mokotow. She had married a Swede years ago but was separated from him. He was in Sweden. Ada had a Swedish passport and a beautiful fifteen year-old daughter who was tall and slim and fair-haired. She went to the Queen Jadwiga grammar school. With her black eyes, reddish hair, a mediocre figure, a flat face – people must have been surprised when

246

they looked at Ada, and wondered what the handsome Swede who had married her had seen in her. She looked Jewish. She was often stopped on the street by informers who whispered, 'You're Jewish. Come along to the police station.' She let herself be taken. To the police station? Certainly. She was quite calm. She had no mean trick in her handbag.

'I handed them my passport with triumph and hatred. Because I loathe those German-serving dogs.'

She was good and she helped Jews as much as she could. She was sincere, uncomplicated, straightforward and trustworthy. People referred to her without any formality. Just Ada. Marysia went to see her. She liked Ada immensely. Could she take Irena in?

'A good friend of mine, Mrs Litwinowicz, is looking for a servant,' said Ada. 'We'll go there at once.'

'What about you?' asked Marysia shyly. 'Have you got a servant?'

'Yes. Jadwiga Hennert, the singer, is my servant.'

Marysia had heard of her. She was Dr Hurwicz's daughter. Ada put her hat on, pulled on her gloves, and they walked along Rakowiecka Street together. Ada told Marysia about Jadwiga Hennert.

'Do you know what? She took poison in my house. And when was it? When I had the house full of guests. Fortunately we saved her.'

It was very inconsiderate. Because, if she hadn't managed to save her, what would have happened next? The police, a report, investigations. It could even be dangerous for Ada despite her Swedish passport. Jews on Aryan papers who wanted to commit suicide shouldn't endanger the people they were living with. They could take poison in the open, or in a quiet avenue of a park, or on the staircase of an unknown house. It might have made Ada angry with Jadwiga Hennert. We wondered whether the Jew Mrs Grabowska told us about who threw himself out of the fifth floor window on Lwowska Street lived in the same house. We were sure he didn't.

Mrs Litwinowicz and Ada met socially and had many acquaintances in common. General Litwinowicz was in Romania. He had left his wife and daughter in poor circumstances. So Irena would have to pay for her keep.

'Believe me, if I could I wouldn't take money for your keep and I'd pay for your work as well. But that's what things are like.'

Irena went over from Zoliborz the next day. At nightfall during torrential rain. She put her wet coat on a stool in an alcove in the kitchen. There was an iron bed there that was going to be her bed. She took a picture of Our Lady out of her pocket and hung it up on a nail. The nail was in the wall and all the previous servants hung their pictures up on it. She came without her things. Just some underwear wrapped up in newspaper. Marysia, who was our family's public face, brought her the old, pink quilt which still remembered her childhood and which father had sent over to the Aryan side from the ghetto together with the other things.

At that time you could still get things taken over, at a price. Carts and lorries with rubbish, goods and food drove in and out of the ghetto. There were people who organized the smuggling of Jewish possessions. Our things didn't get through the first time. A fight followed by shooting broke out next to the German check-point, and so the lorry with our sacks hidden under the rubbish was sent back into the ghetto. But they got through the next day. The best things had disappeared, stolen out of the sacks. Our goods were addressed to a caretaker on Panska Street on the Aryan side. From him they went to other addresses. One sack to Alfred Kaftal on Ogrodowa Street, another to Mrs Krasnodebska, a dressmaker on Narbutt Street, and the third to Mrs Muszol on Marszalkowska Street. Mrs Muszol was a Reichsdeutsch German and she was even related to our family. She was the one Marysia brought the quilt from.

Mrs Litwinowicz had a three-roomed flat. She rented one of them to Lucyna, a secretive girl with slanting Tartar eyes. She dressed like a model, wore dresses that only reached her knees, and had long and lovely legs. She walked lightly and silently through the flat. She didn't walk but glide. She played the part of a vamp or a tigress. A handsome young man called Stefan visited her every evening. She used to fiddle about in the kitchen aimlessly. Usually she stood in the door and watched Irena in silence. Irena felt disturbed by her enquiring slant-eyed gaze. Was she mocking her? Was she putting two and two together, or had she perhaps already guessed her secret?

Mrs Litwinowicz's beautiful daughter Marychna lived in the second room, and Mrs Litwinowicz in the third room.

Irena quickly learnt to cook, make pastry, polish the floors and wash small items of clothing.

'Aniela,' Mrs Litwinowicz said to her, 'nip out to the shop for a packet of candles.'

Irena ran downstairs holding a large basket. She wore a cheap old skirt, a faded blouse, an apron and worn slippers and her hair was

248

plaited and wound round the back of her head. She was a merry girl. It was her mask. She always had a smile and a joke for the caretaker, and a funny story for the washerwoman who came to do the laundry. And so the caretaker was well-disposed towards the freckled girl from the general's lady and the washerwoman found a bosom friend in her.

'Do you belong to the brotherhood, Miss Aniela?' she asked. 'I'm a Child of Mary, you know.'

'Not yet,' replied Irena, 'but I'm thinking about it.'

'Before the war you used to pay a small amount each month and when you died you had a first-class funeral. I had a friend, her name was Pela, and she died after she'd only paid two contributions. They gave her a lovely funeral almost for free.'

She told Irena in the greatest of confidence that she had her suspicions about Lucyna. 'I think she's Jewish,' she whispered in her ear, 'but don't tell anyone for God's sake.'

Lucyna Jewish? Irena was rooted to the ground. No. It's impossible.

'Is that so? So Pela had a funeral for next to nothing?'

'Yes,' she replied and then confided in Irena that she was still a virgin although she was forty-two and had been in love with a plumber who lived in Solec for years. Irena confided in her and told her that she'd met a man who was a glazier and he was no longer young but she thought he'd taken a liking to her. Where had Irena met this man? Where could she meet him? You see, Mrs Litwinowicz's flat was nowhere near as safe as it might superficially seem. You can even say that Irena was sleeping on a volcano. Mrs Litwinowicz's cousin, Miss Wanda Jankowska, was in the underground resistance movement and every day she brought a packet of underground newspapers and hid them in Irena's bed. Two young gardeners came to the kitchen for the newspapers and one of them once gave Irena a beautiful bouquet of flowers. The glazier also came, a man of forty-five.

'He's taken a liking to you', said the washerwoman, very pleased. 'I know him. He lives on Sandomierska Street and he's a widower. I'll get him to come and see you one Sunday. He's a decent man and doesn't drink.'

He really did come. Not for the newspaper this time but to visit. He sat by the window and talked to her while she did the washing-up. Then they both went for a walk in Aleje Niepodleglosci. Irena felt safe and confident with him.

'Let him come,' said Mrs Litwinowicz. 'He can be your official suitor. Let the whole house know about it.'

After that he came every Sunday. He told her about his grown-up children, his family and his work. One day he even suggested that he'd teach her to read, because Irena was pretending to be illiterate. Apart from this official suitor Irena knew a cobbler who would also have willingly walked in Aleje Niepodleglosci with her. But he was shy. He mended her shoes for free and wouldn't take any money from her for anything in the world. Sometimes when they were out walking Irena and the glazier looked into the church.

'Did you go to church?' asked Mrs Litwinowicz. 'Couldn't be better. Did anyone from the house see you, the caretaker's wife or any of the neighbours' servants?'

'The caretaker's wife saw us.'

'That's good. Your position in the house will be safer.'

One day when she went shopping with the basket, Irena bumped into a woman who started laughing. Who was it? The caretaker's wife from the house on Narbutt Street where we lived before the war. Yes, it was her. Wasn't it a mistake to live on Rakowiecka Street and go out in the area which was just next door to Narbutt Street where so many people knew her? When she saw how pale Irena was, the caretaker's wife said, 'Calm down. I won't betray you. I'm only pleased to see you alive and well.'

A few days later she met Mrs Krasnodebska on the same street, our dressmaker from Narbutt Street. She wasn't scared of her. They hugged each other. We trusted her. But she once met the wife of Piotr, our caretaker from Poznanska Street where we lived before the war. She was really scared of her.

'Don't go out so often,' warned Mrs Litwinowicz. 'You're meeting too many people you know. I'll take the vodka round instead of you for a while.'

Irena distributed vodka to houses and restaurants, because Mrs Litwinowicz had to live off something. So she lived off secretly selling vodka which she produced and labelled herself, and off her bridge parlour. She had a gaming-house which masqueraded as a social meeting place. Irena wore a white apron and cap and served tea and sandwiches to the guests. They were exceptionally tasty sandwiches made of ham from the corner shop. One day the whole household went down with trichinosis. Some were more sick than others. Everyone had eaten the leftovers, hadn't they? They'd have been wasted otherwise.

250

The abandoned Jewish child which roamed Rakowiecka Street and usually knocked at the door and received a plate of soup didn't get anything for a day or two. Who was in a state to remember about that? Wanda Jankowska, good soul that she was, nursed all the patients. Marysia heard about Irena's illness via Mrs Muszol and was alarmed. It didn't enter her head that Irena could really be ill. Being ill meant being blackmailed or arrested. She went there at once. When she heard what had happened, she rang Dr Szymonski who was a family friend and a cardiologist and asked him to visit Irena. He went there several times but wouldn't accept any money.

So Irena was fixed up, thanks to Julia and Ada. As time went by she got used to her new ground and stopped being afraid. Her relationship with both Mrs Litwinowicz and her daughter was very good. The only fly in the ointment was Lucyna. She always felt vaguely alarmed in her presence but she couldn't understand why.

The room in Zoliborz was empty again and waiting for father. But it didn't wait long. It was occupied by Dr Leon Szereszewski, my husband's youngest brother. He had Aryan papers in the name of Roman Czyz, an officer in hiding. One evening when he lived on Chlodna Street someone knocked at his door. It was one of the people in the house although Leon didn't know him.

'I've come to warn you,' he said. 'You've got to move away.'

He didn't say anything else. Not a single word. He bowed and went out, closing the door behind him. So Leon moved into the room at Zoliborz. He was fifty-two at the time, tall and handsome with a straight and shapely nose and thick greying hair, there was nothing Semitic about his features. During the First World War he had volunteered while he was still a university student and he was a sergeant. He rarely went out even though his appearance didn't incriminate him. He was sad and depressed. To be on the safe side he didn't live with his wife. They had two sons, one thirteen and one six, and they both lived separately too.

Stefania Szereszewska, Irena Kosinska as she was called in her Aryan papers, knew where we lived and came to see us from time to time on Lwowska Street. She looked a hundred per cent Aryan. She had fair hair, blue eyes and a smooth, pink complexion. She wore large, round, pearl stud ear-rings. She had red lipstick, white shining teeth, and you could smell her perfume from a long way off. She wore a provocatively short, brightly coloured dress with a plunging neckline. She dressed like that on purpose.

'He's depressed,' she said about her husband. 'He can't stand the secrecy of it all. He'd like to go away somewhere.'

She had a room on Chlodna Street and Marysia even stayed the night there once. It wasn't her first room. She lived at Elgiert's for a while too and she wasn't even alone there because her younger son, Piotrus, was with her. Guzik, the former director of Joint, lived there at that time too, and a schoolfriend of Marysia's, Fira Epstein and her mother. She was helped in leaving the ghetto by her children's former governess, a Polish woman called Flora, and her manicurist, Jadwiga, who looked after her furs and the things brought out of the ghetto. Her valuables were brought out by Mrs Muszol.

To be on the safe side they didn't leave the ghetto at the same time. They sent their older son, Rysio, out first. He was red-haired and freckled. On the Aryan side he got into a horse-cab and had himself taken to Flora's. As they were driving along the cab-driver turned round on his box and said, 'I know you've escaped from the ghetto, my lad.' The boy was too surprised to deny it and the driver continued, 'Don't be afraid. You're a brave one. Everything will be all right.' With his red hair and freckles Rysio's appearance was a give-away.

'Weren't we in too much of a hurry to find him somewhere to live,' asked his worried mother leaning her elbows on the desk.

The conditions he lived in were bad. He lived at a teacher's in Saska Kepa. He was the third person in a room where there were two other Jews in hiding as well. He never went out. The others smoked cigarettes and he inhaled the smoke.

'The teacher keeps increasing the price of his lessons and we've got no choice. We have to agree,' sighed Stefania.

'What about Piotrus?' we ask. 'How's he feeling after his operation?'

There was a young Polish doctor in Warsaw who had made his name by operating on Jews. He operated on circumcised children, but adults underwent the operation too. His first patient, his first guinea pig, was Piotrus. The operation was said to be successful. The younger the child, the more successful the operation. Piotrus lived with an unmarried woman who had a villa on Madalinski Street. He was passed off as her nephew and even played in the garden with the neighbours' children. Yes, Piotrus is quite well fixed up, but he doesn't look very Aryan either. He never goes outside the garden.

'Let's talk about the most important thing now,' we interrupt. 'What do you think about leaving for Vittel? Do you believe in it?'

'That's exactly why Leon wants to go and see Edward. Have you got any news? Tell me what you know.'

He wants to see Edward? It must really be important to him if he is going to overcome his caution and go out into the hostile street full of evil eyes. He never goes to see his wife. She was pretending that her husband had deserted her, although that should have seemed strange on account of her exceptional beauty.

'Father mentioned it last time I saw him,' said Marysia. 'There was a German they trusted and he was sent to Switzerland with a huge amount of money. The money was given by the brushmakers on Swietojerska Street. The German is meant to be getting South American citizenship made for them. Father said there'd be papers for the whole family. I asked for papers for Dr Frydman and Anusia and gave him their photos.'

'But I don't want to go away,' says Stefania. 'I don't trust Germans. It's only Leon who really wants to go. I don't want to.'

'I've heard,' says Marysia, 'that Henryk Szpilfogel's aunt in Geneva, Lucja Hersz, is going to send papers for him.'

'I don't want to go,' says Stefania. 'I really don't want to go.'

'Guzik wants us to know that if we decide to go away he'll try to get big reductions for us.'

The only uncle of mine who was still alive, Maurycy Szpilfogel, was seventy years old. In his Aryan papers his name was Jan Wlodarczyk and he lived alone on Emilia Plater Street. His wife and daughter lived elsewhere. Dr Szymonski helped them to find somewhere to live. He had looked after my uncle and had been very friendly. My uncle's appearance was faultless. He was tall, slim and distinguished. No-one visited him apart from Dr Szymonski. However, he had to be consulted in a matter as important as leaving the country. Marysia wanted to talk to him. He didn't have a phone.

Dr Szymonski helped them again. They pretended to meet by accident on a pre-arranged day on Emilia Plater Street. It was just before nightfall, as dusk was falling. They walked along from corner to corner opposite Saint Jozef's hospital a few times. My uncle was undecided. He didn't trust this business, as he called it. At the same time he wanted to have the papers for himself and his family just in case. His family, meaning his wife and daughter Hanna Wyszewianska, Stanislawa Wawrzyniak as she was called in her Aryan papers. His wife and daughter lived separately. His wife pretended to be widowed and was always in mourning. She wore a large black hat and a veil that reached her knees. Hanna lived on Nowogrodzka Street. Of medium height, slim and graceful, elegant and with fine features, she trusted her good appearance.

It wasn't far from Nowogrodzka Street to Mokotowska Street where my second brother-in-law Edward was. Edward's wife, Bronislawa, had fair hair and blue eyes and often visited Hanna. Sometimes they even went out together at nightfall to walk along Marszalkowska Street. One day they were stopped by an informer on the corner of Wspolna Street. He told them to go with him to the police station. 'You're Jewish,' he said straight out to Hanna. She didn't deny it. She didn't lose her head. There wasn't a single German at the police station. Just Poles. She opened her bag, took out 2,000 zlotys and put them down on the table in front of them.

'Can I go?' she asked.

They nodded. When she'd gone they said to Bronislawa, 'Aren't you ashamed to go for a walk with a Jew?' One of them hammered on the table with his fist. 'You're putting yourself in danger. You could quite undeservedly get into trouble out walking with her like that. It's happened before.'

She thanked them for the warning and returned home to Mokotowska Street.

Edward Szereszewski lived at 76 Leszno Street in the ghetto. In the cellar belonging to his flat there was a supply of dyes which my cousin brought from Wola Krysztoporska at the beginning of the war. The dyes were bought by Kosowski who owned a chemical works on Chlodna Street. Edward's wife, Bronislawa, often went from Leszno Street to Chlodna Street to collect the money for them. In July 1942 Mr Kosowski moved his company to the Aryan side, to Dluga Street next to the Hotel Polski. When the resettlement action started Edward rang him and suggested that he buy the rest of the dyes which he had in store. Carts drove up into the courtyard of the house on Leszno Street. When the drivers saw Bronislawa with her fair hair and blue eyes and not at all Jewish looking, they couldn't get over their surprise. 'Are you still here? Haven't you got eyes in your head? Why don't you chuck everything and get on the cart with us?'

'But I've got children,' she said.

Her two children were playing in the courtyard, her six-year-old daughter and her nine-year-old son. Both of them were just as fair as she was.

'Are they your children? We'll take them with us too.'

'But I've got a husband,' she said.

'A husband? That's another matter. A husband's another matter completely.'

She left the ghetto in August through the check-point on Leszno Street. Edward stayed behind and often came to us for the night on Lubecki Street. Crossing the check-point cost 1,500 zlotys. Bronislawa didn't have the money on her. She gave the Jewish policeman a note addressed to my husband at the Jewish Council and asked him to settle the payment. In a gateway on the other side of the check-point she took off the armband with its blue star and threw it away. She didn't take any of her things with her. Only the children, the small girl and the boy. They took a tram to Wspolna Street. The house at 10 Wspolna Street belonged to our family. While the ghetto was still open she ran the house. Everyone knew her there but she went to the caretaker's wife all the same because she didn't have anywhere else to go.

There was a café opposite the house so she sat down by the window and watched everyone entering and leaving the house. She didn't see the caretaker's wife and sent her son to go and get her. He didn't find her as she was at church. She came back an hour later. They all three saw her going into the gateway. She sent her son over again and she came along with him.

'Can we stay with you until we find somewhere to live? she asked.

'Yes, of course. I took over a two-roomed flat a Jewish woman used to live in and you can move in there.'

'But everyone here knows me,' Bronislawa warned her.

'Don't worry. Nobody will give you away.'

She lived there for a month. A week later Edward left the ghetto. He was 54. Of medium height and slim with regular features. One day he went to the check-point on Leszno Street and said, 'I'll give you all the money I've got on me if you let me cross to the other side. I've got a Polish wife and two children and I'd like to see them again.' He spoke in German. They were surprised he knew the language so well.

'Where did you learn German?' asked the gendarme.

'I studied in Germany.'

'What did you study?'

'Philosophy.'

'Where?'

'In Marburg.'

'At Professor Cohen's?'

'That's right.'

'That means we're colleagues,' said the gendarme and shook his hand. But he couldn't let him through because his colleague would never allow it. He said the shift was changing soon. He'd be back at four and would help him through then. He told him to hide somewhere until then. Edward hid in the ruins of a bombed house. He returned to the check-point at four o'clock but the other gendarme wasn't there yet. The others took everything he had on him, his money, some jewels that had been his mother's and his watch. They made fun of him saying, 'Where do you want to go, Jew? You'll die anyway whether it's here or there.'

At last the other man returned. He talked to the others and humoured them and they let him through. When he left the ghetto he lived at Wspolna Street. Their papers were made by a man called Gutgold. He was the husband of a friend of Stefania Szereszewska's. He lived with his wife on Zabia Street and they had a year-old son who was not circumcised. They showed him off lying in his pram ostentatiously naked. The child was their best legitimacy.

'Papers?' said Gutgold. 'They'll cost you a pretty packet.'

Edward's wife took some jewellery out of her bag and put it on the table – a few rings and two or three brooches.

'This is all I've got,' she said. 'I'm giving it to you. I haven't got any money.'

He looked at it carefully, turned it over in his fingers, weighed up its value.

'It's not a lot,' he said. 'There's not much here. But too bad, I'll do it for you.' He believed her when she said she didn't have any money.

He had some papers made out for her in the name of Elzbieta Sieminska, unmarried with two children. Edward's were in the name of Wladyslaw Jablonski. When they had the papers Bronislawa went to Mr Kosowski and received the rest of the money for the dyes. He also gave her 10,000 zlotys as a loan, although she hadn't asked him for it.

'You might need it. You can give it back some other time.'

'Do you happen to know of somewhere to live?' she asked. 'We've been at our caretaker's wife's for a month now.'

He gave her his cousin's address and a letter of recommendation. Her name was Anna Keder and she lived in Bielany. She was separated from her husband. Her husband, an artist, was a Volks-deutsch. Mrs Keder took Edward and his family in warmly and when she heard that Edward was an artist she let him use her husband's workshop.

Marysia was living at Nowy Zjazd at the time. She once went to see them. She found Bronislawa in the kitchen washing Ewa's hair. Then Ewa sat on a stool and Bronislawa combed her long, thick, fair hair. The calm radiating from Bronislawa's face, the graceful child staring out of the window, and Mrs Keder bustling about the kitchen combined to give a feeling of permanence and safety. But the idyll only lasted until Edward admitted to Mrs Keder that he was Jewish. He couldn't lie. Just then red posters had appeared on the streets of Warsaw announcing that anyone hiding Jews would answer with their own heads. Mrs Keder was sensitive and nervous and she was terrified.

'You can't stay here, I'm sorry. I'm very scared. I keep thinking that my husband will want to have his revenge and he'll take advantage of this opportunity.' There were tears in her eyes. 'I'll willingly help you as much as I can.'

She went to Urle with Bronislawa and helped her get Ewa taken in by nuns. She advised Edward to put his name down at an accommodation agency and gave him an address. But for God's sake who used places like that? Mainly Jews. They were given addresses and they rented rooms and then they were blackmailed. Edward put his name down. He took the addresses they gave him but he had the foresight not to rent a room that way. Whenever he looked at a room he said it wasn't suitable. 'I'm an artist and I'm looking for a room with the right light. Have you got any friends where I might find what I'm looking for?'

And that's how he got hold of the address of the room at 18 Mokotowska Street. It was a large five-roomed flat. Two rooms were rented by General Kazbek from Georgia and his wife and sister. They were White Russians who were once wealthy but were now poor. Both the women earned money by making and embroidering women's underwear. Edward rented the third room. The small one next to it was occupied by the owners, Mr and Mrs Lewandowski, and the dining room was for communal use.

So Ewa was in an orphanage run by nuns and Edward and Bronislawa didn't have to worry about her. What about Jozio? What should they do with Jozio? Before Bronislawa left the ghetto my husband gave her the addresses of several of his Polish business

257

associates from before the war. She called on one of them. He advised her to put the boy in an orphanage in Otwock and gave her a letter of recommendation to give the headmaster in which he wrote that Jozio was the son of a high-ranking officer who was at present in London. He was accepted immediately. So Jozio lived in the orphanage and attended the elementary school. One day Bronislawa received a letter from the school headmaster asking her to come and see him. She thought they wanted to expel the boy.

'The boarders live in very bad conditions,' said the headmaster. 'This child comes from a cultured family and it's a pity for him to be wasted. There are three wealthy local families offering to look after him. He'd be well-fed and would lack for nothing.'

She thanked him warmly but didn't accept the proposal, saying that she could never repay the favour. However, she spoke to the boy's teacher, Mrs Balcerkiewicz. She knew she was the poor widow of a policeman and was bringing up three stepchildren. She knew her because she sometimes visited her to find out how Jozio was doing at school. She knew she was kind-hearted. And since she was poor she couldn't have any enemies. Bronislawa asked if she'd take her son in as a lodger. She agreed.

He was one of the best pupils and was good at poetry too. He wrote a poem about the sea which delighted not only the children but even the teachers. A few months later he was confirmed by the bishop together with a group of other children of the same age. The parents were invited to the ceremony and Bronislawa went too.

'What was poor Jozio to do? Not be confirmed?' she asked sitting at our black, galley-like desk. 'He had to dance to their tune.'

'What's his confirmation name?' we asked.

'Dominic.' She was silent for a moment and then she said, 'He's happy at the teacher's. She helps him do his homework and looks after his clothes and food as best she can. The servant, Walerka, is very good to him. But what happened? It turns out that she's Jewish, the sister of Henryk Szpilfogel's wife.'

Jozio had had the same operation as Piotrus. But there were complications as the wound wouldn't heal. He came to Warsaw for dressings for a long time.

'Anyway he comes home once a week specially to have a bath. He won't bath at Mrs Balcerkiewicz's for anything in the world,' said Bronislawa.

She's sitting on the bed. On the small bed Marysia sleeps on. We look at her wavy, fair hair. On the tip of her head she's wearing a tiny, handmade cap. As we look at her we both think it makes her look skittish.

'Does Jozio know about Walerka?' we ask.

'No. How can he? If he knew he might agree to have a bath there. No-one's telling him just to be on the safe side. Do you know what? A Jewish family lived in the house. A father, mother and two children. Someone informed on them and betrayed them. Jozio was watching through the window and saw them being led off.'

Jozio in Otwock, Ewa in Urle. Bronislawa visited her every week. She knew that the Lewandowskis didn't like children and she wanted to keep Ewa in the orphanage as long as possible. Ewa showed her mother round the garden, the corridors, the dormitories and the chapel. 'Look how lovely it is here,' she said. But when her mother was leaving she stood at the gate and cried, 'Take me away from here as quickly as possible.'

One day Ewa fell ill with jaundice. 'She's ill,' Bronislawa told Mrs Lewandowska. 'I don't know if my relations in the country are looking after her properly.' She didn't say that Ewa was in an orphanage because it would seem strange.

'Bring her here,' said Mrs Lewandowska. When she saw Ewa with her grace and her fair plaits, she forgot she didn't like children and even grew to like her. One night the Gestapo came. They were looking for someone who had lived there two years before. They checked Edward's papers and made Bronislawa get out of bed but fortunately they didn't check her papers. Ewa was asleep. They looked at her. Next day everyone knew that a whole family called Sieminski, the same name as Bronislawa had in her Aryan papers, had been arrested in the side annexe.

When the Lewandowskis decided to move out of Warsaw, Edward rented their room as well. It was a narrow room next door and Jozio slept there when he came from Otwock. Edward didn't look as Aryan as his brother Leon. His gait betrayed him. You could see he was Jewish even if your eyes weren't particularly sharp. Which meant he should have gone out on the street as little as possible. He should have stayed at home as much as possible.

'He makes mistakes,' Bronislawa told us. 'When the Gestapo came he spoke German with them.'

'What else?'

'He plays chess with the servant's son. He's a tram driver. No Pole would do that.'

One day a Polish policeman came to the flat. In fact there were

259

two of them, a policeman and an informer. Who had sent them? Who could have sent them. Only the caretaker from Wspolna Street. His wife even warned Bronislawa about him. 'He's my second husband,' she said. 'I married him during the war. I'm even scared of him myself.'

'I know you're Jewish,' the policeman said to Edward. 'You're going to pay me 3,000 zlotys a month. You won't tell anyone about it, not even your wife. It's a secret. And you'll sign a statement saying that you won't bring any charges against me.'

The informer didn't say anything. He just stood and listened. Edward gave the undertaking. And he paid him 3,000 zlotys regularly each month. The informer didn't come any more. Just the policeman. And despite the blackmail Edward didn't move out.

There were many unhappy people who were persecuted by the police or informers. Every so often someone turned up who wasn't to be trusted, who was always hostile and who disturbed our relative peace day and night.

'I met an informer in the gateway in front of the caretaker's flat,' said Mrs Grabowska one day.

I was frying potatoes on the fuel-saving stove just then. Potatoes fried with a piece of finely chopped pork fat were our staple diet. We ate them every day for dinner and supper, and if we had any left over from the day before we had them for breakfast as well.

'How did you know he was an informer?' I asked. But I didn't say it loud, only quietly. I was in the kitchen and in the kitchen you had to whisper.

'You can tell. They have a special look about them. I wonder what kind of deals a pig like that can have with the caretaker or his sons.'

We didn't eat meat every day. In fact we ate meat in exceptional circumstances, for example, when we invited Mrs Grabowska to dinner, which didn't happen often. Marysia bought vegetables, butter, cheese, pork fat and kasha in the market hall on Koszykowa Street near Lwowska Street. She felt confident in the noisy crowd of traders and shoppers. But in fact the market halls weren't safe. Policemen and informers looking for Jews were always milling about in them. Not without reason, because Marysia often met people she knew from the ghetto in that human anthill.

'Do you know who I saw in the market today?' she'd say and tell me who she'd seen.

'Did you go up to him?'

'Of course not! I pretended not to know him.'

One day she met Dr Fejgin's mother, a relative of ours, in the market. 'Do you know Edward and Leon Szereszewski's address?' 'I can't tell you,' said Marysia. 'But I can arrange to meet you and I'll tell them I met you. Do you need money?'

'I only want the address so that I can see them personally.'

One day she noticed a woman selling lemons in the market, a rarity at that time. 'How much are the lemons?' she asked. The price seemed incredibly high. 'Jesus Christ!' she said. She was surprised at herself for saying it. It was probably the first time she'd said something like that. She wasn't in the habit of manifesting her assumed Aryan nature. Some Jewish women overdid it with calling on the saints and Our Lady, and so they gave themselves away because the Polish intelligentsia would never say things like that.

'You haven't had anything to do with him and now you're on intimate terms with him,' replied the trader glancing at Marysia.

The incident gave her a lot to think about and even knocked her off balance for a while. She started doubting her appearance and lost her self-confidence. So she didn't look a hundred per cent Aryan after all. If the market trader sensed she was Jewish, what about other people? Yes, other people sensed it too, or had she forgotten about that already? She was walking along Wilcza Street with Bronislawa one evening. They were looking for a house number in the dark. A passer-by trained the light of his electric torch on them for a second, for just one moment. 'Jews,' he shouted. Fortunately there weren't any Germans nearby. And once under the bridge at Solec; she met Henryk Falencki there and she even had Macius with her. A couple walked past. 'Jews,' they said looking at them.

Now she was thinking about all these incidents as she ate her supper at the black desk – bread, butter, a piece of cheese, and fried potatoes in an aluminium frying-pan. She'd bought the frying-pan with its black handle and two pans, one for soup and one for milk, in the market hall on Koszykowa Street as well.

There were always a lot of peelings in the bin because of those potatoes of ours and it was Mrs Grabowska who emptied the bin. Marysia felt guilty about it. 'Most of the rubbish is ours and I should take it out, not you. You don't eat at home,' she said.

'But I don't want you to spend too much time in the courtyard,' replied Mrs Grabowska.

In the evening we covered the windows with black paper blinds. The light was only on in our room and the kitchen. The kitchen was dark, cold and smoky but we liked being there. However it was right next to the front door and so I had to whisper and walk quietly in there because I wasn't registered.

'I spotted that informer today on Lwowska Street opposite the gateway,' said Mrs Grabowska in the kitchen, looking straight in front of her.

'What can he want?' asked Marysia.

'Maybe he's sniffed out there's been a robbery and he's surprised that the police weren't informed.'

But who could have informed him? Who could have told him about it? The whole business seemed dark and mysterious. Whose side was he on? Was he following the caretaker's sons or Mrs Grabowska? Or did he have his eye on Maria Majewska, her tenant?

'Who am I really?' asked Marysia that evening as she was getting undressed. 'If I'm down as a dressmaker then where's my sewing-machine? It would be good if I had it here.'

Early next morning she went to Alfred Kaftal's on Ogrodowa Street and brought her sewing-machine back with her. Father had had it taken out of the ghetto together with the other things of ours and it had been taken to Kaftal's from the caretaker's on Panska Street.

Marysia always had something to do and went out to town every day. She had to see someone urgently, or go to her sisters, or bring something, or take something to someone. She was always on the move and that might have been suspicious for the caretaker and his sons, because if she was a dressmaker, then when did she sew? I, on the other hand, led a life of contemplation. I was locked in.

I was anxious and worried because I was never sure if Marysia would come back. But the time stretched into infinity when I was alone so I had to fill it. I wrote my autobiography. I amused myself by writing a fictional autobiography of Alicja Majewska née Biernacka, the dead woman whose name I now had. I lived her life, experienced her feelings and felt her ghost behind me. I imagined she was like me, dark, shy and sensitive, a cross-eyed girl with my complexes and inhibitions. I reached back into the earliest years of childhood and poured all my very first memories into her.

My singing nannies, Jozia and Marcela, were Alicja's nannies too. Jozia Kozubka and Marcela the witch whose soul knew how to wander over the world and had to be summoned back to earth. Marcela was the storyteller and Jozia Kozubka was the singer. A singer by God's grace, an inexhaustible treasure. Short, slim, dark-haired, ugly, she sang like a bird from morning to night. She sang because she had a need to sing. In my eyes that inconspicuous girl was the personification of the world of poetry, the world of adventures and mysteries.

During my long, lonely hours at Lwowska Street, I illustrated Jozia's songs with a pencil and crayons. I remembered them and resurrected them from the depths of my memory.

'What are you drawing?' asked Mrs Grabowska. I showed her my drawings. 'They're lovely,' she said.

Every day, hidden behind the curtain, I watched Polytechnic Square. As I stood there I thought to myself that if I watched for hundreds and thousands of years and hundreds of thousands people walked past, even then the people I longed to see would never walk past again. But one day a young woman I was related to, and who I knew was on the Aryan side, crossed the square. I would never have believed that she'd dare to go out on the street because she had Semitic features. She walked towards me not knowing that I was watching her every step.

'Would you believe it,' said Mrs Grabowska that evening, 'I saw that informer again in our gateway today. I went up to him and asked him the time.'

'Why? Why did you ask him?' Marysia didn't have to whisper because she was registered.

'Because I've thought something up. I think it'll be better if I get to know him,' she answered and smiled cunningly.

Locked up in the flat I moved around like a ghost or an apparition. I walked silently from our room to the kitchen, the destination of my silent journey. If anyone rang I stood stock still without moving or breathing and waited until the visitor gave up and left. Sometimes I was so tired of my life-style that I wanted to escape from this cage where time passed by on bitter thoughts. At times like that I swayed as if I were drunk and if I could I would have smashed the walls imprisoning me with my fists. I walked automatically from one black desk to the other, touching their tops and opening and closing their drawers. Every item inside them, even the smallest scrap of material, was connected with our home and had its own eloquence, albeit sometimes tragic.

A coat lay in one of the drawers for a while. It belonged to my brother-in-law Karol Laskowski. When he lived on Walicow Street he gave it to a tailor to be altered. We collected the coat after he died.

The coat with its grey and green weave had come over from the ghetto to the Aryan side together with our things. We gave it to Anusia Laskowska, my niece. Our house at 6 Walicow Street was blockaded on 28 July 1942. Anusia was at Harry's but her mother died during the blockade. Next day I met her on Ciepla Street. 'You haven't got a mother any more,' I said. 'Break it off with that boy of yours and come and live with us.'

'We got married at Professor Balaban's,' she replied.

'We live in Tarasiewicz's house on Grzybowska Street now. We're waiting for you.'

'All right. I'll come.'

She didn't come. She wasn't truthful. We knew you couldn't rely on her word. I found out later that they slept at Walicow Street that night. Next morning they took two suitcases of things with them, gave one of them to the police instead of money, and crossed the wall to the Aryan side. The boy was short and thin and Jewish looking while Anusia looked Aryan. They lived in Radosc near Warsaw. Stefania Szereszewska was there at the time and met them one day.

'Leon's in Warsaw,' she said to them. 'I'd like to send him the stamp album to sell and fifty dollars. I don't know his address but I know Edward's address. Leon will pick the things up from him. Could you arrange it?'

'Of course.'

Harry made Aryan papers for Jews in hiding. Which meant he had contacts. Many people lived off dealings like that. People who made papers, Poles or Jews who didn't look Jewish, were trusted by their clients. They came to where they lived. They knew their address. But we heard rumours that Harry was blackmailing his clients. He was a boy who went off the rails, and with his looks he shouldn't have gone out too much. However, it was unavoidable in his line of business. There was no doubt that he was using Anusia. He was the brains and she the tool.

They didn't give Edward the stamps or the dollars. We heard they'd gone to Krynica. They turned up again some time later. They knew Edward's address. Anusia went to ask him for money and kept coming for more. Edward gave her it because he was afraid of her and he felt sorry for her. One day she said she was pregnant. Edward got her into a clinic on Lwowska Street and even visited her once.

'I'd like to see auntie,' she said. 'What's her address?'

He said he didn't know.

Marysia once met Anusia and Harry on a tram. She sat down next to her and whispered in her ear, 'Leave him. I'll fix you up at a dressmaker's. You can sew, can't you?'

Harry was standing apart and he didn't take his eyes off them, with his black anxious eyes set in a thin, dark face.

'All right,' said Anusia.

'Let me know via the German shop if you decide on it. I'm getting off here.'

'I'd like to see auntie,' said Anusia.

Marysia got off the tram without replying.

Mrs Muszol had a shop selling lamps and kitchenware on Graniczna Street. Marysia left 3,000 zlotys there every month. Anusia came on the first of every month and asked, 'Is there any money for me from Mr Wroblewski?' Then the money was given to her. It had been arranged like that. Anusia wasn't to know of any threads connecting Mrs Muszol to Marysia. That's why the fictional Mr Wroblewski had been made up. Because she might make use of anything to extract money, all kinds of contacts, not so much her as Harry, who always came with her, and waited on the other side of the street.

'He was waiting for her again,' Mrs Muszol's son Mieczyslaw told Marysia. 'Maybe he's afraid she'll run off when she's taken the money.'

Maybe she's afraid of him, maybe he threatens to kill her if she leaves him – that's what I worried about sitting at the black desk at Lwowska Street. Or maybe she loves him so much that . . .

Stefania Szereszewska felt guilty about giving them Edward's address. 'How could I have known?' she said to justify herself. 'I trusted them. Anusia's one of the family after all, isn't she?'

But if Anusia hadn't gone to Harry's that terrible day she'd have died together with her mother. It was also fortunate for her that he persuaded her to leave the ghetto quickly, because even if she'd stayed with us she could have died during one of the actions. I remembered about that on Lwowska Street as well.

'I'll tell you something, Mrs Majewska', said Mrs Grabowska. 'I bought two kilos of pork fat today and gave it to that informer. He won't come any more.'

It never came out from whom that man found out about the robbery. He must have realized something and couldn't understand why the police hadn't been informed. He'd probably been watching the caretaker's family for a long time because it can't have been the first little business they were mixed up in. The pork fat was bought at our expense. We paid for it willingly and sighed with relief.

A young girl like Irena can be fixed up, providing the goodwill is there. It's harder to fix up her mother, particularly if she's got dark hair and a dark complexion.

'What about your mother? Are we going to register her?' asked Mrs Grabowska.

It wasn't the first time she was asking. Registration. That was my nightmare and my obsession. If I registered I'd have to go to the house administrator myself but I didn't trust my appearance yet at that time. It tormented me. I paced from wall to wall in our room thinking about it. I chewed and digested the same thought over and over again. To register or not to register? It seemed as if the matter was hopeless and I'd never have enough strength to make a decision. But I was endangering Marysia and Mrs Grabowska by living there without being registered. I knew it and couldn't bear it. Perhaps I should leave and hide somewhere else?

Mrs Grabowska is always in town and keeps coming home with a new idea.

'I heard there's a woman in Stare Miasto who wants a sub-tenant.'

'Who is she?' we ask.

'She's poor. One room. She'd let you have a corner of it.'

We agree to that. But we want to know the traps and dangers, the bad sides of the arrangement.

'The toilet's in the courtyard.'

The toilet's in the courtyard. That's terrible. The other residents might see me a few times a day. They might watch and wonder about my face and about me.

'What else?'

'There's no tap. The water's in a bucket in the corner of the room.'

'The water's in a bucket. What else?'

'Her son lives with her and he's very ill.'

We don't say anything. We consider it. Marysia gets up off her chair. 'I'll ring Mrs Lubecka. She might be able to help us.' She goes to the shop, the small food shop on Lwowska Street, and rings. 'Could you visit me? I'd like to talk about something with you. Is the child well? Thank God.'

Mrs Zofia Lubecka comes two days later. She sits down on the small bed. She's pleasant, talkative and friendly.

'What do you think?' asks Marysia. 'How does my mother look?'

266

She looks at me. She studies my face, my movements and my figure. Emilia studied Nina in exactly the same way in the attic at Zenon's when she was looking for Semitic features which could betray her.

'Quite well. I'm wondering whether to let your mother have a room in our flat. Your smooth hair and your reserve are good. You'd have to always dress in black and go to church every day. If anyone asked us, we'd say that she's a relation of ours from the country and a bit of a religious fanatic.'

It wasn't possible for me to move in at once. For the sake of Macius' safety. But Mrs Lubecka had given me self-confidence and that was the most important thing at the moment. I even thought I might be able to force myself to go and register.

'Listen,' I said to Marysia one evening, 'why don't I go to the room you rented for father? The name on his papers is Majewski, just like mine. We agreed when we were still in the ghetto that I was going to live with him, that I'd wait for him. Perhaps when he hears I'm already there he'll make his mind up quicker and come over.'

'Leon's living there at the moment. He hasn't found anywhere else yet.'

Could I oppose that? There was nothing I could say.

Shortly afterwards, early in the morning when we were still in bed, the bell rang. Mrs Grabowska was out in town already. Who could be ringing so early? A neighbour? Mrs Grabowska didn't have anything to do with her neighbours. The tax collector? It was too early. Marysia moved the black paper window blind aside, threw a dress over her night-dress and went into the hall barefooted. Remembering not to let any strangers in she quietly approached the door and looked through the keyhole. It was Mrs Grabowska's observation point. The key hung on a nail and the lock was covered with a piece of cloth which you raised and replaced. She saw a policeman in a navy blue uniform. He was ringing more and more insistently. He represented authority, whether she liked it or not. Who knows, he might break the door down if she doesn't open it. The robbery flashed through her mind. Someone must have informed the police. But it wasn't Mrs Grabowska, so perhaps it was the caretaker's sons. Or maybe they'd remembered the woman who was in bed when they put up the net curtain and informed the police that she was Jewish.

'Does Mrs Luczak live here?' asked the policeman when Marysia opened the door.

'No.'

'We'll see about that.'

He crossed from the hall to the reception room, looked at the strange wardrobe and the vase with its peacock feathers, and opened the door to our room. He saw the desk, black and huge, extensive and deep. He sat down at it. Without saying a word he opened it and pulled out the drawers and rummaged among the things. He was clearly looking for something. What was he looking for? I lay in bed and didn't take my eyes off him. What was he looking for? A gun or a radio – we didn't know.

'Has a man spent the night here?' he asked.

'No,' replied Marysia. She was standing next to him with her hair not brushed and wearing her brown and black striped dress. You could see her night-dress underneath.

'What's this?' he shouted fiercely, pulling a pair of men's gloves out of the drawer, grey suede gloves.

'My husband's gloves. I'm keeping them to remember him by. He died in the war. They were his. I'm keeping them.'

Suddenly he turned round and looked sharply at me. 'Who's this?'

'My husband's mother.'

'Is she Jewish?'

'Of course not. She's Catholic. She's Polish.'

'We'll see about that. Get dressed and come with me to the police station. We'll check your papers.'

'Mother's ill and won't go with you. How much do you want? I'll give you 500 zlotys.'

'Give me 3,000.'

'But 3,000 is too much. We haven't got that much.'

'Then I'll take 1,000 and not a penny less. She might be Jewish and we could find it all out in the police station. Not a penny less,' he repeated and threatened her with his finger.

She gave him 1,000 zlotys. She put the money down in front of him on the black desk. His tone changed immediately. He became friendly, even familiar.

'How do I know you won't come again or send someone else here?'

'I won't come on my word of honour. You can trust me.'

We didn't say a word to Mrs Grabowska about this incident. We were afraid she'd ask us to leave. We were terribly anxious. But he didn't send anyone else, and didn't come himself either.

A white armband with a blue star was found behind the cupboard in the kitchen. That dirty, creased rag contained a magical power. It brought us face to face again with the world we had left and which ought to be erased from our minds if we wanted to survive. Woebegone expressions and sad eyes, so characteristic of people in the ghetto, had to be eradicated on the Aryan side. We could not shed tears for our loved ones who were gone for ever. If the tears flowed our eyes would be red and sunken, our faces pale and pre-occupied, and anyone who looked carefully could guess our secret. Self-confidence. That was the quintessence of living in our new surroundings. You must like each passing day and have a spring in your step on the street.

That's what we were thinking one April morning when Fira Epstein was sitting at the desk. She was called Zofia now. Zofia Pawlowska. She lived in Zoliborz. The last time Marysia met her was in Elgiert's house on Wiejska Street. She'd gone there holding Macius by the hand one frosty February morning, when she didn't have anywhere to go. At that time my brother-in-law Leon Szereszewski, Guzik from the Joint and two or three other Jews were all living at Elgiert's. Fira was the servant there. She opened the door when Marysia rang.

'Listen,' she whispered to her, 'I'm getting out of here. I'm going to Zoliborz.'

She gave her the address. She didn't say anything else. Just those few words. She turned round and went back inside the flat. She was wearing a black satin dress, a white apron and a cap.

When life settled down somewhat, when we could let up slightly, Marysia went to Zoliborz. She found the flat where Jan Marcinkowski, the policeman, lived. He was about forty-eight, tall and sinewy with a thin, energetic face. He was a widower and didn't have any children. In his small flat in the side annexe of the house he hid not only Fira who was fair-haired with blue eyes, but also her friend Irka Weinberg, a woman whose appearance was decidedly Semitic. Fair-haired Zofia Pawlowska was thought to be the police-man's niece, or she might even have been his god-daughter. She looked after the flat for her uncle – that's what the neighbours were told, enough to satisfy them. Every morning she took a basket and went out shopping. On Sundays she went to church. She didn't say much. She was careful. She was born in Russia and she still had the accent and intonation of Russian Jews. Irka Weinberg never showed herself. She lived in isolation.

Now Zofia was sitting at our desk. She was wearing a grey costume with a red fox fur over her shoulder.

'My mother was denounced,' she said. 'The Germans came and searched the flat. She was living in a pension in Srodborow. They took her away.' She said all this calmly and drily. The expression on her face didn't change one iota. Her eyes remained dry. 'I'll weep after the war,' she added, looking understandingly at us.

We changed the subject. She'd transferred her mourning for until after the war, so we ought to talk about something else. In the framework of her present life there was no room for despair.

'Listen,' she said, 'have you heard there's a special fund for Jews in hiding? Don't you get anything? So where do you get your money from?'

'From selling the things we managed to place with people. I sold my fur coat for 13,500, then my silver cutlery and my parents' silver cutlery, and I've just sold the piano for 50,000. It was bought by a mill owner.'

'My cousin's got some contacts,' said Zofia, 'and thanks to that I receive a fair bit of money each month for old Mr and Mrs Wyszewianski. If you run out of money ask Guzik.'

'But isn't Guzik going to Vittel?'

'No. Guzik's not going.'

'Because we know he's got a son in Palestine.'

'All the same he's not going.'

That evening I said to Marysia, 'Do you know what I'm thinking about now? It looks suspicious if no-one visits us. But we ought to have Polish visitors, not Jewish ones.'

She didn't answer. She was busy doing something else. She was reckoning up our expenditure: 1,500 every month for Irena, 2,000 for Nina, 3,000 for Anusia. And 2,000 for Macius. What about us? How much do we spend? Then let's say 2,000 for Dr Frydman. But we've still got some money left, thank God.

Not long afterwards, early in the morning, we heard the bell. Mrs Grabowska was out. Marysia opened the door. She saw a Polish policeman, the same one as before. She recognized him at once.

'Does Mrs Kowalska live here?'

'You've been here once already,' she said. 'And you gave your word of honour that you wouldn't come again. But now here I am seeing you again.'

'My apologies. I made a mistake. I won't come again. On my word of honour.'

270

Our youngest daughter Nina was living in Zoliborz at Emilia's, a widow who used to work in the Social Security office but was now out of work. She had two children, a daughter the same age as Nina and a son in the seventh grade in school. There were a lot of Jews in hiding at her place and that alarmed us. We kept thinking that Nina wasn't safe and wondered how and where to fix her up.

Mr and Mrs Wyszewianski, our Hanna's parents-in-law, were in hiding in Emilia's three-roomed flat. Hanna's husband Leon was there for a while too. Also Krysia, the wife of the Wyszewianski's youngest son Michal, called Irena Sopocinska in her Aryan papers. A woman called Basia often dropped in too. Her husband was a highly placed official in the Social Security office before the war and that's how she knew Emilia. Basia came from Sosnowiec. She was christened but her features were extremely Semitic. She talked from morning to night about her ten-year-old daughter who was in hiding at her former servant's.

Emilia didn't take any special payment for hiding all these Jews. All she wanted was to make enough to feed herself and the children. As she had to run around town all the time and do the shopping and settle everything for everyone in the flat, Mrs Wyszewianska looked after the household. Her Aryan name was Mrs Zadorozna. She cooked and baked for eight people in the flat and was helped by our Nina, Irena Sopocinska and sometimes Basia, who never told anyone her Aryan name, just to be on the safe side. They cleaned the saucepans, peeled the potatoes and washed the plates. They spent all day long in the kitchen, isolated from the world by its four walls.

In principle they didn't leave the flat. Everyone apart from Basia stopped going out even though their papers were in order and they were registered. For the first few weeks Emilia took the whole flock to church for mass every Sunday. But then the walks were discontinued because they might be suspect. Such a large group of people with not completely Aryan faces must have been very noticeable.

Emilia wasn't an ordinary housewife but an unusual and exceptional woman. She wasn't interested only in the food and safety of the Jews she had in hiding, but also in lifting their spirits within their tragic reality. She understood like no-one else that these people, tormented with anxiety about the fate of their loved ones and despair over the families they had lost, needed to have an outlet. What sort?

She wanted them to to lose themselves, if only for a moment, in music and art, the most beautiful things mankind has given the

271

world. In music? Yes. She had a grand piano and Leon knew how to play the piano. She made them listen to Beethoven's sonatas every evening. It was an old piano and one or two keys were mute. But they could sing the missing notes to themselves, couldn't they?

Art? Literature to be precise. They read the classics together, *Faust*, Plato's *Dialogues* and the Bible. They read the Bible every evening and she listened with them. Mr Wyszewianski was a Hebrew scholar and he sometimes translated the Polish texts into Hebrew. And in everything they read they found a repetition of their own lives and against the background of the gigantic biblical events their own experiences seemed less tragic.

Kaczynski sometimes came too, a homeless Jewish child who had lost his family and escaped from the ghetto. A boy of twelve, his father had been a cab-driver. He had his own corner in the kitchen where he liked to sit. By a stroke of luck he had managed to rescue a photo and he liked to show it to us. His father on the box of the horse-cab, two boys next to the father, and mother holding a little girl. The photo was his legitimacy. 'That one there, that's me. I'm sitting on the box. It was our own cab,' he said proudly, 'my daddy's and my whole family's.'

He had fair hair with a touch of red. He went to many flats in the house even though he looked Jewish. The house took the proletarian child in and gave him a nickname. He slept on crates in an attic belonging to a worker's family. They didn't have any children and they even wanted to adopt him although he looked Jewish. She was a good-hearted woman and washed his clothes and heated water for him so that he could have a good wash. He told us all this in Emilia's kitchen.

'I'd like to repay them one day,' he used to say.

'Repay? How can you pay them back, poor child?'

'I'd like to pay you back some time too,' he told Emilia.

'He's such a grateful child,' said the workman's wife. 'All he ever talks about is gratitude.'

When he was asleep she stood over him with a lamp and watched him. She always called him Kaczynski. 'Go to sleep, Kaczynski,' she used to say.

'Has Kaczynski been?' Emilia would ask as soon as she entered the flat.

'Yes and he's still here. My husband's teaching him sums now. I gave him a bowl of soup,' replied Mrs Zadorozna.

One day, as he was walking through the courtyard, the other

272

children from the house surrounded him and shouted, 'Jude! Jude!' Then a window opened on one of the top floors and a voice called out, 'Scum! Judases! You're not Polish children, but traitors.'

Kaczynski never played with the children. He avoided them. 'I'm afraid of them,' he said, shrugging his shoulders. He liked talking to adults and having long, serious conversations. He sensed that the children were more dangerous. In the summer, after the ghetto was destroyed, Kaczynski sometimes crossed the walls and ferreted about in the desolate heaps of ruins. Once he found some small knives and forks and gave them to Emilia as a present. She had a subtle nature and accepted them because she didn't want to upset him. She understood that it was his first step towards the repayment he was always talking so much about.

During the Warsaw Rising he accompanied Emilia and her charges to Pruszkow. Women with small children weren't sent to Germany any more by then. A child protected you from being deported. During the selection a young woman whom Emilia knew took Kaczynski by the hand and told the Germans he was her son. She wasn't taken away. After the war we heard that a tailor looked after him in Krakow. He adopted him and even had him christened. Then he was looked after by the Jewish Commission and Kaczynski went to Israel with some other children.

Who was Henryk Falencki, the man who accompanied Irena from Zenon's garret to Mrs Domanska's on Wspolna Street at Marysia's request in February? He was Henryk Frydman from Lodz. He was twenty-six and a doctor in the recuperative sanatorium alongside the institution for the mentally ill in Otwock, Zofiowka as it was called. The sanatorium continued to function until 1942. Marysia was there for a year with Macius when he was ill. She didn't live in the sanatorium the whole time but rented a room in a nearby villa. When she went down with typhus it was Dr Frydman who looked after her.

Twelve hours before they started liquidating the Otwock ghetto in August 1942, Marysia managed to leave it in a car sent from the Warsaw ghetto. She left with a lot of other people but there wasn't enough room for Dr Frydman. My uncle Maurycy Szpilfogel also lived in Otwock at the time, not far away. He got out of there to the Aryan side in Warsaw with his wife and daughter with the help of a friend, Dr Szymonski. They were worried about Marysia and Macius so they asked the doctor to bring them over, and Frydman

273

too because they knew him. Dr Szymonski had a friend, a man called Janusz, and he drove to Otwock but Marysia was already gone. He took Frydman with him.

Both Marysia and Frydman had Aryan papers made by a woman recommended by Halina, Julia's daughter. They were false. Dr Frydman moved in with Janusz on Aleje Jerozolimskie to start with but Janusz didn't want him to stay long. Marysia heard about it and she turned to Halina. Halina and her husband, Kazimierz Cetnarowicz, were active in the scouting movement so Falencki was transferred from one place to the next by girl guides. He pretended to be an officer in hiding, never staying anywhere longer than two nights. That was a terrible time, the constant moves from place to place and long hours spent in churches. In the end a cousin of Cetnarowicz's gave him the address of a widow with two daughters on Bohaterow Street in Saska Kepa. She agreed to rent him a room.

Falencki was a charming man with neutral features. Meaning that he didn't look Jewish but he didn't look a hundred per cent Aryan either. He didn't arouse any suspicions in a crowd on a busy street. He was on a friendly footing with his landlady from the start. Both her daughters were secretly in love with him and very jealous of him and that's why Marysia stopped visiting him. But they didn't know he was Jewish.

He made his own dinners. He gave a few lessons near the house and borrowed books from the library, but apart from that he hardly ever went out. His life might not have been so spartan if he knew about the fund for Jews in hiding and if he had contacts. He was a young and able doctor and would have been given assistance. But he didn't know about it and Marysia didn't know either. Later on we wondered about it. What would have happened if she did know? It wasn't necessary at that time because we still had money, and each new contact, each step, each small carelessness or oversight could be dangerous.

He came to see us on Lwowska Street one Sunday. I knew him from the sanatorium; I went once from the ghetto when Marysia was there. I hardly recognized him. His face had changed and he'd lost weight. He was dressed like the humblest office clerk or a worker, wearing an old brown coat and a cycling cap. He was holding an umbrella. He sat down at our black desk. He smiled confusedly and was shy. It was the confusion and shyness that struck me most of all.

He told us how imaginative some Jews were in order to obtain genuine papers. One Jewish couple got married in a church and so they had a genuine marriage certificate. We were surprised they'd thought of something like that. He told us about a friend who died because of her four-year-old daughter. The child was with her in the kitchen while she was cooking. Suddenly she said to the servant, 'We're Jewish, you know.'

He told us about a Jewish woman on Aryan papers who fell ill and called the doctor. 'You've got to go to hospital,' he told her.

'I can't.'

'Why not?'

'Because I'm Jewish.'

Then – this is what he'd been told – the doctor went and rang the police station.

He told us about his room. Although his landlady and her daughters were very friendly, they suspected for a while that he was Jewish. They told him so but he laughed, and to get rid of their suspicions completely he said, 'Well then, I'm prepared at any time to prove I'm not Jewish. All you have to do is agree.' But of course they couldn't agree to his proposal, could they?

He had dinner with us. We invited Mrs Grabowska too and she didn't take her eyes off him. She watched him with her sharp, wise eyes and listened to his voice attentively. She knew he was Jewish. Until now she'd never been in the company of Jews. She'd traded with them and bought from them but people like that were completely different according to her. The ones here weren't really any different from Poles. Their behaviour, their appearance and their way of talking were the same. When Falencki said good-bye and the door closed behind him she said, 'He's a good man, I'm sure.'

She didn't say anything else and sat there lost in thought. He had charmed her.

That was the framework containing Henryk Frydman's life. What about the other young Jews we knew? They struggled through the dangers of the Aryan side more successfully or less so, just like him. Maryla Kalisz's brother was a boy of eighteen who looked Jewish. He hid in a cupboard in his sister's room on Natolinska Street and went out in the evenings. After the curfew he'd meet a friend near the house and they'd walk along Aleje Ujazdowskie, talking loudly in German. They spoke German well so they pretended to be German. No-one ever stopped them, so we heard. We wondered who the friend was. Maryla and her brother came from Lodz. They had a lot of friends, including the sons of German factory owners in

275

Lodz. These young boys even visited Maryla in Warsaw at the beginning of the war. They may have been in touch with her later and may have helped her brother.

When Nina was working as a clerk in the Council in 1941 when it was still on Grzybowska Street, a group of Germans with SS men once came there. They were noisy and cracked their whips and behaved arrogantly and impertinently. To her great surprise Nina recognized a young Jewish boy whom she'd known before the war. He was born and brought up in Berlin and spoke excellent German. He had an aunt in Poland whom he used to come and visit with his mother. Nina didn't let on that she recognized him. From the way he looked at her she guessed that he recognized her too. His father was an engineer and had been deported to Stutthoff by the Germans. His mother and aunt were in Warsaw. We never managed to puzzle out whether the boy disguised himself so brilliantly in order to help the two women in their poverty, or whether he sold out and joined the enemy.

A young doctor called Süsswein was in hiding with his wife in Zoliborz. He was tall with black hair, black eyes and a dark complexion. One day the house where he lived was blockaded. The Germans were looking for Jews. Although Süsswein had Aryan papers his looks would have betrayed him. Then he had a brilliant idea: he ran into the bathroom, lathered his face and started shaving. The thick, white foam covered his dark, eastern face. He looked different than his normal self and that's why he felt more confident. When the Germans came to the flat he faced them fearlessly.

He lived with an Orthodox priest. The priest didn't know he was Jewish and would probably have started suspecting if he'd stayed at home all the time. So he rented a room a few streets away from a woman who had a millinery workshop and he went there in the mornings and came back at four. He pretended to be working. He told the woman he was writing a thesis and didn't have the conditions to work at home.

He died tragically. During the Warsaw Rising he was working as a doctor. One day a young messenger was killed by a bullet, she was hit just as she was trying to cross the road. Her distraught mother begged them to bring her daughter's body back but nobody volunteered because the area was under fierce fire. Süsswein went and he was hit just as he was returning holding the dead girl.

Leon Wyszewianski, our Hania's husband, also died in tragic circumstances. At the beginning of January 1944 he lived alone in

276

Zoliborz in a flat which housed a secret vodka distillery. A few young Poles came there at night to work. The business flourished until in the end someone noticed what was going on and denounced them. The Polish and German police suddenly arrived and took seven people to Pawiak. Leon was pulled out of bed and taken away in his pyjamas. A Jewish woman who lived there was also taken away. The other people were got out afterwards by the underground resistance but Leon and the Jewish woman didn't come back.

I should now say something about Bronislawa Szereszewska's mother, Mira Konstantynowska. She left the ghetto half-way through September 1942 when Edward and his wife were living in Bielany. On the Aryan side, she fixed herself up with somewhere to live in one of the bachelor rooms on Aleje Jerozolimskie. A bachelor room, that was her start. The occupants of the room often changed, although the tenants were usually Jews. She got in touch with Bronislawa and being taught by her experience she didn't approach Gutgold for papers, but was given Mrs Jachimowicz's address and went to her instead. She collected her baptism certificate in person from the church in the name of Janina Zawadzka .

She was fifty-seven at the time. She was tall and slim and her appearance didn't arouse suspicion. So she walked freely along the streets of Warsaw and looked every passer-by openly in the face. But in order to survive she had to speak as little as possible. You could only recognize she was Jewish by her accent. She dressed quite strangely for Mira Konstantynowska but it was what she imagined Janina Zawadzka should look like. She used a lot of rouge and lipstick and painted her eyebrows black. She wore a flat black hat with a bunch of white flowers and a short, tight costume. She looked like an aging woman of questionable reputation and a rich past.

When Edward and his wife moved from Bielany to Mokotowska Street she visited them every day. She looked after the household for them and cooked for them in the first few weeks even though there was a servant in the flat whom the Lewandowskis couldn't or wouldn't take with them. Silent Mrs Zawadzka enjoyed the work and didn't want to give it up. She came from a family of orthodox Jews so it's not surprising that she was particularly attached to Jewish dishes. The Lewandowskis' servant must have been surprised when she made onion rolls or chulent. The servant had sharp eyes after all. Once when Mrs Jachimowicz came, the one who made Aryan papers, she said, 'She's Jewish. What does she come here for?'

Mira Konstantynowska was now called Zawadzka and so she

couldn't be Bronislawa's mother because her name was Elzbieta Sieminska and she was single. They said she was her aunt. But Bronislawa sometimes addressed her as mother when she entered the kitchen and that must have surprised the servant as well. Bronislawa told her that, 'She brought me up from when I was small and so she's like a second mother to me. It's quite natural.'

March passed, April came and Easter was approaching. Marysia met father in the bank again.

'Can I stay with you for a few days?' he asked. The question surprised her and she didn't answer. Seeing her hesitation he said, 'No, it doesn't matter.'

'But daddy, you've got a flat in Zoliborz and papers and we could see you every day.'

He didn't reply. He was perturbed and wanted her to go.

'I'll let you know,' she said. 'I'll ask.'

She came home extremely confused. How was she to tell Mrs Grabowska? She still hadn't forgotten the robbery and she was afraid of the caretaker's sons. We didn't say a word to Mrs Grabowska. We didn't want to overtax her patience. Next day Marysia phoned the ghetto and told father it wasn't possible. It didn't cross our minds that it was rumoured that the ghetto was going to be liquidated. We thought that father wanted to visit us again.

On 18 April the Jewish work team marched past our window towards Mokotow at seven in the morning as usual and returned at five. But to my immense astonishment I saw the team again that day, going in the direction of Mokotow again in the early evening. None of them was wearing their armband. They didn't have their white armbands on their sleeves. They were carrying rucksacks. When Marysia came home I told her what I'd seen and asked what she thought it meant. She didn't pay any attention because her thoughts were elsewhere. 'Mrs Poniatowska has died. I'm going to her funeral tomorrow,' she said.

So she'd died. I suddenly remembered what she'd said when she was almost unconscious and Marysia visited her, just the one word, 'Father'. We didn't know if it was a warning or a question. She knew that father was in the ghetto and she knew how much we missed him and worried about him.

'You slept uneasily last night,' I told Marysia next morning. 'You were moaning and crying in your sleep. What's wrong?'

278

She was in a hurry and kept looking at her watch. She was going to the Powazki Cemetery for the funeral. When she was in the tram she saw that the ghetto was surrounded by police and soldiers. At the cemetery she found out what was happening.

'Father is dead or he's going to die,' she called out when she came home. 'I saw smoke over the ghetto.'

She didn't shed a single tear. She put off her mourning until after the war.

The first person who came to us was Dr Szymonski. He lived on Lwowska Street, just next door, and knew our address. He came to comfort us.

'Don't despair,' he said. 'You might find him in a camp somewhere. We'll send someone to Poniatowa and Trawniki.'

See someone? Travel somewhere? Fly somewhere? Marysia was the one who did all the running around. She went to Mr Kowalski first. He lives closest. He works in the bank. He lives with his mother on Marszalkowska Street, on the corner of Wspolna Street. He knew father from before the war and she sometimes went to the bank to ask his advice on money matters. Why did she go? 'The ghetto's burning,' she said. That's all she wanted to say and she left immediately afterwards. She didn't stay a single moment.

Where will she go now? To Mr Sztark the engineer, a friend of father's. Yes, she'll go there. She goes to Zurawia Street. 'Would you like to come and visit my mother, Mr Sztark?' She didn't even say the ghetto was burning. He can hear just like she can and he can see the smoke above the houses just like she can, can't he? She gives him our address. He promises to come.

What did Dr Szymonski say? He mentioned camps in Poniatowa and Trawniki. Who can we send there? Who can we discuss it with? With Wiktor. With the office boy from father's office on Czacki Street before the war. Wiktor is a young man, tall and handsome. He's twenty years old, I don't think he's any older. Father thought well of him. Marysia knows his address. He lives on Bielanska Street. But he doesn't. He doesn't live there any longer. 'Where does he live now?' she asks the woman who opens the door. '4 Graniczna Street.' So she goes to Graniczna Street. She walks. She prefers to walk, today she prefers to walk.

'The ghetto's burning,' she says to Wiktor. 'My father's still there. He might have been sent to Poniatowa or Trawniki. Can you go there? You might manage to sort something out.'

279

'Mr Szereszewski stayed in the ghetto? He could have come here. I hid a Jew here for a while.'

Marysia looks round the empty room. 'Where did you hide him?'

'In the divan bed.'

'I had a room for him in Zoliborz, and papers, but he didn't come. Will you go?'

'Yes.'

Marysia returns to Lwowska Street. She nips into the shop and rings Mrs Lubecka. 'Is that Mrs Lubecka? Oh, Mrs Lubecka,' she starts but when she catches the owner of the shop looking at her sharply she says in a different voice, 'How's the child?'

Finally she enters the gateway and crosses the courtyard. The caretaker lives in the courtyard, his window is at the same height as the courtyard. A wide window. An observation point. The caretaker and two of his sons are standing in the window. Everyone who crosses the courtyard is entered into their memory like on a negative – their clothes, what they look like, their faces, everything. Does Marysia remember that?

A week passes and then the next. Wiktor came back a long time ago. He came back with nothing. Every day we see a glow in the sky above the ghetto. From morning till night we hear explosions, the rattle of machine-guns and cannon fire. At that tragic time, when we could see the burning ghetto night and day, we saw one face only and it was the synthesis of all that horror. Now we were alone – me, my three daughters and Macius.

'We must ask father what he thinks.' How often we'd said it! Now the words dissipate and disappear. The ghetto was our base, but we won't have any more contact with it now. Now we're going to have to rely on our own instinct.

Mr Sztark comes. He keeps his word. He comes to comfort us.

'Your children are with you,' he says to me.

But his words don't sink in even though they're friendly and sympathetic. My children are with me? Shouldn't we go to Irena and Nina and suffer with them? So Marysia goes. First to Irena on Rakowiecka Street and then to Nina in Zoliborz. That day, when she went to Zoliborz, she only got as far as Miodowa Street in the tram. The tram didn't go any further because the rails ran under the walls of the burning ghetto. From Miodowa Street you took a cart. The carts were full. So Marysia gets on a cart. Suddenly she sees that the young man sitting next to her is looking at her carefully. She feels uneasy. She thinks he must be an informer and wonders how much money he'll want.

'Are you going to Zoliborz? Can I ask where you're getting off? Because I might be getting off at the same place and we could go together. Can we meet and go to a café?'

She didn't want to. She didn't feel like any meetings. She opened her bag and checked to see if she had any money. It was bound to end like that. So long as he didn't want more than she had with her. He looked like a clerk or a teacher. It never even entered her head that he might be quite innocent and just liked the look of her. Something as straightforward as that was simply out of the question. A hunted Jewish woman on Aryan papers always scented a trap everywhere.

'You don't want to? Pity because you're very nice.'

It's all just a game, thought Marysia. The most important thing is for him to leave me alone as quickly as possible. The cart stopped. She got off and started weaving along the side streets and turning round to see if he was following her. She met him again twice. Once on Krolewska Street and once on Marszalkowska Street. Both times he asked if they could meet in a café or in the park. She refused. She was afraid. Her fear turned out to be groundless. It probably didn't enter his head that she might be Jewish.

About the end of May Bronislawa's mother went to discuss something with Mr Kosowski who owned a chemicals factory. She went to the Hotel Polski. The entrance door was open. There was a crowd of well-dressed Jews, men and women, in the courtyard, and German policemen among them too, but they weren't hitting anyone or pushing anyone or shouting at anyone. She was highly intrigued and surprised, and asked Mr Kosowski who they were.

'They're Jews. They're going abroad to be exchanged.'

She flew back home as if on wings and related what she'd seen. Everyone was very excited. Even the usually sober Bronislawa was tempted by the chance and went to the Hotel Polski to put down her name and her mother's, children's and Edward's. A few days later she went to the hairdresser who always did her hair. 'Would you like to have your palm read?' he asked her. 'I know someone who's said to be miraculous.'

She made a note of the address and went there the same day. The man looked at her palm. 'You're going on a long journey, but I can see a cross. That's death. Don't go.'

When the papers in all our names arrived at the beginning of June Bronislawa decided not to go because she remembered what the man who read her palm had said. After his initial excitement Edward had recovered and cooled down but Leon insisted on going. He went to see Guzik, whom he knew well from the time when they lived in Elgiert's pension together. Guzik demanded some money. 'What?' shouted Leon furiously. 'For the papers in my name? Not a penny. The money's already been paid. Have you gone mad?'

That's how things stood when Stefania Szereszewska visited us on Lwowska Street one day with her dog.

'Can you imagine what an adventure I've had?' she asked and laughed. 'I was waiting for a tram at the stop. There was a young man in high boots next to me. The tram didn't come for ages so he suggested we take a horse-cab. For a joke I asked him if he had enough money and he said, "I've got lots of money. I make it on the Jews."'

'Do you still take the dog for a walk?' we ask.

'Yes. Guzik said to tell you that your papers have arrived.'

'We're not going.'

'You're not going? You might do if you saw what I see from my balcony. I live on Chlodna Street, don't I? And if you heard what I hear every day. My landlady stands on the balcony for hours. She watches the ghetto burning and she's pleased. "They deserved it," she says. "Aren't you pleased, Mrs Kosinska?" I can't stand it. I'm selling my things already, my pillows, and the coats and bed-linen we don't need. We won't be able to take anything with us.'

But even so it was clear she didn't want to go. After she'd gone we wondered if she had any forebodings.

The so-called departure to Vittel excited the Jews in hiding. Everyone knew about it. Everyone knew that there was a registration office on Chmielna Street. Everyone knew that the people accepted were living in the Royal Hotel. The first transport had set off from there. The next left from the Hotel Polski. Everyone also knew that Guzik was the go-between in the discussions between the Germans and the Jews. These departures were a sickness and everyone who couldn't cope with the secrecy of being in hiding submitted to it in the first place. And everyone who had lost their flats or felt unsafe where they lived also felt they were a lifeline.

Our papers were ready. They arrived from Switzerland and were waiting for us in the consulate. We had Ecuadorian citizenship. Papers for Anusia Laskowska and Henryk Falencki arrived at the same time. We were informed about it. But no-one went for them. They were probably sold to someone else later.

Leon Szereszewski and his wife Stefania and their two sons Rysio and Piotrus left for Vittel, as they said, on 7 July. Bronislawa's mother wanted to be there when they were leaving. She thought she'd see them one more time. She went to Dluga Street. A huge crowd was standing on the pavement opposite the Hotel Polski. She waited with the crowd but didn't see them. She couldn't see them. They left the courtyard in covered lorries.

A poorly dressed woman who looked like a servant was standing next to her holding a bunch of carnations in her work-worn hands. She must have been waiting for someone as well. Perhaps she wanted to say goodbye to a child she had looked after. When the lorry passed her she threw the flowers inside. 'Look! Look! See how she is serving the Jews,' someone shouted from the crowd. 'They're better than you, you scum,' the woman said gritting her teeth. Bronislawa's mother heard all this. She was standing right next to her and touching her with her shoulder. She got into the tram and went to Mokotowska Street with a heavy heart. She sensed that they were heading for destruction.

My cousin Henryk Szpilfogel also went because he didn't have anywhere to stay. His wife and daughter lived somewhere else and they remained in Warsaw. The young lawyer Jozef Zysman didn't have anywhere to go either, but he delayed his departure. Not everything had been completely settled yet and the next transport was already leaving. When everyone's papers were being checked it turned out that he didn't have any. People like him who lived in the hotel but whose cases weren't finalized yet were sent to Pawiak and shot.

Irena and Nina had somewhere to live, thank God. We did as well. We rented two rooms and paid 450 zlotys a month for them. Mrs Grabowska hadn't asked us to leave yet. One of her tenants was registered and so she wasn't responsible for her. If the flat was searched she could say she didn't know she was Jewish. But the second tenant was living there unregistered. She was in hiding. The landlady's own head was at stake. When it suddenly turned out that Macius couldn't stay with the Misses Lubecki any longer the situation became even more complicated. Marysia rang every few days to ask if the child was well and if everything was all right. One day Wanda Lubecka told her, 'It's not all right, my dear. We want you to come and take Macius away.' She immediately went to Nowy Zjazd extremely worried.

'What's happened?'

'The caretaker came here. He said that the wife of one of the professors suspects that Macius is Jewish. "Why else would his mother have run away?" she said. "I don't want him to be in this house." The caretaker said that he didn't think it up because he's convinced they're going to lose the war and he wants to be in order.'

Miss Lubecka was furious when she told Marysia about it. She said that the house was full of academics and the woman felt bothered by a child who wasn't even living in her own flat. But there was nothing she could do. So Marysia brought Macius to Lwowska Street. Now he's in the reception room next door and looking at everything. He might even be scared. Perhaps he doesn't feel as safe as on Nowy Zjazd. He got used to it there but here that old woman with piercing eyes might make him feel shy and frightened.

He drinks everything in with his inquisitive eyes. The vase with peacock feathers, the two black desks, the barometer and the strange cupboard with all its bottles. He even ventures to the kitchen, which is as far as the flat extends. He looks at the walls, the cupboard, the stool, the rubbish bin and the sink with the leaking tap.

'In the other place you were called Swiecicki,' says Marysia. 'Your name here is Majewski.'

He doesn't reply. He doesn't ask her to explain. But she knows he's understood and accepted her words without question. Like all Jewish children on the Aryan side, he knew how to observe the rules of life underground.

'Don't make a noise and don't run around because the people underneath will be surprised and will want to know who's stamping on their heads. You can draw, write and play as best you can.'

'Can you buy me a surplice?' the child asks shyly.

'What for?'

Macius goes over to the corner, lifts up his hands and prays like a priest during mass. He served as an altar boy for a while with Jerzyk Kumaniecki. Father Kozubski, who was professor of theology at Warsaw University, gave them surplices to wear and told them to ring the bell in Saint Anne's Church on Krakowskie Przedmiescie. He was a friend of Jerzyk's father, Professor Kumaniecki, who was a neighbour of the Misses Lubecki. Macius was looked after by Mrs Kumaniecka and he played with Jerzyk and even started going to school with him.

'I can't buy you one. You'll have to play at something else.'

But she's got to buy a new bed at once. Or borrow one, except there's no-one to ask. Ada Albin has already lent us one. It was for the room we rented for father in Zoliborz because there was no bed there. So Marysia goes to Graniczna Street and buys the cheapest bed she can find. Macius will sleep on the short bed which is a child's bed anyway. At the same time Marysia gets hold of a blank birth certificate. 'Bronislawa's going to fill it in,' says Marysia, 'I've already rung her.'

Fortunately Mrs Grabowska accepted the presence of Macius almost indifferently. She knew that Marysia had a child and she might have taken it into account that she might want to have him with her one day.

When Bronislawa came she filled in the certificate: Maciej Majewski, name of father, Ryszard, name and surname of mother, Maria Barbara Grabczewska. Marysia took the certificate to the house administrator. She said that she'd brought the child back from the country and wanted to register him. Bronislawa brought her daughter Ewa with her and she brought Macius a book as a present, *Doctor Doolittle and His Animals*. It was the first reading book of his own he'd ever had. He could read already. He read it from beginning to end over and over again and never tired of it. The pictures in the book delighted him. He stopped talking about a surplice. He was one of those children it's easy to amuse with a book and a pencil.

When Henryk Falencki visited us again one day Macius was sitting reading by the window as usual. Falencki liked the child but he hadn't seen him for a long time. 'How are you Macius?' he said and kissed his hand in greeting.

Mrs Grabowska was just passing and was surprised and touched to see a man do something seemingly so unmanly. She said to Marysia, 'Mr Falencki must really be a good man.'

This time he told us that Lucyna had returned from Pawiak! Lucyna, Eugenia Gotheil as she really was, was the sister of Marian Glass who was a colleague of Ryszard's. She was suspected of being Jewish and taken to Pawiak with her six-year-old daughter. She didn't admit it. In prison she demonstrated exceptional courage and strength of character. In the end she was set free for lack of proof.

'Let's go and see her,' Falencki suggested. 'I've got her address.'

They both went. There were loads of visitors. All her friends and

285

acquaintances had come to see her and congratulate her when they heard about her miraculous return from Pawiak.

'I shouldn't have done it,' said Marysia later. 'It was really dangerous, us going and all those people. Is this the right time to go visiting?'

To go visiting? Definitely not. I don't even know if it was the right time to go for a walk with a little Jewish boy even if he did have fair hair. Macius wore a blue cap that hugged his face tightly. When Marysia went into a shop with him the shop-keeper said, 'What a nice little girl. Her fringe really suits her.'

Marysia was seriously considering dressing him up as a girl to make it safer. It wasn't her idea. She'd heard of people doing it.

Then Falencki stopped coming. In the autumn of 1944, during the Warsaw Rising, he was taken to Pruszkow and worked there for some months as a doctor. In January 1945 he was denounced and shot by the Germans, a few days before the Red Army arrived.

In the night of 13 May we were woken by the sound of bombs exploding. We jumped out of bed and hurriedly got dressed. It was a raid – Soviet bombers. We didn't turn the light on. We could hear chairs being shuffled in Mrs Grabowska's room and then her footsteps and then something heavy falling on the floor.

'Don't turn the light on,' she called. 'I'm going to the cellar. Are you coming too?'

'No, we're not going.'

Mrs Grabowska goes down to the cellar. We hear her footsteps growing fainter all the time. Go down to the cellar? It would be mad. No-one knows us. Everyone will be looking at us. Everyone in the house will be in the cellars now including the caretaker and his sons. We go into the hall. We move three chairs aside and sit down with our backs to the wall. We think it's the thickest wall in the whole flat and we think it'll protect us. The two doors that open into the hall are firmly closed.

So we sit there with Macius sitting between us. Every time we hear a loud explosion we think that being killed by a bomb isn't that terrible, it's the best of all ways to die. One of the bombs hit a house on Szosty Sierpnia Street. Next day we heard that many people died in the rubble. The explosion was so near and so loud that we felt it in our rib cages.

Suddenly Mrs Grabowska came back from the cellar. She went to the kitchen, brought out a stool and sat down next to us. Since we

286

were in the hall where there were no windows and the light couldn't be seen outside, she lit a candle. In the flickering light we could see that she was holding a plaster figure of St Anthony and squeezing it hard.

'St Anthony, our guardian, have mercy on us and intercede for us with the Mother of God,' she prayed.

We sat there for several hours. She was praying aloud and we were lost in our own thoughts. May father watch over Irena and Nina and may he protect them at this difficult time. Because we knew for sure that they hadn't gone down to the cellar either.

The next day was warm and sunny. We opened the window and standing hidden behind the net curtain we watched the passers-by. We tried to guess from their faces the extent of last night's disaster. Bronislawa came at midday. She called Marysia into the kitchen and they whispered together for a long time. I wondered if anything had happened and if they were hiding anything from me. I went into the kitchen too.

'Tell me, has anything happened to Irena or Nina?' I asked.

'No,' replied Bronislawa. 'Nothing's happened to them.'

'She was in Mokotow today,' said Marysia after she'd gone, 'at Mrs Sabart's. And she heard the news on the radio from England.'

'You mean she was at the administrator's and there was a Polish programme on the radio just then?'

'That's how it was. Mrs Sabart turned the radio on and Bronislawa heard it.'

'What did she hear?'

'That Marek Lichtenbaum, Gustaw Wielikowski, Alfred Sztolcman and Stanislaw Szereszewski died in the ghetto.'

'They died?'

'They were shot.'

'When did it happen?'

'On 23 April.'

The news deprived us ultimately and finally of any hopes and illusions we were still subconsciously harbouring.

The days were sunny, the sky was blue and the trees were becoming green. But in the north of the city you could still hear explosions and shots and the smoke still wound its way upwards in wide swathes.

A light and sunny spring day has its own laws and requirements. Straw hats trimmed with ribbons and flowers appeared on the streets. Marysia bought a hat on Krucza Street with a velvet ribbon and a white veil which covered her forehead. The hat matched her face and hair. She felt good in it. She put it on and went to collect her identity card feeling self-confident.

'I can't issue you with it,' said the clerk, 'because the marriage certificate is a fake. Your witnesses will have to come.'

'I haven't got any.'

He pointed to the people milling around. Their occupation was providing testimonies in return for money. 'You've got your witnesses here.'

They're a suspicious bunch of people, she thought, just waiting to be able to blackmail their customers.

'I don't want them. I don't want to have anything to do with them.'

'Today is the last day for collecting identity cards here,' said the clerk. 'You'll have to collect it from the Germans on Danilowiczowska Street.'

'I can't go there. It's out of the question,' said Marysia.

The clerk thought about what she'd said. Maybe she had something on her conscience or she was giving him to understand that she was Jewish. He nodded at a man sitting at a table in the corner of the room. 'Ask him. He'll do it for you.' The man at the table must have belonged to the underground resistance. He gave Marysia the identity card without a word.

Handing the papers in was child's play, the skill lay in collecting the identity card. My marriage certificate was fake as well. In order to avoid fake marriage certificates, almost all the Jewish women in hiding claimed to be single. But the certificate had been drawn up for me because I intended to live with my husband. My papers, like Irena's and Nina's, were handed into the office on Krakowskie Przedmiescie by Mrs Jachimowicz who specialized in papers.

Nina went to collect her identity card with Emilia. Nina had dark hair so how could she have the courage to go on her own? But next to Emilia's Aryan appearance Nina's exotic features became pastel, they faded and disappeared. They got into a cart in Zoliborz and drove round part of the ghetto walls. The ghetto was still burning. From Miodowa Street they walked to the office. Everything went well. Nina was fingerprinted and she was given an identity card. They returned to Zoliborz the same way.

Next day Emilia accompanies Mrs Zadorozna to collect her identity card. Mrs Zadorozna is an imposing woman with a distinctive face. Her beauty is dangerous and should be disguised. So she puts on a large black hat and pins a mourning veil to it. Emilia buys a bunch of lilac. They get into a horse-cab. They drive along in the horse-cab and anyone looking at them will think that the woman in deep mourning is going to her husband's fresh grave in Powazki Cemetery with the flowers. So they arrive at Krakowskie Przedmiescie and enter the office.

Who will I go with for my identity card? On my own? I'd never dare. I'll go with Ada, Mrs Ada Albin, the Swedish woman. She comes. We cross the courtyard laughing loudly and a bit falsely. You have to pretend to be confident and in a good mood in front of the caretaker's window. It's a dangerous game and also I'm not sure if my companion is the right person because Ada looks more Semitic than I do. We get on the tram. In the crowd I won't attract any attention. The courtyard was dangerous. Crossing those few steps under fire from the caretaker's watchfulness was terrible. The caretaker of the house where I wasn't registered.

Irena went to collect her identity card with Marysia. Fira Epstein went with Mrs Jachimowicz. Falencki went on his own. So did Bronislawa's mother. She was so brave that she even went to the church for her baptism certificate on her own. But Mrs Jachimowicz had arranged everything beforehand and she received the document with no questions asked.

My brothers-in-law Edward and Leon were delivered their identity cards at home. They paid specially for it. My husband's identity card with his most recent photo stayed in the office. No-one ever collected it.

The school holidays began in June. Jozio, Bronislawa and Edward's son, came home from Otwock because it would be strange if he stayed in Otwock during the holidays, wouldn't it? Jozio and Ewa were always out on the streets. They couldn't be kept inside. So to be on the safe side, and also because the place in Mokotow wasn't secure, they decided to go somewhere outside Warsaw. Bronislawa found Olszanka in an advertisement. The owner of a small pension there had advertised some vacant rooms.

She went there at once with Stefania. They both had light-blonde hair and didn't look Jewish at all, so that only the most skilled eye could detect any Semitic features. The owner of the pension, Mr Strojnowski, was pleased to rent Bronislawa a room. A few days later she went there with the children. Bronislawa also invited Stefania and she went too. She was her guest in Olszanka for two weeks, almost to the day when she left her room on Chlodna Street to move to the Hotel Polski. Stefania was feeling so bad at the time that a change of surroundings could only do her good.

One day Bronislawa's mother, Janina Zawadzka, went to Olszanka. She'd had a perm before coming. What on earth was she thinking of? Bronislawa nearly fainted when she saw her mother. She looked just like a Jewish woman from a small town. The very same evening a gardener sitting in the kitchen said in front of everybody, 'Who's that Jewish woman?'

'You're talking rubbish,' said the maid. 'That's Mrs Sieminska's mother.'

'What have you gone and done?' Bronislawa asked her mother in despair.

'I thought it would be better,' she explained. She went back to Warsaw quicker than planned because she didn't want Bronislawa to have any difficulties on her account.

When she went to Mokotowska Street the next day she saw that a young clerk who was a relative of the Lewandowskis had moved into the room Jozio slept in. The girl had turned up one evening. She was in the underground resistance and perhaps she'd had to find somewhere else to live. The room was empty and Edward let her live in it.

Janina Zawadzka lived on Pius Street at the time in a flat with a Jewish woman called Ewa. She looked Aryan and worked in a bank. Her friend, a colleague from work, came every evening and spent the night with her. One day a Polish policeman came to the flat and said to the owner, 'I've come to warn the woman who lives here with you. Her friend's wife has found out about her and has informed the German police. Don't ignore what I've just said.'

When he left she rang Ewa and told her not to return to the flat. Ewa understood at once. Her sister had died the week before and the tragedy had made her careful and alert. She'd go and sleep somewhere else. But how could she go without a night-dress and a change of clothes?

She took a young girl with her and said to her, 'I'll wait for you in the entrance and you bring me my things.' And that's where she was arrested. The Germans were waiting for her there.

Janina Zawadzka shouldn't stay in the flat a moment longer. The Germans might come for Ewa's things. That's how it was: the possessions of any Jews they found on the Aryan side belonged to them. She fled. She left the flat in the greatest hurry. Her life was in danger and she was saving it. She went to Mrs Muszol in Sulejowek where there was a temporary stopover for people who suddenly had nowhere to live. This was in December 1943. Marysia had been living in Sulejowek for a few months at that time.

At Christmas Edward went to Olszanka. 'It would be odd if my husband didn't come at Christmas, wouldn't it? What would it look like?' said Bronislawa. He didn't want to go but she talked him into it. How she regretted it later! This was because the next day one of the guests, a teacher, said, 'Mrs Sieminska's husband is a Jew.'

On 1 February 1944 Kutschera was killed, the man in charge of the SS and the police. The raids and round-ups on the streets of Warsaw assumed terrifying proportions. A mute anxiety hung over the city like a thunder-cloud. Bronislawa was in Sulejowek that day. Marysia had invited her and Ewa. Janina Zawadzka warned Edward not to go out that day because Kutschera had been killed. She told him there'd been a lot of arrests and the atmosphere was very uneasy. Edward didn't pay any attention. 'I'll be back in fifteen minutes,' he said.

It was twelve o'clock. She sat down by the stove and waited. Fifteen minutes passed. An hour passed. Edward wasn't back. She was terrified. She said to Mrs Lewandowska's relative, the bank clerk, 'Mr Jablonski's not back. He was only meant to be gone fifteen minutes. I'm going to get Mrs Sieminska. We'll be in the courtyard opposite in the evening. We'll wait for you. We won't come into the flat. Will you come?'

'Yes,' she replied. Her face was as white as a sheet.

Janina went to Sulejowek. Bronislawa was sitting in the window and suddenly saw her mother approaching along the snowy path. She immediately realized that something bad had happened. She trembled.

'Edward left the house and hasn't come back. We've got to go to Zoliborz at once. We'll give Emilia some money. She's got contacts. I've arranged with Barbara that we'll be in the courtyard opposite this evening.'

'Oh God. Who can have denounced him?'

'Might have been a policeman or the caretaker at Wspolna Street.'

Mrs Zawadzka didn't even take her coat off. They both left at once. Ewa stayed in Sulejowek. They arrived in Zoliborz after five, gave Emilia ten thousand zlotys and asked her to do everything possible, and everything impossible too. In the evening they stood in the courtyard leaning against the garage wall and watched the dimly lit entrance. Would the girl come? And what would she say?

She came. They saw how she looked round to see if she was being followed and then entered the darkness of the empty courtyard.

'They were looking for Mr Jablonski's wife,' she whispered breathlessly. 'An informer and a smartly dressed woman.'

She told them that Mr Jablonski didn't have a wife, just a friend who visited him. Then the informer took out the photo of Bronislawa that Edward always had on him and said, 'We know he's got a wife.' He pointed to his colleague, 'This woman was detained with him but she's been set free. He said he wanted to talk to his wife and only to tell her what to do to get him out.'

'I'm going,' said Bronislawa.

'Don't go,' advised her mother. 'It's a German trick.' She gave the girl 5,000 zlotys. He might take the money. He might want to help. The next day they came again, the informer and the smartly dressed woman. The girl wanted to give him the money but he wouldn't accept it. 'I'm looking for his wife,' he said. 'I'll only tell her.'

Bronislawa didn't return to Mokotowska Street. She moved in with Mrs Pienczykowska, Dr Szymonski's sister, on Chmielna Street. She used the spare room. She stayed another six weeks in Warsaw. She received a note from Emilia saying that Edward died on 1 February. Nothing else. Now she knew for sure that the informer was a German agent. He had been looking for her to make a deal when Edward was already dead.

Then Bronislawa took the children to a forester's lodge in Krzeszow. The owner, Mrs Rogozinska, was a school friend of Mrs Pienczykowska's. She knew they were Jewish. She stayed there until the end of the war. In the meantime her mother moved to Olszanka. They lost sight of each other for many months. When the war finished they were both on their way to Wola Krysztoporska and met by chance on the road out of Piotrkow.

I lived at Lwowska Street until the beginning of June 1943, until the day I received my identity card.

Mrs Grabowska had a confessor in the church on Zbawiciela Square. She went there once a week and sought his advice in everything.

'There are two women living with me, a mother and daughter. They're Jewish. I want to get the mother taken in somewhere.'

'Nuns are the best,' advised the priest. 'The Ursulines or the Felicians. The Felicians have got a place on Leszno Street now.'

'Shall I tell the Reverend Mother the truth?'

'Don't say anything. I'll take the lie on my own conscience. Give the woman these books to contemplate from me.'

Mrs Grabowska took the tram to Leszno Street at once. She was an old woman and not scared of round-ups. She went to Leszno Street, the street which used to be Jewish. The ghetto walls bristled with glass and stood there just like before. On Leszno Street opposite Zelazna Street there was a gate in the wall. When it was opened she saw an endless pile of ruins. Everything was immobile and silent. The houses had stopped burning and not the slightest trace remained of the smoke which until recently had billowed so endlessly.

A cross of light-coloured wood with Christ stretched out on it hung above the entrance to the institution. She looked at the cross, lowered her head devoutly and went up the white marble stairs. She entered the office. The Reverend Mother was sitting at a desk.

'I've come on behalf of my tenant, Maria Majewska,' said Mrs Grabowska. 'Her mother has got a bad heart because of her terrible wartime experiences. She'd like the sisters to look after her.'

'Tell her to come with her mother,' said the nun. 'We've always got room.'

Mrs Grabowska bowed and left. On the staircase she saw a sign above a door that said 'Chapel'. She opened the door quietly and crossed herself religiously. She looked at the altar decorated with flowers, knelt and said three, short, heartfelt prayers asking for Alicja Majewska to be accepted into the institution.

5 • *The Cross and the Mezuzah*

The institution for invalids and the incurably sick, run by the Felician Sisters, was located at Szosty Sierpnia Street at first. Then the Germans requisitioned the building for a hospital and when the ghetto was liquidated they gave the nuns the former Jewish students' hostel on the corner of Leszno Street and Zelazna Street. I went there with Marysia.

'You're not Jewish or a convert, are you?' asked the Reverend Mother in her office.

'God forbid! I'm a good Catholic.'

'You're a widow? What happened to your husband?'

'They picked him up on the street. He had some underground newspapers on him.'

'When did it happen?'

'On 28 April.'

'Mother's been depressed since then,' said my daughter, 'and wants to stay here with you until the end of the war.'

'She calls me mother but she's my daughter-in-law. My only son died in the war and left a wife and son.'

'In principle we only accept people over the age of sixty-five,' said the nun looking at me inquiringly. 'You're too young for us. But sometimes we make exceptions.'

I was accepted and paid her the amount required, 500 zlotys. Then she stood up. She was tall and stout with a wide, honest face. She came from Poznan, I could tell from the way she spoke. She wore a long, brown habit with a rosary for a belt. A large cross hung on her breast. Her face was framed with stiff, white linen and she had a black veil.

'I'll show you the chapel,' she said.

The chapel was right next door, opposite the staircase. A figure of Our Lady with a gold crown and a blue cloak stood on a pedestal a little lower down. She opened the chapel door. There was a stoup next to the door. She touched the holy water delicately with her fingers and crossed herself. I did the same. Then she knelt, bowed low and touched the floor with her forehead. When she was standing beside me again she said proudly, 'This is our chapel.'

She could rightly be proud. It was her own work. The Felicians' first chapel had been left behind in the other building and the one here had been made out of the canteen of the former students' hostel. The nuns had brought the pews, hassocks, figures and pictures with them. The altar was a sea of flowers and shone with the whiteness of the cloth with its wide lace border. Among the flowers were life-size figures of Jesus and St Joseph holding the Infant Jesus.

It was very strange for me. I didn't know whether to kneel and recite a Hail Mary. Or only to kneel and cross myself. I stood by the stoup not knowing what to do and at a complete loss. Wasn't I giving myself away by standing in this holy place? Perhaps I should have fallen to my knees and cried out my sorrow in the silence of this sanctuary. I was claiming to be depressed after all. How should a depressed good Catholic behave in a chapel full of flowers when she's standing next to a nun who's fallen to her knees and touched the floor with her forehead?

I kissed her hand and went downstairs. Marysia was sitting on a cane sofa on the landing. I sat down next to her. A bell rang. Nuns in brown habits and black veils appeared from the corridors, from the upper and lower floor, from all directions. They all wore a cross on their breast. They all had their eyes lowered and their hands hidden in the long sleeves of their habits. They were going to the chapel to say the rosary. A lot of old women were also going in the same direction. Most of them were wearing a hat even though they lived in the building. There were a few men too.

I noticed a large girl with a paralysed hand. A white-haired woman in a wheelchair pushed by a nun. A young girl with rapturous eyes. A midget, yes a real midget, with bulging eyes. A woman creeping along with a terrible face. And another girl, sixteen at most, suffering from chorea and supported by a nun.

Sister Amarylis took me to the room I was going to live in and showed me my bed. Her name was Amarylis. She bore her poetic name with dignity and understanding. Her face was pale and contemplative. If she looked up you could see that her eyes were seeing things not of this world. Deep peace and silence surrounded her. The room was large, with a Venetian window and whitewashed walls. There were four beds in the four corners of the room. Next to each bed stood a bedside table or a small table with a drawer and one chair. There was also a chest of drawers with four drawers and a wardrobe for coats and dresses. Above the chest of drawers a picture of the Holy Family. Only one bed was occupied, on the left side by the window. On it lay a woman of over fifty who was clearly ill.

'Are we getting up today, Mrs Tarlo?' asked the nun.

She didn't reply at all. She was staring at me as if I was a picture. She didn't take her eyes off me. As soon as the nun left the room I unpacked my suitcase. I put my underwear and odds and ends into one of the drawers in the chest of drawers and hung my coat and dresses up in the wardrobe. I found a nail in the wall above the bed, took a picture out of my suitcase and hung it up on the nail. The woman didn't take her eyes off me the whole time.

I thought worriedly that it might have been another mistake not to take the picture Mrs Grabowska wanted to give me. It was a large picture in a gilded frame, there was nothing on it, just a red heart pierced with arrows.

'Have you seen our lovely chapel yet?' the woman asked suddenly.

There was a crafty look on her face and her eyes shone cunningly. I've no idea what she thought about me. She was watching me like a detective. Maybe she'd already guessed everything but was just delaying now in order to stun me.

'Yes. I've been to the chapel already,' I said.

'When you go for the rosary after dinner please say three Hail Marys for me.'

I nodded my head and carried on arranging my things. I put a pot of butter and a loaf of bread into the drawer of the table. I made the bed. I didn't know how to behave. Should I go to the chapel or not? Mightn't I do something wrong there? No. I won't go. I'll lie down on my bed. I'm meant to be depressed so I can be indifferent to everything.

At four o'clock a bell rang. I could hear footsteps in the corridor. I lay on the bed and felt the other woman staring at me all the time. Then the door opened and a thin and unusually tall nun came in. When she saw me lying down she said, 'You should go down to the chapel, Mrs Majewska. You'll feel better at once.'

I got up, put on my hat even though the chapel was in the same house, just one floor lower, and looked for my prayer-book. And when I was rummaging in my corner I could hear the same voice saying to the other women who had stayed in their rooms, 'You should go down to the chapel. You'll feel better at once.'

'Tarlo. My name's Tarlo,' I suddenly heard the woman say. She was introducing herself.

'Majewska,' I replied. 'Alicja Majewska.'

And I waited. I turned pale and waited. She was sure to ask which Majewskis. The ones with the pencil factory or the ones that Erazm Majewski comes from? Because she knows both. But she didn't ask anything.

A lot of people came from outside to the rosary masses which were celebrated all through June. I didn't pay it any particular attention. When I entered I touched the holy water with my fingers, crossed myself and sat down as far from the altar as possible. The girl with chorea was sitting on the end pew and right next to me was one of the lay servants. I'd seen her in the corridor carrying brushes and buckets. There weren't many nuns. I repeated, 'Pray for us' with all the others, and sang with the others too. There were three rows of pews. In the middle row sat an old woman in a black coat and a worn black felt hat on her head. She had a Jewish nose and looked like a town Jewess. She sat huddled up and slept all through the mass. She immediately attracted my attention.

The entrance to the chapel was from the staircase. The wide curved stairs were faced with marble. Three floors of corridors ran from each side of the staircase. The rooms on the first two floors were for the nuns and female residents, and the third floor was for men. When mass was over I went up to the second floor and turned into the dark corridor. Half-way along the corridor was a door with a smashed frame and that was the room I lived in.

'Praise the Lord,' I said as I opened the door.

'For ever and ever,' replied Mrs Tarlo.

She looked at me cunningly. I opened the drawer in the table and my heart missed a beat. Only half the loaf was left and the pot of butter was almost empty. I was so astonished that I couldn't think clearly. Did I really bring only half a pot of butter and half a loaf of bread? Why did I think I'd brought a whole loaf? With my heart beating I found my needles, thread and scissors and started sewing. Mrs Tarlo didn't say a single word to me and I was silent too. At six o'clock a nun with an apron entered and brought supper on a tray. Oatmeal in a mess tin, tea and bread and jam. When I'd finished eating I put the dishes on a table in the corridor. I took Mrs Tarlo's empty mess tin as well.

297

At eight o'clock I started getting ready to go to sleep even though it was still light. I took my towel and went to the washroom. Where the doors of other rooms were open I could see other women also getting ready for the night. As I was going to the washroom which was at the end of the corridor next to the entrance to the kitchen, I saw the Jewish-looking woman who'd been snoozing all through mass in the chapel coming out of there. She was wearing a very worn, loose black dress. Her hair was frosted with silver and combed upwards into a small bun. She was leading a blind woman much taller than herself by the hand. She was leading her carefully, attentively and affectionately, like you lead a child that can't walk. She opened the door to the room opposite ours, led her companion in first, then entered herself and closed the door.

When I returned to our room Mrs Tarlo was standing by her bed in her night-dress. The window was wide open. I could see the ruins of the ghetto slowly being absorbed by darkness. We could hear the sounds of the street, people walking past, the rattle of carts and the knocking of tram wheels. Suddenly I see that she's bending over, taking a chamber-pot from under the bed and pouring its contents out of the window onto the street.

'Mrs Tarlo,' I say to her, terrified, 'there aren't as many German patrols anywhere in Warsaw as on our street. The Germans will come and blow us sky-high.'

'I shit on them, missus, on your Germans, I shit on them, that's what.'

That's what she said. I didn't know whether to go out on the corridor and fetch a nun and tell her everything or to sit quiet and not say anything. I was becoming more and more afraid of the woman. I knelt down by the bed, said a prayer and crossed myself. I could feel Mrs Tarlo looking at me all the time I was praying. I didn't know how long evening prayers ought to take. Was it enough just to say 'Our Father'? I wasn't even sure if I should mumble the prayer or say it silently.

I undressed, got into bed and covered myself with my quilt. I suddenly felt alarmed at the strangeness of my surroundings. All alone. All alone in a sea of strangeness. Will I succeed in fighting off this feeling? Will I get over it and get used to this air, so different from the air in my lungs? As I lay there in that strange bed staring at the cold white wall with the strange and terrible woman next to the window, I started thinking about my three daughters who were living in three different parts of Warsaw.

298

First of all my thoughts ran to Zoliborz, to Nina. She was twenty. In her Aryan papers she was called Jadwiga Tokarska. She was in hiding at the Kedzierskis. I hadn't seen her for many months. That lovely girl with hair black as ebony looked Malayan or Hindu. She never left the flat as her unusual looks would be too prominent. She was registered as a knitter. What's Nina thinking about this June evening? All alone. She's all alone too in the sea of strangeness surrounding her.

What's Irena doing and what's she thinking about on Rakowiecka Street in Mokotow? She's Mrs Litwinowicz's servant and Girl Friday. In her Aryan papers her name is Aniela Gologowska. Mrs Kedzierska and Mrs Litwinowicz both know the girls are Jewish. But no-one else should know. I hadn't seen Irena for as long as Nina but I had news about the two of them from Marysia who visited them.

Who is Marysia thinking about this very minute on Lwowska Street? She must be thinking about me, about how hard it is for me on this first day in these strange surroundings in the house opposite the gate to the ghetto.

The next day I got up early. The lay servant brought us hot water in jugs and poured it into the bowl which I kept under my bed. As I was washing, doing my hair and getting dressed, I could feel Mrs Tarlo looking at me. Then I said a prayer, made my bed and opened the door. I was struck by a strange sight. I saw lots of old women walking towards the lavatory, each holding a chamber-pot. The strangest thing was that the women weren't abashed or shy. They were carrying their pots carefully with a serious look on their faces. Mrs Tarlo wasn't among them. Mrs Tarlo had emptied the contents of her pot out of the window onto the street.

Sister Prospera brought breakfast. Coffee, bread and jam. At eight o'clock the bell rang for the first mass. I put on my hat and jacket, the same short, black jacket that still had the mark from where the white armband with the blue star had been. I wore the armband for so long in the ghetto that sometimes when I was on the Aryan side I was terrified that I'd forgotten to put it on. I took my prayer-book and went out because I wanted to be one of the first in the chapel. I sat down on a pew by the window and watched everyone coming in.

Behind the pews was a small room connected to the chapel by an arch and in it stood an harmonium. A young organist sat down at the instrument and the nuns stood by him in a semicircle. They sang

299

hymns accompanied by the harmonium. Then the organist sang 'Blessed Mother of the Saviour' solo in a beautiful and dignified voice. Then an old, stout priest in a golden chasuble celebrated the mass. There were two small altar boys, eight years old perhaps.

In the third pew I noticed a middle-aged woman in black wearing a large felt hat and sitting with her back to me. She was praying fervently and swaying. I didn't pay it any attention as I was preoccupied with other things. I got up when everyone else got up and made the sign of the cross when everyone else did. I sang with the others and quickly learnt the simple hymn tunes.

The nuns took communion first. Then a lot of people from the chapel. One of the nuns brought the girl with chorea up to the altar. Her eyes rolled and she walked with difficulty. Every muscle on her face quivered and was distorted when, with her head nodding, she finally managed to kneel down. The woman from the third pew who swayed while she was praying also took communion.

I watched the altar boys and thought about Macius. He had served at mass too thanks to Father Kozubski. The priest knew that Macius was Jewish and wanted to protect him. So he gave him a white surplice and a bell. The young curate also knew about Macius but he found it worrying and one day he said, 'He's a Jewish child so what's he doing serving at Holy Mass.'

'What about it?' All children are the same before God,' replied Father Kozubski.

At half past eight the first mass finished and the next one started. It was celebrated by a young priest who didn't live in the institution but came specially from town. The more devout women attended both masses. Many people got up and left, and others only came for the second mass. I stayed for both because I wasn't sure if it would go down well if I only attended one.

I was hungry. When I returned to my room I opened the table drawer and my heart froze. Not a crumb of bread was left and all the butter had gone. I didn't say a word. I only looked at Mrs Tarlo. Her hands were lying on her quilt and she was holding an alarm clock in one and a photo of her children in the other. There was an ironic and cunning look on her face. She didn't look away.

Just then the door opened and Sister Franciszka came in with a new resident who was going to live in our room. She showed her the bed in the corner opposite Mrs Tarlo and went out immediately. The new woman stood in the middle of the room. She was a young woman of thirty-five, of medium height and slim. She had light, fair hair cut short. She wore a black eye patch, a black hat and a light coat. She was holding a large parcel wrapped up in newspaper.

She started moving nervously around in her corner and glancing at us all the time. She unpacked the parcel and took her coat off. She was wearing a long-sleeved, navy blue, dotted dress and high heeled shoes. She was a young woman, young and mobile, and I couldn't see anything wrong with her. So what category of resident was she?

'Missus,' Mrs Tarlo said to her from her bed, 'can you lend me five zlotys?'

I saw she was surprised. She'd only just come. She hadn't taken her hat off yet and here they were borrowing money from her already.

Yes, of course,' she replied. Her voice sounded nice. Young and melodious. She took a worn purse out of her pocket and obligingly handed Mrs Tarlo the money.

'Are you Zofia Loziewicz?' someone outside asked. She ran to the door, clacking her heels. As she passed me she introduced herself to me.

I heard a quiet whispered conversation outside. She returned shortly but the eye patch was gone. I couldn't see anything wrong with her eye. It wasn't red or swollen.

'I was hit in the eye in a crowded tram,' she told Mrs Tarlo, 'but I can't wear an eye patch all the time, can I?'

Now when she'd taken it off I noticed she had a big nose. But in general she was a good-looking woman. Her solicitude towards Mrs Tarlo was unlimited. She picked her handkerchief up from the floor and fluffed up her pillows, while Mrs Tarlo smiled cunningly and allowed herself to be served.

When Sister Prospera brought in the dinner tray Mrs Tarlo said, 'I've got a nice boy for you. I'll write to the Pope and he'll come and marry you.'

What was that? Did I hear right? Is that how you talk to a nun? It was iconoclastic. The nun left the room with her eyes lowered and without saying a word. But what did Zofia Loziewicz think? She took it as a good joke because she smiled at Mrs Tarlo and nodded her head understandingly.

Dinner consisted of pearl barley soup and a meat ball with potatoes. I took the mess tin out to the corridor and then returned to the room and lay down. I started thinking about something important. Before I came here Marysia taught me to remember I was depressed and to cry a lot. I was to cry all the time so they'd leave me in peace and wouldn't ask about anything. I might decide to pretend to be simple-minded or a religious fanatic. In that case I ought to take the lives of the martyrs from the library. I was to decide on my own what role to play. I was to sense which role would protect me best.

'Mrs Loziewicz, can you come out for a moment?' I heard the same voice in the corridor again.

'I'm coming, Mrs Mech,' she replied.

For the rosary she put the black eye patch on again. She sat down next to the old woman who snoozed all the way through. She sang fervently and when she returned she told Mrs Tarlo she'd said a Hail Mary for her.

After dinner it was humid and stormy. The clouds sailed across the sky chased by the wind and illuminated by the reflection of sudden, short flashes of lightning. The last resident of our room arrived that stormy evening. She was given the bed opposite me, in the other corner next to the door. She was a woman of seventy-seven, slim and desiccated with a lovely old face. She held herself as straight as a die. When she took her hat and coat off I could see that she was dressed like a peasant with a tight jacket and a skirt. She immediately put on a wide striped apron. Her daughter brought a basket with her things and a bag with a few provisions. I saw her put a pot of plum jam into her bedside table. We curiously watched her arrange her things in the chest of drawers and her food in the bedside table. She was a simple peasant and gave the impression of being very calm and quiet.

'What's your name?' she asked.

'Majewska.'

'My name's Karolina Sztuczke.'

Her mouth was toothless. Her head with her white hair parted in the middle reminded me of an old print. Although it was early she went to bed and covered herself with the quilt she'd brought. She said her prayer in a loud whisper and then fell asleep. We fell asleep shortly afterwards too. Outside the window the storm raged and it poured with rain as if the sky had opened. We were woken by Karolina Sztuczke shouting, 'Praise God all you spirits! In the name of the Father, the Son and the Holy Ghost. Amen!'

I sat on my bed and by the light of the lightning I saw a naked woman crawling across the room. She was quickly scurrying away from Karolina Sztuczke's bed. Karolina jumped out of bed and ran into the corridor. She was wearing a short night-dress. She lifted her hands up and from behind she looked like a girl of twelve.

'What's happened?' asked Sister Franciszka who was just passing. She was holding a candle because there was no light. She was on duty that night and was coming from the kitchen with a bottle of hot water. Karolina Sztuczke was so frightened that she couldn't speak. She grabbed the nun by the sleeve of her habit and pulled her into the room. They both stood in the middle of the room, the tall nun holding a lighted candle and small, thin Karolina clutching her tightly.

There was lightning and then thunder. Sister Franciszka saw Mrs Tarlo squatting naked by the chair next to her bed.

'You won't get anywhere,' she said to her in her calm voice, 'go to bed.'

Karolina Sztuczke went up to her bedside table and opened the door. 'She's eaten all my jam,' she shrieked. She started crying like a helpless, wronged child.

The scene was so grotesquely funny that I was choking with laughter. I've never laughed so much. That's how it seemed at any rate. Zofia Loziewicz sat on her bed looking like a ghost. She told me the next day that she was scared of being hit on the head with the chair or the alarm clock that Mrs Tarlo didn't let go of even while she was creeping round the room.

'Sleep well,' said Sister Franciszka, 'and praise the Lord.'

We woke up at six o'clock and what did we see? Mrs Tarlo was sitting cross-legged on her bed cutting up her bed-linen into fine strips with a pair of scissors. A whole heap of finely cut strips lay on the floor. She'd already cut up the sheet and quilt cover and was now cutting up the pillowcases. She didn't pay us the slightest attention. While we were at mass she got dressed, took the alarm clock and photo and slipped out of the institution. Sister Franciszka immediately rang her son and daughter and told them everything that had happened. I told her that Mrs Tarlo had got up to terrible things and had emptied her chamber pot out of the window.

'Don't worry, Mrs Majewska,' she replied. 'When the men go soft in the head they pee out of the window onto the street. Then we know what to do. We don't let them into the chapel any more.'

When she was talking about these normal human activities I felt very close to her. She was no longer the praying nun always listening to another world and gazing into it, just an ordinary woman. From that moment I started observing the sisters from a different

303

angle. I looked for their human faults and defects and waited for them to say ordinary, plain, and sometimes even trivial, things.

Mrs Tarlo came back in the afternoon. She was holding her alarm clock in one hand and the photo in its frame in the other. She was smiling cunningly just like before. The cab-driver who brought her waited and waited. She didn't pay him. Suddenly we heard a loud noise on the stairs, the knocking of heavy boots, and he came in and demanded payment. Mrs Tarlo's children came in just then. Her son and daughter. The son paid the cab-driver. He entered the office and talked with the Reverend Mother. Then they took their mother away. Mrs Tarlo's bed stood empty.

One day Zofia Loziewicz said, 'Would you like me to draw you? I'm an artist.'

I said yes. She took a piece of white paper and started drawing the shape of my face. She lifted the crayon to her face and used it to measure with, narrowing her eyes when she was doing so, while I sat in the chair and looked at the ruins of the ghetto through the window.

'Those eyes of yours. Spanish or Creole. No, eastern rather.'

And suddenly she stopped drawing, the hand holding the crayon hung in the air and I sensed that she'd guessed.

Zofia Loziewicz was out and about every day. Sometimes she even went out twice. I never went out. Sometimes she put the eye patch on, and sometimes she went out without it. I saw her one day as she was getting ready to go out, but without putting her black eye patch on, and said, 'It's much better with the eye patch. Much safer.'

She looked at me and smiled. I immediately regretted saying it but couldn't take it back. If Zofia Loziewicz had any suspicions about me, what I'd just said gave her a good card. I'd betrayed the secret I should have guarded.

At this time it was dangerous to go out onto the street. There were round-ups and houses were being blockaded. German patrols stopped trams and picked everyone up out of them, men, women and youngsters. From time to time they blockaded houses under the pretext that they were looking for Jews or political activists. It was very dangerous for priests to go out on the street. They were arrested, particularly the young ones. So our young priest who came to celebrate the second mass wore ordinary clothes, a coat and cap. He usually changed into his cassock in the sacristy where the confessional was and left it hanging there on a nail. He had beautiful

304

hair, a tremendous head of hair. To be on the safe side he didn't have a tonsure. He was tall and well built and his face reminded me of Kosciuszko.

Early one morning when Sister Prospera brought the tray with the coffee jug and we were drinking coffee and eating bread and jam, I said, 'That young priest is putting his life in danger when he comes here for the second mass every day. Couldn't the old priest who lives here celebrate the second mass as well? If there have to be two masses, why must there be two priests and not one?'

'Ils ne font jamais deux fois la même chose,' said Zofia Loziewicz in French.

The blood rushed to my face and I couldn't breathe. I glanced at Karolina Sztuczke. She was slowly cutting the crust off a slice of black bread. She couldn't eat crusts. Zofia Loziewicz ate them.

'Mrs Majewska,' said Karolina Sztuczke calmly, 'you've forgotten that there's only one day in the year when the same priest can say three masses in a row. But on an ordinary day he can only say one because he's got to have an empty stomach. He takes communion when he celebrates holy mass, so how could he do the same thing twice?'

'I was only joking,' I said in a strangled voice.

'Yes, yes, Mrs Majewska dear,' concluded Karolina Sztuczke.

But if a younger, more intelligent woman was sitting there instead of Karolina, not as simple minded as she was, she could have made use of my words immediately. Knowing my secret she could blackmail me by threatening to tell the nuns who I was. I looked up and looked at Karolina Sztuczke's hands. I looked at her old, veined hands, at her work-worn fingers, her yellow nails, at every vein of those hands which held my fate. Then I looked at her face lowered over her knitting. It looked like it was hewn out of old yellow wood. I saw her lowered eyelids covering her indifferent faded pupils. I wasn't afraid of Karolina Sztuczke.

At that time I went out every day. I walked along Leszno Street. I went out with Karolina. I held her arm and walked along the street, hiding in the shadow of her Aryan old age. We stopped in front of the displays in the windows of the miserable haberdashery shops. We looked at collars, pins, braces and two or three men's shirts with blue and grey stripes. Sometimes we crossed the street and walked alongside the wall. Behind it was the burnt out ghetto, an enormous heart which had stopped beating.

What about Zofia Loziewicz? What was Zofia Loziewicz thinking about at her table, looking out of the window and chewing her crusts? She couldn't be in any doubt about me now. But I knew that she was Jewish too. I'd known the truth on the first day, when I saw her with a black eye patch covering a good eye and part of her face. Did I have any reason to fear Zofia Loziewicz?

She was now on the best of terms with the nuns, particularly the Reverend Mother. On pieces of white card the size of a postcard she painted for the good sisters Our Lady with the Infant Jesus or Our Lady ascending to heaven surrounded by angels. They all wanted to have a hand-painted picture. The Reverend Mother was grateful to her for repainting the statue of Our Lady which stood on a pedestal on the staircase. She painted the cloak blue, the stars and crown gold, and the dress white. She worked from morning till night. I saw her every time I passed. She always wore the same dotted navy blue dress and I never saw her in anything else. The first two days she was working she wore the eye patch, then she stopped wearing it. She became more and more self-confident.

A lot of people from outside attended mass in the chapel, mainly requiem masses for their relatives. You were likely to meet someone you knew from before the war at any time. One day I saw the head-mistress of my daughters' school at a requiem mass. I walked past her pretending I didn't know her. What would have happened if she'd greeted me and used my real name? I had to be careful always and everywhere.

Jewish women on Aryan papers who went out onto the street found all sorts of ways of masking themselves. I heard of one who always took a long roll of oilcloth with her every time she went out. Another held a huge bunch of flowers and took a horse-cab. One of my relatives, a woman who looked a hundred per cent Aryan, dressed provocatively. She wore large studs in her ears and had a tiny dog on a lead. Another woman wore a long mourning veil in memory of her mother for years.

Wasn't Karolina Sztuczke my mask? I wouldn't go out on the street for all the world with Zofia Loziewicz or the old woman who looked Jewish and slept during mass. But I'd willingly go out with the girl with the paralysed hand or with a nun, or the priest or even one of the lay servants. It wouldn't make the informers suspicious about me. But I still didn't have the courage to go out on my own and I still hadn't chosen the best role to play in the institution either. I wasn't above suspicion yet. I didn't receive any letters and no-one visited me apart from Marysia. She pretended to be my daughter-in-law.

'You've got a good daughter-in-law, Mrs Majewska,' Karolina Sztuczke often said. 'Yes, my dear, not like me.' She was thinking about her daughter-in-law who rarely visited her and had neither the time nor the heart for her.

Being visited by people whose appearance was faultless could strengthen my position. It was very important. So Marysia asked Mrs Grabowska to visit me one day. She came one morning and sat down with me on the cane sofa in the corridor. I could tell that she was uneasy pretending to be a relative or a friend. The conversation didn't flow. She called me Alicja, and Mrs Majewska too. She quickly said goodbye and then forgot her umbrella and had to come back for it. All the same I was seen sitting with her by Sister Prospera, Sister Franciszka and Sister Amarylis. A few old women saw us too, the one who swayed while she was praying, Mrs Szaniawska who was nearly a hundred, and the old woman who helped blind Mrs Niemirowska to the lavatory, the one who dozed during mass. That wasn't much good.

So a few days later Marysia asked the very aristocratic-looking Mr Sztark with the walrus moustache to visit me. He did in fact come. He entered the room and greeted me, and we went out into the corridor and sat down on the cane sofa. A lot of people saw us because the sofa was right next to the chapel door. That wasn't all. He went to see the Reverend Mother in her office, kissed her hand, introduced himself and asked her to take special care of me as I was the wife of a colleague of his. 'I used to work with Mr Majewski,' he said. 'He was an engineer just like me. A very good man.' He was very moved – he was telling the truth, after all. All he changed was the name. His visit made a big impression and after that no-one could have any suspicions about me.

When the weather got colder Karolina Sztuczke started complaining about a draught from the floor. She moved her armchair to the window because it was too dark for her by the bed, jumped onto the seat and sat down on the arm of the chair. She sat like that for days on end, looking like a sitting hen. Zofia Loziewicz sat next to her and painted her pictures while I darned the nuns' black veils. One day I had told Sister Franciszka that I wanted to work – to work in the kitchen or mend the linen. I couldn't sit doing nothing because I had too many memories.

She brought me the priest's underwear to mend and for a few days I patched and darned his fustian shirts and long johns. Then I went to the kitchen and helped the nuns check the cherries, bilberries and tomatoes. They sang the litany while they worked and I sang with them. When Zofia Loziewicz also came to the kitchen to help the nuns I withdrew. I could see her exaggerated fervour and I felt it could even be harmful.

I met Anna Bialkowska when she was using the bidet in the washroom. As I was walking along the corridor I noticed that the door was open and there was a woman on the bidet. She waved at me. 'Help me get off the bidet,' she said.

She was a large, stout woman, younger than me. Her black hair was smoothly combed into a knot. She had regular features, shining teeth and a charming smile. She used two walking sticks because there was something wrong with her legs. She swayed from side to side when she walked. She used the familiar Polish form of address from the very start.

'Tell me, my dear, who lives in your room?'

'Zofia Loziewicz, Karolina Sztuczke and me.'

'What about the fourth bed?'

'Mrs Tarlo used to be there but she's gone now.'

'Then I'll move in with you because my room is full of old women.'

She moved in the next day and took Mrs Tarlo's bed. Opposite our room lived blind Mrs Niemirowska with the old woman who dozed during mass and whose name was Mrs Mech. From the time Anna Bialkowska moved into our room, Mrs Mech stopped coming. She didn't knock at the door any more and ask, 'Is Mrs Loziewicz there?' Before that she used to visit frequently. She sat next to Zofia on the bed and they whispered together for ages. Once when they were sitting next to each other whispering I noticed that their noses were identical. They weren't put off by Karolina or me. I even suspected that Zofia Loziewicz had told Mrs Mech who I was. I could tell by the way she looked at me and I was afraid that she wanted to confide in me and would become too familiar. Now she didn't come any more. She was scared of Anna Bialkowska.

The room next to Mrs Niemirowska was occupied by the woman who swayed while she was praying. Her name was Mrs Kowalska. She was said to be an old maid and extremely devout. She used a walking stick and told us she was seventy. She didn't look that old.

She had black hair and black eyebrows and looked fifty at the most. She invited me to her room one day. I've never seen so many holy pictures in my life. She also had hearts of Jesus pierced by arrows and there were even some oil lamps burning above some of the pictures.

'I'm an old maid, Mrs Majewska, and very religious.'

She used a stick as well, like Anna Bialkowska, and waddled like a duck.

'Who's moved in with you?'

'Anna Bialkowska.'

'I must make her acquaintance. The woman who lives with me, do you know who she is? She's a fortune-teller. All the women here come to see her. You know, Mrs Majewska, I like it when she tells my fortune, even though I'm very religious.'

Although Zofia Loziewicz had seen through me and guessed who I was, I carried my secret like a pregnant woman carries her baby. I carried it constantly and warmed it incessantly, in the chapel or on the dark corridor or the light staircase. It followed me along Leszno Street like a ghost or a soul doing penance, I sensed it in me night and day, and it was the essence of my every moment. But from the time when Anna Bialkowska moved into our room I stopped thinking about the role I was meant to play. I rejected all roles as unnecessary requisites. Because with Anna Bialkowska so close, in the same room, I would have been lost whatever part I played.

Here was an opponent who made me quail. Wise, young, penetrating and bold. She had aristocratic connections. In the second year of the war she was taken to Ravensbrück concentration camp and cleaned the latrines there. The cold and terrible damp affected her legs. Thanks to her distant relatives she got out after a while and spent a year in the Red Cross hospital in Warsaw unable to use her legs. She came to us straight from the hospital. She still swayed when she walked but at least she could walk.

She was bluff, loud, and self-confident. She addressed everyone in the familiar way, even the nuns. She was a Calvinist. In principle the institution only took in Roman Catholics, but they made an exception for her. She might have been related to Countess Sobanska, one of our benefactors. She supported the National Democrats and had ultra right-wing views. I realized that the very first evening when she mentioned politics while talking to Zofia Loziewicz. That evening Zofia was playing the part of an anti-Semite who was nevertheless a supporter of Josef Pilsudski.

I had the feeling that Anna Bialkowska might be the most dangerous of the lot. If she started to question me about the Majewskis I'd be lost. If I played the part of a religious fanatic she'd sense the deception immediately. Would I have got away with the careless question I asked Karolina, the one that compromised me completely in Zofia's eyes, if she'd been there? So I stopped being devout. I stopped working in the kitchen and darning the priest's drawers. I only attended one mass and didn't always go to mass after dinner. I stopped reading the lives of the martyrs and took two novels out of the institution's library instead, one in English and one in French.

The library had hundreds of books of all sorts in various languages. A lot of the crates still hadn't been unpacked. All the books had been donated. Many of the invalids brought their furniture with them as well as their books. They lived in the institution for many years. Until they died. When they died everything went to the institution.

Miss Maria Sokolowska was in charge of the library, a good and helpful woman. She was a member of the League of Mary and had a special badge which she showed me. She was so devout that before the war she went to Rome every year on a retreat. She came from eastern Poland and was fifty-eight. Until now this unusually devout woman, whom I sometimes saw lying in a cross in front of the altar, had only picked religious books out for me. She must have been surprised when I opened the catalogue myself and asked for some fiction, and when it became clear that I knew foreign languages.

A few days after Anna Bialkowska moved into our room a bombshell burst. Zofia Loziewicz was summoned to the office. 'Mrs Loziewicz,' said the Reverend Mother, 'you concealed the fact that you're Jewish. Your papers are in order and no-one knew, but your secret has come out now and we can't keep you here any longer.'

'Mrs Majewska,' said Mrs Kowalska to me in the corridor, the one who swayed while she was praying, 'come and sit down on the sofa with me. They told her she's got to leave tomorrow. Someone rang from town and informed on her. They can't keep her any longer. But they're taking her to Otwock, to another place they've got. Sister Franciszka is going with her.'

'Mrs Majewska,' said Mrs Mech, the one who dozed during mass, 'could you come to my room? Mrs Niemirowska is out at the moment. Do you know who set her up like this? Her husband. She

310

had a Polish husband who wanted to get his own back on her. Did you guess that Zofia is my daughter?'

I didn't want to listen any longer. I didn't want to! I always had the feeling that there was just one thing Mrs Mech wanted and that was to sit down with me in some dark corner and tell me her secrets. And then she'd want to know mine, and that's why I avoided her.

Anna Bialkowska spent all that day in bed. It was windy and raining and her legs were very painful on days like that. She took an old pullover out of her suitcase and unravelled it. A few balls of multicoloured wool lay beside her.

'What a kettle of fish,' she said to me. 'I didn't like that Zofia right from the start. Such a busybody. And I suspected she was Jewish too.'

Karolina Sztuczke didn't say anything about the whole business. I don't even know if the whole tragic affair penetrated to her. She was already in bed and was repeating a prayer in a loud whisper. She said, 'Amen' and then very quietly, 'yes, yes, Mrs Majewska dear,' and fell asleep.

Zofia Loziewicz didn't sleep in the institution that night. But she came next morning at eight o'clock for the first mass and took communion. I saw her one more time standing on the landing. She was going to Otwock with Sister Franciszka and was waiting for her. She didn't have a suitcase, only a parcel wrapped up in newspaper and tied with string. She was wearing her black eye patch.

One of the old women who carried their chamber pots to the lavatory each morning always greeted me warmly. The few words she said to me were in good Polish but she definitely had a foreign accent. She lived in a narrow little room at the end of the corridor with 94 year-old Mrs Szaniawska. I was so engrossed in myself, so preoccupied with guarding my secret – even though I often slipped up – that I was never curious about the other residents. I was glad that no-one was over interested in me and I was left in peace. One day Mrs Kowalska told me that the woman was Princess Uchtomska.

'Is she really a real princess?'

'Yes. A real princess. She's Russian. A very decent woman.'

I'd never talked to her for long, just said good morning or good evening if I happened to meet her on the corridor in the evening.

Zofia Loziewicz hadn't reached Otwock yet, she was still on her way there, when someone new took her bed. Jozefina Gadomska. She was seventy-six, an old maid and a teacher. She had aristocratic

311

connections too, just like Anna Bialkowska. Tall and hunched with beautiful, thick white hair, but extremely short-sighted. She was a rabid supporter of the National Democrats and loathed Jews.

She hung a tiny picture above her bed, really tiny, but she was terribly devout all the same. Much more so than Mrs Kowalska. Devotion surrounded Mrs Gadomska like a halo. You could tell by her eyes and gait and movements that her whole being and all her thoughts were directed towards God. Mrs Kowalska, despite her pictures and her swaying way of praying, was in fact a completely secular and down-to-earth woman. If she didn't remind you from time to time that she was very devout you wouldn't have believed it. Our old priest was her confessor and she went to communion.

She went out in the company of Mrs Szaniawska, the 94 year-old who lived with Princess Uchtomska. There was a small shop on Leszno Street that sold sausages, and meat too. Mrs Kowalska used to buy a steak and fry it with onions on a stove in the corridor. The nuns didn't like it. They didn't let the residents cook on stoves. But Mrs Kowalska would die if she didn't have her steak and onions. That's how she was.

Mrs Gadomska was my opponent too, although on a lesser scale than Anna Bialkowska. I blessed the moment when it came to me in a flash that I had to stop reading religious books, because a woman as intelligent and erudite as Mrs Gadomska would have found me out in a few minutes. So I went to bed that night with tears in my eyes and a heavy heart, because of what had happened to Zofia Loziewicz, and because I was convinced I'd be summoned to the office in a day or two and I'd hear the words, 'Mrs Majewska, you concealed the fact that you're Jewish. Your secret has come out and we can't keep you here any longer.'

I was so upset by the affair and so convinced that the same would happen to me that I was again gripped by the terrible anxiety which I had almost completely managed to rid myself of.

I noticed objects and things I hadn't paid attention to before. The door to our room had panels and was boarded up with hardboard. There were rust coloured stains on the door and you could see similar stains in the darker corners of the room which weren't cleaned so often. Suddenly I realized that the house used to be Jewish and located in the Jewish district which had been surrounded by the ghetto wall and then narrowed down later. The door panels had been smashed with the butts of German rifles during the last blockade. The rusty stains were the blood of Jews who had been dragged through the door or killed in the room.

Once when I was walking along the dark corridor I looked up and saw a sign on the door of the store-room where the nuns kept sacks of kasha and flour, oil and fat. It was a rectangular sign made of white yellowed card. A few Hebrew letters were written on it. I read the word 'kich'. The sign must have hung there before the war when the Jewish students' hostel was housed in the building. The room was a kitchen then. From then on I always looked up and looked at the letters whenever I passed.

One day when I was in the kitchen I saw some papers with writing on lying scattered on the floor. I picked one of them up. It was a document from the office of the lawyer, Szymon Szteinberg. I knew him, and his wife was a distant relative of mine. I couldn't understand what these documents from Szteinberg's office were doing here since he lived on Koszykowa Street at the beginning of the war and was killed there by a bullet or a piece of shrapnel.

'What are these papers doing here?' I asked one of the nuns.

'There are whole crates of them in the attic. I took some because I needed some kindling in the kitchen.'

'Maybe they used to belong to Jews,' said Sister Alfreda. 'At first when we moved in here there were still a lot of Jews hiding in the attics. They ran away when they saw us. I even came across one recently when I was taking the washing off the line. He looked like a ghost.'

In the chapel during morning mass I looked at the altar decked with flowers, and then at the plants and all the greenery surrounding the statues of Jesus and St Joseph. Weren't they now hiding here from the Germans in among all the greenery? If they were alive today they'd be killed for sure. So they're in hiding, just like I am. When the organist sang 'Ave Maria' in his deep tenor voice I bit my lips and the tears flowed slowly down my face. When Karolina Sztuczke saw it she didn't know why I so was so upset but she wanted to comfort me and so she said with a sigh, 'Yes, yes, Mrs Majewska dear.'

In the library good Mrs Sokolowska said to me when she was changing my book, 'Dear Mrs Majewska, I know you have a weight on your mind. You should take communion. I know that a lot of people don't go to communion because of objections they can't over-come, but it really calms you down.'

She was the one woman I could definitely have entrusted with my secret, knowing that she'd help me and protect me with all her heart and strength. There were times when I was tempted to confide in her, but what for? From the fervent way she prayed I could see that she was carrying a burden too, because it wasn't prayer but expiation. So what was the point of adding more bitterness to her bitter chalice?

'I can't,' I said quietly.

Then I went back to our room. Anna Bialkowska and Mrs Gadomska were both lying on their beds and they looked at me. Didn't the fact that I went out with Karolina Sztuczke give them food for thought? They were both so sharp and wise and they must have talked about me sometimes as they lay on their beds opposite one another. Why did I go out with Karolina and not anyone else? Why not with Mrs Kowalska or Mrs Szaniawska, or the princess or even the fortune-teller. Without a shadow of doubt they all stood higher in the social hierarchy than that simple peasant woman. What was the connection between Alicja Majewska and Karolina Sztuczke? I was hypnotized by those two distinctive personalities, like a bird which has stopped defending itself.

When the days became colder and colder and there was a terrible draught from the floor Karolina moved her armchair to the window like before, jumped onto the seat and sat on the arm of the chair. And when she was sitting on the armchair in her apron between those two scornful aristocrats she sighed from time to time in her simple way and said, 'Yes, yes, Mrs Majewska dear.' And the other two lifted their eyebrows in astonishment, one bent over her prayer-book and the other in her glasses over the pullover she was unravelling.

'Mrs Gadomska, I can't stand it, I'll throw her out of here, that Karolina,' said Anna Bialkowska.

'She wipes her nose with her hand,' muttered Mrs Gadomska.

'I can't stand the prattling way she recites the litany.'

Throw Karolina Sztuczke out? Get her moved to another room? It was nothing. It was a trifling matter. At four o'clock in the afternoon when Karolina was at mass in the chapel a nun moved all her things to another room, including her sheet, pillows and quilt. She didn't even forget her bowl and chamber-pot. She also moved her armchair so she wouldn't be wronged. She didn't ask her opinion at all. But that was normal in the institution. The nuns moved the residents from room to room as they saw fit.

'She's sad, do you hear, Mrs Gadomska?' said Anna Bialkowska that evening. 'She's sad they've taken Karolina Sztuczke away from her. But she had lice, do you understand. Sister found in her bed the louse ridden rags her son brought her to mend. You don't know what lice are. You haven't seen anything yet. Lice and shit, that's what Ravensbrück was!'

She always expressed herself coarsely and bluntly. That was her way. 'Sister, take that shitty liquid away and bring me another coffee from the kitchen! Alicja, you must be surprised at the way I talk. But I was in Ravensbrück and cleaned out latrines. Shit was an everyday thing for me and as common as air – like bread and salt.'

She talked like that in front of Mrs Gadomska and also in the presence of the Reverend Mother, Sister Bogumila, whom she was very friendly with. In fact no-one found it shocking. Times were terrible. The previous day the Germans had hanged seventeen young priests on a balcony on Leszno Street. If you leaned out of the window far enough you could see the balcony. There were crowds of people standing underneath.

The gate in the wall surrounding the ghetto on the other side of Leszno Street opposite Zelazna Street was broken. One day I saw a team in striped prison uniforms mending the gate. The nuns said they were Greek Jews.

A few houses were still standing whole and untouched in the sea of ruins, each one a long way off from the next. It was said that the property on Dzika Street where the Jewish Council used to be hadn't been burnt down and that a huge concentration camp was there now.

The road leading to Pawiak went through that gate. I sometimes woke in the night and heard the rumble of lorries coming from Zelazna Street in the direction of the ghetto. I could hear voices from the lorries – everyone who had been arrested was repeating the same sentence. Perhaps they were saying their surnames. Perhaps they wanted the people standing shaking by their windows to know who had been picked up that night. I used to get out of bed too. I approached the window and looked out through the crack. I stood there like that in my night-dress shaking with terror and pity.

'What are they saying?' whispered Anna Bialkowska.

'I can't distinguish the words.'

She got up from bed too and came up to me, leaning on her stick. When the last lorry passed she sighed, 'They'll never come back.'

In July, in my first few weeks in the institution, when I was standing at the window one day I saw lorries driving through the

315

gate. They were full of men and women, mostly young, although there were some children as well. They were all well-dressed. Some of the women wore hats. Expensive leather suitcases were standing next to them. About eight lorries drove past and all of them drove through the gate leading to the ghetto.

'Who are those people in the lorries?' I asked one of the nuns.

'Jews,' she replied. I found out later that they were Jews from the Hotel Polski.

In the ruins not far from the wall stood a nearly untouched house where the Germans had a billet. For a long time, every day at seven in the morning, a Jewish work team came to the house from the depths of the burnt-out ghetto. Young men and women, about twelve in all. One of the women brought a small girl with her. I watched them working around the house from the window. Some of them brought up the coal, others dug, and the women must have done the cleaning. In the evening they returned to the depths of the ghetto. One day the team didn't come. I didn't see it again.

At the beginning of my stay Sister Franciszka came into the room. She stood by me, extremely tall. 'I heard,' she said, 'that the Germans dug out a bunker in the ghetto and found a fourteen-year-old girl still alive there. They were astonished she was still alive. They pulled her out and shot her.'

Every Sunday I listened to the priest's sermon. He often referred to the events which had so recently and so tragically taken place. He talked about the annihilation of the Jews. 'Everything that has happened to the Jews is atonement for the terrible sins they committed. It was God's punishment. The Germans are only the instruments of God's punishment.'

You can imagine how I suffered sitting next to Karolina Sztuczke and listening to these sermons. I was scared of the priest. Because if that's what he thought, then he wouldn't lend me a helping hand if he knew I was Jewish. But perhaps he suspected me already. I didn't go to confession and take communion. Perhaps he was already observing me without my knowing it.

He didn't look like a person with such radical views at all. In my imagination he should have been a thin ascetic, a second Savonarola. But he was a stout man with a jovial face who liked to laugh. He had the manners of a lord. One day I was behind him in the corridor when I wanted to enter the office and he let me past with a charming bow. I don't know if he knew that every first Sunday of the month I brought myself to an immense effort. I left my breakfast untouched on the table and left the institution on my own, holding a prayer-book and telling one of the nuns that I was going to confession and would be back in an hour or two.

I walked to the church of St Charles Boromese on Chlodna Street. I sat down on a pew and thought about my daughters, then after a while I went back. I didn't necessarily have to go to to our priest for confession. I was still young enough to have my own confessor elsewhere in the city. Once I was in the church when it was completely empty. Mass had just finished and no-one stayed behind. I sat down on a long, low pew near the confessional. I didn't notice it was a pew for people waiting to go to confession. Suddenly I trembled and turned my head. Someone was looking at me. A priest was sitting in the confessional waiting for me. Perhaps he was even annoyed at wasting his time for nothing.

I got up and approached the altar and knelt down. I put my hands together and leaned my head against a large brass candlestick standing next to me. In front of me was a blackened with age wooden cross with Christ stretched out on it. So I knelt in front of the altar under the huge cross all alone in the church, sensing the priest's questioning look on my back. He must have known who I was.

At that time it often happened that even Jews with good Aryan papers suddenly found themselves without anywhere to live. A blackmailer might be after them or their landlady might want them out. If they had money they could move to a spare room they had already paid for. But if they didn't have anywhere else to live, or friends who'd put them up for a night or two, then they roamed around and usually spent the night in a church where it was safest.

After a while I got up off my knees and walked towards the door, followed by the priest's stare. The heels of my worn shoes clattered loudly on the stone floor and the echoes reverberated off the walls. I walked along Chlodna Street in fear and dread thinking that every man coming the other way was an informer who'd stop me and take me to the police station. I didn't have Karolina Sztuczke beside me to make me feel safe and secure.

Zelazna Street, with its small colonial store, was just next to Leszno Street. 'They've got a phone in there, Mrs Majewska,' Mrs Mech told me once with a faint smile, winking knowingly. Leszno Street. And here's the entrance to our institution with the cross above the door. 'Listen, Mrs Gadomska,' said Anna Bialkowska, 'I know who will live here in Karolina's place. Princess Uchtomska.'

Mrs Gadomska was so short-sighted that there wasn't even a centimetre's distance between her eyes and her prayer-book. She literally lay on it. She just shrugged her shoulders and kept on praying. That evening Princess Uchtomska was already installed in our room. One of the nuns followed her carrying two suitcases, her bedding and an armchair. She went back again and returned with her bowl and chamber-pot. Then she dragged in a tiny black cupboard containing nothing but drawers. The nun slid one of the suitcases, the bowl and chamber-pot under the bed. She made the bed and placed a flowerpot on the bedside table. The armchair went beside the bed. Princess Uchtomska had been moved.

The nun said, 'Praise the Lord' and made as if to go but then she turned back from the door. She pulled a drawer out of the chest of drawers and took the suitcase from under the bed and transferred all the princess's things from the suitcase to the drawer herself. The whole move took ten minutes. Anna Bialkowska and Mrs Gadomska lay on their beds watching the move with great curiosity. One was unravelling a pullover, the other was reading her prayer book. The princess was embarrassed and her cheeks were flushed. We had all seen her poor possessions, her scratched bowl and blue chamber-pot with white dots.

'My dear Mrs Majewska, could you put my small suitcase on top of the cupboard, please?' she asked me.

I picked up the small leather case. It was quite heavy. What could be in it? I put it on the cupboard next to a candlestick without a word. The princess hung a small picture in an oval frame on a nail, a black Our Lady of Czestochowa. Karolina Sztuczke's picture had hung there before, a heart of Jesus pierced with arrows. She placed a thick French missal bound in black on the bedside table. She prayed in French. She was a real Russian princess. She had fled to Poland from Russia after the October Revolution in 1917. She had been a refugee in Poland for twenty-five years.

Her invalid husband had been in the institution for 12 years and died eight years ago. The princess and her husband converted to Catholicism because only Roman Catholics were allowed to live here. Since the prince's death Princess Uchtomska had been living on the nuns' charity. As far as a bed and food were concerned she was treated exactly the same as the other residents, no better and no worse. But because of her royal title she had a special privilege: she had a place of her own in the chapel and no-one else could sit in it. Next to Sister Angela, the director .

318

The princess was seventy-four. She was short and stocky. Her glasses hung on a silk cord and she kept putting them on and taking them off when she was praying from her French missal in the chapel. She always wore a tiny black felt hat with a black veil half-way down her forehead. She resembled an old Jewish woman with that stocky figure of hers. I'd never dare go out on the street with her.

Anna Bialkowska liked the princess. Maybe not just out of snobbery. She had over a hundred women to choose from to replace Karolina but picked her out. Mrs Gadomska's attitude was slightly scornful and she called her 'the Muscovite'. 'That Muscovite,' she used to say, 'I don't know where she goes.' She couldn't stand her. But she didn't breathe a word to Anna Bialkowska because she knew that if she did she might be thrown out of the room she liked so much.

Princess Uchtomska was frequently visited by other refugees from Russia. Most of them lived in Praga where they had an Orthodox church and a priest. They used to bring her a few cream cakes in a box, a piece of sausage, or butter or cheese. They sat with her on the cane sofa in the corridor and spoke Russian.

One evening when we were all in bed Anna Bialkowska and Mrs Gadomska brought up the Jewish question.

'Deceitful parasites and hostile to everyone. They always keep themselves apart so they never become sons of the earth where they live,' said Mrs Gadomska.

'Why?' asked the princess in a quiet voice. 'I had a friend in Petersburg who was a Jew. She was really charming. She was so broadminded.' She fell silent. Perhaps she was thinking of those far-off days when, wearing a dress with a train, she received guests in her little palace.

'Horrible egoists,' said Anna Bialkowska. 'They'd let themselves be hung for a penny.'

'No,' protested the princess. 'My husband and I once had an adventure in Russia. We were travelling to the Crimea via Kishiniov and got out of the train in Kishiniov to stretch our legs. When we returned we found we'd been robbed. We didn't have any money or tickets because everything had been in our suitcases. We didn't even have our papers with us. The train left and we stayed on the station. We were very worried. We didn't know anybody in Kishiniov and no-one knew us. We had to get hold of some money from someone to continue our journey. There was a man standing listening with the others and he took his purse out of his pocket and told us to take as much money as we needed. He was Jewish, a lawyer from Petersburg. He didn't know us. He'd never seen us before.'

That's what Princess Uchtomska told us. The fact that she had defended the Jews didn't harm her reputation in the least or break the trust the nuns had in her. But could I have related a story like that? In those terrible times when the Poles were also suffering (not as much as the Jews, it's true, but they were cruelly persecuted all the same), Jews were almost universally loathed. Zofia Loziewicz had assumed an anti-Semitic mask thinking she had a better chance of surviving that way. I didn't say a word since I couldn't defend the Jews. If I defended them openly I'd be suspect. But wasn't I also suspect if I didn't say anything?

Every day that passed contained so many traps and snares. I had to be on my guard over everything I said and did, and even more so now that I was under fire from these two wise and experienced women. At the same time I was anxious about my three daughters too. Had the day passed well for them? Might they slip and fall?

I was really shattered by the business with Mrs Zawadzka which happened at that time too, and by the business with the old woman who didn't want to die.

'Alicja,' said Anna Bialkowska coming into the room, 'hold me because I'm going to burst. I made Mrs Kowalska's acquaintance. Do you know how she introduced herself? "I'm an old maid and very devout." She's got a screw loose.' That was Anna Bialkowska's favourite expression. 'Now, Mrs Gadomska,' she continued, 'hold onto your bed with both hands because you'll burst when you hear what I'm going to tell you. It's a bombshell. Maria Zawadzka is Jewish! The whole place is talking about it.'

Maria Zawadzka is Jewish? I felt I was going white. I was more likely to believe that our priest was Jewish. I sat down at the table with my back to them so that they couldn't see my terrified face. My hands were shaking when I opened my book and pretended to be reading. But suddenly I jumped up from my chair. If I heard something so unusual and didn't react, wasn't I making myself suspect in the eyes of these women? If Zawadzka was caught out, then how could clumsy, careless Majewska who doesn't know how to extricate herself from difficult situations protect herself with all the mistakes she kept making? I left the room, sat down on the sofa in the darkest corner of the corridor and with my heart beating I sat in solitude contemplating the incredible news.

Maria Zawadzka was a real zealot in our institution. She had even founded an association for the contemplation of Christ's wounds. Blind Mrs Niemirowska who lived with Mrs Mech, old Mrs Szaniawska, Mrs Gozdawska from Poznan who talked about nothing but bishops, Mrs Kowalska and her room-mate, another blind woman, young Miss Szymanska and her friend Mrs Grabska all belonged to the association. They tried to induce me to join their circle but I politely refused. Mrs Gadomska and Miss Sokolowska weren't members either so I could not be one too without arousing suspicion.

Maria Zawadzka was fifty. Her figure and face were rough hewn, her thick, white curly hair was cut short and her voice was thick. She looked ordinary, a hundred per cent Aryan. She was energetic, good-tempered and extremely helpful, and cherished Christian virtues. She and Miss Sokolowska went round all the rooms on the three floors every day, including the men's part, and did small bits of shopping for the bedridden or the ones who could still get around in the institution but didn't go out any more.

No-one prayed as devoutly as Maria Zawadzka. She took communion every day, just like the nuns. At a certain moment, while celebrating holy mass, the priest used to lift himself up towards heaven, as it were, and she was the only one who stood up in her religious fervour and did the same. She had a room of her own. She and Miss Sokolowska. No-one else was afforded such privileged treatment. Her room was right next to the office, a few steps away from the chapel. She often invited me in. She was an educated woman – she knew French and even Italian. I sang French ballads for her and she was moved to tears by them.

If Mrs Kowalska had a gallery of holy pictures, then Maria Zawadzka had a whole museum of them. Tables joined together and covered with white cloths in imitation of an altar were arranged along the whole wall by the door and on them were countless cribs, figures of the saints in various sizes, crosses and rosaries, and missals and religious books. Pictures hung on all the walls. A hassock stood next to the bed. Her room had the atmosphere of a church. Her room was a church. So the rubber hot-water bottle, which hung on a nail by the screen, was out of place in these surroundings. She suffered from rheumatism.

That day, immediately after mass, as she was going round the rooms where the bedridden women lived, she came across someone who had just come to the institution. The woman looked at Maria

Zawadzka and shouted, 'I know her! She's Jewish! She comes from a Jewish house! I did their washing and I know her!'

Maria Zawadzka turned as white as a sheet, ran out of the room, looked for the Reverend Mother, Sister Bogumila, and threw herself at her feet. Crying, choking and nearly unconscious, she told her what had happened. Then Sister Bogumila rushed into the room like a fury, her habit flapping and her cross and rosary beads jingling. 'Listen you, you hell-raiser.' Perhaps she wanted to call her a bitch, but could she of all people say that? 'You monster. If you open your mouth once more and say one more word about Mrs Zawadzka you'll die and perish and you'll be damned and swallowed up by hell. And you won't receive absolution in this world or in the next either. You're nearly dead already, you viper.' That's how she spoke to her in her fury, completely ignoring the other invalids lying next to her and half dead with fright.

Later the nuns tried to cover up the whole business. 'It's completely untrue,' they told everyone. 'That old Mrs Pikulska has gone mad. She doesn't know what she's saying. She was very ill when she came here and she'll go to Jesus soon.'

'Alicja,' said Anna Bialkowska, 'did you hear?' The nuns say that the old bitch Mrs Pikulska has gone soft in the head. But if it's really true then Maria Zawadzka must be terrified.'

Old Mrs Pikulska did go to Jesus shortly afterwards. The priest gave her extreme unction and absolved her. She died in the night.

There wasn't a day or night when we didn't suddenly hear a bell. It was the priest going to the dying with Our Lord and holding the holy oils. If I met him I knelt on one knee and made a sign of the cross. If Princess Uchtomska met him she bowed deeply. Mrs Kowalska did the same. Maria Zawadzka knelt on both knees. Mrs Mech got out of the way as quickly as possible. Even Anna Bialkowska made the sign of the cross and devoutly bowed her head.

He went to the mortally ill. They kept dying but new patients came from the city and surrounding area in their place. Sometimes they were so ill when they arrived that they died a few days later. A certain Prince Mirski died after eight days. The doctor was rarely called. It wasn't done like that. The priest was called instead. And the sick died – or should have died – reconciled to God and resigned, in peace and quiet.

One of them rebelled. 'I want a doctor,' she shouted. You could hear her a long way off. The nuns were troubled and surprised. 'She should be pleased she's going to Our Lord,' they said.

But when I heard her shouting I wondered what I'd do if I was very ill. Wouldn't I call for a doctor? Would I have enough strength to play my part to the end, the role of a God-fearing Catholic? Or was the woman who rebelled Jewish as well? I knew the story of a relation of ours, an old woman who was in hiding in the country with the family of a Polish friend of her son's. She became very ill so they called the priest. She was on the verge of dying. When she caught her breath she called out, 'Shema, Israel.' He gave her the holy oils. She died. He closed her eyes. 'I think,' he said as he was leaving, deeply moved, 'that Catholic wasn't completely Catholic.'

The thought of that unfortunate woman who didn't want to die made me break down. I fell onto my bed and hid my head in my pillow.

'Alicja, my dear Alicja,' said the princess. 'What's the matter with her? Why's she crying?' she asked helplessly.

'Alicja, how can you? How can you, for no reason?' said Mrs Gadomska.

'Alicja, aren't you ashamed?' thundered Anna Bialkowska. 'Why are you crying? Is it private matters or things in general? If it's things in general then you know it's all shit, don't you?'

In the end I got up, smoothed out my skirt which had got creased when I was lying down and left the room. I went along the dark corridor, then down the well-lit staircase one floor lower. I passed the chapel and stopped in front of the door, the low small door leading to the sacristy. A forgotten mezuzah hung on the doorpost. I stood by the door and leaned against the post, and the mezuzah hung above my head like an exclamation mark. Formerly there used to be scores of mezuzoth in this three-storey building. They were all removed when the rooms and corridors were painted but this one had been forgotten. It was just as yellow as the post so it was almost invisible.

Perhaps when the building was part of the ghetto or even earlier when it was a Jewish students' hostel, the small room used to be a cloakroom or store-room. It was right next door to the chapel and connected to it. The wall had been removed and replastered in the shape of an arch. Now it was the sacristy. The priest came out of there in his golden chasuble. The harmonium the organist played when he sang to the nuns was in there. The confessional was there too.

The nuns went to confession there and the girl with the paralysed hand whispered her sins resoundingly. Mrs Gadomska, blind Mrs Niemirowska, Karolina Sztuczke and fanatical Mrs Kowalska went there. The midget knelt in the confessional and the ecstatic girl burnt herself out completely there. The monstrous woman with the terrible face dragged herself in there. And the girl with chorea, and the rolling eyes, and the quivering head, stretched out her poor hands there because she was unable to say the words. And that was her confession.

A wardrobe containing the priest's robes stood in the sacristy. Also a chest, and in it altar cloths with wide lace borders, and a few pews which didn't fit into the chapel. A wooden cross blackened with age hung on the wall. Every time the priest or a nun opened the sacristy door, the mezuzah looked at the cross and the cross at the mezuzah. And so these two symbols hung facing each other in peace and quiet. The cross and the mezuzah. The mezuzah and the cross.

All the nuns, including the director and the Reverend Mother, had strange names that you wouldn't come across in everyday life. They assumed these names when they entered the order. Most of them were from Poznan and the surrounding area and came from the families of wealthy peasants or city folk who were impressed at having a daughter who was a nun. When they entered the order they rejected their old names and surnames and assumed new ones. Blind, deaf and disabled girls were not received into the order.

When they entered the chapel, all dressed alike and with their eyes lowered and hiding their hands in the wide falling sleeves of their habits, they fell on their knees in front of the altar and touched the floor with their forehead. I couldn't tell them apart when I first came. They were all the same. I didn't see them as women, just as shapes. As time went by their differences started to emerge. I knew their names. And I knew their place in the great mechanism of our institution. Much later I learned the fundamental aspects of their characters. The misty shapes were slowly transformed into ordinary women with virtues and vices.

The nun who looked after the residents on our corridor was Sister Amarylis. The job used to belong to Sister Franciszka but when she left for Otwock taking Zofia Loziewicz with her, her responsibilities were taken over by Sister Amarylis. In the evening she went round all the rooms holding two huge kettles and pouring some hot water into a hot-water bottle for every resident. The rooms had central heating but it hardly ever worked. We were frozen and our fingers were swollen from the cold.

'Amarylka,' said Anna Bialkowska, 'pour some water into my bottle. If the top comes off and it wets my bed, it'll be your fault.'

She always talked to her like that. She called her Amarylka because she could get away with everything.

'Now tell me, dear, what your name was when you were at home. Were you called Wladzia or Basia or Marynia?'

The nun didn't reply and smiled discreetly. She knew Anna Bialkowska and didn't take her abrupt expressions or troublesome questions seriously. She just said, 'Praise the Lord' and left the room.

There was hardly ever a night when someone's hot-water bottle didn't leak. The tops didn't fit, they were either too big or too small. Last night it happened to the princess, tomorrow it'll be Mrs Gadomska. It made us laugh and was a kind of distraction.

The women on the other corridors envied us our Sister Amarylis. She was so ethereal and peaceful. Particularly the women on the corridor where Mrs Zawadzka and Miss Sokolowska lived. Sister Germana was in charge of the corridor there, a short, dry, ascetic and extremely devout nun. She was friendly with Mrs Zawadzka who suited this rough sister spiritually. Because of Sister Germana the women had to attend mass and observe all the religious practices. She washed and ironed beautifully so she was also responsible for the altar cloths, while Sister Amarylis was in charge of decorating the altar. The altar was decorated according to the time of year and the religious festivals. Sometimes it was only decorated with white or red flowers. Sometimes with gladioli, at other times with roses or lilies. No-one was so well-suited to the job as that quiet nun with the poetic name.

Sister Rafaela and Sister Benedykta worked with the bedridden. Sister Benedykta was a qualified hospital attendant and could give injections, apply cupping glasses and even use leeches. She was the most beautiful of the nuns – she was tall and stately with a noble face and reminded me of a Renaissance woman. Loquacious Sister Gencjana and merry Sister Alfreda ran the kitchen. If you closed your eyes it was easy to imagine the black-eyed, stocky and good-natured Sister Alfreda loading sheaves of corn onto a wagon, pitch-fork in hand. Or sitting on a stool with her skirt tucked up, milking a cow. Or chasing chickens in the yard. I couldn't understand what had induced this happy peasant girl to enter the order and submit to a strict rule.

When I first lived there, when I was keen and worked in the kitchen, two or three nuns would sit down to sort through a box of cherries or cranberries. If Sister Alfreda was there she preferred to talk than to sing the litany. When she smiled you could see her excellent teeth.

'When we lived at Szosty Sierpnia Street,' she said, 'and we were crossing Polytechnic Square, the boys pointed at us and do you know what they said? "Look! The black crows are coming."' She was doubled up with laughter. That's what Sister Alfreda was like.

Sister Floryna was in charge of the technical side. She looked after the shopping, heating and repairs. She was an engineer of a nun. If the electricity failed, then she pulled up a ladder, rolled up her sleeves, took out the fuses and fiddled with them until she fixed the light. I often saw her doing something like that. She would suddenly change from gazing into another world and approach things of this world, grabbing a hammer, nails and pliers, and getting down to work. The plaster came off the wall and she stood on the ladder hammering.

'Mrs Gadomska, I'd give my back teeth to see what their knickers are like,' said Anna Bialkowska one day.

'You should go along when they're sorting the underwear,' replied the princess. 'They do our washing as well as their own. You might satisfy your curiosity.'

'No, princess. They're so shy. I know them. They hide their underwear so no-one can see it.'

One evening our light-bulb went. It was black as hell because the windows were covered. We had thick, black paper blinds which we lowered in the evening. Anna Bialkowska shouted and ran out onto the corridor.

'Hey! Wikcia! Michalinka!' she called to the lay servants. 'Is Sister Floryna there? Run and get her as fast as you can.'

Sister Floryna was just coming back from the boiler room. The central heating was her responsibility. If there was any coke available it was her job to stoke the boiler. She placed the table in the middle of the room, jumped on it, lifted her hands, unscrewed the light-bulb and screwed in a new one. Suddenly the light came on. She was still standing on the table with her hands in the air. And when she was standing there like that, we saw that she was wearing long drawers that almost reached her ankles, white fustian ones. We could see them under her habit. Anna Bialkowska laughed like mad for three days. I laughed too and so did Princess Uchtomska. Even Mrs Gadomska laughed in her noiseless way, hiding her head in her shoulders and blinking her short-sighted eyes.

The Felician Sisters' main convent was in Krakow and that's where the Mother Superior who was in charge of the whole order throughout Poland lived. Our director, Sister Angela, went there from time to time. Every so often one of our nuns went there and one or two came to us from Krakow or other places. It all happened according to the Mother Superior's orders. One day Sister Fabrycja turned up. She worked for the first few days helping Sister Prospera. Then she stopped working. She'd had a serious operation but she didn't like talking about it. She walked along the corridors with nothing particular to do. She came to our room too and talked for ages about this and that. Then she went to hospital and didn't come back any more.

It was the same with Sister Prospera. She was a young nun, not yet twenty-five. She was short, quiet and lost in thought, with blue eyes and lovely red cheeks.

'Haven't we got a lovely sister,' said the women on our corridor. 'Her face is like an apple.'

But her lovely red cheeks turned out to be deceptive. One day she went to hospital and didn't come back. She had tuberculosis of the intestines.

'Alicja,' said Anna Bialkowska, 'they usually die of tuberculosis, you know. Even though they eat better than we do and have special food, but it's the way of life. Sister Bogumila has got bad lungs too and that's a great shame because she's such a good person.'

Anna Bialkowska's greatest friend was Sister Bogumila. You often saw them walking along the corridor together talking. Sister Bogumila was very energetic and nearly as tall as Sister Franciszka whom the Reverend Mother ordered to run the convent in Otwock.

What about the lay servants? Wikcia and Michalinka were old maids, just plain peasant girls who'd worked for the nuns for thirty years. Apart from that there were also three young girls from town to help, Irka, Wladzia and Miecia. Irka was lame. In the evenings the organist went to the kitchen. He was a short, stocky young man with glasses. You could hear laughter in the kitchen. Sometimes you could hear Sister Alfreda's merry voice in among Irka's, Wladzia's and Miecia's

The old women had been in bed for a long while and the noisy laughter and joking kept them awake, but they never complained. They craved for laughter in the saintly atmosphere of the institution.

I'd never ever swap rooms with the old women down on the next corridor whom Sister Germana looked after. No-one stopped them from sleeping. They could burn out in religious ecstasy as much as they wanted under the watchful eye of that nun. That's what old Mrs Kosinska down there did, the one who looked Jewish. I always looked into her room when I went down there. Mrs Kosinska's bed stood right next to the door. She lay there from morning till night holding a rosary and muttering the litany staring at the ceiling.

I never saw her talking about ordinary things or smiling. She was so old that she couldn't walk on her own. When I first went there she still went to the chapel leaning against Sister Germana's arm. The old woman looked so very Jewish that it seemed really strange when she took communion and made the sign of the cross. Then she didn't go to the chapel any more. She just lay there. Shortly afterwards another woman occupied her bed.

One day when our old priest was celebrating mass a woman I'd never seen before entered the chapel. She entered awkwardly because mass had already started. She didn't have a coat or hat on but she was wearing a smart dress of violet wool. She was about sixty-five with beautifully done white hair, regular features and a neat figure. She was every inch a lady. I could tell that she was terribly confused. She didn't know whether to kneel or sit. She could see that nearly all the women were wearing a hat while she was bareheaded. She didn't have a missal. In the end she found a place and sat down. She was so agitated that her face flushed red.

Her name was Mrs Makowska and she'd just arrived that day. She was allocated a place in one of the rooms under Sister Germana's care. I could immediately tell that she was Jewish. It wasn't because of her face, because her features were completely neutral, but her manner and behaviour. Later on she wasn't any different from the rest of us. She wasn't late, she wore a hat and coat and held a missal. She got up together with the others at the right times and quickly learnt to sing the hymns.

There was one thing I often thought about. I knew I wasn't the only Jew in the place. How did Mrs Makowska, old Mrs Kosinska, Mrs Mech and Mrs Kowalska get into the institution? Mrs Makowska could have got in the same way as I did. We both had neutral features and our identity cards were in order. The director could easily fail to recognize us. But Mrs Kosinska's and Mrs Mech's Jewish faces were absolutely obvious and so how could Reverend Mother possibly ask them that ritual question about whether they were Jews or converts?

That was it. They were converts. In the first year of the war a lot of

Jews were converted. Not only assimilated Jews but simple people too, often ones who spoke bad Polish. Every so often the Jewish Council issued long lists of people who had stopped being members and we often came across the names of many of our friends and even people related to us. At the time no-one knew that the Germans would persecute all Jews and being converted wouldn't make any difference. When that became clear many converts returned to the Jewish Council again. So these women might have been converts placed in the institution by the priests who had christened them.

Half-way through December 1943. The rooms and corridors were piercingly cold. Sister Floryna didn't get any coke rations. The central heating was off. Everyone had forgotten about Zofia Loziewicz. The business with Mrs Zawadzka had quietened down. One day I came across Mrs Mech in the corridor. 'Mrs Majewska, could you come into my room for a moment? Mrs Niemirowska is at Mrs Kowalska's.'

Could I refuse? But the fact that she'd stressed that Mrs Niemirowska wasn't there meant that she hadn't forgotten who I was and that she wanted to tell me something in secret. About her daughter Zofia perhaps, or about herself. I didn't trust her because she was old and couldn't control her words and feelings any longer. That's why I avoided her.

'Mrs Majewska,' she said, closing the door, 'I've got a small leather suitcase here. Could you put it under your bed?'

Sometimes when I was walking along Leszno Street with Karolina Sztuczke I caught sight of Mrs Mech coming the other way. Then I started walking faster and held Karolina more firmly under the arm and turned quickly into a side street to avoid meeting her. I didn't do it because I didn't like Mrs Mech, it was just a sub-conscious safety reflex. You couldn't have two Jews together because the mutual proximity made the Jewish features slumbering in each of them unexpectedly gather strength. That's what people thought.

Could I not take the suitcase? I couldn't. I took it without saying a word and left the room. Then when I slid it under the bed I wondered why for God's sake she'd given it to me. She lived with a blind woman. There were only two of them in the room. Was the blind woman to know that Mrs Mech had a suitcase under her bed? Or was she scared of the nuns or the cleaners? But the suitcase was locked. She gave it to me locked too. The Germans never came here.

329

So why? The only thing I could think of was that the old Jewish woman was so used to putting all her things into safer hands than her own all the time that she wasn't thinking clearly any more. She had forgotten that her things were safe here. Perhaps she thought she was more suspect than I was. That my shares stood higher. That no-one else knew about me apart from her, whereas perhaps other people already knew about her.

'You, Alicja, why do you say "I'm reaching the window" instead of "I'm going up to the window?" Don't you know that's what Jews say?'

How can I know if Anna Bialkowska suspects anything yet. God! How could I have forgotten myself so far and say 'reaching' instead of 'going up to'? There really were specific words only Jews used. Clever Poles could tell they were Jews because of it. After that comment I felt very depressed. In addition the smart leather suitcase under my bed gave me no peace. It was so different from my own worn, plain cardboard suitcase.

'I'll tell you something, Mrs Gadomska, and you listen too, Alicja,' said Anna Bialkowska one day. 'You know that I spent over a year in the Red Cross hospital. While I was there a Jewish woman rushed into our ward one day shouting. There were fourteen beds on the ward and fourteen women on them. Some teenager or other denounced her to the German police. Instead of hiding somewhere she started running between the beds like a startled hen. In the end she crouched down next to someone's bed shaking all over. But everyone could see her! Then the Germans came in and took her away.'

She told us the story simply and plainly, without any comments. Without criticizing the teenager and without sympathy for the hunted woman. And that's exactly why it terrified me. How could she so easily accept the tragedy she had witnessed? The hunted Jewish woman was shot a few hours later, wasn't she? But her death wasn't important to Anna Bialkowska. I worriedly thought that she definitely knew. She told us the story deliberately. 'You listen too, Alicja,' she'd said.

On the other hand, she didn't have the use of her legs so could she have helped the hunted woman? Everything happened so quickly. Could she have hidden the woman in her bed? But I didn't want her to help her, I didn't require that. I only wanted her to feel sorry for the woman, that's all I wanted. But there wasn't a shred of pity in her words. That's why I went to bed with a heavy heart that night.

When I looked at the cold white wall I doubted whether even here I'd win the battle for survival. And when I was looking at the wall in front of me so worriedly I thought about my three daughters in three different parts of Warsaw again.

Is Nina well at the Kedzierskis' in Zoliborz? Yes, Nina's well but she had a terrible fright recently. There was a blockade in their house, they were looking for Jews and they even took an old man from the flat opposite. Mrs Kedzierska quickly tore Nina's dress off her. She pushed her into bed, covered her with a quilt, tied a towel round her head. She placed a bottle of medicine and a thermometer on the bedside table. The Germans were already entering. 'She's ill,' she said. 'Krank. Tyfus.' Then they moved back and left the room. They were scared of typhus. When was that? When did it happen? Maybe it happened at a time when I was laughing.

Is Irena well in Mokotow? Yes, Irena is well and she went out in the morning with a basket to do the shopping as usual. She went out with a basket as usual and she was wearing a green woollen headscarf. And when she was buying beetroots and cabbage a woman called out, 'Look, people, that girl is Jewish.'

People were already starting to look. They were already starting to gather round the girl holding the basket – round the frightened girl, round my daughter whom I couldn't help in that terrible moment. Then another woman who was just as much a stranger as the first one and was also buying vegetables, said, 'What's she talking about? I've known her for years and I know her parents too.'

Then everyone started to move away. The woman said to the troubled girl, 'Don't worry child. Everything will be all right.'

She'd never seen her before. Why on earth did she follow that instinct and not the other one? She knew that Irena was Jewish, just like the first woman did, but she didn't destroy her, she saved her. What day did it happen? What time was it?

And now Marysia. Marysia and her son aren't in Warsaw. They're in Sulejowek with a German woman called Mrs Muszol who had a Jewish husband and two grown-up children, a son and a daughter. Her husband died in the ghetto. She had Aryan papers made for the children in the names Mieczyslaw and Maria Rozycki. They pretended to be her sister's children. A relation of ours, Leon, was a student and engaged to her daughter, Marylka. Marylka lived in Sulejowek in a small house she'd rented and her fiancé was in hiding there.

The mother lived on Marszalkowska Street and had a kitchenware shop on Graniczna Street. The son worked in the shop. He looked Aryan. The flat in Marszalkowska Street was a large one. Two rooms had been requisitioned. A German woman called Natalia lived in one of them. Two Jewish Gestapo women lived in the other. Our things from the ghetto were in the flat. It wasn't far from Lwowska Street to Marszalkowska Street. So Marysia sometimes went there for a pillow or a quilt to take to her sisters. Sometimes Natalia opened the door. Marysia was very scared of her. Sometimes one of the Jewish Gestapo women opened the door. That was even more dangerous.

One day Mrs Muszol opened the door. 'A disaster has happened,' she whispered to Marysia. 'Leon left the house and came across a patrol and they shot him. He's dead. Marylka is going out of her mind. Go with me to her and comfort her.'

Marysia went to Sulejowek the same day and took Macius with her. Could Marylka live in the house alone after losing Leon? No, she couldn't.

'Marysia, move in with Marylka. She likes you. Keep up the rent on Lwowska Street and it'll be there in case you need it,' said Mrs Muszol.

So she'd lived in Sulejowek since October. Now it was half-way through December and Christmas was approaching. I had no idea how to behave at Christmas. I was scared about doing something silly which might be the end of me. Marysia was even more scared and decided to take me to Sulejowek for Christmas.

'Oh no!' Princess Uchtomska suddenly shouted. 'The top's come out of my hot-water bottle and it's all over my bed. Dear Mrs Majewska, please help me.'

She got out of bed and stood there helplessly in her long, white, flannel night-dress. I took a sheet out of her drawer and started to help her remake the bed.

'I don't know how it happened. I can't understand how my only pair of black jersey knickers has got wet.'

'The radiator's warm today,' I said. 'Why don't you hang them up and they'll be dry by morning?'

She hung them carefully on the radiator. I saw her smooth them out with her hand. Then she folded the wet sheet in four and hung it next to the knickers. When she returned to bed she straightened the curlers next to her ears, turned off the light and lay down.

I whispered to her so as not to wake Anna Bialkowska and Mrs

Gadomska, 'What about the bladder complaint I've heard so much about? Couldn't your friends from Praga buy you some warm knickers instead of cakes?' We spoke French. I called her 'Princesse' and she addressed me as 'ma chère Alice'.

'Ma chère Alice,' she whispered back, 'I couldn't tell them about it. Believe me, I couldn't possibly tell them.'

I often thought about this woman, so quiet, so calm and even-tempered. Even-tempered but not resigned. Polite and courteous, undemanding, without a trace of snobbery. She had converted to Catholicism out of common sense as she wanted to ensure that her invalid husband had a roof over his head. She practised religion with dignity, not for herself but for the nuns who'd taken her in. There wasn't an ounce of devotion in her. What on earth had happened to her imperious manner? In which cell of her being was it still kept?

The fact that she liked to speak and pray in French didn't signify anything. French was her natural second language. She spoke it from childhood as fluently as Russian. That night I understood. 'Ma chère Alice, believe me, I couldn't possibly tell them.'

Next morning when I opened my eyes I heard Mrs Gadomska's voice. 'What's that I can see? The black knickers on the radiator again. Is the Muscovite here? No, she isn't. I tell you, Anna Bialkowska, I can't stand her,' she stopped, unable to finish. She loathed the princess.

'That's enough!' shouted Anna Bialkowska. 'Those aren't Christian feelings.'

I could see Mrs Gadomska blushing. She had red stains on her face, just like Mrs Makowska. That morning she brushed her beautiful white hair longer than usual and wasn't in the mood for talking. She crossed the room slowly, hiding her head in her hunched shoulders. First along the dark corridor, then down the well-lit staircase and then she stopped in front of the door to the sacristy. That's where she waited for the priest because she went to confess her morning outburst. While she was waiting she leaned her head against the doorpost. The mezuzah hung above her head like an exclamation mark.

Nowhere in the world were there as many fleas as in our institution. Our sheets, pillowcases and night-dresses were covered in fleas. There were more of them in the chapel than anywhere else. The nuns often kneeled and their long, woollen habits were full of them. Wherever you looked you could see women scratching themselves. They'd be singing hymns and suddenly clutch their knee or scratch their hip. It was a real plague.

'Do you know what, Alicja?' said Anna Bialkowska, hunting a flea on her quilt, 'I sometimes think that Mrs Sokolowska's surname isn't her real name. I think she's a countess from eastern Poland. What do you think?'

I didn't say anything. I found the conversation troublesome. I felt as if I was walking along a slippery plank.

'If you think, Alicja, that Mrs Grabska, the friend of blind Miss Szymanska, is really called Grabska, then you're mistaken. I was told that her husband is a colonel who's in Romania. She changed her papers for safety's sake.'

'One of my cousins has been using a false name since the war started,' said Mrs Gadomska.

'Got you, you bitch!' shouted Anna Bialkowska. She opened the window and threw the flea out on the street. 'I can tell you,' she continued, 'that almost half the people in this place aren't using their real names.'

So that's it, I thought. That's the reason why I was never asked which Majewskis I was from. It was an unspoken agreement. Fortunately it wasn't only Jews who changed their names and assumed false ones, but Poles too. The names were ordinary ones. Zawadzka, Majewska, Jablonska, Kosinska, Malinowska. Hundreds of thousands of people in Poland had the same name. That's why it was good.

But why had Anna Bialkowska brought up the subject this morning? I thought she was looking at me in a special way. Yesterday she told us about the hunted Jewish woman. Now she's telling me about assumed names. Who can guarantee that tomorrow she won't say, 'Alicja, I've found you out and I know who you are. Put your cards on the table! Say what you're really called and who you are. You know what I'm capable of, don't you?'

Or perhaps she was talking about it just to reassure me. Perhaps she didn't know I was Jewish but assumed that I had reasons for changing my name, like Mrs Grabska. She might have wanted me to rest assured that no-one would ask me about anything because there were a lot of people like me here. In spite of everything, in spite of her obsessive behaviour and her impulsive and ruthless nature, and even despite her radical opinions, my heart went out to that woman and it was for a simple reason – she had three daughters, just like me.

334

Ewa the eldest was twenty-four and a splendid girl, as fit as a fiddle. She had Tartar features and was just like her mother – energetic, lively and enterprising. She worked on the trams, selling tickets. She started work at five in the morning. She wore a uniform and a cap. She sometimes dropped in, stayed a bit and then left. She was always in a hurry.

'Do you know what she told me, Alicja? That a colleague of hers on the trams knows where there's a Jew in hiding. He wants to take her into a partnership. They can make a lot of money. But I squashed her. "For Christ's sake, keep away from things like that and don't touch that kind of money with a barge-pole." Tell me, what on earth's come into her head?'

The second daughter was called Joasia. She was nineteen. She was naïve, irresolute and a bit anaemic. She had six front teeth missing but new ones had been fitted.

'Have you any idea how it happened, Alicja? During the bombing at the beginning of the war we were taking cover in a shelter and someone went by with an iron bar. It was awful. Such a young child.'

Joasia didn't work. She lived at her aunt's.

The third one, Basia, was seventeen. She was a waitress in a small café on Wspolna Street.

Marysia came to take me with her to Sulejowek two days before Christmas.

'You've got a very good daughter-in-law, Alicja,' said Anna Bialkowska. 'No-one's invited me for Christmas.'

I said goodbye to my room-mates. I went into Mrs Mech's and Mrs Niemirowska's room as well.

'Mrs Majewska,' said Mrs Mech. 'Are you going to Sulejowek? We've got a villa there.'

She wanted to talk to me about it and about other things too but I didn't have time and Mrs Niemirowska was in the room. I also said goodbye to Sister Amarylis and to Mrs Kowalska who was just passing in the corridor.

The trip to Sulejowek wasn't a good idea. But it didn't have any tragic consequences, thank God. Sulejowek was full of Jews in hiding. Not only Sulejowek but other suburban places too, Lesna Podkowa, Swider, Chylice, Skolimow and Milanowek. We knew people who were in hiding in all these places. The house in Sulejowek that Mrs Muszol had rented for her daughter was quite far from the station. We passed lots of houses, many of them empty because it was winter. It seemed to us that Jews were in hiding in all of them. I looked at the locked doors and the windows with their blinds lowered and saw emptiness everywhere. But didn't it only seem to be empty and silent? Someone might have been living and suffering in a small room or a disguised garret or cellar.

Marylka's house was a one-storey building with several rooms and a small garden. It was far from the shop. Marylka did all the shopping alone on a sleigh which she pulled along on a piece of string. She was a lovely girl with black hair and black eyes, just like her father. That's why she was scared to live in Warsaw. She pretended to be a Volksdeutsch. She was friends with two German officers who visited her. One was called Schmidt and the other Hartwig. From what Marylka said they even gathered that she had a Jewish fiancé who had died in tragic circumstances. She introduced Marysia to them as a friend of hers.

The visits from the Germans were a kind of shield protecting the dubious people in the house. If you hadn't got anywhere to live you could sleep there before finding a place. If you were surrounded or hunted you could take shelter there and have a moment's respite. The appearance of people staying in a house visited by the Germans won't have aroused any suspicions. The house seemed safe.

Mrs Muszol came for Christmas Eve with Jozef, a friend who worked in her shop. He was younger than she was. He had been a soldier in Pilsudski's legions in the First World War and subscribed to the cult of Pilsudski. His favourite occupation was playing patience while singing legionary songs. He was Jewish but never talked about it.

Mrs Muszol was a stout woman with prematurely white hair and regular features. She was quiet and very restrained. Many Jews owed her their lives and possessions. She led a double life: as a German Reichsdeutsch who was born in Berlin she received German officers in her house in Sulejowek, while there were always Jews in hiding in her flat on Marszalkowska Street. There was an accommodation agency where she gave Jews advice and money in the shop on Graniczna Street.

Now, at the end of December, there was a Jew in hiding in her cellar who had managed to escape from a bunker in the ghetto. It was absolutely incredible. The man had spent several months underground and so his face was completely yellow and he gave off a specific rotten smell. You couldn't stand beside him because of it.

Mrs Muszol spent all week in Marszalkowska Street with her son Mieczyslaw, who was short and blonde just like her, and they both went to Sulejowek every Sunday. Always with Jozef. They sometimes brought Jozef's five year-old daughter who lived with a Polish family on Piekna Street with them and then Macius was pleased because he had someone to play with. Mieczyslaw was twenty-four. His fiancée also came for Christmas Eve. She had Aryan papers and lived at a dressmaker's where she worked as a servant and helped with the sewing and earned her keep that way. The dressmaker didn't know she was Jewish.

Natalia came too, the German woman Marysia was so scared of. She was Mrs Muszol's subtenant and it didn't do not to invite her.

The two Jewish women in the Gestapo had moved out by then. Who were they? They were attractive young Jews who were destined to die, but the Germans had spared their lives on condition that they worked for them by denouncing Jews in hiding. The Germans paid them and they dressed smartly.

The two German officers, Schmidt and Hartwig, were also invited for Christmas Eve.

Marylka put two tables together and covered them with white table-cloths. She and Marysia prepared everything. It was very ceremonial. We shared the traditional Christmas wafer and sang carols. Mrs Muszol sat in the place of honour and watched everyone with her wise eyes and smiled. After the meal Jozef twirled his walrus moustache and chatted with Marylka. Mieczyslaw joked with his fiancée. The two officers sat stiff and serious on each side of Natalia.

Natalia was the queen of the evening. She wore a simple black long-sleeved dress pinned at the neck with a white cameo. Her smoothly brushed hair was done in a bun. Her hair was like bronze. She had brown eyes and white skin. She was delicately holding a wine glass in long shapely fingers with well manicured nails. She was talking with ease and charm. Her German was faultless and her accent excellent. She gave the impression of being very distinguished. She had good manners, didn't give herself airs and didn't flirt. In the simply furnished room with its bare walls and low ceiling she looked very unusual.'

I sat at the festive table opposite the German officers and that beautiful girl who scared me, and bitterly regretted leaving Warsaw.

Marysia and Macius sat next to me. We formed a family. Natalia looked at us and although there was no hostility in her eyes, there was curiosity and that scared me more than anything. Won't she share her observations with Hartwig sitting next to her? Who can guarantee that she won't bend her head towards him and whisper, 'Have a look at that woman. Who does she remind you of?' And he'll put on his monocle and look at me attentively. 'You're right,' he'll say, 'she's Jewish. What's she doing here?'

Good God, what did I come for? I've endangered my daughter and her child, and Mrs Muszol too to some extent.

I dreaded Natalia, but who was she? A few days later, after she'd gone, I was told her story. She came from Minsk Mazowiecki, a small town near Warsaw, from a poor Jewish family. She was twenty-four and married. After losing her parents and her husband she managed to escape to the Warsaw ghetto and went over to the Aryan side. She roamed the streets in poverty, then she got hold of some pullovers and sold them in Hale Mirowskie market. A German airman saw her there and took her with him. He had Aryan papers made for her. Then he rented a room for her on Marszalkowska Street at Mrs Muszol's.

It was a repeat of the Pygmalion story. The girl only spoke Yiddish and Polish. No-one knew if she'd even finished elementary school. She quickly learnt excellent German and learnt songs and arias which she sang tunefully from records. She dressed and did her hair just like a typical German. She was beautifully built, big and strong. You sometimes see Jewish women like that. She could only be Jewish or German. There's no way she could be Polish.

When I met her she worked for the Germans as the director of a former Jewish factory. When she travelled by train she always sat in the carriages reserved for Germans. She never stopped playing her new role. She never mentioned her former life even though they knew all about her in this house. It was said she was the airman's fiancée, that he'd promised to marry her. He wrote about her to his family, he even wrote that she was Jewish and all the same the family didn't object.

It was a strange Christmas Eve. It turned out that apart from Mrs Muszol and the two officers everyone else was Jewish. I went back to the institution with a sigh of relief and that really astonished me. I suppose it was because my stay in Sulejowek seemed more dangerous than my stay here. Although the relationship Mrs Muszol had established with the two German officers protected the house, I didn't feel good there. I never went further than the garden. So when I returned and opened the door of our room I caught myself thinking that I had come home. Wasn't it my home now? I stood in the door and breathed a sigh of relief.

'Alicja,' Anna Bialkowska called out. She didn't say anything else. She bent down, slid her suitcase out from under the bed, rummaged in it and pulled out two men's shirts, one striped and the other checked. 'Look,' she said, 'Sister Bogumila gave me them as a present. I'll make a night-dress out of them. What do you think, Alicja?'

She sewed for two days. When she finished she put the night-dress on and walked round the room in it. The back was striped and the front was checked but it didn't bother her at all.

'They belonged to someone who died,' she said and laughed.

At that time she started going out on the street with the help of a stick. When she felt better she even visited the aunt who Joasia lived with. One day she went out quite early and was gone all day.

'What's happened to Anna Bialkowska?' the princess kept asking. She rummaged anxiously in her corner, looked out onto the corridor, even went downstairs once and sat on the cane sofa for a long time. But she froze and came back.

'She must be having a good time somewhere,' said Mrs Gadomska. I could sense the worry in her voice. The day was ending. It was foggy and grey but she was still sitting by the window, bent low over her prayer-book.

It was after six when Anna Bialkowska came back at last. She sat down heavily on her bed without taking her coat off. She was very tired and her face looked strangely different.

'Do you know what happened, Mrs Gadomska? The Germans caught Joasia yesterday in a round-up on the street. They took her to Pawiak. I arrive at aunt's and she's not there. Where's Joasia? She's not here. Can you imagine what I've been up to, princess? I pulled out all the stops, every one of them, and Joasia's back now. She spent a day and a night in Pawiak. I've been absolutely terrified.'

Whenever I thought of Anna Bialkowska's daughters I couldn't help feeling jealous. It wasn't ordinary jealousy but bitter sorrow that her daughters visited her and she kept in touch with them and wove their lives into her own. And that they didn't have to hide like mine did. Now I saw an exhausted mother who had almost lost her child, because Joasia's return was a miracle. At that moment she wasn't the omnipotent Bialkowska but weaker than all of us. I went

339

up to her, undid the buttons of her brown coat, took the coat off her and hung it up in the wardrobe. I did it to comfort her.

The following day huge wagons with antique furniture, pictures and crates containing old china, drove up in front of the institution. They belonged to Countess Sobanska, our benefactress. She'd brought them from her landed estate, afraid they'd fall into the hands of the Germans. She thought they'd be safer here. All these invaluable treasures were stored up in the attics. Everything was seen to by our administrator, an old aristocrat who lived in the institution. For hours we could hear the shouts of the men carrying the furniture and crates upstairs, and their heavy boots. Then everything was quiet again.

Countess Sobanska arrived a few days later. She was a tall, thin woman of over 60. She was very respectfully brought in to holy mass in the chapel by our director and our Reverend Mother. She sat down next to Princess Uchtomska. I watched her from a distance. Anna Bialkowska was in the chapel as well that day.

'Listen, Alicja,' said Anna Bialkowska, smiling in her own charming way. 'I've got a friend. His name is Marian and he's thirty-six. And this Marian is smart and handsome and he wants to marry Joasia. You know her, Alicja. She's a real blockhead. Why does Marian want to get married now at this terrible time and why does he want to marry Joasia? Because he's gone crazy. He wants to have a child. Can you understand it? Who would agree to it at this terrible time? Yes, Joasia. She's quiet and obedient. And I'll tell you something else in confidence. He's a Frankist. He's got Jewish blood. He's also a practising Catholic. Not in an ordinary way but like Zawadzka. He's a friend of the bishop's. You'll see him today because he's coming to see me.'

She got up and crossed the room, swaying but without her stick. She wanted to try out if she could walk without it. Then she sat down on her bed again and started winding some wool into a ball.

'There's another consideration,' she continued. 'I haven't got a penny and Marian is independent. Joasia can't work hard, she can't even work at all. Joasia needs a protector. She's indolent and anaemic. She went to the doctor with her aunt recently and he ordered her to eat six onions a day. She'll smell of onions like a Jew.' She lifted her skirt up to her knees, pulled down her stocking, caught a flea and threw it out of the window without stopping talking for a moment. 'I tell you about my greatest worries and you say

340

nothing. I wouldn't even tell the princess, and you say nothing. You say nothing.'

Marian came at five o'clock.

'This is Alicja Majewska,' she introduced me.

He bowed and kissed my hand. He was a very handsome man with the manners of a great gentleman. He had a noble face. After a while I went out of the room and left them alone. In the evening Anna Bialkowska said, 'He wants to get married at once. He hasn't got time for any fuss.' She lowered her voice, 'He's in the underground resistance movement.' There was no-one in the room but she lowered her voice all the same.

Then the door opened and Sister Bogumila looked in. She nodded at Anna Bialkowska who immediately went out into the corridor. She wasn't gone ten minutes before she was back again. She was swaying because she wasn't leaning on her stick. She was holding her stick upturned like a sceptre.

'I want Alicja. I want Alicja.' I went pale. Accustomed to bad news I did not expect anything good.

There were two small rooms on the third floor, just above the chapel. A woman with subcutaneous lice had lived in one of them. It was an oriental disease with no known medication in our country. The nuns looked after her for ten years. She never left her room and no-one had seen her face apart from the nuns. Then her family took her in and her room was vacant. Sister Bogumila, the Reverend Mother, was a friend of Anna Bialkowska's and she immediately told her about it.

'There's a room vacant on the third floor. And a small hall with a cupboard and a stool with a bowl. But you can't live there alone. You've got to choose a companion.'

She went to look at the room immediately. She opened the cupboard and looked inside. She opened the window and tried out with her hand the springs of the armchair standing by the wall. Everything was to her liking.

'Who will you choose?' asked Sister Bogumila.

'Alicja Majewska.'

I met Mrs Mech in the corridor and said quietly, 'I'm moving. What about your suitcase?' She was alarmed. She thought I was leaving the institution. 'I'm moving to the third floor. Shall I give the suitcase back?'

'No, Mrs Majewska. Please keep it.'

So I took Mrs Mech's suitcase with me and put it on the cupboard in the dark hall. Everything happened at lightning speed. Wikcia cleaned the room and we were moved in 15 minutes.

'Alicja, I'm delighted with our room. You know the nuns don't let us cook on stoves and rightly so, because one of those old women might burn the house down. But who's going to look in here? We'll get hold of an electric ring and a frying-pan and we can cook and fry what we want. I feel like Robinson Crusoe. You're probably missing the princess and Mrs Gadomska already if I know you.'

She went to the kitchen and said to Sister Gencjana, 'Sister, have a look in your box-room. I need a shitty electric ring that used to belong to one of your dead residents. And a frying pan. An ordinary steel frying-pan.'

She brought both items back triumphantly. She immediately knocked a nail into the wall in the hall and hung the frying-pan up, then placed the electric ring on a stool between the beds. The beds stood in a row by the wall, hers by the window and mine by the door. Then she sat down with complete unconcern in the armchair that the woman with subcutaneous lice had used. She looked at me and said with a smile, 'I know you through and through. I bet you'll never sit in this armchair. It disgusts you. But I'm sitting on it like a throne. Do you know why? Because I sat on shit in Ravensbrück.'

She took a piece of Greek tulle perhaps a metre long out of her pocket. It was dyed purple. She unfolded it on her knees. 'I got it from Sister Gencjana. Some crazy old woman dyed this nice tulle this wild colour. What could I make out of it?'

'If it weren't for the colour I could cut out some bras for Joasia. I've even got a pattern in my suitcase.'

'Yes, please do. She can have them for her trousseau. She won't have anything else.'

I laid the tulle out on the table and used the pattern to cut out four bras. Next day Anna Bialkowska borrowed a hand sewing-machine from her friends.

'It fits together like a watch,' she said delightedly, sewing the pieces together. 'You're so clever.'

The whole move, the whole sudden and unexpected undertaking, made a huge impression on me. I was surprised. I wasn't surprised about being moved without being asked, because that was normal. Had anyone asked Karolina Sztuczke or even Princess Uchtomska what they thought? But why had Anna Bialkowska chosen me and not anyone else? Why not the quiet and distinguished princess. She really liked her. As far as Mrs Gadomska went, she didn't have a chance. Anna Bialkowska couldn't stand zealots.

I could only explain it by of the fact that I was younger than the others. She couldn't stand zealots and old women. She called the women on our corridor 'old bags' and on other corridors 'old cows'. According to her all old women were cunning and crafty creatures full of spleen which had collected during the course of their long lives and had intensified because of the afflictions of age. She advised me to be on my guard against 'the old cows', the best proof being old Mrs Pikulska who came within a hair's breadth of finishing Maria Zawadzka off. She didn't have a grain of respect for old women either. She said they were crazy and were all soft in the head, the best proof being the woman who had that lovely tulle and had dyed it purple like a nobleman's jacket and so poor Joasia would have to have strange underwear in her trousseau.

Although I guessed the reason, I felt as if I'd wronged Princess Uchtomska and Mrs Gadomska. When I went back to the room to get something, Mrs Gadomska was lying on her bed with her face to the wall and wouldn't even look at me. I knew she was suffering. Parting from the princess was very painful. I was really going to miss the short conversations we had as we lay on our beds facing each other when the other two were already asleep. She was the same age as my mother whom I'd lost in the ghetto and she had defended the Jews that memorable evening. I sometimes craved to take her worried head in both my hands and whisper in her ear the secret I was guarding so jealously before all the world.

On the day of Joasia's wedding Anna Bialkowska got up earlier than usual, carefully dressed and did her hair and fried herself two finely chopped onions for breakfast. 'You know, ever since the doctor ordered Joasia to eat six onions a day I can't stop thinking about onions. I haven't any secrets from you so I'll tell you I bought some onions. We've got two doors separating us from the corridor so we can go ahead and fry them.'

She was standing next to the electric ring holding the frying-pan by its handle and a wooden mixing spoon in her left hand. I was suddenly impelled by a feeling I couldn't explain and went up to her and put my hands on her shoulders. 'I wish Joasia happiness, just as if she was my own daughter,' I said.

She turned her head. I could tell she was touched. We stood next to each other for a moment. I could see from the way she smiled and the way she looked at me that she liked me.

'Listen, Alicja, call me by my name. Call me Nuna. Everyone calls me that. Please do.'

I was silent. I was scared of this confidence. She was still dangerous. I wondered what would happen if I told her I was Jewish. She was friendly now. But if she knew, how would she react? She waited. Seeing that I wasn't replying, she gathered that I didn't consent, that my friendly gesture wouldn't be repeated, and that I'd retreat to my own thoughts which she had no access to.

Late in the evening when we were in bed Anna Bialkowska liked to talk and she had a ready listener in me because I never contradicted her. She often brought up Jewish questions. I didn't know if she did it because she suspected or if on the other hand, because she had no suspicions about me. She once listed many of the aristocratic families in Poland with Jewish blood.

'You've no idea how many aristocratic families are related to Jews.' She was quiet for a moment. Then she suddenly started talking about me. 'I think that you couldn't possibly be Jewish. You're not practical and not canny and everyone can shit on you. Women like that aren't Jewish.'

She was quiet again. Maybe she was waiting for me to say something or contradict her in some way. She said that I couldn't be Jewish so she had obviously thought about it. There must have been times when she suspected me and looked for typically Jewish characteristics in me. She didn't find them so she abandoned her theory.

When she said I couldn't be Jewish wasn't she asking me to confirm it? Wasn't she begging me to confirm it? She must have wanted to hear me say, 'What? Do you think I'm Jewish? What on earth are you talking about?' But my throat was strangled and I didn't say a word.

'Alicja, do you know what our partisans do? When they get hold of a group of Jews they hand them over to the Germans. They once picked up four hundred of them in the quarries near Busko. The partisan comes out of the wood. The German officer faces him. The group of Jews is handed over. The officer salutes, the partisan salutes and then goes back to the wood.'

Isn't she getting at me cunningly, I thought to myself? I didn't say that the partisans did or didn't do the right thing. Again my throat was strangled and I couldn't say a single word. I remembered Zofia Loziewicz. What chutzpah she had.

344

'Alicja, they say that 100,000 Jews are in hiding in Warsaw alone. As soon as the war is over they're going to come out and murder all the Poles.'

I smile pityingly in the darkness. If our servants Wikcia and Michalinka had said something like that it would be understandable. But Anna Bialkowska? It was impossible. But she said it all the same. And I heard the words and received them in silence.

The day after that conversation, when I returned to our room from the chapel, I saw a woman I didn't know. She was a slim, fair-haired woman of about thirty. She was crying. She sat on the armchair the woman with lice had used and Anna Bialkowska sat on a chair next to her.

'This is Miss Lewandowska. This is Mrs Majewska.'

When Miss Lewandowska said goodbye and left she said to me, 'Do you know of anywhere where Marysia Landau can live? That woman is her teacher. Marysia's parents were killed in a village outside Warsaw while she was in Warsaw. She didn't know about anything. When she came back she was told what had happened. She returned to Warsaw and went to Miss Lewandowska. I know Marysia. She's such a good child. She's twenty. We must find her somewhere to live.' She had tears running down her face and she wiped them with her hand.

'I don't know of anywhere,' I said.

I went pale. I was standing in front of her in my jacket and hat and I don't know what made the bigger impression on me, her tears or what she told me.

'Sit down Alicja. Why are you so pale? I know the girl and I knew her parents. I'm going out and I'll move heaven and earth to find her somewhere to live.'

She put her coat on, wrapped a scarf round her neck, leaned on her stick and went out. She came back a few hours later.

'I found somewhere. And I've already let Miss Lewandowska know.' She sat down and started thinking. Then she said, 'You know, Miss Lewandowska is a Frankist. She's got Jewish blood. Perhaps that's why she was so upset about Marysia Landau.'

I thought to myself that she hadn't got any Jewish blood in her veins, but all the same, she'd been running round all over on her bad legs for so many hours, looking for somewhere for this Jewish girl to live. Going upstairs and downstairs, knocking with her stick and stepping carefully on the slippery pavement. I was suddenly very touched and I also thought to myself: who knows? Perhaps she'd do the same for me. And from then on I stopped being afraid of Anna Bialkowska.

Princess Uchtomska was the first to visit us. Although she lived one floor lower, she came wearing her hat, that felt hat of hers with the black veil half-way down her forehead. Anna Bialkowska received her with all the honours. She opened her hands wide and swayed as she seated her in the chair that used to belong to the woman with lice. We'd been in our room for ten days but I still hadn't stopped thinking about the former resident. I kept looking suspiciously at the walls and floor and all the furniture and even the window pane. I never sat on the armchair. Now when the princess sat down on it I felt guilty, as if we'd played her a nasty trick.

'Alicja, look, the princess has come to see us. Very nice on her part. Now we can expect other visits. Miss Sokolowska, Mrs Zawadzka and Mrs Gadomska.'

'I don't live with Mrs Gadomska any more. I was moved somewhere else today.'

'Where to? Who do you live with?'

'I live with Mrs Makowska. And two others. There are four of us altogether. On Sister Germana's corridor.'

When I sat next to the princess and looked at her I wondered if Anna Bialkowska was aware of the wrong she'd done her. Her and Mrs Gadomska. She'd broken up the harmony of the room and both women had definitely been wronged. I didn't know the women who had taken our places. They might have been from the city. But I gathered that the nuns must have sensed Mrs Gadomska's dislike of the princess and that's why they moved her to smart Mrs Makowska's. They thought she'd be an appropriate companion.

Mrs Gadomska had lost Anna Bialkowska. She was scared of her but they both came from the same background, they had the same politics and they might well have had the same relations. She had also lost me, and she liked me. You could tell by her eyes. She was a lonely, hungry soul. She swallowed warmth just like a thirsty person drinks water. What about Princess Uchtomska?

'But Miss Sokolowska lives on the same corridor and you'll be next door to her. She's an extraordinary woman,' Anna Bialkowska said to the princess to comfort her.

The princess smiled. 'Alice,' she said and stretched her hand out to me. She immediately withdrew it. She was not generous in showing her feelings. She was as balanced as a well set precision instrument. And that's how she wanted to remain to the end. But when I sat right next to her, near her knees, and looked at the small network of wrinkles under her eyes and at the hand she had withdrawn, I thought that her balance might have been disturbed just now.

Our next visitor was Mrs Zawadzka. Anna Bialkowska seated her in the armchair the woman with lice had used, just like the princess. Miss Zawadzka was wearing her hat and she was holding a large shopping bag. She was going to town after her visit to do some shopping for the residents who were very ill. She continued to cherish Christian virtues. The business with Mrs Pikulska had been forgotten. She was calm and cheerful and since she couldn't hear well in one ear she talked very loudly. When she left Anna Bialkowska said, 'If you want to know what I think, I find zealots like that very suspicious. The nuns don't like them because they tread on their toes and enter their territory. They don't like it when someone's more devout than they are. Everything should be done in moderation and without excess.'

Then Mrs Kowalska came and manoeuvred in our tight room between the chair and the stool and finally anchored herself in the armchair like the other guests.

'You've got a sweet room,' she said to start with.

'But you can't complain either, Mrs Kowalska. There are only two of you in your room,' replied Anna Bialkowska.

'Yes, but it's not the same. Because we've got a room, but this is a separate apartment. I wonder what Karol and Malgosia would say if they saw such a lovely little place.'

Anna Bialkowska knew Karol and Malgosia. Karol was a tall, well-built man and Malgosia was small with a round face. They both looked after Mrs Kowalska with great kindness. When she had flu they came every day and were very worried about her. She lay under her picture gallery in a white gown and they sat anxiously next to her bedside table with the cross on it. They kissed her hands and stroked her head, and Karol even came twice a day for a while. He was a tall, strong man and he risked his life in coming because there wasn't a day that passed without a round-up on the streets.

It must have all seemed strange to the fortune-teller who lived with Mrs Kowalska. She knew they were her friends' children. Mrs Kowalska had once shown her friends a lot of kindness and the children were now showing their gratitude. But their gratitude was completely over the top. Anna Bialkowska often visited Mrs Kowalska. When she saw Karol and Malgosia sitting so close to each other and so worried she had the idea of bringing them together. She even told Mrs Kowalska.

When Mrs Kowalska said goodbye and left, Anna Bialkowska saw her to the stairs and then to her room because they still had something to tell each other. When she came back she said, 'That Mrs Kowalska, I find her suspicious. She's got a funny accent. She says everything is sweet. Karol's child, our room and Mrs Makowska's violet dress. When we were going downstairs she told me she used to go to Karlsbad every year before the war. Who used to go to Karlsbad before the war? Rich Jewish women. Mrs Kowalska's Jewish, I'm telling you. Karol and Malgosia are her children. I can see now that Malgosia is very like her. And there I was wanting to be a matchmaker.'

I laughed to myself as I listened to her. I thought of the times when all four of us lived together. Sometimes I was out and then she probably said to the princess and Mrs Gadomska, 'You know, if you ask me, Alicja is a mystery to me. When we mention Jewish matters she never takes the subject up. She hasn't done it once. On the other hand I can't find a single thing that's typically Jewish about her. So who is she, for God's sake?'

Today I realized that I wasn't alarmed at what she said. It was like water off a duck's back. I wasn't afraid of her at all. Even if she suspected me I was sure that she'd never ask me straight out if I was Jewish. She was too well-mannered to do that.

Marysia came in April, just before Easter. She wanted me to go to Sulejowek again but I refused. Marysia came to Warsaw once or twice a week to visit her flat on Lwowska Street. She wanted the caretaker to know that she still lived there and hadn't moved out for good and that she'd only taken the child somewhere outside Warsaw temporarily. Sometimes she even called in to see him on purpose, and asked about something completely trivial.

'I won't go,' I said, 'because I feel safer here than in Sulejowek. I can't forget that man who was watching me so attentively in the garden.'

'But what if you make a mistake with the Easter customs and prayers? Catholics always go to confession and communion before Easter.'

'I'll go to the church on Chlodna Street again and sit there for an hour or two.'

I went there a few days later. In my black costume and grey hat and holding my prayer-book I didn't arouse anyone's suspicions. But all the same my heart beat anxiously and when I walked along Zelazna Street I kept glancing right and left. A German patrol leading a man and a woman came out of Ogrodowa Street opposite me. They were walking along calmly, surrounded by Germans. They must have been Jews. They passed me and walked down Zelazna Street, probably to the Gestapo on Aleja Szucha.

As I was looking at them Mr Welt passed me, our neighbour from the house on Narbutt Street. His wife was Polish. She was his second wife. He recognized me. He looked at me at the same time as I was automatically looking at him. Our eyes met. Although he was a Christian Jew, he was in as much danger as I was, on the Aryan side with Aryan papers.

I stopped for a moment on the corner of Zelazna Street and Chlodna Street. Just for a short moment, in order to sigh and then walk on. That was where the bridge over Chlodna Street had been in the ghetto. Crowds of people had passed this way. Aryan Chlodna Street was underneath and above it a crowd of Jews flowed over the bridge. I suddenly wondered if my pale face wouldn't give me away. Chlodna Street was full of informers and they were bound to notice an apparition of a woman, a woman from that bridge.

So I walked towards the church of St Karol Boromese that morning and I was afraid. But was I the only one? All Jews on the Aryan side were scared to go out on the street. Even the ones who looked a hundred per cent Aryan, even that fair-haired relation of mine who wore large earrings and had a tiny dog on a lead. Even she was afraid. She admitted it when you talked to her. Even Marysia who circled between Irena, Nina and me with her straw hat over her fair hair was afraid. Even she was afraid to go out on the street.

But you couldn't show the world your fear. You had to hide it in the deepest recesses of your soul. A carefree face, a light and springy step and relaxed eyes – that's how you had to walk along the street if you didn't want to give yourself away. Sometimes you saw a best friend or a relative you hadn't seen for a long time coming towards you. Or even your brother or sister. For safety's sake you had to pass them indifferently without admitting to knowing them by even the tiniest movement or smile or even a flicker of the eyelid. Because danger was lurking everywhere at all times.

A few weeks later the May masses started. I attended them from time to time. Whenever I went I saw our neighbours from the third floor, Mr and Mrs Binder. They lived in a little room with a hall just like ours. Mrs Binder was an attractive, stout woman of about fifty. She came down to the chapel in a black straw hat with a wide brim. She always sat one pew in front of the back row next to the door. Mrs Grabska, blind Miss Szymanska's friend, sat behind her.

The loudest singer was Basia with the paralysed hand, and then Mrs Binder. Her husband sat on the last pew by the window together with two or three men the nuns allowed to come to the chapel because no suspicious symptoms of illness were visible yet. He sat there staring glumly. He didn't have a missal, he didn't pray and didn't sing. I never heard his voice. But his wife's voice spread all over the chapel. He was of medium height, stocky and cross-eyed. You could see suffering on his face. He was carelessly dressed and looked Jewish. He never said anything.

Mrs Binder was like a rose. She was all wreathed in smiles. She spoke excellent Polish. She went out on the street, did the shopping and willingly talked to other women who were more poorly dressed and simpler than she was. It was said that her husband had a very bad heart and his wife had to look after him. That's why they were taken in and given a separate room. Mr Binder never opened his mouth, not even in the Reverend Mother's office the day they were accepted. His wife did all the talking. When the Reverend Mother asked the ritual question about whether they were Jews by any chance or converts, Mr Binder turned pale. Mrs Binder replied, 'God forbid! We're Catholics.'

So they were accepted and paid the sum required, 1,000 zlotys. I suspected that Mr Binder was Jewish but I wasn't sure about his wife. I was surprised that they picked a name for their identity cards that didn't sound completely Polish. It might have been because they retained their real name.

I didn't really pay them too much attention. I was friends with white-haired Mrs Dziekonska from Sister Germana's corridor. She came to the chapel in a wheelchair pushed by that severe nun. She lived next to Miss Sokolowska. She was subtle and poetic and shared a room with a simple and common woman called Mrs Kaczorowska. It made her suffer to have such a badly matched room-mate but she didn't dare tell the nuns because it wasn't Christian to dislike your neighbour. She suffered in silence.

She had one son who was in Turkey. He got there after the September Campaign. All she knew was that he was in Turkey but she didn't have any news from him. Every day at three o'clock –

always at the same time – she opened the window. She lifted herself up in her wheelchair and stretched out her hands. 'My son,' she called to him in her mind, 'my son in Turkey far away. I bless your every heart beat, every flicker of your eyelid and every step you take.'

'And he can hear me, Mrs Majewska,' she said, nodding her head. 'At three o'clock my son opens the window, leans out and listens to my voice. And when he misses me very much he can make out every word I say.'

Her room-mate, Mrs Kaczorowska, sat on her bed and recited the litany. She heard every word Mrs Dziekonska said and smiled ironically. She had a class hatred of her and demonstrated it in all sorts of ways. She wouldn't pick anything up that Mrs Dziekonska dropped even though she knew she couldn't bend down. She didn't put her mess tin out in the corridor together with her own and didn't help her from her bed to her wheelchair. Did Sister Germana know about it? She might have known, but in her ascetic severity she might have treated Mrs Kaczorowska as a scourge from God. She might have wanted the two of them to overcome their mutual dislike in accordance with the commandment to love your neighbour as yourself.

When I left Mrs Dziekonska's room I glanced through the open door into the room where Mrs Kosinska used to live, the old woman with a Jewish face. She used to recite the rosary from morning till night, immersed in prayer. She wasn't there any longer. Surprisingly enough I saw a much younger but unmistakably Jewish woman lying on her bed. I'd never seen her in the chapel. She must have been pretending to be ill because she didn't know what to do during mass. I found out later that she was called Mrs Kozubowska and had a young daughter who visited her.

I met the girl one day. She was sitting on the cane sofa next to the chapel. She was no more than twenty. I sat down next to her. She was wearing a brick-red dress and earrings. Her face was round, childish and sad, her hair curly. The child's coming too often, I thought as I sat there next to her. She must be living in poor conditions if she comes running to her mother all the time. She's putting herself in terrible danger. And she really doesn't look very Aryan. She was the same age as my Nina, whom I missed terribly. I looked at the girl's hands entwined around her knees. She was wearing a thin gold ring on her finger and I looked at the blue veins on her hands. I couldn't get up and leave her. I didn't have the strength.

351

Princess Uchtomska lived on Sister Germana's corridor now. I called in one day. She was sitting on her bed and the small suitcase which she had once asked me to put on the cupboard was lying on the armchair next to her. I sat down beside her and looked into the suitcase. There were two green malachite inkstands with a heavy base, a press, two candlesticks and a cigarette box. Each object was engraved with her coat of arms. She handed me each object in turn. When I had attentively and respectfully looked at everything she wrapped it all up in paper and replaced it carefully in the suitcase.

'Chère Alice, could you please put the suitcase on the cupboard?'

I took the suitcase by the handle and put it on the cupboard, next to the candlestick.

It was raining and so her companion, Mrs Makowska, was wearing the violet woollen dress which looked so lovely against her white hair. 'You've got a sweet dress,' Mrs Kowalska once said to her on the corridor. With that one seemingly innocent sentence Mrs Kowalska displayed her cards. Because the adjective 'sweet' was never used by Poles to describe children or objects. When Mrs Makowska heard it, she knew for sure that Mrs Kowalska was Jewish. She smiled knowingly.

Anna Bialkowska's middle daughter Joasia came frequently. She was tired and pale and complained of nausea and headaches. All she wanted was to be with her mother all the time.

'Didn't I tell you, Alicja? At such a terrible time like this, when there are notices on every street corner with the names of everyone who's been shot. At a time like this.'

She was very sorry for Joasia who was still so childish and helpless. Sometimes Joasia came and Anna Bialkowska wasn't in the room. She might have been at Mrs Kowalska's, or she might have been sitting in one of the corridors, and talking quietly with the Reverend Mother. Or she might have gone to the shop to sell her sweets. She manufactured sweets in our room and sold them in town. She got hold of a mincer and a large saucepan. She bought sugar and potatoes and various oils and flavourings. She made a mixture of sugar and potatoes in the saucepan, minced it, divided it up and flavoured and coloured it. Then she made balls out of the mixture and wrapped them up in paper. I helped her. After a few days the sweets went bad and cracked. She stopped using potatoes and started making sweets out of beans.

'Alicja, it's a brilliant recipe but I can't give it to you because it's a trade secret.'

In the institution she sold them to the administrator. He praised them very highly. Joasia sat in the chair that the woman with lice had used and waited for her mother. I looked at her sunken eyes and her pale cheeks.

'You're putting yourself in danger, coming here so often,' I said.

'But I must be with my mother now.'

When I looked at Joasia I missed my daughters. By this time I dared to go and visit them.

'Which niece did you visit today, Alicja? Jadzia or Aniela?'

I told her a lot about my nieces, too much perhaps. I said that they had lost their mother and father and I was all they had in the world.

'You must love them a great deal because you talk about them so warmly.'

Then I interrupted what I was saying. Hadn't I given myself away? She was so wise. Didn't she realize it was strange how I changed from being usually so quiet to suddenly becoming a stormy stream? So I fell silent. I didn't want to talk about them any more.

'Why don't they ever come and see you here?' she asked. She was holding a pastry board on her knees borrowed from Sister Gencjana and was making balls out of the pink sugar mixture and laying them out evenly on it.

'They're out on the streets in their own neighbourhood for long enough. I don't want them to come.'

She understood and nodded her head. She didn't want Joasia to visit her so often either.

'She comes here because she knows I can't go and see her on my bad legs. But I'm going to Busk to get better. Marian's giving me the money.'

Suddenly the door opened and one of the nuns came in and said, 'Mrs Bialkowska, something terrible has happened. Mrs Grabska and Miss Szymanska have been run over by a lorry and killed. On Bielanska Street.'

Anna Bialkowska put the pastry board aside on the bed. She got up and went out of the room. When she came back she said, 'See, what kind of a pair was that? One was old and the other was blind and they were both out on a busy street. They wanted to cross the road.'

For two days everyone talked about Mrs Grabska and Miss Szymanska. A requiem mass was said. Then nothing more was said about the business. Death was a normal everyday occurrence in this house and everyone had come to terms with it, and sometimes longed for it impatiently.

One May morning I went to where Mr and Mrs Kedzierski lived in Zoliborz. I hadn't seen Nina for fourteen months. I found her in an apron and brush in hand, cleaning the flat. I suddenly thought that she had changed. I looked at her more closely. She had dyed her hair dark red.

'How are you, darling?'

She grabbed the bucket and brush and took them to the kitchen.

'I was doing the cleaning because they can't have a servant on account of me.'

She took me to her room. I looked at the walls, the ceiling, and at every piece of furniture and thought to myself that she had been here all alone during the air raids. In the dark. In the deserted flat. She never went to the shelter because she was afraid of people she didn't know.

'I'm so happy to see you,' I said.

'I've had my hair dyed. Emilia thinks it will be better like this.'

After Nina moved out Emilia continued to look after her and visit her, and her lovely daughter also visited. The fact that someone came to see Nina was enormously important at that time. Poles who visited Jews increased their chances of survival and strengthened their position, above all in the eyes of caretakers and fellow residents.

Emilia was surrounded by mystery. She came from a Jewish family in a small town in eastern Poland. When she was sixteen she fell in love with a Pole, went to Warsaw with him, converted to Christianity and married him. Perhaps her attitude to Jews was a form of penance for what she'd done when she was young. The price she was now paying, the debt she was repaying for her mother's tears, her father's despair and the family she had deserted. One evening she told Nina all about it when she was visiting her.

Next Sunday I went to see Irena on Rakowiecka Street. I couldn't even greet her because her washerwoman friend was there in the kitchen.

'Mrs Majewska,' she said to me, 'Mrs Litwinowicz hasn't come back yet. But would you like to wait?'

When the washerwoman left I sat down in the alcove in the kitchen and we talked while she cooked the dinner. Jews hiding on Aryan papers made the best servants. They had all the virtues – they were honest, hard-working and dedicated. It was a matter of life and death, and having somewhere to live was a guarantee of survival. That's why they did everything they could to please their employers. And that's also why exemplary servants could be suspect. Mrs Litwinowicz was a wise and experienced woman, and as she wanted to create the best possible conditions for the girl who was in hiding with her, she deliberately blackened Irena in front of the neighbours.

'She stole the ten zlotys I left on the table under the candlestick and I suspect that she stole my night-dress as well. She's dirty. The corners are full of cobwebs and she wipes the tumblers with a dirty cloth. The only reason I keep her is because she's so amusing. Apart from that she's crazy. She told them to put her down as a nurse on her identity card. Her a nurse! She once worked as an assistant in a hospital in Lwow and emptied the chamber-pots.'

Maybe that's how Irena's position in the house was safeguarded. The caretaker sat in his doorway and smiled at her indulgently. And he even invited her in for a glass of vodka from time to time.

Half-way through June Macius fell seriously ill.

'I must go back to Warsaw,' said Marysia. 'I don't know any doctor I can trust in Sulejowek.'

She picked him up and carried him to the station. When she arrived in Warsaw, she took a cab and had herself taken to her room on Lwowska Street. Mrs Grabowska opened the door.

'What's happened?' she asked.

'Macius is ill. I had to come back with him.'

She undressed him and put him to bed. Then she had to ring for the doctor. But who should she ring? Any doctor would know he was Jewish as soon as he examined him. Dr Szymanski was a trusted friend of the family and he recommended a doctor. She rang him immediately from a shop with a phone. The doctor came the same day. He examined the child but didn't take the quilt off him while he was doing so.

'It's scarlet fever. He's got to go to hospital.'

'It's impossible, doctor. He's Jewish.'

'In that case we'll look after him at home.'

But Mrs Grabowska was terribly scared of the illness, fearing she'd be infected. The doctor gave her special tablets and calmed her down and probably looked after her more than the sick child. He came several times because there were complications. Marysia paid him very little for his visits. He didn't ask for more.

At that time I went there every day. I got on the tram on Zelazna Street and got off at the Polytechnic. Then I turned into Lwowska Street and entered the house she lived in. I crossed the courtyard with my head held high and walking nonchalantly. Weren't the caretaker and his two sons surprised that I came every day?

I usually sat down next to Macius' room with the door open. Then Marysia went out. In order to entertain him I told him all about our institution.

'On the roof there's a terrace and on the terrace there are hens and ducks. There's a bench that the nuns sit on. Some narrow stairs lead from the attic to the terrace.'

'I'd like to see the hens and ducks. What can you see from the terrace?'

'The whole of Warsaw.'

'I'd like to see Warsaw from there.'

I looked at him and thought how pale he looked and how sunken his eyes were. I also thought how lonely he was and I wondered how his sad childhood would influence his life, if he survived the war.

'Well then, Alicja, are you going to Marysia's again?' asked Anna Bialkowska. 'You go there every day.'

She knew that Marysia wasn't in Sulejowek any more and that she'd come back with her sick child. But I didn't tell her that he had scarlet fever. I just couldn't.

'Yes. I go there every day.'

'I'm going to Busk soon and you'll be alone.'

In the evening when she was washing herself in the dark hall she placed the candle on Mrs Mech's leather suitcase and not on the cupboard as usual. It was a candle stub and it quickly burnt down and left a dark stain on the leather. The next day I met Mrs Mech in front of the chapel.

'Mrs Majewska, I'll take the suitcase back today.'

'Good. I'll bring it to you.'

'No. Karolina Sztuczke will sit down on the sofa in front of the door and you can give it to her.'

I thought to myself that she'd really got used to being conspiratorial. I could have taken her the suitcase myself at any time. I wasn't scared of anyone any longer. Even if Anna Bialkowska had noticed me carrying the suitcase and had asked whose it was I could have replied quite fearlessly, 'It's Mrs Mech's and I'm just taking it back.'

Anna Bialkowska knew by then that Mrs Mech was Jewish. 'The nuns know very well that Mrs Mech is Jewish,' she once said to me. 'She must just sit quiet. Anyway she's a decent woman and looks after blind Mrs Niemirowska.'

I did what Mrs Mech wanted. When I saw Karolina in front of the door I handed her the suitcase. But why did Mrs Mech pick Karolina for the mission? Because she knew that Karolina in her simplicity wouldn't be curious about what was going on. Over the next few days, every time I met Mrs Mech I heard, 'Mrs Majewska, how could you ruin the suitcase like that? There's a dark stain on the leather and I can't get it off.'

Could I tell her Anna Bialkowska had done it? I accepted the accusation, feeling as if I'd really done something bad.

By now I was sure that the nuns knew they had Jews in hiding in the institution. I became fully aware of it when a tall, thin woman with a typically Jewish face entered the chapel for morning mass one day. She sat down on a pew and was so terrified that she didn't make the sign of the cross when she came in or during mass. Later I saw her several times on Sister Germana's corridor. She was gloomy and silent. I didn't know her surname. Perhaps her Polish was bad and so she preferred not to talk. She was definitely a peasant woman, I could tell by the way she moved and behaved. I was sure that the nuns had accepted the woman knowing very well who she was.

But what about Zofia Loziewicz? Why had she been expelled? Because someone had rung from outside. No-one outside should ever know that the nuns were hiding Jews.

'They know Mrs Makowska is Jewish too,' Anna Bialkowska said to me one day. Then she said, 'I can't stand her.'

Why? There was probably something about Mrs Makowska that irritated her. I thought it was the fact that Mrs Makowska dressed carefully and looked after her nails and hair, while Anna Bialkowska dressed very plainly and brushed her hair back smoothly and didn't pay any attention to her appearance.

The German armies started retreating in July. There were rumours about preparations for an armed Rising. Anna Bialkowska and Sister Bogumila had been whispering about it on the corridor for ages.

'She's a brave one, is Sister Bogumila. She supports a Rising. But don't tell anyone for God's sake.'

We talked about it in the greatest secrecy although I knew that Anna Bialkowska's son-in-law and Emilia's seventeen-year-old son and my Irena's admirer were in the underground resistance. We heard that all the cellars were linked by tunnels and you could cross from one end of the city to the other without showing your head on the street. Arms had been hoarded and soldiers, doctors and nurses mobilized for a long time. But no-one knew when the Rising would start. The atmosphere was tense. Everyone was waiting.

I could stand in the window for hours and watch the motorized German armies retreating. Leszno Street was one of their arteries. The army was followed by wagons and carts harnessed to horses, ordinary peasant vehicles carrying women and children. Cows and horses were tied behind the vehicles and some of the women walked alongside in order to relieve the horses. On the wagons I saw pigs, geese, sacks of corn or flour and sometimes even furniture. The inhabitants of entire villages or perhaps even whole districts were on the move. They drove along Leszno Street endlessly, day and night.

One night at about four o'clock I was woken by a loud stamping of feet. At first I thought it was the army passing by under the window. I got out of bed and carefully moved the black paper blind aside. Dawn was already breaking. I leaned my head out and saw an incredible sight. Thousands of people in striped prison uniforms were coming out of the open gate leading to the ghetto and were flowing down Zelazna Street towards Chlodna Street like a stream. They were walking in even rows, eight to a row. Among them I saw a young boy of perhaps eleven, also in stripes. One man dropped his mess tin. It fell on the asphalt street with a clatter. He didn't pick it up but just walked on. There must have been a few thousand people. Behind them about a dozen horse wagons with suitcases and other baggage. The concentration camp on Gensia Street was being evacuated, so it was said.

On the other side of Leszno Street opposite our institution and inside the ghetto wall stood an untouched building. It used to be a school before the war. Now it was said to be a German staff head-quarters and looked like a fortress. Lorries had been taking crates and furniture out of the building for many days. The next building, outside the ghetto wall, must have housed a factory because at certain times you could see a lot of women and children in the windows. They were watching the evacuation and laughing, clapping their hands and singing patriotic songs. One of the officers threatened them with a revolver.

I lived alone now. Anna Bialkowska had gone to Busk. One morning I left the institution to go to Marysia's. The tram stop was on Zelazna Street, just past Chlodna Street. While I was standing at the stop waiting for the tram I noticed Nina's old nanny on the corner of the street with her back to me. I recognized her immediately and was terribly scared. I backed into Chlodna Street and stood looking at a shop window. When I went to the stop a quarter of an hour later she was gone. Emilia was at Marysia's.

'I was at Nina's yesterday and she sends you her love.'

Emilia was wearing a striped summer dress and a large straw hat on her head. She had come to tell Marysia that if she needed a spare flat she could arrange one in Zoliborz. Marysia thought about the suggestion for a long time.

'In the last few days,' she told Emilia, 'they've starting saying in the house that I'm Jewish. I'm scared to stay here. I should really move somewhere else but I'd like to be with my mother during the Rising. How long will it last? Everyone thinks it'll be two weeks. The Russians are nearly at Warsaw, aren't they?'

'Ask the Reverend Mother,' Marysia said to me, 'to let me and Macius stay with you during the Rising.'

So they suspected her in the house. I knew how terrible the consequences could be. The very same day when I got back to the institution I went to the office and with tears in my eyes I asked if my daughter-in-law and her son could live with me during the Rising.

'We don't want to split up. We want to stay together,' I said.

She gave her permission. Like everyone else she thought that the Rising would last no longer than two weeks. It was strange the way everyone believed it would be two weeks. People even arranged to meet in such and such a place in two weeks' time.

'But she must provide her own food,' said the Reverend Mother.

I went to Marysia's again next day and told her what had been arranged.

'The whole house is now talking about me being Jewish. Mrs Grabowska tells me what they're saying.'

On 30 July at about noon Marysia and Macius came to our institution. She brought a suitcase and a basket with food. She moved into Anna Bialkowska's corner and immediately made some soup for herself and Macius on the electric ring.

'When's the rising?' I asked quietly.

'In the next few days,' she replied in a whisper. 'I was told by someone who's in touch with the underground resistance.'

On 1 August the first shot was fired at three o'clock near our institution. Old Mrs Witkowska went out to town at six in the morning to look after someone's flat and couldn't get back. She was cut off and was forced to stay in the flat she was looking after. If she'd risked it and tried to come back via streets where the fighting was in progress she'd have been shot. The same happened to the Reverend Mother, Sister Floryna and Walenty, the manservant, who went shopping in the afternoon. They didn't come back, they were cut off. They probably took shelter in the nearest church or in another institution in a district where the fighting hadn't started yet.

Our institution was a small island in the whole of Warsaw. Life might still have been pulsing in other districts but on this island it died completely. The streets were deserted and there was no traffic. All you could hear was the whistle of shots, the buzzing of planes and distant explosions.

Our window looked out over the former ghetto, at the house where there was said to be a German staff headquarters. The Germans placed a machine-gun on the roof of the house and fired into the windows of our institution. When the first shot was fired into our room Marysia, Macius and I ran out onto the staircase.

'Let's sit here behind the wall. We'll put a cupboard in front of the door and leave a narrow gap.'

We entered the hall carefully and moved the cupboard in front of the door. But the shots pierced the cupboard, flew across the staircase and disappeared through the tall window. While we were standing there not knowing where to take shelter from the shots the administrator quickly ran upstairs and said, 'It's not safe here.'

We followed him to the attic. It was like a box-room, full of old furniture – trunks, chairs and armchairs. There was an easel in the corner and on it a painting someone had once started. Everything was covered with dust and cobwebs. The wooden ceiling sloped. A tiny, narrow window looked out over the courtyard. Rays of light entered at an angle and the dust quivered in them, layers of dust which were raised when we entered. Because it was cramped there and the tiny window only gave a half-light, or else because of the dust dancing in the sharply delineated narrow shaft of light, we had the illusion of safety. Our beating hearts slowly calmed down. This

360

cosy corner was the first stop at which we fought for our lives during those dangerous days.

The priest was sitting on the armchair and talking with a tall man we didn't know who was standing next to the easel. He was on our street when the Rising started. He was cut off from his neighbourhood. When he heard the rattle of machine-guns he ran into our doorway. He didn't know how and when he'd be able to get out of here and rejoin his family. When the priest saw us coming in he stirred. He opened his hands wide like a host receiving visitors with all the honours. We sat down on a crate. The administrator sat down next to the priest in another armchair and they immediately started talking politics.

'It definitely won't last long,' they said, 'the Russians are just outside Warsaw.'

'What about those 100,000 people that the Germans need to dig trenches? Just think. 100,000 people! They won't get them.'

Then they fell silent and listened to the noise from outside. It was getting louder. Shells exploding, the rattle of bullets and the sound of window panes smashing as they fell and hit the pavement. The priest stretched out his arm and hugged Macius and held him close. He put his hand on his fair hair and after every louder explosion it seemed as if he wanted the silent child to help calm the beating of his heart. Or perhaps he thought that the child was afraid and would be calmer with him than with his worried mother.

He didn't say a word to him. He could have told him to say a prayer. He could have asked him if he said his prayers regularly. He didn't say anything. Maybe the terrible shooting aroused his paternal instinct and he wasn't a priest, only a father feasting his heart and eyes on Macius' delicate beauty. I sat next to him, surprised. When I saw him hugging the boy so warmly I thought about the sermons I'd heard so often and listened to with a trembling heart.

'Everything that's happened to the Jews is a punishment and penance for their sins. The Germans are only the instrument of punishment.'

And here he is hugging this Jewish child.

I worried about Irena and Nina too and mentally said goodbye to them. I didn't know if I'd ever see them again. Then I wondered where Marian was at this crucial time. What street was he on duty on? He was close to me and I was afraid for him. As if he was a member of my family and we were joined by bonds of blood. I also

361

thought about Emilia's son, seventeen and still at school. He was also on duty with a machine-gun or waiting round a corner clutching a grenade. And I thought about the glazier who visited Irena. What street is he standing on now with his machine-gun?

When the first shots came through the windows into the rooms at the front, the women who lived there started shouting. They ran out onto the corridor in disarray and called the nuns, like children call their mothers. When the sister in charge didn't return Sister Bogumila took over the reins of government. She took over calmly and with dignity. She started with moving all the beds from the front rooms into the corridors. It was packed tight with the beds arranged next to each other in two rows, and so she told the women to lie down because she didn't want them moving around and making each other nervous. So, sick or not, they were all lying down, and the nuns walked along the narrow gap between the beds.

She foresaw that things would get worse and so she started making preparations to move the bedridden, of whom there were about a hundred, men and women, to the spacious basements which were reached from the courtyard. 'The beds will stand next to each other. The women in one part and the men in the other.' That's what she ordered. She also ordered the altar to be taken from the chapel and placed in the basement and some pictures hung on the wall above it.

In the evening when it got dark and the shooting stopped we came down from the attic. I squeezed into our room and took the aluminium pan which was standing on the electric ring. Groping in the dark I came across the bag of sugar and so I took that too. Then I went downstairs and made my way through the beds towards the kitchen followed by Marysia and Macius. I met Miss Sokolowska who was helping the nuns move the sick.

'Is that the little boy?' she asked. 'What's your name?'

'Maciej Majewski,' he replied.

She stroked his fair hair. 'He looks like a little lord,' she said to me quietly.

Mrs Kowalska nodded to me. She was lying on her bed and eating soup out of a mess tin. Two paraffin lamps lit the corridor. A bedside table stood next to Mrs Kowalska's bed and on it was a cross with a rosary hung round it. The cross glistened in the dim light and the beads quivered in the air which was thick from the breath of the women lying down and the steam from the hot soup. 'Sit down on my bed for a moment,' she said. 'Is that the little boy? You're all together, while Karol and Malgosia aren't with me and I don't know what's happening to them.' She took my hand. 'What a pity Mrs Bialkowska's not with us. She'd give us all courage.'

At this critical time I was really sorry that Anna Bialkowska had gone to Busk to get her bad legs better. But if she hadn't gone would Marysia and Macius be with me?

Mrs Gadomska was lying opposite Mrs Kowalska with her prayer-book right in front of her eyes. The bed behind hers in the row was Karolina Sztuczke's. She called out to me. When I went over to her she had forgotten she had called me. She started reciting the litany. But her faded pupils were staring at me. Her face looked as if it was hewn out of wood yellow with age and was turned towards me. I waited in case she wanted to say something. She'd got smaller and shrunk in the course of that one day.

I didn't want to stay any longer. I kept thinking about where we were going to spend the night. We couldn't move our beds out onto the corridor because right next to the door was the staircase.

'Could I have some soup for my daughter-in-law and her son, please? She couldn't make any today because of the shooting coming in through the window,' I said to Sister Gencjana in the kitchen.

It wasn't in the agreement I'd made with the director. She had allowed Marysia to stay on condition she provided her own food. But could I foresee that our room would be under fire right from the start? It was beyond our control. That's why I asked for the soup in a strangled voice, handing her the pan just like a poor woman asks for alms. Sister Gencjana ladled some soup out of her pot and poured it into the pan. She also gave me two pieces of bread.

'May God repay you,' I said, and not 'thank you'.

Wikcia and Michalinka were washing mess tins. 'Where are you going to live now, Mrs Majewska?' they asked.

I stood with the pan of soup in my outstretched hand. 'I don't know.'

They glanced at each other. Wikcia said, 'We'll let you have our room and we'll go somewhere else.'

'Wikcia!' I couldn't say anything more. I couldn't find the words to thank her.

Wikcia led us to her room holding a lighted candle stub. The room was on the first floor. The front corridor turned into the side annexe of the building and then into the opposite annexe. Doors led off from it to the smaller rooms where the servants lived. We pulled our shoes off and lay down on the flea-ridden beds without getting undressed at all and fell asleep immediately.

Next morning Marysia crawled into our old room on all fours and pulled the suitcase out from under her bed. She crawled away with it and carefully went down the stairs which were covered with splinters of broken glass. The cannonade started again at twelve o'clock. Through the window we could see a lot of people running across the courtyard towards the cellars. We went down as well.

The house was a huge closed block consisting of a front, a back and two side annexes. The courtyard was paved with small, yellow, rectangular bricks. In the middle of the courtyard was a walled circle and in the circle was grey earth where flowers should have grown. Now all you could see there were weeds, dried out in the sun. Also two low graves with hurriedly made crosses. Two women from our institution had died in the night and were buried there.

We ducked and quickly ran across the courtyard and took cover in the hall of the side annexe. We sat on the floor for a while and then, exhausted, we entered a flat on the ground floor through the open door. A young couple lived there. A lot of people we didn't know were in the flat. We sat down. No-one paid us any attention. Through the open door leading into the next room we could see a wide bed covered with a bedspread. On it were lots of multi-coloured cushions and among them a teddy bear.

A little kitten was running around the flat mewing piteously. Then it jumped onto the bed and cuddled up to the teddy bear. Within the tragedy that the huge city was experiencing the small creature was experiencing its own tragedy as well. It had lost its mother. Lost, terrified and searching for warmth it was looking to a soft toy for protection, care and consolation .

We spent the night and many of the following days and nights in the cellar. We came up from the cellar to Wikcia and Michalinka's room and then went down again. About a dozen steps led to the cellar and down there were crates and stools and even an old arm-chair. By the wall a table littered with things. Blankets and quilts lay on the floor. High up there was a small, long window. A door led into another cellar. The residents of the house, including a lot of strangers who had been cut off from their own homes, and a few people from our institution took cover in the cellars.

The bricks had been taken out of one of the walls, making a huge, dark, oval hole. It formed a tunnel linking the cellars of other houses. One night a group of insurgents came out of the hole and quartered themselves in our house. We now knew that the Germans were using incendiary bombs and systematically setting fire to houses one after the other. But everyone believed the Russians would come. They were so close, just outside Warsaw.

That night we spread a coat on the table and Macius slept on the coat and Marysia and I sat next to him. Mr and Mrs Binder sat next to us. They were our neighbours. The priest and the administrator sat on armchairs. Scores of people sat and lay on the floor all huddled together in a heap. The priest made a speech. He comforted and calmed everyone. He mentioned the Jews and voiced his opinions ruthlessly and directly. 'Trust in God, my children. Poland will continue to exist. But remember to guard against Jewish miasmas everywhere, in art, poetry and literature.'

Weren't we and the Binders sitting next to us a secret Jewish community in this sea of strangers? Just like the Marranos in Spain. In our battle to stay alive we had to accept in silence what the priest said. That night the Binders guessed we were Jewish. We didn't deny it. We didn't turn away and didn't harden our faces under their questioning looks.

'We're from Lodz,' said Mrs Binder quietly.

We nodded our heads. The story of their life was encompassed in those few words. At midnight one of the nuns came and brought some soup in a watering can. She was holding a ladle and a stack of mess tins in her other hand. First of all she gave some soup to the priest and the administrator, then gave some to us and the Binders and then distributed the rest to everyone else.

The nun was followed by an old woman from the institution. She must already have been soft in the head because she had a bag containing lots of empty bottles. She started moving around the cellar rattling the bottles and then finally she found a place for herself next to the tunnel. She sat down on the floor, put her arms round her bag and hugged it tight. She was guarding her property. If you'd tried to take the bottles off her she'd have felt lost and naked, just as if someone had taken your money and you were left with no support.

Suddenly a strong blast of air from a nearby explosion hit the window. A column of dust and lime poured over the cellar. Macius jumped off the table and shook the dust and pieces of lime off him.

365

The priest stretched out his hand. 'Did it frighten you, Macius?' he asked. He drew him close. 'Are you scared?' No. He wasn't scared now. He was a brave boy. He was scared when he lived on Nowy Zjazd and Lwowska Street with his mother. When his mother went out and left him all alone. He knew what a round-up meant. He'd heard the word. He knew his mother might not come back. He stood by the door in the hall all the time she was gone. He understood that his life was bound up with hers.

The priest took the child's head in his hands and brought it towards himself, smiling kindly. The boy leaned against the priest's knees and watched the spiders swinging in their webs beneath the low ceiling. He was tired. It wasn't his first night in the cellar. I looked at the two of them and wondered whether the priest knew or not. Didn't he suspect anything? He lived in the institution, so could he really not know about the Jewish women in hiding there, and the Jewish men too? There were thirty men in the place after all and there could well be some Jews among them.

If he knew, why did he preach those sermons of his? Why did he terrify people who didn't know what tomorrow had in store and whose thoughts were still so inseparably linked to their experiences in the ghetto, like an unborn child to its mother? Why did he torment them if he knew? I could imagine Sister Bogumila kneeling in the confessional and whispering, 'It's my Christian duty to rescue Jews.' She was sure to say that. Even if the others didn't she did. So did he know or didn't he?

The priest repeated the child's name tenderly. He put one hand lightly on his head in a gesture of benediction. His hand hung for a moment in the air and then descended as lightly as a caress. He didn't ask if he was obedient and loved Jesus, like priests often do. The two of them hugged each other and listened to the shots and the noises of exploding buildings, and at every louder explosion they shuddered simultaneously.

Just then we heard a loud stamping of feet somewhere deep underground and suddenly a unit of insurgents appeared out of the darkness of the tunnel. The old woman with the bottles who was sitting next to the tunnel shouted and they quickly crossed the cellar and disappeared out of the open door. There were a few dozen of them. Some had rifles, some had revolvers and some had Molotov cocktails. They also carried machine-guns and had grenades tied to their belts. They were very young. There was one Jew among them. He was stocky and strong and must have been a craftsman.

They walked in single file. They had to stoop in the tunnel and straightened themselves up in the cellar.

Then some nurses crossed the cellar. Young girls of about sixteen. They were carrying stretchers. At the very end a messenger, a small boy of ten. I wondered if we were watching a film or if we were in the theatre. Perhaps we were the audience and the stage was in front of us. The underground army passed. It had appeared from under the earth and disappeared into the darkness of the night. We could hear the stamping of feet for a bit longer and then everything became quiet.

At dawn one of the nuns brought us some coffee in a jug and said, 'They're standing in every gate and in every entrance. They say they're going to attack the house opposite today. They say they'll take the fortress today, as they put it.'

We left the cellar and sat on the stairs. Tired, sleepless and shivering with cold, we watched the grey smoke of fires flowing upwards. A few insurgents were standing and sitting next to us. Like thoughtless children: they examined each other's rifles and fastened and unfastened the grenades on their belts. We suddenly heard with surprise the sounds of a piano coming from the front ground-floor flat. Then loud singing. They were singing *Warszawianka* and the song about the heart in a rucksack which was so popular at the time. We listened to the noisy playing and singing with beating hearts. On the other side of the street, over the wall of what used to be the ghetto, a German patrol was keeping watch. If the insurgents were planning an assault on that fortified building in a few hours' time, then they had betrayed their presence by the noise they made. The Germans would be on their guard already and might even bring in reinforcements.

At eight o'clock we attended mass in the cellar on the other side of the courtyard. The altar, pews and confessional had been moved there. About a dozen soldiers went to confession before the battle. The shelter was down here. The chapel was in the shelter and next to it, in the wide, dark space which used to be a store-room, about a hundred sick people lying in bed. The midget came out of the open door of this huge shelter and knelt on the concrete floor by the altar. She was followed by the girl with the paralysed hand and the girl with the ecstatic face. They both knelt by the altar. Then the monstrous woman dragged herself in and crouched down beside them. Finally one of the nuns came in holding the girl with chorea. The girl was nodding her head and walking strangely. Every muscle on her face twitched when, rolling her eyes and waving her hands, she sat down at last and made the sign of the cross with a disobedient hand.

The soldiers on the pews watched this human debris. They saw the terror on their faces and the way their bodies shook at every shot, they saw their terrified eyes looking through the small window at the sky with its billows of dark smoke. It was a pathetic sight, this fear of death on the part of creatures so very disabled by fate. They didn't leave the shelter for a single second and hid under the thickest walls when they heard the buzzing of a plane.

We also hid in the shelter for one night with these women, next to the bedridden. But we preferred the cellar the priest was in. He must have preferred it too. He was a good-natured man who liked the course of everyday life and ordinary, unforced conversation. So as soon as mass was finished we went down to the other cellar, and the priest and institution administrator came along a moment later.

'Who is this Bor-Komorowski? I've never heard of him before,' said the priest.

'Nor have I,' said the administrator, 'but he must have a good head on his shoulders if he's commanding the Rising.'

Then another unit came out of the tunnel and joined the first one. At twelve o'clock the soldiers opened the gate and started their attack. They took a ladder along and placed it against the wall of the former ghetto, but they were repulsed. They retreated leaving the gate open and built a barricade in the courtyard by the open gate. They used whatever there was at hand – barrels, crates and benches. They fetched wardrobes, stools and sofas from flats. The Germans were shooting through the open gate, killing one and wounding a few more. The barricade was badly built so everything kept falling off it.

'Why didn't they build the barricade before attacking, when the gate was closed?' asked someone. 'Why didn't they foresee that they might have to retreat? Now the Germans can come in at any time and kill the lot.'

They immediately dug a grave in the courtyard, next to the two graves of old women from our institution, and buried their dead comrade. No-one had time to erect a cross. We were sitting in the cellar when the wounded fighter was carried in on a stretcher. He was screaming terribly. The hospital was on Ogrodowa Street next to the junction with Biala Street. He had to be taken to the hospital through our tunnel and through dozens of tunnels and cellars. The empty stretcher had passed through the tunnel but now it was too narrow to take a stretcher with a wounded person on it. It didn't fit. The tunnel had to be widened. They threw themselves at it. One had a hammer, one a shovel, and one just smashed the bricks with a piece of stone. At last the stretcher passed through.

The attack was unsuccessful. The insurgents retreated leaving the gate wide open, while the Germans kept shooting through it with machine-guns. The nun who brought a watering can of soup a few hours later couldn't cross the courtyard. She came through the flats in the adjacent annexe.

'They say the houses next to our building are on fire,' she said. 'Someone climbed up on the roof and put his hand on the wall of the neighbouring house and the wall was hot. There's a machine-gun on the window sill in Mrs Majewska's room.'

Things were different in other parts of the city. On Chlodna Street some SS men, who were surrounded by insurgents, blew themselves up in the building they were in. We heard the explosion. We were more scared that night in the cellar than the night before. There were so many dangers lurking. Machine-gun fire and bullets, bombs and incendiary bombs from low flying planes, houses on fire all around, the Germans who would probably shoot all the residents because the insurgents were in the house. And in addition the fear when a woman we had started an innocent conversation with in our cellar said, 'Your daughter-in-law looks just like you. It's very strange.' That was an additional fear, as if the others weren't enough.

That night Marysia lay down on a table next to her son and fell asleep. She was exhausted. They both slept oblivious to the shooting and explosions. I sat beside them and thought about my other two daughters in Mokotow and Zoliborz. My thoughts raced from Mokotow to Zoliborz as fast as a shot. Where are Irena and Nina at this moment? What cellars are they sheltering in?

At dawn, when cold mist crept in through the open window, I looked around with dull eyes. A man we didn't know got up from the floor, took his coat off and covered Marysia with it. The messenger, a small boy of ten, kept moving around our cellar. He would disappear into the tunnel and then slide out of it some time later. He was bringing instructions. He wasn't much taller than Macius.

'Look at that soldier, Macius,' said the priest. He stretched out his arm and pointed with his finger.

We all looked at the boy and couldn't tear our eyes off him. He was exposed to such danger. Sometimes he had to run across the street in order to cross from the cellar of one house to the cellar of the next, because not all houses had underground connections. A small boy like that could do it quicker and more unnoticed than an adult. Marysia's son stood leaning against the priest's knees with his head on his shoulder and watched the small messenger with delight. He was a hero, wasn't he? I thought that out of the whole group of insurgents that one person would stay in his memory for ever.

'Let's use him to send a letter to Ogrodowa Street,' I said to Marysia. 'Write a note.' I asked the boy if he'd be on Ogrodowa Street. 'Can you get to 60 Ogrodowa Street?'

'Yes, I'll be there and I can take a letter.'

Marysia's former teacher lived on Ogrodowa Street. He and his wife were friends of ours. The boy disappeared into the darkness of the tunnel and brought us a reply a few hours later. They wrote that the houses all around were on fire.

The insurgents left our house that night. One by one they entered the tunnel they'd come from and then they were gone. They left behind a fresh grave in the courtyard and some dead comrades by the wall of the former ghetto. They crossed the cellar quickly, and again it seemed to us that we were the audience in a theatre and were looking at the stage. First the soldiers, including the Jew, then the nurses, and finally the small messenger. There were no insurgents in the house now. The gate was open. The Germans were on the other side of the street in their fortress.

Despite the shooting and the explosions we could hear from the city it seemed as if a threatening ominous silence was hanging in the air. We expected a catastrophe at any moment, terrible revenge on the part of the Germans.

'They won't spare anyone. That's sure,' said the priest.

'As sure as amen after a prayer,' said the administrator.

Binder was sitting next to us and he started to cry. He couldn't stand the tension. His shoulders shook, he took his handkerchief out of his pocket and covered his face with it. 'Now, now, calm down,' said his wife. She was worried about his heart. Always so quiet and reticent – no-one had ever heard his voice – he suddenly broke down. It was terrible.

Everyone came over from the neighbouring cellars to ours. It became cramped and stuffy. In the face of the direct danger threatening them they wanted to be near the priest. No-one believed they'd survive. Everyone listened. In a moment the sound of German hobnailed boots would be heard in the courtyard. In a moment they'll come down the steps to the cellars. In a moment everyone's heart will burst in the explosion of firing.

No-one slept on the blankets in the corners of the cellars that night. A group of women was loudly reciting the litany. A weeping mother was pressing her baby to her breast. A young married couple was embracing. The old woman with the bottles, who had always sat so calmly next to the tunnel, was now pacing nervously about the cellar because she couldn't find a place for herself. One of the nuns came at dawn. 'Sister! Sister! What's the news?' asked the priest. 'Have the Germans entered? Are they here already?'

'There's no-one here. The gate's open.'

She was as white as a sheet. Her eyes were lowered. It looked as if she was asleep. She was standing in the doorway and barely moving her lips. She looked like a ghost. The shiny cross on her dark habit swung like a pendulum. She brought with her the fear of the bed-ridden who were hiding in the other shelter and of the people on the corridors who never came down to the shelter. She brought with her the fear of the midget and the monstrous crawling woman and the girl with chorea.

The gate was wide open. The insurgents had gone but all the same the Germans didn't come. They didn't come at noon. The sun set, evening drew on but they didn't come. No-one shot at the windows through the open gate either. But we could feel their presence. We had the impression that someone's eyes were following us incessantly. They were lurking in their fortress. They were waiting. Perhaps they were suspicious? Perhaps they scented a trap? Perhaps they thought that a few thousand insurgents were hiding in the house and were going to attack them again with reinforcements?

One by one the people sheltering in the cellars started going up to the courtyard. They didn't trust the silence but through the windows they saw the nuns moving around and that gave them courage. Two or three braver children even started to chase each other among the graves. At dusk the old woman, who had sat steadfastly in the cellar until now rattling her empty bottles, shuffled through the courtyard to the shelter in the basement. The residents of the side and opposite annexes started going back to their flats. We left the cellar too followed by the Binders and, using the courtyard entrance, we made our way to Wikcia and Michalinka's room.

371

Cinders and ashes fell into the courtyard from low billows of smoke and were blown in one direction by the wind. We could see that the neighbouring house on Zelazna Street and the adjacent house on Leszno Street were on fire. Ours was the corner building and it was the only one still standing untouched in this sea of flames.

'We're here in this room very close to you,' said Mrs Binder.

We took our shoes off and went to bed in our clothes. The beds were filthy. There were fleas on our pillows and cockroaches on the walls. But we craved sleep just like you crave water when you're thirsty. Towards morning we were woken by the sound of hooves on the bricks of the courtyard. Fearing something bad we hurled ourselves at the window with our hearts beating. The courtyard was full of horses, and on them the army – the *Wehrmacht*. They were elderly soldiers, family men.

Some of them were sitting on their horses, others were walking around the courtyard and looking into the staircases of each annexe. The nuns were among them and were speaking German. They came from Poznan and the surrounding area so their German was just as good as their Polish. We could see they were scared but they didn't let it show. They tried to speak and behave normally. They succeeded with difficulty because they didn't know how this visit would turn out, but of course they feared the worst. Sister Bogumila's height and Sister Rafaela's beauty obviously made an impression on the commander because he was extremely polite.

Then the soldiers jumped onto their horses, rode round the walled circle containing the graves with a loud stamping and rattling and disappeared out of the gate. All the residents breathed a sigh of relief. On the whole it was a good-natured visit. These German soldiers seemed to be made of a different clay. Some of them, the ones who had gone downstairs and come across the chapel, had kneeled devoutly in front of the altar and prayed.

Is that the end of it? Have they gone and won't come back? Will we be able to eat some soup at last without fear? After two weeks of endless tension, hope that the Russians would come, disappointment and surprise that events had turned out differently than expected – that the help anticipated had not been forthcoming, after two weeks as long as eternity didn't we deserve a sigh of relief?

It was only a reconnaissance. An advance party which had entered enemy territory to see and examine if the insurgents had really left the building. They made their report. The way was open and the Germans were no longer in any danger. After a while we could hear a whistle in the courtyard. The characteristic whistle of the SS which was so familiar to the Jews in the former ghetto as well as to the Polish population. The SS had entered the courtyard, in boots, with rubber truncheons, with a unit of gendarmes. They summoned all the residents of the house and everyone who had taken shelter here on the first day of the Rising.

There was a group of about fifty people. They were surrounded by gendarmes and ordered to march through the gate to Leszno Street, which was on fire. That was the first selection. A moment later the whistle could be heard again. Now they summoned the nuns, the priest, the organist, the lay servants and everyone not connected with the institution who had found themselves in the place on the first day of the Rising. They were given half an hour. This category would have included Karol and Malgosia if they'd come to visit Mrs Kowalska. It included Mrs Idzikowska's daughter who had come to visit her mother and had been cut off. It also included Marysia and her son.

I was terrified that I'd have to be separated from them. I started looking for Sister Bogumila. I found her in the shelter, in the huge basement where the beds of all the very ill residents were grouped. It was stuffy there and although it was early a paraffin lamp was burning. The light barely reached this place from the small window. I saw a few nuns in the semi-darkness and recognized Sister Bogumila. I threw myself at her.

'Sister!' I called with tears in my eyes. 'Can you save my daughter-in-law? Can you give her a habit to wear and hide the child among the sick?' I pointed to all the sick women lying one next to the other. Then one of them got up from her bed and sat down. It was the Jewish woman who had come to the institution last. The one who had behaved so clumsily in the chapel and was always silent because her Polish was bad. My hand stopped at this woman. She was the one I wanted to hide the child with.

'No,' said Sister Bogumila drily. She was always so polite and always had a smile for me, but now she pushed me aside. 'No,' she said again. 'You can stay because you're one of our residents, but your daughter-in-law is young and so she can go and work for them!'

Oh God, I thought exhausted, I'll fall and die at her feet. Then she'll let the two of them stay.

'Couldn't I get a note or certificate saying she works here in the kitchen?'

373

'I won't give you any certificate,' shouted the nun. 'She can go. She's not one of ours. There's no room for her here.'

'You should go with your daughter-in-law,' said Sister Rafaela calmly.

It seemed as if I was hearing her voice from very far off because it was so smothered by the gloom and reek in the basement. I stood there without a word, struck by what she'd said. Then I was surrounded by silence. I ran to Wikcia and Michalinka's room.

'Sister Bogumila won't hide you. I'm going with you. I'm just going to say goodbye,' I said to Marysia.

I went to Sister Amarylis' corridor where I used to live. I slipped along the narrow gap between the women lying on their beds. They were now all fearfully pale and wasted.

'I'm going with my daughter-in-law. I'm leaving the institution. I've just come for a moment to say goodbye.'

I was crying and kissing their hands. Mrs Gadomska, blind Mrs Niemirowska, Karolina Sztuczke. She looked at me with her faded pupils. She was nodding her head. I wasn't sure if she realized that our paths were parting for ever.

'Mrs Majewska,' said Mrs Gadomska, 'may God lead you.'

'Who's come? What's happened?' asked blind Mrs Niemirowska.

'Mrs Majewska's leaving with her daughter-in-law,' explained Mrs Mech. 'Didn't you hear the whistle? The Germans are in the courtyard. The SS.'

I said goodbye to sobbing Mrs Kowalska, to old Mrs Szaniawska and to the fortune teller even though I'd hardly spoken to her all the time I was there. I glanced at the board with the word '*kich*' above the store-room door, at the Hebrew letters of the word I'd looked at so many times. Then I ran down the stairs covered with glass to Sister Germana's corridor where Princess Uchtomska lived. She was in bed. How she'd changed. Next to her was Mrs Makowska, completely unlike her former self, so fastidious about her appearance. Then Mrs Kozubowska who was visited by her very young daughter in a brick-red dress. Mrs Kozubowska with her Semitic face was now thin and scared and her features were even more obvious.

I reached the princess. 'I'm going, I'm going with my daughter-in-law. I'm leaving the institution.' I took her head in both hands just like I'd often imagined, her troubled head in both my hands. Should I tell her? Now, when I know I'll never see her again, should I tell her who I am? Mrs Dziekonska's bed was right beside the princess.

Her face was framed by her white hair and seemed whiter than the pillow it lay on. I kissed her hands and asked her, 'Are you afraid?'

'I'm only afraid of fear,' she replied, 'and that's an enemy I'll never let near me.'

That's what she said, but I didn't believe her. They were all afraid, every single one of them. The old and sick and the ones most maltreated by fate. They shuddered for their lives, they fought to their last breath.

Then I ran down the stairs over the crackling glass to the first floor and stood by the small door next to the chapel. The upper part of the door was shattered and blown out by a shell. I could see the ruined sacristy through the gap. The cross was hanging untouched on the wall by the window. The yellow mezuzah hung on the door-frame. Untouched. They hung opposite each other, the cross and the mezuzah. The mezuzah and the cross.

Time was running out but how could I go without saying goodbye to Maria Sokolowska and Maria Zawadzka? I knew where they were. I ran to the chapel in the basement and both of them were kneeling there, lost in prayer.

'I'm going with my daughter-in-law,' I said to them. 'Goodbye and may God have you in his care.'

They tore themselves away from their meditation and looked at me with eyes that were still looking into another world. They were returning very slowly from heaven to earth. This wasn't the place for questions and explanations, for surprised cries, even for farewell kisses. I only placed my hands on their shoulders and my eyes met their dilated pupils.

Now to the Binders, our companions from the cellar. As I was running up the stairs it started to rain and we didn't have an umbrella. The child's just been ill, I thought, he's just had a bad bout of scarlet fever and he'll get wet in the rain. God only knows how long we'll be walking. The Binders were sitting in the small room, huddled up to each other and shrunken, black like two birds.

'I'm going with my daughter-in-law, but it's raining and we haven't got an umbrella. The child's been ill and we don't know what's in store for us.'

'I'll give you an umbrella,' said Mr Binder. He was very moved when he gave it to me. 'I don't need it here,' he added.

It was the first time I had heard his voice. He hadn't said a word in the cellar.

Finally I rushed to Wikcia and Michalinka's room and started getting my things together.

'Don't take a lot,' said Marysia. 'Every gram weighs and will be a nuisance. I'm going now.'

I stood the umbrella in the corner. I put some underwear, some bread and some sugar into a bag. Instead of a blanket I put a winter coat over my arm. I heard the whistle again. I started to move round the room nervously. I put my hand out to open the door but it opened of its own accord. Suddenly Countess Sobanska our foundress was right opposite me and behind her was the administrator. Without a word, in a terrible hurry, without taking their clothes off, they lay down in Wikcia and Michalinka's flea-ridden beds. The beds we had slept in with the linen still warm from our bodies. They covered themselves with the quilts, right up to their necks, and then threw their shoes onto the floor. I gathered that they wanted to pretend to be sick in order to avoid deportation. I was so astonished that I forgot to take the umbrella. It stayed in the corner.

When I was going downstairs I remembered Mr Binder's umbrella. I couldn't go back as Marysia had already gone. There wasn't a single second to spare but the umbrella was as important to me as life itself.

A German soldier was coming upstairs towards me. At the same time I heard the whistle in the courtyard again.

'My umbrella,' I said to the soldier in Polish.

'What did you say?' he replied in Polish, in a Silesian accent.

'I've left my umbrella in the corner of the second room along the corridor.'

'I'll look for it and bring it to you,' he said.

The courtyard paved with small, yellow bricks. In the middle a walled circle and in the circle grey earth where grass or even flowers should have grown. Now it contained graves, six crosses on six mounds. Five old women from our institution, and the sixth grave belonged to the insurgent. In the courtyard 16 nuns, the priest, the organist and the lay servants, all in a row. Next to them Marysia with her son, Mrs Idzikowska's daughter and three men whom I recognized from the cellar. They hadn't come out at first but stayed hidden. Then they were scared that the Germans would search the cellars and shoot them if they found them. So they came out.

I started saying goodbye to the priest and the nuns. I thanked them warmly for looking after me and everything good they had done for me while I was in the institution. Macius stood lost next to the priest and nuns. He turned pale and shivered when the priest placed both his hands on his head and blessed him for the journey into the unknown. First he lifted his eyes towards the billows of thick smoke, the grey smoke with red reflections which sailed endlessly across the sky, then he closed his eyes and prayed silently. I knew that he was summoning all the heavenly powers, God, the saints and archangels, and was begging them to pour their grace onto the child's head. He made a triple sign of the cross over him, bent over and kissed him tenderly.

I suddenly remembered Isaac in the Bible, the one who was cheated. Hadn't we cheated our old priest? In this case wasn't our child like Jacob, who received the blessing that wasn't intended for him and would carry it with him all his life, just like Jacob?

'Schnell! Schnell!' shouted one of the Germans. I started to look around to see if the soldier was coming with Mr Binder's umbrella. I wanted to prolong the moment. Marysia took the child by the hand and they both went quickly towards the gate. One of the Germans hit me on the back with a whip and pushed me in their direction with his fist.

There were seven of us in the group. The three men from the cellar, Mrs Idzikowska's daughter and the three of us. There weren't many of us so we were only escorted by one soldier, an elderly soldier with a rifle. We passed through the gate with our shoes clattering and this clatter was echoed loudly from the yellow walls of the house all riddled with shells. Then we went out onto Leszno Street and it was one sea of flames.

It was 14 August 1944 at eleven in the morning.

At the beginning of May 1945, when we returned from the camp and were staying in Krakow, I met a nun on the street wearing the habit of the Felician Sisters. I went up to her and asked, 'Sister, what happened to the Felician Sisters in Warsaw? They had an institution on Leszno Street. I lived there for a while.'

'The nuns and priest were allowed to go to Krakow. The lay servants were taken to Germany.'

'What about the the rest? The 180 old and sick people.'

'They shot them all and set fire to the house. The house burnt down with all of them in it.'

Oh God, I thought. So who was saved? Anna Bialkowska, because she went to Busko to cure her legs, old Mrs Witkowska who left at dawn on 1 August to look after someone's flat, and me.

'When did it happen, Sister?'
'It happened on 14 August, at twelve o'clock, at noon exactly.'

6 · *Journey into the unknown*

We walk along the middle of Leszno Street on asphalt which has gone soft from the heat. Around us houses are burning silently. There are no women running quickly or men with buckets and no crying, frightened children to be seen. We don't see anyone. Smoke is billowing out of empty windows. A burnt out wall falls softly down. Then the inside of the flat appears – a picture, a sink, a yellow chest of drawers, a towel on a nail. There are no people to be seen at all. The houses are burning in solitude.

We walk along the middle of this tragic street in the unbearable heat. The three men from the cellar, the young woman who'd come to visit her mother and wasn't allowed to stay there, and the three of us, Marysia, seven-year-old Macius and me. Corpses are lying in front of house gates, blackened and shrivelled. Sometimes a wild cat runs across the street and disappears into the ruins. Sometimes we look up and see birds lost in the grey billows of thick smoke. Apart from the crackle of cracking walls and the sound of falling bricks nothing disturbs the silence of this August noon.

The German soldier escorting us drags his feet indifferently. He has a featureless face and is short and stocky. He's quite old and is carrying the rifle on his shoulder as if it were a rake or a pitchfork. He's no soldier, just a peasant who's been torn away from his field. We're not scared of him. So later when we're passing the hospital on Plocka Street someone in the group says, 'If we hid in the hospital he wouldn't even shoot,' and stops, makes a movement as if to go and then glances at the soldier. It's tempting to hide in the hospital.

We see a small gate and low iron railings. Behind them a garden and a paved path. Then a door. Not a gate, just a closed door. It's not very risky, although we don't know if the door will open when we turn the handle. But if it did open we could hide there and stay. The soldier won't chase us if we escape because he knows that the others will run off and hide in the ruins. But no-one tries. We walk on and regret missing the chance. We were prepared so many times to give away half our life in order to obtain our goal. Then it turned out that a step like that might have cost our life.

I'm wearing a headscarf and a short, black jacket, the one with the impression of the armband I wore in the ghetto. Marysia is also wearing a headscarf. She's got her apron on under her coat. We look like any other women. We think that's what we look like. What about the child? He's pale and undernourished. He follows us silently and patiently. The biting smoke makes him cough too and he sees the blackened corpses and the lost birds in the grey sky. Suddenly we see a sentry post in front of us, in it Germans, or are they Ukrainians? No-one knows. They order us to halt. Will they turn us back? Or arrest us? Or kill us?

We see a small group of about six people in front of the sentry post. We approach them and all stand there together craning our necks to catch what they're saying. They're not saying anything. They let them pass through the narrow gap one by one, men first. They search them deftly with their fingers and take their watches. Then the women. They take their wedding rings and brooches. We take off our wedding rings and hide them in our pockets. We pass through last.

The child is shuffling along behind us and because the gap is narrow he's holding onto the back of Marysia's coat. Marysia in her headscarf with the checked apron visible under her coat. What can a woman like that have on her? Behind her the mother in a headscarf. She's not even wearing a wedding ring so what can a woman like her possibly have? Ordinary colourless women, no different in the way they look or dress than a thousand others. That's what they think. An older woman, her daughter and a child. We pass through to the other side. The Germans don't take anything off us.

The sun ascends higher and higher. The burning city is behind us now. Kilometres of streets behind us. But we walk and walk. Now we're in the suburbs. Wooden houses with railings and behind the railings gardens and orchards. And the road is worse because it's sandy. At a bend in the road on the very edge of the city there's a tall church spire. The sun is piercingly reflected from the gilded cross on the steeple and the huge windows in the red brick walls. It's the church of St Stanislaw Kostka, our journey's end. Round the church and inside it countless crowds. On the pews, on the floor, on the altar steps. Some people have got bundles, others have got

380

nothing. Mothers with babies, old people, children, young people. From all walks of life – beggars, fine ladies in hats, women in headscarves, bareheaded women, workers, traders, well-dressed men and paupers.

We sit down on the altar steps by the door under a huge cross with an outstretched Christ. Christ's face is bent and suffering. His feet touch our backs. We sit under the cross hugging our knees. Our bundles are next to us and we don't take our eyes off them. This handful of things in old bags is part of ourselves, as it were, the extension of our personalities. And as we sit there watching the motley crowd swaying in front of our tired eyes, a woman approaches us and sits down on the altar steps as well.

'Where are these people from?' we ask. 'What streets?'

'From all over. I'm from Gdanska Street. The Germans burnt our houses. We've been here since morning.'

We chat. She's not young. Her hair is going grey and there's a network of wrinkles under her eyes. She's suffered a lot in her life because two of her children died and her husband disappeared without trace. But she had a flat of her own on Gdanska Street, thank God, and even rented a room out. 'But now everything's burnt, lady.'

She tells us about her misfortune. We listen and sympathize. In fact we are drawn to this woman because we feel safer by her side. We feel more self-confident in her presence. But suddenly we lose our self-confidence and fear overcomes us because two German officers enter the church. They stop and look around as if they're looking for someone and then walk on. Slowly they approach us. Two excellently dressed officers. They jingle their spurs. One of them is wearing a cape lined with scarlet. They look at us. They whisper something to each other. Marysia turns her head away.

'Why don't you look at me? Am I so terrible?' one of them asks.

'There must be Hungarian blood in your veins,' says the other one, the one in the cape. 'I can tell by your eyes. Are you from Hungary?'

From Hungary? God in heaven! He's recognized us by our eyes. If these two Germans have guessed we're different, then it'll be that much harder to protect ourselves against the Poles and foil their watchfulness.

'Yes,' I say. 'My grandmother was Hungarian.'

'I thought so at once,' he says. He beckons me with his finger. 'Come with us.'

'My mother won't go but I will,' says Marysia and gets up from the altar steps.

They turn towards the door. Marysia follows them together with a dozen or so other people. A few workers, an old woman, a trader and a man wearing a railwayman's uniform. At first we wait calmly. I give Macius some bread and a piece of sugar. But when an hour has passed and Marysia hasn't come back my anxiety mounts with every second. 'Look after the things,' I tell the child and run out in front of the church. But then I'm terrified and imagine that I lose him or that he gets deported. So I go back. Now I take the things and the child with me and we stumble round the church. I ask if anyone knows what happened to the people the officers took away. But no-one knows.

The square round the church has been dug up revealing soft deep sand. My heart's in despair as I flounder through the sand dragging the tired child behind me. It's not sand, but the sea. It's not a crowd of people I'm tearing my way through, but alienation. A sea of alienation. We're going to drown in it. We can't be rescued. Barbed wire all around the square. I see a small gate. Next to it a soldier on guard with a rifle. He's alone. There's no-one by him. I keep sinking in the sand and looking back at the child but I approach the soldier. When I reach him I put our bundles on the sand. Now my hands are free and I can undo my blouse and take out the brooch hidden in my bra.

'Some officers came and took people from the church,' I say to the soldier. 'Including my daughter. She hasn't come back yet. Here's a gold brooch, find out what's happened to her. Her name is Maria Majewska.'

I stand in front of him with my hand outstretched. In the palm of my hand my mother's ruby brooch with a pendant on a thin chain.

'A brooch?' he says. 'You want to give me a brooch? I'm not a cursed SS man. They take brooches. I've got a wife and five children at home. It's them I miss and not your brooch I need. I'll be relieved in a moment so I'll ask what's happened to them and I might hear something.'

'I'll wait for you in the church by the altar near the door. You'll find me there. Do you remember what she's called?'

'Maria. Marija.'

We return to the church and sit down again on the steps under the huge cross. The clock strikes three. It now seems as if something's changed. It doesn't feel lazy and sleepy any more. People are getting up, walking around, packing things and putting on their rucksacks. It looks as if they are going somewhere very soon. Going somewhere? What'll happen if Marysia doesn't get back in time and they make the two of us march off? Then we'll lose each other and never find each other again. I am again overcome by terrible anxiety. What shall I do? Shall I wait for the soldier? Shall I look for somewhere in the church to hide and conceal myself?

I'm in complete despair and have no idea what to do when suddenly I notice a Jewish family sitting not far from us by the wall. Father, mother and son of about ten. I'm astonished and terrified. My astonishment is immense because the family is typically Jewish, not only in their features but also in their gestures and movements and the way they behave, and even in their clothes. They must have been driven out of a house together with the residents or with the people from the flat where they were in hiding. Then the house was burnt. I look at them. They got out, but how many others didn't get out at all? They might have thought it was a blockade. They didn't come out when the Germans blew the whistle. They didn't trust their appearance. They hid in wardrobes, hide-outs or cellars. Then the Germans burnt the house and what happened to them?

But what about these people here? The unshaven father in his long grey jacket. The mother with a silk scarf on her head and her wide face and round surprised eyes. How could she not be surprised? There were so very many people here everywhere, while she had probably been hiding in a cellar or a tiny room with a wardrobe covering the door. The wardrobe had double doors but no-one else knew about it. What about the boy? He had black hair, black eyes and sticking out ears. I look at them and wonder if they've got identity cards. Have they got any documents at all? Probably not. And they'll speak Polish badly too.

When gendarmes appear in the church door and people get up and start getting ready to go, the Jews get up off the floor and start clumsily gathering their things together. I'm terrified that the father and son will put their caps on. The whole crowd in the church is moving, everyone is on their feet, stirring themselves, moving around and calling to each other. I look at Macius worriedly. He's pale and anxious but he's not crying. It's me who can't stop myself from sighing and lamenting.

A woman passes by and advises me to leave all my food behind, if I've got any. The Germans will take it off me. Food? Some sugar and dry bread. That's all the food I've got.

We're still sitting, although other people are leaving the church. Half of them have gone already. Soldiers and gendarmes are getting them up and making them hurry. They'll come for us soon and then what'll happen? As I wait and look out for the soldier I see Marysia coming towards us.

'Calm down! I'm here, aren't I?'

'Where were you? Why were you so long? Ten minutes longer and I'd have gone with the child and you wouldn't have found us.'

'Yes, that's just what I was scared of.'

She tells me that she was in an office. With eight other people. They all had to say in turn what they knew about the Rising. They deliberately picked people from all walks of life. It took so long.

'What did they ask?'

'About the insurgents. I pretended to be stupid. "Did you see any insurgents?" "I saw one." "Where was it?" "In the courtyard." "What was he doing?" "He was carrying a bucket." "How do you know he was an insurgent?" "Because that's what people said." Then I clutched my head and shouted, "What am I going to live off now? My sewing-machine is burnt."'

I tell her about the soldier at the gate.

'Wasn't he calling you. Didn't you hear anyone calling "Marija"?'

No, she didn't. But there were a thousand people there so how could she hear?

'Don't think about it any more,' she says. 'It'll soon be our turn to be chased out of the church.'

I also tell her about the woman who advised me to leave any food I had. 'Don't believe her, it's a lie,' she replies. 'How much food have we got after all? We haven't got any.'

I point the Jewish family out with my eyes. They're moving now. First the father. Then the mother and boy. Aren't the people who hid this family here somewhere in among this huge crowd? They might be nearby but not letting on there's any connection between them. Maybe it's this delicate web of a covenant, this fluid flowing along the nave of the church, that gives them confidence and courage.

Now it's our turn. We move towards the door with the crowd. 'Schnell! Schnell!', shout the Germans. We leave the church, then cross the square, pass through the gate and walk along field tracks. Macius walks along with us, calm and silent. At last we reach the railway ramp. There's no train. We sit down on the concrete platform and wait. We're all very tired. The platform is full of people.

We look round and see a cripple. A man with no legs. The

Germans drove him out of his home with all the rest before setting fire to it, and we can't understand how he managed the long and tiring journey from Warsaw. Did he crawl the whole way? We look round further and see a beggar. An old man of about eighty. He's standing under an iron post and he's even begging here, out of habit. Even here among these shattered, downtrodden people. He stretches out his hand and moves his toothless mouth. Perhaps he's saying his prayers.

The Jewish family is sitting on the concrete platform. The mother is holding a basket and they're calmly eating food out of it. The father is wearing a black felt hat and the boy a cap pulled low over his ears. They're so naïve that they're eating with their heads covered, and so different that we expect a disaster to happen any second. Someone might shout and point them out to the Germans, or the Germans themselves might recognize them and take them away. But no-one seems to be paying them any attention. I wonder how it's possible and if they're wearing caps which make them invisible. But after all I can see them, can't I?

I can't take my eyes and thoughts off them. I watch them and weave the story of their sad life on the Aryan side. Perhaps they were hiding in an old house in the suburbs which had a cellar under the kitchen of the ground floor flat. You opened the flap in the floor, a square flap, and some steps led down to it. Or maybe they hid in the attic. Some kitchens had a door opening into a small attic. An attic like that belonged to the tenant. Maybe that's where they spent long tiring hours, freezing in winter and tormented by the heat in summer.

While I'm thinking about all this the train approaches and stops by the ramp. Everyone gets into the wagons. The cripple has been lifted up under the arms and helped up. He crouches down among the seats. The old beggar with the outstretched hand is put in by the crowd and stares unconsciously through the window blinking his half-blind eyes. The train whistles and moves forward. No-one knows where to. It travels slowly, stopping at every station. Some people jump off. We see a man jumping off at Ursynow and no-one shoots at him.

'People are jumping off. Let's jump too,' I say.

'They're on their own,' replies Marysia, 'but there's three of us.'

All the same we have a great desire to jump off in Ursynow. The train is moving slowly, so slowly that you could swear the driver is doing it deliberately to enable people to escape. Crowds are standing on the platforms of the small stations and watching the trains deporting the population of Warsaw. If you jump out you'll easily be able to hide among them because they understand and pity us. We look at Macius and know he won't want to jump from the train. He accepts the existing state of affairs. He's calm and cool. He's looking out of the window at the fields, trees and houses we pass. He hasn't seen all this for ages.

Pruszkow. The train stopped. We got off and mingled among the enormous crowd. It was a huge camp for the deported inhabitants of Warsaw. The selection took place here. Everyone capable of work left for Germany from here. Some people stayed in Pruszkow for three or four days or even more. They slept squashed on the dirty concrete floor. But some people bought themselves out and escaped from the camp. I noticed a girl giving the gendarme a ring. He slipped it into his pocket and turned round, and she followed him. He will have taken her out.

'You see it does succeed sometimes,' I said to Marysia.

'I'm not bold enough to do it yet,' she replied. 'I might be in three or four hours.'

We didn't even stay two hours in Pruszkow. A selection was in progress when we arrived. People were segregated to the right and the left. The ones on the right were to go to Germany. Older people were detained and then located in towns and villages. I was terribly scared because they might separate us. Marysia passed through first holding Macius by the hand. She was young and looked healthy. There was no doubt that she was fit for work. I followed her quickly and energetically with my heart beating. I never normally walked like that. It was artificial and dictated by fear and despair. The German pointed to the right with his whip. I was fit for work.

Before we realized that we wouldn't be separated the train had already arrived and we were loaded into cattle wagons. There were 1,500 people in the transport. We were all given a loaf of bread for the journey. We entered the end wagon and spread our coat out against the back wall. People were so squashed that we could hardly move. We sat on our bread. When the train shuddered and set off into the unknown everyone in the overcrowded wagon made the sign of the cross. We made the sign of the cross too, including Macius.

What about them? The Jewish family. Did they remember to make the sign of the cross? I saw them clambering into the wagon. The father climbed up first and gave the mother his hand. She couldn't manage it and people pushed her up from behind. Then they both pulled the boy up. Who was in their wagon? The same mixture as in ours from Gdanska Street and Hrubieszowska Street. There were shop owners, traders, caretakers, thieves, prostitutes.

The door of our wagon was wide open. Some people sat in the door with their legs dangling down outside. A few children squeezed through the crowd, huddled together into a group and watched the passing scenery. The sun was setting and dusk was slowly falling. I knew for sure that at this moment the pious Jew was silently reciting the evening prayer. And I shuddered with fear lest he was swaying while whispering the words. It was a terrible riddle which I couldn't solve. I even thought that perhaps they didn't completely comprehend the danger they were in, so they remained themselves out of boundless naïvety. Maybe that's what aroused deeply hidden emotions in the hearts of the people around them and made them keep silent.

Macius is also among the children crowded round the open door. His fair hair covers his ears. He's got a fringe. He looks like a page, a little page in medieval times. Against the background of the dirty cattle wagon, among the other children with their common faces, his poetic striking beauty is as dangerous as the swaying of the Jew in silent prayer. A woman sitting next to us is looking at him in a peculiar way. She's got a towel tied round her head and is wearing a robe made out of the lining of a coat, and old worn slippers. She's holding a boy of four with measles on her knees. Although it's a hot day the child is dressed in warm clothes. The fever makes him cry and mutter. Her two daughters are sitting in the wagon door. The younger one has a childish face and is slim, fair-haired and beautiful.

'Halka!' shouts her mother from inside the wagon, 'wet a hand-kerchief in water and wipe the sweat from the child's forehead or else he'll die on you.'

Then she tells the people sitting near her, 'He's her illegitimate child, dear people. But do you think she cares for him? The child says "mummy" to me and doesn't even look at her. She's not a mother but a bitch.' She raises her voice and now addresses the furthest corners of the whole wagon. 'I'm a person who likes to save, you know. I packed all my dresses and shoes into suitcases and took them down to the cellar. I wore the lilac lining of an old coat in the house and a pair of worn slippers fit for the dustbin. And that's how the Germans took me away. Look at me. All I do is bring shame on my children, my poor Broncia and the other one.' Everyone looks at her. She really is dressed strangely for a journey into the unknown.

'And just before we left she hit me on the head with a rolling pin. I wrapped a towel round the bruises and I look like a Turk. And this poor bastard has got the measles and he'll either live or die.' She leans over the child and kisses him with limitless tenderness. 'If it wasn't for me and poor Broncia this puppy would have been long gone. We'd give our last drop of blood for him. We stand on our heads to amuse him. But God cheated her when it came to good looks. He gave one of them too many and the other too few. And what does she do, my poor Broncia? Her fingers are pricked all over because she's a sempstress. And what does Halka do? She dances in the ballet. Now you're thinking this bastard comes from the director of the ballet, aren't you? No way.'

Now everyone looks at Halka and her lovely face. She's gazing at the scenery. Her eyelids don't even quiver in reaction to what her mother is saying. She's distant and indifferent. Her mother might just as well be talking about a stranger no-one's interested in, not about her.

A young woman who looks like the personification of despair is sitting on a bench opposite the open door. They say she's the wife of a procurator and is going into the unknown with her servant. The servant is sitting next to her in a black dress and black hat and with her hair brushed back smoothly. The woman left her blind twelve year-old daughter in the house. The Germans didn't let her take the girl with her and the house burnt down with the girl in it.

'Can you imagine it?' says the servant to the woman sitting next to her on the right. 'They didn't let us take our girl, the beasts. And they set fire to the house.'

A few minutes later the whole wagon has heard about the tragedy. Now everyone is looking at the pathetic face of the unfortunate mother. While her glassy extinguished eyes are staring at the red glow of the setting sun.

So where are we going? A dour man whose face is covered with soot says we're going to Auschwitz. And they'll probably finish us off there. 'They'll do what they did to the Jews,' he says. The man sitting next to us on the bare boards and leaning against the same swaying wagon wall is one of the three men we know from the cellar on Leszno Street. He's about forty. He found his niece in Pruszkow, a girl of fifteen. She's with us now.

'They're either taking us to a concentration camp or a labour camp,' he says. 'If it's a labour camp then what do they need so many children for?'

True. What do the Germans need so many children for? We stop looking at each other. We're all lost in thought. Food is so hard to get and so how long will the Germans want to keep feeding our children? There's a long silence while we all listen to the fearful beating of our hearts.

Suddenly the train stops. The evening is warm and quiet. It's as light as day from the stars in the sky and the white light of the moon. Beyond the railway track is a field and then a wood. The train guards jump down from the train and run along the wagons telling everyone to come out and relieve themselves. People get out and hide behind sheaves of corn, although a lot of them don't even hide at all. We jump down as well. It's so light that I can clearly see people running from sheaf to sheaf and then into the wood. No-one shoots at them. And just like on Plocka Street in Warsaw we are overcome by an enormous desire to run away. 'Let's run away,' I say, 'this is still Poland. We'll hide behind the sheaves and then go into the wood. If we come across a cottage they'll put us up for the night.'

We're standing between the rails under the buffers of the end wagon. If the train moved backwards suddenly it could have killed us. We're ready to leave and lose everything we've got in the wagon – coats, food and everything. Because perhaps they really are taking us to be destroyed in Auschwitz. Suddenly one of the guards is standing in front of us with a rifle. I tear the brooch off my bra and hand it to him on my outstretched palm. I can't speak. I lift up my other hand and with a circular movement I point to the field and the wood darkening nearby. He threatens us with the rifle. 'Los!', he yells. 'Los und schnell!'

The child begins to cry. 'Don't let's run away,' he says. He's trembling all over because he's so scared of running away. We return to the wagon. Night falls. Our first night in the shaking wagon. It's so cramped that we sit with our legs doubled up, leaning against each other. Can you sleep with your legs doubled up? We don't sleep, just doze. We keep waking and wondering what the Germans want so many children for. We worry about it. Maybe they'll separate the children from their mothers and fathers. We're afraid to talk about it. We're afraid to even whisper about the possibility. We're afraid to even think.

We crossed the border a long time ago. These are German fields,

389

woods, villages and towns. What's left of our home, of our real home, the one where we were a family? Nothing is left apart from the few rags in our bags. We don't sleep, just doze. If we stretch our legs out we knock the child with measles or the woman with the towel on her head sleeping huddled up beside him. We shouldn't get on the wrong side of this woman. We've got to be careful with her. She's headstrong and knows no restraint. She says what comes into her head. We've heard her lay bare her soul, her worries, her disappointments and her impulsive nature in just a few sentences. She's a dangerous neighbour. We're afraid of her.

She might suddenly say something about us. About us or our child. We've already caught sight of that unfriendly look of hers directed at ourselves. 'Educated women,' we can hear her mutter. If we attract attention to ourselves we might lose. We've got to be grey, we've got to melt into the crowd like animals which use mimicry as a disguise.

The end wagon where we are is shaking most of all, and we're leaning against the very end. It's dawning and the sun is rising. The child with measles relieves himself into a tin and then the tin is passed from hand to hand. Finally a hand pours the contents out through the open door. Other women in the wagon ask the grandmother if she'll lend them the tin for their children. 'Why not?' she replies. 'Is it made of gold?' So the other children pee into the tin and then the adults.

When the sun has risen and the train stops at a siding people jump out of the wagons with a sigh of relief. They can go and relieve themselves in the bushes, drink some fresh water, and perhaps even wash at the well. We get up off the floor with the others and make towards the door on swollen legs. The woman with the towel on her head talks to the child. 'What would happen to you if you didn't have a grandmother who loves you more than her own life? I'll carry you outside into the fresh air and you'll freshen up.' She picks the child up and jumps down. We jump down after her.

People look for bricks and flat stones and build primitive stoves. They make a fire of sticks and couch grass and light it. The smoke lifts upwards in a grey smudge. They make coffee or soup. Some use saucepans, others use tins. How we'd love to drink something warm! We walk along the rails looking for an empty tin. But we can't find one. Can't we go up to someone who's making coffee or soup and ask for a drop for the child? He's so pale and tired. But we're afraid to. It's safer not to be noticed. So we stand on the rails and look longingly at the red flames escaping from among the stones and at the people crouching around them warming their frozen hands. Two German railwaymen are standing nearby and looking at our train. We go up to them.

'Do you know where they're taking us?' They don't know. 'Some people are saying that they're going to separate us from the children. We're scared of that. Do you know anything about it?'

'Of course they won't. You can be sure of that. We've never heard anything like it,' they say.

One of them has got a bag hanging over his shoulder. He takes out his sandwiches, wrapped in paper. He undoes the paper carefully so as not to lose a single crumb and gives Macius a slice of bread and margarine. He holds the bread in his calloused hand, yellow from grease. And the small, slender, childish hand takes hold of the bread.

Then we return to the wagon and move off. We travel all day and in the evening we stop at a siding again. We're in a holiday resort. We don't know what it's called and we can't see anyone to ask. Small houses stand hidden in gardens and empty. The doors and windows are closed. The paths are overgrown. We walk alongside the train on a gravel path and our Macius is running with some other children. We can't stop talking about the train guard who said, 'Los und schnell' and didn't take the brooch. It was so incredible that we're still astonished. After all, he could have taken the brooch and chased us into the wagon.

While we're talking we suddenly hear a little girl shouting, 'Jew! Jew!' We're terrified. What's that she's saying? Did Macius hear? If he did, how did he react? We cross the rails. We take him by the hand. 'Come to the wagon at once,' we say. He doesn't resist. We don't know if the little girl is watching us. Our wagon is a long way off. The last wagon of the train. It's empty. Everyone's gone to get some fresh air, stretch their legs, have a drink and fill their bottles with fresh water from the well. Everyone apart from the procurator's wife. She's sitting in the same place, in the same position. And her extinguished eyes are still staring into the sky.

After many stops in sidings, or in fields outside towns whose names we don't know, one of the men sitting in the wagon door says, 'Do you know what? I recognize these fields and that red church past the wood. We're going back. I swear to God and the saints that we're going back.'

We become anxious. We all rush to the door. We can hear people saying that they recognize the place too and that we've been this way before. 'What can it be, for God's sake?' they ask.

'We're going round in circles. It's a ghost train,' says someone.

We passed through Erfurt long ago, we've been in Karlsruhe twice, we've passed Darmstadt and we stop in a siding near Dresden. People jump off the train again. The woman with the towel on her head tells the child not to run so fast because he'll sweat. He's well now and is running around with all the other children whenever we stop.

There's a pump at this stop. And if you have the patience to wait your turn you can even wash yourself. I wash myself and brush my hair. I put my blouse and comb on a stone. I return to the wagon in a hurry because I think they're calling. When the train moves off I see that I've forgotten to take the comb and it's still on the stone. It belonged to my mother. I worry about it being a bad omen. I sigh and swallow my tears. My anxiety is boundless. Isn't this train a monster driven by evil spirits and racing without compass along unknown ways in an unknown direction?

But there's another reason for my anxiety too. I've stopped trusting in our appearance. If that young girl guessed the truth, then what do the others think? Next time we stop we don't go far from our wagon so as not to stand out. We reckon that the people in our wagon have got used to us. We sit down close to the wagon on the grass, preferably in the shade of a tree, and talk quietly about the danger we managed to get ourselves out of. How could it happen? How could the child have guessed? And we come to the conclusion that perhaps a lot of people suspect us but aren't saying anything. Our endless conversations on the subject and our belief in bad omens make us sad and depressed. We don't expect anything good from fate and as time goes by our hope of survival is dashed in our hearts.

One day we again stop past a larger station whose name we don't know. It's twelve o'clock. Even the roof of the wagon doesn't protect us against the burning sun. Some railway workers cross the rails. Italians. They're carrying a bucket of soup. Dinner for themselves and their comrades. They stop. They see our tired, hungry faces, the sunken eyes of our children. 'Porca miseria,' they say. They lift up the bucket and give us their soup. It's our first soup for many days. We have soup for the second time in Hof–Hof in Bavaria. We get there the next day. This time we stop at the station. German women in white aprons from an aid committee are standing next to large pots and ladling the soup into cardboard cups. Thick pea soup.

'Poor people,' they sigh. 'We know you're running away from the Russians.'

We look at them in surprise. So that's the official version of our journey. We ran away from the Russians. We approached the German authorities of our own free will and asked them to evacuate us. We've come of our own unforced free will. No-one set fire to our homes.

Now on Hof station we all move about the platform freely. We can't see any train guards any longer. It's not Poland, so there's no point in escaping, is there? An unknown land and unknown people. Now we keep to the train which is the last link connecting us to the country where our homes were. I walk freely along the wide platform. An officer comes towards me with a huge Alsatian on a lead. 'Such den Jud,' he suddenly shouts. He lets the dog off its lead and it bounds forward in great leaps.

When I was still in the ghetto I heard about dogs that were specially trained to hunt Jews. They could recognize Jews by their smell, so it was said. I never believed those rumours. Now when I was face to face with reality I was terrified. In a moment the dog will tear me apart. Should I turn back and run? But then I'll give myself away. So I keep on walking with a pale face but a sure and elastic step, as if I were hurrying to work. The dog runs past me with its tongue hanging out. I can feel its hot breath. Then I turn back. I enter the wagon and tell Marysia what happened. She's surprised and wants to see the dog so she goes to the door to look for it. But it's gone.

Suddenly we hear a terrible scream. A child screaming. A sound which tears your soul. 'Mame! Mame!' We rush to the door again. We see the Jewish boy with the big ears. The boy from Warsaw. He's lost his way. He's lost the wagon his mother is in. He doesn't shout 'Mummy', but 'Mame', like Jews do. He runs backwards and forwards, terrified. After a while, fifteen minutes or so, we see him passing our wagon with his father. He's crying and the tears are flowing down his face. His father is waving his hand explaining something to him and trying to calm him down. While he was walking along the platform in the heart of this hostile land, the dog specially trained to hunt Jews ran along beside him like an arrow. But he was bending over the child and didn't notice anything and kept on talking.

Two days later the ghost train arrived at Hof again, having encircled Germany. And for the second time we receive soup in

393

cardboard cups on the same platform from the women in the aid committee. And we hear the same words again about running away from the Russians. From Hof the train goes to Munich, from Munich north to Hannover. From Hannover it turns south and on the fifth or sixth day it stops in Linz. We spend the whole day here. We're going to have a shower. From where the train stopped it was a long way to the showers. We walked through the streets of the town in a long column. The inhabitants looked at us with interest. The streets were winding and clean. Little houses with red roofs, a well-tended garden surrounding each house.

How we'd like to stay here! 'Can we stay with you?' we ask the German women we pass. 'Can we get work?'

'Sorry, no. We haven't got any work for you.'

We didn't yet know that we were the property of the German Reich. We weren't allowed to leave the transport and make our own arrangements. That would be desertion.

A huge barrack stood in a sparse pine wood. The showers were in the barrack. Up to a thousand people could shower there at one time. Special ovens disinfected the clothing. Orderlies checked if we were clean. Anyone with lice had their heads shaved. A lot of women came out with their heads shaved. People sat under the pine trees and waited their turn. Some were waiting and others must have already had their shower. There was no control and no compulsion. We didn't at that time know that many of the people sitting under the pine trees didn't have a shower at all. They had the foresight to rescue their things and, in some cases, their lives. After all, there might have been some Jews among them.

But we entered the door of the building like birds into a snare. Could we have known what was happening inside? Unfortunately we didn't have the wise shrewdness of the people sitting under the pine trees, neither their shrewdness nor their caution. We had a circumcised child with us, so we should have twisted and turned and asked people, and maybe we'd have found someone who'd have told us that it wasn't compulsory to have a shower.

So we entered the women's section. We immediately found ourselves in a dense mass of naked bodies with uniformed guards in among the huge crowd. We stopped undecided and terrified. The guards ordered us to undress and a moment later our things disappeared into the disinfection ovens. We still had our bags with us. We threw towels over our shoulders and made our way to a huge compartment where the showers were, Marysia carrying the child and I behind her with the bags and the soap. I put the soap down for a moment, for a tiny moment, and in the twinkling of an eye it disappeared. We didn't have any soap any longer.

'Stop,' shouted the guard and directed the crowd of naked women to the control point to have their heads checked for lice. I stood in the queue and behind me stood Marysia holding her naked son. She pressed him close and wanted to keep holding him like that. I passed through first.

'Stop,' they said to Marysia. 'That's not allowed. Let go of the child and go through separately.'

She put the child down and her heart died in her. He was alone. How defenceless he was in his nakedness. On the edge of life and death. Those few steps – weren't they an eternity for our thudding hearts? That moment when he stood alone and trembling in front of the stout German guards and hundreds of naked women, was it a moment or eternity? What was he thinking about? Did he understood the danger he was in? Did he realize that he might have been saying goodbye to life?

Was it not strange and incomprehensible? He passed through. Not a single voice was lifted against him. No-one pointed at him. Didn't they see? Didn't they guess the truth? They must have seen and known. Only perhaps a deeply hidden emotion was aroused in their hearts and made them keep silent. Marysia picked him up again and we went to the huge compartment with water pouring from the ceiling. 'What was it?' I whispered in her ear, weeping. 'What was it? Tell me. He's miraculously escaped death, hasn't he?'

The guards mingled with the women and no-one was embarrassed. They were an inseparable part of the showers, just like the taps, the pipes, the drains. Our bags lay in the neighbouring compartment. When we were getting undressed I slid the bracelet that was pinned to my bra into a thermos. And all the time I was showering I was haunted by the thought that someone might steal our thermos.

'Let's go and get dressed,' I said. 'God only knows if we'll find our things.'

We went into the next compartment. The disinfected clothes had already been placed there. We had been given numbers but who paid any attention to that? A pile of dresses, shoes, underwear and coats lay on the floor. Naked women were running around it. They threw other people's things aside and trampled on them, hunted, lost their tempers and quarrelled. We only found one of our shoes, and our bags disappeared. I ran from one end of the compartment to the other looking for the thermos with the bracelet. It was nowhere to be found. I went up to a guard. 'Our bags and shoes have disappeared. I had a thermos and there was a gold bracelet in it.'

'What? The bracelet's disappeared? What colour was the thermos?'

'Blue.'

He was terribly excited. 'Johann! Kasper! Eine goldene Kette! Herr Gott!'

They threw themselves into the battleground of scattered things. A thermos with a bracelet should not disappear on German soil! They were as dogged as if their lives depended on it. The deeply rooted characteristics of the German race were suddenly aroused in them: their systematic way of doing things and their liking for order.

We thought we were in hell. Naked, despairing women were running around the room screaming, while others who were already dressed were leaving the showers with huge bags. Did the woman with the towel on her head, the one from our wagon, come out of here in her lilac overall? Of course not. She didn't look like she had any scruples. Now was the time when people with property lost out and people with nothing got rich at their expense. Macius started to cry pitifully. He was standing on the threshold and the door suddenly slammed. A huge bruise appeared on his forehead but we were still feverishly looking for our shoes.

'Here it is!' shouted one of the guards. 'Here's the bag with the blue thermos.'

They handed us the half empty bag. All that remained was a bit of food in the bottom. There was no spare underwear and no towel.

'Is the bracelet there?' asked the guards. They all three surrounded us.

I took the thermos and turned it upside down. The water poured out and the bracelet fell out. They sighed with relief and laughed.

'Something like that couldn't possibly go missing,' they said.

So the thermos turned up and in the end, when we'd completely lost hope, Marysia's other shoe showed up, and my shoes and Macius's. We also found our coats and clothes. We lost most of our food, Macius's pullover, Marysia's underwear and her only towel.

'What are you going to wipe yourself with?' I asked her worriedly. 'There's a piece of cloth here.'

'But it's not mine.'

'So what?'

'It's disgusting,' she said.

Tired and mangled we left the barrack at last. The Jewish boy was sitting crying on a heap of rags just beside the door. Had he lost his parents again? We sat down under a pine tree and watched him. We saw his mother coming out of the showers and then shortly afterwards his father came out of another door. He didn't have his hat. They only had one bag. So they found one another again and all three of them sat down under a tree. I couldn't tear my eyes off them. Wasn't it strange that we were meeting this Jewish family so many times during our journey? This invisible thread would be sure to break at some stage and then we'd never know what happened to them.

The sun was setting when we returned to the train. During our absence the wagons had been swept, scrubbed and disinfected. Over a dozen more wagons were attached too. We now had strangers for our neighbours, people we were seeing for the first time, while many of our previous companions went elsewhere. The woman with the towel on her head, her daughters and the child weren't with us any more. The sad procurator's wife and her servant weren't there either, but the man we knew from the cellar on Leszno Street and his fifteen-year-old niece sat down next to us like before.

And we rattled along again all night long through places we didn't know. Through the open door we could see fields, woods, linesmen's buildings, churches, houses with red roofs, and lonely spreading trees. At dawn we arrived at a station siding. We jumped down into yellow heaps of deep, dry sand. People immediately started gathering pieces of wood and dried up plants. They constructed tiny stoves out of bricks and stones, and cooked. Then they put the fires out and a thin, white smudge of smoke rose from the ashes. Some people took their shoes off and walked barefoot. The fifteen-year-old girl from our wagon did the same. Sinking into the sand she stepped on some hot ashes and burnt her feet terribly. She was carried into the wagon nearly unconscious.

At this desert of a station some of the people from our transport approached the locomotive and one man who could speak German started talking to the driver. 'I've heard we're near Berlin. Why have we circled around the country for so long? We've been travelling five days and six nights.'

'Because no concentration camp wanted to take you,' replied the driver. 'They're all full.'

'Really?'

'Yes. We've been from camp to camp.'

'What's going to happen now?'

The driver shrugged his shoulders. He didn't know. The news was handed from mouth to mouth and within a few minutes the whole transport knew. But there was no time to be surprised or comment on it because the train guards ordered us to take our things out of the wagons. The locomotive whistled and the empty train shuddered and moved off. We stood on the sandy dunes and looked back at the train which was the last link connecting us with home. We all looked in the same direction and felt that the earth was slipping away from under our feet.

After a while some huge lorries drove up and took us to a transit camp. It stood on a wide, sandy plain beside a sparse pine wood. On the plain there were about a dozen wooden barracks covered with shiny, black roofing felt. Here and there, by the walls or on the slope of a small hill, was grass and clumps of weeds. No trees or bushes were visible at all. In the middle a huge sandy square. The barracks are grouped round the square.

The camp is surrounded by thick barbed wire. On one side is a gate and then a road. The road leads down to a German village and up into unknown and distant parts. The gate is open. You can go down to the village if you like. People come and go. They don't run away. There's a windmill on the hill and we can watch its sails turning. Couples are formed here on the road. If a woman has the charm of youth, if she doesn't talk a lot but only listens kindly, then a man forgets about his wife back home.

The soup is thick and fat. It's made of tinned meat. Everyone gets a brown enamel bowl with two handles and a tin spoon. You can wash in the same bowl. Even wash a few clothes. Everyone receives half a litre of soup in the brown bowl and black coffee in a brown mug. A slim, quiet, silently stepping young man from Hrubieszowska Street called Madejski registers for this nourishing soup in two barracks, in one as Madejski and in the other as Sicinski. He'll receive two portions.

Who's brave enough to run away now? No-one runs away even though the future is uncertain.

There's a letter-box on the barrack wall next to the gate. Can we write a letter and post it? Do they empty the letter-box? The German in charge of the camp laughs. You can write letters. Write as many as you like. No-one has got any writing paper, or envelopes, or German stamps. But we've got two postcards from Poland. Two very old postcards without stamps, with 'Postcard' written on them in Polish. We've got a pencil too and there's a table you can sit at in the barrack. We want to write a letter. We want someone to know about us. But we can't write to friends in burning Warsaw. We've got to send the letter somewhere else. Where to?

We have a distant relation in Geneva called Lucja Hersz. Her husband is a university professor. But we can't address the letter using that surname. Hersz sounds Jewish. We've got to be careful and think of everything. Careful, that's the most important thing. Look like everybody, move like everybody, don't stand out in the grey crowd by the way we behave or dress. Do women from Hrubieszowska Street write letters to Geneva? We decide to write all the same.

Lucja Hersz has got a daughter called Joanna. She studied philosophy with Professor Oltramare. This is the roundabout route we use to send some news of ourselves. We write the address: for Joanna, Professor Oltramare, University, Geneva, Switzerland. I write: dear Joanna, do you still remember me after all these years? My husband, Stanislaw, always talked about you. I'm here together with Marysia and her little boy, Macius, and we send best wishes. Alicja Majewska. Marysia writes on the second card: dear Joanna, I'm here with my mother and my son, Macius. We haven't any news of my sisters. Please send our best wishes to the whole family. Maria Majewska.

We don't have any stamps. But if our cards reach Joanna she'll give them to her mother. From the names we give she ought to guess who it is. That's what we think. We don't have much hope but we post the cards in the letter-box bearing the inscription *Reichsdeutsche Post* all the same. We were terribly excited. We'd sent news of ourselves into the wide world. We thought that other members of our family in Poland might write to Lucja Hersz too. And this sign of life might get through to Irena and Nina. We didn't know anything about them.

We all had to sign a declaration saying that we had run away from the Russians of our own free will. Everyone signed – we had to. Madejski even signed twice. Once in our barrack as Jan Madejski, and then in the barrack opposite as Mieczyslaw Sicinski. In the evening people racked their brains until late at night over why they had been made to sign. But although they puzzled over the question for a long time they didn't reach any conclusions. Then they put the lights out and went to sleep on their bunks, on mattresses stuffed with scraps of paper. There weren't enough beds so a lot of people slept two to a bed.

Marysia slept on the bottom bed with Macius and above her an older man who wore a railwayman's uniform. I slept on the bed opposite together with a girl from Hrubieszowska Street. Madejski slept above us. The girl was called Helena. She was tall, slim and black-haired. 'Am I disturbing you, Mrs Majewska? Are you comfortable?' she used to say. She tried to take up as little room as possible on the bunk and squashed herself up to the wall. She slept so quietly and peacefully that I could hardly hear her breathing. 'No, dear child, you're not disturbing me,' I often wanted to say. I was surprised that my heart was so tender towards this girl I didn't know and about whom I knew nothing.

Madejski was quiet and calm by day, but at night he tossed and turned on his bed and showered us with scraps of paper. He sometimes shouted in his sleep and then he panted as if he was being chased by a pack of hounds. 'He's a well-known thief from Hrubieszowska Street,' Helena told me quietly. She whispered it in my ear so that Madejski wouldn't hear.

'Do you know what Helena told me? Madejski's a well-known thief from Hrubieszowska Street. He walks in such a strange way that you can't hear him. He suddenly appears and then suddenly disappears again. Who knows, perhaps he's a safe-breaker.'

I started to worry about our things, the things we had left after the shower in Linz. About Macius's coat with the velvet collar, about his gaiters, about our coats. Even about our shoes which we took off when we went to bed. What'll happen if Madejski steals our shoes one night and disappears?

If a woman is afraid of loneliness and piercing cold in the hours before dawn and a man has two strong hands and understands her complaints and sorrows, then what more do you need? An engineer called Zawadzki was taken from his office by the Germans together with his clerk Marta. His wife stayed at home and might have been travelling in a different transport. Kwiatkowski was taken alone because his wife and children were in the country, while Weronika Cichocka had a husband and child in Brwinow but she was deported from Warsaw where she was visiting relatives.

Many men and women were cut off like that from their families in the transit camp. They didn't know what tomorrow would bring and whether they'd ever see their spouses and children again.

Kwiatkowski was a dour man but he was often seen sitting under the windmill with Weronika Cichocka. Zawadzki was often seen walking up the road with Marta. That was where couples came together, on that sunny road. They promised each other constancy and assistance in time of need. And that they would comfort and sustain each other so long as they were on German soil. Their promises went no further. Because they were promises and not vows, and their limits were defined by scruples.

But what could link that sixty-year-old man from Georgia with Maria Michalska who was twenty? He was thin, small and muscular and had an ugly face, while she was tall and healthy, and full of life. She was with her mother, a woman who was still young but exceptionally fat. Mother or not, here in this forgotten corner and faced by an uncertain future, she had nothing to say. Mothers weren't sure of their children or children of their mothers. The only thing that was sure was the present moment. Every approaching night brought the threat of separation. Anyone might suddenly hear a whistle and be deported into the unknown darkness of this hostile country.

Every day at the same time you could come across the Georgian and young Maria sitting by the edge of the wood on a small hill above the road. He was carefully dressed, with glasses on a black string, and looked like an intellectual. He spoke Polish with a Russian accent. She was wide-hipped and spreading, wore a dress with colourful flowers, and listened to his promises in silence. The poetic nature of the place with its early evening silence, purple heather, scent of thyme and the red rays of the setting sun helped him win the village beauty over. He brought along the dark bottled beer you could buy in the camp. And bread and pork fat, bought on the side. Most people in the transit camp were hungry. We received only one portion of nourishing soup per day, and apart from that bread and black coffee morning and evening. Obviously the Georgian had money.

Every day at sunset we went out on the road too. French prisoners of war worked for the local farmers and used the road. They wore shabby coats with a triangular sign and a letter on their shoulders. In the distance we could see the Georgian and Maria sitting near the wood and we talked about that strange couple.

'Why do you think it is?'

'He's got money and perhaps she's hungry.'

At first they used to return to the camp holding hands. Then they walked arm in arm. Now she was doing a lot of lively talking while he listened in silence. Their roles were reversed as time went by. We didn't really pay a lot of attention to the Georgian or Weronika Cichocka or Zawadzki and Marta. Their business and their problems passed us by. We peeped into the lives of these people by chance and without design. We had problems of our own.

One day as evening was falling we were all three sitting close together on Marysia's bed. Macius was leaning against her shoulder and dozing. I looked at his eyelashes, his pale cheeks, the blue veins of his hands plaited together and wondered if he'd survive this war. And if he survived and grew up, what would make up for his hungry and dangerous childhood?

We talked quietly about Irena and Nina whom we'd left behind in burning Warsaw. I felt guilty about not thinking of them more often. We were so beset by dangers of all kinds that we even forgot to think about them. I suddenly looked up. Madejski wasn't asleep but was leaning over and staring at us. What was he thinking about? What was this mysterious man thinking about and what had he surmised watching us from above in his bed?

We worried about it for a few days. But then other worries came along and that one was extinguished and erased. Our life was full of all sorts of difficulties which we kept having to overcome. There was a boy of six in our barrack. He was called Leszek and he sometimes played with Macius. 'Leszek's wearing my pullover,' he said one day. I went outside and saw it was true. 'What should I do? Leszek's mother must have taken the pullover in Linz. We've got so few clothes. Shall I tell her?'

'God forbid! We can't say anything. She won't admit it or give the pullover back. We'll just attract attention to ourselves needlessly.'

We looked longingly at the pullover for a few days. Then we stopped thinking about it. We were thinking about something completely different, about working for the farmers. The camp commander allowed us to go out for seasonal work, planting and weeding. A lot of people did it. They weren't paid for the work but they were well fed and usually brought some potatoes or tomatoes back with them. What was most important, their camp portion of soup went to their family. They left at six in the morning and returned after sunset, completely exhausted.

They returned at exactly the same time as the young people in the camp gathered on the hill behind our barrack led by the young priest and sang religious songs until late at night. The priest had an ordinary face. He wore a cassock with a jacket on top and a cap. He looked half clerical and half secular. He probably lost his coat and hat in Linz. If he'd lost his cassock as well he'd have looked like a peasant as he was stocky with strong hands for work. I was surprised that he hadn't cast off his cassock for safety's sake.

I knew the religious songs too as I had learnt them in the institution. When the music and words entered the barrack through the open window the older women sitting inside took them up and sang mournfully, thinking about their exile and their burnt down homes in distant Warsaw.

'With the smoke of fires, with the dust of fraternal blood,

To You, Lord, sounds this voice.'

That was the one they sang most often. Because of the analogy, the truth and reality it contained. It was sung emotionally and tearfully, a reminder of the billowing black smoke and the softly falling burning walls. They didn't sing patriotic songs. The Germans might think the young people were insurgents. Insurgents were always sent to concentration camps. We were only the civilian population of Warsaw. We had come to Germany of our own free will.

One day at six in the morning Marysia went to work in the fields with the other labourers. All day long, with short breaks, she weeded cabbage patches. She pulled the thin weeds out easily and effortlessly but there were also deeply rooted ones that she couldn't manage. A young man called Ziolkowski worked in the row next to her. He pulled out all the more obdurate weeds for her. She received bread and liver sausage for breakfast, and thick soup for dinner, tea and supper. She didn't bring any potatoes or tomatoes back with her. In fact she only worked for her keep. But that day Macius and I had extra soup. So the only positive outcome of that hard day's work was a bowl of soup and the fact that Marysia met Stanislaw Ziolkowski.

The land-owner, a real land-owner who owned the property, came to the field they were working in, in riding boots, a leather jacket and a Tyrolese hat. Two women went up to him and asked, 'Could you give us permanent work? We'd like to work in the fields or in the kitchen.'

'No, I can't do that. You belong to the Reichsbahn [State Railway].'

To the Reichsbahn? We belong to the Reichsbahn. It's as if we were the Reichsbahn's slaves. In the evening the whole camp knew.

People said to each other, 'We belong to the Reichsbahn.' It was strange and incomprehensible. When they started registering us one evening something should have dawned on us. But no-one understood what the connection with the Reichsbahn was. Two Germans in uniforms went round from barrack to barrack with an interpreter writing down our names and occupations. If you had an identity card you showed it. Some people didn't have any documents at all. Particularly the women. They'd been caught suddenly and thrown out of their flats without their identity cards. The Germans didn't bother with any interviews. Just three words: occupation, name, family name. And also 'fertig' [finished]. Yes, they said that too.

A lot of the men were wearing railwaymen's uniforms. The Germans believed they were railwaymen even if they didn't have any papers. Kwiatkowski said he was a railwayman but Zawadzki gave his occupation as mechanical engineer. Everyone knew that the Germans were deliberately destroying the intelligentsia – engineers, doctors, and lawyers – so we were surprised that Zawadzki admitted his real occupation.

When they asked the Georgian his occupation he hesitated for a moment. Then he said, 'Glazier'. We noticed his hesitation. He was more careful than Zawadzki. He kept his real occupation a secret. Then the priest approached the table. When they asked him his occupation he told them he was an agricultural worker. Helena, the girl I shared the bed with, was written down as a knitter. Marysia and I told them we were dressmakers. 'Fertig', said the German.

Madejski was last. He took his time approaching the table. Helena winked at me. From the ensuing silence I gathered that the whole barrack knew about Madejski's occupation. 'Occupation?' asked the German. 'Cobbler,' replied Madejski. It was the first time we had heard his voice. Everyone was looking at him. He fiddled about nervously, coughed and returned to his bed. He jumped up onto it in the twinkling of an eye and with incredible agility. A rain of fine paper scraps showered down onto the bed below.

I often met Barbara Gorska in the camp, a handsome woman of about thirty with a pale face. I used to meet her in the barrack when I went for the soup, in the beer queue and in the lavatory. One day she told me she had a six-year-old daughter in Skolimow. 'I had a dress shop in Warsaw but my daughter was in Skolimow.' Another time she confided in me that the Germans had taken her away straight out of bed. 'Would you believe it, I didn't have time to get dressed. I threw a dress over my night-dress. I didn't even have time to put my knickers on. Fortunately it happened in August when it's warm.'

I rarely saw her alone. When she sat on the grass behind the barrack she was accompanied by two or three men. She had a personal magnetism emanating from her which acted in a specific way. The strangest thing was that she wasn't very lively or coquettish, or flirtatious. She seemed rather quiet and distant, and even sleepy. She looked as if she came from an intellectual background. She was of medium height, slim and had a pleasant voice. She didn't know a word of German. A German used to come and see her, bringing a sack. We gathered he brought her pork fat and sausage and maybe even butter. He wore civvies. Where had she managed to meet him? It was hard to guess.

She was one of those diligent women who try with all their might to regain everything they've lost. Since she'd been taken away from Warsaw almost naked she decided to get hold of some clothes as quickly as possible. She got hold of a blue and white checked sheet for example and made herself a blouse out of it. She might have got the sheet from the German as well. One day I met her in the lavatory again. That camp lavatory with its wet, rotting floor.

'I'll tell you something in secret,' she said to me. 'They're going to pick a small group of a hundred people and send them somewhere. I don't know where yet. They're sending the rest to Hamburg, the women and children and people with no occupation. Someone special is going to come and take the hundred with him.'

I returned to the barrack at once. 'Do you know what I found out?' I said to Marysia. 'They're going to pick out a hundred people who've got an occupation and the rest will go to their deaths in Hamburg.'

'To their deaths? Why?'

'Because they'll die there in the bombing.'

'Who told you about it?'

'Gorska. A German is going to come and take the group with him.'

'Yes, I saw a uniformed man I didn't know on the square. Maybe it's him.'

We were very worried. We could see people whispering together in corners. The 'special' German kept appearing and then leaving again. He wore a hat with gold braid and he had gold braid on his sleeve. We stopped going onto the road. We racked our brains as to

405

how to get into the small group and not go to Hamburg. We noticed that the Georgian and Maria also stopped going for walks. Kwiatkowski and Weronika, Zawadzki and Marta, didn't leave the barrack for days on end. A strange tension hung in the air. Something was going on behind our backs and something was shortly going to happen.

On the surface life went on just like before. But it was different all the same. The news wasn't broadcast, perhaps they didn't want to give rise to dissatisfaction or panic. If it weren't for my accidental acquaintance with Gorska we would only have found out about it afterwards. I sometimes wondered what had made Gorska tell me. Loyalty? She'd only known me a short time but perhaps I'd mentioned that my daughter and her child were with me. Was it that? She belonged to the chosen group for sure. Her heart beat calmly.

But our hearts beat anxiously. 'I'll talk to him,' I said to Marysia, 'and ask him to take us.'

'It won't do any good. It's all been settled.' I was surprised that Marysia was being so lethargic now and I didn't understand why.

He didn't come all day. He came at eleven at night. I waited in the square until eleven. When I saw him in the darkness I followed him. He was walking from the gate towards the barracks. He didn't hear my footsteps and shuddered when I spoke to him. 'Herr *Lagerführer*, please enter me and my daughter on the list. We're dressmakers.'

'Surname?'

'Majewska.'

'No, the list is closed.'

I returned to the barrack. Marysia was waiting for me.

'I talked to him. He said the list is closed.'

'There you are. Too bad. We'll go to Hamburg.'

'We must go to the main barrack and look round,' I said. Although it was about midnight no-one in the main barrack was asleep yet. The light was on and people were milling around just like in the daytime.

'Ziolkowski's sitting there by the window,' I said to Marysia. 'The one you worked with in the field.'

'I'll talk to him.'

When she came back she said, 'Do you know what he told me? We've got to give that special man something and then he'll take us.'

Give him something? That means that Ziolkowski must have

given him something, and the Georgian, and Gorska and Kwiatkowski.

'If that's the case, then I'll give him the bracelet. I'll wait for him in the square until he comes out of the barrack.'

I waited for him until three o'clock. I stood in the darkness with my eyes fixed on the main barrack. I could see the light was still on through the black curtains.

'Please don't be angry with me. I'm Majewska and I spoke to you here. We really want to go with the group. We're dressmakers, my daughter and I. I've got something here which I'd like to give you as a souvenir. It's a bracelet.'

'Oh,' he said carelessly and waved his hand, 'it's not necessary. But if you insist then I'll take it. We're leaving in a lorry at six o'clock. In three hours' time. Will you be ready? Come earlier and I'll get you onto the list.'

The lorry drove up at six o'clock. The German in the hat with the gold braid was standing next to it and reading out the names from a sheet of paper. People approached in turn and clambered up onto the lorry. I could see Gorska, Ziolkowski, Kwiatkowski and Weronika, Zawadzki and Marta and Madejski on the lorry. The Georgian and Maria Michalska's names were read out. Then he read out, 'Michalska Estera.' It was Maria's mother. But what a name! I shuddered when I heard it. Was she Jewish? I glanced at her with interest. Her face was perfectly calm. She replied to the name like a one hundred per cent Aryan. She was extremely fat. The Georgian and young Maria pulled her up onto the lorry with great difficulty.

We were last on the list. 'Majewska Alicja. Majewska Maria and child.' We stood there helpless. How were we to get up? It was impossible to clamber up without someone's help. Then Madejski jumped down from the lorry at lightning speed and with incredible agility. Before we knew it he was standing next to us. I leaned against his shoulder and he helped me jump onto the wheel and then up higher and then I grabbed hold of people's outstretched hands. Then, when he picked Macius up and held him carefully, but clumsily like a person not used to carrying children, I was sure that he would never do us any harm. I was ashamed of guarding our coats and shoes so carefully in case he stole them.

The lorry moved off. I kept thinking about Madejski. He was sitting in front of us. I looked at him. He didn't say a word. Helena had often told me about his past. How many times he'd been in prison and how he escaped. Who his friends and enemies were. About him being a safe-breaker.

'Where are we going?' I asked Gorska.

'To Wansee, I think.'

To Wansee? Wansee was a lakeside holiday resort near Berlin with the most beautiful villas and gardens round the whole lake. We believed in Wansee. We didn't yet know that our German convoy had been joking and we were going somewhere completely different. The lorry took us to the railway station. Then we went by electric train and suddenly found ourselves in a sea of ruins, in a huge, dead city.

'Where are we?'

No-one knew. After a while the answer was passed from person to person. 'In Berlin'.

So we were in Berlin, not at Wansee. We thought it would be impossible to survive here. We could see thousands of bombed houses from both sides of the train and the sight was so oppressive that the women turned pale and wrung their hands while the men were dourly quiet. The compartment became silent.

We reached Spindlersfeld camp in the suburbs of Berlin, in Koepenick. Reichsbahn camp or Communal camp, Berlin-Koepenick, Grünauer Strasse 210 – that was our official address. It wasn't a large camp, just one barrack made of plywood. Next to it were the burnt out ruins of a barrack for Italian workers which had been hit by a bomb. All around were unploughed fields. On one side a railway embankment. Also there was a canal about fifty paces from the barrack. Barges and boats passed by all day long. Sometimes a boat sailed past with a smoking chimney and the captain's whole family on it. Wife and children, dog and cat, and washing drying in the sun. It was seen off by sad eyes looking out of the barrack window.

When we followed our German convoy to the barrack a man and a woman jumped up from a wooden bench leaning against the wall and stood looking at us with a smile. They were Lagerführer Schmidt and the camp cook, Gertrude Lund.

A long corridor divided the barrack into two halves. On the right hand side – the kitchen, the food store, the wash-rooms, lavatories and two rooms, and on the other side – the office, sick-room, the clothes store, the cook's room and three rooms. Each room contained bunks and an iron stove.

Lagerführer Schmidt's smile was intended not for us, but for our German convoy with the gold braid on his hat. They shook hands very warmly. Schmidt gave his left hand because his right hand was paralysed. Then they entered Schmidt's room in the barrack and closed the door. After their confidential conference they came out in front of the barrack again. 'Heil Hitler,' said the convoy. He nodded at us and off he went, his task completed.

There were large rooms for married couples and a small room for single women. There are six single women to be in three bunk-beds in a row, one behind the other. They have three beds and three narrow cupboards made of rough wood. One cupboard for two people. Three grey blankets on each bed. No sheets. Straw mattresses. Straw pillows. One blanket to put on the mattress, two to cover yourself with. The iron stove is by the door.

Zofia Centkiewicz and Lucyna Wisniewska took the first bunk by the door. Zofia underneath because she was older and young Lucyna could sleep on top. On the second bunk Pelagia Mankowska on the bottom and Barbara Gorska on top although she was older than Pelagia. She preferred it that way. The third bunk by the window was for us. Me on the bottom and Marysia and Macius on top.

'Married couples here,' shouted Lagerführer Schmidt. 'Each with his legal wife.' He laughed insincerely. When he walked he used a cane, and a small, yellow mongrel milled round his feet. He was of medium height and thin and nervous. He hid his restless eyes behind glasses. He had an earthy complexion, with sunken cheeks and a long nose, and quick and restless movements. He wore the uniform of a German railwayman, navy blue with red edging. The couples in that room also included Kwiatkowski and Weronika, and Zawadzki and Marta. And the parents of Leszek who wore Macius's pullover. Old Mrs Zielinska with her railwayman son was in there too. The Georgian and young Maria received a separate room which was entered from outside. At first no-one paid any attention to this special distinction. There were eight children in our group, two pregnant women and a few older people. Families from our transport were not separated. We had come 'voluntarily' and so we had special privileges.

When we'd all found a bunk Lagerführer Schmidt made a speech. While he was speaking he turned away, held his collar, leaned on his cane or chased away the dog which was licking his boots. 'This is the railway's camp. You're going to work for the railway. Some of

409

you at stations, some on the rails and some on the engines. Some of the women will clean the trains and the dressmakers will make uniforms in the workshops. One of you will work with the pans in the kitchen and a few women will help the cook, Mrs Lund.'

He allocated jobs to all of us. Lucyna from our room, Weronika and Marta will clean trains. Zofia, Pelagia and Barbara Gorska will make uniforms at Warschauerbahnhof. The Georgian and young Maria will go to the Tiergarten station to glaze windows. Lotta the Volksdeutsche will be our interpreter and will stay in the barrack to help the Lagerführer. Mrs Michalska, young Maria's mother, will help the cook. What about the Majewskis? Both Majewskis. Both Majewskis will go to the kitchen too. Michalska, Majewskis, and two others, Natalia and Waclawa, wives of railwaymen. Natalia is pregnant.

They immediately start peeling potatoes. Johann gets the fire going under the pan. The cook runs around the kitchen and shouts for Johann. Johann is a giant of a boy with a face covered with pock-marks. A leucoma on his right eye. He looks like a bandit and was picked up from Hrubieszowska Street with his fifteen-year-old daughter. 'Johann!' shouts Mrs Lund. 'Schnell! Schnell!'

'My name is Konstanty,' he mutters. 'Where's that wretched inter-preter? She should tell her.'

Schmidt is followed by his dog Stutzi and the cook by her cat Metzi. The whole barrack shouts, 'Stutzi! Metzi!' We'd all like to stroke the little mongrel and we all have a friendly caress for the grey cat.

Reinhold is in residence in the clothes store. He's tall and slim and in civvies. He speaks Polish with a Masurian accent so he's immediately nicknamed Mazur. Apart from blankets he issues us all with a brown enamel bowl with two handles and a brown mug. The bowl for soup and the mug for coffee. And two tin spoons, one big and one small.

There's a serving hatch in the kitchen for ladling out the soup. We all come up to the hatch in turn and place our bowl on a shelf. The cook pours the soup from the huge pan into the bowl with a half litre ladle. They distribute bread, jam and margarine. In the evening they place a pan of coffee made of roast acorns in the corridor by the kitchen door. You can drink as much as you like. The coffee isn't rationed.

The bulbs of the electric light in the corridor are wrapped in blue paper. Men and women weave along the corridor until late at night.

Everyone is lively and excited. What's it going to be like at work? Will they treat us well? Will we be hungry?

All the barrack windows are carefully blackened. The shelter is in the field. Not far, not more than a hundred paces away. A long, deep, camouflaged ditch. There's even a ceiling made of boards and supported by poles and with a dimly-burning electric light.

Silence slowly descends in the barrack. 'They're going to wake us at half past four,' we tell each other.

'Who'll wake us? Schmidt?'

'No, someone else.'

Lucyna was one of the six women in our dormitory. The seventh person was Macius. Lucyna was an attractive blonde of about twenty, good-hearted and calm. She was by nature indolent and in need of support and friendship. Zofia, whom she met in the wagon, or maybe back in Warsaw, could have been her mother. So Lucyna transferred to Zofia all her love for the mother she left behind in a small flat in Praga in Warsaw. While Zofia was separated from her only daughter and so she surrounded Lucyna with maternal warmth. They came together by chance and decided to stay together. Slow, kind Lucyna needed a wise, clever and self-confident companion like that.

'Lucyna? What are you thinking of? Why are you wriggling around so much? You'll fall down on top of me. The boards won't stand it and you'll crush me to death.'

That's how Zofia grumbled, taking off her glasses and putting them carefully away into their case. She was short-sighted with a face well marked by time, a rough-hewn figure with a pair of strong legs and springy calves. 'Do you know, Lucyna? At the selection in Pruszkow the Germans didn't look at me at all. They looked at my legs just like you examine a horse to see if it's got strong fetlocks.' She spoke Polish with an eastern accent. When she smiled she showed long, yellow teeth and her clever, shrewd eyes looked out from behind her glasses.

Pelagia on the lower bunk asked Barbara Gorska to lie still because blades of straw were falling all over her. Pelagia was low, stocky and stout and her head was hidden in her shoulders. She had long hands and pock-marks on her face. White strong teeth. Black hair. Mongolian features. A beautiful, captivating smile which changed her face out of all recognition. She would jump onto a stool as agile as a monkey and crouch down. She ate her soup like that. She crouched on her bed and tidied her things. She slept naked. That was Pelagia. The gutter was her father and a den of thieves her mother. She used vulgar expressions. She had no shame or scruples. 'I used to go to a bar on Chlodna Street,' she told us at the very outset, 'we drank vodka and ate herrings. I went with Germans and had lots of things.'

She loathed Barbara Gorska right from the start. This hatred hatched out in the crooked labyrinths of her unconscious. In the most secret recesses of her primeval nature. 'For God's sake, don't twist and turn because you're sprinkling me with straw. If you keep doing it I'll break your head open with a plank. Dirty Jew!'

That's what she said. The blood ran to our hearts. Jew? What did she mean by that? Did she mean it as a contemptuous insult because a Jew was outside the law and outside life itself, or did she sense that Gorska was Jewish? We looked at Gorska. She was lying on her back with her head facing the plywood ceiling. She was looking at the dark circle on the ceiling, at the moving shadow cast by the electric light on its cord. She didn't say anything. She didn't become furious and didn't deny it. Pelagia's words flowed off her like water off a duck's back, as if they weren't intended for her. A shared cupboard and a shared bunk. A terrible neighbour. Wouldn't Gorska have preferred to go to Hamburg if she'd known what was in store for her?

The nights were warm so we put two blankets on the mattress and covered ourselves with the third one. Macius was asleep on the top bunk and Marysia dozed next to him. Someone put the light out. 'Don't kick,' whispered Marysia. Macius was sleeping uneasily and waking her. What on earth was he dreaming about? Perhaps he was running away from someone because he was thrashing about on the bed. Sometimes he cried or sat up and looked around in surprise. He slept with his mother. I don't know if he could have slept on his own at that time. He was unusually calm and collected during the day but at night he rebelled against this reality which wasn't cut out according to the measure of his strength.

At half past four when we were all fast asleep the light suddenly came on and the guard entered the room. He yelled at us to get up at the top of his voice, just like soldiers are woken. His name was Hofman. He had light-blonde hair and a long, narrow face. He wore glasses and had sad, tired and indifferent eyes. He had lost his left hand at Stalingrad and had an artificial hand with a black glove. He was so tall that he seemed to be on stilts. He could clearly see the women lying on the top bunks, Marysia, Lucyna and Gorska.

412

Suddenly the mysterious force which emanated from Gorska charmed him. He approached her bed and stood there in silence and stayed like that. She felt the man looking at her and slowly turned her head and looked at him.

In the morning when I was crossing the corridor I glanced through the open doors into the rooms. They were empty. There was no-one there. Empty? Kwiatkowski was lying on his bed. In a black suit, with his shoes off and smoking cigarettes. And Ziolkowski was sitting by the window winding his watch. Those two hadn't gone to work. Those two preferred not to work. I saw them in the same places again the next day. When I entered the kitchen I saw Schmidt. He rushed into the room followed by Stutzi. He passed Kwiatkowski indifferently and stood in front of Ziolkowski. 'You damned wretch!' he bellowed. He hit him across the face with all his might. 'Go to work! Understand!'

Ziolkowski understood and went to work from then on. But Kwiatkowski lay on his bed. In his black suit and with his shoes off. He lay there smoking cigarettes. He had bad eyes and was excused work. So it was said.

'There are strange things going on in our barrack,' I said to Marysia. 'The Georgian and Maria have got a room all to themselves even though four more people could fit into it and we're all terribly squashed. Schmidt hit Ziolkowski but passed Kwiatkowski indifferently. No-one believes he's got bad eyes.'

It was strange in the kitchen as well. After two weeks Schmidt was still joking with Natalia and Waclawa but when he passed me and Marysia he frowned and looked the other way. The cook wasn't as effusive to us as she was at the beginning either. She said that I peeled the potatoes too slowly, and one day when Marysia cut her hand while washing-up she told her that she wasn't suitable for the kitchen. We sensed insinuations in the air. The work in the kitchen had its advantages and it meant a lot to us. We were with Macius and we could keep an eye on him in the event of an air raid. So we were very upset by Mrs Lund's comments.

Mrs Lund was a doctor's widow. She was a tall, blonde woman of about fifty, deaf in one ear. She liked to talk. Her son had died of pneumonia. 'I haven't got anyone close left now, you know,' she used to say. 'I haven't got a flat either because it was bombed. I've been bombed out. And you know, before the war I worked for many years in the home of a rich Jewish family in Berlin.' I wondered why she was telling us this and whether she wasn't looking at us while

413

she was talking. 'And when they were expelled from their flat I cried terribly because I was very fond of them.'

Natalia and Waclawa didn't say a word. They didn't want to take the subject up, so it seemed to us. Mrs Lund's story was calculated to create an effect but it was interrupted and just hung in the air, as it were. All that remained was the beating of our hearts, nothing more. She told Natalia to grate some large potatoes because Schmidt liked potato pancakes. 'And Frau Alice will go with me to the stores to help me weigh the margarine.' Both Schmidt and the cook addressed all the young women by their first names, but they called me Frau Alice.

In the stores she placed a ten gram weight on the scales together with the margarine. In that way, if she was meant to weigh eighty grams she in fact weighed seventy. 'Ten grams is hardly anything at all, but after a hundred times I get two kilograms of margarine for myself,' she told me. I realized that the guards took part of our rations home with them as well. There were two of them, one with no right hand and one with no left hand. Schmidt was also taking things home in that leather case of his which he never ever parted from.

Schmidt had porridge with milk for breakfast every day. The guards ate the porridge too. We longed for Macius to have some nourishing porridge once a day too. Every child in our camp received a cup of milk at eleven o'clock, but never any eggs, meat or fruit. We gave Macius thin slices of sausage from our portions and most of our margarine and jam. But it was not enough. We worried immensely about him being undernourished. We couldn't manage, we didn't have any contacts yet for buying food on the side. There was just one thing I did – I had an oval, black, agate brooch with a lacy metal edging. I gave it to the cook as a souvenir in return for a bowl of porridge every morning from Lagerführer Schmidt's pan.

The atmosphere in the kitchen thawed immediately. She didn't talk about me peeling the potatoes slowly any more or Marysia being unsuitable for kitchen work. 'Frau Alice, I saw you take a powder compact out of your pocket today. A real beauty. I've wanted one like that for a long time.' The cat was on her knees and she was feeding her out of a beautiful china bowl. With gold edging and a rose painted in the bottom. 'That's Rosenthal,' I said. I didn't want to give her the compact.

Pelagia was thrown out of her job sewing buttons onto uniforms in the tailoring workshops at Warschauerbahnhof after three weeks. She was given penal work to do and now worked at clearing bomb rubble. She came into contact with Germans and had lots of possibilities. In these difficult times she brought rolls made of white flour back to the barrack. She once brought half a kilogram of semolina in a cotton sack. And once even a piece of strong, white parachute silk.

'What can I make out of it, Mrs Majewska?' she asked, as pleased as a child.

'A blouse. A beautiful blouse, if you can cut it out.'

I lent her some scissors. She cut it out on the bed, crouching and jumping from place to place. She gave me a small scrap for a handkerchief.

She assiduously brought back from town everything she could get hold of. A bra, a night-dress, a pair of knickers. If she brought back some rolls she gave Macius one. Crouching on a stool – we didn't have chairs, only tall, rustic style stools – she would stretch out her hand and give him a roll on the palm of her hand. 'Here you are, eat it. It's made of real white flour.' If she cooked some semolina she gave him some in a bowl too. She smiled charmingly, in her own way, and her slanting eyes looked like two slits when she smiled. She pulled him to herself, hugged him, smoothed his hair, pressed his head to her breast and kissed his cheeks.

'You're an intelligent girl, Pelagia,' Marysia once said, 'but don't you know you shouldn't kiss children.'

She blushed and took offence. She was quiet for a long time. Then she lifted her head wilfully, turned to Macius and looking at Marysia, she said, 'My beautiful little Jewish prince'.

That's what she said. Exactly that. Those five terrible words. Marysia went pale. She looked confusedly at Macius not knowing how he'd react and then at Pelagia, waiting to see if she'd say something else. She didn't say anything else. She ate her semolina in silence and then went to wash her bowl.

We were shattered. What could Pelagia's words mean? Did she know? Wouldn't she want to make use of what she knew? It all depended on how touched she was by what Marysia had said. Because there was no doubt that the lives of the three of us were now in this girl's hands. But there hadn't been any discord between us until now, in fact she got on well with us. She was at war with Gorska. She ignored Lucyna and Zofia because they treated her contemptuously. We were the only ones who were friendly to her.

415

Because despite her brutality and ruthlessness we sensed the goodness, tenderness and longing in her primeval nature.

She talked a lot about her brother, the priest, and we listened patiently. She was proud of him. Whatever she was talking about, she always returned to him. It made her feel higher in the social hierarchy. She wanted respect for herself in the eyes of her listeners, and even thought she was envied for having a brother who was a priest.

We lived in fear for a week or two because Pelagia wasn't as friendly to us as she used to be. She ate her soup in silence and tried not to look at us or Macius. Then she jumped onto her bed and spent a long time sliding together the boards from Gorska's bed above her head which had moved apart. While she was doing it she muttered to herself, 'The wretched woman moves the boards apart on purpose in order to sprinkle her rubbish on me.'

After a while the incident was forgotten. And Pelagia gave Macius rolls or sweets just like before. She was impelled by an instinct which she couldn't understand. Yes. It seemed as if the incident was forgotten. Everything pointed that way. Nothing disturbed the current of our days and nights. But I was terrified to hear her say one day, 'I love you because you're pretty, my little Jewish darling.'

We had all been using the outdoor latrine for many weeks. The lavatories in the camp were closed. It was impossible to teach people not to stand on the seats but to sit on them. Every morning all the lavatories, so clean and shining on the day we arrived, were terribly fouled. There was no use Schmidt being irritated and cursing. In the end the entrance to the lavatory was boarded up. The latrine was different. The floor was wet, the door didn't close and there weren't even any partitions. One long partition divided the men's part from the women's.

So it was desperate if you had a bad stomach or a bad bladder and had to run to the cold latrine on a rainy night. Your candle stub went out at the first blast of wind and so you ran in darkness and tripped over the ruins of the burnt out barrack. You lit the candle in the latrine and there was always someone else there standing on the seat.

When Marysia got dysentery she was isolated in the small sickroom. She stayed there for two days and two nights. Then Barbara Gorska received the room. For her exclusive use as a work-room because she was a dressmaker. Hofman was in love with her and

416

got hold of a hand sewing-machine from somewhere. Schmidt permitted it to be placed in the sick-room and Gorska made his wife a dress in two nights. Then she made a blouse for the wife of the second guard – he was called Roerich – and a night-dress for Hofman's wife.

There were two guards, one was on duty during the day and the other at night. They changed over every now and then. They were invalided out of the army with the rank of corporal. Roerich had two nicknames, Rerys and Lapka. He was always hanging around in the barrack with a cup or a soup bowl. They were both young men and treated us decently. The day guard's duties included standing guard at the gate. He was meant to check if everyone going to town had the letter P sewn onto their clothes. The order was generally disregarded and few people sewed the letter on. The guard rarely interfered. The night guard sat in Schmidt's room, burnt briquettes or coke in the stove and woke people up for work at various times.

When Gorska had made clothes for the guards' wives and Schmidt's wife, she got hold of two blue and white checked sheets. She made herself a fashionable floor length dressing-gown, wide and cloche shaped. When she returned from work she wore the dressing-gown in the corridor and when she went to collect her rations from the kitchen. Such elegance looked grotesque against the background of the cockroach infested barrack. All the same she aroused jealousy in the hearts of the young women and magnetically attracted the men's eyes.

If Gorska sewed at night, then when did she sleep? She slept for an hour or two on the bed in the sick-room, and apart from that she slept in the tram and the electric train which took her to work and back. She often missed her stop and woke suddenly to find that she was far away in a neighbourhood she didn't know at all. But Gorska was in the management's good books, which is not what you could say about the kitchen helpers Alicja and Maria Majewska. Schmidt bared his teeth in a smile when he passed Gorska in the corridor, mindful of the dress she had made for his wife, but he furrowed his eyebrows threateningly when he saw the Majewskis.

'Why is it?' asked Marysia in surprise. 'What's happened? Why was it all right at first and bad now? Shouldn't we bribe him? Give him something?'

'Bribe him?' I asked terrified. 'Give him a bribe? We can rot in prison for bribery and then what'll happen to the child?'

'Maria!' we hear Schmidt shouting in the corridor. His voice was so loud it made the windows ring. 'He's calling me,' she said. 'I'm going to the office.' She went and came back a few minutes later. 'Do you know what he said? I'm going to work at Goerlitzerbahnhof as from tomorrow. The guard will wake me at half past three.'

'Why so early? He wakes everyone else at half past four.'

'Because it takes an hour to get there on the train. Don't worry. It'll be better like this. We're too visible in the kitchen. A lot of people are probably envious thinking that we have God knows what advantages there. I'm young and I should be working outside. The most important thing is for you to stay and look after Macius.'

The door opened at half past three and Hofman entered. He didn't put the light on in the room, just left the door open. He approached Marysia's bed and shook her pillow. 'Get up, Maria,' he said quietly so as not to wake the others, 'it's half past three.'

She slid down from the top bunk in a stupor. She put her shoes on. They were all torn but she didn't have any others. She put on her coat, too thin for cold autumn nights. She spread a few slices of black bread with jam and wrapped them up in paper. She went to the kitchen and brought some coffee in a pan. She sat down at the table dressed ready to go out and had something to eat. In the half-light she could see our sleeping shapes. Pelagia's naked breasts, Zofia's hand hanging down and Lucyna's profile faintly delineated against the black wall.

Then she went out. Her quick steps thumped loudly in the long, empty, dimly lit corridor. The door of the sick-room was ajar and she saw Gorska sitting at the sewing-machine and Hofman's pained face bent over her. Darkness engulfed her in the yard. She joined her shift, the few other people who worked at the same station. A fine rain started to fall. She bent her head against the wind and wound the scarf more tightly round her neck.

What had happened to Hofman? He didn't eat, didn't sleep, lost weight and was fading away. It was no secret that he was in love with Barbara Gorska. Didn't he follow her incessantly with his eyes? Couldn't we sense that he'd go to hell at a nod of her head? Didn't he kiss her hand to say good night? Against the background of our dismal reality, that courtly gesture alone demonstrated how bound up he was emotionally. But it was a tragic love because it was unrequited, and you can understand the tragedy of it. When his hand was amputated he experienced a nervous shock and lost his

418

self-confidence. He was an invalid and thought that women didn't find him attractive any longer.

But he had a pleasant and good-looking wife who was in the first few months of pregnancy. She came to our barrack sometimes and they went home together. She quickly realized what was happening. When they were quarrelling she used to throw the night-dress Gorska had made at him.

Did Hofman know that the German who used to come to the transit camp came to our barrack as well? He came carrying the same canvas sack, and in the sack was food, which was to hard to come by. Butter, pork fat, sausage. When he came Gorska put her coat on without a word and went out to town with him. But before she left she would open her cupboard with a key and place the paper wrapped parcels inside. She locked the cupboard using a padlock she'd bought on Alexanderplatz. She was the first to lock her cupboard. Lucyna and Zofia were the next. What for? We thought it was because of Pelagia. Only later did we realize that it was probably because of us. We had a child who was undernourished. And maybe what they thought was that you never know what his mother might do to get hold of some food for him. They had foresight and were being careful.

One day we received a parcel from Switzerland. It was Lucja Hersz's reply to the letter we had sent from the transit camp. We were really moved. What could such a small, light parcel contain? We thought it was tea, because what else could it be? The sender wasn't Lucja Hersz or her daughter Joanna. The sender was a Maria Lubinska. We understood that Lucja had deliberately not given her real name out of regard for our safety. We turned the parcel over on all sides. Before we opened it we examined every letter and every seal, and the string, the paper, and the stamps, because this was the world and it had come to us. The parcel contained a watch. A luminous ladies' watch. Intended for sale and sent to us with that in mind. We immediately sold it to Gorska for a kilogram of butter and a kilogram of pork fat. That way we could feed Macius better for a while.

Reinhold the storekeeper, Mazur as we called him, allocated us a few things. Every woman received a pair of warm knickers, thick cotton stockings and a checked cotton dress which we wore instead of a night-dress. But Marysia happened to get a real night-dress from Mazur and immediately sold it to Gorska for a piece of butter.

All the women in the barrack wore camp underwear, apart from

419

Lotta, our interpreter, who considered herself a cut above us. Mazur also promised us some wooden-soled shoes for winter and wooden clogs for use in the camp. None of this concerned Lotta. Could you imagine Lotta wearing shoes with wooden soles? Lotta was forty. She was a stocky brunette, quite good-looking and kind. We all tried to get on well with her. Whenever Lucyna received a food parcel she always put an onion aside for Lotta.

Lotta lived with Olek. He was twenty-eight-years old and worked on the railway. A handsome, tall and healthy man. She prayed to God for the set-up to last for ever – barrack, corridor, bunk and Olek. Although Schmidt favoured her she didn't have a room of her own. The Georgian and young Maria were the only ones to have a separate room in the barrack. It was rumoured that Gorska had enchanted Olek. They worked at the same station and were said to meet there in secret. Pregnant Natalia whispered about it to Waclawa as she was peeling potatoes in the kitchen. Roerich said to the cook, 'I'd never let myself be charmed by that terrible woman, that's for sure.'

Lotta felt like a lioness whose cub has been taken away from her. She aged suddenly in the course of a single night. She didn't talk to anyone. Huddled up and lost in thought she prepared to attack. One day she was near the office door when Hofman's pregnant wife came out sobbing. 'That Polish bitch' she kept repeating in a strangled voice. She'd come to Schmidt to complain about Gorska and tell him that her husband, who had always been so attentive, had become indifferent to her. Schmidt listened in grim silence and considered what to do. He'd already heard the rumours about Olek and Gorska. Before Lotta entered he managed to take a few gulps from the bottle he kept hidden in his desk. He was a solitary drinker, a fact he kept secret.

The room the married couples lived in presented the strangest picture in the world. It consisted of dozens of tiny houses, as it were, all separate, but all on top of each other. The couples got hold of curtains, blinds or scraps of colourful material which they used to separate themselves from their neighbours, wanting to create at least the illusion of privacy. These unfortunate couples longed to have even an old wooden cell of their own, and when Gorska arbitrarily appropriated the light, clean sick-room she became a bone of contention and the object of their deadly hatred.

But all the same, when she walked along the corridor in the evening in her long cloche dressing-gown and with an artificial flower in her skilfully pinned hair, clattering her clogs and with a mysterious smile on her lips, all the men looked at her. And obedient to the fluid which emanated from her, weak and enchanted, they weren't surprised at Hofman who was mortally sick with love.

The yard outside the barrack was surrounded with barbed wire. A sentry-box by the gate and in the sentry-box a guard. Then the spreading, unploughed fields. Heaps of briquettes and coke lay in the yard and even in the field outside the barbed wire. We looked at them and said, 'At least we won't freeze in winter'. The track across the fields was uneven and full of puddles when it rained and led to Grünauer Strasse, a city street with houses, a carriageway and a tram. The stop was very near. People from our camp took the tram to their work places from that stop.

The nights were now long and the evenings were long. You left the camp in darkness and returned in darkness. Everything was blacked out. It was easy to trip and fall. One of our workmen, an older man called Debczak, fell under a tram. He was hit on the head and was never the same again. If the journey to work was so dangerous, the work itself was that much more dangerous. Whether in the dark on stations, or in locomotives, or on the rails. Zielinska cleaned trains. She fell under a locomotive and was killed instantly. She was a quiet woman, no longer young. She lived in the married couples' room with her railwayman son. Everyone was sorry and her son was shattered. After her death a new railway worker was needed and Schmidt designated Marysia to take her place.

Marysia reported to the railway office at the station. 'Please give me indoor work. I'm scared of the cold. My hands are frost-bitten.'

'What can you do?'

'I can speak and write German . . . ' then she hesitated. 'I was educated at university,' she continued.

They were surprised and started looking at her more carefully. 'Let's see your handwriting.'

They dictated a few sentences in German. She wrote them down quickly in beautiful handwriting.

'You'll work here in the office.'

The next day she went to work in my shoes and I wore the wooden clogs. She gave Madejski her shoes to mend – he worked as a cobbler and mended railwaymen's shoes. At nine o'clock in the evening Madejski brought the shoes. When he stood in the doorway with a shy smile, coughing and not looking straight at us, we felt guilty because all day long we'd been worried that he'd sell the shoes and we wouldn't see them again.

'How much do I owe you?' asked Marysia, with a sigh of relief.

'Nothing. I took the leather from the workshop.'

'But I want to pay for your work at least.'

'Don't mention it.' He waved his hand. 'And this is for the child.'

He took a tiny, green malachite figure of Buddha out of his pocket and clumsily gave it to Macius. He must have found it ferreting in the ruins of a bombed house.

Even if Madejski had accepted a few marks from Marysia, what could he buy? A small beer, shoe-laces, a dozen safety pins. He could go to the barber. The shops were empty. Food was rationed. In the huge shop on Alexanderplatz, apart from sewing requisites, there were a few books and a huge selection of gramophone records. The mark, the paper German mark, didn't count as money at this time. The unit of currency was the cigarette.

There were about fifty tiny wooden houses between our barrack and Grünauer Strasse. People whose flats had been bombed lived there. One of these tiny houses belonged to an elderly woman who lived on her own. I went there one day. I had ten cigarettes in my pocket. Marysia got them from Ziolkowski. He sold them to her at cost price. I bought a pair of warm knickers for Marysia from the woman for ten cigarettes.

Once we broke a spoon. Our tin camp spoon that we used for eating soup. Marysia stopped a German woman on the street and asked her to sell her a spoon. 'I can't get one anywhere in the shops and how can you live without a spoon?' The woman waved her hand and moved away. But a moment later she turned round again. She took Marysia to her flat and gave her a spoon. 'Here you are,' she said, 'you can have it.'

A young girl from Denmark lived in a wooden hut next door to the house where I bought the knickers. She had come to Berlin before the war and worked as a waitress in a café. She was doing well and even had a bike of her own. Now she was a prostitute. It surprised me that her neighbours knew what she did but were friendly to her all the same. She sold me a short, red skirt of thick wool that she didn't wear any more. For eight cigarettes. I bought the skirt because I needed material for trousers for Macius.

What else could you buy for German marks? A small helping of plain cooked cabbage. And a cinema ticket. The cinemas still played in bombed Berlin. And I even went with Macius to the Sunday morning children's performance once. The cinema was outside Koepenick in a long, wooden hut. There were a few hundred children. They came on their own. Only about a dozen adults were present. I was scared to talk to Macius in Polish in front of the other children. They clapped every soldier and every cannon on the screen.

We returned along empty Grünauer Strasse. The pavements and carriageway where the tram drove were wide but the street wasn't completely built up yet. Here and there you could see empty fields or a garden surrounded by railings. A lot of ruined houses. Along the sides of the streets heaps of rubble, and among the rubble, rags, old pans, bits of wood and rusty tins. I couldn't pass a rubbish heap without looking. I glanced at every empty tin. That was as a result of the train journey when we longed to heat some water in a container when the train stopped.

On the street stood a low bunker with a flat roof, said to have been built so strongly that it was bomb-proof. There were a few hundred cabins in the bunker. They were rented out and women went there for the night with their children and returned home in the morning. In the evening we watched mothers pushing their children in prams towards the bunker from our barrack window.

I had the letter P sewn onto the lapel of my jacket. A dark letter on a yellow background. Not everyone sewed the letter on. Many people rebelled against it. Marysia and I wore the letter the longest. We felt safer under the protection of that distinct dark P. On our coat sleeves you could still see signs of the armband with the blue star we wore in the ghetto.

I unstitched and washed the skirt and then made Macius a pair of trousers. He didn't want to wear red trousers. We told him that French soldiers wore trousers exactly the same colour red. If a French soldier can wear red trousers, then he can too. That argument convinced him.

Where else could you go with German money? To the zoo at Tiergartenbahnhof. Marysia went there one Sunday with the child. They paid the entrance fee and looked at the animals in cages. So Macius didn't have too many amusements. He went to the cinema once and to the zoo once. That was all. What about the other children in the barrack? There weren't any children his age. They were all either older or younger.

He started being friends with a German boy. His name was Hans

423

and he was nine years old. His mother lived in one of the little wooden houses, right next to the Danish girl's hut. Her husband and oldest son were away at war. She had a few children. Hans came to our barrack every day for kitchen scraps as the family kept chickens and rabbits. Sometimes he brought his sister or brother along. He said he didn't go to school regularly. He went for two hours, and not every day. Many schools had been destroyed by bombs and the teachers were away at war. He was a calm, intelligent boy. He played with Macius and other children in the camp although, according to the regulations, it was forbidden for German children to play with children in camps. One day he gave Macius a tiny bit of soap, and in those times soap was priceless. Another time, to Marysia's astonishment, he told her what the BBC was broadcasting.

That was exactly the time when lice showed up in our flea and cockroach ridden barrack.

'Lice in our barrack!' said Lucyna terrified. 'Those two who work at Schlesingerbahnhof have got lice in their clothes.'

'Mazur in the clothes-store is giving out some lotion,' said Zofia. 'Everyone can get it. For head lice.'

We got some too. But while the other women weren't in a hurry to use it on their heads, we used it all the time for fear of head lice. That meant we were suspected of having lice. Macius as well. A veritable campaign against Macius's hair started up. He still had a fringe and his hair covered his ears. 'Those big ears of his might give him away,' said Marysia. 'Better keep them covered.'

Schmidt summoned her to his office and yelled, 'If you don't get your son's hair cut I'll take the scissors and do it myself. He's sure to have lice.'

'But I wash his hair every day and rub the lotion into his hair every evening.'

'That proves he's got lice. I'm giving you two days to think about it. What's going on for God's sake? Why isn't his hair cut short like all the other boys?'

That sentence prevailed. If the other boys had short hair, then Macius shouldn't look different. He should be like the others. Maybe looking different was more dangerous than big ears.

'Tomorrow afternoon,' Marysia told me, 'take him to the barber. There's one on our street next to the bombed house.'

I went the next day and paid the barber in German marks. When Marysia returned from work she looked at Macius and said, 'He hasn't got big ears at all. It was all unnecessary.'

She returned from work at about six now. If there was an alarm and bombing she got back later. The station where she worked and the other railway stations were bombed frequently. Work was interrupted and then resumed. Sometimes she had to take cover in a shelter or under a bridge on her way home. Sometimes she came back at one in the morning.

There was a workman in our barrack who worked at the same station. He was called Alfred Tchorzewski. He had a wife and two children in Warsaw. If he finished his work earlier he didn't return to the camp even though he was tired and hungry. He waited for Marysia. He didn't want her to return on her own in the darkness. Shy, quiet and unkempt, he was completely absorbed in the home he missed so much.

Marysia got to know him one sunny Sunday when she took our bunk to pieces and carried it outside the barrack. She brought two buckets of hot water from the kitchen and poured it over the boards to kill the cockroaches. When the boards dried she couldn't put the bed together again. Tchorzewski helped her do it and set the bed up in our room. That was the beginning of their acquaintance.

'You understand how important it is that you work in the kitchen,' Marysia often said to me. 'You take Macius to the shelter. If you weren't there he'd run round the yard collecting coloured strips of cellophane from the incendiary bombs.'

Two bags stood in our cupboard. In them were our most vital belongings. We took them to the shelter during alarms.

'Remember the bags,' Marysia told me. 'I heard that a barrack was bombed and burnt down while the people were at work. They didn't have anything to wear afterwards.'

So when I went with the churns to the shop to buy milk and Macius was on his own I told him, 'There might be an alarm while I'm not here. At least take one bag to the shelter and then something will be saved if the barrack catches fire.'

One day there really was a bombing raid while I was out and I returned terrified. How's Macius? Is the barrack standing? Has it burnt down? The barrack was untouched. A few women were just leaving the shelter with their children. Macius wasn't among them. He wasn't in the shelter at all. He was in the yard cuddling a small teddy bear. He'd been given it when he was a baby and never parted from it. He had it in the ghetto and on the Aryan side. We were superstitious at that time so the toy was our mascot. We

425

ascribed it mysterious but propitious properties. 'Make me lucky with the teddy because I'm going to work,' Marysia used to say if Macius wasn't asleep when she was leaving.

'Did you go to the shelter? Did you take any of our things?' I immediately asked.

'No,' he said. 'But I took my teddy and everything had to be all right.'

If the alarm was at night not everyone went down to the shelter. Tchorzewski never went down. Nor Ziolkowski. No-one ever saw the Georgian in the shelter, or Kwiatkowski, although he didn't work. People were tired after work and preferred to sleep. Or perhaps they were convinced that the shelter was no good and that's why they never went down. Women went down with their children and wives with their husbands. Sometimes there were two alarms in one night. Or even three. The third time everyone was tired and no-one went down. The guard shouted, slammed the doors and tried to chase us all down in vain.

We always went down because of Macius. But he didn't want to get down from his bed. He was asleep. No way did he want to get down. Then Marysia smacked him. There was a stick by the bed and in her despair she beat him with it at night when fire was falling from the sky and everything around that could still burn was in flames. In the end, swaying in the dark, falling and losing our way in the dense mist caused by the bombers, in rain or in storm, we reached the shelter at last. We returned after half an hour to fall asleep for a moment and then get up – Marysia and her shift at half past three and the rest at half past four.

'Get up, Maria. Get up,' said the guard in a loud whisper. If it was Roerich he left the room immediately. If it was Hofman he always stopped if only for a second by Gorska's empty bed. He was thinking about her and remembering how she would slowly turn her head towards him and smile mysteriously. Gorska was no longer in the light, clean sick-room nor in our room. She fell out of favour and was exiled, transferred to another camp near Berlin. Lotta the interpreter was relieved. So was Hofman's pregnant wife. Schmidt swore on his honour that Gorska would never set foot in his camp again.

We didn't work on Sundays. Sunday was a day of rest. Hardly anyone went out to town. People generally stayed in the barrack. A few women went to church. Including Mrs Malinowska, a woman of fifty who cleaned the offices at one of the stations. Her husband had bad lungs and haemorrhaged from time to time. He was meant to be a metalworker but made saucepans out of aluminium most of the time. He sold them to people in the barrack, but he gave Marysia one. Mrs Malinowska went to church regularly each Sunday. Mrs Zielinska used to go too before she was killed by the locomotive.

Schmidt didn't care for it. 'On Sundays everyone should sleep from morning till night in order to work better afterwards,' he used to say. He encouraged people to sleep and not to go to church.

No-one was interested in religion. No-one ever talked about it. No-one ever sang religious songs either. Marysia hung a picture of Our Lady above her bed but then she noticed that no-one else had done so. Neither Pelagia nor Lucyna and not even Zofia either. She was the only one with a holy picture in the whole barrack. In our room only Pelagia slept all day on Sundays. The rest talked. It was a day for talking, which we didn't have time for on workdays.

'Just think,' I said. 'The letter reached Lucja Hersz but it didn't have a stamp. How did she find us since we didn't know what camp we'd go to? We only wrote that we were in the transit camp.'

'The postal clerk can't have been a Nazi,' replied Marysia. 'He affixed a stamp and let the letter go. Or he let it through without stamps. As for our address, she might have got it from the Red Cross. We wrote our names and surnames.'

'She's sent a parcel so she might write soon. I'm afraid of that happening because Lotta censors the post and she'll read it. Mrs Hersz might write about something we're concealing. For example she might ask about my daughters, while I tell everybody that I had just the one son who died.'

Lucyna was sitting on Zofia's bed and making a little sack out of a coloured cloth. She cleaned trains and brought bits and pieces back from work. Every now and then she'd break off from her sewing and look at a photograph lying by the side of the bed. It was taken in a cemetery. A gravestone with a cross and a clear inscription: Jan Centkiewicz. Zofia was standing next to the gravestone in deep mourning. 'It's my husband's grave,' said Zofia. She liked showing people the photograph.

Zofia was in general a good-tempered woman. She ate well as she made dresses and blouses for the Ukrainian cooks in other camps in her spare time and received food from them instead of money. Every evening she peeled some potatoes and put them in her bowl. She covered them with water and added some fat from a tin. She covered the bowl securely and placed it on the iron stove. The bowl stood there all night long. In the morning Zofia ate the potatoes and gave Lucyna some too.

'It smells tasty, what you cook up,' said Pelagia crouching on her stool.

Zofia dismissed her words in complete silence. She didn't say anything. She held the girl in complete contempt while we got on with Pelagia. Didn't wise Zofia find that suspicious?

Fortunately we didn't suffer from the cold. We burnt the briquettes which we brought in from the yard in a bucket. If the stove went out I'd bring some glowing ashes on a shovel from the kitchen or from another stove.

There was another worker to help with the pans in the kitchen now. Konstanty wasn't there any longer. The new man was called Feliks Kaczynski. But although his name was Feliks, Mrs Lund called him Johann.

On Sundays we sat on our beds and laughed about it. And we always recalled the one incredible dinner we once received. Just once, shortly after our arrival, we were given real Viennese cutlets. Why? No-one could understand it. Perhaps they were expecting a Red Cross Commission or maybe a visit from someone from the neutral countries. It was a riddle. But we talked about the dinner for months. It was a real event in our camp lives.

We sometimes had fried flounders for dinner. How tasty they were, those large flat fish with the white bellies and light brown skin with dark spots. Our weekly rations were microscopic. Portions of sausage, cheese, margarine and plum jam, all of the highest quality, but so small. Once we were given snails for dinner. Sea snails in cardboard cups. No-one wanted to eat them. People protested and demanded something different. They went to sleep hungry. And? Would Schmidt throw out a hundred helpings of snails?

There was worker called Wegliszewski in the barrack. He lived with a woman who had a tragic look on her face, like Marlene Dietrich. They lived in a room with Lotta and Olek and could tell us a thing or two about them at the time when Olek and Gorska used to meet at the station. To the surprise of the whole camp Wegliszewski ate all the untouched helpings of snails. 'I like eating,' he said, patting his stomach. He was about fifty. He was unshaven, dirty and unkempt and always wore his coat in the barrack but he was good-natured and amusing.

'I like eating,' he said when he was on his fiftieth helping.

'Shall we bet on it?' Ziolkowski asked Kwiatkowski. 'Will he burst or not?'

Everyone watched Wegliszewski and laughed. Everyone apart from his woman. She held a cigarette delicately in her hand and let out the smoke, blinking her eyes. She held him in complete contempt. .

On Sundays I worried most. Everything looked black and I had no faith or hope.

'Macius was very ill in the ghetto and then he had that scarlet fever on the Aryan side,' I said to Marysia. 'Look what he's eating. A glass of milk a day and no meat, eggs, fruit or vegetables ever.'

'But he's alive,' replied Marysia.

There was nothing I could say to that. We looked out of the window at Macius standing by the barbed wire. He wore a navy blue cap, a beige coat with a velvet collar and from under his coat you could see his red trousers, made from the Danish girl's skirt. I told Marysia about that girl. Whenever I passed by the wooden houses and looked into her hut she was always lying there with a man. The man was asleep. She was looking out of the window and I always caught sight of her face. She had short, fair, smoothly brushed hair, a pale, quiet and sad face, and she moved slowly and shyly. She dressed carelessly. Her name was Ingeborg.

I sometimes saw her sitting on a bench next to someone's house and talking quietly with some older women. The women never mentioned what she did. Their friendship with her was quite touching. The most they said was that she was ruining her health. I explained it by the fact that the terrible pile of ruins which was now Berlin had levelled all classes. And also by the fact that the girl's appearance and behaviour remained at striking odds with her profession.

When Lucyna, Zofia and Pelagia weren't in the room we talked about Gorska.

'I'm convinced she's Jewish,' said Marysia. 'If Pelagia guessed that Macius is Jewish then she mightn't have been wrong about Gorska.'

'But she doesn't know a word of German.'

'Perhaps she's just pretending.'

She intrigued us. I watched her attentively. I listened to the intonation of her voice, I examined her eyes, her gait, her back, her hair. Nothing escaped the alertness of my gaze. If I could I would have stolen into her soul. There were days when I was convinced she was Jewish and then other times I thought it was impossible.

One evening as I was crossing the corridor I stopped in front of the office. The door was closed. It was pay-day. I could hear raised voices. It was Schmidt and Zofia. They were talking loudly in German. German? Zofia was simply speaking Yiddish, like Jews from eastern Poland. What about Schmidt? Perhaps he thought that it was a dialect, there were dozens of dialects after all, and some of them were hard to understand. But Alicja Majewska standing in front of the door understood every word the Jewish woman was saying. And as in a flash of lightning I realized that the bowl of potatoes which Zofia placed on the hot stove every evening and cooked all night long was chulent, the traditional Jewish dish.

What about that photograph in the cemetery? A man with a moustache in an oval frame on the gravestone. The shining cross above the Grecian urn. The dates of birth and death and the inscription saying 'in holy memory of Jan Centkiewicz'. A brilliant ruse. The most amusing of masks. That and the Aryan papers must have cost a pretty penny. We often sat on my bed on Sunday afternoons and talked about it. We had experience of all sorts of masks, but Zofia's was the best of the lot. It was unique. And it was definitely worth the money it had cost.

Zofia became an inexhaustible subject for us. We watched with interest to see the methods she used and the strategy she assumed to play her role. We deliberated on her moves and decided whether they were mistakes, or if they proved her ingenuity and intelligence. Her friendship with Lucyna was undoubtedly a good move. Against the background of the fair-haired girl, in the light of her blue eyes, Zofia's Semitic features were toned down. Lucyna was her shield and she used it skilfully.

In the evenings we heard their conversations. 'Lucyna? Are you asleep? I've just remembered a dream I had last night and I wonder what it might mean. I dreamt of a house like the one on Graniczna Street, and the mice were moving out of it.'

'The mice?' answered Lucyna, surprised. 'How do you know they moved out?'

'Because they were carrying cases. And the caretaker was chasing them with a spade.'

'A fire!' said Lucyna. 'Well, what do you want? Surely the Germans have burnt the house on Graniczna Street down.'

Delving into dreams and looking for what they meant, investigating dreams and troubling your head with them – this wasn't a Jewish characteristic. It was the specific characteristic of small town gossips. And if Zofia deliberately delved into dreams and thought up visions and charms for Lucyna, it was definitely in her favour. But wasn't she overstretching the bow with her contempt for Pelagia? She must have been incredibly self-confident, but perhaps she was over-confident.

I sometimes caught in Pelagia's eyes a poisonous look directed at Zofia and heard a mocking giggle after she'd heard a weird dream. Pelagia's pillow met my pillow on our respective bunks. That evening when the light was out Pelagia lifted up her head and whispered two terrible sentences into the darkness of the room. 'She's a Jew. It's Rojza from Graniczna Street.' That was her revenge for Zofia's contempt.

The Malinowskis' daughter, Jadwiga, arrived from Poland. She came voluntarily to her parents and that's why she immediately received a good job at one of the many stations. She worked in the parcels shop. She repacked spilled and badly wrapped parcels. And she sometimes brought her parents back some apples or even sweets. She was twenty. Her father was handsome and her mother had regular features, but she wasn't pretty. But she had a beautiful, trained voice and was very self-confident.

She made herself a loose, wide coat with a shawl collar and a muff out of a grey camp blanket, and a large flat beret from the scraps left over. She bought a feather on Alexanderplatz and put it on the beret. This was an elegance which our flea-ridden barrack, full of cockroaches, could well appreciate. She went to work dressed like that and even to the shelter during alarms. They always went to the shelter, Mr Malinowski with a heavy suitcase, Mrs Malinowska with a bundle of bedding, and Jadwiga with her muff. The Malinowskis were the only people in the barrack to have any bedding.

'What's happened, Mrs Malinowska?' I asked her one day as she was running along the corridor holding a wet towel.

'My husband's lungs are haemorrhaging.'

I was scared. But I noticed that neither she nor her daughter were very worried. 'It used to happen at home too,' they said.

I looked into the room Mr Malinowski was lying in. He was sixty-three, with thick white hair and a thick white moustache. That's what Poles must have looked like in olden times. You could imagine

431

him dancing the polonaise, with the traditional coat and a sword in his belt. He could have been the sword-bearer or cup-bearer or equerry at the royal court. But now he was lying in a plywood barrack. And from under his white eyebrows his eyes looked out through the window at the barbed wire. Past the barbed wire was the canal with its barges.

Jadwiga sang for us from time to time. Our camp was greatly privileged to have a singer. Since she dreamed of fame and thousands of admirers, and a triumphal procession through the capitals of the world, she only sang operatic arias. This wise girl took life soberly and looked at everything and everyone from the height of her voice, but funnily enough she didn't understand how much the repertoire was out of keeping with the reality of our barrack. An ordinary folk-song would have touched her audience to the quick, but these strange, grand arias with words no-one could understand flowed over our heads like rain-water. But everyone listened. Enchanted not by the words and maybe not even the tune, but by the very sound and modulation of her voice.

One day a new group of railwaymen came to our camp. And who was in the group? Konrad. Handsome Konrad. When he came to the barrack for the first time, when he leaned against the door-frame and took in the miserable room and Jadwiga singing with her hand against a bunk with one glance of his impudent eyes, she probably felt that the floor had swayed under her feet. She fell silent.

In the first week of our stay in the camp we were all taken to a distant suburb. It was so long ago! First of all they got hold of passes for us allowing us to travel outside the Berlin administrative area. We took the electric train, and Mrs Lund stayed behind and looked after the camp.

There was a pine wood with lots of wooden barracks. I saw a crowd of Italian women from one of the barracks with towels on their shoulders. They must have been coming back from the showers. They were talking loudly in Italian. It was a transit camp and a registration point. We were registered and photographed. There were crowds waiting their turn. We spent many hours without food. There wasn't even anywhere to sit down. We sat on the ground. On the grey, soft dust. Not on the grass because there wasn't any. Every blade of grass had been trampled by thousands of feet.

As we sat there in the dust, tired and sleepy, we suddenly saw a column of people, all men. They were marching quickly, six or eight to a row. When they passed us we could hear, 'Zielonka, Zielonka, Zielonka'. It made a huge impression on us. We gathered that they'd been taken from Zielonka outside Warsaw. And that they wanted to tell us so that we'd know and remember. When about a hundred men had passed, the next rows said, 'Praga, Praga, Praga'. They couldn't stop and talk to us. They were convoyed by Germans and were walking very quickly just like a unit of soldiers. They came from all sorts of backgrounds. Some were well-dressed, others were in rags. Workers, students, porters, clerks, craftsmen. We all felt depressed when we heard them rhythmically repeating, 'Wawer, Wawer, Wawer'.

Then we went to the office located in one of the barracks. We signed a declaration saying we had come of our own free will. There was a special statute for volunteers and on that basis we had special privileges. What did they consist of? We were a labour camp, and not a concentration camp. We were able to move freely within the city of Berlin and we had the right to receive medical assistance.

While we were signing the declarations a few Italian soldiers came in. They were unshaven and their uniforms were very worn. They obviously wanted to ask about something because they were standing there very confused. One of the clerks asked what the Italian monkeys wanted. Italian soldiers were no longer allies and people were hostile to them. I sometimes met them on the Berlin streets, dirty and hungry, picking up dog-ends and looking for scraps in the rubble.

After standing in the sun and sitting in the dust for many hours our turn came. We were photographed in a small booth with a number pinned to our chests. Marysia and I were so tired that our photos bore no resemblance to our true selves. We looked like corpses. Then they made identity cards which also served as workbooks. The photograph was stuck on the first page. The numbers came out most clearly of all on the photos. They were really obvious.

One day Lotta stopped me on the corridor and said, 'Mrs Majewska, there's a letter for you.' She handed me a postcard. There were Swiss stamps on it. I went into the room and shut the door behind me. I didn't want anyone to see my emotion. We were the only ones in the whole barrack who didn't receive any letters. From family or friends. Warsaw was burnt down. But there were other towns and villages in Poland apart from Warsaw and life went on normally there. Someone, somewhere, should have shown an interest in us. If no-one did we became suspicious.

No-one in Poland. And then suddenly someone writes from Switzerland. A neutral country, true, but who were we if we got letters from Switzerland? Our aim was to be the same as everyone else and melt into the grey crowd. But neither Johann from the boiler nor the Malinowskis nor Lucyna received letters from abroad. That's why I thought that Lotta had looked at me in a particular way when she gave me the postcard. Part of her job was to censor letters. She must have read the postcard and might have told Schmidt what it said.

The card was from Lucja Hersz in Geneva, but signed Lubinska. The same person who'd sent the parcel with the watch. 'Dear Alice, I was so pleased to hear your news. Thank God you're all well. But you didn't say anything about your daughters. How are they?' Daughters? I turned pale. Every Jew on Aryan papers had a prepared story. Long or short, more or less complicated. You had to remember your story well so as not to get mixed up and make a mistake. According to my story I didn't have any daughters. I was a widow and my only son had died in the war. I was with my daughter-in-law and her son. Everyone in the camp that we were friendly with knew all this very well. Lotta too.

That's why letters were dangerous. The other side wasn't always initiated and could make trouble. We had a friend near Piotrkow Trybunalski, a Polish woman who'd known our family for many years. We often wanted to write to her and ask about Irena and Nina but we were afraid to. Precisely because of that. We were definitely in Lotta's hands now. Slowly but surely she might unravel the whole truth and get our secret out of us. What could we buy her silence with?

I'd brought a winter coat from Warsaw instead of a blanket. A coat made by a good tailor. It was brown and narrow-waisted with a wide belt. On cold and windy days I often wore it to fetch some briquettes from outside in a bucket. Lotta would sit in the window and look out. I caught her looking at me.

'Mrs Majewska, would you like to sell me your coat?' she asked.

'No, I can't sell it. I'll freeze without it.'

But what'll happen if Lotta now asks, 'Mrs Majewska, do you still not want to sell your coat?' and smiles ambiguously.

And me? Will I tell her again I'll freeze without it? No. I won't say that now.

What else did Lucja Hersz write about? In the evening when Marysia came back from work we pondered over every letter and every word. Because there was something else in the card which was really important. 'A commission is to go soon and bring children from the camps to Switzerland. Would you like Marysia's son to go?'

Would we like it? In our imagination we could see him sitting at table in a Swiss house. A glass of milk in front of him. Rolls. Butter. An apple. Chocolate. Let him go! Where's the commission? We must reply immediately and tell her yes, we want him to go. We beg you. Our hearts were too joyful to hide the news from Macius. He didn't really have to know about it for the time being, did he? It was all so far off. But we told him. He was afraid. He cried. He couldn't stand the thought of being separated from us and was frightened.

We avoided Lotta. We watched her anxiously. But nothing happened. She kept quiet. Perhaps she hadn't noticed. Or maybe she was suffering so much because of Olek's unfaithfulness that she was indifferent to everything else. Mrs Michalska was also indifferent to everything, the fat mother of young Maria, the Georgian's friend. Nothing interested her. Intrigues, romances and quarrels flowed off her like water off a duck's back. There was only one thing she thought about day and night: to return to Poland. While she was chopping garlic or cutting up the potatoes she told me in confidence, 'I'm from the landed gentry. My family is trying to get us released. We're going home soon, my daughter and I.'

She received a letter the same time as I did. She was called Estera, a strange name. 'Does it surprise you?' she asked me in the kitchen. 'That's what my mother called me. It was her wish. Children died in our family.'

The letter was from Poland. From her husband. A registered letter. In the letter a document issued by the German authorities. They could go home on the strength of that document. Mrs Michalska couldn't wait for Maria to come back from work at four o'clock. In the meantime she packed her things. At half past four she sent a boy to fetch Maria. She came at once. 'Maria,' said her mother and stood there with her hand outstretched and the letter shaking in her fingers. She couldn't catch her breath. 'The letter's come. We can go tomorrow.'

435

'The letter?' Maria was silent for a long while. 'You go, mummy, because father is at home on his own. But I've got to stay. I'm staying.'

'Mrs Majewska, he's the first man in her life. He's a Georgian and he's enchanted her. How can I go and leave her? He'll never let her go.'

Maria returned to her room. Two bowls of soup were standing on the table. The Georgian was waiting for her. They ate the soup in silence. Maria chewed her bread and looked at the miserable bed, the lousy camp bowl, the plywood walls, at the window through which she could see a fine rain falling, and at the old, ugly man watching the emotions coming and going on her face. He sensed her tumult with every nerve and although she didn't say anything he understood the battle she was waging.

At seven o'clock she ran along to her mother. She hugged her and put her head on her shoulder. 'I'll go with you. What's in store for me here?'

'And she sat with me like that for two hours, Mrs Majewska, laughing and crying in turn. She's like a child. She's big and strong but she's like a child. And we talked about our home and our dog and the people in our part of the world.'

At nine o'clock Maria jumped up from her stool. 'But my documents are still in the cupboard. How can I go without them? I'll nip over and get them and be back at once. I'll leave everything else because there's nothing I care about. But how can I go without my documents?'

She left the barrack in the rain and ran into her room. She opened the cupboard, took out the papers and slipped them into her pocket. It was dark in the room. She thought no-one was there. When she turned round she suddenly saw him. He was standing by the window and the moonlight was falling on his face. His eyes were lowered and he wasn't looking at her at all. But he stretched out both his hands in front of him. She was already standing on the threshold with her hand on the doorhandle. And when she saw those outstretched hands she fell into them like a bird. Next day Mrs Michalska left on her own.

So Marysia went to work at the station every day. She left the barrack in the misty darkness of the night and returned at dusk. Night swallowed her up and night returned her. But I didn't know what she did in the daytime. I had to recreate her world, weave it and summon it up on the basis of what she told me. Sometimes she had a lot to say about it and at other times she ignored my questions.

I knew that the station-master was called Koska. That he came from an aristocratic Austrian family. He was calm and level-headed and never raised his voice. He treated his subordinates and even his foreign workers politely. He was a helpful man and if he could be of assistance he did it willingly. In the room she worked in there were two clerks, Merzicky and Bitter. They did the book-keeping and Marysia counted the stokers' and drivers' hours.

'Are they polite to you?' I asked.

'Yes. They give me sweets and call me Marianna. "Go to the Reichsbahn headquarters with a report, Marianna."'

So she went. And people at headquarters asked her strange questions. They wanted to know what the Polish Jews had been like. Was it true they had all sold currency on the black market? What had happened to the Jews in Poland? From their questions she gathered that news of the extermination had reached them. Their interest, their dogged questioning and their sensitivity about the matter proved it. But she was afraid to take the conversations up. She didn't know if the questions were meant to catch her out or if they were just posed out of curiosity.

'I didn't know any Jews,' she replied evasively. 'I once had a friend at school who was Jewish. But I didn't know any Jews and I don't know anything about them.'

That's what she said. Any Polish woman could say the same thing in her place.

'I gave Bitter two cigarettes and he gave me an onion,' she said one day. Another time she said, 'I've got something for Macius. Bitter gave me a cake that his wife baked. Do you know who she is? Hitler's cook.'

Hitler's cook. Our astonishment knew no bounds.

Both Bitter and Merzicky knew that she had a son and a mother. Bitter wrapped the cake in grease-proof paper and then in newspaper and gave it to her for her son. She thanked him. She put the cake into her worn bag, laughing to herself. Wasn't it odd that her child was going to eat a cake baked by Hitler's cook?

'You've no idea how proud he is of his wife. When he talks about her he seems contemptuous, not just of me but even of Merzicky too.'

What did I know about Merzicky? Only that he and his wife had

437

lived near Poznan for many years. And that he didn't have any children, to his great sorrow.

So contact had been made. When the rains came and all Marysia had was a pair of low, thin shoes she asked Bitter if he could get hold of some galoshes or boots for her. 'I'll pay you in cigarettes,' she told him.

He brought her some boots his wife didn't wear any longer. Marysia bought some cigarettes from Ziolkowski – he always let her have them at cost price – and gave them to Bitter in exchange for the boots. The boots were worn and too big. We could see they'd tear soon. We examined them with great interest. Hitler's cook had worn them and now Marysia was wearing them. Wasn't it odd?

'What else do you do on that station?' I asked.

Sometimes she interpreted. She didn't speak Russian or Ukrainian but she understood and was always able to interpret. 'Marianna,' they called, 'come and interpret what this Ukrainian woman is saying.'

Ukrainian women were being trained on the station to stoke boilers. Filling a heavy shovel with coal and throwing it into the locomotive isn't work for a woman. One of them rebelled and spat at the old foreman. She beat her breast and by her movements she gave them to understand that she couldn't carry on, that she was exhausted. The foreman struck her on the face. Twice. She swayed and fell but she was picked up and put back on her feet. She calmed down immediately, in a single moment. She turned away, clambered up still swaying onto the locomotive, and picked up the shovel.

When the heavy rains started and were then followed by early snowstorms Marysia was already wearing the boots but she didn't have a warm coat or any stout footwear. Ziolkowski promised to try and get hold of a warm coat. He was out and about in Berlin and carried on some dealings that he didn't talk about openly. One evening he brought Marysia a man's winter coat which he sold her at cost price. He didn't want to make a profit on it because of the day when they had both weeded the cabbage patch together. She managed to buy some shoes from Mrs Lund. Flat, black lace-ups, the sort that older German women usually wore.

When the new group of railwaymen arrived from Poland, including handsome Konrad, about a dozen of them were sent to the station where Marysia worked. Among them was Pawluk and his wife. Everyone in the barrack knew that Marysia worked in the

438

station office. Some people asked her to get hold of uniforms for them. Mrs Pawluk asked her to help her get a job in the stores.

'Mrs Majewska,' she whispered to her, 'it means a lot to me because I can't move about. My leg's pinned.'

She moved as if to lift up her skirt and show the pin but she stopped. The pin was in her knee or hip but she only limped a little. She was a tall, handsome woman, energetic and wise. She loathed Jews with all her heart. When she latched onto the subject she could keep going endlessly. Thanks to Marysia's good works she did receive a job in the stores. Her gratitude and attachment knew no limits. Once she even brought a handful of rice in a bag for Macius when he was ill. It was priceless at that time.

Marysia also got hold of uniforms for all the railwaymen from Koska. And what happened? Seven of them escaped to Poland. It was easy for them because they had uniforms. The escape definitely played a big part in undermining her position in the office. She wasn't trusted like before. One day a girl from Poland showed up in the office. She'd come to Germany voluntarily. She was smartly dressed and ate bread and pork fat. She had a lot of clothes and a lot of food. But no clue about office work. She knew nothing.

Marysia immediately understood that the girl had been sent to replace her. She accepted the situation. The war was finishing, you could feel it in the air and in the increasingly heavy atmosphere in the office. She started slowly and patiently teaching the girl clerical work. The girl gave her bread and pork fat, payment for the lessons really.

Who knows? Perhaps Marysia survived this difficult time because of it. We gave Macius almost all our rations of fat and sausage. We wanted him to survive. In fact there was a certain nonsense in it, because if we'd died first, what would have happened to him?

'I think they'll throw me out of the office soon and transfer me somewhere else,' said Marysia one evening.

'Why do you think that?'

'Because I've taught the girl and they trust her more than they do me. She came on her own. Not with a transport but on her own. Voluntarily.'

And sure enough she was transferred shortly afterwards to the turntable which turned the locomotives onto the right tracks. It was electric, but after bombing raids there was often no power, so then she pushed the turntable together with the other workers.

Her base was now a tiny, wooden hut among the network of rails. An iron stove burnt there day and night. She warmed her red and swollen frozen hands above the stove. She ate her hard bread thinly spread with jam and drank black coffee out of a bottle in there. She cooked beetroots she brought from the camp in a tin on the stove. The German railwaymen sat next to her and once one of them said, 'You have to admire and respect the Allies because they're fighting and dying to pull us out of this shit.' His name was Kraus and he'd worked on the station for twenty-seven years.

When I wailed about her work, like mothers do, and regretted that she wasn't in the office she said, 'But this is more interesting. I meet different people here. And there's another thing – in the office I struggled to stay awake, while here I'm on the move all the time.'

One day she was hit by the winch handle. She fell and fainted. She was hit on the head between her eyes and in her chest. She was standing by the turntable and pushing it together with the others. There'd just been a raid. The light had stopped working. And then suddenly the power came back on and the winch started up. They carried her to the office. A worker she knew was there when the accident happened. An Italian from near Milan. He clenched his fists and ran around the platform shouting, 'Barbarians! Barbarians! Giving work like that to women!' In the evening she returned to the barrack with Alfred Tchorzewski.

All the workers in our camp were insured, just like the Germans. If you were ill and your temperature was over 38 degrees, you went to the doctor in Adlershof camp and got sick leave. If there was something wrong with your eyes you were sent to the eye clinic and received free glasses. When Marysia twisted her ankle on the station in the dark she had an X-ray.

There was also a dentist you could go to after work. Marysia went too for a while because her front tooth was hurting. The dentist liked jokes. 'Well then,' he used to say, 'is it true that all the Jews in Poland suddenly died? They got flu and died? Just like that? All of them at once? How could it happen? Tell me something about it.'

One day Mr Debczak got hit on the head. He was standing at the stop in the dark and didn't notice the tram coming. He was taken to hospital and stayed there for two months. He came out a changed man. He sometimes talked to himself or giggled and didn't always make sense when he talked. He had a deep scar from his eye to his ear, but he was alive and even went to work. Everyone had thought he'd die.

440

The Luczaks' beautiful daughter was five months' pregnant. She had an abortion. She didn't pay anything. It was the same with Weronika, the one who lived with Kwiatkowski. She wanted to find out if she was pregnant and asked me to go to the gynaecologist with her. He lived in Koepenick. 'Please come, Mrs Majewska. I'm scared to go on my own.'

I took her arm and we walked along Grünauer Strasse with our heads bent against the strong wind. Suddenly she said, 'I want to tell you something. Make a confession. Kwiatkowski isn't my husband. I've got a husband and two children in Brwinow near Warsaw. Please judge me charitably, Mrs Majewska.'

Miss Luczak was said to be unmarried, but was anyone bothered? Just as religious matters didn't fit into the frame of our barrack, so things to do with morality didn't either. The couples generally lived calmly and decorously together although they accepted it as a foregone conclusion that their ways would part after the war. That's why I was so surprised and touched by what Weronika said.

If a woman got pregnant, she had an abortion. It was even recommended. But Natalia, who worked with me in the kitchen, was eight months' pregnant when she came and she was with her husband. She was left in peace. She had the baby in hospital and brought it back to the barrack.

One night Macius suddenly got an inflammation of the ear and was moaning and crying with pain. I made some bags out of handkerchiefs and we gave him compresses with hot sand. 'I'll take him to Adlershof tomorrow,' I said. Our stove went out that night but the one in Schmidt's office was alight. Hofman was on duty there. It was he who heated the compresses and brought them along to our room at intervals all through the night, saying, 'Maria, here I am again.'

And what did we do? We were tired and worried and we took the man's heartfelt words as deserved tribute and I don't even know if we thanked him.

The campaign against me started at about this time. On the part of Lagerführer Schmidt and the camp cook, Mrs Lund. He ordered me to be woken at half past two in the morning to light the fire for the coffee pan. Johann had done it before, but I was to do it now.

'Ugh,' he said, walking around the kitchen and furrowing his eyebrows threateningly, 'this woman is no good. She can't even light the fire under the pan. She's not suitable for kitchen work. She can go to the station.'

No-one was treated with any ceremony in the camp and so two days later I was already at Grünau station. I was given a broom and cloths. I swept the platforms and washed the stairs and windows. I swept the platforms in the smart brown coat made by a good tailor in Warsaw which Lotta had her eye on. On the coat was my dark P. The Germans were surprised when they saw me.

A young girl called Jozefka from our barrack worked at the same station. When an electric train came in her duties included checking the compartments to see that no-one had left anything behind. She was meant to take everything she found to the office. I once went to the stores with Jozefka to get some coal. Two buckets of coal. Each of us was carrying a bucket. When we'd taken the coal and were going back, she met someone she knew and stopped for a chat. I waited for her a little way off.

'Do you know what he said?' she laughed loudly. 'He said you're Jewish. "What are you talking about," I said. "She's from our camp and I've known her for months."'

I was terrified. At the same time I was astonished at how astute the man was. He'd guessed my secret just by glancing at me, and at a distance too. I supposed he must have had a primeval nature like Pelagia, who'd also seen through us immediately. Not only us either.

Shortly afterwards Jozefka stole a packet of wool left on the train. The theft came out. She was sent to a penal camp and we didn't see her again. Theft of every kind was punished by the Germans with great severity, including being sent to penal camps. Sometimes there were court-martials. Three people were hung once in Adlershof camp, two women and a man. It must have been quite some theft. A few curious people even went to look at the three unfortunate corpses.

I went to the station alone now. I brought the coal for the stove on my own. But when I went to the store I was always afraid of meeting Jozefka's friend with the penetrating eyes.

To get warm I used to go to the hut with an iron stove. I ate my hard bread and jam and heated the coffee from my bottle in a tin in there. The railwaymen and ordinary workmen warmed themselves at the stove too. They came for a few moments or for longer. Sometimes they only came to warm some coffee. Sometimes only to warm their hands. There was a Russian workman who came too. I talked to him in Russian. He came from the Smolensk area. He was twenty years old and the son of a peasant.

'What do you do?' he asked.

'I'm a teacher,' I replied.

'An educated woman carrying coal? I won't stand for it,' he shouted and grabbed the bucket and brought the coal from the store himself instead

Electric trains left the station every three minutes. They stopped silently, the doors opened automatically and the passengers waiting on the platforms got in. The train set off three minutes later. Dog-ends remained on the platforms. Small boys rushed to pick them up. Oh no, not only small boys but prisoners of war as well, French or Italian. Some even managed to jump into the compartment during the three minute halt and pick the dog-ends up off the floor in there.

One day I was summoned to the office. It had two rooms with a tall, tiled stove in each room. A clerk was sitting at a table. He barely glanced at me. 'Light both the stoves,' he said. I fetched some kindling and a bucket of coal. I started lighting the stove but the fire kept going out. The clerk looked up.

'What was your occupation?'

'I was a teacher.'

'And you never lit the stove?'

'Never.'

My heart thumped in fear. Will he shout at me? Will he smash the table? He got up silently. He crouched down and lit the stove himself. He lit both stoves himself. I stood behind him and watched. He must have been a good man. All manifestations of human feeling made a deep impression on me, especially then.

At four o'clock when work was finished I got on the tram with some other women from our barrack who cleaned the trains. The tram was packed. We were all standing. Suddenly an old German women shouted out, 'Get up, German women! They're tired. They work for us. Let them have our seats.' There was so much feeling in her voice that two or three did get up, but we were surprised because it was so exceptional and we didn't dare sit down. Especially as according to the law we were obliged to give up our seat in trams and trains to any German who was standing. But in the end we did sit down. We talked about it for a long time afterwards.

After three weeks of work in the open air, in the wind and rain, I was convinced I wouldn't last out any longer. I was also constantly worried about Macius. I knew he didn't go down to the shelter during raids. And that he hardly ever ate anything warm all day long. Then I was transferred to another station. Mrs Malinowska, the mother of Jadwiga the singer, was also a cleaner there. The first day I helped her. We were closely followed by a half crazy shrew of a German woman who grabbed our sleeves, pushed us against the doors and said, 'Follow me. I'll show you a wagon on the sidings. Do you know who's there? Sweet little French girlies.'

Next day I was summoned by the station-master. 'What am I going to give you to do? They sent you here and I don't know what to do with you. You can dig out the garden together with the Ukrainian women who work there.'

I thought of my one and only pair of old shoes and heard the rain beating against the window and said, 'Couldn't you give me something else to do? I know four languages.'

'No, I can't.'

That day I returned to the barrack completely exhausted. I decided to make a last-ditch attempt – go to headquarters and speak to the Reichsbahn director. Marysia was appalled at the state of me, mental and physical, so at the same time she tried through Koska to get me transferred back to the camp. Not to the kitchen, but as a cleaner and to look after the children. But we didn't know when the answer would come. I felt I was dying. I was ill but I didn't have a temperature, so according to the regulations I couldn't have two days' sick leave. My lungs hurt but there was no temperature. So according to the regulations I was fit for work.

In the night, lying on my bunk, I looked at the window which was cut off at a sharp angle by the bunk above. I thought that I was sure to die and wondered what would happen to Marysia and Macius. I was completely obsessed by the idea of going to railway headquarters. It was madness. But I was impelled by forces I was unable to comprehend and so I didn't go the station at dawn but to the headquarters of German railways.

When I left the barrack I stopped on the bridge for a moment and leaned against the balustrade. Could I not stop myself? A barge was sailing along the canal just then. The captain at the wheel with his pipe. A dog huddled up at his feet. On a line behind his back shirts fluttering in the wind. It always moved me and calmed me down to see that. Maybe because the barge was sailing into the unknown, or maybe because the scene contained a simple accessible poetry which spoke to everyone in distress.

The enormous Reichsbahn building was untouched inside. I thought to myself that I was at a turning point in my life. If I succeeded, I'd live. If I didn't succeed, I'd die. I wouldn't stand the work on the stations, that was definite. Suddenly I felt immensely lonely in this huge bombed city of Berlin. The door to the hall was open. When I entered I saw the porter's back disappearing. He couldn't have noticed me. To the right was the counter where he usually stood. A notice on the wall: 'No Foreigners or Camp Inmates'.

Stairs leading upstairs. As I went up I thought to myself that with the dark P on my coat I didn't have the right to enter the building. I'd be arrested, or killed even. A door in front of me. On it a sign saying 'German Railways Inspector'. I knocked. A man of about forty-five was sitting behind the desk. He was handsome with dark hair. When I entered he looked at me.

'What do you want?' he asked.

'I'm Polish and I'm in the railway camp. I work on a station but I can't manage the work. Now I've been allocated to dig out the garden. I'm a teacher. I can speak and write French, Russian, German and Polish. Would it be possible for me to be given other work?'

He got up from behind the desk and came a few steps nearer. What was he thinking? I stood in front of him with my heart beating, the dark scarf on my head and the letter P sewn onto my coat. I'd said everything. I didn't have a single word to add. He was sure to ask how I got there. Didn't I see the notice on the wall? Where was the porter? No admittance. I heard his calm and courteous voice.

'Would you like to work as a translator?'

'Yes.'

'What's your name and address?'

'Alicja Majewska. Reichsbahnlager Spindlersfeld, Koepenick, Grünauer Strasse 20.'

'Thank you. That's all.'

During the war I had often expected something terrible to happen. I would be prepared for a catastrophe, certain that I wouldn't survive, that some hostile forces would knock me down and destroy me, and later my fear would turn out to have been unfounded. It was the same now. I left the room. Slowly, step after step, I went downstairs gripping the bannister tightly. No-one chased me out. But what an effort it was! What a terrible weakness in my knees. The porter was standing in the hall and looking at me with surprise. I passed him engrossed, indifferent and distant. But I sat down immediately afterwards, I had to sit down on the first pile of rubble, right next to the pavement. I took a piece of bread out of my pocket and ate it, weeping.

The same day Marysia met the Georgian in the soup queue. He was standing in front of her and holding two bowls, his own and Maria's. 'You've no idea how much we're suffering lately because of Schmidt,' she said. 'They're throwing my mother from station to station like a ball. And I was so keen for her to stay in the camp.'

'You should give Schmidt something.'

'Do you think so? We've often thought about it but we were afraid that he'd have us imprisoned for bribery.'

'You're very naïve. Nearly everyone in the barrack bribes Schmidt. Would I have a room of my own if I didn't pay for it? What about Kwiatkowski? He hasn't worked a single day yet, has he? Every so often we give him something as a souvenir.'

'Thank for very much for what you've told me. But it's a pity I found out so late.'

In the evening I gave Marysia the ring which used to belong to my mother. She went into the corridor and waited until Schmidt was alone. Then she knocked at the door. She immediately said, right at the start and without beating about the bush, that she had some-thing she wanted to give him as a souvenir. From Maria and Alicja Majewska. And from little Majewski too, she added with a smile. She placed the gold ring with its four small emeralds and four diamonds on the table in front of him. He picked it up with a calm and easy movement.

'Yes, it's very nice. I'll remember you.'

Late in the evening, when we were all in bed, when the light was out, we suddenly heard a crash, bang, smash. Had a bomb hit the barrack? No, it was Lucyna falling onto Zofia's bed with her mat-tress, blankets and broken boards.

'Help,' shouted Zofia. 'I'm dying.'

Her voice was strangled. She only just managed to get out from under the mattress that Lucyna was sitting on. It was Zofia's head she was sitting on. The whole of Lucyna's bed was one big wreck. We jumped up and got Zofia out from under the mattress and from under Lucyna.

'Didn't I tell you? Didn't I say you toss and turn too much? Boards aren't made of iron. I often looked and wondered if they'd withstand the weight.'

'It's not my fault, Zofia,' said Lucyna with tears in her eyes. 'I'm black and blue as well.'

'All right then, all right. Too bad, we'll have to sleep together tonight.'

They threw the mattress onto the floor and lay down on Zofia's bed together. They both wrapped their heads in wet towels. At half past three in the morning the door opened and in came Roerich. He tripped on the mattress and swore. 'Who's sleeping on the floor?' he asked. He took out his pocket torch and shone it. Shadows fluttered over the walls. A bowl which hung on the hook of his false hand suddenly clattered in the silence. He crossed Lucyna's mattress and approached our bunk. 'Get up, Maria,' he said. He shone his torch again for a second on her pale face and rung the bowl as if it were a bell. We lifted ourselves up and rubbed our eyes. Naked Pelagia, Lucyna, Zofia and I, all broken and aching.

I went to the kitchen and brought some warm water to wash with from the pot which always stood on the stove. I poured as much cold water into the pot as I'd taken warm water out. That's what Mrs Lund taught us and I always did it. She looked at me in an unfriendly way all the same. I poured the water into the bowl we kept under the bed and washed myself. Then I went to the kitchen again. I went back for some porridge from Lagerführer Schmidt's pan. It was for Macius. Even though I'd bought the right to it with my mother's brooch she still had an unfriendly look for me this morning.

I placed the porridge on the table in our room next to the slices of bread which were to last Macius until we returned. Then I put some more briquettes into the stove. I was worried that he'd eat cold porridge. He wouldn't warm it up. I quickly wrapped some bread and jam in newspaper, poured some coffee into a bottle, put my coat and headscarf on and left the barrack. I went to the station.

The boy of sixteen whom Mrs Michalska used to send for her daughter was called Manius and she sent him because she had 'never set foot in their place'. His name wasn't really Miller. When we were being registered Miller, the railwayman, said he was his brother. We didn't even know if Miller was his real name. He might have deliberately chosen a German-sounding name so that people thought he was Volksdeutsch. No-one knew what was in his mind and what his plans were. He was a tall, handsome and well-nourished man and he looked after Manius. They both worked in the ironworks. One day he ran away. He got on a locomotive going in the direction of Poland and ran away. He was wearing the new uniform Marysia had got. He might have paid the driver something but then again he might not have given him anything. He didn't mention his plan to anyone, not even Manius. He went out one morning and didn't come back. He ran away.

'It wasn't hard for him to do,' said the people in our barrack. 'he was wearing a railwayman's uniform. But why didn't he take Manius with him?'

Fair-haired Manius wandered around the barrack, lost and neglected. 'Just like a lost sheep,' said Mrs Malinowska.

'Do you know who he's like, Konrad?' said Jadwiga. 'Jontek – deserted Jontek in the opera *Halka*.'

Manius could be heard crying at night. He sniffed and blew his nose and tossed on his bunk. 'Don't cry,' people said. 'He might come back. Or send you some money and you can join him.' They said it to comfort him although they didn't believe it. And they added, 'Manius, why are you so worried? After all he's not dead but alive. So he'll be in touch.'

Manius listened but didn't hear. He grew thin and wasted, and stopped going to work. It gets dark at four o'clock in December. At four o'clock Manius went out of the barrack. I was standing leaning against the door-frame and I watched him walk away into the distance. He stopped for a moment on the bridge. He couldn't not stop. A barge was passing just then. I thought the sight of it would calm him down, that he'd cry and then return. But he turned off into the field and walked straight ahead, unevenly and with difficulty. Mrs Malinowska called out to him. He didn't hear. He was crossing the field and becoming smaller and less visible all the time. A fine rain started and then wet snow and Manius melted into the grey mist.

The letter arrived at twelve noon. With a seal. With many seals. The letter was from the headquarters of the German Reichsbahn to Lagerführer Schmidt. Registered. Important. Confidential.

At six o'clock when I was walking down the corridor I met Schmidt. He was walking quickly and Stutzi was running behind him. 'Frau Alice,' he said, 'come to the office, please.' He didn't address me any differently even during the height of the campaign against me. I knew that Schmidt's attitude to me would change after he got the ring and he wouldn't make any impertinent or biting remarks. But the work I was doing was beyond my strength and made me so exhausted and over-sensitive that I entered the office with a faint heart full of uncertainty and fear.

'Frau Alice, I've received a letter. As from Monday you'll work at Schlesingerbahnhof as a translator.'

The letter came unexpectedly quickly, after just a few days. Schmidt smiled kindly. He was pleased. He drummed on the table with the fingers of his good hand while the other one hung down lifelessly. He was pleased, but of course the transfer wasn't his doing at all. It was the reply to that desperate step of mine which he knew nothing about. But that's how it was and it looked as if he'd conjured up the promotion. He looked at me as if we had a shared secret which only the two of us were privy to. I was afraid he was so pleased he'd get up from his chair and slap me on the back. I knew that his good mood was because Marysia and I had learnt to toe the line at last.

He'd shown us patience for quite a long time. The German in the hat with the gold braid, who brought us to the camp, must have told him about the present he'd received from us. Would he have allocated us to the kitchen if he didn't know? But since we'd given the other man a present, Schmidt expected one too. We had no idea how widespread bribery was among the Germans. We couldn't imagine that Schmidt would take a bribe. It was precisely because he didn't get one that he threw Marysia and then me out of the barrack.

I returned to our room, sat down on my bunk and started thinking. I sat for a long time staring at the window with its black paper blind, deaf and indifferent to everything. The effort was too big. I'd paid for this good fortune with too much strength. There wasn't a single cell in all my being with room for joy. Then I got up with difficulty, dragged myself over to the door and opened it. Some children were running along the corridor, stamping loudly. Our Macius was among them too. He was wearing the red trousers. He'd grown used to them now.

The barrack stood on short poles with an empty space under the floor. That's why the stamping of the children's feet caused thousands of echoes which rebounded off the walls and made an incredible noise. People complained about their running around. But it didn't make any difference if you threatened the children or tried gentle persuasion – they were starved of play and wanted to stamp as loudly as possible.

I touched his arm. 'Go to bed early tonight,' I said. 'Have a good sleep because there might be a raid again tonight.'

I went to the kitchen and took some warm water for him to wash with from the pan. Pregnant Natalia was grating potatoes.

Mrs Lund was frying potato pancakes for Schmidt. Mindful of the way she'd looked at me and the unfriendly look in her eyes I immediately turned to go. But she stopped me. 'I won't let you go, Frau Alice,' she said. 'You must try a bit of pancake.'

There was as much kindness in her words and voice as Schmidt's behaviour had displayed. I wondered if it was possible that she'd already been ordered to treat us differently. I sensed that something had been played out behind our backs. Something was decidedly different – the hostility had disappeared. And all thanks to the ring which I had such difficulty in parting with.

We had only just gone to bed, Zofia had just placed her chulent on the stove and Lucyna hadn't finished the story about her aunt in Skierniewice, when we heard the gong in the corridor. It was our alarm signal. We had to go down to the shelter as quickly as possible. It was nine o'clock or a little later, and pouring with rain. We didn't want to leave our warm beds. But when we heard the rumble of planes quite close and the muffled explosions, we jumped down. Someone in the corridor shouted, 'They're attacking the railway embankment!' Someone else shouted, 'A bomb's fallen into the canal!' Someone else said, 'The house at the end of the field is on fire, but how are we to go out in this downpour?'

People were panic-stricken. Perhaps it was because the heavens were opening. Nearly everyone rushed to the shelter. Only a few stayed behind. But the thing is that no-one wanted to go to our proper shelter in the downpour and we all sheltered somewhere completely different. Right next to the barrack was a cellar, overgrown with grass and weeds. The steps had rotted away a long time ago and you had to go down a steep slope. The soil was clay, there was no door, and the rain-water poured in down the slope. When people heard the rumble of planes right above their heads they rushed to the cellar. They stood in water, terribly squashed, shoulder to shoulder. The children were terrified and cried loudly.

It was one of the biggest raids on Berlin. All around were the glow of fires and smoke trailing low across the horizon. Marysia came back from work at two in the morning. The track had been destroyed so she had to walk seventeen kilometres.

'Fortunately I had some sugar in my bag and Tchorzewski was with me,' she said. 'Won't Macius catch cold?' she asked worriedly.

He was in bed covered with blankets and his wet shoes and socks were drying in front of the stove. We sat next to him and listened to his breathing. The child was the be all and end all of our lives. The subject of our conversations, the source of our worries, the incentive for our hopes and desire to live. Didn't we go down to the shelter because of him? Because here, in Berlin, we measured everything according to his measure. That's the reason why my life and Marysia's were so valuable – if there were two of us, his chances of survival were doubled. That's why I fought so desperately when I saw that I was in danger. Because it wasn't me who was in danger, but him.

'I didn't have time to tell you,' I said to Marysia, 'a letter came from the Reichsbahn headquarters. They're transferring me to Schlesingerbahnhof. I'm going to be a translator there.'

She sighed with relief. It was undoubtedly a victory. But only partial. In her heart of hearts she wanted me to be given work in the barrack. Then I wouldn't lose so much strength and energy travelling in the cold, bad weather, and I could keep an eye on Macius, which was the most important.

'I'll talk to Schmidt tomorrow,' she said. 'I'll ask him to write to the people in charge and tell them he needs a woman to help in the camp. We'll see how he repays us for the ring.'

We were whispering. Very quietly so that no-one could hear.

The next day was Sunday. The day for tidying up and washing the floor. Not the whole floor but the part around the bunks because the floor was divided into as many sections as there were bunks. Our floor was divided into three. There was never any trouble with Lucyna and Zofia. Every Sunday Lucyna scrubbed the two metres of floor belonging to her and Zofia. Zofia was excused the work. The slow and lethargic Lucyna was in Zofia's debt in every way. She always asked her advice. And didn't she eat her chulent every day?

Every Sunday Marysia scrubbed our two metres of floor. It didn't surprise anyone. She was my daughter-in-law and did it for the two of us. It was different with Pelagia and Barbara Gorska, when she still lived with us. 'That bitch tosses about on her bed,' said Pelagia, 'and moves the boards apart under her mattress on purpose. She makes it dusty and scatters straw all round. If the clot makes a mess then she should scrub two metres of floor, shouldn't she?' She raised her voice. She turned to Lucyna, to me and to Zofia as if she wanted us to be her witnesses. 'Shouldn't she?' she asked. We didn't know what to say because Gorska was in the room and the words were in fact addressed to her. Except that Gorska had her own way of dealing with Pelagia – silence. She didn't say a word.

451

There was an argument between Pelagia and Gorska about the floor nearly every Sunday. Macius could hear Pelagia's coarse words while he was sitting at the table drawing or looking at maps cut out of the newspapers. 'Shouldn't she?' she asked threateningly looking round and sometimes she stared unseeingly straight at him. He went pale because he couldn't stand arguments. Even when he was tiny he always used to cry during an argument.

Then when it was quiet and peaceful he traced his finger over the maps and read out the towns, rivers and mountains. He knew where the retreating Germans were, he knew the names of the generals on both sides, and knew the planes and their names. He knew too much. He was too intelligent and that could be suspicious. Pelagia crouched on her stool and delightedly watched him trace the French frontier, and when he looked up she smiled at him in her own charming way.

When Gorska was expelled from our camp Jadwiga took her bed over. Jadwiga didn't want to scrub the piece of floor either.

'Why?' asked Pelagia, her eyes flashing.

'I don't make it dirty. I'm not here all day. I only sleep here,' replied Jadwiga.

'Is that so? Then I won't scrub it either.' But she didn't raise her voice. She didn't swear. She respected Jadwiga's talent.

So no-one wanted to scrub that section of floor, neither Pelagia, nor Gorska, nor Jadwiga. The dirty, muddy boards looked odd among the clean ones. Marysia couldn't stand the sight of it and so in the end she scrubbed that piece too.

We replied to Lucja Hersz. We replied to her question about Macius and the commission. So many giddy hopes were hidden in what she had written about Macius going to Switzerland. We even talked about it in front of him and dreamed about it out loud to encourage him. But our efforts were in vain. He didn't want to go.

After a while when we recovered we started thinking differently. What children was the commission coming for? The ones who lived in bad conditions in camps. Why draw attention to ourselves? Why should it be Macius who goes to Switzerland? Wouldn't it be suspicious? These considerations made our hopes slowly shrink and fade, like plants nipped by the frost.

'Dear Mrs Lubinska, thank you for thinking of us. Macius is eating well and has got everything he needs.' That's what we wrote back in the end.

There was an iron stove that burnt briquettes in the middle of the room in the railway office on the Schlesingerbahnhof, just like in every other office. At seven o'clock in the morning on a frosty December day, I went up to the stove for the first time to warm my frozen hands. I stretched out both my palms above the glowing hot-plate and they watched me. Three of them were sitting at desks. One by the window, the second on the right-hand side of the room and the third on the left-hand side. There was a radio on the desk by the window. A typewriter stood on a small table. They immediately asked me, 'Are you from Warsaw? Tell us then, we heard that whole streets were on fire, house after house. Is it true that the Germans set fire to Warsaw?'

I was silent.

'She's afraid,' they said. 'Don't be afraid of us. You can tell us the truth. No-one will know apart from us.'

'The Germans set fire to Warsaw,' I said.

'Yes, it's very sad. But you'll be all right on the station with us. We'll respect you. We'll show you the stores and teach you to type.'

I thought to myself that they were strange Germans. The German clerk who worked in the next room also asked me about Warsaw burning. She had to know who started the fire, the Germans or the Russians.

Russian, French and Polish workers came to the office and I inter-preted for them. The work amused me. In fact it wasn't work at all. At half past one they turned the radio on and all three sat down close together next to it. The clerk from the next room came too. She sat down near them and listened attentively to the quiet and secret programme. I was hammering out a German poem on the type-writer for practice.

'It's the BBC from London,' said the station-master looking at me alertly. 'But Alicja won't betray us, will you Alicja?'

I smiled. His words made an incredible impression on me. They were spoken with embarrassment as if he was making excuses and asking me to be discreet. He wasn't ordering me but asking me. We're among the civilian population of Berlin, I thought to myself, and I can see human feelings towards people from camps. What's the explanation? Was it like this two or three years ago?

The German owner of the small canteen on Grünauer Strasse, where we sometimes called in for a beer, and who listened to our story with such sympathy. The German boy who played with Macius. The clerk who lit the fires for me. The old woman in the tram. And now these friendly words coming from the station-master. Wasn't this the end of the war? Couldn't we feel it in the air? Wasn't the end approaching? Wasn't it quite close now?

Marysia sometimes told me about Bitter, the husband of Hitler's cook. She didn't work in the office now but on the turntable, but she saw him from time to time. 'He's fading,' she said, 'he's fading with every passing day. He's fading like the flame of a lamp when it's got no fuel.'

'No,' repeated the station-master. 'You can rest assured that Alicja from Warsaw won't betray us.'

I began to pay particular attention now to how they treated the workers. I thought they'd be indulgent or even familiar. But they were every inch sticklers for authority. Energetic and firm. They punished all offences. In the presence of the workers from many countries who passed through the office they didn't betray their thoughts by a single movement or word. That's why I was surprised that they put their cards on the table in front of me. After all I was one of their many workers, wasn't I?

It must have been a deep, mysterious intuition, the same as Pelagia had, when she guessed that Macius was Jewish. They guessed that there was no way I could betray them and that they could trust me whole-heartedly, although they had no grounds for trusting me.

Eight days later a letter came to Lagerführer Schmidt. It was the reply to the submission Koska made after Marysia had spoken to him. But oddly enough Koska had got the names the wrong way round and his submission was granted, but not for me. Marysia was appointed camp helper in our barrack.

'Maybe we should leave it like it is and not put it right?' I said. 'You have to travel a long way to work and you could look after Macius here better than me. I'll stay at the station, they treat me as an equal there. They trust me.'

'But I'm young and it'll be odd if I work in the barrack. Anyway it's only a mistake because it meant you and not me. We should put it right.'

The mistake was put right. After Marysia talked to Schmidt he wrote to the appropriate authorities asking for me to be allocated to his camp as a camp assistant. I wasn't a young woman. No-one was surprised at the transfer. So I became a camp assistant and quickly learnt my new duties. At six o'clock every morning I went to the wash-room with a bucket, brush and cloth. I washed the floor and cleaned the lavatories, if they weren't boarded up. Then together with fourteen year-old Jasia who helped me carry the churns I took the tram to fetch the milk. I also cleaned Schmidt's room. Jasia had done it until now. 'But I suspect she's got lice,' he said. 'You'll do it from now on, Frau Alice.'

One day, when I brought some ashes on a shovel from the kitchen to light the stove, I found Schmidt's wife sitting at the desk. I'd heard she was born in Lwow and could speak Polish. I glanced at her hands. She had my mother's ring on her finger. She was pregnant. A young woman with dark hair. A box of tobacco stood in front of her. She was making cigarettes. The ring on her finger shone and glittered.

I was also to scrub the long corridor which divided the barrack into two. It had never been scrubbed. It had to be done before Christmas. It was heavy work and I started it one evening. I brought a bucket of water, a brush and a cloth and started scrubbing. Marysia ran out of the room, took the brush off me and started scrubbing. When she was tired, Mrs Pawluk took the brush and then Jasia, Lucyna and even Pelagia. The brush and cloth went from hand to hand until the whole corridor was scrubbed.

My duties also included looking after eight children. In fact there were nine children because Natalia's baby had been born. But she looked after the baby herself while working in the kitchen. These were Jasia, Kazia and Miecia; the three daughters of Mrs Pawlowska who cleaned trains. Mrs Chojnacka's daughter Olesia. Two year-old Kasia. Three small boys – Macius, Leszek and Tomek.

If there was a raid I went down to the shelter with the children. At eleven o'clock I gave them a mug of milk in the kitchen. On sunny days I took them for a walk along the canal to Adlershof camp. Sometimes we walked across the field to the railway embankment. Sometimes we went to the bridge and stood there for ages watching the barges. On rainy days I brought the children into our room. They drew, sang and even danced. I told them about the kings of Poland, taught them arithmetic and told them about birds, animals and plants.

Jasia looked after the food for her sisters and Olesia. Leszek's food was on the cupboard in his parents' room. Every so often I gave him a slice of bread and pork fat. Tomek and little Kasia's mothers worked in the kitchen so they could see to their children's food themselves. Sad Hofman photographed the children and gave the mothers the photos. He also photographed our barrack surrounded

455

by barbed wire and gave the photo to everyone who wanted it as a souvenir.

When I went outside the camp I wore the wooden-soled shoes we'd been allocated. Inside the camp I wore the white wooden clogs. I clattered loudly in them as I lugged buckets of water and cleaned out the lavatories in the dim daylight entering through the opaque glass. I tied a dark scarf round my head and a wide blue apron over my pullover and dark jacket. While I was cleaning the lavatories I always remembered what Anna Bialkowska had said. 'You haven't been through anything. You don't know about anything. But I was in a camp and cleaned out lavatories.'

Two days before Christmas Johann, Frau Lund's helper, the one who looked after the stove in the kitchen, went to the pine wood near Adlershof and brought us back a Christmas tree. On Christmas Eve the tree was decorated with coloured paper and gold tinsel and even sweets and nuts, and was placed in the married couples' room. All the bunks were moved aside and some space for dancing was left near the tree. Mazur brought a gramophone from town and placed it on a kitchen stool which was covered with a clean cloth.

That day we all received one egg. We immediately boiled ours for Macius. When everyone had gathered in front of the Christmas tree, washed and dressed in their best clothes, we sang carols. We also sang 'Heilige Nacht' and we were very moved even though it was German, because we all thought about our homes and families.

Mazur was said to be the *éminence grise* of the camp, its eyes and ears, and he wasn't trusted even though he spoke Polish. He stood between two railwaymen with his hands on their shoulders. He was tall, slim and handsome, and always wore civvies. This evening he was ostentatiously friendly to everyone.

Mr Luczak's wife was said to have been a performer and she recited a poem. Then Jadwiga Malinowska sang an aria. When her voice was pouring over the barrack in a wide wave, Schmidt came along with his dog and stood by the door, with that smile of his on his face. You could tell by looking at him that he'd already been at the bottle. There was no vodka to be seen anywhere but all the same Johann was drunk. When Jadwiga stopped singing the gramophone was wound up and Johann started dancing with Frau Lund. He opened the ball. Then the others started dancing too.

He was a God-given dancer, that Johann. As wide as a door and as light as a feather. That hand of his, those fingers, that little finger pointed saucily upwards! His face was dour and gloomy and he kept his head in his shoulders, his eyes hard and wild. But he held her delicately all the same as if she was a lily. But what did she know and what did she understand, this German cook he was holding in his arms? The Georgian was with young Maria, Mazur with Lucyna, Dyksa with Basia, Wegliszewski with his woman, Olek and Lotta, and Jadwiga in the arms of handsome Konrad.

Sad Hofman wove among the dancing pairs and after a while Schmidt shut himself up in his office and we didn't see any more of him. At twelve o'clock Johann was completely drunk and was kissing Mrs Luczak's hand and crying, 'Mummy', while his fifteen year-old daughter Cecylka was in the room next to ours singing her favourite song:

'Heute nicht arbeiten
Maschinea kaputt
Alexanderplatz
Alles, alles gut.'

Suddenly the door opened and Schmidt was standing there. He was drunk. He took his revolver out of his pocket and fired at the ceiling. The girls who were already asleep woke up screaming. Cecylka was the cheekiest girl in the whole of Berlin. She snatched the smoking revolver out of his hand. Then she hit him on the head with the bowl she ate her soup out of. 'You big pig,' she said when he tried to kiss her and she hit him with her fist in his stomach with all her strength. In the end she threw him out, straight into the arms of the guard. Next day he didn't remember a thing. He wasn't angry with Cecylka. He was the same as ever.

I missed my daughters terribly. I didn't even know if they were alive. I hadn't had any news of them during the Rising. We heard from our neighbours in the barrack that 250,000 people had died in Warsaw. Perhaps that's what their friends and relations wrote. I couldn't sleep at night. I sighed and wept. I said to Marysia, 'Maybe I should pluck up the courage and write to Mrs Zeromska.'

I assumed that if my daughters were alive they'd write to her too. But we were afraid to write. Mrs Zeromska wasn't initiated into our story and might get us into trouble when she replied. In our over-sensitive imagination we exaggerated everything. We struggled and grappled with our desire to write. But in the end we did write: dear Mrs Zeromska, do you know what happened to my nieces Aniela

Gologowska and Jadzia Tokarska? If there's any news please let us know.

After a while we received a reply: dear Mrs Majewska, I received my third card from Jadzia Tokarska today. It's the third time she's written to me for news in the hope that she'll find her family through me. She knows that Aniela is working in a hospital at Okecie. They've already found each other. She's very worried about you. I'll write to her again today.

Then a card came from Nina, dated 11 January 1945: my darlings, I really don't know what to do first – whether to be happy or to worry about you. I can't believe you're in Berlin. Sometimes I think it's a dream. Aniela's address is Hospital No. 2, The Barracks, Pruszkow, near Warsaw.

That's how I found Irena and Nina. I was happy. Whatever I was doing, carrying milk churns, or a bucket of coal, or washing floors, I didn't stop thinking about it. But at first when the news came that they were alive, I didn't feel anything apart from limitless exhaustion. I didn't have the strength to be glad. My anxiety had been too great. I only relaxed a few hours later. My soul was like a wound spring that uncoiled slowly and absorbed the happy news.

One morning when I was working on Grünauer station sweeping the platforms I saw a train passing. The sight of it shook me to the core. It was early. The sun hadn't risen yet. Mist and greyness was all round. The moon was sailing along the sky and the stars were shining. Suddenly the train passed along one of the platforms like a ghost, made up of cattle wagons only. In the open doors and inside the wagons I could see women sitting and standing. It was a transport being taken somewhere. But the look of the women, their faces and their features were familiar to me. They were Jews! They were Hungarian Jews or Jews from somewhere else. They collided with me, passed me and disappeared without a word and without trace. I stood there for a long time with my broom in one hand and my wooden dustpan in the other and watched the train disappearing into the distance.

Now, half-way through January, when I'd been working as camp assistant for a long time, and should have thrown everything that happened on the station outside the bounds of my memory, I kept thinking about those Jewish women. Because people started talking about huge transports of Hungarian Jews being deported to Auschwitz.

'I've heard that you can now get as many apples, oranges and lemons in Auschwitz as your heart desires,' said Pelagia.

'And I've heard that you can buy silk dresses and beautiful underwear and even furs there as cheap as anything,' added Lucyna.

Zofia didn't say a word. She only lifted her head in that way of hers and the light from the lamp was reflected in her glasses. She knew very well what happened in Auschwitz, just like we did.

Until now no-one ever talked about Jews in our barrack. With the exception of Mrs Pawluk, who'd let herself be chopped up out of friendship with Marysia, the word 'Jew' never fell from anyone's lips. This with the exception of Pelagia, who'd once called Gorska a Jew in her rage, and had also called Zofia Rojza from Graniczna Street such, and lovingly called Macius 'my little Jewish darling'.

No-one spoke about the Jews, but everyone came from Warsaw and had seen the glow of fires in the Jewish district for three weeks, hadn't they? Why? Was it a secret agreement? Or perhaps they believed that as the Germans had burnt the ghetto and had erased and destroyed all the Jews, they could remove them from their minds too. So Pelagia's remark and Lucyna's comment, and other things we heard in passing about the deportation of Jews, were for us like a return wave of our silent despair. The wheel had turned. And so we suffered and were tormented and died a second time.

I didn't receive any more letters from Nina. The Russians had advanced and I lost my daughters again. It was as if a huge wall, a wall from the ground to the sky, had cut me off from them.

I had three cards from Nina and one from Mrs Zeromska. That was the sum of our correspondence. We didn't receive the food parcel Nina sent. It would have been immensely important for us. As time went by the food got worse and worse. We received fewer and fewer potatoes for dinner, the bread was old and mouldy, and the soup was meagre and contained no fat.

We all lost weight and lost our strength. A huge barrel of small salt herrings put us back on our feet again. You could buy kilograms of them very cheap. We soaked them in water all day long. The herrings were fat and tasty but they ran out quickly and we all regretted not buying more. People started getting hold of passes to travel outside Berlin in order to get hold of some food. They took things they could barter for food. They brought back potatoes, peas, kasha, and sometimes even pork fat. It was forbidden to bring food into the camp but the guards turned a blind eye.

Mrs Paszkowska once brought back some meat from a burnt out butcher's stall. The people who worked on the stations brought some rye back from bombed wagons. The grain was dark and looked like roasted coffee. Machines similar to coffee grinders turned up in the barrack and the grain was ground and cooked on a small stove in the kitchen. We bought some of the grain too. From time to time a lorry drove up and unloaded heaps of carrots and beetroots onto the ground. Half were stolen to cook or eat raw before they were even carried down to the cellar.

At this critical period when bread took over from cigarettes as the unit of currency, one man in the camp bought a new, warm coat for his young son for a loaf of bread. We had a cobbler in the camp. He was called Kuczynski. He was given tools, some hide and scraps of car tyres. He set up a workshop and mended shoes. He accepted bread in return for mending shoes, even though it was forbidden. He used better materials when you gave him some bread, so it was said. When he was to nail some rubber soles to my shoes, I secretly took him a slice of bread from my ration under my apron.

Then a transport was brought from Auschwitz, mainly women and children. They were located in the barracks belonging to the 'Todt' organization near our camp. This organization employed non-Jewish labour throughout the occupied territories, mainly to construct fortifications, airfields and so forth. People said they foraged in the bins for peelings. We saw them from a distance, hanging their washing on the barbed wire. The Russians kept advancing so the Germans started evacuating endangered camps. The inmates brought to our camp didn't have enough food. What was it like in their camps then, if it was so bad in our labour camp?

'Do you know what happened? All the washing those poor people hung on the barbed wire was stolen in the night. Nothing but rags. Who could have wanted them?'

The evacuated women learnt that we were Polish and started coming to our barrack. They told us about the stolen washing. But not only about that. 'The Jews hit us on the face,' they said and, 'The ones who worked in the kitchen used to steal and then sell what they'd stolen.'

'They hit you on the face!' shouted Mrs Pawluk, enraged. 'They're the worst of the lot. I'd never give a Jew a crumb of bread or a sip of water. I really loathe them.'

We could hear her because she was shouting loud enough for the whole corridor to hear. We also heard what the other woman said.

At that critical time we received a food parcel from the Red Cross, arranged by Lucja Hersz again. We opened it with trembling hands. A bag of sugar, a bag of rusks, two flat boxes of tinned fish. Marysia immediately took one tin and gave it to Schmidt as a present. She handed it to him triumphantly and asked him to accept it as proof that the Majewski family remembered him. She opened the second tin. She cut half a loaf of our bread into tiny pieces, the bread which was now money, and spread them with tinned fish. Then she went round the barrack and offered the bread to everyone until it was all gone. We didn't even get to try the fish.

'I hadn't any choice. Did you hear what that woman said? She infected everyone with hatred of the Jews. They might start looking more closely now. Who knows?'

In the meantime the Russians were still advancing. We foresaw a period of hunger and, fearful for Macius, we started hoarding supplies. In fact the food we hoarded couldn't even be called supplies. Pieces of dry bread which we stole from ourselves, some burnt grain, a bag of sugar, a small sack of peas. This valuable food was the first thing we took to the shelter now. We watched it like hawks. Lucyna, Zofia and Pelagia did the same. They didn't take bags with things down to the shelter any longer. They took food.

'Mrs Majewska,' they asked, 'if there's a fire, if the barrack catches fire, then please throw the bags on top of the cupboard out of the window.'

They were never sure when they left for work that the barrack would be in one piece when they returned. Wasn't the barrack next to ours where the Italians used to live burnt down by an incendiary bomb? Didn't we walk over the ruins? It was March and spring was coming. Tiny lilac flowers swayed in the wind among the charred timbers. Grass and weeds poked through the gaps in the rubble and when I saw life being renewed I wondered if the barrack had burnt down at night or in the daytime. Had no-one remained in it? Maybe there'd been a few exhausted people in it who didn't want to go down to the shelter and they got hit by the bomb.

There was a tailor in our barrack called Kozub. Kozub was a mystery to me. He was young, tall and decently dressed and had Semitic features. He didn't know a word of German. 'I don't know and don't understand a single word of German,' he used to say. He lived in a small room with the cobbler Kuczynski. One mended shoes and the other sewed and pressed with a flat-iron, with a thimble on his finger and a threaded needle in the lapel of his jacket. He made the cook a pair of trousers. She wore them in the kitchen and the whole barrack admired them.

I often looked at Kozub and wondered if he was Jewish and had bought Aryan papers with a common name. He could have been a tailor who spoke good Polish. But perhaps he spoke Yiddish even better. And if he started speaking German, the German words and phrases would have got mixed up with the Jewish ones and he could have given himself away. What about Gorska? Perhaps her mother tongue was Yiddish too. Maybe that's why she claimed not to know any German. Not everyone could get away with it like Zofia. Not everyone had her nerve and impudence. Not everyone would dare talk to Schmidt in Yiddish.

If Kozub was Jewish then he played his part brilliantly. He wore a brown coat with wide, padded sleeves and a green felt hat. He hadn't worked at the station right from the very start. Mazur got hold of a sewing-machine and an iron for him. He mended the guards' trousers, remade suits and altered uniforms. Sometimes he was given other jobs. Once he brought back a cart of beetroots from Adlershof. Kozub was always in a good mood, but wasn't friends with anyone. He didn't have a camp wife and that was also strange. If he was talking to anyone when we were in earshot we listened to his voice and the way he accented the words, the way he asked questions and replied to them. We observed his walk, the movements of his hands, even his behaviour during raids. Because he always went to the shelter. In his smart coat and green hat, and carrying a suitcase, he was one of the first to go down. In the cellar he stood leaning against one of the posts which held the roof up and nervously smoked cigarettes. Perhaps he'd suffered so much that he wanted to stay alive at any price.

As time went by there were no more alarms. They stopped announcing alarms because there was a constant alarm. You suddenly heard the rumble of planes and the crash of bombs falling from the sky. If it happened at night or even during the day, and Schmidt was in the camp, he took his radio down to the shelter. We listened to the code but we had no idea what was happening. We only knew that Berlin was divided into squares and the radio was informing what sector the bombers were in.

Schmidt didn't usually spend the night in the camp. At about eight o'clock he went home to his wife and left the barrack in the guard's hands. As he walked along the corridor towards the door with his well-filled brief-case under his arm, people passed him and smiled to each other, pointing the brief-case out with a wink. At half past eight they entered his office and turned the radio on. They caught a programme in Polish from London. The cook and the guard who sat in her kitchen must have known about it. Maybe they didn't go to the office at that time on purpose. Schmidt and Mazur may well have known too. But they kept quiet about it. Times were such that they had to keep quiet. You could even sense that they were trying to get into our good books. They wanted us to like them and be friendly.

How far away were the Russians? We knew they were advancing on Berlin. And that the Americans and English were approaching from the west. We lifted up our heads. The times when we had stroked Schmidt's dog and petted the cook's cat seemed incredibly far away.

Barbara Gorska returned suddenly. She returned to the camp with a suitcase and a blanket thrown over her shoulder. It was late evening. Schmidt couldn't throw her out so late. So she stayed.

'That bitch has come back again,' said Pelagia.

But Barbara's bed in our room was already occupied by Jadwiga, so where was Barbara going to sleep? There was another bed free in the room where the mothers and children and saucy Cecylka, Johann's daughter, slept. It was the most cockroach infested room in the whole barrack. She went there. Schmidt wasn't going to tolerate her return. He was afraid that it would seethe in the barrack again so he decided to act energetically. A transport was going to Erfurt. It was said that unproductive elements were being sent west in those transports. Schmidt sent Gorska, Ziolkowski, whose earnings he suspected, and a few more nitwits, as he called them, and idlers who didn't want to work. Perhaps they didn't want to give him anything as a bribe. And strangely enough, the Georgian and young Maria volunteered for the transport.

'What? Are you going to Erfurt?'

'Yes, we're going to Erfurt. But we'll try to go further to a small town on the Swiss border and then try to get to Switzerland from there. We haven't any secrets from you,' said the Georgian. 'That's our plan.'

He had a rucksack on his shoulders and a walking-stick in his hand. He turned round into the grey morning mist. The sun hadn't risen yet. We'd just returned from the shelter. Maria walked two steps behind him, obedient and silent.

At the beginning of April when I was returning along Grünauer Strasse with the milk churn I saw Vlassov's army. I placed the milk churn on the pavement and watched the procession riding past. Vlassov was riding in a carriage. He was gorgeously dressed. On his head a tall hat with a velvet brim the colour of wild strawberries and a wonderful coat lined with sheepskin. I felt as if I was in the theatre watching the stage. That's what Pugachov must have looked like, and he must have ridden in a carriage surrounded by Cossacks as well, holding a baton.

The German newspapers sounded the alarm. 'Defend every inch of soil,' they exhorted. 'German people! The Russians are Huns – bandits and rapists.' But the Germans were exhausted and didn't believe the papers, saying they were spreading news like that on purpose.

One day an army marched past along Grünauer Strasse. Everyone watched curiously, but turned their heads away and laughed. They were clearly laughing at this strange army which was made up of the oldest reservists to be conscripted into the Home Guard. The soldiers were all over sixty and dressed in old, faded, ill-fitting uniforms. It wasn't an army, just a grotesque imitation.

One day we woke up – the sun hadn't risen yet and it was still grey and misty – and saw the Home Guard in front of our barrack. Some were fat, some thin, some had moustaches, others were clean-shaven. But they were all old. They dug deep ditches behind the wire and deep holes along the road which our people walked along to go to work. The first evening Gorska fell into a hole because she came back late that day and there was no light. She was stuck in the hole for over an hour until finally someone came along and helped her out. Barbara had returned to our camp again. She bribed or charmed the train guard and came back when she was half-way to Erfurt. Schmidt didn't bother doing anything about it now. The course of events had decided his battle with the woman.

So the soldiers dug deep holes along the road leading to Grünauer Strasse, and in the ditches they had gouged out in the field beyond our enclosure they placed plywood figures representing soldiers in caps, with only the heads visible. They sometimes came to the wash-room in our barrack to wash their hands. They smiled at us. They were talkative and sympathized with our predicament. 'Yes,' they said, 'you'll go home soon. It's all rubbish.'

From these preparations, manoeuvres and exercises, we gathered that the Russians were near and that we'd hear the sound of cannons shortly. There'd be a siege. Who knows how long it would last? What will happen if the Russians come when Marysia's at work? Maybe the Russians will take the suburb of Koepenick, and Gerlice will be cut off. We were worried about all this. We were afraid of being separated. What should we do?

Our people kept telling us something new when they returned from their various stations. We'd been hearing about sabotage for a long time. It wasn't always bombs that destroyed the grain wagons. Now, in the final days, the sabotage increased and assumed hitherto unknown proportions.

'Tell me what'll happen if your station is cut off,' I often asked Marysia.

'I'll sense it. The trick is to sense it in good time. I've hardly ever had any sick-leave. Only once when I twisted my ankle. Even when the winch hit me on the turntable I went to work the next day. And when the right moment comes I'll say I'm ill.'

'Yes. But when?'

'When we hear the cannons.'

Marysia's work at the station had the advantage of enabling her to come into contact with people. So she could buy some food from time to time. There'd been no fat in our food for a long time now. We ate watery, turnip soup every day. We wanted to stock up with some fat in case there was a siege.

'The Italian baker from near Milan, who once brought me a cake, will sell me a kilogram of pork fat and a bottle of oil in return for a gold watch. I told him to come here.'

I still had a gold watch sewn into the padded sleeve of my winter coat. He came that evening, sat down on our bed and took his parcel out from under his jacket. I gave him the watch. The pork fat was yellow and rancid. He couldn't vouch for the oil. 'It might be poisonous,' he said.

'But at least he told us,' said Marysia when he'd said goodbye and gone. 'He's a decent man. He didn't have to say anything. We'll be careful with the oil.'

We put the pork fat and the bottle of oil wrapped in Macius's shirt into our bag and watched it like hawks. On the way to the shelter, tripping over a stone or clod of earth in the dark or sliding down the clay slope, we squeezed the bag tight so as not to break the bottle containing the oil.

But I was sorry to part with the watch. It had been my mother's. I knew that these were times when you measured everything with a

465

different measure, when values had a different price and the normal order of things was transformed. So why was I sorry? Had I bartered the watch together with my memories? No, the memories stayed with me. I thought they stayed with me. But wouldn't they die if they weren't kept alive by something miraculously saved from these irretrievable times? Never mind what. A ring, a watch, a brooch, anything. Something that connected us to the past, that was a bridge between the endlessly sad present and the better past which had slipped away.

One rainy afternoon in the second half of April we heard the cannons.

'They're pounding Alexanderplatz,' said the people who worked there.

'Then I'll go to the doctor tomorrow,' said Marysia. 'The time's come.'

She went to see the doctor on duty at Adlershof camp. She said she had backache and couldn't work. She told him she'd never been off sick until now. He examined her and signed her off for two weeks. We were relieved and glad as we were certain that the Russians would enter Berlin during those two weeks.

It looked as if the Germans had lost their heads completely. They started bringing enormous quantities of planks and poles to the field between our barrack and the shelter. They brought workers over from Adlershof, bearded Russian peasants.

'What are you building?' we asked.

'Barracks. A lot of new barracks. The people in Adlershof are moving here.'

'Moving here? But the Russians are so close. You can hear the cannons. They'll enter Berlin in a week or two.'

'They'll enter and we won't even know when, Mrs Majewska. We'll just see them one day,' said Mrs Malinowska, lugging her bedding to the shelter. Our life was now a constant hike between barrack and cellar. No, not a hike but a sprint – hurried, exhausted and hungry. A lot of people kept their things in the shelter all the time.

The days and nights were as like as peas in a pod. We didn't react to the shudders and explosions any more. After spending the night in the cellar we penetrated the mist in the pale light of dawn, dragging our tired legs. We returned to the barrack. Still standing? Yes, still there despite everything. But the guards and Schmidt and

Mazur weren't with us any longer. Only the cook was left. No-one went to work any more.

'Go to Erfurt,' Schmidt advised us when he was leaving, 'evacuate yourselves to Erfurt.'

He was holding the radio under the arm of his good hand. He didn't forget to take the radio and his brief-case. He didn't take the dog. It stayed in the camp.

Roerich, the guard, and Mazur hadn't been seen for a few days now. They both did a flit. Suddenly Hofman turned up and spent the whole night in the shelter with us. He was wearing civilian clothes. A long, black coat and a cap. He looked extremely strange and poor. He didn't have any authority any longer. We didn't know why he'd come, what had impelled him.

We didn't know? But Gorska was back in the barrack and he was condemned to circle in her orbit like a planet round the sun. He was despondent because of the events of the last few days and resembled a shadow. He didn't talk to her and didn't even look at her. It was enough for him to breathe the same air. Even if there'd been no other signs we'd have known from looking at him that the fate of Berlin was a foregone conclusion. We told him that Schmidt had taken the radio. 'He took the radio,' they said, 'and without it we won't hear the code and we won't know where the bombers are.' They laughed. 'Shit,' he replied.

Kozub gave him a cigarette. Now, in the murky light of the dim bulb, it was Kozub who looked more like the person in charge. Kozub, Johann, Parzynski, Konrad. The guard in civvies looked like a pauper. But they didn't have anything against him. Towards morning when it got light he took the track across the field to Grünauer Strasse. We didn't see him again.

We were afraid that the barrack would catch fire during the incessant bombing so all the food supplies from the camp stores were taken down to the cellar. We took suitcases and sacks of clothes down to the cellar too. Everything lay heaped up in all the corners. We now spent day and night in the shelter. The barrack stood lonely and deserted, like a nest when all the fledglings have been taken out. There wasn't a single soldier from the reserves in the holes and ditches.

On 25 April at dawn Dyksa, who was our plumber, went towards the back door, which was never used. He came back at once. He was as white as a sheet. 'There's a Soviet soldier standing by the door,' he said.

A soldier was standing there in a lambskin cap and leaning against the barrel of his rifle. He didn't say a word. He just stood and looked at us. And we looked at him. Then someone ran outside into the field. Others followed him. They came back a few minutes later and said that lorries were standing in front of the barrack and there were Soviet soldiers everywhere. 'They gave us some saccharine and tinned salmon,' they added.

There was immense joy in their voices. It had happened. They were here. In fact this decisive moment was the one we were scared of most of all: the moment when the Soviet soldiers arrived. Because they might shoot at us before we managed to tell them who we were. Or they might blow up our cellar with grenades thinking that the German army was in hiding down there.

It's a joy that makes our hearts burst! A slant-eyed soldier is standing in the shelter, alien, unshaven, in a thick, wadded jacket and thick gloves. He's smiling at us. So they're here. It's happened. We're alive. Oh happy hour! How can we make it memorable? Something has to be done to give vent to the overwhelming joy. Something has to be done to manifest the loathing of the Germans. We hear the sudden barking and howling of a dog – they've killed Schmidt's dog. Then Metzi the cat flashes past in the long cellar corridor. They throw themselves at her too.

They pulled the sacks of flour and kasha brought down here from the stores out of the shelter onto the muddy entrance slope. They kicked them open and their insides poured out in a white ribbon, and as the pearly grain spilled out they shouted, 'We never ever saw that beautiful kasha'.

Mrs Lund stood beside the open sacks. She had aged. She was trembling and terrified. 'Have you seen Metzi?' she was asking.

'No, I haven't,' replied Mrs Parzynska. 'I hope she goes and dies,' added her husband.

'Take it!' said the cook in a strange voice and pointed at the kasha. 'Take as much as you want.'

But no-one took it. 'We're going home!' they shouted. 'To Warsaw!'

They were shouting like children do when they want something. You felt as if Warsaw was just over the other side of the railway embankment or on the other side of the canal.

Some of them went to the small wooden houses where the bombed out Germans lived and came back with small handcarts.

They loaded their things onto them and immediately set off for Warsaw. On the spot. Without wasting a single second. Natalia the railwayman's wife went like that, the one who worked in the kitchen and had recently had a baby. She put the baby in a pram she took from a German. Waclawa and her husband and son, Parzynski and his wife, and Kuczynski and Kozub went with them. Followed by Johann and his daughter Cecylka, and Wegliszewski and his woman.

They didn't take just carts from the Germans. Hens too. They cooked them hurriedly in the kitchen for the journey. God alone knows what else they took. Mrs Matuszewska showed everyone a huge doll. It was beautifully dressed with a hat, shoes and a pink dress and was as big as a year-old baby. No-one had ever seen a doll like it.

They left in small groups, in eights or twelves. The Russian soldiers stood round and watched in silence. Were they Russian? They had protruding cheek-bones, slant eyes and yellow skin. A sledge harnessed to a dozen dogs appeared from round the corner of the barrack. A man in a thick sheepskin with Mongolian features was running alongside it.

'Frau Alice,' said the cook, taking me by the hand. 'Frau Alice, take me with you.'

She was swaying and wringing her hands. But no-one paid her any attention. She kept entering the barrack and then reappearing, alien, pained, lonely. The barrack was battered but still standing. Soldiers and our people were milling about inside. Lucyna and Zofia had already gone. Pelagia was getting ready to leave. She brought a pan with boiled chicken into the room. 'I stole two hens,' she said. She smiled charmingly at Macius, poured some chicken broth into a bowl for him and gave him a piece of meat, as hard as leather.

'I took a pram for my things from a German woman as well,' she said. 'I'm off now.'

Alfred Tchorzewski was still in the barrack. Marysia called him out into the corridor.

'When are you going?'

'Tomorrow at seven in the morning. I've got a bike.'

'We'd like to go with you,' she said.

'All right. But you can't spend the night here.'

'Why not?'

'Because they're all drunk.'

'Then we'll go to Mrs Ulrich's, the German woman in one of the wooden houses. We'll meet you tomorrow morning.'

A couple of hundred metres away from the camp a unit of German soldiers had left about twenty bikes behind. Someone told us and our people threw themselves at them. Tchorzewski got hold of one. It was a means of transport and therefore priceless. He didn't take a single thing more from the Germans.

We were suddenly overcome by fear of the Soviet soldiers. We decided to leave the barrack immediately. We took the bag of food – the oil, pork fat and rusks. We left the peas and burnt rye in the cupboard. We took a few blankets to use as payment for a bed for the night. As we were running quickly along the corridor Marysia fell into a shell hole. Her right leg got stuck.

'Have you broken your leg?' I shouted.

'No.'

I wondered what would happen if she really had broken her leg. At a moment like this. The Malinowskis were standing in front of the barrack with Jadwiga who was still wearing her beret with the feather and her muff. We told them we were going to spend the night at Mrs Ulrich's. As we were going towards the gate loaded with our bags and blankets we saw a Soviet officer on a horse. The gate was open. Above it was a roof made of planks. In order to pass through the rider ought just to have bent his head. He didn't do that. He smashed the gate down. At that moment we understood what victory means.

Ingeborg was sitting in front of Mrs Ulrich's house. When she saw us she came up to us and stretched out both hands in front of her. Gold rings shone on every finger. 'They gave them to me,' she said. She took us to her wooden hut. A large Persian carpet was standing there rolled up. 'They gave me that too. They bring me everything they take from people,' she smiled sadly.

'Mrs Ulrich,' we asked, 'can we spend the night here? We'll give you two blankets.'

She nodded her head and pointed to a bed which was covered with a pile of blankets.

'We've nothing else to pay with.'

'Lie down on the bed here. I'm going to sleep in the cellar. The two Dutchmen are down there too.'

The Dutchmen were her tenants. We were surprised that they were sleeping in the cellar.

When it got dark we lit a candle. We started moving the blankets and getting the bed ready for the night. Suddenly there was a knocking at the window.

'Mrs Majewska,' we heard the voice of Jadwiga Malinowska, 'we're going to Warsaw tomorrow morning. First thing. Terrible things are happening here.'

'Where are you spending the night tonight?'

'Tonight? Nowhere. We'll sit down in a hole somewhere.'

At about nine o'clock the door opened and two Soviet officers entered. One of them had dishevelled hair, his cap had slipped down to the back of his head and he was holding an empty bottle. He was drunk. He immediately stretched out on the bed. The other one sat down at the table and asked us who we were and what we were doing here. I replied in Russian that we were Poles from the camp behind the wire and that we wanted to sleep here and then leave for Warsaw in the morning.

In the meantime the one lying on the bed got up, went up to Marysia and told her to go out with him. She was surprised and said, 'I'm Polish. We waited for you like for saviours. Please leave us alone.' He didn't listen. He handed her Macius's coat which was lying on the chair. He was so drunk he was swaying. Marysia turned to the other soldier and said, 'Please tell him. Please explain.'

He shook his head. 'I won't manage him. He's drunk too much. I'll go and get someone.' He went out and the door closed behind him.

The drunken officer took his revolver out and put it to Marysia's temple. He was still holding Macius's coat in his other hand. The child was frightened and started to cry. I was terrified. I ran out onto the dark street and started calling for help. A patrol was passing just then. Two soldiers and an officer. I grabbed the officer's sleeve and pulled him towards the house. I spoke to him in Russian. He ran after me immediately, surprised that I could speak Russian. When he entered the room the drunken officer jumped out of the window and disappeared into the night.

'You're Polish?' asked the officer in surprise. 'But why aren't you wearing your colours?'

'We didn't know we should.'

'You must understand they're drunk with victory and that's why they've gone wild.' He saluted and left.

One of the Dutchmen came up a few minutes later. He was pale and terrified.

471

'What happened?' he asked.

'Take us down to the cellar with you,' said Marysia.

We left the door open. We left all our things, even the leather bag containing our papers and some money. The shelter proper was underneath the cellar. The Dutchman opened the flap and jumped in through the opening into a hole strewn with pillows and quilts. No-one said a word. We were afraid to move. We could hear the footsteps of soldiers entering and leaving the house. We heard steps above our heads and even conversations. Our hearts thumped when they came into the cellar. Fortunately they didn't find the flap.

When the sun rose, Mrs Ulrich went out first, followed by the Dutchmen. They helped us out of the shelter. We stood in the door of the house terrified. All the contents of the cupboards and drawers were lying on the floor. We started collecting our things. I found a pair of stockings in one corner and Macius's shirt somewhere else. The leather bag lay under the table. The papers were still there but they'd taken the money, some scissors, and some sugar cubes. I found our pork fat, the bottle of oil and bag of rusks.

We thought about Tchorzewski all night in the cellar. He said he was leaving at seven in the morning, but wouldn't he change his mind? Or perhaps he wasn't in the barrack any longer but had left the previous day? At six o'clock I ran along to the camp. A ribbon made of a white and red scrap of material we found among Mrs Ulrich's scattered things was sewn onto the lapel of my jacket. I didn't meet anyone on the way there. Huge lorries were standing next to the barrack with lots of drunken soldiers everywhere. Was it the army, the regular Russian army? No, this was Asia, this was the steppe.

Tchorzewski was standing beside his bunk packing a suitcase.

'We're going to Warsaw with you,' I said. 'We'll wait for you in Mrs Ulrich's house.'

'Good. I'll be at the gate at seven.'

He was dressed for the journey to Warsaw like the worst pauper. A torn, dirty, faded, striped pullover, torn trousers and crooked old shoes. I'd have to tell Marysia. We must dress like that too so as not to attract attention to ourselves. So I rushed into our room and took the two aprons I wore when I was cleaning so we could put them on for the journey. Tchorzewski accompanied me to the camp gate. In the distance I could see Marysia and Macius standing in front of the house. On the bridge I felt a weakness in my knees. I sat down in the sand and dust. I sat like that for a moment with my head against a concrete post, staring into the water of the canal.

Tchorzewski was at the gate punctually at seven. He had the bike and his suitcase was strapped on to it. Marysia gave him a mug of hot coffee and a rusk with pork fat. He ate it standing up and then tied our bags to the bike. Our headscarves and aprons made us look like peasant women. We agreed to pose as a family, to make it safer. Tchorzewski would be Marysia's husband, Macius their son, and I the mother. We returned to the house for a moment. We said good-bye to Mrs Ulrich and the two Dutchmen. One of them ran out after us and gave Marysia a grey blanket with pink checks.

'It's for the journey,' he said. 'It'll be useful for the child.'

When we passed the wooden hut I knocked at the window to say good luck to Ingeborg.

We walked along the track towards Grünauer Strasse. Anyone looking at us can see a man and his wife, their child and the mother. All four poorly dressed, tired and pale. All they have is a suitcase and a few bundles strapped to a bike. The mother has got a coat thrown over her shoulder. The wife is holding the child by the hand. The husband leads the way pushing the bike in front of him. White and red ribbons are fastened to their clothes. They're from a camp and are returning to their own country. Everyone knows that.

So we walk along the street. A terrible hurricane has been this way and in its wake it has left straw, ruins, rubble, asphalt riddled with holes, dead horses and the blackened corpses of German soldiers. The Soviet army, the infantry and cavalry, is advancing, followed by endless supply columns. Sometimes a cavalryman hurtles along the pavement. Sometimes a burnt out tank bars the way. Or we have to make our way round a deep bomb crater.

Here's the bunker where the German mothers sheltered against the bombs with their small children. Four hundred young mothers had cabins there. The soldiers are said to have rushed in and raped them. Where's the shop where I collected the milk for the camp? The door is smashed, the shop is plundered and there's no-one to be seen inside. On this April morning there's not a single German woman or girl to be seen. They're all hidden in cellars, in attics, in inaccessible hide-outs.

The soldiers enter flats and plunder them. They take carpets, furs, and furniture and load them onto lorries. Lines of lorries with carpets and furniture stretch eastwards from Berlin. If the carpets

473

and furniture could speak – who knows? They might say they come from Jewish homes and are now on their return journey.

We continue walking along a wide street with a few buildings and we see that people are coming out of various narrower streets and joining into groups, bigger or smaller, just like streams running into a river. They're all going in one direction. East. Most people have got a cart and on the carts are their personal belongings. They speak Russian, Ukrainian, Italian, French and Polish. They're wearing ribbons of various colours in their lapels.

Female Soviet soldiers stand at street intersections and control the traffic. Strong and stocky with faces tanned by the sun and wind. The camp inmates look with astonishment at the huge posters, at the portraits of Stalin and the written slogans. Every few dozen steps there's a poster. I can see an animal with bared teeth on one, and under it the words 'we'll kill the beast in its lair'.

Macius is holding his mother's hand and is calm and quiet. Nothing surprises him, he doesn't ask any questions. The unknown journey ahead of us, the nights to be spent in strange places, the long walk, the rain, the piercing morning cold – he doesn't think about any of that at all. Macius isn't a child walking along the streets of Berlin now, but our companion. Even the body of a baby which some unfortunate mother has left lying under a fence doesn't make any impression on him. He seems indifferent to everything around him. Alfred Tchorzewski too. He wheels his overloaded bike with calm and level steps. He is silent.

This silent walk has its own deeply rooted reasons. We are weak and exhausted. The sleepless nights and the dramatic events of the last two days have taken our strength away. And perhaps we unconsciously sense that if we keep silent our strength will last longer. In our condition everything is tiring – even a word crossing our lips.

Berlin is a city with many stations, many districts and suburbs. You travel from one district to another by train. So it's not surprising that even though we walked for hours and frequently stopped to rest, we were still in Berlin. We thought we'd never get out of that magic circle.

When we came to a well or a tap we rested. Then Marysia cut a slice of yellow pork fat and gave it to Macius on a rusk. After that she gave some to Tchorzewski, the captain of our expedition. We ate our rusks with devotion. We drank water with solemnity. We rested on the kerb of the pavement, or on a stone wall, or on the grey trunk of a fallen tree. Then we continued wordlessly. We knew the measure of time. We sensed instinctively when we should get up and move off. Tchorzewski in front. Without a cap, with his untidy fair hair that hadn't been cut for ages. He pushed the bike and didn't turn round. And we followed him, trusting and disciplined, staring at his dusty head. Old men sitting on steps or old women in wide aprons looked at us, blinking their watery eyes in the sun, as we disappeared into the distance.

Other people were walking in front of us and behind. In groups of ten or fifteen. Everybody had one and the same thought: don't take the wrong turning, don't lose the way, take the right road. Our group was the smallest. Only four people. There was just one thing we longed for – not to get lost in this network of roads, to find the right road which would take us home. Although, of the four of us, only Tchorzewski had a home. Where was ours?

Strings of military vehicles passed us. We were tired and so we decided to try our luck. When a jeep with two Soviet soldiers drove up we raised our arms. The jeep stopped. We sat in the back and pulled the bike in. 'We must pay them,' I said. I had a thin, gold watch-chain sewn into the hem of my skirt. I unstitched the hem and pulled out the chain.

'I only want to give them a bit. After all we haven't any money,' I said.

We didn't have pliers or a hammer or scissors so Tchorzewski bit the chain off. The soldiers drove up to a popular holiday spot and stopped. They weren't going any further. Then I gave them a bit of the chain. 'Take it for giving us a ride,' I said.

They laughed and played with the chain as if it was a toy. Then we understood they hadn't counted on being paid. But the months in the camp had taught us that you have to pay for everything, even for indifference. We were slowly switching over to a new way of thinking. Even now, after being liberated, we didn't believe in disinterested friendliness.

Now we walked along a wide, asphalted street. Railings on both sides. Behind the railings villas with gardens. Suddenly two soldiers with rifles stood in front of us. They stopped us. They took the bike without saying a word and threw the suitcase and bundles onto the ground. Marysia said to them in Russian and Polish, 'Don't take our bike. It's all we've got. This is my husband and this is our child and mother. We've got no home.'

'We've been ordered to requisition bikes,' they said. 'But God be with you. You can continue.'

475

To avoid it happening again, Tchorzewski took some parts off the bike to make it look broken. A star flashed in the sky. Above us was a thickening greyness, under our feet a narrow path, to our right and left wide, empty fields. From time to time we saw a herd of cows being led by Soviet soldiers. Black and white Dutch cows taken from the Germans.

In front of us and behind us like an endless trail of ants hundreds and thousands of camp inmates, men and women, pulling carts with their possessions on them. Some were tired and threw their things away. We saw parts of sewing-machines lying along the road, pillows, coats, dresses, underwear and whole suitcases thrown in'o fields. They must have been plundered from deserted German houses. When they became a burden they were thrown away with no regrets.

The skirts we were wearing were worn and falling apart. Tchorzewski was just as poorly dressed. Perhaps he didn't have anything better in his scratched, cardboard suitcase. Marysia and I could have changed our clothes from head to toe and put these dresses on. We didn't do it out of some deep-seated reason. We believed that these German things would bring us no luck, and Tchorzewski thought so too. We looked with curiosity at the Ukrainian women who passed us in rich Persian lamb coats. Also plundered from German homes, no doubt.

'They're Jewish furs that are going back east now,' we said to each other and winked.

But when I saw an umbrella lying in a field I couldn't resist the temptation. It was old and very threadbare. But priceless for us. It was the end of April. The rainy season. That day was miraculously fine without a single cloud in the sky. But it might change any minute. To thunder and lightning or a hailstorm or a torrential downpour. Even that old umbrella would come in useful.

Among the things scattered along the road we came across a hand cart. Someone had left it, perhaps they'd found a better one. It was broken but could be mended. Tchorzewski had some nails in his pocket so he knocked them in with a stone. We put the things we were carrying onto the cart. Also my brown winter coat and the umbrella. Marysia took the shaft while Macius and I pushed it from behind.

So we were moving forward all the time – towards Warsaw. Night was falling and there weren't many people left on the road. Some had lain down for the night under roadside trees.

476

Others passed us, while we passed others still, more tired than we were.

'Isn't the cart going to get in the way?' asked Marysia. 'The jeep that gave us a lift wouldn't have taken us with the cart. Isn't it better to leave it?' she said in a monotonous voice, staring at Tchorzewski's back.

'We can always leave it. Let's keep it for a while yet,' he replied.

It was completely dark when we came to a village. We followed a herd of cows. Straight to the cowshed. The cowshed contained an area with a concrete floor covered with straw. Its main purpose was as a store for chaff or other cattle feed. The cows stood behind a partition and we could hear them clanging their chains, lowing and mooing.

A lot of other people were already lying asleep on the floor, tired out by the walking just like we were. Tchorzewski collected a handful of straw into a corner, laid the bike down beside him and covered it with the straw. He also took the things off the cart and placed them next to us. We lay down to sleep. Marysia was afraid of the cold coming up from the concrete floor and so she made Macius a bed on the cart. She put a coat and blanket down for him to lie on. But he didn't want to sleep there. He was afraid that someone would wheel him out together with the cart while he was asleep.

When it was light we got up off the floor. The soldiers were just milking the cows. A middle-aged soldier stood leaning against the doors of the cowshed. He was immensely tall and was wearing a lambskin cap.

'Could I have some milk?' asked Marysia. 'I've got a child with me.'

'Why not?' he said. 'Go to the cowshed and milk a cow. Take as much milk as you need.'

'Alfred,' she called to Tchorzewski, 'I'll go to the yard to look for a bowl or pan. We'll milk the cow.'

He stood in front of her, untidy, with straw in his hair, dirty and shaking with cold.

'Maryska,' he said hesitantly. The name passed his lips with difficulty. He touched her sleeve. 'I've never milked a cow. What shall we do?'

She took a cigarette out of her pocket, the soldier gave her a light and she inhaled the smoke. She looked, blinking her eyes, over the stable roof, at the pinkening dawn. Tchorzewski stood in front of her, clumsy and touching in the role of husband which he couldn't

477

play. He was a bad actor. The expression on his face was silly and he forgot his part easily.

The Soviet soldier with the thin hawk-like face and hair dusted with grey stood next to her and smoked his cigarette. He watched the strange couple. 'Is he your husband?' he asked. He was silent and then continued, 'I think he's not your husband. He's a worker and you're an intellectual. But what business is it of mine?'

'Well now,' she said sharply to interrupt this dangerous conversation, 'I'll go and milk the cow.'

She borrowed an enamel bowl from someone, sat down on a stool next to the cow and pulled her teats once and then a second time. When the cow lowed she took fright and spilled the milk she'd just milked. Seeing that it was no good, she took her last cigarette out of her pocket and gave it to the soldier milking beside her. She asked him for some milk. He willingly gave her some from his bucket. We were dreadfully parched and drank it straight out of the bowl, one after the other. It gave us new strength.

The soldiers gave us some black, army bread. They were cooking a chicken in a pot in the yard. I asked for a piece for the child. The pot was standing on a stove improvised out of bricks and the smoke and sparks rose and billowed over the large yard.

We wrapped our headscarves round our heads, pulled them low over our eyes and set off. The cart rolled along with a clatter on its twisted, badly fitting wheels. Tchorzewski in the lead with the bike, behind him Marysia at the shaft and Macius and I at the back. We guarded the oil so that it wouldn't spill and the rusks so that they wouldn't disappear. The rusks were the object of our incessant care. We brought them back to Poland with us.

We went out onto the road. There was a bridge right in front of us and the mayor's house just next to it. Heaps of clothes and linen lay in the shrubs in the garden surrounding the house. Broken china, crystal vases and blue Delft dishes. We trampled on woollen pullovers. We picked up a spoon, a tiny plate and a piece of coloured rag all covered in dust and put them on the cart as token spoils. Then we walked along the road for a long time. We passed huge posters with portraits of Stalin. We passed a small cemetery and saw the conical graves of fallen Soviet soldiers.

Carts rolled along behind us and in front of us. In an instant we were dragged and crowded into the trail of ants. We became one of the thousands of links in an endless conveyor belt. After a few hours we stopped. We didn't know what to do. A sandy track ran diagonally across a field away from the road. Some people were continuing along the road while others were turning into the field.

'It's a short cut,' they said. 'Just under three kilometres. The track leads to the same road.'

'Are you sure?' asked the others. 'Isn't it better to walk along the road?'

What on earth made us choose that supposed short cut? Was it a road? The Sahara, more like. Our route so far had been a trifle, nothing in comparison with these few kilometres of soft, loose sand. Pushing the bike and cart became a torment. The cart kept breaking and Tchorzewski had to knock nails in and keep tying it up with string. He straightened himself up from the work, sweating and exhausted. We could see that more and more things were thrown into the field as there was no tree or bush to rest under during the hot midday.

Why didn't we throw our things off? All we had with us was rags, and Tchorzewski's rolled up jacket tied to the saddle was an old rag too. But the thought didn't even enter our heads. We were attached to these things. We had taken them from home. We'd carried them to the shelter so many times. We didn't have the strength to part with them.

Emptiness is all around. Crows circle over our heads and drop softly onto the field. Not many people are walking along the sandy track. The groups are further apart than on the road. The ones in front of us might be stronger than us and reach their destination quicker and then we'll be alone. Will the track ever end? It'll never end and the effort will kill us. Suddenly we saw a long row of poplars in the distance. The people in front of us gesticulated and shouted, 'It's the road. It's the road.'

The cart trundled forward more blithely. We could see our destination now. Marysia, dusty and bent double, and Macius and I behind. And suddenly something strange happened. Macius, who was always so calm and collected and bore all discomforts so bravely, now became angry. He pushed me away and wanted to push the cart himself. Was he being difficult? Or was it because he could see how tired I was and wanted to spare me but didn't know how to express it any differently.

We got there at last. A large German village. No civilians to be seen. Only in front of one house we saw a doddering old couple sitting on a bench. They weren't scared of anyone. Age was their shield. In every house the door and windows were wide open.

Crowds of Soviet soldiers everywhere, male and female. A board nailed to a wooden pole. On the board in enormous letters the new name of the village: Pavlovo.

The village lay on the sandy track but the main road ran just outside it. We drank some water from the well, straight out of the bucket. We sat down on the edge of the track opposite the sign saying Pavlovo, ate a piece of bread and pork fat, rested and set off again.

Supply columns stretched all along the road. Peasant carts harnessed to a pair of small, strong horses. They were generally empty and were driving in the opposite direction, towards another front perhaps. They were driven by bearded peasants wearing caps made of cloth or fur with earflaps and thick overcoats. We looked longingly at them.

'Father,' I said to one of them, 'we're tired and your cart is empty. Take us a little way, please take us.'

He consented. 'Faster! Faster!' he called. 'Hurry up!'

We clambered up onto the cart immediately, at lightning speed. We sat down on some straw. Together with the bike and cart. When the horses moved, we didn't have the strength to speak. We sat hunched and dozing. The sun and blue sky above us, the flight of the birds, the spreading distance of the fields – none of it existed for us. Sometimes the horses stopped suddenly. For some reason there was a hold-up and the string of vehicles stopped dead. Then we opened our eyes.

If only we could sit on this bundle of straw until the end of the world. Life can roll on, but without us, without our participation. Who needs us? What are we needed for? Aren't we lost scraps on the immense roads of this alien land? We've been fighting for our lives so long and with such determination. Where will the battle end at last?

Despite these sad thoughts which accompanied the rumble of wheels and the clatter of hooves, we longed for four walls. A roof and four walls, a corner of our own, a final halt. A bed and a wardrobe, a table and a chair. One window. Silence outside. And our own pan on our own stove. Glowing coal for warming our frozen hands in winter. And what else? A pot of butter, a glass of milk, a loaf of bread, a bag of sugar. What more do you need?

I looked at Tchorzewski. I knew that although he was a weak-willed man with no initiative who let himself be carried along by events like a leaf by the wind, all the same he was our guardian and faithful companion. He shared our meals, dozed exhausted next to us and drank water from the same well. What would happen if he knew? What would he do if he learnt the truth about us? I answered the question myself. Nothing. I was sure that his behaviour and attitude wouldn't change one iota.

Before evening fell, at sunset, we arrived in the outskirts of Landsberg. Swaying on legs like wood, we went up to a one-storey house on a narrow street near the road. Someone was sitting in the window. It looked as if he was resting after a hard day.

'Could we spend the night here somewhere?' we asked in German.

He was about forty. He had a moustache and his hair was brushed upwards into a crew cut. He looked at us. We stood by the low garden fence, dusty and dirty. He noticed the red and white ribbons on our clothes. He replied in Polish, 'Spend the night?' He described a semi-circle with his hand. 'Aren't there enough empty houses here?'

Yes, the houses on the other side of the street looked uninhabited. A white sheet on every house. No woman or child or even dog to be seen.

'You can sleep in any house you like. They're all open and empty. But the soldiers may trouble you in the night. At the end of this street there's a yellow house where some German women resettled from Bessarabia live. Go there for the night.' He saw that we were still standing holding the fence and added, 'I'm the mayor. A Soviet colonel lives with me. If you come tomorrow morning you'll get a bowl of soup from his kitchen.'

We should have left then. We had in front of us the prospect of a bowl of soup and we knew where to spend the night. The yellow house stood at the end of the street, surrounded by an orchard. Through a green thicket we could see a square of wall and a chimney on a red roof. At that moment it was our destination. But we didn't move. The sun had set now and with the piercing chill we were overcome by such exhaustion that we sat down on the ground exactly where we were standing. We only moved when night fell.

We knocked at the door of the yellow house but no-one opened it. It was getting darker all the time so we opened the door ourselves. A long table stood in a room with two windows and about thirty women and children were sitting at it. The table stood by the windows and a candle was burning in a tin, stuck into sand. The floor was scattered with straw covered with coats and blankets. We could see through a door into a second room which was also full of straw.

'Can we spend the night here?' we asked in German.

'Yes, you can,' replied a red-haired woman.

They were eating supper. Mothers were holding their children on their knees and feeding them. Slices of black bread lay on a tray. A large pan of kasha or potatoes stood in the middle of the table. The red-haired woman got up from the bench and a second woman with a child got up after her. She was probably no more than eighteen but a mother already. Her face was still childish and she moved with an indescribable charm. All the women were wearing peasant clothes. Tight jackets and long gathered skirts. They were farmers from the German colonies, evacuated by the Germans. They spoke Russian as fluently as German.

'You can sleep here in this corner on the straw,' said the red-haired woman. She took us to the other room and showed us the corner.

I touched her sleeve with my fingers. 'Tell me,' I said, 'how come you've managed to keep such a beauty safe? How is it that she hasn't been carried off yet?'

'We hide her away and watch her like hawks. She never leaves the house. If anyone comes in she hides immediately. My mother-in-law opens the door.'

She pointed to a haggish old woman of at least eighty who was sitting at the table. We lay down on the coats and blankets on the straw and fell asleep instantly. At two in the morning we were woken by the rumble of a car. Then we heard hammering on the door. In the pale moonlight I saw the haggish old woman clattering towards the door in wooden clogs. I heard a voice say, 'Don't be afraid, don't be afraid.' Then, 'Zdravstvujtje [Good day]. Are there are any nice little ladies here?'

The red-haired woman who was sleeping next to us jumped up from the floor. But the officer was already walking round the house, shining his torch into all the corners. He had a revolver in his other hand.

'God be with you,' said the woman. 'There are no young ladies here! Just old women and children.'

'All right, all right. I just dropped in for a moment. I'm drunk,' he said, shot at the ceiling twice and left.

'Go back to sleep,' said the woman. 'We've got used to it.'

She unfastened her jacket and scratched her bare breast because the straw was full of fleas. Then she covered herself with a rag, turned to the wall and added, 'And our beauty and the younger women sleep in the attic. You go up a ladder through an opening in the hall. We hide the ladder under the straw.'

At sunrise we got up from the floor and cleaned the straw off our clothes. The haggish old woman stood in the door and watched us putting our things on the cart. Perhaps she didn't trust us. Perhaps she was afraid we'd steal a pan or a rag. She stood in the light of the first rays of the sun nodding her head and chewing bread in her toothless mouth. As soon as we moved off a soldier came up to us and put his hand on the bike.

'We need it,' he said. 'I'm requisitioning this bike.'

We were experienced by now. We wrung our hands and begged the soldier to have pity and not take the sum of our belongings off us. This theatrical despair was always successful. Tchorzewski never said a word. He stood with his head down, his hands dangling, unhappy and deathly tired. 'Thank God it worked this time as well,' he said.

We stopped in front of the mayor's house. We looked after the bike while Tchorzewski entered the kitchen and asked the house-keeper for the soup we'd been promised the day before. He brought the soup in a large chipped enamel bowl with lumps of lamb fat swimming in it. We sat down round the bowl. We ate the soup in turn, passing our one and only spoon from hand to hand. It was really life-giving, hot and greasy.

'That's enough,' said Marysia, 'or else we'll get ill and die. You shouldn't eat such greasy food on an empty stomach.'

The mayor stood behind us, looking at us attentively.

'What do you do?' he asked.

Tchorzewski was the first to reply. 'I worked in a precision instruments factory in Warsaw. For the Germans I worked on the railway.'

'We're dressmakers,' said Marysia.

He liked what he heard. 'Listen. Stay here. In this town. In Landsberg. I'll give you a beautiful, brick built house that used to belong to Germans. With furniture and bedding.'

'No. We can't. Our families are in Warsaw. Our brothers and sisters.'

'Brothers and sisters? Bring them here then. They'll have everything their hearts desire here.'

'We'll think about it,' said Tchorzewski gloomily. He got up off the steps, picked up the bowl and went to thank the housekeeper who was standing in the door. Next to the house fourteen young girls were sweeping the street. Seeing us looking at them the house-keeper said, 'They were raped and became infected. They were cured in hospital by a Soviet doctor and have returned to work now.'

They all looked indifferent and tired. They were singing a tango. Their work was lazy, their movements heavy and slow. Our thoughts returned at lightning speed into the past. To the ghetto. We remembered the teams of Jews sweeping snow on the streets. But all the same there were tears in our eyes when we looked at these abused women. There were girls of fifteen among them. The most terrible thing of all was the song they were joylessly singing. We started hurriedly arranging the bags on our cart as if we were afraid the mayor would detain us by force. Suddenly a lorry drove past. We raised our arms to stop it. It stopped. One of the soldiers jumped down.

'Take us a little way,' we requested.

'We can't. It's forbidden.'

'Why? Please take us. Just a little way.'

'We're carrying corpses. It's forbidden. That's regulations.'

He took a cigarette out of his pocket. The mayor gave him a light. He lit up, jumped onto the lorry and drove off. The mayor didn't detain us. 'God be with you,' he said and nodded his head in farewell. The cart creaked and we set off on a path alongside the road in our accustomed order.

'Macius, throw something behind you for luck,' said Marysia. 'Have you got anything in your pocket?'

'I've got a pencil.'

'Throw it. We might have a lucky day today because of it.'

He stopped for a moment, took the pencil out of his pocket and threw it behind him onto the road. We walked. Our steps were regular and measured. Not too fast and not too slow. We were silent, lost in our own thoughts. We were subconsciously saving our strength. We didn't have too much of it. Three or four kilometres later the cart broke. Tchorzewski strapped the bag with food to his bike and we divided the rest of the things up between us.

The sun was hot, it was nearly noon, and even what little baggage we had was hard to carry. So every now and then we sat down in the ditch and rested. We kept hoping a lorry would drive past and give us a lift for part of the way. In the meantime we were alone among the endless fields full of greenery bursting into life. In front of us was the long ribbon of road disappearing into the distance and behind us the empty town of Landsberg. Suddenly we felt alarmed at this silence and emptiness all around. We were in the middle of a huge circle in which all human sounds had died. We listened but could hear nothing apart from the chirruping and buzzing of insects.

'Is this the right road?' asked Tchorzewski worriedly. 'Aren't we going the wrong way? We haven't seen anyone for a long time and I can't see anything moving on the road.'

He stopped the bike and looked round questioningly. At that moment we each thought of that bowl of soup. Shouldn't we return to Landsberg? In our quandary and indecision we remembered the soup and the straw on the floor where we could spend another night.

We had definitely gone to pieces without the cart. It had been our support. I looked anxiously at the child. Whenever I didn't know what to do and felt dejected, I looked at Macius. Wasn't he the fourth equal partner in our group? Didn't the same dangers threaten him? Didn't he struggle with tiredness, didn't he long for hot food, wasn't he overcome with sudden anxiety about the uncertainty of this alien world just like us? So let him have his say too. I waited for what he'd say. For a complaint, a demand, a fancy even, but all that came was a rough movement, an impatient expression on his face or silent expectation.

As we stood there despondent and not knowing what to do, whether to continue or turn back, we heard the rattle of wheels and a small peasant wagon harnessed to a single horse turned out of a side track onto the main road.

'Take us with you, please. We've gone the wrong way.'

He took us back to Landsberg and set us down in exactly the same place we had started from that morning, outside the mayor's house. A huge lorry was standing there just then, loaded with tyres. A mountain of lorry tyres, and underneath them, rifles.

'Are you going in the direction of Warsaw?' we asked the soldiers.

'Yes, we are.'

'Will you take us?'

'Can you climb up onto the tyres?'

Can we climb up! The child was up there in an instant. But what about me? 'Alfred, hold the child or he'll slip down into that hole,' shouted Marysia. Then Tchorzewski climbed up, pulling the bike behind him. Quickly and deftly because this really was an

485

exceptional opportunity. He gave Marysia his hand and they both sat down on a tyre. Then me. Even I scrambled up quickly, just in case the driver changed his mind. The mayor was watching out of the window. He saw us getting down from the peasant wagon and saw us climbing up onto the loaded lorry. He was saying something to us and waving his hands but his words didn't reach us. Perhaps he wanted to talk us into staying. To stagger us with a new proposal.

'Can you throw something, Macius?' asked Marysia. 'Have you got another treasure in your pocket?'

'I've got the figure Madejski gave me.'

'Throw it. It'll bring us luck, you'll see.'

He took out of his pocket the figure made of green stone, the tiny Buddha which Madejski had found in the ruins of a bombed house and hurled it over his shoulder into the roadside dust. He didn't look back. You mustn't look back. The game or the spell gave us courage, and surely gave confidence to the tired child.

The lorry set off. At first it seemed as if the mountain of tyres was slipping down with us on it and we were just about to fall into the ditch. The two Soviet soldiers sitting in front wouldn't even notice if we did fall. The tyres shook and rocked under us and only seemed to stay put thanks to our weight. We sped past the same lanes and gardens that we remembered from the morning. The same dog jumped out of its kennel. The well we had drunk from flashed past and was hidden behind the branches of the trees. The same bucket was still standing on its casing.

Then we saw the broken cart once more which Tchorzewski had rolled into the ditch, and the sunny turn in the road where we had stood undecided listening to the silence and emptiness. And the sandy track where we saw the thin horse pulling the rattling wagon.

'We were going the right way, after all,' said Tchorzewski suddenly. 'Perhaps we shouldn't have gone back. We'd have been picked up by the same lorry.'

'You never know,' I said. 'It might not have stopped when it was speeding along. It was standing still in front of the mayor's house. We were able to ask the driver.'

Then we fell silent. It was difficult to open our mouths and we were reluctant to speak. Tired and hungry, we nodded our heads sleepily and our ears were filled with the whistling of the wind. We kept shuddering and waking out of our lethargy and looking

486

around in surprise. Now in the fields we could see wrecked tanks and huge bomb craters. A battle had been fought here. Then we drove over a wooden bridge into a town that was completely burnt down A ghost town. It seemed as if there wasn't a single inhabitant left. Burnt out houses from end to end.

'What's this town called?'

'Kostryn,' replied the driver.

'This is the place where our camp cook's sister lived. She used to talk about it.'

The sun was moving westwards when we stopped in the main square. Among the lorries stood a supply truck which was just about to move off. A few soldiers were still loading crates and blankets.

'Where are you going?'

'To Poznan.'

We hurl ourselves at the supply truck like wolves onto their prey. We transferred our bags instantly and jumped onto the wheels. Tchorzewski threw the suitcase and bike across. But he didn't have time to get up. The truck moved off and he was dangling on the back. All we could see was his terrified face and two hands clutching the edge of the flap.

'My husband! My husband!' shrieked Marysia. She jumped up, then swaying and waving her hands she made a few steps and then knelt down and grabbed him by his hands. 'Alfred! Alfred!' she shouted.

'Stop! Stop!' shouted Macius. He was as pale as a sheet and crying. But he wasn't able to pretend. Even at this tragic moment he couldn't say the word 'father'. What he should have shouted was, 'My father! Save my father.' Then one of the soldiers grabbed Tchorzewski by the head and another by the hands and they pulled him up onto the truck. He fell down like a sack. But then he picked himself up and sat down next to Marysia.

Shortly afterwards it started to drizzle. I wanted to keep Macius dry so I opened the umbrella I had found in the field. It was coming in useful for the first time. Tchorzewski sat indifferently on a crate hugging his knees with his hands. The rain drops flowed down his face like huge tears. The soldiers covered themselves with canvas sheets. One of them took Marysia by the hand, sat her down beside him and covered her with his canvas. And then they started to sing. In the quiet hum of the rain, in the rattling of the wheels, in the beating of our hearts and the thickening dusk.

The soldier next to Marysia was called Vasyl. He was the lead singer. His voice was clear, high and dreamy. Then he sang solo and there was an indescribable poetry in it. He sang to the German fields and the misty night, or perhaps only to the woman sitting next to him. The songs told of the triumph of youth, the joy of victory, yearning for love and regret for each passing moment.

'Where will you go in Poznan? Where will you sleep?' Vasyl asked suddenly.

'We've got relatives in Poznan,' we replied.

'But you can't walk along the streets at night. It's past curfew. Come with us to our barracks. You can sleep there.'

'No. We'll sleep in the police station. Drop us off there, please.'

'You silly things,' he said. 'It's good fun in the barracks. We play the harmonica, drink vodka, dance, sing and have a laugh. You'll have fun with us too.'

'No.'

'Silly things.'

We reached the outskirts of Poznan at half past eleven. The truck suddenly stopped in a deserted street full of orchards surrounded by tall railings.

'Get down,' they said, 'you can't go any further. We're not allowed to take civilians.'

They throw our bags and Tchorzewski's suitcase down into the dust and helped him take the bike down.

Thank you,' we said, 'Spasibo, gjeroje.'

We stood there listening for a moment longer. They had driven off. They had disappeared into the darkness. As we stood there on the street, lost and not knowing where to go, jolted by the ride and disorientated by the darkness, two policemen suddenly appeared in front of us. Two Polish policemen shone torches into our eyes.

'What's this? What birds are these?' said one of them.

'Where have you come from? Fallen from the sky, have you?' asked the other.

They looked suspiciously at the bags we were still picking up in the darkness.

'Thieves or what? What are these things and whose are they? Don't you know it's long after curfew? You deserve to be arrested!'

They didn't let us get a word in edgeways. We didn't know how to address them and how to appease them.

'Please, officer,' said Tchorzewski at last, 'we've come from

Berlin, from a camp. We just arrived a moment ago. The soldiers set us down right here off the supply truck.'

'Come along to the station. We'll check your papers.'

We were surprised at being greeted so suspiciously and roughly on Polish soil. The war was over for us, wasn't it? Did we look like bandits? Do you set out on a robbery with a child and two women who can hardly drag themselves along?

'Is it far?'

'Not far. Just round the corner.'

Then we arrive. There's a wooden bench in a hall permeated with tobacco smoke. We sit down. 'Papers!' they say to us. We search in our pockets and hand them our identity cards from Warsaw and our camp papers. They take them away, leaving us alone. We lie down for the night. A blanket on the floor for Tchorzewski, Marysia and Macius. They put coats under their heads and fall asleep instantly.

They leave the bench for me. I sit on it, and then lie down but I can't get to sleep for a long time. I look at the walls, the window through which the trees are humming, the door, the ceiling, at the whole place, all so inhospitable and unfriendly. I wonder why we don't admit to being Jewish. Why don't we throw the mask off? The Germans have gone now after all. The war is over, but it hasn't even entered our heads to tell people who we really are. Not only the Soviet soldiers and the policemen but even Tchorzewski.

I lie on the hard bench. Cocks are crowing in a yard somewhere, dogs are barking, the whistle of a train pierces the silence of the night, but I'm still looking into the future and it now seems so full of worries that it's as if the war isn't over for us at all.

At six o'clock the door of a neighbouring room opens and a young man in civvies enters. He gives Marysia and me our papers and says, 'You two are Jewish, aren't you?' He looks at us mean-ingfully and smiles. He smiles and winks. We think to ourselves that until recently he was an informer. He looks just like the informers on Chlodna Street in Warsaw used to. His eyes are so experienced and practised that no-one and nothing can hide from him.

'Who? Us? Are you mad? Us Jewish?' Marysia jumps up from the floor.

Tchorzewski's got up now. And Macius.

'Maryska,' says Tchorzewski calmly, 'don't pay any attention to what he's saying.'

Why is she so irritated? Why is she behaving like that? It's the memory of former times. She's reacting as if the war is still on. She straightens her skirt, pulls a comb out of her pocket and combs her hair.

'Can we sit here for a few more minutes? We haven't eaten anything since yesterday afternoon.'

'Yes, you can,' he replied. He stood in front of us with his hands in his pockets, a cigarette in his mouth and an ironic look on his face. He was watching us. He didn't believe a single word Marysia said. He was clearly amusing himself at our expense. We took out the black bread the soldiers had given us and cut a slice of pork fat for each of us with Tchorzewski's penknife. First a slice for Tchorzewski.

'Here you are,' said Marysia and looked at him warmly.

Then we left the police station and went towards the railway station. We decided to go to Krakow because we knew the address of Mrs Frumik, where Nina had lived. She'd sent the address to us at the camp in one of her letters. 'You'll find out where I am from Mrs Frumik,' she wrote.

'This is where our ways part,' we said to Tchorzewski. 'You're going to Warsaw and we're going to Krakow.'

We kept seeing Soviet soldiers. Huge lorries were driving in all directions. The city looked like an army camp. Marysia suddenly glanced at a sign in front of one of the houses. 'Dr Stabrowski lives here!' she exclaimed. 'He looked after Macius when he had scarlet fever. Let's go up and see him.'

I sat down on a bench with Tchorzewski and she took Macius by the hand and entered the gate. While they were going upstairs they sat down for a moment on the window sill between the first and second floors. 'Macius,' said Marysia, 'have you got anything left you can throw for good luck? We haven't arrived yet. Our journey isn't over yet.'

'I've got a paintbox.'

'Throw it. We'll get to Krakow quicker if you do.'

'I'll leave it on the window sill,' he said. He didn't want to throw it. It was his last toy and was precious to him. He placed the box on the window sill.

'Well?' we asked when they returned. 'Was he there?'

'He's away but his wife was there. She gave us breakfast and three hard-boiled eggs for the journey.'

We set off again. We asked the way from time to time and then reached the railway station at last.

'This is where we say goodbye,' said Tchorzewski, 'because we're going to different platforms.'

We said goodbye warmly. Marysia wrote down his address and said, 'I'll come and see you when I'm in Warsaw.'

We pushed our way through the crowds of people and went to look for our platform. Suddenly we noticed Tchorzewski running towards us with his suitcase in his hand. He was pale and out of breath. The sweat was pouring down his face. 'What's happened?' we asked.

'Two soldiers came up to me and took my bike off me,' he said, catching his breath.

Marysia was close to tears. 'If I'd been there,' she said, 'I'd have wailed and managed to get it back this time too.'

The train to Krakow was in the station already. It was so crowded, so packed, that it was impossible to get into the compartments even if we'd tried to get in through the window. We walked dejectedly along the platform, convinced that the train would set off any minute and we'd stay behind just like the hundreds of other people we could see sitting on suitcases and bags, resigned and passive. We moved along from wagon to wagon until we reached the locomotive. Behind it were the post van and luggage compartment. We went up to the driver.

'We've got to go to Krakow today. We'll give you some gold if you can squeeze us in somewhere?'

'Let's see it,' he said.

I took one of the pieces of chain that Tchorzewski had bitten off with his teeth out of my pocket and held it out on the palm of my hand for him to see. He didn't muck around or make a fuss or pretend he was offended. He dealt with the matter briskly. He picked the chain up with two fingers, looked at it and quickly slipped it into his jacket pocket.

'I'll put you in the luggage compartment. It's full of people but you might fit in without being smothered.'

He helped us up onto the high steps and threw our bags in behind us. We squeezed into a corner crammed with crates, trunks and people, and sat down on the floor tucking our legs under us. The compartment was almost the same as the one we left Warsaw in for our journey into the unknown. People were sitting and lying in an indescribable crush, just like they were then. Except that now we were returning. And the wheel had come full circle.

We arrived at Krakow towards morning. The reason it took so long was because we stood for hours in sidings waiting for military

491

transports to pass. Dawn was breaking. In the grey half-light of the new day the stars were shining and the moon was sailing along through the clouds. It was still curfew so it was forbidden to be out on the streets. We had to wait a few hours in the station waiting room. We left the station at seven o'clock. We walked slowly, dragging our tired legs. People turned to look at us. Some stopped and asked, 'Where are you from?'

'We're returning from a camp.'

'What camp?'

'In Berlin.'

From Berlin? No-one had been seen returning from Berlin yet. Berlin is under siege, isn't it? It hasn't fallen yet.

'But our camp was in Koepenick, in the suburbs, and the Russians took it.'

'How long have you been travelling?'

'Three days and three nights.'

They don't believe us. We can tell by their eyes. I take a piece of cloth out of my bag and show it to them – the letter P on a yellow background. Will they believe us now?

Oddly enough, their disbelief starts to affect us too. Are we really coming back from Berlin? Is it possible? What's the date today? 29 April. We spent three nights travelling and one night in Mrs Ulrich's cellar. The Russians took Koepenick at dawn of the 25th. But is it all true? If it is, then where is everyone from our camp now? What roads are they travelling along now?

'Is this the right way for Zygmunt August Street?' we ask.

'Yes. Straight on and then right.'

'Anyway, even if we find Mrs Frumik she won't let us into the house,' I say.

'Why not?' asks Marysia.

'She'll be afraid we've got lice. People from camps often have lice.'

'But we can ask. We can stand on the threshold and ask about Nina.'

Is this Zygmunt August Street? Yes, this is it. What about number 5? Yes, there it is. And flat number 1. We ring. Mrs Frumik opens the door.

'I'm the mother of Jadzia Tokarska who lived with you. And this is her sister. We've come back from the camp. Have you had any news from Jadzia?'

We stand on the threshold. We don't even say that we've come from Berlin. We know she won't believe us.

'Jadzia's in Warsaw! She lives in Praga, on Stalowa Street. She works in one of the ministries. Her sister's in Warsaw too and lives on Narbutt Street. Do come in, please. You must lie down and rest. I'll make some tea.'

We cross the threshold. I look at this woman who took my daughter in once. I think to myself that after all the war might really be over for us too.

The Library of Holocaust Testimonies

Out of the Ghetto

Jack Klajman

Jack Klajman was an eight-year-old in Warsaw when Germany invaded Poland. He survived the bombing of his home, the daily risks and hardships of smuggling across the walls of the Warsaw Ghetto and the deaths of his parents and siblings. He was a participant in the Warsaw Ghetto uprising, fled the ghetto through the sewers and survived on the streets of Warsaw posing as a Catholic boy. Written from the perspective of the child, this autobiography chronicles Jack's tragic, but compelling story.

2000 208 pages illus 0 85303 389 7 paper

Have You Seen My Little Sister?

Janina Fischler-Martinho

A vividly-told account of the author's childhood experiences of the Krakow Ghetto, this work details the loss of all her immediate family, except her older brother, with whom she escaped from the Ghetto during its final liquidation, via the sewers. An important theme in this moving tale is that of memory and loss; whilst memory may be painful, it is the only memorial to many of those who have been consumed by the *Shoah*.

1998 296 pages
0 85303 334 X paper

The Children Accuse

Maria Hochberg-Mariańska and Noe Grüss

This most unusual book contains evidence collected by the author in 1945 in Poland from children and teenagers who surfaced from hiding in forests and bunkers, and told the story of their survival as it happened. The interviews, expertly translated from the original Polish, document life in the ghettos, in camps, in hiding, in the resistance and in prison.

1996 316 pages 0 85303 312 9 flapped paper

My Heart in a Suitcase

Anne L. Fox

Immediately after Kristallnacht in 1938, the author, then aged twelve, was sent to safety in England. This book tells of her experiences in adjusting to an unfamiliar environment, living with Jewish and Gentile families on a primitive farm and at a progressive boarding school.

1996 reprinted 1997 170 pages illus 0 85303 311 0 flapped paper

A Cat Called Adolf

Trude Levi

This is one Holocaust memoir which does not stop at survival but goes on to describe the lasting effects upon those survivors of their persecution, betrayal and suffering.

The author's wish in telling her story is that the lessons of the Holocaust are never forgotten and that the events she has recorded are never allowed to happen again.

> 'The reader cannot help but marvel at her resilience and adaptability.'
>
> *Jewish Chronicle*

1995 reprinted 1995, 1996 176 pages illus0 85303 289 0 flapped paper

A Child Alone

Martha Blend

This book describes the author's background in pre-*Anschluss* Vienna, through its annexation by Hitler, her passage to England as a *Kindertransport* nine-year-old and her gradual assimilation into England and English culture during and after the war years.

> 'compelling detail, giving an insight into how the Kindertransport children transcended the horrors of separation, guilt and uncertainty to lead full, if . not altogether happy lives.'
>
> Riva Klein, *The Times Educational Supplement*

1995 168 pages illus 0 85303 297 1 flapped paper

An End to Childhood

Miriam Akavia

Written as fiction but based on fact, this book describes the efforts of a young Polish brother and sister to survive in secrecy and constant anxiety in Lvov, at a time when Jews were being rounded up and sent to the Ghetto – or worse.

> 'This deeply moving book vividly recreates the complex perils of occupied Poland. Fear is tangible.'
>
> *Jewish Chronicle*

1995 124 pages illus 0 85303 294 7 flapped paper

495

I Light a Candle

Gena Turgel with Veronica Groocock

Out of the ashes of the Nazi concentration camps came an extraordinary love story which caught the public's imagination at the end of World War II. This autobiography tells how the author survived the camps and met her husband, a sergeant working for British intelligence when he arrived to round up the SS guards for interrogation.

1995 reprinted 2000 160 pages illus 0 85303 315 3 flapped paper

From Dachau to Dunkirk

Fred Pelican

Born in Upper Silesia, the author was imprisoned before the war for the 'crime' of being a Jew. He subsequently served in the British Army, was nearly captured in Dunkirk and ended the war as an interpreter at BAOR (British Army on the Rhine) Headquarters, helping to investigate war crimes.

1993 224 pages illus 0 85303 253 X

My Lost World
A Survivor's Tale

Sara Rosen

An account of how a young girl from Krakow was able to survive the Tarnow ghetto and escape to Bucharest, this book tells the story of what was once the largest Jewish community in the world.

> 'The Holocaust wiped out not just a way of life, a tradition, and Rosen's story is in remembrance of this. She escaped through a series of risky adventures and was among one of the first survivors to enter Palestine.'
>
> *Jewish Chronicle*

1993 reprinted 1996 320 pages 0 85303 254 8 flapped paper

My Private War
One Man's Struggle to Survive the Soviets and the Nazis

Jacob Gerstenfeld-Maltiel

The author experienced the first 21 months of Soviet rule in the Polish town of Lvov and then, from June 1941, the nightmare of Nazi genocidal policies. He survived in a most unusual way, by disguising himself as a civilian auxiliary of the German Army.

> 'His closeness to the events he describes enables him to provide a wealth of detail. He recreates the unbearable tension of life.'
>
> *Jewish Chronicle*

1993 336 pages 0 85303 260 2 flapped paper